연설문 독해완성과 문제풀이

연설문 독해완성과 문제풀이 [동영상 강좌]

초판 1쇄 인쇄　　　2014년 12월 19일
초판 1쇄 발행　　　2014년 12월 26일

지은이　　김 재 성
펴낸이　　손 형 국
펴낸곳　　(주)북랩
편집인　　선일영　　　　　　　편집　　이소현, 김진주, 김아름, 이탄석
디자인　　이현수, 신혜림, 김루리　　제작　　박기성, 황동현, 구성우
마케팅　　김회란, 이희정
출판등록　2004. 12. 1(제2012-000051호)
주소　　　서울시 금천구 가산디지털 1로 168, 우림라이온스밸리 B동 B113, 114호
홈페이지　www.book.co.kr
전화번호　(02)2026-5777　　　　　　팩스　　(02)2026-5747

ISBN　　979-11-5585-440-2 13740(종이책)　979-11-5585-441-9 15740(전자책)

이 도서의 국립중앙도서관 출판예정도서목록(CIP)은 서지정보유통지원시스템 홈페이지(http://seoji.nl.go.kr)와
국가자료공동목록시스템(http://www.nl.go.kr/kolisnet)에서 이용하실 수 있습니다.
(CIP제어번호 : CIP2014037313)

연설문 독해완성과 문제풀이

[동영상 강좌]

동영상 강좌로
영어독해를 완성

학교, 학원, 공부방 보충교재용

김 재 성 지음

북랩 book Lab

이 책의 학습방법은 다음과 같습니다.

[학습방법 1 - 기초반]

1. 제시된 지문을 읽으면서, 모르는 부분은 밑줄을 그으면서 독해를 시작하세요.

2. 다시 한 번 독해를 하면서, 밑줄 쳐진 부분을 전체 문장과 비교하여 이해해 보세요.

3. 지문해석을 보면서 이해가 안 된 부분과 문법분석을 비교하면서 공부해 보세요.

4. 지문 동영상 강좌로 최종 이해를 합니다.

　(제 강의 목소리를 똑같이 따라하면서 학습하시면 효과가 배가 됩니다.)

5. 제공된 문제를 꼼꼼히 풀어 봅니다.

6. 문제 동영상 강좌로 마지막 100% 이해를 합니다.

7. 제공된 동의어와 반의어를 발음기호에 따라 정확히 읽고 쓰면서 최종 마무리를 합니다.

8. 다음날 같은 지문을 빠르게 복습하면서 반복하여야 됩니다.

[학습방법 2 - 중급반]

1. 제시된 지문을 읽으면서, 모르는 부분은 밑줄을 그으면서 독해를 시작하세요.

2. 지문 동영상 강좌로 반복학습 합니다.

　(제 강의 목소리를 똑같이 따라하면서 학습하시면 효과가 배가 됩니다.)

3. 지문해석을 보면서 이해가 안 된 부분과 문법분석을 비교하면서 공부해 보세요.

4. 제공된 문제를 꼼꼼히 풀어 봅니다.

5. 문제 동영상 강좌로 마지막 100% 이해를 합니다.

6. 제공된 동의어와 반의어를 발음기호에 따라 정확히 읽고 쓰면서 최종 마무리를 합니다.

7. 다음날 같은 지문을 빠르게 복습하면서 반복하여야 됩니다.

[학습방법 3 - 고급반]

1. 제시된 지문을 읽으면서, 모르는 부분은 밑줄을 그으면서 독해를 시작하세요.

2. 지문해석을 보면서 이해가 안 된 부분과 문법분석을 비교하면서 공부해 보세요.

3. 제공된 문제를 꼼꼼히 풀어 봅니다.

4. 지문 동영상 강좌로 최종 이해를 합니다.

　(제 강의 목소리를 똑같이 따라하면서 학습하시면 효과가 배가 됩니다.)

5. 제공된 동의어와 반의어를 발음기호에 따라 정확히 읽고 쓰면서 최종 마무리를 합니다.

6. 다음날 같은 지문을 빠르게 복습하면서 반복하여야 됩니다.

독자 여러분의 독해실력이 쑥쑥 향상되시길 간절히 기원합니다.

학습 시 궁금한 사항과 질문은 제 카페에 오셔서 무엇이든 물어 보세요.

http://cafe.daum.net/kimteach116

동영상 원본 구입을 원하시는 분은

http://eng119.co.kr 에서 구입하실 수 있습니다. (단, 파일은 이메일로 전송됩니다.)

감사합니다.

차례

Farewell to the Old Guard

by Napoleon Bonaparte

[난이도 ★★☆☆☆]

동영상 강좌 http://youtu.be/BRaN3GAWO0U

April 20, 1814.

Following the failed invasion of Russia and defeat by the Allies

Soldiers of my Old Guard:

I bid you farewell. For twenty years I have constantly accompanied you on the road to honor and glory. In these latter times, as in the days of our prosperity, you have invariably been models of courage and fidelity. With men such as you our cause could not be lost; but the war would have been interminable; it would have been civil war, and that would have entailed deeper misfortunes on France.

I have sacrificed all of my interests to those of the country.

I go, but you, my friends, will continue to serve France. Her happiness was my only thought. It will still be the object of my wishes. Do not regret my fate; if I have consented to survive, it is to serve your glory. I intend to write the history of the great achievements we have performed together. Adieu, my friends. Would I could press you all to my heart.

📎 본문분석

Following the failed invasion of Russia and defeat by the Allies
- 러시아 침공 실패와 연합군에 퇴패한 후 / following[=after ~이후]

Soldiers of my Old Guard:
- 나의 근위대 병사들이여

I bid you farewell.
- 저는 여러분에 작별을 고하고자 합니다.
- bid A(사람) B(인사) : A에게 B를 말하다 = bid B[인사] to A[사람]

①For twenty years ②I ④have constantly accompanied you ③on the road to honor and glory.
- ①20년 동안, ②저는 ③명예와 영광의 길을 ④여러분과 항상 계속해 왔습니다.
- for[전치사: ~동안], during[전치사: 때를 나타내는 명사가 온다. ex) during life 일생동안] / have accompanied[현재완료 계속용법, ~와 동반하다] / constantly[부사로 accompanied 동사를 수식] / you[목적어] / on the road[전치사구: 길 위에, 여정에] / to[=forward ~로 향하는]

②In these latter times, ①as in the days of our prosperity, ③you ⑤have invariably been models of ④courage and fidelity.
- ①우리 번영의 시대와 같은 ②요즈음, ③장병 여러분들은 ④용기와 충성심의 ⑤변함없는 모범이 되어 왔습니다.
- latter[late의 비교급, 이후의, 요즈음의] / times[=ages, days 시대] / as[전치사: ~같은] / prosperity[prɑspérəti] 번영 / invariably [invέəriəbli] ad. 변함없이 / have been[현재완료의 결과로 해석] / model [mάdl]n. 모범, 본보기. / of courage[of+명사=형용사구 courageous] / of fidelity[of+명사=형용사구]

①With men such as you ②our cause could not be lost; ④but the war ⑤would have been

interminable; ⑥it would have been civil war, ⑦and that ⑩would have entailed ⑨deeper misfortunes ⑧on France.
- ①여러분과 같은 병사들과 함께 ②우리의 대의는 잃을 수가 없었습니다.;④그러나 전쟁은 ⑤지루했던 것 같았습니다; ⑥전쟁은 내전인 것 같았습니다, ⑦그리고 그것은 ⑧조국 프랑스에 ⑨더더욱 깊은 불행을 ⑩수반한 것 같았습니다.
- with[더불어] / such as[~처럼] / could[can의 과거형] / be lost[수동태: ~을 잃다] / would have been [과거를 추측: ~였던 것 같다] / interminable [intə́ː rmənəbəl] a. 끝없는; 지루하게 긴 / civil warp[내전]
- entail [entéil] vt. 일으키다, 수반하다. / deeper(deep의 비교급: 더욱 깊은) / entail A on B : A를 B에 남기다

①I ④have sacrificed ②all of my interests ③to those of the country.
- ①저는 ②모든 저의 이해관계를 ③조국에 ④바쳤습니다.
- have sacrificed[현재완료: 결과] / all of + 복수명사 / sacrifice A to B : A를 B에 바치다 / those[=my interests]

I go, but you, my friends, will continue to serve France.
- 저는 떠납니다. 저의 동료인 여러분은 계속해서 조국 프랑스에 봉사를 하게 될 겁니다.
- go[=leave 떠나다] / you, my friends[동격] / will[설득조의 명령, 부탁: ~해 주세요.] / continue to do [계속해서 ~하다] / serve[봉사하다]

Her happiness was my only thought. ①It ④will ②still be ③the object of my wishes.
- 조국의 행복은 저의 유일한 생각이었습니다. ①그것은 ②앞으로도 여전히 ③저의 소망의 목표일 ④것입니다.
- her[=France 국가는 여성명사] / only[유일한] / it[=her happiness] / still[부사: 여전히, 변함없이] / object[목표, 목적]

②Do not regret ①my fate; ③if I ④have consented to survive, ⑤it ⑦is to serve your glory. ⑧I ⑪intend to write ⑩the history of the great achievements ⑨we have performed together.
- ①저의 운명을 ②안타깝다 하지 마세요.; ③만일 제가 ④생존한다면, ⑤그것은 ⑥여러분의 영광에 ⑦기여하는 것이 될 것입니다. ⑧저는 ⑨우리가 함께 쌓아온 ⑩위대한 업적의 역사를 ⑪쓰고 싶습니다.
- [명령문] do not regret[후회하다] my fate[운명]; if[가정법: 만일 ~라면] / consent to [~에 동의하다] / survive [생존하다] / it[=my survival] / is to[be to의 용법의 예정: ~일 것이다] / intend to[~할 의도이다, ~하고 싶다] / achievements [that 목적격 관계대명사 생략] we have performed[목적어는 achievements]

🖊 동의어/반의어
- **consent**[kənsént] 동의하다 v. assent[əsént] ant. refusal[rifjúː z-əl] rejection[ridʒékʃ-ən]
- **perform**[pərfɔ́ː rm] v. portray[pɔː rtréi], achieve[ətʃíː v], effect[ifékt] ant. fail[feil]

Adieu, my friends. Would I could press you all to my heart.
- 안녕히 계십시오. 제 친구 여러분. 제가 여러분 모두를 제 가슴에 꼭 안아 봤으면 좋을 텐데!
- Would that + 과거/과거완료[~라면 좋을 텐데] / Would it were so [true]. 그렇다면[정말이라면] 좋을 텐데.

✹ 다음 글을 읽고 물음에 답하시오. [1~8]

Following the failed invasion of Russia and defeat by the Allies
_____Ⓐ_____
I bid you ① **farewell**. During/For twenty years I have constantly accompanied you on the road to honor and glory. In these latter times, as in the days of our prosperity, you have invariably been ② **models** of courage and fidelity. With men such as you our cause could not be lost; but the war would have been ③ **interminable**; it would have been civil war, and that would have entailed deeper ④ **misfortunes** on France.
I have sacrificed all of my interests to those of the country.
I go, but you, my friends, will continue to serve France. Her/His happiness was my only thought. It will still be the object/objection of my wishes. Do not ⑤ **expect** my fate; if I have consented to survive, it is to serve your glory. I intend to write the history of the great achievements we have performed together. Adieu, my friends. _____Ⓑ_____ .

1. 위 글의 빈칸 Ⓐ에 들어갈 제목으로 가장 적절한 것은?

① Saddest Thing in Defeat
② A Nation in Danger
③ The Way Never to Return
④ My Incapability and Your Suffering
⑤ Soldiers of my Old Guard

2. 위 글에 나타난 지은이의 심정은?

① indifferent   ② gloomy
③ desperate   ④ thankful
⑤ boring

3. 위 글에 나타난 'I'와 일치하지 않은 것은?

① A conqueror   ② A failure
③ An imperialist   ④ A humanitarian
⑤ An ambition

4. 위 글에서 네모상자 안의 적절한 단어는?

① During	Her	object
② During	His	objection
③ For	Her	object
④ For	His	objection
⑤ For	Her	objection

5. 위 글에서 밑줄 친 ①~⑤중, 문맥상 단어의 쓰임이 어색한 것은?

①   ②   ③   ④   ⑤

6. 위 글의 주제로 가장 적절한 것은?

① Despite defeat let the country be prosperous
② The chance will come again, so don't forget me.
③ Wars will never happen again in France.
④ My ambition will go on with my friends in France.
⑤ We witnessed the sever scene of the wars together.

7. 위 글에서 밑줄 친 빈칸 Ⓑ에 가장 적절한 표현은?

① May you not forget me
② My tears are falling down as I say a goodbye
③ The wars with me were so great
④ Would I could press you all to my heart
⑤ Follow me and go forward again

8. 위 글과 일치하지 <u>않은</u> 것은?

① 나폴레옹의 작별인사이다.

② 이 연설은 러시아 침공 후, 행해진 것이다.

③ 병사들의 용기와 충성심에 감사하고 있다.

④ 조국 프랑스의 번영을 위해 늘 봉사정신을 잊어서는 안 된다.

⑤ 다시 기회는 오므로 새로운 역사를 함께 써 나아가자.

1. ⑤   2. ④   3. ④   4. ③
5. ⑤ expect→regret   6. ①
7. ④   8. ⑤

[난이도 ★★☆☆☆]

동영상 강좌 http://youtu.be/utppk44ejiQ

Stanford Report, June 14, 2005

'You've got to find what you love,' Jobs says.

This is a prepared text of the Commencement address delivered by Steve Jobs, CEO of Apple Computer and of Pixar Animation Studios, on June 12, 2005.

📎 **본문해석+문법분석**

Stanford Report, June 14, 2005

- 2004년 6월 14일자 스탠퍼드대학 뉴스 / [According to) Stanford Report (on) June 14th, (in) 2005.

①'You③'ve got to find ②what you love,' ④Jobs says.

- ①'여러분들은 ②자신이 좋아하는 것을 ③찾아야만 합니다.' ④잡스는 주장합니다. / You've got to[=You have to(must):~해야만 한다] what you love[목적어: 여러분이 좋아하는 것]

①This ⑥is a prepared text of ⑤the Commencement address delivered ④by Steve Jobs, ③CEO of Apple Computer and of Pixar Animation Studios, ②on June 12, 2005.

- ①이 연설문은 ②2005년 6월 12일 ③애플컴퓨터와 픽사 애니메이션 스튜디오의 최고 경영자인 ④스티브 잡스가 ⑤스탠퍼드대학 졸업식장에서 연설한 ⑥원고입니다. / This[이 원고를=This manuscript] is a prepared text [준비된 글] of the Commencement address[졸업식 연설] (which was) delivered by Steve Jobs, CEO [동격]

📎 **단어분석**

commencement [kəménsmənt] n. (the ~) (대학 따위의) 졸업식 (행사 기간) / **deliver** [dilívər] vt. (의견을) 말하다; (연설을) 하다.

📎 **동의어/반의어**

commencement n. creation[kriː éiʃən], dawn[dɔː n]새벽, genesis[dʒénəsis]발생, 기원 창세기, start[stɑː rt], graduation[grædʒuéiʃən], initiation[iniʃiéiʃən]착수, 비법전수, 입회식 ant. end[end]

I am honored to be with you today at your commencement from one of the finest universities in the world. I never graduated from college. Truth be told, this is the closest I've ever gotten to a college graduation. Today I want to tell you three stories from my life. That's it. No big deal. Just three stories.

The first story is about connecting the dots.

I dropped out of Reed College after the first 6 months, but then stayed around as a drop-in for another 18 months or so before I really quit. So why did I drop out?

📎 **본문해석+문법분석**

①I ④am honored to ③be with you today at your commencement ②from one of the finest

universities in the world. - ①저는 ②세계적으로 가장 유수한 대학 중 한 곳에서 ③여러분의 졸업식에 참여하는 것이 ④영광입니다. / I am honored[수동태: ~한 영광을 받다] / one of + 복수명사[유수한 대학 중 한 곳]

I never graduated from college. - 저는 대학을 졸업하지 못했습니다. / graduate from[자동사: ~을 졸업하다]

①Truth be told, ②this ④is the closest I've ever gotten ③to a college graduation. - ①사실, ②이번이 ③대학졸업식에 ④가장 가까이 있는 것입니다. / Truth be told=As truth should be told=Truly speaking / this is the closest[최상급: 이번이 가장 가까운 곳] / get to[~에 도달하다] / I've ever gotten to[현재완료경험: 지금껏 도달했던 것 중]

①Today ②I ⑥want to tell ③you ⑤three stories ④from my life. - ①오늘 ②저는 ③여러분들에게 ④제 인생에서 터득한 ⑤3개의 이야기를 ⑥들려줄까 합니다. / three stories (which have been experienced) from my life[인생에서 경험한 3가지 이야기]

That's it. No big deal. Just three stories. - 그것이 전부입니다. 굉장한 것도 아니며, 단지 3가지 이야기 뿐입니다.

The first story is about connecting the dots. - 그 첫 번째 이야기는 점과 연결된 것에 관한 것입니다. / is about[전치사]+~ing[connecting~연결에 관한 것]

①I ③dropped out of Reed College ②after the first 6 months, but then ⑦stayed around ⑥as a drop-in ⑤for another 18 months or so ④before I really quit. ⑧So ⑨why did I drop out? - ①저는 ②첫 학기 6개월 만에 ③리드대학을 중퇴했습니다. ④완전히 그만두기 전, ⑤18개월쯤 ⑥중퇴자로 ⑦방황하였습니다. ⑧그럼 ⑨왜 제가 중퇴했을까요? / drop out[~을 중퇴하다] / stay around[배회하다, 방황하다] / as [전치사: ~로써] another 18 months or so[또 다른 18개월 쯤]

🔖 **단어분석**

honor [ɑ́nər] vt. ① 존경[존중]하다(respect) ② ~에게 수여하다(with). / **deal** [diː l] n. 관계. 협정. 대우.

🔖 **동의어/반의어**

<u>**graduate**</u> n. alumna[əlʌ́mnə] n. (특히 대학의) (남자) 졸업생, 동창생 / **bachelor**[bǽtʃələr] n. ① 미혼[독신] 남자. [cf.] spinster. ② 학사 / **grade**[greid] vt. 등급[격]을 매기다, 유별하다, (답안 등을) 채점하다. / **measure**[méʒə r] vt. 재다, 계량[측정, 측량]하다. ~ 을 판단하다, 평가하다.

It started before I was born. My biological mother was a young, unwed college graduate student, and she decided to put me up for adoption. She felt very strongly that I should be adopted by college graduates, so everything was all set for me to be adopted at birth by a lawyer and his wife. Except that when I popped out they decided at the last minute that they really wanted a girl. So my parents, who were on a waiting list, got a call in the middle of

"You've got to find what you love"

by Steve Jobs at Stanford University

the night asking: "We have an unexpected baby boy; do you want him?" They said: "Of course." My biological mother later found out that my mother had never graduated from college and that my father had never graduated from high school. She refused to sign the final adoption papers. She only relented a few months later when my parents promised that I would someday go to college.

📎 **본문해석+문법분석**

It started before I was born. - 이 이야기는 제가 태어나기 전에 시작되었습니다. / It[=adoption양자를 삼는 일] / before[시간의 부사절:~하기 전]

①**My biological mother** ②**was a young, unwed college graduate student, and** ④**she decided to** ③ **put me up for adoption.** - ①저의 생물학적 어머니(생모)는 ②젊고 미혼인 대학생이어서 ③저를 양자로 보내기로 ④했습니다. / biological mother[생모] / decide to do[to부정사를 목적어로 취함: ~하기로 결심하다] / put me[대명사] up for adoption[나를 양자로 보낼 것을 알리다]

①**She** ④**felt very strongly that** ②**I** ③**should be adopted by college graduates,** ⑤**so everything** ⑧ **was all set for me to be adopted** ⑥**at birth** ⑦**by a lawyer and his wife.** - ①그녀는 ②제가 ③대학졸업생 부모에게 양자로 가야만 한다고 ④집착하여서 ⑤모든 것이 ⑥태어날 때 ⑦한 변호사 부부에게 ⑧이미 가기로 결정되었습니다. / felt very strongly that[~에 강하게 느끼다. 집착하다로 해석함] / should[조동사로 의무: ~해야만 하다] / everything was all set[모든 것이 준비되었다] / 주어가 everything이므로 to be adopted[수동태]로 쓰임 by의 의해 수식

①**Except that** ②**when I popped out** ③**they** ⑥**decided** ④**at the last minute that** ⑤**they really wanted a girl.** - ①그것 외에도 ②내가 태어났을 때, ③그들은 ④마지막 순간에 ⑤여자아이를 원한다고 ⑥마음을 바꾸었습니다. / except that[전치사 구나 절: 그것 외에도] / pop out[세상에 나오다] / decide that[절을 받음: 마지막 순간에 마음이 변하다]

①**So** ②**my parents, who were on a waiting list,** ④**got a call** ③**in the middle of the night asking:** "⑤**We** ⑥**have an unexpected baby boy;** ⑦**do you want him?"** ⑧**They said: "Of course."** - ①그래서 ②대기명단에 있던 저희 부모님은 ③한밤중에 ④전화를 받으셨습니다. ⑤저흰 ⑥기대하지 않은 남자아이를 받았어요. ⑦그 아일 원하시나요? ⑧그들은 승낙하였던 것입니다. / who[주격 관계대명사로: 대기 명단에 있던 제 부모(선행사)] / asking[a call을 수식함: ~요구하는 전화]

①**My biological mother** ④**later found out that** ②**my mother had never graduated from college and that** ③**my father had never graduated from high school.** - ①저를 낳은 어머니는 ②제 어머니가 대학을 다닌 적도 ③제 아버지가 고등학교를 졸업한 적도 없다는 사실을 ④나중에야 알았습니다. / later found out that[that이하의 사실을 나중에야 알게 되었다]

①**She** ④**refused** ③**to sign** ②**the final adoption papers.** - ①그녀는 ②마지막 양자서류에 ③서명을 ④거절했습니다. / refuse to sign[refuse는 to 부정사인 sign을 목적어로 받음: ~하는 것을 거절하다]

⑤**She only relented** ①**a few months later when** ②**my parents** ④**promised that** ③**I would someday go to college.** - ①몇 달 후 ②제 부모님이 ③절 앞으로 대학에 진학시킬 것이라고 ④약속한 후에야 ⑤마음이 풀렸던 것입니다. / only relented when[~했을 때서야 마음이 풀리다]

단어분석

unwed a. 미혼의(unmarried) / **adoption** [ədápʃən] n. 양자결연 / **put up for** 팔려고 내놓다. / **refuse** [rifjúːz] vt. 거절하다. / **relent** [rilént] vi. 누그러지다. 가엾게 여기다.

동의어/반의어

relent v. **give in, relax** 완화하다. / **soften** [sɔ́(ː)f-ən] vt. 마음을 누그러지게 하다. / **submit** [səbmít] vt. 복종시키다. 제출하다. / **yield** [jiːld] vi. 산출하다(produce), (이익 따위를) 가져오다. 포기하다.

동영상 강좌 http://youtu.be/rNNpfr5HptY

And 17 years later I did go to college. But I naively chose a college that was almost as expensive as Stanford, and all of my working-class parents' savings were being spent on my college tuition. After six months, I couldn't see the value in it. I had no idea what I wanted to do with my life and no idea how college was going to help me figure it out. And here I was spending all of the money my parents had saved their entire life. So I decided to drop out and trust that it would all work out OK. It was pretty scary at the time, but looking back it was one of the best decisions I ever made. The minute I dropped out I could stop taking the required classes that didn't interest me, and begin dropping in on the ones that looked interesting.

본문해석+문법분석

And 17 years later I did go to college. - 그리고 17년이 지나 저는 대학에 정말로 들어갔습니다. / did [강조용법: I really went 약속을 지킴]

①**But I ③naively chose ②a college that was almost as expensive as Stanford, ④and all of my working-class parents' savings ⑤were being spent on my college tuition.** - ①그러나 저는 ②스탠퍼드처럼 거의 비싼 대학을 ③섣불리 선택했습니다. ④그리고 저의 맞벌이 부모님의 저축 모두는 ⑤제 대학등록금으로 쓰이고 있었습니다. / a college that[관계대명사: ~한 대학] / as expensive[동급비교: 형용사] as[~처럼 비싼 등록금의] / all of[~의 모든] / parents'[복수형으로 끝날 경우 소유격은 ' apostrophe: 아포스트로피만 붙임] / were being spent[과거 수동진행형: 쓰이고 있었다]

After six months, I couldn't see the value in it. I had no idea what I wanted to do with my life and no idea how college was going to help me figure it out. - 6개월 후, 저는 대학에서의 가치를 찾을 수가 없었습니다. 저는 제 인생에서 무얼 하고 싶은지 대학이 제가 인생을 이해하는 데 도움을 줄까에 회의를 느꼈습니다. / the value in it[=college 대학에서의 가치] / had no idea[몰랐다] / figure it[=my life] out[내 인생을 이해하다]

①**And here I ④was spending all of the money ②my parents ③had saved their entire life.** - ①그리고 이곳 대학에서 저는 ②제 부모님이 ③그들이 평생 모아둔 ④돈을 낭비하고 있었습니다. / here[=at the

15

college 이곳과 같은 대학] / was spending[과거 진행형: 낭비하고 있었다] / all the money (which/that) [목적격 관계대명사, saved의 목적어는 선행사인 all of the money임] (during) their entire life[평생 동안]

①So I decided to drop out and ③trust that ②it would all work out OK. ④It was pretty scary at the time, but ⑤looking back ⑥it ⑧was ⑦one of the best decisions I ever made. - ①그래서 저는 중퇴를 결심했고 ②이 모든 것이 잘될 것이라 ③믿었습니다. ④그 당시엔 아주 무서웠습니다만 ⑤그때를 돌이 켜보면 ⑥그것은 ⑦제가 내린 결정 중 최고의 것 중 ⑧하나였습니다. / I decided to drop out and (decided to) trust / would[will의 과거로 시제의 일치] / work out OK[일이 잘되다] at the time[그 당시에] / looking back[동명사로 주어:~과거를 돌이켜 보는 것은] / one of the best decisions[복수명사: 최고의 선택 중 하나] (that/which) I ever made[제가 지금껏 내린 최고의 결정]

①The minute I dropped out ②I ④could stop taking ③the required classes that didn't interest me, and ⑥begin dropping in on ⑤the ones that looked interesting. - ①제가 중퇴를 하는 순간 ②저는 ③흥미 없는 필수과목을 ④수강할 필요가 없었고 ⑤흥미로울 것 같은 과목들을 ⑥잠시 듣기 시작했습니다.

🔖 **단어분석**

naive 순진한 / **trust** [trʌst] vt. 신뢰하다 / **minute** [mínit] n. 순간(moment) / **drop in** (1) 잠깐 들르다; 불시에 방문하다(on; at). (2) 우연히 만나다(across; on; with)

🔖 **동의어/반의어**

naive a. ingenuous[indʒénjuː əs], innocent[ínəsnt], gullible[gʌ́ləbəl], trusting[trʌ́stiŋ], ant. wise[waiz]

It wasn't all romantic. I didn't have a dorm room, so I slept on the floor in friends' rooms, I returned coke bottles for the 5¢ deposits to buy food with, and I would walk the 7 miles across town every Sunday night to get one good meal a week at the Hare Krishna temple. I loved it. And much of what I stumbled into by following my curiosity and intuition turned out to be priceless later on. Let me give you one example:

🔖 **본문해석+문법분석**

It wasn't all romantic. I didn't have a dorm room, so I slept on the floor in friends' rooms, I ③returned ②coke bottles for the 5¢ deposits ①to buy food with, and ⑧I would walk the 7 miles ⑦across town ⑥every Sunday night ⑤to get one good meal a week ④at the Hare Krishna temple. I loved it. - 그것 은 꼭 낭만적인 것만은 아니었습니다. 저는 기숙사 방이 없었습니다. 그래서 친구들 집 바닥에서 잠을 잤습니 다. ①저는 음식을 사기 위해 ②5센트가 적립되어있는 콜라병을 ③가져다주고 ④해어 크리쉬마 사원에서 ⑤매주 한 번의 맛있는 음식을 얻기 위해 ⑥일요일 밤마다 ⑦마을을 가로질러 ⑦7마일을 걷곤 했습니다. 저는 이것이 좋았습니다. / wasn't all[부분부정: 꼭 ~한 것만은 아니었다] / coke bottles for the 5¢ deposits[5센트가 적 립되어 있는 콜라병] / to buy food with[전치사 with의 목적어는 the 5¢ deposits] / would[과거에 ~하곤 했다]

And ②much of what I stumbled into ①by following my curiosity and intuition ④turned out ③to

be priceless later on. **Let me give you one example:** - 그리고 ①저의 호기심과 직관력에 의해 ②제가 좌절했던 많은 것들은 ③이후 아주 귀중한 것으로 ④입증되었습니다. 제가 한 예를 드리겠습니다. / much of + what[불가산 명사] ~ into[목적어는 what] / by[수단을 나타내는 전치사] / turned out to[~로 입증되다]

📎 **단어분석**

dorm [dɔː rm] n. dormitory 기숙사 / **stumble** [stʌmb-əl] vi. 넘어지다, 우연히 만나다(across; on, upon) / **curiosity** [kjùəriásəti] n. 호기심 / **intuition** [ìntjuíʃən] n. 직관(력) / **priceless** [práislis] a. 아주 귀중한

📎 **동의어/반의어**

priceless a. costly[kɔː stli], inestimable[inéstəməbəl], precious[préʃəs] ant. worthless[wə́ː rəlis]

Reed College at that time offered perhaps the best calligraphy instruction in the country. Throughout the campus every poster, every label on every drawer, was beautifully hand calligraphed. Because I had dropped out and didn't have to take the normal classes, I decided to take a calligraphy class to learn how to do this. I learned about serif and san serif typefaces, about varying the amount of space between different letter combinations, about what makes great typography great. It was beautiful, historical, artistically subtle in a way that science can't capture, and I found it fascinating.

📎 **본문해석+문법분석**

②**Reed College** ①**at that time** ⑥**offered** ④**perhaps** ⑤**the best calligraphy instruction** ③**in the country.** - ①그 당시 ②리드대학은 ③미국에서 ④아마도 ⑤가장 권위 있는 서예 강좌를 ⑥개설하고 있었습니다. / at that time[그 당시] / offered[=provided제공하다]

①**Throughout the campus** ②**every poster,** ③**every label on every drawer,** ④**was beautifully hand calligraphed.** - ①캠퍼스 어디든 ②포스터와 ③서랍 위에 라벨 모두 ④아름다운 붓글씨로 써져 있었습니다. / throughout[내내, ~의 도처에] / every+단수명사

①**Because** ②**I had dropped out and** ③**didn't have to take the normal classes,** ④**I** ⑦**decided** ⑥**to take a calligraphy class** ⑤**to learn how to do this.** - ①왜냐하면 ②저는 중퇴하였고 ③일반강의를 수강할 필요가 없었기 때문에, ④저는 ⑤이것이 어떻게 되는지를 알기 위해서 ⑥서예 강좌를 수강하기로 ⑦결정했습니다. / had dropped[과거완료: 더 이전에 일어난 사실] / didn't have to[=didn't need to: ~할 필요가 없었다] / decided to take[decided는 to부정사를 목적어로 취함]

①**I** ⑥**learned** ②**about serif and san serif typefaces,** ④**about varying the amount of space** ③ **between different letter combinations,** ⑤**about what makes great typography great.** - ①저는 ②세리프와 산 세리프 서체에 관해서, ③다른 글자 조합 사이의 ④공간의 다양성에 관해서, 그리고 ⑤멋진 인쇄술을 위대하게 만드는 것에 관해서 ⑥배웠습니다. / learned의 목적어는 about serif ~, about varying, (and) about what[의문사] makes A B

①It was ③beautiful, historical, ④artistically subtle ②in a way that science can't capture, and ⑤I found it fascinating. - ①그것은 ②과학이 이해할 수 없는 방식에서 ③아름답고, 역사적이고, ④예술적인 미묘한 것이어서 ⑤저는 이것의 매력에 빠졌습니다. / it[=calligraphy] / in a way that[관계대명사: capture의 목적어인 a way를 수식] / found it[목적어] fascinating[목적격 보어] 5형식 문장

🔖 **단어분석**

calligraphy [kəlígrəfi] n. 서예 / serif, seriph [sérif] n. (인쇄활자) 세리프 / typeface [táipfèis] n. (활자) 서체, 체. / vary [vέəri] vt. 다양하게 하다. / typography [taipágrəfi] n. 활판 인쇄, 조판 / subtle [sʌ́tl] a. 미묘한

🔖 **동의어/반의어**

subtle a. implied[impláid]암시하는, indirect[indirékt]간접적인, insinuated[insínjuèit]은근히 심어준, astute[əstjú: t]기민한, 교활한, discriminating[diskrímənèiti식별하는, keen[ki: n], sly[slai], wily[wáili]잔꾀를 쓰는, delicate[délikət], intricate[íntrəkit]
ant. obvious[ábviəs], undiscerning[ʌndisə́: rniŋ], guileless[gáillis], blatant[bléitənt] 주제넘게 구는

동영상 강좌 http://youtu.be/xX4q9NLz1HE

None of this had even a hope of any practical application in my life. But ten years later, when we were designing the first Macintosh computer, it all came back to me. And we designed it all into the Mac. It was the first computer with beautiful typography. If I had never dropped in on that single course in college, the Mac would have never had multiple typefaces or proportionally spaced fonts. And since Windows just copied the Mac, it's likely that no personal computer would have them. If I had never dropped out, I would have never dropped in on this calligraphy class, and personal computers might not have the wonderful typography that they do. Of course it was impossible to connect the dots looking forward when I was in college. But it was very, very clear looking backwards ten years later.

🔖 **본문해석+문법분석**

①**None of this** ④**had** ③**even a hope of any practical application in my life.** - ①이 어떠한 것도 ②제 인생에 ③심지어 실질적인 응용할 희망을 ④주진 못했습니다. / None[「~ of+단수(대)명사」 조금도 ---않다] / any ~ in my life[실생활에 활용]

①**But ten years later,** ④**when** ②**we** ③**were designing the first Macintosh computer,** ⑤**it all** ⑦ **came back** ⑥**to me.**
- ①그러나 10년이 지나, ②저희가 ③첫 번째 매킨토쉬 컴퓨터를 디자인하고 있을 ④때, ⑤이 모든 것이 ⑥저에게로 ⑦돌아왔습니다. / it all came back to me[이 모든 것이 돌아왔다. 현실에 적용되었음을 의미]

①And ④designed ②it all ③into the Mac. - ①그리고 우리는 ②이 모든 것을 ③맥 안으로 ④디자인해 넣었습니다. / designed A[it all] into B[the Mac] : A를 B 안으로 디자인해 넣다.

It was the first computer with beautiful typography. - 그것이 아름다운 인쇄체를 갖은 첫 번째 컴퓨터였습니다. / It[=the first Macintosh computer]

①If I ④had never dropped in on ③that single course ②in college, ⑤the Mac ⑧would have ⑥ never had ⑦multiple typefaces or proportionally spaced fonts. - ①만일 제가 ②대학에서 ③그 유일한 과정을 ④잠시 듣지 못했더라면, ⑤맥은 ⑥결코 ⑦다양한 인쇄체 또는 균형 잡힌 공간의 글꼴을 ⑧갖지 못했을 것입니다. / [가정법 과거완료(과거 사실에 반대)] If I had never dropped[had+과거분사] ~, the Mac would have never had[조동사(would, might, could, should)+have+p.p] : ~ 했었더라면, ~ 했을 것이다 [과거 사실에 반대]

①And ③since ②Windows just copied the Mac, ⑥it's likely that ④no personal computer ⑤would have them. - ①그리고 ②윈도우가 단지 맥을 베꼈기 ③때문에, ④어떠한 컴퓨터도 ⑤그것들(멋진 인쇄체)을 갖지 못할 것 ⑥같습니다. / since[=because] / would[가정법: ~일 것이다] / them[=multiple typefaces or proportionally spaced fonts]

①If I had never dropped out, ②I ④would have never dropped in on ③this calligraphy class, and ⑤personal computers ⑧might not have ⑦the wonderful typography ⑥that they do. - ①만일 제가 중퇴하지 않았더라면, ②저는 ③이 서예 수업을 ④잠시 듣지도 못했을 뿐더러, ⑤개인용 컴퓨터도 ⑥그것들이 갖고 있는 ⑦경이로운 서체를 ⑧갖지 못했을 것입니다. / [가정법 과거완료 표현-과거사실에 반대] If I had ~, [가정법 과거-현재 사실에 반대] might not have[혼합가정법] / they do[=have]

①Of course ④it was impossible ③to connect the dots looking forward ②when I was in college. - ①물론 ②제 대학시절엔 ③점들을 미래와 연결하는 것은 ④불가능했습니다. / it[가주어] ~ (for me)[의미상의 주어] to connect[진주어] / the dots looking forward[미래를 향한 점들]

But it was ①very, very clear ③looking backwards ②ten years later. - 그러나 ①아주 분명했던 것은 ②10후에 ③과거로 복귀하고 있었다는 것입니다. / very, very[부사: 강조용법]는 looking[동사]를 수식

🐚 단어분석

multiple [mʌ́ltəp-əl] a. 복합의, 다양한 / **proportional** [prəpɔ́ː rʃənəl] a. 비례의, 비례하는(to)

🐚 동의어/반의어

proportional a. consistent[kənsístənt], harmonious[haː rmóuniəs], complementary[kàmpləméntəri]보충하는, proportionate[prəpɔ́ː rʃənit] ant. asymmetrical

"You've got to find what you love"

by Steve Jobs at Stanford University

❋ 다음 글을 읽고 물음에 답하시오. [1~5]

This is a prepared text of the Commencement address delivered by Ⓐ **Steve Jobs**, CEO of Apple Computer and of Pixar Animation Studios, on June 12, 2005.

I am honored to be with you today ① **at your commencement** from one of the finest universities in the world. I never graduated from college. Truth be told, ② **this is the closest I've ever gotten to a college graduation**. Today I want to tell you three stories from my life. That's it. ③ **No big deal**. Just three stories.

The first story is about connecting the dots. I dropped out of Reed College after the first 6 months, but then stayed around as a drop-in for another 18 months or so before I really quit. So why did I drop out?

④ **It started before I was born**. My biological mother was a young, unwed college graduate student, and she decided to put me up for adoption. She felt very strongly that I should be adopted by college graduates, so everything was all set for me to be adopted at birth by a lawyer and his wife. Except that when I popped out they decided at the last minute that they really wanted a girl. So my parents, who were on a waiting list, got a call in the middle of the night asking: "⑤ **We have an unexpected baby boy**; do you want him?" They said: "Of course." My biological mother later found out that my mother had never graduated from college and that my father had never graduated from high school. She refused to sign the final adoption papers. She only relented a few months later when my parents promised that I would someday go to college.

1. 위 글의 제목으로 가장 적절한 것은?

① Unhappy period in youth
② Adoption in the long way
③ Regret as a drop-out
④ Home without affection
⑤ Three stories at the commencement

2. 위 글의 분위기에 어울리는 단어는?

① interesting　　　② enthusiastic
③ disappointing　　④ gloomy
⑤ indifferent

3. 위 글에서 밑줄 친 Ⓐ와 관계가 없는 것은?

① An addressor at the graduation ceremony
② A successful entrepreneur
③ A drop-out at the college
④ A adopted son
⑤ A man grown in affluent home

4. 위 글에서 밑줄 친 ①~⑤중, 우리말 해석이 어색한 것은?

① 여러분의 졸업식장에서
② 이번이 제가 대학졸업식으로 온 가장 가까운 곳
③ 흥미진진한 이야기
④ 이야기는 제가 태어나기 전부터 시작되었다.
⑤ 반갑지 않은 사내아이가 태어났다.

5. 위 글을 통하여 알 수 없는 사실은?

① Who is CEO of Apple Computer?
② How many topics does he present?
③ How was his domestic background?
④ How was his school performance?
⑤ What was his biological mother like?

And 17 years later I did go to college. But I naively chose a college that was almost as expensive as Stanford, and all of my working-class parents' savings were being spent on my college tuition. After six months, I couldn't see the value in ① it. I had no idea what I wanted to do with my life and no idea how college was going to help me figure it out. And here I was spending all of the money my parents had saved their entire life. So I decided to drop out and trust that ② it would all work out OK. ③ It was pretty scary at the time, but looking back ④ it was one of the best decisions I ever made. The minute I dropped out I could stop taking the required classes that didn't interest me, and begin dropping in on the ones that looked interesting.
_____ Ⓐ _____. I didn't have a dorm room, so I slept on the floor in friends' rooms, I returned coke bottles for the 5¢ deposits to buy food with, and I would walk the 7 miles across town every Sunday night to get one good meal a week at the Hare Krishna temple. I loved ⑤ it. And much of what I stumbled into by following Ⓑ _____ turned out to be priceless later on. Let me give you one example:

6. 위 글의 주제로 가장 적절한 것은?

① In the end of wandering something was found for his future.

② Education should equally spread to all.

③ Drop-out is sometimes necessary for a genius.

④ Home environment is so important in the childhood.

⑤ Divorce should be prevented as soon as possible.

7. 위 글에서 밑줄 친 ①~⑤중, 각각 가리키는 것이 올바르지 않은 것은?

① my college tuition

② their entire life

③ to drop out

④ the drop-out

⑤ the wandering time

8. 위 글에서 밑줄 친 빈칸 Ⓐ에 적절한 표현은?

① It was a good time for change

② It wasn't all romantic

③ I had many good friends

④ I was happy at that time

⑤ The study was too hard to follow school

9. 위 글에서 밑줄 친 빈칸 Ⓑ에 적절한 표현은?

① my entertaining journey

② my endless thought

③ my curiosity and intuition

④ my hard study

⑤ my endurance and observation

10. 위 글과 일치하지 않은 것은?

① 내가 입학한 대학은 스탠퍼드처럼 유명한 곳이었다.

② 저의 부모님의 평생 번 돈은 내 학비로 쓰였다.

③ 나는 대학에 대한 가치를 찾을 수 없었

"You've got to find what you love"

by Steve Jobs at Stanford University

다.

④ 나는 대학을 중퇴한 것에 후회하지 않는다.

⑤ 방황 속에서 터득한 경험은 후에 귀중한 것이 되었다.

❋ 다음 글을 읽고 물음에 답하시오. [11~15]

Reed College at that time offered perhaps the best calligraphy instruction in the country. Throughout the campus every poster, every label on every drawer, was ① **beautifully** hand calligraphed. ____Ⓐ____ I had dropped out and didn't have to take the normal classes, I decided to take a calligraphy class to learn how to do this. I learned about serif and san serif typefaces, about ② **varying** the amount of space between different letter combinations, about what makes great typography great. It was beautiful, historical, artistically subtle in a way that science can't capture, and I found it ③ **fascinated**.

None of this had even a hope of any practical application in my life. But ten years later, when we were designing the first Macintosh computer, it all came back to me. And we designed it all into the Mac. It was the first computer with beautiful typography. If I had never dropped in on that single course in college, the Mac would have never had multiple typefaces or ④ **proportionally** spaced fonts. And ____Ⓑ____ Windows just copied the Mac, it's likely that no personal computer would have them. If I had never dropped out, I would have never dropped in on this calligraphy class, and personal computers might not have the wonderful typography

that they do. Of course it was impossible to connect the dots ⑤ **looking** forward when I was in college. But it was very, very clear looking backwards ten years later.

11. 위 글의 주제로 가장 적절한 것은?

① To learn study earlier would be more helpful.

② The Mac would be the most significant computer later on.

③ The experiences in the past would be great results.

④ There are many science can't prove in the world.

⑤ Time doesn't wait for a man.

12. 위 글에서 작가의 심정으로 가장 적절한 것은?

① desperate   ② satisfied

③ undeterminable   ④ discouraged

⑤ confused

13. 위 글에서 밑줄 친 ①~⑤중, 어법상 어색한 것은?

①   ②   ③   ④   ⑤

14. 위 글에서 밑줄 친 빈칸 Ⓐ, Ⓑ에 적절한 단어는?

① Though   because

② If   when

③ Because   since

④ Since   though

⑤ When   now that

15. 위 글의 내용과 일치하는 것은?

① 대학들 사이에 서예 강좌의 열풍이 불었다.

② 인쇄체 글꼴은 큰 매력이 없었다.

③ 작가는 과학이 증명할 수 없는 멋에 빠져 있었다.

④ 맥과 윈도우는 각각의 독특한 특성을 갖고 있었다.

⑤ 지은이는 대학시절부터 점과의 연결에 관심이 많았다.

1. ⑤	2. ④	3. ⑤	4. ③	5. ④
6. ①	7. ②	8. ②	9. ③	10. ①
11. ③	12. ②	13. ③	14. ③	15. ③

"You've got to find what you love"

by Steve Jobs at Stanford University

동영상 강좌 http://youtu.be/HzaM-bJj63M

Again, you can't connect the dots looking forward; you can only connect them looking backwards. So you have to trust that the dots will somehow connect in your future. You have to trust in something — your gut, destiny, life, karma, whatever. This approach has never let me down, and it has made all the difference in my life.

🔖 **본문해석+문법분석**

①**Again,** ②**you** ④**can't connect** ③**the dots looking forward;** ⑤**you** ⑦**can only connect** ⑥**them looking backwards.**

- ①다시 말해, ②여러분들은 ③미래로 향하는 점을 ④연결할 수는 없습니다. ⑤여러분은 ⑥과거로 향하는 점⑦만을 연결할 수 있습니다. / the dots (which are) looking forward[미래로 향하는 점들] / them[=the dots] (which are) looking backwards[과거로 향하는 점들]

①**So** ②**you** ④**have to trust that** ③**the dots will somehow connect in your future.** - ①그래서 ②여러분은 ③그 점들은 미래엔 여하튼 연결될 것이라고 ④믿어야만 합니다. (확신과 신념을 갖으라는 의미)

①**You** ⑦**have to trust in something** — ②**your gut,** ③**destiny,** ④**life,** ⑤**karma,** ⑥**whatever.** - ①여러분은 ②용기, ③운명, ④인생, ⑤인연, ⑥무엇이든지를 ⑦믿어야만 합니다. / whatever[복합관계대명사: 무엇이든]

①**This approach** ②**has never let me down, and** ③**it** ⑤**has made all the difference** ④**in my life.** - ①이 접근법은 ②저를 낙담시킨 적도 없고 ③이것은 ④제 인생에 ⑤모든 것에 영향을 미쳐왔습니다. / this approach[위 문장의 모든 것을 믿는 일] / has never let[현재완료 경험: ~ 한 적이 전혀 없는] / it[=this approach] / has made all the difference[모든 것에 영향을 미쳐왔다]

🔖 **단어분석**

somehow [sʌ́mhàu] ad. 여하튼, 어쨌든 / **trust** [trʌst] vi. 신뢰하다(in). 기대하다(to). / **gut** [gʌt] n. (pl.) (구어) 용기, 배짱, 결단력 / **destiny** [déstəni] n. 운명 / **karma** [káːrmə] n. 인과응보, 인연. / **approach** [əpróutʃ] n. 접근(of; to), (문제 따위의) 접근법, 해결 방법. / **make a [the] difference** (1) 차이를 낳다; 차별을 두다(between). (2) 효과를 내다, 영향을 미치다; 중요하다(to)

🔖 **동의어/반의어**

difference n. cdistinction[distíŋkʃən], variation[vὲəriéiʃən], deviation[dìːviéiʃən]벗어남, 탈선, discrepancy[diskrépənsi]불일치, disparity[dispǽrəti], divergence[divɔ́ːrdʒəns], argument[áːrgjəmənt], quarrel[kwɔ́ːrəl]싸움, 말다툼 ant. similarity[siməlǽrəti], harmony[háːrməni]

My second story is about love and loss.
I was lucky — I found what I loved to do early in life. Woz and I started Apple in my parents garage when I was 20. We worked hard, and in 10 years Apple had grown from just

the two of us in a garage into a $2 billion company with over 4000 employees. We had just released our finest creation — the Macintosh — a year earlier, and I had just turned 30. And then I got fired. How can you get fired from a company you started? Well, as Apple grew we hired someone who I thought was very talented to run the company with me, and for the first year or so things went well. But then our visions of the future began to diverge and eventually we had a falling out. When we did, our Board of Directors sided with him. So at 30 I was out. And very publicly out. What had been the focus of my entire adult life was gone, and it was devastating.

📖 본문해석+문법분석

My second story is about love and loss. - 저의 두 번째 이야기는 사랑과 실패입니다. / about[전치사: ~에 관한]

I was lucky — I found what I loved to do early in life. - 저는 운이 좋았습니다. - 저는 어린나이에 제가 하고 싶었던 것을 찾았습니다. / [목적어인 명사절]what I loved to do[목적어는 what] / early in life[어린 나이에]

①Woz and I ④started Apple ③in my parents garage ②when I was 20. - ①우즈와 저는 ②제 나이 20세 때 ③저의 부모님 차고에서 ④애플컴퓨터를 시작했습니다. / Apple[애플 컴퓨터]

①We worked hard, and ②in 10 years ③Apple ⑦had grown ④from just the two of us in a garage ⑥into a $2 billion company ⑤with over 4000 employees. - ①우리는 열심히 일했고 ②10년 만에 ③애플은 ④차고에서 2명으로 시작하여 ⑤4,000명 이상의 직원을 둔 ⑥20억 달러의 회사로 ⑦성장했던 것입니다. / in[=after~만에] / had grown[과거완료: 성장했다] / from just two of us[단지 우리 두 사람에서] / into[~으로]

①We ④had just released ②our finest creation — the Macintosh — ③a year earlier, and ⑤I had just turned 30.
- ①우리가 ②우리의 가장 최신 작품인 매킨토시를 ③년 일찍 ④막 출시하자 ⑤저는 곧 30세가 되었습니다. / [29세에 매킨토시를 출시했음을 의미.] / had just released[과거완료: 완료]

And then I got fired. How can ①you ③get fired ②from a company you started?
- 그리고 나서 저는 해고되었습니다. ①당신은 ②당신이 설립한 회사로부터 ③해고당할 수 있나요? / got + 과거분사[fired] : 해고당했다.

①Well, ②as Apple grew ③we hired ⑤someone who I thought was very talented ④to run the company with me, and ⑦for the first year or so ⑧things went well.
- ①글쎄요, ②애플사가 성장함에 따라, ③우리는 ④저와 함께 회사를 운영할 ⑤아주 재능 있는 사람을 ⑥고용했습니다. 그리고 ⑦1년쯤 ⑧일을 잘되었습니다. / someone who[주격관계대명사] (I thought[생략가능]) was ~

"You've got to find what you love"

by Steve Jobs at Stanford University

①But then ②our visions of the future ③began to diverge and ④eventually we had a falling out.
- ①한편 ②미래에 대한 우리의 비전은 ③어긋나기 시작했고 ④결국 우리는 추락을 했습니다.

①When we did, ②our Board of Directors ③sided with him. ④So at 30 I was out.
- ①우리가 추락했을 때, ②이사진은 ③그의 편을 들어줬고 ④저는 30세에 쫓겨났습니다. / did[= had a falling out] / sided with[~편을 들다] / out[=fired]

And very publicly out. ①What had been the focus of my entire adult life ②was gone, and ③it was devastating.
- 그리고 아주 공개적으로 쫓겨났습니다. ①제 모든 성인인생의 초점을 두었던 것이 ②사라졌고 처참했습니다. / (I was) very publicly out. / [주어]What had been ~ life[제 모든 것을 걸었던 것] was gone[=disappeared] / it[앞의 사실을 말함]

🔖 단어분석

loss [lɔ(ː)s] n. U 분실, C 손실, 손해, 실패, 패배. / **garage** [gərάːʒ] n. 차고, 주차장 / **diverge** [divə́ːrdʒ] vi. (진로 등을) 벗어나다(from). (의견 따위가) 갈라지다(from). / **falling** [fɔ́ːliŋ] n. U 낙하, 추락 / **devastating** [dévəstèitiŋ] a. 황폐시키는, 파괴적인

🔖 동의어/반의어

devastating a. calamitous[kəlǽmitəs], cataclysmic, disastrous[dizǽstrəs], ruinous[rúːinəs], desolating[désəleitiŋ], humiliating[hjuːmílièitiŋ], mortifying[mɔ́ːrtəfain], overwhelming[òuvərhwélmiŋ]
ant. helpful[hélpfəl], constructive[kənstrʌ́ktiv], encouraging[enkɔ́ːridʒiŋ]

I really didn't know what to do for a few months. I felt that I had let the previous generation of entrepreneurs down - that I had dropped the baton as it was being passed to me. I met with David Packard and Bob Noyce and tried to apologize for screwing up so badly. I was a very public failure, and I even thought about running away from the valley. But something slowly began to dawn on me — I still loved what I did. The turn of events at Apple had not changed that one bit. I had been rejected, but I was still in love. And so I decided to start over.

🔖 본문해석+문법분석

①I ④really didn't know ③what to do ②for a few months.
- ①저는 ②몇 달 동안 ③무엇을 해야 할지를 ④정말 몰랐습니다. / know의 목적어 what do to / for + 숫자, 시간

①I ⑤felt that ②I had let the previous generation of entrepreneurs down - that ④I had dropped the baton ③as it was being passed to me.
- ①저는 ②기업가의 구세대는 끝났고 ③저에게 이전되고 있었던 ④경영권을 포기해야겠다고 ⑤생각했습니다. /

let A down : A를 내려놓다[포기하다] / the baton[지휘권, 경영권] / it[=the baton] was being passed to me[과거 진행형: 나에게 계승되고 있었던 경영권]

①**I met with David Packard and Bob Noyce and ③tried to apologize ②for screwing up so badly.**
- ①저는 데이비드 패커드와 밥 노이스를 만났고 ②심하게 혼란을 가중시킨 것에 ③사과하려고 노력했습니다. / apologize for A[A를 사과하다] / so badly[심하게]는 screwing up를 수식

①**I was a very public failure, and ②I even ④thought ③about running away from the valley.**
- ①저는 공개적인 실패자였고 ②저는 심지어 ③이 실리콘벨리를 도망칠까도 ④생각했습니다. / a failure[a+추상명사=보통명사화 됨: 실패자]

①**But something slowly ②began to dawn on me — ③I still ⑤loved ④what I did.**
- ①그러나 뭔가가 서서히 ②저에게 떠오르기 시작했습니다. - ③저는 여전히 ④제가 했던 것에 ⑤애착을 갖고 있었습니다. / loved의 목적어 what I did[내가 했던 것]

①**The turn of events at Apple ③had not changed ②that one bit.**
- ①애플사에서의 사건의 반전은 ②조금도 ③바뀌지 않았습니다. / that[부사: 그 정도로] one bit[조금도]

①**I had been rejected, but ②I was still in love. ③And so ④I decided to start over.**
- ①저는 거절당했지만 ②여전히 열정을 갖고 있었습니다. ③그리하여 ④저는 다시 시작하기로 마음먹었습니다. / had been rejected[거절당했다] / still in love[여전히 정열 속에] / start over[처음부터 다시 시작하다]

📎 **단어분석**
baton [bǽtən] n. 사령장 / **dawn** [dɔːn] vi. 날이 새다. (생각이) 떠오르다(on, upon)

📎 **동의어/반의어**
dawn n. aurora[ərɔ́ːrə], cockcrow[[kɑ́k-kròu], daybreak[déibrèik], daylight [deílàit], morning[mɔ́ːrniŋ], advent[ǽdvent]도래, 출현, emergence[imɔ́ːrdʒəns]출현, inception[insépʃən]시작 v. appear[əpíər]출현하다, arise[əráiz], commence[kəméns]시작하다, emerge[imɔ́ːrdʒ]나오다, unfold[ʌnfóuld]펼치다 ant. dusk[dʌsk]땅거미, conclusion[kənklúːʒən]결론, elude[ilúːd]교묘히 피하다

I didn't see it then, but it turned out that getting fired from Apple was the best thing that could have ever happened to me. The heaviness of being successful was replaced by the lightness of being a beginner again, less sure about everything. It freed me to enter one of the most creative periods of my life.

📎 **본문해석+문법분석**
①I ④didn't see ③it ②then, but it turned out that ⑤getting fired from Apple ⑦was the best thing ⑥that could have ever happened to me.

"You've got to find what you love"

by Steve Jobs at Stanford University

- ①저는 ②그때 ③그것[기회를]을 ④보진 못했습니다만 ⑤애플사에서 해고당한 것은 ⑥저에게 일어날 수도 있었건 ⑦최고의 기회였습니다. / it[=the best thing, 다시 일어서기] / it[가주어] turned out[~가 입증되었다] that[진주어] / could have ever happened to me[나에게도 일어날 수도 있다는 가능성]

①**The heaviness of being successful** ③**was replaced by the lightness of being a beginner again,** ② **less sure about everything.**

- ①성공의 중압감은 ②모든 것이 덜 확실한, ③다시 시작하는 초심자의 가벼움으로 바뀌었습니다. / was replaced by[~의해 대체되다] / a beginner, (who was) less sure[덜 확실한(부담이 덜한)]

①**It** ③**freed me to enter** ②**one of the most creative periods of my life.**

- ①그것[초심자의 마음]은 ②제 인생의 가장 창의적인 시기 중 하나로 ③저를 이끌었습니다. / freed me to enter[내가 ~로 들어가게 해방시켜 주었다] / one of 복수명사[~ periods]

📖 **단어분석**

successful [səksésfəl] a. 성공한, 출세한 / **replace** [ripléis] vt. ~에 대체하다.

📖 **동의어/반의어**

successful a. flourishing [fləː ririʃ], prosperous[práspərəs], thriving[θráiviŋ], eminent[émənənt]저명한, conquering[káŋkəriŋ], triumphant[traiʌmfənt]승리를 거둔, 성공한, victorious[viktɔː riəs], effective[iféktiv], fruitful[frúː tfəl], productive[prədʌktiv] ant. failing[féiliŋ], obscure[əbskjúər], unsuccessful[ʌnsəksésfəl], futile[fjúː tl]

✻ 다음을 읽고 물음에 답하시오. [16~19]

 Again, you can't connect the dots looking forward; you can only connect them looking backwards. So you have to trust that the dots will somehow connect in your future. You have to trust in something — your gut, destiny, life, karma, whatever. This approach has never let me down, and it has made all the difference in my life.

My second story is _____ⓐ_____.
I was lucky — I found what I loved to do early in life. Woz and I started Apple in my parents garage when I was 20. We worked hard, and in 10 years Apple had grown from just the two of us in a garage into a $2 billion company with over 4000 employees. We had just released our finest creation — the Macintosh — a year earlier, and I had just turned 30. And then I got fired. How can you get fired from a company you started? Well, as Apple grew we hired someone who I thought was very talented to run the company with me, and for the first year or so things went well. But then our visions of the future began to diverge and eventually we had a falling out. When we did, our Board of Directors sided with him. So at 30 I was out. And very publicly out. What had been the focus of my entire adult life was gone, and it was devastating.

16. 위 글의 제목으로 가장 적절한 것은?

① My difficult start in Apple

② The big failure in business

③ My pleasure and setback

④ The way to cope with any adversities

⑤ Dots only for looking backward

17. 위 글에서 밑줄 친 빈칸 ⓐ에 적절한 표현은?

① about success with enthusiasm

② about the beginning of my Apple company

③ about how to create new items for success

④ about making good friends in business

⑤ about love and loss

18. 위 글에 나타난 지은이의 상황과 어울리지 않은 것은?

① calamitous   ② catastrophic

③ disastrous   ④ humiliating

⑤ constructive

19. 위 글과 일치하는 것은?

① Dots should only be connected with the future.

② The writer puts emphasis on reality in life.

③ For the start the writer would be assisted by many good friends.

④ The addressor would be happy with someone who was hired for the company.

⑤ After fired, the author didn't care about his situation.

"You've got to find what you love"

by Steve Jobs at Stanford University

✻ 다음을 읽고 물음에 답하시오. [20~24]

I really didn't know what to do for a few months. I felt that I had let the previous generation of entrepreneurs ① **down** - that I had dropped the baton as it was being passed to me. I met with David Packard and Bob Noyce and tried to ② **apologize** for screwing up so badly. I was a very public failure, and I even thought about running away from the valley. But something slowly began to ③ **dawn** on me — I still loved what I did. The turn of events at Apple had not changed that one bit. I had been ④ **rejected**, but I was still in love. _____

I didn't see it then, but it turned out that getting fired from Apple was the best thing that could have ever happened to me. The heaviness of being successful was replaced by the lightness of being a beginner again, ⑤ **better** sure about everything. It freed me to enter one of the most creative periods of my life.

20. 위 글에서 밑줄 친 빈칸에 가장 적절한 표현은?

① And so I decided to start over.
② Something difficult in life delayed me opening the new.
③ The love is most important in the world.
④ Being fired is the saddest thing in the business.
⑤ My second start wasn't easy.

21. 위 글에서 밑줄 친 ①~⑤ 중, 문맥상 단

어의 쓰임이 <u>어색한</u> 것은?

①　　②　　③　　④　　⑤

22. 위 글에 나타나 있는 지은이의 상황에 어울리지 <u>않은</u> 것은?

① a failed entrepreneur
② a expected successor
③ a public failure
④ a new beginner
⑤ a past attached generation

23. 위 글로 보아 지은이의 성격으로 가장 적절한 단어는?

① arrogant　　② inflexible
③ conventional　　④ creative
⑤ critical

24. 위 글과 일치하지 <u>않은</u> 것은?

① 해고된 후, 몇 달 동안 방황을 하였다.
② 그는 곧 경영권 승계를 받을 예정이었다.
③ 자신의 과오를 시인했다.
④ 애플사의 태도는 점차 누그러지고 있었다.
⑤ 훌훌 털고 새롭게 시작하였다.

16. ③　17. ⑤　18. ⑤　19. ②　20. ①
21. ⑤ better → less　22. ⑤　23. ④
24. ④

Harvard Commencement Address

by Bill Gates

[난이도 ★★☆☆☆]

동영상 강좌 http://youtu.be/gwkguBE8LJQ

---

①President Bok, ②former President Rudenstine, ③incoming President Faust, ④members of the Harvard Corporation ⑤and the Board of Overseers, ⑥members of the faculty, ⑦ parents, ⑧and especially, the graduates

---

- ①복 총장님, ②전임 루덴스타인 총장님, ③신임 포스트 총장님, ④하버드 사단법인 여러분 ⑤그리고 감독 위원 여러분, ⑥교수진 여러분, ⑦학부모님, ⑧그리고 특히 졸업생 여러분
- former[이전, 전임] / incoming[후임의]
- incoming [inkʌmiŋ] a. 다음에 오는, 뒤를 잇는; 후임의. / corporation [kɔːrpəréiʃən] n. 법인
- **corporation** n. business[bíznis], establishment[istǽbliʃmənt], firm[fəːrm], organization[ɔːrgənizéiʃən]

---

①I've ④been waiting ③more than 30 years ②to say this: ⑤"Dad, I always told you ⑥I'd come back and get my degree." ①I ③want to thank Harvard ②for this timely honour. ①I'll ③be changing my job ②next year ... and ⑥it will be nice ⑤to finally have a college degree ④on my resume.

- ①저는 ②이 말씀을 드리려 ③30년 이상을 ④기다려 왔습니다: ⑤"아빠, 제가 늘 말씀 드렸죠. ⑥다시 돌아와 학위를 받을 거라고(졸업을 할 거라고)." ①저는 ②이 때맞춘 영광을 ③하버대학에 감사드리고 싶습니다. ①저는 ②내년에 ③제 직책을 바꿀 것입니다 ... 그리고 ④제 이력에 ⑤대학졸업장을 마침내 포함하는 것은 ⑥멋진 일이 될 것입니다.
- I have been waiting[현재완료 계속: ~기다려 왔다] / (for) more than 30 years[30년 이상 동안] / told you I would[told와 시제의 일치:~일 것이다] / thank A[Harvard] for B[this timely honour] 오늘의 영광을 하버드대학에 감사드립니다. /
- **timely** [táimli] a. 적시의, 때맞춘(seasonable)

---

①I ④applaud the graduates today ③for taking a much more direct route ②to your degrees. ①For my part, ⑥I'm just happy that ②the Crimson ⑤has called ③me ④"Harvard's most successful dropout."

- ①저는 ②여러분들이 학위를 받는데 ③훨씬 빠른 지름길을 택한 것에 대해 ④오늘 졸업생 여러분을 칭찬하고 싶습니다. ①제로서는, ②하버드 학생들이 ③저를 ④"하버드의 가장 성공한 중퇴자"라 ⑤부르는 것이 ⑥전 아주 행복합니다.
- applaud A[the graduates] for B[taking ~] : A가 B한 것에 칭찬하다 / taking A to B[A를 B로 가져가다] / the Crimson 하버드대학의 공식학교 색상, 여기서는 하버드 학생들 / call A B[5형식: A를 B라 부르다] / most successful[최상급: 가장 성공한]
- **applaud** [əplɔ́ːd] vi. 성원하다. 기리다. vt. ~에게 박수갈채하다 / **dropout** [-àut] n. 중퇴자
- **applaud** v. clap[klæp], congratulate[kəngrǽtʃəlèit], extol[ikstóul], laud[lɔːd], praise[preiz]   ant.

boo[buː] criticize[krítisàiz]

①I ⑤guess ②that ⑤makes ③me ④valedictorian of my own special class ... ①I ③did the best of ② everyone who failed. But ①I ⑤also want to be recognised ④as the guy who got ②Steve Ballmer ③to drop out of business school. I'm a bad influence. ①That's ②why I ④was invited to speak ③at your graduation.

- ①저는 ②그것이 ③저를 ④저의 특별학급의 고별사를 읽는 대표로 ⑤만든다고 ⑥생각합니다. ①저는 ②실패한 사·람들 중 ③최고였기 때문입니다. 그러나 ①저는 ②스티브 발머를 ③경영학교에서 중퇴하도록 ④시킨 자로 서 ⑤인식되기를 또한 원합니다. 저는 나쁜 실세입니다. ①그것이 ②왜 제가 ③여러분 졸업식장에서 ④연설 하기 위해 초빙 받은 이유이기도 합니다.

- that[=Harvard's most successful dropout] / make A B[5형식: A를 B로 만들다] / do[did] the best of[~중에 최고이다] / to be recognised[수동태: 인식되어지다] / as[전치사: ~로써] / got[사역동사] + 목 적어[Steve Ballmer] + to[부정사] : 스티브 발머를 경영학교에서 중퇴하도록 시켰다 / That's why[결과: 그것이 ~였기 때문이다] / was invited[수동태: 초대받았다]

- **valedictorian** [væ̀lədiktɔ́ːriən] n. (졸업식에서) 고별사를 읽는 학생. / **recognize** [rékəgnàiz] vt. 알아보 다, (공로 따위를) 감사하다. / **Steve Ballmer** 빌 게이츠 뒤를 이어 2000년부터 2013년까지 마이크로소프트 (MS) 최고경영자(CEO)로 재임한 임물 / **influence** [ínfluːəns] n. U,C 영향(력), C 영향력이 있는 사람[것]

- **influence** n. authority[əθɔ́ːriti], leverage[lév-əridʒ], might[mait], sway[swei] v. bias[báiəs]편견을 갖다, incline[inkláin], prejudice[prédʒudis], sway[swei], convince[kənvíns], persuade[pəːrswéid], arouse[əráuz], impel[impél], inspire[inspáiər], motivate[móutəvèit]

※ 다음 글을 읽고 물음에 답하시오. [1~3]

President Bok, former President Rudenstine, **incoming/outcoming** President Faust, members of the Harvard Corporation and the Board of Overseers, members of the faculty, parents, and especially, the graduates

I've been waiting more than 30 years to say this: "Dad, I always told you I'd come back and get my degree." I want to thank Harvard for Ⓐ **this timely honour**. I'll be changing my job next year ... and it will be nice to finally have a college degree on my resume.

I applaud the graduates today＿＿＿＿ Ⓑ ＿＿＿. For my part, I'm just happy that the Crimson has called me "Harvard's most successful dropout."

I guess that makes me valedictorian of my own special class ... I did the best of everyone who failed. But I also want to be recognised as the guy who got Steve Ballmer to **drop/dropping** out of business school. I'm a bad influence. That's **because/why** I was invited to speak at your graduation.

1. 위 글에서 밑줄 친 Ⓐ가 가리키는 것은?

① to meet many cherished people
② to graduate from the college
③ to address at the commencement
④ to leave out for an adequate job
⑤ to say of regret for the past experience

2. 위 글에서 네모상자 안의 적절한 단어는?

① incoming   drop   because
② incoming   dropping   because
③ incoming   drop   why
④ outcoming   dropping   why
⑤ outcoming   drop   why

3. 위 글에서 밑줄 친 빈칸 Ⓑ에 적절한 표현은?

① for following my past trail as dropouts
② for doing the successful business
③ for taking a much more direct route to your degrees
④ for doing great performance in school
⑤ for dropping out of school

1. ③   2. ①   3. ③

동영상 강좌 http://youtu.be/MzdP8VXDSb8

①If I ③had spoken ②at your orientation, ⑥fewer of ④you ⑤might be here today. ① Harvard ③was just a phenomenal experience ②for me. Academic life was fascinating. ①I ③used to sit in ②on lots of classes I hadn't even signed up for. And dorm life was terrific. I lived up at Radcliffe, in Currier House.

- ①만일 제가 ②여러분의 오리엔테이션에서 ③연설했다면, ④여러분들은 거의 ⑤오늘 이곳에 ⑥있지 않을 것 같습니다. ①하버드는 ②저에게는 ③단지 놀라운 경험이었습니다. 학업은 매혹적이었습니다. ①저는 ②제가 수강신청하지 않은 많은 과목을 ③듣곤 했습니다. 그리고 기숙사 생활은 아주 좋았습니다. 저는 쿠리어 하우스에 있는 라드크리프에서 남부럽지 않게 생활했습니다.

- [가정법 과거완료] If had+p.p[과거분사] ~, [가정법 과거] fewer of you[부분부정: 거의 ~ 않은] - 혼합 가정법 / used to[(과거에) ~ 하곤했다] / sit in on[수강하다=take] / classes (that/which) I hadn't even signed up for[전치사 for의 목적어는 classes] / live up (to)[남부럽지 않게 생활하다]

- **orientation** [ɔː rientéiʃən] n. 오리엔테이션, (적응) 지도(신입생[사원] 등의). / **phenomenal** [finámənl / -nɔm-] a. 놀라운 / **fascinating** [fǽsənèitiŋ] a. 매혹적인. / **terrific** [tərífik] a. 아주 좋은, 멋진.

- **phenomenal** a. amazing[əméiziŋ], astonishing[əstániʃiŋ], extraordinary[ikstrɔː rdənèri], marvelous[mɑː rv-ələs], sensational[senséiʃənəl], spectacular[spektǽkjələ r], exceptional[iksé pʃənəl], outstanding[àutstǽndiŋ] ant. average[ǽvəridʒ], common[kámən / kɔ́m]

There ④were always lots of people ①in my dorm room ②late at night ③discussing things, ⑤ because ⑥everyone knew ⑧I didn't worry about ⑦getting up in the morning. ①That's ③how ②I came to be the leader of the anti-social group. ①We ④clung to each other ③as a way of validating ③our rejection of all those social people.

- ①제 기숙사 방엔 ②밤늦게까지 ③여러 가지를 토론하고 있었던 ④늘 많은 학생들이 있었습니다. ⑤왜냐하면 ⑥그 사람들은 ⑦제가 아침에 일어날 ⑧걱정을 하지 않았기 때문입니다.(늦게 일어나다). ①그것이 ②제가 반사회 집단의 리더가 된 ③방법입니다. ①우리는 ②모든 그러한 사회 사람들에 대한 우리의 거부를 ③정당화 시키는 방법으로서 ④서로를 집착했습니다.

- [도치문] there is[was, are, were] + 주어 / lots of[=many 많은] / people (who were) discussing[의 주어는 people] / , because[앞에 ','는 계속적인 용법으로 해석] / worry about[be worried about ~관해 걱정하다] / That's how[the way]+절[그것은 ~한 방법이다] / came to[=became ~가 되다] / clung to[cling to의 과거: ~집착하다] / as[전치사: ~로서] / a way of validating[~을 정당화하는 방법]

- **discuss** [diskás] vt. 토론[논의]하다(debate), 의논하다. / **anti** [ǽnti] n. a. 반대(의견)의. / **cling** [kliŋ] vi. (p., pp. clung [klʌŋ]) (습관·생각 따위에) 집착[애착]하다, 고수하다. / **validate** [vǽlədèit] vt. (법률상) 유효하게 하다, 확인하다.

- **cling** v. adhere[ædhíər], cleave[kliː v], cohere[kouhíər], clasp[klæsp, klɑː sp], clench[klentʃ], clutch[klʌtʃ], grip[grip], be faithful[féiθfəl], cherish[tʃériʃ] ant. separate[sépərèit], release[rilíː s]

Radcliffe was a great place to live in. There were more women up there, and most of the guys were science-math types. ③That combination ⑥offered ④me ⑤the best odds, ②if you know ①what I mean. ①This ④is where I learned the sad lesson that ②improving your odds ③doesn't guarantee success.

- 라드크리프(제 기숙사)는 거주할 만한 곳이었습니다. 그곳에 더 많은 여학생들이 있었고 대부분의 학생들은 과학과 수학형 이었습니다. ①만일 제가 의미하는 것을 ②당신이 알고 있다면, ③그 결합은 ④저에게 ⑤최고의 좋은 가능성을 ⑥제공한 것입니다. ①이곳은 ②여러분의 가능성을 끌어 올리는 것은 ③성공을 보장하지 않는다는 ④슬픈 교훈을 터득한 곳이기도 합니다.

- a great place to live in[to부정사의 형용사적 용법: ~살만한 좋은 곳] / more women than men[남자들보다 여자들이 더 많음] / most of guys[대부분의 학생들] / science-math types[과학적이고 체계적인 성격] / offered A[me] B[the best odds: 저에게 최고의 조건을 제공했다] / [조건절] if ~[만일 ~라면] / the sad lesson that[동격절: ~라는 슬픈 교훈]

- **combination** [kàmbənéiʃən] n. 결합 / **offer** [ɔ́(ː)fər] vt. 제공하다. (신 등에) 바치다. (감사·존경 따위를) 표현하다. / **odds** [ɔdz] n. pl.불평등[불균등] (한 것). 유리한 조건 / **improve** [imprúːv] vt. 개선하다, 향상시키다(in) / **guarantee** [gæ̀rəntíː] vt. (p., pp. ~d; ~ing) ~을 확실히 하다, 보장하다.

- **guarantee** v. certify[sɔ́ːrtəfài], endorse[endɔ́ːrs], support[səpɔ́ːrt], vouch[vautʃ] for, affirm[əfɔ́ːrm], attest[ətést] to, confirm[kənfɔ́ːrm], witness[wítnis], insure[inʃúər], prove[pruːv], secure[sikjúər]
  n. pledge[pledʒ], promise[prámis], warranty[wɔ́(ː)rənti], word[wəːrd]

※ 다음 글을 읽고 물음에 답하시오. [4~7]

ⓐ If I had spoken at your orientation, fewer of you might be here today. Harvard was just a phenomenal experience for me. Academic life was fascinating. I used to sit in on lots of classes I hadn't even signed up for. And dorm life was terrific. I lived up at Radcliffe, in Currier House.

There were always lots of people in my dorm room late at night discussing things, because everyone knew I didn't worry about getting up in the morning. That's how I came to be the leader of the anti-social group. We clung to each other as a way of validating our rejection of all those social people.

Radcliffe was a great place to live in. There were more women up there, and most of the guys were science-math types. That combination offered me the best odds, if you know what I mean. ⓑ This is where I learned the sad lesson that improving your odds doesn't guarantee success.

---

4. 위 글의 제목으로 가장 적절한 것은?

① The happiness in much Discussion
② The long life in College
③ Good friends in College
④ More classes taken, more benefits comes out.
⑤ My Dorm Life in Harvard

5. 위 글에서 밑줄 친 ⓐ와 의미가 같은 것은?

① As I didn't speak at your orientation, most of you might be here today.
② Though I didn't speak at your orientation, most of you might be here today.
③ Because I spoke at your orientation, most of you might not be here today.
④ When I hadn't spoken at your orientation, fewer of you might be here today.
⑤ While I hadn't spoken at your orientation, many of you might be here today.

6. 위 글에서 밑줄 친 ⓑ가 가리키는 것은?

① My sad lesson was a good way of solution.
② To guarantee success we should learn sad lesson.
③ Success always causes some sad lesson.
④ The best situation doesn't always offer the best success.
⑤ It's important to get a good place to succeed.

7. 위 글과 일치하지 않은 것은?

① 하버드는 저에게는 단지 놀라운 경험이었고 학업은 매혹적이었다.
② 기숙사 방엔 밤늦게까지 여러 가지를 토론하기 위해 늘 많은 학생들이 있었다.
③ 우리는 모든 그러한 사회 사람들에 대한 거부를 정당화시키는 방법으로서 서로를 집착했다.
④ 그곳에 더 많은 여학생들이 있었고 대부분의 학생들은 과학과 수학형이었다.
⑤ 집안의 좋은 조건은 성공을 보장하지 않는다는 슬픈 교훈을 터득한 곳이다.

---

4. ⑤   5. ①   6. ④   7. ⑤

①**One of my biggest memories of Harvard** ②**came in January 1975,** ③**when I** ⑦**made a call** ④**from Currier House to a company** ⑤**in Albuquerque, New Mexico** ⑥**that had begun making the world's first personal computers. I offered to sell them software.**

- ①하버드에서의 저의 가장 큰 추억 중 하나는 ②1975년 1월이었습니다. ③그때 저는 ④제 기숙사에서 ⑤뉴멕시코주에 알부퀘큐에 소재한 ⑥한 첫 번째 개인용 컴퓨터 제조회사로 ⑦전화를 걸었습니다. 저는 개인용 컴퓨터에 소프트웨어를 끼워 팔 것을 제안했습니다.
- one of + 복수명사[~중에 하나] / came[~일이었다] / made a call[전화를 걸었다] / from A[Currier House: 기숙사에서] to B[a company: 한 회사로] / that[관계 대명사: 선행사는 a company] had begun making[만들기 시작했던] / sell A[them=personal computers] B[software] : A에게 B를 팔다.
- **memory** [méməri] n. 기억, 회상. / ╪personal [pə́ːrsənəl] a. 개인의, 직접의.
- **personal** a. confidential[kɑ̀nfidénʃəl], intimate[íntəmit], private[práivit], individual[ìndəvídʒuəl], ant. public[pʌ́blik], general[dʒénərəl]

---

①**I** ⑤**worried that** ②**they** ③**would realize I was just a student in a dorm and** ④**hang up on me.** Instead they said: "①**We're not quite ready,** ②**come see us in a month,"** ③**which was a good thing,** ⑥**because** ④**we** ⑤**hadn't written the software yet.** ①**From that moment,** ⑥**I worked day and night** ⑤**on this little extra credit project that** ④**marked** ②**the end of my college education and** ③**the beginning of a remarkable journey with Microsoft.**

- ①저는 ②그들이 ③제가 기숙사에 있는 학생에 불과해 ④전화를 끊을까 ⑤걱정했습니다. 대신 그들은 말했습니다; "①우리는 전혀 준비되어있지 않으니 ②한 달 후 만나자"고, ③다행스럽게도 ④우린 ⑤아직 소프트웨어를 작성하지 않았기 ⑥때문입니다. ①그때부터, ②저의 대학교육의 끝과 ③마이크로소프트와의 주목할 만한 여정의 시작을 ④알리는 ⑤이 작은 특별한 영예로운 프로젝트는 ⑥저를 밤낮으로 심혈을 기울이게 만들었습니다.
- I worried that[목적어인 명사절] they would[시제의 일치: ~을 것이다] realize (that) I was just a student in a dorm[기숙사의 학생의 불과하다] hang up on me[전화를 끊다]. / which was a good thing[다행히=fortunately] / from that moment[그때부터] / day and night[온종일=all day long, around clock] / ~ project that[주격 관계대명사, 선행사인 project를 수식]
- **quite** [kwait] ad. 완전히, 아주, 전혀(completely), 매우(very). / **mark** [mɑːrk] vt. 구분하다, 명시하다. / **credit** [krédit] n. U 신용, 영향력, 명예 / **remarkable** [rimɑ́ːrkəb-əl] a. 주목할 만한, 놀랄 만한.
- **remarkable** a. exceptional [iksépʃənəl], extraordinary[ikstrɔ́ːrdənèri], fabulous[fǽbjələs], incredible[inkrédəbəl], ant. ordinary[ɔ́ːrdənèri]

What ①**I** ③**remember** ②**above all about Harvard** ⑥**was being** ⑤**in the midst of** ④**so much energy and intelligence.** ①**It** ⑥**could be** ②**exhilarating,** ③**intimidating,** ④**sometimes even discouraging,** ⑤**but**

always challenging. ①It ②was an amazing privilege - and ③though ④I left early, ⑤I ⑨was transformed by ⑥my years at Harvard, ⑦the friendships I made, ⑧and the ideas I worked on.

- ①제가 ②하버드에 관해 우선적으로 ③기억하고 있는 것은 ④너무나 풍부한 정렬과 지성의 ⑤산실이 되고 있 었다는 것⑥입니다. ①그것(하버드)은 ②기분을 돋구어주고, ③위협적이고 ④때론 아주 절망적이지만 ⑤늘 도 전적이었던 것 ⑥같습니다. ①하버드는 ②놀라운 특권이었고 ③비록 ④제가 일찍 떠났을지라도, ⑤저는 ⑥하버 드에서의 내 몇 년, ⑦내가 가꾼 우정, ⑧그리고 제가 심혈을 쏟은 사고에 ⑨의해 인격이 형성되었습니다.
- What I remember[주어: 제가 기억하는 것] above all[무엇보다도, 우선적인] / It[하버드] could[과거를 추측: ~이었을 것 같다] / though[양보절: 비록 ~ 일지라도] / I was transformed by[~에 의해 인격이 혼성되었다] / friendship (that/which) I made[의 목적어는 friendship] / the ideas (that/which) I worked on[심혈을 기울였던 아이디어들]
- **in [into] the midst of** 한창 ~중에(during). / **intelligence** [intélədʒəns] n. U 지성, 지능; 지혜 / **exhilarating** [igzílərèitiŋ] a. 기분을 돋우어 주는, 상쾌한. / **intimidate** [intímədèit] vt. 위협하다, 협박 하다. / **discouraging** [diskə́ːridʒiŋ] a. 낙담시키는, 실망적인 / **challenging** [tʃǽlindʒiŋ] a. 도전적인, 매력적인 / **amazing** [əméiziŋ] a. 놀랄 정도의, 굉장한(astonishing). / ╪ **privilege** [prívəlidʒ] n. U,C 특권 / **transform** [trænsfɔ́ːrm] vt. (외형) 변형시키다(into)
- **intimidate** v. browbeat[bráubìːt], coerce[kouə́ːrs], extort[ikstɔ́ːrt], alarm[əláːrm], dismay[disméi], scare[skɛəːr], terrify[térəfai] ant. cower[káuər] 움츠리다, bolster[bóulstər] 기운 을 북돋다.

One of my biggest memories of Harvard came in January 1975, when I made a call from Currier House to a company in Albuquerque, New Mexico that had begun making the world's first personal computers. I offered to sell them software.

I worried that they would realize I was just a student in a dorm and hang up on me. Instead they said: "We're not quite ready, come see us in a month," which was a good thing, because we hadn't written the software yet. From that moment, I worked day and night on this little extra credit project that marked ___Ⓐ___ of my college education and ___Ⓑ___ of a remarkable journey with Microsoft.

What I remember above all about Harvard was being in the midst of so much energy and intelligence. It could be ___①___, ___②___, sometimes even ___③___, but always ___④___. It was an amazing privilege - and though I left early, I was transformed by my years at Harvard, the friendships I made, and the ideas I worked on.

8. 위 글의 제목으로 가장 적절한 것은?

① The Growing Business at the Campus
② The Microsoft : My Ambitious Dream
③ Good Friendship at School
④ My Unforgettable Memories
⑤ The Adversities in Opening Business

9. 위 글에서 지은이의 캠퍼스 생활을 한 단어로 요약할 수 있는 것은?

① successful   ② transitional

③ unbearable   ④ cowardly
⑤ gutless

10. 위 글에서 밑줄 친 빈칸 ①~④에 들어갈 적절한 단어로 알맞지 <u>않은</u> 것은?

① exhilarating   ② intimidating
③ discouraging   ④ challenging
⑤ boring

11. 위 글에서 밑줄 친 빈칸 Ⓐ, Ⓑ에 각각 절적한 단어는?

① the appreciation   the prosperity
② the end   the beginning
③ the performance   the encouragement
④ the dislike   the affection
⑤ the jump-up   the long way

12. 위 글과 일치하지 <u>않은</u> 것은?

① 하버드는 너무나 풍부한 정열과 지성의 산실이었다.
② 작은 특별한 영예로운 프로젝트를 위해 밤낮으로 심혈을 기울였다.
③ 한 회사에 자신이 완성한 소프트웨어를 팔 것을 제안했다.
④ 기숙사에 있는 학생에 불과해 전화를 끊을까 걱정했다.
⑤ 하버드에서의 몇 년, 우정, 그리고 제가 심혈을 쏟은 사고에 의해 인격이 형성되었다.

8. ④ 9. ② 10. ⑤ 11. ② 12. ③

On Surrender to US Army

by Chief Josheph of the Nez Perce

[난이도 ★★☆☆☆]

동영상 강좌 http://youtu.be/QpZJ3Y8eWvY

In 1877

Chief Joseph of the Nez Perce - On Surrender to US Army

Tell General Howard I know his heart. What he told me before, I have it in my heart. I am tired of fighting. Our Chiefs are killed; Looking Glass is dead, Ta Hool Hool Shute is dead. The old men are all dead. It is the young men who say yes or no. He who led on the young men is dead. It is cold, and we have no blankets; the little children are freezing to death. My people, some of them, have run away to the hills, and have no blankets, no food. No one knows where they are - perhaps freezing to death. I want to have time to look for my children, and see how many of them I can find. Maybe I shall find them among the dead. Hear me, my Chiefs! I am tired; my heart is sick and sad. From where the sun now stands I will fight no more forever.

Chief Joseph - Thunder Traveling to the Loftier Mountain Heights - 1877

🔖 **본문분석**

Chief Joseph of the Nez Perce - On Surrender to US Army

- 미 인디언 네즈퍼스 족장 조세프 - 미군에 항복

- surrender to(~에 항복)

- **surrender** [səréndər] vt. 양도[명도]하다. 포기하다.

🔖 **동의어/반의어**

- **surrender** n. capitulation[kəpìtʃəléiʃən], relinquishment[rilíŋkwiʃmənt], resignation[rèzignéiʃ-ən], submission[səbmíʃən] v. abdicate[ǽbdikèit], give up[givəp], relinquish[rilíŋkwiʃ], concede[kənsíːd], ant. resistance[rizístəns], retain[ritéin] withstand[wiðstǽnd]

Tell General Howard I know his heart. ①What he told me before, ③I have it ②in my heart.

- 하워드 장군에게 고합니다. 저는 당신의 마음을 압니다. ①당신이 전에 말한 것을 ②가슴속에 ③간직하고 있습니다.

- tell A B(A에게 B를 말하다) / [문장 안에서] what(의문사)+주어+동사 / I have it(=what he told me before)

I am tired of fighting. Our Chiefs are killed; Looking Glass is dead, Ta Hool Hool Shute is dead.

- 저는 전투에 신물이 납니다. 우리 참모진들은 모두 죽었습니다.; 글래스를 찾는 일도 끝났습니다. 타 훌 훌 셔트도 죽었습니다.

- tired of(~가 지겨운) tired by[from/with] ~로 지친 / be killed(죽음을 당하다) / dead [ded] a. 죽은, 활기 없는

🔖 **동의어/반의어**

dead a. deceased[disíːst], departed[dipáːrtid], extinct[ikstíŋkt], late[leit], anesthetized[ənésəətàizd] 마취가 된, insensitive[insénsətiv], numb[nʌm], inanimate[inǽnəmit], inert[inɔ́ːrt] 생기 없는,

lifeless[láiflis], stagnant[stǽgnənt] 괴어 있는, 썩은, 불경기의, exhausted[igzɔ́ːstid], obsolete[ὰbsəlíːt] n. casualties, deceased[disíːst], fatalities ant. alive[əláiv] survivors[sərváivərs]

The old men are all dead. It is the young men who say yes or no. He who led on the young men is dead.

- 연장자들은 모두 죽었습니다. 삶과 죽음을 선택할 사람들은 젊음이들 뿐입니다. 그 젊은이들을 이끌었던 사람은 죽었습니다.
- the old men과 the young men이 대조를 이루는 문장. / [강조용법] it is [강조어구] who[that] ~는 바로 [강조어구]이다 / say yes or no(사느냐 죽느냐의 선택을 하다로 해석) / led(lead의 과거형 ~을 이끌었다)

It is cold, and we have no blankets; the little children are freezing to death.

- 날씨는 춥고 우리는 덮을 담요도 없습니다.(모든 것이 불타 없어짐을 의미). 어린 아이들은 얼어 죽어가고 있습니다.
- [무생물 주어] it / no[형용사로 전체 문장을 부정] / freeze [friːz] v. froze[frouz]; frozen[fróuzən])vi. 얼다, 얼어붙다(to).

🖋 동의어/반의어

- **freeze** v. chill[tʃil], harden[háːrdn] 무감각하게 하다, solidify[səlídəfai] 응고시키다, arrest[ərést], halt[hɔːlt], paralyze[pǽrəlàiz], stop[stɑp] n. frost[frɔːst], ceiling[síːliŋ], control[kəntróul], restriction[ristríkʃ-ən] ant. thaw[θɔː] 녹다

My people, some of them, have run away to the hills, and have no blankets, no food.

- 제 부족민 중 몇몇은 언덕으로 달아났습니다. 그리고 담요나 음식도 없습니다.
- some of 복수명사[그들 중 몇몇] / run away to[~로 달아나다]

No one knows where they are - perhaps freezing to death. I want to have time to look for my children, and see how many of them I can find.

- 아무도 그들이 있는 곳을 모릅니다. - 아마 동사하였을 것입니다. 저는 내 부족 아이들을 찾을 시간을 원합니다. 그리고 몇 명을 찾을지 알고 싶습니다.
- where[의문부사]+they[주어]+are[동사] / have time to look for[~을 찾다, 형용사적 용법, ~찾을 시간] / see[want to see] how many of them[그들 중 몇 명을]

Maybe I shall find them among the dead.

- 아마도 저는 죽은 사람들 중 몇을 찾게 될 것입니다.
- shall[주어의 강한 의지] / among[전치사 (셋 이상) ~사이에

Hear me, my Chiefs! I am tired; my heart is sick and sad.

- 제 참모들은 들어라! 나는 지쳤다; 내 가슴은 병들고 슬프다.
- my Chiefs[자신의 참모들을 일컬음] / sick[형용사] and[등위 접속사] sad[형용사]

From where the sun now stands I will fight no more forever.

- 태양이 떠있는 곳에서(이 순간부터) 나는 영원히 더 이상의 전투를 하지 않을 것입니다.
- from[전치사] where[의문사]+the sun[주어]+now[부사]+stands[동사] / will (의지미래) ~하려고[하겠다고] 하다. / no more[더 이상] / forever[부사 영원히]

🐚 **동의어/반의어**

forever a. eternally[itə́ːrnəl], everlastingly[èvərlǽstli], perpetually[pərpétʃuəli], constantly[kάnstəntli], continually[kəntínjuəli], incessantly[insésənti], unendingly, unremittingly[ʌnrimítiŋli] ant. never[névəːr] sporadically[spərǽdik-əli]

Chief Joseph - Thunder Traveling to the Loftier Mountain Heights - 1877

- 추장 조세프 - 1877년 천둥이 지나는 더욱 고결한 장 정상에서
- travel [trǽv-əl] vi. (멀리 또는 외국에) 여행하다, (빛·소리 등이) 전해지다(over a scene, topic).
- **travel** v. commute[kəmjúːt], jaunt[dʒɔːnt], , tour[tuəːr], voyage[vɔ́idʒ], wander[wάndəːr]

Chief Joseph of the Nez Perce - On Surrender to US Army

(a) Tell General Howard ⒜ I know his heart. What he told me before, I have it in my heart. I am tired of fighting. Our Chiefs are killed; Looking Glass is dead, Ta Hool Hool Shute is dead. (b) The old men are all dead. It is the young men who say yes or no. He who led on the young men is dead. It is ① cold, and we have no blankets; the little children are ② freezing to death. My people, some of them, have run away to the hills, and have no blankets, no food. (c) I want to have time to ③ look after my children, and see how many of them I can find. Maybe I shall find them among the dead. (d) Hear me, my Chiefs! I am tired; my heart is sick and ④ sad. From where the sun now stands I will ⑤ fight no more forever.

(e) Chief Joseph - Thunder Traveling to the Loftier Mountain Heights - 1877

1. 위 글의 주제로 가장 적절한 것은?

① It's time to find the lost after the war.
② It's unavoidable to wage a war in human history.
③ Merciless defeat has no more escape except give-up.
④ The cruel reality in wars should not be forgotten.
⑤ Wars are another turning point for new jump-up.

2. 위 글에서 밑줄 친 ⒜의 'I'와 관련이 없는 것은?

① a tribe header
② a surrender after wars against the US army
③ a frustrated commander to seek for the rest of his tribe
④ a tyranny escaping for his own life
⑤ a generous chief of the Nez Perce

3. 위 글의 상황과 어울리지 않은 것은?

① desperate   ② gruesome
③ appalling   ④ horrible
⑤ appealing

4. 위 글에서 밑줄 친 ①~⑤중, 문맥상 단어의 쓰임이 어색한 것은?

①   ②   ③   ④   ⑤

5. 위 글의 역사적 배경에 가장 적절한 것은?

① a civil war
② a segregation time
③ an independent war
④ the World War I
⑤ a frontier age

6. 위 글에서 (a)~(e)중, 아래의 문장이 위치할 곳은?

No one knows where they are - perhaps freezing to death.

① (a)   ② (b)   ③ (c)   ④ (d)   ⑤ (e)

7. 위 글과 일치하지 <u>않은</u> 것은?

① 마지막까지 부족을 지키려는 부족장의 심정이 잘 그려져 있다.

② 어느 인디언 부족의 멸망을 알려주고 있다.

③ 전투에서의 패배의 쓰라진 상처를 잘 설명해 주고 있다.

④ 승리한 미군의 사기충전을 생생히 묘사하고 있다.

⑤ 미국의 한 슬픈 역사를 보여주고 있다.

1. ③	2. ④	3. ⑤	4. look after → look for
5. ⑤	6. ③	7. ④	

Encourages His Soldiers

by Giuseppe Garibaldi

[난이도 ★★☆☆☆]

동영상 강좌 http://youtu.be/XEBuBFR_AUI

Giuseppe Garibaldi Encourages His Soldiers (1860)

We must now consider the period which is just drawing to a close as almost the last stage of our national resurrection, and prepare ourselves to finish worthily the marvelous design of the elect of twenty generations, the completion of which Providence has reserved for this fortunate age.

🖎 본문분석

Giuseppe Garibaldi Encourages His Soldiers (1860)

- 주세페 가리발디는 병사들에게 용기를 북돋아 준다.
- **encourage** [enkə́ː ridʒ] vt. 용기를 돋우다, 장려하다.

🖎 동의어/반의어

<u>encourage</u> v. cheer[tʃiər], hearten[háː rtn], inspire[inspáiər], stimulate[stímjəlèit], persuade[pəː rswéid], sway[swei], advocate[ǽdvəkit, -kèit], sanction[sǽŋkʃən], foster[fɔ́ː)stəː r, fás-], further[fə́ː rðəː r], promote[prəmóut], spur[spəː r], succor[sʌ́kər] ant. dishearten[dishá́ː rtn], discourage[diskə́ː rididʒ], prevent[privént], hinder[híndər]

①We ④must now consider ③the period which is just drawing to a close as almost ②the last stage of our national resurrection, and ⑧prepare ourselves to finish worthily ⑦the marvelous design of the elect of twenty generations, the completion of which ⑤Providence ⑥has reserved for this fortunate age.

- ①우리는 ②우리 조국의 부흥의 마지막 무대에 ③거의 다가가는 이 시점을 ④지금 고려해야만 합니다. 그리고 ⑤전지전능하신 신이 ⑥이 행운의 시대를 완성하기 위해 보존한 ⑦20세의 젊은이들의 선택한 경이로운 계획을 ⑧가치 있게 끝낼 준비를 해야만 합니다.
- must[조동사:~해야만 하다] / the period which[주격 관계대명사: 선행사 the period를 수식 ~한 단계(시대)] / draw to a close[정점에 다다르다] / as[전치사:~로서] / the last stage of our national resurrection[조국의 마지막 단계(무대)] / and (we must) prepare ourselves to[~을 준비하다] / finish worthily[부사로 finish동사를 수식: 가치 있게 끝마치다] / the elect[뽑힌 사람들] / Providence[하느님, 신] / the completion of which[관계대명사의 선행사는 the completion] / has reserved[목적어는 the marvelous design] / for this fortunate age (of the completion)

- **resurrection** [rèzərékʃ-ən] n. U 재기, 부활 / **marvelous** a. 불가사의한, 믿기 어려운(improbable). / **completion** [kəmplíː ʃən] n. U 성취, 완성 / **reserve** [rizə́ː rv] vt. 비축하다. 준비[마련]해 두다.

🖎 동의어/반의어

<u>marvelous</u> a. fabulous[fǽbjələs], fantastic[fæntǽstik], outstanding[àutstǽndiŋ], remarkable[rimáː rkəb-əl], spectacular[spektǽkjələː r], superb[suː pə́ː rb], wonderful[wʌ́ndəː rfəl] ant. terrible[térəb-əl]

Yes, young men, Italy owes to you an undertaking which has merited the applause of the universe. You have conquered and you will conquer still, because you are prepared for the tactics that decide the fate of battles. You are not unworthy of the men who entered the ranks of a Macedonian phalanx, and who contended not in vain with the proud conquerors of Asia. To this wonderful page in our country's history another more glorious still will be added, and the slave shall show at last to his free brothers a sharpened sword forged from the links of his fetters.

🖋 본문분석

①Yes, ②young men, ③Italy ⑥owes ④to you ⑤an undertaking which has merited the applause of the universe.
- ①그렇습니다. ②젊은이들이여. ③이탈리아는 ④여러분들에게 ⑤이 우주의 찬사를 받을 만한 책임을 ⑥맡기고 있습니다.
- owe A to B[A는 B의 덕분이다] / which[관계대명사: 선행사는 an undertaking ~할 책임]
- owe [ou] vt. ~의 은혜를 입고 있다. / undertaking [ʌndərtéikiŋ] n. 사업, (떠맡은) 일. / merit [mérit] vt. ~할 만하다(deserve). / applause [əplɔ́ːz] n. U 박수 갈채, 칭찬.

①You have conquered and ②you will conquer still, ③because ④you ⑥are prepared for ⑤the tactics that decide the fate of battles.
- ①여러분들은 정복했고 ②여전히 정복해 나갈 것입니다. ③왜냐하면 ④여러분들은 ⑤전투의 운명을 결정할 전술로 ⑥무장되어 있기 때문입니다.
- have conquered[현재완료 결과] / will conquer still[앞으로도 변함없을 의미] / because[계속적인 용법: 왜냐하면 ~이기 때문이다] / are prepared for[~가 준비되어 있다] the tactics that[주격 관계대명사로 선행사는 the tactics(~라는 전술)]

🖋 동의어/반의어

conquer v. defeat[difíːt], subdue[səbdjúː], vanquish[vǽŋkwiʃ], surmount[sərmáunt], triumph[trái iəmf] over ant. surrender[səréndər]항복하다 yield[jiːld]

①You ⑤are not unworthy of the men ②who entered the ranks of a Macedonian phalanx, and ④ who contended not in vain ③with the proud conquerors of Asia.
- ①여러분들은 ②마케도니아 방진 형태로 들어가 ③아시아의 자부심의 정복자들과 ④당당히 맞선 ⑤귀중한 병사들입니다.
- not unworthy[가치가 없지 않은, 귀중한] / enter the ranks[열로 들어가다] / the men who entered ~, and who contended[~로 들어가 만족한 병사들] / not in vain[부사구: 가치 없지 않은, 당당히] / contended with[~와 경쟁하다]
- rank [ræŋk] n. U, C 열, 행렬, (특히 군대의) 횡렬 / phalanx [féilæŋks, fǽl-] n. (pl. ~es, phalanges [fælǽndʒiːz / fə-]) ① (고대 그리스의) 방진(方陣)(창병을 네모꼴로 배치하는 진형). ② 밀집 대형

----

②**To this wonderful page in our country's history** ①**another more glorious still** ③**will be added,** ④**and the slave** ⑨**shall show** ⑤**at last** ⑥**to his free brothers** ⑧**a sharpened sword** ⑦**forged from the links of his fetters.**

- ①또 다른 더욱 영광스런 정적이 ②우리 조국의 역사의 이 경이로운 페이지에 ③여전히 첨부될 것입니다. ④그리고 노예들도 ⑤마침내 ⑥속박에서 벗어난 형제들에게 ⑦족쇄의 사슬로 만들어진 ⑧날카로운 칼을 ⑨보여주게 될 것입니다.
- add A to B : A를 B에 더하다 / [도치문] ~ will be added to this ~ history / shall[말하는 사람의 의지: ~하리라, ~이리라] at last[부사구: 마침내] / show to A B: A에게 B를 보여주다 / sword forged the links of his fetters[족쇄의 사슬로 만든 칼]
- **still** [stil] n. 고요, 정적 / **forge** [fɔːrdʒ] vt. (쇠를) 불리다. / **fetter** [fétər] n. 족쇄(shackle)

To arms, then, all of you! all of you! And the oppressors and the mighty shall disappear like dust. You, too, women, cast away all the cowards from your embraces; they will give you only cowards for children, and you who are the daughters of the land of beauty must bear children who are noble and brave. Let timid doctrinaires depart from among us to carry their servility and their miserable fears elsewhere. This people is its own master. It wishes to be the brother of other peoples, but to look on the insolent with a proud glance, not to grovel before them imploring its own freedom. It will no longer follow in the trail of men whose hearts are foul. No! No! No!

---

①**To arms, then,** ②**all of you!** ③**all of you!** ④**And the oppressors and the mighty** ⑥**shall disappear** ⑤**like dust.**

- ①전투준비, ②제군 여러분! ③병사 여러분! ④그리고 압제자와 독재자들은 ⑤먼지처럼 ⑥사라지게 합시다.
- the+형용사(mighty)[복수보통명사: 독재자들] / like[전치사] dust[먼지처럼]
- **To arms!** 전투준비. / **disappear** [dìsəpíər] vi. ∼ 사라지다

📖 동의어/반의어

disappear v. dissipate[dísəpèit], evaporate[ivǽpərèit], vanish[vǽniʃ], depart[dipáːrt], withdraw[wiðdrɔ́ː] ant. materialize[mətí-əriəlàiz] 실체화하다, 실현되게 하다. appear[əpíər]

---

①**You, too, women,** ④**cast away** ③**all the cowards** ②**from your embraces;** ⑤**they** ⑧**will give** ⑥**you** ⑦**only cowards for children,** ⑨**and you who are the daughters of the land of beauty** ⑪**must bear** ⑩**children who are noble and brave.**

- ①여성 여러분들도 또한, ②두 팔로 ③모든 겁쟁이들을 ④쫓아내세요. ⑤그들은 ⑥여러분들에게 ⑦아이들과 같은 겁쟁이에 ⑧불과합니다. ⑨그리고 아름다운 조국의 딸들은 ⑩당당하고 용맹한 아이들을 ⑪낳아야만 합니다.
- cast away A from your embraces[두 팔로 안아다 버리다] / give you only cowards for children[아이들에게 겁을 주는 나약한 겁쟁이들] / you who[주격 관계대명사: ~한 딸들의 여러분] / bear[아이를 낳다]

47

- cast away (걱정 따위를) 떨쳐버리다, 잊다. / embrace [imbréis] n. 포위. / noble [nóub-əl]a. (-bler; -blest) 귀족의, 고귀한, 고결한

Let ④timid doctrinaires ⑤depart ①from among us ③to carry ②their servility and their miserable fears elsewhere.
- ①우리들 사이에 ②그들의 굴욕과 가련한 공포를 ③쫓아내도록 ④소심한 공론가를 ⑤배척합시다.
- let[사역동사:~시키다]+목적어+depart from[원형동사:~쫓아내다] / to carry[to부정사의 부사적용법 목적: ~하기 위해서] ~ elsewhere[다른 곳으로]
- **timid** [tímid]a. (~er; ~est) 겁 많은, 소심한 / **doctrinaire** [dáktrənéər] n. 공론가 / servility [səː rvíləti] n. U 노예근성, 비굴 / **miserable** [mízərəbəl] a. 불쌍한, 비참한, 가련한(pitiable)

📖 동의어/반의어

miserable a. disconsolate[diskánsəlit], forlorn[fəː rlɔ́ː rn]버려진, 고독한, heartbroken['-bròukən], wappalling[əpɔ́ː liŋ], contemptible[kəntémptəbəl], deplorable[diplɔ́ː rəbl], sorry[sɔ́ː ri] ant. happy

동영상 강좌 http://youtu.be/7BMgcHtQKKI

This people is its own master. ①It ③wishes ②to be the brother of other peoples, but ⑤to look on ④the insolent with a proud glance, ⑦not to grovel ⑥before them imploring its own freedom.
- 이 사람들은 이 땅의 주인입니다. ①이 나라는 ②다른 민족들의 형제가 되기를 ③소망합니다. ④그러나 뽐내며 눈짓하는 거만한 사람들을 ⑤무시하고(원치 않고), ⑥자신들의 자유를 애원하는 자들 앞에서 ⑦비굴하지 않기를 소망하고 있습니다.
- it wishes to be ~, but (it wishes) to look on ~, (it wishes) not to grovel로 연결된 문장임. / but[=only] / the insolent[거만한 사람들] with a proud glance[뽐내며 흘깃 쳐다보는]
- **insolent** [insələnt] a. 거만한(arrogrant), 무례한(impudent) / **grovel** [grɔ́vəl] vi. 굴복하다, 비굴한 태도를 취하다. / **implore** [implɔ́ː r] vt. 애원[탄원]하다; (아무에게) 애원하다.

①It will ③no longer ④follow in ②the trail of men whose hearts are foul. No! No! No!
- ①이 땅은 ②마음이 비열한 사람들의 자취를 ③더 이상 ④따르지 않을 것입니다. 그렇습니다!
- no longer[부사: 더 이상 ~이 아닌] / men whose[소유격 관계대명사] hearts[그들의 마음이] are foul[비열한 사람들] / follow in[~을 따르다] / 앞 문장에서 no longer가 부정이므로, No!는 '그렇습니다'로 해석
- **trail** [treil]n. 자국, 지나간 흔적 / **foul** [faul] a. 더러운, 비열한

📖 동의어/반의어

foul a. loathsome[lóuðsəm], odious[óudiəs], offensive[əfénsiv], repugnant[ripʌ́gnənt], repulsive[ripʌ́lsiv], gross[grous] ant. pleasing[plíː ziŋ], pure[pjuər], clean[klíː n] tasteful[téistfəl]

Providence has presented Italy with Victor Emmanuel. Every Italian should rally round him. By the side of Victor Emmanuel every quarrel should be forgotten, all rancor depart. Once more

I repeat my battle-cry: "To arms, all-all of you!" If March, 1861, does not find one million of Italians in arms, then alas for liberty, alas for the life of Italy. Ah, no, far be from me a thought which I loathe like poison. March of 1861, or if need be February, will find us all at our post-Italians of Calatafimi, Palermo, Ancona, the Volturno, Castelfidardo, and Isernia, and with us every man of this land who is not a coward or a slave. Let all of us rally round the glorious hero of Palestro and give the last blow to the crumbling edifice of tyranny. Receive, then, my gallant young volunteers, at the honored conclusion of ten battles, one word of farewell from me.

---

①**Providence** ④**has presented** ②**Italy with** ③**Victor Emmanuel. Every Italian should rally round him.**

- ①전능하신 신께서 ②이탈리아에게 ③빅터 엠마누엘을 ④내려 보내셨습니다. 모든 이탈리아인들은 그 주위로 모여야만 합니다.
- present A with B : A에게 B를 보여주다[내려 보내다] / should[조동사: ~해야만 한다] / round[전치사: ~주위로] / Victor Emmanuel : 이탈리아의 왕(1759~1824)

①**By the side of Victor Emmanuel** ②**every quarrel** ③**should be forgotten,** ④**all rancor depart.**

- ①빅터 엠마누엘 옆에선 ②어떠한 불평도 ③없으며 ④모든 증오도 ⑤없게 됩니다.
- by[전치사: ~옆에] / be forgotten[주어인 every quarrel의 사물이므로 수동태: 분명히 잊혀지다] / all rancor (should) depart[자동사: 사라지다]
- **quarrel** [kwɔ́ː rə] n. 싸움, 불평(against; with) / **rancor**[rǽŋkə r] n. U 깊은 원한, 적의

🖋 동의어/반의어

rancor n. animosity[æ̀nəmásəti], enmity[énməti], hostility[hɑstíləti] ant. goodwilll[gúdwíl]

---

①**Once more** ③**I repeat** ②**my battle-cry:** ④**"To arms, all-all of you!"** ⑤**If March, 1861,** ⑦**does not find** ⑥**one million of Italians in arms,** ⑨**then alas** ⑧**for liberty, alas for the life of Italy.**

- ①다시 한 번 ②나의 함성을 ③반복합니다. ④병사들이여 무기를 드세요! ⑤만일 1861년 3월이 ⑥무장한 100만 이탈리아 병사를 ⑦찾지 못한다면, ⑧자유와 이탈리아의 운명도 ⑨사라질 것입니다.
- if[조건절: 만일 ~라면] / Italians in arms[무장한 이탈리아 병사들] / alas[근심을 나타내므로: 사라지게 될 것이다로 해석]
- **báttle crỳ** 함성; (주장·투쟁 따위의) 표어, 슬로건. / **alas** [əlǽs, əláː s] int. 아아, 슬프도다.

Ah, no, ②far be from me ①a thought which I loathe like poison. ③March of 1861, ④or if need be February, ⑧will find us all ⑤at our post-Italians of Calatafimi, Palermo, Ancona, the Volturno, Castelfidardo, and Isernia, and ⑥with us ⑦every man of this land who is not a coward or a slave.

- ①제가 독소와 같이 진저리를 내는 생각을 ②갖지 않지 않도록. ③1861년 3월, ④또는 만일 2월이라도, ⑤우리의 후세와 ⑥우리와 함께 ⑦겁쟁이나 노예가 아닌 이 땅의 모든 사람들을 ⑧찾게 될 것입니다(기

억하게 될 것이다).

- a thought which I loathe like poison (should) be far from me[나로 부터 멀리 떨어지다]
- **loathe** [louð] vt. 몹시 싫어하다, 질색하다. / **if need be [were]** (문어) = **when [as, if] the need arises** 필요하다면, 일에 따라서는, 어쩔 수 없다면(if necessary).

🔖 동의어/반의어

loathe v. abhor[æbhɔ́ːr], abominate[əbámənèit], despise[dispáiz], detest[ditést] ant. love[lʌv]

Let ①all of us ③rally ②round the glorious hero of Palestro and ⑤give the last blow ④to the crumbling edifice of tyranny. Receive, then, ⑥my gallant young volunteers, ⑦at the honored conclusion of ten battles, ⑧one word of farewell from me.

- ①우리 모두 ②영광스런 영웅 팰레스트로 주위로 ③모입시다. 그리고 ④폭정의 무너지는 건물에 ⑤마지막 한방을 날립시다. 그리고 ⑥나의 용감한 젊은 지원병들은 ⑦10개의 전투의 명예로운 끝에서 ⑧나와의 작별하게 될 것입니다.
- round[=around, 주위로] / give the last blow[마지막 한방을 먹이다] / Receive의 목적어는 one word of farewell from me[나와의 작별]
- **rally** [ræli] vt. (공통의 목적을 위해) 불러 모으다. / **blow** [blou] n. 강타(hit), 급습 / **crumbly** [krʌ́mbli] a. (-blier; -bliest) 부서지기 쉬운 / **edifice** [édəfis] n. (큰) 건축물, 건물 / **tyranny** [tírəni] n. U 폭정 / **gallant** [gǽlənt] a. 용감한 / **volunteer** [vὰləntíər] n. 지원자, 지원병, 의용병

※ 다음 글을 읽고 물음에 답하시오. [1~4]

Giuseppe Garibaldi ① **Encourages** His Soldiers (1860)

We must now consider the period which is just drawing to a ② **close** as almost the last stage of our national resurrection, and prepare ourselves to finish worthily the marvelous design of the elect of twenty generations, the completion of which Providence has reserved for this fortunate age.

Yes, young men, Italy owes for/to you an undertaking which has merited the applause of the universe. You have conquered and you will conquer still, because/if you are prepared for the tactics that decide the fate of battles. You are ③ **not unworthy** of the men who entered the ranks of a Macedonian phalanx, and who contended ④ **in vain** with the proud conquerors of Asia. ⑤ **To** this wonderful page in our country's history another more glorious still will be added, and the slave shall show at last to/with his free brothers a sharpened sword forged from the links of his fetters.

1. 위 글의 주제로 가장 적절한 것은?

① The fate of Italy is dependant upon Soldiers.
② In the battle don't be afraid or escape.
③ Wars are sad but we must defeat enemies.
④ After triumph, let's go home as soon as possible.
⑤ Protect your friends as long as the enemy is strong.

2. 위 글에서 밑줄 친 ①~⑤중, 문맥상 단어의 쓰임이 어색한 것은?

①   ②   ③   ④   ⑤

3. 위 글에서 네모상자 안의 적절한 단어는?

① for	because	to
② to	because	to
③ for	because	with
④ to	if	with
⑤ for	if	with

4. 위 글과 일치하지 <u>않은</u> 것은?

① 이글은 전장에서 병사들의 사기를 진작시키고자하는 연설문이다.
② 국가 부활의 마지막 단계에 도달하였다.
③ 신은 우리와 함께 하신다.
④ 연설자는 병사들의 용기와 전술에 확신을 갖고 있다.
⑤ 노예해방을 위한 전쟁이다.

※ 다음 글을 읽고 물음에 답하시오. [5~10]

To arms, then, all of you! all of you! And the oppressors and the mighty shall disappear like dust. You, too, women, cast away all Ⓐ **the cowards** from your embraces; they will give you only cowards for children, and you who are the daughters of the land of beauty must bear children who are noble and brave. Let timid doctrinaires depart from among us to carry their servility and their miserable fears elsewhere. _____ It wishes to be the brother of other peoples, but to look on the insolent with a proud glance, not to grovel before them imploring

51

its own freedom. It will no longer follow in the trail of men whose hearts are foul. No! No! No!

Providence has presented Italy with Ⓑ **Victor Emmanuel**. Every Italian should rally round him. By the side of Victor Emmanuel every quarrel should be forgotten, all rancor depart. Once more I repeat my battle-cry: "To arms, all-all of you!" Ⓒ **If March, 1861. does not find one million of Italians in arms, then alas for liberty, alas for the life of Italy.**

5. 위 글의 분위기로 가장 적절한 것은?

① disappointing
② calmly
③ darkening
④ unshaken
⑤ indifferent

6. 위 글에서 밑줄 친 Ⓐ와 일치하지 <u>않은</u> 것은?

① They indicate the enemies.
② They feel afraid of our arms.
③ They are not brave.
④ They shall be defeated soon.
⑤ They feel proud of themselves.

7. 위 글에서 밑줄 친 빈칸에 가장 적절한 표현은?

① It will be they who will lose the battle
② You should go home right now
③ This people is its own master
④ This war is so serious for our country
⑤ Let's take some time to consider how to win

8. 위 글로 미루어 밑줄 친 Ⓑ가 의미하는 것은?

① A king
② A wise soldier
③ An enemy
④ An addressor
⑤ Providence

9. 위 글에서 밑줄 친 Ⓒ가 의미하는 것은?

① If this war is defeated, Italy will not be independent.
② The liberty for Italy is too long way to go.
③ We are faced with easy phase to win the battle.
④ The Goddess of victory will be with our.
⑤ March in 1861 is too terrifying.

10. 위 글과 일치하지 <u>않은</u> 것은?

① 병사들이여! 무기를 들고 싸워라!
② 압제자와 독재자들은 한낱 겁쟁이들에 불과하다.
③ 겁 많은 공리주의자들의 배척하자.
④ 아녀자들도 전쟁에 동참해야만 한다.
⑤ 위대한 Victor Emmanuel을 믿고 따르라.

1. ①	2. ④ in vain → not in vain				
3. ②	4. ⑤	5. ④	6. ⑤	7. ③	
8. ①	9. ④	10. 없음			

Nobel Peace Prize Acceptance

by Martin Luther King

[난이도 ★★☆☆☆]

동영상 강좌 http://youtu.be/9h_8_CufCJs | in Oslo December 10, 1964

Your Majesty, Your Royal Highness, Mr. President, Excellencies, Ladies and Gentlemen:

I accept the Nobel Prize for Peace at a moment when 22 million Negroes of the United States of America are engaged in a creative battle to end the long night of racial injustice.

I accept this award on behalf of a civil rights movement which is moving with determination and a majestic scorn for risk and danger to establish a reign of freedom and a rule of justice. I am mindful that only yesterday in Birmingham, Alabama, our children, crying out for brotherhood, were answered with fire hoses, snarling dogs and even death. I am mindful that only yesterday in Philadelphia, Mississippi, young people seeking to secure the right to vote were brutalized and murdered. And only yesterday more than 40 houses of worship in the State of Mississippi alone were bombed or burned because they offered a sanctuary to those who would not accept segregation. I am mindful that debilitating and grinding poverty afflicts my people and chains them to the lowest rung of the economic ladder.

Therefore, I must ask why this prize is awarded to a movement which is beleagured and committed to unrelenting struggle; to a movement which has not won the very peace and brotherhood which is the essence of the Nobel Prize.

Your Majesty, Your Royal Highness, Mr. President, Excellencies, Ladies and Gentlemen:
- 폐하, 왕실 관계자 여러분, 대통령, 각하, 신사 숙녀 여러분
- **majesty** [mǽdʒisti] U 위엄(dignity), 주권(sovereignty), (M-) 폐하. / **royal** [rɔ́iəl] a. 왕족의, 황족의 / **excellency** [éksələnsi] n. (E-) 각하(장관·대사·총독· 지사 기타 고관에 대한 경칭)

I accept the Nobel Prize for Peace / at a moment when 22 million Negroes of the United States of America are engaged in a creative battle / to end the long night of racial injustice.
- 저는 노벨평화상을 수락합니다. / 미합중국의 2천 2백만 흑인들이 ~ 창의적인 전투에 바쁜 이 와중에 / 인종차별의 긴 밤을 끝내기 위한
- 저는 미합중국의 2천 2백만 흑인들이 인종차별의 긴 밤을 끝내기 위한 창의적인 전투에 바쁜 이 와중에 노벨평화상을 수락합니다.
- at a moment when[시간의 부사절로 ~하는 순간에] / are engaged in[~에 종사하다, are busy ~ing] / to end[to부정의 부사적 용법 목적: ~하기 위해서]

- **accept** [æksépt] vt. 받아들이다. / **engaged** [engéidʒd] a. 약속이 있는, 활동 중인, 종사하고 있는 / **creative** [kriːéitiv] a. 창조적인, 독창적인(originative) / **racial** [réiʃəl] a. 인종(상)의, 민족(간)의 / **injustice** [indʒʌ́stis] n. U,C 부정, 불법, 비행. [cf.] unjust.

I accept this award / on behalf of a civil rights movement / which is moving with determination

and a majestic scorn for risk and danger / to establish a reign of freedom and a rule of justice.

- 저는 이 상을 수락합니다. / 시민운동을 대신하여 / 결단과 장엄한 멸시를 받으며 위험으로 치닫고 있는 / 자유통치와 정의의 법칙을 확립하기 위해

- 자유통치와 정의의 법칙을 확립하기 위해 결단과 장엄한 멸시를 받으며 위험으로 치닫고 있는 시민운동 을 대신하여 저는 이 상을 수락합니다.

- on behalf of[~을 대신하여] / a civil rights movement[시민운동] / which[주격관계대명사로 movement 를 수식] / is moving for risk and danger[위험으로 치닫고 있는] / with determination[with+추상명사 =쿠사구 determinatively] / (with) a majestic scorn[부사구: 장엄한 조롱을 받으며] / to establish[to부 정사의 부사적용법의 목적: ~확립하기 위해서]

- **determination** [ditə̀ːrmənéiʃən] n. U 결단(력) / **majestic** [mədʒéstik] a. 장엄한, 위엄 있는 (dignified), 웅대한, 당당한 / **scorn** [skɔːrn] n. U 경멸, 멸시, 비웃음, 냉소 / **risk** [risk] n. U,C 위험, 모험 / **danger** [déindʒər] n. U,C 위험 (상태), 위난(peril) / **reign** [rein]n. 통치, 지배 / **establish** [istǽbliʃ] vt. 확립하다, 설치[설립]하다.

I am mindful / that only yesterday in Birmingham, Alabama, / our children, crying out for brotherhood, were answered / with fire hoses, snarling dogs and even death.

- 저는 걱정이 됩니다./ 알라바마의 버밍햄에서 어제만 하더라도 / 형제애[노조]를 울부짖던 우리의 아이들 이 답변을 받았습니다. / 소방호수의 물세례와 으르렁 위협하는 개들 그리고 심지어 죽이겠다는 위협으로

- 알라바마의 버밍햄에서 어제만 하더라도 노조를 울부짖던 우리의 어린 아이들이 소방호수의 물세례와 으 르렁 위협하는 개들과 심지어 죽이겠다는 위협의 보복을 받은 것이 저는 걱정이 됩니다.

- only[단지 ~만 하더라도] / our children[주어], (who were) crying out[울부짖다], were answered[답변 을 받다, 보복을 받다]

- **mindful** [máindfəl] a. 주의 깊은(of) / **brotherhood** [brʌ́ðərhùd] n. U 형제의 관계, 협회 / **snarl** [snɑːrl] vi. 으르렁거리다; 고함치다.

I am mindful / that only yesterday in Philadelphia, Mississippi, / young people seeking to secure the right to vote were brutalized and murdered.

- 저는 염려가 됩니다. / 미시시피의 필라델피아에서 어제만 하더라도 / 투표권을 쟁취하고자 하는 젊은이들 이 잔인하게 맞고 살해당했다는 소식

- 미시시피의 필라델피아에서 어제만 하더라도 투표권을 쟁취하고자 하는 젊은이들이 잔인하게 맞고 살해 당했다는 소식에 저는 마음이 아픕니다.

- young people (who were) seeking to / the right to vote[to부정사의 형용사적 용법: 투표할 권리] / were brutalized[수동태: 잔인하게 폭행을 당하다] / were murdered[살해당하다]

- **secure** [sikjúər] vt. 안전하게 하다, 굳게 지키다. 확고히 하다. / **brutalize** [brúːtəlàiz] vt., vi. 잔인 하게 하다[되다]. / ⊤ **murder** [mə́ːrdər] vt. 살해하다.

And only yesterday / more than 40 houses of worship in the State of Mississippi alone / were bombed or burned / because they offered a sanctuary to those who would not accept segregation.

- 그리고 단지 어제만하더라도 / 미시시피주만 해도 40여 곳의 예배당이 폭파되었고 불태워졌습니다. / 왜 냐하면 그들이 인종차별을 피하고자하는 사람들에게 은신처를 제공해 주었기 때문에

- 그리고 단지 어제만하더라도 인종차별을 피하고자하는 사람들에게 은신처를 제공해 주었다는 명목 하에 40여 곳의 예배당이 폭파되었고 방화되었습니다.

- more than[~이상] / houses of worship[예배당] / alone[~만 하더라도] / were bombed[수동태: 폭파를

당했다] / (were) burned[방화 되었다] / they[=more than 40 houses of worship] / offer A[a sanctuary] to B[those who(~하는 사람들)] A에게 B를 제공하다. / would[~하고 싶어했다]

- **worship** [wə́ːrʃip] n. U 예배, 숭배, 존경 / **bomb** [bɑm] vt. 폭격[폭파]하다. / **burn** [bəːrn] v. (p., pp. burned, burnt) vt. 불태우다, 태우다. / **sanctuary** [sǽŋktʃuèri] n. 거룩한 장소, 교회, 은신처/ **segregation** [sègrigéiʃ-ən] n. U 분리, 격리, 인종 차별(대우)

I am mindful / that debilitating and grinding poverty / afflicts my people and chains them to the lowest rung of the economic ladder.

- 저는 걱정스럽습니다. / 쇠약해지고 쓰라린 가난이 / 제 동포들을 괴롭히고 그들을 경제계층의 최하위 단계로 얽어매는

- 쇠약해지고 쓰라린 가난이 제 동포들을 괴롭히고 그들을 경제계층의 최하위 단계로 얽어매는 것이 저는 걱정스럽습니다.

- debilitating and grinding과 poverty는 능동적인 관계이므로 ing형 형용사 / chains A[them=my people] to B[the lowest ~] A를 B로 쇠사슬로 얽어매다.

- **debilitate** [dibílətèit] vt. (사람·몸을) 쇠약하게 하다. / **grinding** [gráindiŋ] a. (맷돌로) 타는; 가는; 삐걱거리는; (일이) 힘드는, 지루한; 괴롭히는; 압제의, 폭정의; 매우 아픈[쑤시는]. / **afflict** [əflíkt] vt. 괴롭히다(distress) / **chain** [tʃein] vt. 속박[구속]하다, 감금하다. / **rung** [rʌŋ] n. (사회적 지위 등의) 단계.

Therefore, I must ask / why this prize is awarded to a movement which is beleaguered and committed to unrelenting struggle; / to a movement which has not won the very peace and brotherhood / which is the essence of the Nobel Prize.

- 그러므로, 저는 묻고 싶습니다. / 왜 이 상은 잔인한 투쟁에 공격당하고 헌신하는 운동에 수여되는지를; / 진정한 평화와 조합을 얻지 못하는 운동에 / 노벨평화상의 본질인

- 그러므로, 저는 왜 이 상은 잔인한 투쟁에 공격당하고 헌신하는 운동에 수여되는지와 노벨평화상의 본질인 진정한 평화와 조합을 얻지 못하는 운동에 수여되는 지를 묻고 싶습니다.

- Therefore[결과로서] / ask why[ask의 목적어] / is awarded to a movement[운동에 수여되다] which [주격 관계대명사] is beleaguered (to unrelenting struggle)[무자비한 투장으로 공격받는] and committed to unrelenting struggle[무자비한 투장에 헌신한] / the very peace[진정한 평화] / which[의 선행사는 the very peace and brotherhood]

- **award** [əwɔ́ːrd] vt. 수여하다, (상을) 주다. / **movement** [múːvmənt] n. (정치적·사회적) 운동 / **beleaguer** [bilíːgər] vt. 포위 공격하다. 괴롭히다. / **committed** [kəmítid] a. 전념하는, 헌신적인 / **unrelenting** [ʌnriléntiŋ] a. 무자비한 / **essence** [ésəns] n. U 본질, 핵심

✹ 다음 글을 읽고 물음에 답하시오. [1~3]

Your Majesty, Your Royal Highness, Mr. President, Excellencies, Ladies and Gentlemen:

I accept the Nobel Prize for Peace at a moment when 22 million Ⓐ**Negroes** of the United States of America are ①**engaged in** a creative battle to end the long night of racial injustice.

I accept this award ②**on behalf of** a civil rights movement which is moving with determination and a majestic scorn for risk and danger to establish a reign of freedom and a rule of justice. I am mindful that only yesterday in Birmingham, Alabama, our children, crying out for brotherhood, were answered with fire hoses, ③**snarling** dogs and even death. I am mindful that only yesterday in Philadelphia, Mississippi, young people seeking to secure the right to vote were brutalized and murdered. And only yesterday more than 40 houses of worship in the State of Mississippi alone were bombed or burned because they ④**offered** a sanctuary to those who would not accept segregation. I am mindful that debilitating and grinding poverty afflicts my people and chains them to the ⑤**lowest rung** of the economic ladder.

Therefore, I must ask why this prize is awarded to a movement which is beleaguered and committed to unrelenting struggle; to a movement which has not won the very peace and brotherhood which is the essence of the Nobel Prize.

1. 위 글의 제목으로 가장 적절한 것은?

① The Greatest Prize in the World
② The Mindfulness of My Brothers
③ The Qualification for the Nobel Prize
④ The Hope for New Era
⑤ The World Peace

2. 위 글에서 밑줄 친 ①~⑤ 중, 의미가 <u>다른</u> 것은?

① busy
② representative of
③ barking
④ provided
⑤ most dejected level

3. 위 글에서 밑줄 친 Ⓐ의 상황과 어울리지 <u>않은</u> 것은?

① They are treated in racial injustice.
② They are campaigning for a civil rights.
③ They are crying out for freedom and justice.
④ They are securing the right of vote and brotherhood.
⑤ They are on the modest level of economic ladder.

1. ② 2. ② 3. ⑤

After contemplation, I conclude that this award which I receive on behalf of that movement is a profound recognition that nonviolence is the answer to the crucial political and moral question of our time - - the need for man to overcome oppression and violence without resorting to violence and oppression. Civilization and violence are antithetical concepts. Negroes of the United States, following the people of India, have demonstrated that nonviolence is not sterile passivity, but a powerful moral force which makes for social transformation. Sooner or later all the people of the world will have to discover a way to live together in peace, and thereby transform this pending cosmic elegy into a creative psalm of brotherhood, If this is to be achieved, man must evolve for all human conflict a method which rejects revenge, aggression and retaliation.

The foundation of such a method is love.

The tortuous road which has led from Montgomery, Alabama, to Oslo bears witness to this truth. This is a road over which millions of Negroes are travelling to find a new sense of dignity. This same road has opened for all Americans a new era of progress and hope.

After contemplation, / I conclude / that this award which I receive on behalf of that movement / is a profound recognition / that nonviolence is the answer to the crucial political and moral question of our time / -- the need for man to overcome oppression and violence / without resorting to violence and oppression.

- 숙고한 후, / 저는 결론을 내렸습니다. / 그 운동을 대신하여 제가 받는 이 상은 / 뜻 깊은 치하라고 / 비폭력은 우리시대의 중대한 정치적 도덕적 문제에 대한 해답이라는 / 즉 인간이 억압과 폭력을 극복할 필요성 / 폭력과 억압에 의지하는 것 없이

- 숙고한 후, 저는 그 운동을 대신하여 제가 받는 이 상은 비폭력은 우리시대의 중대한 정치적 도덕적 문제에 대한 해답이라는 것과 인간이 폭력과 억압에 의지하는 것 없이 억압과 폭력을 극복할 필요성에 대한 해답이라는 뜻 깊은 치하라고 결론을 내렸습니다.

- I conclude that[명사절로 목적어임] / this award which[목적격 관계대명사] I receive[의 목적어는 this award: 내가 받는 상] on behalf of[~을 대신하여] a profound recognition과 that절은 동격절임[~라는 뜻 깊은 치하] / the answer to[~대한 답변] / the need for man to overcome[인간이 ~을 극복할 필요성] / without resorting to[~에 의존 없이]

- **contemplation** [kὰntəmpléiʃən / kɔ̀ntem-] n. U숙고, 기대, 계획 / **conclude** [kənklúː d] vt. 끝내다, ~에 결말을 짓다. / **profound** [prəfáund] a. 뿌리 깊은, 뜻 깊은, 심원한. [opp.] superficial. / **recognition** [rèkəgníʃ-ən] n. U 승인, 허가, 치하, 표창, 감사, 보수 / **nonviolence** [nɑnváiələns] n. 비폭력(주의), 평화적 수단(에 의한 저항), 비폭력 데모 / **crucial** [krúː ʃəl]a. 결정적인, 중대한 / **moral** [mɔ́(ː)r-əl, mɑ́r-]a. 도덕(상)의, 윤리(상)의, 훈계[교육]적인 / **overcome** [òuvərkʌ́m] (-came [-kéim]; -come) vt. 극복하다. / **resort** [rizɔ́ː rt] vi. 의지하다, 도움을 청하다, 호소하다(to)

Civilization and violence are antithetical concepts. / Negroes of the United States, following the people of India, / have demonstrated / that nonviolence is not sterile passivity, / but a powerful moral force which makes for social transformation.

- 문명과 폭력은 정반대의 개념입니다. / 인도 국민 다음으로 미국의 흑인들은 보여주었다. / 비폭력은 단순한 무저항이 아닌, / 사회변혁을 위해 필요한 강력한 도덕적 힘이라는
- 문명과 폭력은 정반대의 개념입니다. 인도 국민 다음으로 미국의 흑인들은 비폭력은 단순한 무저항이 아닌, 사회변혁을 위해 필요한 강력한 도덕적 힘이라는 것을 보여 주었습니다.
- following[~ 다음으로=after] / have demonstrated[현재완료 결과: ~을 보여 주었다] / that[demonstrated의 목적어인 명사절] / not A[sterile passivity], but B[a powerful moral force] which[주격 관계대명사] make[의 목적어는 a powerful moral force]

- **antithetic, -ical** [æntiθétik] a. 정반대의, 대조적인 / **concept** [kánsept] n.개념, 생각 / **demonstrate** [démənstrèit] vt. 증명하다, (모형·실험에 의해) 설명하다. / **sterile** [stéril]a. 메마른, [opp.] fertile. [cf.] barren. 단조로운, 빈곤한 / **passivity** [pæsívəti] n. U 수동(성); 복종, 무저항 / **transformation** [trænsfə : rméiʃ-ən] n. 변형, 변화, 변질 / oppression [əpréʃən] n. C,U 압박, 억압, 탄압, 학대.

동영상 강좌 http://youtu.be/_fYEXhwsq58

Sooner or later / all the people of the world / will have to discover a way to live together in peace, / and thereby transform this pending cosmic elegy / into a creative psalm of brotherhood. / If this is to be achieved, / man must evolve for all human conflict a method / which rejects revenge, aggression and retaliation.

- 조만간 / 세상 모든 사람들은 / 평화롭게 함께 더불어 사는 방식을 발견해야만 할 것입니다. / 그리하여 이 절박한 우주적인 만가를 형제애의 창의적인 성가로 바꿔야만 할 것입니다. / 만일 이것이 성취되기를 원한다면, / 사람들은 모든 인간의 분쟁을 위한 원한, 공격 그리고 보복을 거절하는 방식을 개발해야만 합니다.
- 조만간 세상 모든 사람들은 평화롭게 함께 더불어 사는 방식을 발견해야만 할 것입니다. 그리하여 이 절박한 우주적인 만가를 형제애의 창의적인 성가로 바꿔야만 할 것입니다. 만일 이것이 성취되기를 원한다면, 사람들은 모든 분쟁을 없애기 위해 원한, 공격 그리고 보복을 거절하는 방식을 개발해야만 합니다.
- will have to[해야만 할 것이다] / a way to live together[to부정사의 형용사적 용법: 함께 사는 방식] / in peace[부사구: 평화롭게=peacefully] / transform A[this pending cosmic elegy] into B[a creative psalm of brotherhood] A를 B로 변형시키다 / If[조건절] is to[~하고 싶다] / be achieved[성취되다] / evolve의 목적어는 a method[방식을 개발하다] / which[주격 관계대명사의 선행사는 a method]

- **transform** [trænsfɔ́ : rm] vt. 변형시키다(into). 바꾸다 / **pending** [péndiŋ] a. 미정[미결]의, 절박한 / † **cosmic**[kázmik] a. 우주의, 정연한. [cf.] chaotic. / **elegy** [élədʒi] n. 비가(悲歌), 엘레지, 애가, 만가 / **psalm** [sɑ : m] n. 찬송가, 성가(hymn), 성시(聖詩) / **evolve** [iválv] vt. 발전시키다. 전개하다, 안출[고안, 개발]하다 / **conflict** 갈등 / **revenge** [rivéndʒ] n. U 보복, 복수(vengeance) / **aggression** 공격 / **retaliation** 보복, 앙갚음

The foundation of such a method is love. / The tortuous road which has led from Montgomery, Alabama, to Oslo / bears witness to this truth.

- 그러한 방법의 토대는 사랑입니다. / 알라바마의 몬트고메리로부터 오슬로에 이르는 구불구불한 도로는

이 진실의 산 증인입니다.
- such+a/an+(형용사)+명사[그러한 ~] / road which has led[~을 이어져 있는 도로] from A to B[A로부터 B까지]
- **foundation** [faundéiʃ-ən] n. 설립, 기초, 토대 / **tortuous** [tɔ́ːrtʃuəs] a. (길·흐름 따위의) 구불구불한, 부정한, 불성실한 / **witness** [wítnis] n. 증언, 증인, 목격자. bear witness to [of] ~을 입증하다.

This is a road over which millions of Negroes are travelling / to find a new sense of dignity. This same road has opened for all Americans a new era of progress and hope.
- 이것은 수백만 흑인들이 여행하는 도로입니다. / 존엄의 새로운 감각을 찾기 위해 / 이와 같은 길은 모든 미국인들을 위해 진보와 희망의 새로운 시대를 열어 놓았습니다.
- 이 도로는 존엄의 새로운 감각을 찾기 위해 수백만 흑인들이 여행하는 도로입니다. 이와 같은 도로는 모든 미국인들을 위해 진보와 희망의 새로운 시대를 열어 놓았습니다.
- millions of Negroes are travelling (over a road) / to find[to부정사의 부사적용법: ~찾기 위해] / has opened a new era
- **dignity** [dígnəti] n. U 존엄, 위엄; 존엄성; 품위 ② U (태도 따위가) 장중함, 위풍

✽ 다음을 읽고 물음에 답하시오. [4~7]

After contemplation, I conclude that this award which I receive on behalf of that movement is a profound recognition that _____Ⓐ_____ is the answer to the crucial political and moral question of our time -- the need for man to overcome oppression and violence without resorting to violence and oppression. Civilization and violence are antithetical concepts. Negroes of the United States, following the people of India, have demonstrated that _____Ⓐ_____ is not sterile passivity, but a powerful moral force which makes for social transformation. Sooner or later all the people of the world will have to discover a way to live together in peace, and thereby transform this pending cosmic elegy into a creative psalm of brotherhood, If this is to be achieved, man must evolve for all human conflict a method which rejects revenge, aggression and retaliation. _____Ⓑ_____.

The tortuous road which has led from Montgomery, Alabama, to Oslo bears witness to this truth. This is a road over which millions of Negroes are travelling to find a new sense of dignity. This same road has opened for all Americans a new era of progress and hope.

4. 위 글의 주제로 가장 적절한 것은?

① We should pave new roads for speedy traffic.

② By way of love we can solve our problems.

③ More specific instruction is needed for nonviolence.

④ The world peace should come in by everybody's open mind.

⑤ Civilization and violence are not to be avoided throughout ages.

5. 위 글에서 밑줄 친 빈칸 Ⓐ에 공통으로 적절한 단어는?

① thankfulness   ② cooperation

③ humanity   ④ nonviolence

⑤ affection

6. 위 글에서 밑줄 친 빈칸 Ⓑ에 가장 적절한 표현은?

① We should think of others' problems

② We should be ready for other's oppression

③ The method is to ignore of other's indifference

④ The foundation of such a method is love

⑤ The new construction of roads of love isn't ready

7. 위 글과 일치하지 <u>않은</u> 것은?

① 비폭력은 우리시대의 중대한 정치적 도덕적 문제에 대한 해답이다.

② 문명과 폭력은 정반대의 개념이다.

③ 조만간 세상 모든 사람들은 평화롭게 함께 더불어 사는 방식을 발견해야만 할 것이다.

④ 모든 미국인들을 위해 진보와 희망의 새로운 시대를 열어 도로는 만들어 놓아야만 한다.

⑤ 사람들은 모든 분쟁을 없애기 위해 원한, 공격 그리고 보복을 거절하는 방식을 개발해야만 한다.

4. ②   5. ④   6. ④   7. ④

Tribute to Dogs

by George Graham Vest

[난이도 ★★☆☆☆]

동영상 강좌 http://youtu.be/EAWH1cB9vWM

George Graham Vest - Tribute to Dogs (c. 1855) after winning a case against a man who killed a dog

----

🔖 **본문분석**

George Graham Vest - Tribute to Dogs (c. 1855) after winning a case against a man who killed a dog

- 조오지 그래햄 베스트의 개를 죽인 사람에 대한 재판에서 이긴 후, 개에 대한 찬사

🔖 **문법분석**

- tribute to[~에게 찬사] / after (he won=winning) a case against a man[한 피고인에 대한 재판에서 이긴 후]

🔖 **단어분석**

- **tribute** [trībjuː t]n. ① U,C 공물, 조세; 과도한 세[관세, 부과금, 임대료], 터무니없는 징수금; 납공[납세] 의무. ② C,U 찬사, 칭찬[감사, 존경]을 나타내는 말[행위, 선물, 표시].

Gentlemen of the Jury: The best friend a man has in the world may turn against him and become his enemy. His son or daughter that he has reared with loving care may prove ungrateful. Those who are nearest and dearest to us, those whom we trust with our happiness and our good name may become traitors to their faith. The money that a man has, he may lose. It flies away from him, perhaps when he needs it most. A man's reputation may be sacrificed in a moment of ill-considered action. The people who are prone to fall on their knees to do us honor when success is with us, may be the first to throw the stone of malice when failure settles its cloud upon our heads.

🔖 **본문분석**

Gentlemen of the Jury: ③The best friend ①a man ②has ④in the world may ⑤turn against him and ⑥become his enemy.

- 배심원 여러분께: ①사람이 ②사귀는 ③친구는 ④도대체 ⑤배신하며 ⑥적이 되는지요.

🔖 **문법분석**

- the Jury[재판에서 배심원] / The best friend (that/whom/who 생략) / in the world[도대체] / may[가능성: ~인 것 같다] turn against[등을 돌리다, 배신하다] and become[~가 되다]

----

④His son or daughter that ①he ③has reared ②with loving care ⑤may prove ungrateful.
- ①자신이 ②애지중지하게 ③양육한 ④자식은 ⑤은혜를 모르는 것 같습니다.

Tribute to Dogs

by George Graham Vest

🪶 **문법분석**

- His son or daughter [that생략가능: 목적격 관계대명사, 목적격 whom이나 주격 who도 가능] he[=a man 일반적인 사람, 우리] has reared[현재완료 결과: ~양육한] with loving care[with+명사=부사구 lovingly carefully] may prove ungrateful[prove+형용사 2형식: 은혜를 모르는 것으로 입증되다]

🪶 **단어분석**

- **rear** [riər] vt. ① 기르다; 사육[재배]하다; 육성하다. [SYN.] ⇨ GROW. / **ungrateful** [ʌngréitfəl] a. ① 은혜를 모르는, 감사할 줄 모르는. ② (일이) 일한 보람이 없는, 헛수고의; 달갑지 않은, 불유쾌한. ⑭ ~ly [-fəli]—ad. ⑭~ness —n.

🪶 **동의어/반의어**

- **ungrateful** a. fruitless[frúːtlis], unappreciated[ʌnəpríːʃièitid], unrequited[ʌnrikwáitid]일방적인, unrewarded[ʌnriwɔ́ːrdid], thoughtless[θɔ́ːtlis], ant. rewarding[riwɔ́ːrdikdiŋ] appreciative[əpríːʃətiv]

---

①**Those who are nearest and dearest to us,** ②**those whom we trust with our happiness and our good name** ④**may become traitors** ③**to their faith.**

🪶 **본문분석**

- ①우리와 가장 가깝고 귀중한 사람들, ②우리가 진정 믿고 있는 사람들이 ③믿음에 반하는 ④배신자가 되는 것 같습니다.

🪶 **문법분석**

- Those who[주격 관계대명사: ~하는 사람들] are nearest[최상급: 가장 가까운] and dearest[최상급: 가장 사랑스런] to us[우리에게], those whom[목적격 관계대명사: ~하는 사람들] we trust with our happiness[with+명사=부사구: 우리가 만족스럽게] and (with) our good name[with+명사=부사구: 우리의 명예를 걸고] / traitors to[=against ~에 반하는 배신자]

🪶 **동의어/반의어**

- **traitor** n. betrayer [bitréiər], informer [infɔ́ːrmər], judas [dʒúːdəs], renegade [rénigèid], turncoat [tɔ́ːrnkòut] ant. patriot [péitriət]

The money that a man has, he may lose. ①**It** ④**flies away from him,** ②**perhaps** ③**when he needs it most.**

🪶 **본문분석**

- 자신이 갖고 있는 돈을 그는 잊어버리는 것 같습니다. ①그 돈은 ②아마 ③그가 절실히 필요로 할 때, ④그에게서 멀리 달아납니다.

🪶 **문법분석**

- The money that[목적격 관계대명사, has의 목적어는 the money] / he may lose[의 목적어는 the money] / It[=the money 불가산 명사] flies away from[~로부터 달아나다] when he needs it most[그가 돈을 가장 절실히 필요로 할 때]

---

①**A man's reputation** ③**may be sacrificed** ②**in a moment of ill-considered action.**

- ①한 사람의 명성은 ②잘못된 행동을 하는 순간에 ③사라지는 것 같습니다.

🍃 문법분석

- be sacrificed[수동태: 희생양이 되다, 사라지다] in a moment[~의 순간에] of ill-considered action[잘못된 행동의]

🍃 단어분석

- **reputation** [rèpjətéiʃ-ən] n. U,C 평판, 세평. 명성. / **sacrifice** [sǽkrəfais] vt. 희생하다, 단념[포기]하다 (for; to). / **moment** [móumənt] n. 순간, (어느 특정한) 기회, (보통 the ∼) 지금.

🍃 동의어/반의어

  reputation n. character[kǽriktər], fame[feim], name[neim], position[pəzíʃən], prestige[prestíːdʒ], rank[ræŋk], standing   status [stǽndiŋ stéitəs]

----

③The people who are prone to fall on their knees ②to do us honor ①when success is with us, ⑤may be the first to throw the stone of malice ④when failure settles its cloud upon our heads.

🍃 본문분석

- ①우리가 성공할 때, ②우리의 위신을 세워주기 위해 ③자신의 무릎을 꿇기 쉬운 사람들은 ④실패의 그림자가 우리 앞에 있을 땐, ⑤악으로 가장 먼저 돌변하는 사람들인 것 같습니다.

🍃 문법분석

- The people who[주격 관계대명사: ~하기 쉬운 사람들] are prone to fall on their knees[무릎을 꿇다, 굴복하다] to us honor[부정사의 부사적 용법: 우리의 명예를 세워주기 위해서] [삽입 부사절]when success is with us[우리가 성공할 때] may be[본동사] the first (people) to throw the stone of malice[악담하다, 배신하다] [시간의 부사절]when failure settles its cloud upon our heads[실패가 우리 머리 앞에 드리울 때]

🍃 단어분석

- **prone** [proun] a. ~하기 쉬운, ~의 경향이 있는(to) / **malice** [mǽlis] n. U (적극적인) 악의, 원한

🍃 동의어/반의어

- **malice** n. animosity[ænəmásəti], malevolence[məlévələns], rancor[rǽŋkəːr], spite[spait], spleen[spliːn] ant. affection[əfékʃən]

The one absolutely unselfish friend that man can have in this selfish world, the one that never deserts him, the one that never proves ungrateful or treacherous is his dog. A man's dog stands by him in prosperity and in poverty, in health and in sickness. He will sleep on the cold ground, where the wintry winds blow and the snow drives fiercely, if only he may be near his master's side. He will kiss the hand that has no food to offer. He will lick the wounds and sores that come in encounters with the roughness of the world. He guards the sleep of his pauper master as if he were a prince. When all other friends desert, he remains. When riches

Tribute to Dogs

take wings, and reputation falls to pieces, he is as constant in his love as the sun in its journey through the heavens.

----

②**The one absolutely unselfish friend that man can have** ①**in this selfish world,** ③**the one that never deserts him,** ④**the one that never proves ungrateful or treacherous** ⑤**is his dog.**

🔖 본문분석

- ①이 이기적인 세상에서 ②사람이 사귈 수 있는 아주 이타적인 친구는, ③결코 친구를 버리지 않고, ④은혜를 모르거나 배신하지 않은 ⑤자신의 개일 뿐입니다.

🔖 문법분석

The one (who is) absolutely unselfish friend[주어] that[주격 관계대명사] have[목적어는 friend], in this selfish world[부사구: 이 삭막한 세상에서], the one[동격절=friend] that never deserts him[자신을 버리지 않은 친구], the one[동격절] that never proves[동사+형용사] ungrateful or treacherous is[본동사] his dog.

🔖 단어분석

- **treacherous** [trétʃ-ərəs] a. 배반하는(to), 믿을 수 없는, 위험한

🔖 동의어/반의어

- **treacherous** a. chancy[tʃǽnsi]위험한, dangerous[déindʒərəs], perilous[pérələs], risky[ríski], unstable[ʌnstéibəl], perfidious[pərfídiəs], traitorous[tréit-ərəs], unfaithful[ʌnféiəfəl] ant. safe[seif] faithful[féiəfəl]

----

①**A man's dog** ④**stands by him** ②**in prosperity and in poverty,** ③**in health and in sickness.**

🔖 본문분석

- ①한 주인의 개는 ②좋을 때나 나쁠 때나 ③건강할 때나 아플 때나 ④늘 주인 옆에 서 있습니다.

🔖 문법분석

- stand by[전치사: ~옆을 지키다] in prosperity[부사구: 좋을 때에] in poverty[부사구: 가난할 때에, 나쁠 대에] in health[부사구: 건강할 때에] in sickness[부사구: 아플 때에]

🔖 단어분석

- **prosperity** [prɑspérəti] n. U 번영, 성공. [opp.] adversity. / **poverty** [pávərti] n. U 가난, 빈곤([opp.] wealth). 결핍, 부족(of; in).

🔖 동의어/반의어

- **prosperity** n. abundance[əbándəns], affluence[ǽflu(ː)əns], fortune[fɔːrtʃ-ən], opulence[ápjələns], riches[rítʃiz], wealth[welə], accomplishment[əkámpliʃmənt], success[səksés], victory[víktəri] ant. poverty[pávərti] failure[féiljər]
- **poverty** n. destitution, impoverishment, indigence[indidʒəns], penury[pénjəri], privation[praivéiʃən], dearth[dəːrə], insufficiency[insəfíʃənsi], meagerness[míːgəːrnis], paucity[pɔːsəti], scarcity[skéəːrsəti] ant. wealth[welə] abundance[əbándəns]

----

⑤**He will sleep on the cold ground,** ③**where** ①**the wintry winds blow and** ②**the snow drives**

fiercely, ④if only he may be near his master's side.

📖 본문분석

- ①찬바람이 불고 ②눈이 심하게 몰아치는 ③곳에서, ④만일 그가 주인 옆에만 있을 수 있다면, ⑤개는 차가운 땅바닥에서 자려 할 것입니다.

📖 문법분석

- will[의지와 고집을 내타냄: 자려할 것이다] ~, where[관계부사로 on which: 그 땅 위에서] ~ the snow drives fiercely[심한 누보라가 치다], if[조건절: 만일 ~한다면]

📖 단어분석

- **drive** [draiv] v. (drove [drouv], driven [drívən]) vt. 쫓다, 몰아내다, 휘두르다. / **fierce** [fiərs] a. (fiercer; -est) 몹시 사나운(savage), 모진(raging), 격심한(intense).

---

①He ③will kiss ②the hand that has no food to offer. ①He ⑤will lick ④the wounds and sores that come ③in encounters ②with the roughness of the world.

📖 본문분석

- ①개는 ②먹이를 주지 못하는 주인의 손에 ③키스를 할 것이다. ①그는 ②모진 세상과 ③만날 때 ④주인의 상처를 ⑤핥아 주려 할 것이다.

📖 문법분석

- the hand that[주격 관계대명사] has no food to offer[부정사의 형용사적 용법: 제공할 음식]. the wounds and sores[상처와 고통] that[주격 관계대명사] come in encounters[우연히 만나다] with[부사구: 모진 세상] the roughness of the world

📖 단어분석

- **encounter** [enkáuntər] n. (우연히) 만남, 조우 / **wound** [wuː nd, (고어·시어) waund] n. 부상, 상처. (정신적) 고통, 상처. / sore [sɔː r] n. 상처, 종기(boil). 옛 원한. / **rough** [rʌf] a. 거친, 텁수룩한, 털이 많은. ③ 울퉁불퉁한, (날씨 따위가) 험악한.

📖 동의어/반의어

- **encounter** n. appointment[əpɔ́intmənt] confrontation[kànfrəntéiʃən], fight[fait], meeting[míː tiŋ], rendezvous[rándivu], battle[bǽtl], brush[brʌʃ], clash[klæʃ], skirmish[skɔ́ː rmiʃ] v. affront[əfrʌ́nt], confront[kənfrʌ́nt], face[feis] , meet[miː t], endure[endjúər], experience[ikspíəriəns], suffer[sʌ́fər] ant. retreat[ritríː t]퇴각하다, avoid[əvɔ́id escape[iskéip]

---

①He ④guards ③the sleep of his pauper master ②as if he were a prince.

📖 본문분석

- ①그는 ②마치 자신이 왕자인 것처럼, ③가난한 주인의 잠자리를 ④지킨다.

📖 문법분석

as if[접속사(가정법): 마치 ~인 것처럼]

Tribute to Dogs

by George Graham Vest

🔖 **단어분석**

- **pauper** [pɔ́ː pər] n.극빈자, 빈민, 거지

When all other friends desert, he remains. ①When riches take wings, and ②reputation falls to pieces, ③he ⑤is as constant in his love ④as the sun in its journey through the heavens.

🔖 **본문분석**

- 모든 다른 친구들이 떠날 때, 그는 홀로 남습니다. ①부가 쌓일 때나, ②명성이 산산조각이 날 때도, ③그는 ④하늘에 유유히 떠있는 태양과도 같이 ⑤그의 사랑은 변함이 없습니다.

🔖 **문법분석**

- deserts[=leaves] / falls to pieces[명성이 조각조각이 되다, 실패하다] / as constant[형용사] in his love as[동급비교: ~처럼 ...한] / as the sun in its journey through the heavens[천국을 여행하는 태양처럼(하늘에 유유히 떠있는 태양과도 같이)]

🔖 **단어분석**

- **desert** [dizɔ́ː rt] vt. 버리다, 돌보지 않다(abandon). (신념 따위를) 버리다. / **take wing(s)** 날아가다; 비약적으로 신장하다, 기세가 더하다; 도망치다.

If fortune drives the master forth, an outcast in the world, friendless and homeless, the faithful dog asks no higher privilege than that of accompanying him, to guard him against danger, to fight against his enemies. And when the last scene of all comes, and death takes his master in its embrace and his body is laid away in the cold ground, no matter if all other friends pursue their way, there by the graveside will the noble dog be found, his head between his paws, his eyes sad, but open in alert watchfulness, faithful and true even in death.

---

①**If fortune ④drives the master forth, ②an outcast in the world, ③friendless and homeless, ⑤the faithful dog ⑧asks no higher privilege than that of accompanying him, ⑥to guard him against danger, ⑦to fight against his enemies.**

🔖 **본문분석**

- ①만일 운명이 ②세상에서 버림받은 ③친구도 집도 없는 ④주인으로 만들지라도, ⑤그 충실한 개는 ⑥주인을 위험으로부터 지키기 위해, ⑦주인의 적과 싸우기 위해 ⑧주인과 함께하는 특권 이상을 요구하지도 않습니다.

🔖 **단어분석**

outcast [áutkæst / -kàː st] n. 추방당한 사람, 집 없는 사람, 부랑자; 폐물.

🔖 **문법분석**

- if[조건절: 만일 ~라면, 양보절로 해석 가능: ~일지라도] / the master와 an outcast는 동격 / (who is) friendless and homeless[주격관계대명사와 동사가 생략됨: an outcast를 수식함] / ask no higher privilege

[더 높은 특권을 요구하지 않다: 합당한 대가를 요구하지 않다] / that[=privilege 주인을 따르는 대가] ~, to guard[부정사의 부사적 용법으로 원인, 이유: 위험으로부터 주인을 보호하기 때문에]; to fight against[~에 대항하여 싸우다]

📎 **단어분석**

- **privilege** [prívəlidʒ] n. 특권. / **accompany** [əkʌ́mpəni,] vt. ~에 동반하다, ~에 수반하여 일어나다. ~의 반주를 하다(on). / **guard** [gɑːrd] vt. (위험 따위에서) 보호하다, 지키다(from; against).

📎 **동의어/반의어**

- **privilege** n. advantage [ædvǽntidʒ], entitlement, liberty [líbəːrti], license [láis-əns]   v. empower [empáuər], entitle [entáitl], grant [grænt], permit [pəːrmít], sanction [sǽŋkʃən]   ant. penalty [pénəlti] prevent [privént]

---

①And when the last scene of all comes, and ②death takes his master in its embrace and ③his body is laid away in the cold ground, ④no matter if all other friends pursue their way, there ⑤by the graveside will ⑩the noble dog ⑪be found, ⑥his head between his paws, ⑦his eyes sad, ⑧but open in alert watchfulness, ⑨faithful and true even in death.

📎 **본문분석**

- ①그리고 마지막 순간이 닥칠 때나 ②자신의 주인이 죽을 때나 ③자신의 몸이 차가운 땅에 파묻힐 때, ④모든 다른 친구들이 자신의 길을 갈지라도, ⑤주인의 무덤 옆에는 ⑥자신의 발톱 사이로 머리를 대고, ⑦슬픈 눈으로, ⑧경계하면서, ⑨자신이 죽을 때까지도 충실하고 진실한 ⑩그 고귀한 개가 ⑪있을 것이다.

📎 **문법분석**

when[시간의 부사절: ~할 때] ~ and his body is laid away[수동태: 자신의 몸이 파묻힐 때], no matter[양보절: 비록 ~일지라도] ~, there[도치문] will be found the noble dog by the graveside / (with ~한 채로) his head ~ / (with ~한 채로) his eyes sad, but (with ~한 채로) open ~ /

📎 **단어분석**

embrace [imbréis] n. 포옹. / **lay away** 파묻다

67

❋ 다음 글을 읽고 물음에 답하시오. [1~4]

Gentlemen of the Jury: The best friend a man has in the world may turn against/for him and become his ① enemy. His son or daughter that he has reared with loving care may prove ungrateful/ungratefully. Those who are nearest and dearest to us, those whom we trust with our happiness and our good name may become ② traitors to their faith. The money that a man has, he may lose. It flies away from him, perhaps when he needs it most. A man's ③reputation may be sacrificed/sacrifice in a moment of ill-considered action. The people who are prone to fall on their knees to do us ④ dishonor when success is with us, may be when ⑤ failure settles its cloud upon our heads.

1. 위 글의 주제로 가장 적절한 것은?

① Who you have to trust is only you, so don't make friends anymore.
② The proper punishment would be necessary for children not to respect their parents.
③ The wild world doesn't make us believe each other.
④ In the emergency the money would be significant above all.
⑤ Today's friends will be tomorrow's enemies, which needs to be careful to make friends.

2. 위 글에서 네모상자 안의 적절한 단어는?

① against   ungrateful   be sacrificed
② for   ungratefully be sacrificed
③ against   ungrateful   sacrifice
④ for   ungratefully sacrifice
⑤ against   ungrateful   sacrifice

3. 위 글에서 밑줄 친 ①~⑤중, 문맥상 단어의 쓰임이 어색한 것은?

①   ②   ③   ④   ⑤

4. 위 글에서 밑줄 친 빈칸에 가장 적절한 표현은?

① the man who praises his friend
② the last man to blame for his mistake
③ the person to help the failure
④ the second to ask why he has failed
⑤ the first to throw the stone of malice

❋ 다음 글을 읽고 물음에 답하시오. [5~10]

①The one absolutely unselfish friend that man can have in this selfish world, ②the one that never deserts him, the one that never proves ungrateful or treacherous is his dog. A man's dog stands by ③him in prosperity and in poverty, in health and in sickness. ④He will sleep on the cold ground, where the wintry winds blow and the snow drives fiercely, if only ⑤he may be near his master's side. He will kiss the hand that has no food to offer. He will lick the wounds and sores that come in encounters with the roughness of the world. He guards the sleep of his pauper master ____Ⓐ____ he were a prince. When all other friends desert, he remains. When riches take wings, and reputation falls to pieces, he is as constant in his love as the sun in its journey through the heavens.

_____Ⓑ_____ fortune drives the master forth, an outcast in the world, friendless and homeless, the faithful dog asks no higher privilege than that of accompanying him, to guard him against danger, to fight against his enemies. And when the last scene of all comes, and death takes his master in its embrace and his body is laid away in the cold ground, no matter if all other friends pursue their way, there by the graveside will the noble dog be found, his head between his paws, his eyes sad, but open in alert watchfulness, faithful and true even in death.

5. 위 글의 주제로 가장 적절한 것은?

① A faithful animals should be reared at home.
② The sanitary places are necessary for dogs to grow properly.
③ To choose a correct dog is essential for his master's health.
④ Nobody can't be believed except for dogs.
⑤ Because of dogs' faithfulness dogs' popularity increases more and more.

6. 위 글에서 밑줄 친 ①~⑤중, 가리키는 대상이 나머지 넷과 <u>다른</u> 것은?

①   ②   ③   ④   ⑤

7. 위 글에서 '개'의 특징과 어울리지 <u>않는</u> 단어는?

① unselfish   ② ungrateful
③ faithful   ④ accompanying

⑤ watchful

8. 위 글의 분위기는?

① surprising   ② disappointing
③ believable   ④ exciting
⑤ boring

9. 위 글에서 밑줄 친 빈칸 Ⓐ, Ⓑ에 적절한 단어는?

① though   As if
② because   However
③ when   Even though
④ as if   If
⑤ while   Though

10. 위 글과 일치하지 <u>않는</u> 것은?

① 충실하고 믿음직한 개의 특성을 잘 설명하고 있다.
② 작가는 사람보다 개에 더 많은 애착을 느끼고 있다.
③ 작가는 수의사로 개에 대한 많은 정보를 갖고 있다.
④ 개는 죽음에 직면해서도 주인을 배신하지 않는다.
⑤ 개는 주인에게 바라는 것이 없다.

1. ③	2. ①	3. ④dishonor → honor	
4. ⑤	5. ④	6. ③	7. ②	8. ①
9. ④	10. ③		

[난이도 ★★☆☆☆]

동영상 강좌

St. Francis of Assisi - Sermon to the Birds (1220)

My little sisters, the birds, much bound are you to God, your Creator, and always in every place ought you to praise Him, for that He has given you liberty to fly about everywhere, and has also given you double and triple raiment; moreover He preserved your seed in the ark of Noah, that your race might not perish out of the world; still more are you beholden to Him for the element of the air which He has appointed for you; beyond all this, you sow not, neither do you reap; and God feeds you, and gives you the streams and fountains for your drink; the mountains and valleys for your refuge and the high trees whereon to make your nests; and because you know not how to spin or sow, God clothes you, you and your children; wherefore your Creator loves you much, seeing that He has bestowed on you so many benefits; and therefore, my little sisters, beware of the sin of ingratitude, and study always to give praises to God.

본문분석

St. Francis of Assisi - Sermon to the Birds (1220)

- 아시시의 프란시스 성자의 소녀들에게 설교

단어분석

- sermon [sə́ːrmən]n. 설교. [cf.] preachment.

----

①My little sisters, the birds, ④much bound are ③you ②to God, your Creator, and ⑤always in every place ⑧ought ⑥you ⑦to praise Him, ⑨for that ⑩He ⑬has given ⑪you ⑫liberty to fly about everywhere, and ⑯has also given ⑭you ⑮double and triple raiment;

- ①나의 귀여운 어린 자매들이여, ②창조주인 하느님에 ③너희들은 ④단단히 묶여 있을지니, ⑤늘 어디서나 ⑥너희들은 ⑦하느님을 찬양⑧하여라. ⑨그에 대한 보답으로 ⑩하느님은 ⑪너희들에게 ⑫어디든 날아갈 수 있는 자유를 ⑬주셨고 ⑭너희들은 ⑮두 배 세배 옷을 ⑯받았기 때문이니라.

단어분석

- My little[어린] sisters와 the birds[귀여운 여자아이] 동격 / [도치문] you are much[부사로 bound를 수식] bound to[bind의 과거분사: ~에 묶여 있는] God와 your Creator[창조주]는 동격임 / [도치문] you ought to[조동사≒should ~해야 한다(권유, 충고)] / praise[칭송하다] Him[=God] / for[전치사 ~을 위해] / that[지시대명사]로 He has given ~와 동격을 이룸 / He[=God] has given[현재완료 결과] you[간접목적어] liberty[직접목적어] to fly[to부정사로 liberty를 수식하는 형용사적 용법 ~날아갈 자유] about[주위를 날다] / everywhere[부사, 어디든] / has given[현재완료, 결과] / double[두 배] / triple[세 배] / raiment 옷

----

①moreover ②He ⑤preserved ④your seed ③in the ark of Noah, that ⑥your race ⑧might not perish ⑦out of the world;

- ①더욱이 ②하느님은 ③노아의 방주에 ④너희들의 씨앗을 ⑤보존하셨으니 ⑥너희는 ⑦세상에서 ⑧굶어 멸망하지 않

을지어다.

🖎 문법분석

- **moreover** [mɔːróuvəːr] ad. 그 위에, 더욱이, 또한. / He[=God] / preserved your seed[싸앗을 보존하다] / (so) that[계속적인 용법 : 그러므로, 그리하여] / might not[조동사(가능성): ~하지 않을 것이다] / perish out of the world 세상에서 사라져 멸망하다

🖎 단어분석

- **preserve** [prizə́ːrv] vt. 보존하다. / **ark** [ɑːrk] n. 〖성서〗 (노아의) 방주(方舟)(Noah's ～). / **perish** [périʃ] vi. 썩어 없어지다, 사라지다, 타락하다.

🖎 동의어/반의어

- **perish** v. depart[dipáːrt], expire[ikspáiər]끝나다, pass away, decline[dikláin], ebb[eb]점점 쇠하다, fade[feid], subside[səbsáid], wane[wein] ant. revive[riváiv] vt. ① 소생하게 하다; (~의 의식을) 회복시키다; 기운 나게 하다. ② (잊어진 것·유행·효력·기억·관심·희망 따위가) 되살아나게 하다, 부흥시키다.

---

⑥still more are ①you ⑦beholden ⑤to Him ④for the element of the air which ②He ③has appointed for you;

- ①너희들은 ②하느님이 ③너희들을 위해서 정해주신 ④공기로 인해 ⑤그에게 ⑥훨씬 더 많은 ⑦은혜를 입고 있느니라.

🖎 문법분석

- still[부사: 비교급 수식] more[훨씬 더] / beholden[은혜를 입은] to[전치사: ~에게] / the air which[관계대명사] ~ appointed[목적어는 the air] - beholden[bihóuldən] a. (문어) 「서술적」 은혜를 입고, 신세를 지고. / element [éləmənt] n. 요소 / ✝appoint [əpɔ́int] vt. 지명하다, 지시하다.

🖎 동의어/반의어

- **appoint** v. commission[kəmíʃən], designate[dézignèit], name[neim], nominate[námənèit], select[silékt], arrange[əréindʒ], determine[ditəːrmin], establish[istǽbliʃ], set[set] ant. dismiss[dismís] 떠나게 하다, 해임하다 cancel[kǽnsəl]

---

①beyond all this, ②you sow not, ③neither do you reap; and ④God feeds you, and ⑤gives you the streams and fountains for your drink;

- ①무엇보다도, ②너희가 씨앗을 뿌리지 않으면, ③너희는 거두지 못하게 되느니라. ④하느님이 너희에게 일용할 양식을 주시고, ⑤마실 물로 시내와 샘을 주셨느니라.
- beyond all this[이 모든 것을 넘어, 무엇보다도] / (if) you sow not[=you don't sow] / sow[씨앗을 뿌리다] / neither[또한 ~도 아닌] do you reap[=or also you don't reap] / feed[양식을 주다]
- **sow** v. plant[plænt], scatter[skǽtəːr], seed[siːd], strew[struː] 흩뿌리다, disperse[dispə́ːrs], disseminate[disémənèit], spread[spred] , foster[fɔ́ːstəːr], incite[insáit]자극하다, 선동하다, invoke[invóuk]기원하다, 호소하다. ant. harvest[háːrvist], gather[gǽðər] prevent[privént]

---

②the mountains and valleys ①for your refuge and ⑤the high trees ④whereon ③to make your nests;

- ①은신처를 위한 ②산과 계곡을 주셨고 ③너희들의 보금자리를 위한 ④그 위에 ⑤높은 나무를 주셨느니라.
- **refuge** [réfjuːdʒ]n. 피난소, 은신처. /****nest** [nest] n. 보금자리, 둥우리. / whereon [hwɛ-ərɔ́n] ad. (고어) ① 「의문사」 무엇의 위에, 누구에게. ② 「관계사」 그 위에(on which).

🖎 **동의어/반의어**

- **refuge** n. escape[iskéip], haven[héivən], resort[riːsɔ́ːrt], retreat[ritríːt], sanctuary[sǽŋktʃuèri] shelter[ʃéltəːr]

and ③because ①you ②know not how to spin or sow, ④God ⑥clothes ⑤you, you and your children;

- 그리고 ①너희들이 ②직물을 짜고 바느질하는 방법을 모르기 ③때문에, ④하느님은 ⑥너희와 너희 자식들에게 ⑥의복을 주셨느니라.
- you know not[=you don't know] / how to[~하는 방법]
- **clothe** [klouð] vt. ~에게 옷을 주다. / spin [spin] v. (spun [spʌn], (고어) span [spæn]; spun; ~ning) vt. (실을) 잣다, 방적하다.

---

wherefore your Creator loves you much, seeing that He has bestowed on you so many benefits;

- 그러므로 너희 하느님은 너희를 너무 사랑하셔서 너희들에게 너무나 많은 혜택을 하사하셨느니라.
- wherefore[관계부사: 그러므로] / seeing that[~이므로] / bestowed on A[you] B[so many benefits]
- **bestow** [bistóu] vt. 주다, 수여[부여]하다, 증여하다. / **benefit** [bénəfit] n. 이익, 은혜.

---

and ①therefore, ②my little sisters, ③beware of the sin of ingratitude, and ⑤study ④always to give praises to God.

- ①그러므로 ②나의 어린 누이들은 ③은혜를 모르는 죄를 경계하고 ④늘 하느님을 찬양하는 것에 ⑤애쓸 지어다.
- **beware** [biwéər] vi, vt. 조심[주의]하다, 경계하다. / **study** [stʌ́di] vt. 배우다, 공부하다. ~에 마음을 쓰다.

St. Francis of Assisi - Sermon to the Birds (1220)

My little sisters, the birds, much bound are you to God, your Creator, and always in every place ought you to praise Him, for that He has given you liberty to fly about everywhere, and has also given you double and triple raiment; moreover He preserved your seed in the ark of Noah, that your race might not perish out of the world; still more are you beholden to Him for the element of the air which He has appointed for you; beyond all this, you sow not, neither do you reap; and God feeds you, and gives you the streams and fountains for your drink; the mountains and valleys for your refuge and the high trees whereon to make your nests; and because you know not how to spin or sow, God clothes you, you and your children; wherefore your Creator loves you much, seeing that He has bestowed on you so many benefits; and therefore, my little sisters, beware of the sin of ingratitude, and _____.

1. 위 글의 주제로 가장 적절한 것은?

① The Almighty gave us all things we need.
② Food we are fed with is a gift by God.
③ God's love was to preserve seeds in ark of Noah.
④ You little sisters should love each other.
⑤ Only to give praises to God is a reward for gratitude.

2. 위 글의 분위기로 가장 적절한 것은?

① regretful   ② complex
③ appreciative   ④ understandable
⑤ liberal

3. 위 글에 나타난 단어의 관계가 나머지 넷과 다른 것은?

① sermon = preachment
② Creator = heavenly Father
③ liberty = freedom
④ bestow = receive
⑤ ingratitude = thanklessness

4. 위 글에서 밑줄 친 빈칸에 가장 적절한 표현은?

① study always to give praises to God
② always go church to pray for your sin
③ love your neighbors even though they don't love you
④ remember his warnings in order not for revenge
⑤ fly all around the world

5. 위 글과 일치하지 않은 것은?

① 늘 하느님께 감사하는 마음을 지녀야만 한다.
② 하느님은 노아의 방주 안에 씨앗을 저장했다.
③ 씨앗을 뿌리지 않아도 하느님은 늘 일용할 양식을 준다.
④ 직물을 짜고 꿰매는 법을 몰라 하느님은 옷을 주셨다.
⑤ 하느님은 우리를 너무나 사랑하셔서 많은 것을 주셨다.

1. ⑤   2. ③   3. ④   4. ①   5. ③

독해 The Votes for Women Speech

by Mark Twain

[난이도 ★★☆☆☆]

동영상 강좌 http://youtu.be/KNSIXBHfi8A

Ladies and Gentlemen - It is a small help that I ① can afford, but it is just ② such help that one can give as coming from the heart through the mouth. The report of Mr. Meyer was admirable, and I was as interested in it ③ as you have been. Why, I'm twice as old as he, and I've had ④ so much experience that I would say to him, when he makes his appeal for help: ⑤ "Don't make it for today or tomorrow, but collect the money on the spot."

We are ⑥ all creatures of sudden impulse. We must ⑦ be worked up by steam, as it were. ⑧ Get them to write their wills now, or it may be too late by-and-by. Fifteen or twenty years ago I had an experience I shall never forget. I got into a church which was crowded by a sweltering and panting multitude. The city missionary of our town - Hartford - made a telling appeal for help. He ⑨ told of personal experiences among the poor in cellars and top lofts requiring instances of devotion and help. The poor are always good to the poor. When a person with his millions gives a hundred thousand dollars it makes a great noise in the world, but he does not miss ⑩ it; it's the widow's mite that makes no noise but does the best work.

I remember on ⑪ that occasion in the Hartford church the collection was being taken up. The appeal had so stirred me that I ⑫ could hardly wait for the hat or plate to come my way. I had four hundred dollars in my pocket, and I was anxious to drop it in the plate and wanted to borrow more. But the plate was so long in coming my way that ⑬ the fever-heat of beneficence was going down lower and lower - going down at the rate of a hundred dollars a minute. The plate was passed too late. When it finally came to me, my enthusiasm had gone down ⑭ so much that I kept my four hundred dollars - and stole a dime from the plate. So, you see, time sometimes leads to crime. Oh, ⑮ many a time have I thought of that and regretted it, and I ⑯ adjure you all to give while the fever is on you.

⑰ Referring to woman's sphere in life, I'll say that woman is always right. For twenty-five years I've been a woman's rights man. I have always believed, long before my mother died, that, with her gray hairs and admirable intellect, perhaps she knew ⑱ as much as I did. Perhaps she knew as much about voting as I.

I ⑲ should like to see the time come when women shall help to make the laws. I should like to see that whiplash, the ballot, in the hands of women. As for this city's government, I don't want to say much, except that it is a shame - a shame; but ⑳ if I should live twenty-five years longer - and ㉑ there is no reason why I shouldn't - I think I'll see women handle the ballot. If women had the ballot to-day, ㉒ the state of things in this town would not exist.

㉓ If all the women in this town had a vote today they would elect a mayor at the next election, and they would rise in their might and change the awful state of things now existing here.

문법 분석

① ~할 여유가 있다.

② such + 명사 that[관계 대명사] : 가슴에서 우러나 말로 전달되는 것과 같은 도움

③ as you have been (interested in the report) 여러분들이 그 보고서에 흥미를 가져왔듯이.

④ so[부사] ~ that[관계 대명사] I would say[의 목적어인 that의 선행사 much experience] 제가 그에게 말하곤 했던 많은 경험.

⑤ 일을 내일로 미루지 마세요. on the spot : 현장에서, 즉시.

⑥ 갑작스런 충동의 생명체 = 충동적인 사람들.

⑦ work up 자극을 주다. as it were 말하자면.

⑧ get[사역동사] them[목적어] to write their wills now 그들이 지금 유언장을 쓰도록 시키다.

⑨ tell about[of] ~에 관해 말하다.

⑩ it = a great noise(떠들석함, 관심) 그는 다른 사람의 관심을 놓치려 하지 않다.

⑪ 그런 때(그런 경험) : 소란을 떨거나, 조용히 기부한 위의 두 경우를 일컬음.

⑫ 거의 기다릴 수 없었다. 안절부절하다.

⑬ 헌금의 열기가 점점 수그러지고 있었다.

⑭ so much that 절 : 너무 ~해서 ...하다. 나의 열정이 너무 가라앉아 나는 4백 달러를 헌금하지 않았다.

⑮ [도치문] many a time I have thought of that[지시대명사]

⑯ adjure A[you all] to B[give] : A에게 B하라고 간청하다. 여러분 모두에게 열정이 있을 때 기부하라고 간청드립니다.

⑰ [분사구문] As[If] I refer to ~.

⑱ A as much as B : B만큼 A한, 제가 아는 것만큼 그녀(어머니)는 알고 있다.

⑲ would like to ~하고 싶다.

⑳ [전치사] except (for) ~ 제외하고 / except that 절

㉑ [가정법 미래] 혹시라도 ~한다면, 혹시라도 제가 25년 더 산다면

㉒ 그렇게 되지 않응 이유가 없다. 분명히 25년 더 산다.

㉓ 큰 변화를 예고함.

㉔ [가정법 과거, 현재 사실에 반대] 이 마을에 모든 여성들이 오늘날 선거권을 가진다면, 그들은 다음 선거에서 새로운 시장을 선출할 것이다. - 선거권이 없어서 선출할 수 없다.

동영상 강좌 http://youtu.be/KNSIXBHfi8A

---

①Ladies and Gentlemen - It is ③a small help that ②I ④can afford, but ⑤it is ⑧just such help that ⑦one can give ⑥as coming from the heart through the mouth.

- ①신사 숙녀 여러분 - ②저는 ③약간에 도움을 ④줄 여유 밖에 없지만, ⑤그것은 ⑥입을 통해 가슴에서 뿜어져 나오는 것과 같은 ⑦사람이 줄 수 있는 ⑧바로 그런 도움입니다.

①The report of Mr. Meyer was admirable, and ③I was as interested_in it ②as you have been. ④ Why, I'm twice as old as he, and ⑥I've had so much experience that I would say to_him, ⑤when

he makes his appeal for help: ⑦"Don't make it for today or tomorrow, ⑧but collect the money on the_spot."

- ①메이어씨의 보고서는 감동적이었고, ②여러분들도 그래왔듯 ③저도 그것에 흥미를 느꼈습니다. ④왜, 제가 그의 나이보다 두 배나 많을까요, 그리고 ⑤그가 저에게 도움을 호소 할 때, ⑥전 많은 경험으로 그에게 말하곤 했답니다.: ⑦"오늘 또는 내일 조급해하지 마세요, ⑧그러나 즉석에서 돈을 모으세요. 라고)."

①We are all ②creatures of sudden impulse. ④We ⑥must be worked up ⑤by steam, ③as it were. ⑩Get ⑦them ⑨to write their wills ⑧now, ⑪or ⑫it may be too late by-and-by. ⑬Fifteen or twenty years ago ⑮I had an experience ⑭I shall never_forget.

- ①우리 모두는 ②충동의 생명체입니다. ③말하자면, ④우린 ⑤증기(정열)에 의해 ⑥자극 받아야만 합니다. ⑦그들에게 ⑧지금 당장 ⑨유언장을 쓰도록 ⑩시키세요, ⑪그렇지 않으면 ⑫너무 늦은 이별이 될 것 같아요. ⑬15년이나 20년 전에, ⑭전 결코 잊지 못할 ⑮경험을 했습니다.

①I ③got into a church which was crowded by ②a sweltering and panting multitude. ④The city missionary of_our town - Hartford ⑤made a telling appeal for help. ⑥He ⑨told of personal experiences ⑧among the poor in cellars_and top lofts ⑦requiring instances of devotion and help.

- ①저는 ②더위에 땀에 흘리면서 헐떡이고 있는 군중들로 ③붐비는 전 한 교회 안으로 들어갔죠. ④우리 마을 하트포트의 시 전 도사는 ⑤도움을 요청하는 확실한 부탁을 했습니다. ⑥그는 ⑦헌금과 도움의 여러 시례를 바라면서 ⑧지하실과 맨 위층에 있는 가난한 사람들에게 ⑨자신의 여러 경험담을 들려주었습니다.

①The poor are always good to the poor. When ②a person with his millions ③gives a hundred thousand dollars ④it makes a great noise in the world, but ⑤he_does not miss it; it's ⑦the widow's mite ⑥that makes no noise but does the best work. ⑩I remember on that occasion ⑨in the Hartford church ⑧the collection was being taken up.

- ①가난한 사람들은 늘 유유상종이죠. ②백만 달러를 갖고 있는 자는 ③10만 달러를 기부할 때, ④그것은 세상을 떠들썩하게 하지만, ⑤그는 그것을 놓치지 않으려 합니다.; ⑥요란하진 않지만 최고의 것을 하는 것은 ⑦바로 미망인의 작은 금액입니다. ⑧헌금이 모아지고 있던 ⑨그 하트포드 교회의 ⑩그때가 기억이 납니다.

①The appeal ②had so stirred me that ④I could_hardly wait for ③the hat or plate to come my way. ⑤I ⑥had four hundred dollars in my pocket, and ⑦I was anxious to drop it in the plate and ⑧wanted to borrow more. But ⑨the plate was so long in coming my way that ⑩the fever-heat of beneficence ⑪was going down lower and lower - ⑬going down at the rate of a hundred dollars ⑫a minute.

- ①그 간원은 ②너무 절 너무나 감동시켜 ③내 쪽으로 오는 헌금 모자나 접시를 ④거의 기다릴 수가 없었습니다. ⑤전 ⑥주머니 속에 4백 달러를 갖고 있었고, ⑦전 그 돈 전부를 접시에 넣을까 갈등을 하면서 ⑧나중에 더 빌리기를 원했습니다. 그러나 ⑨그 헌금접시가 나에게 오는 시간 너무 오래 걸려, ⑩자선의 열광된 심정은 ⑪조금씩 사라지고 있었습니다. - ②분 당 ③100달러의 비율로 내려가고 있었죠.

①The plate was passed too late. ②When it finally came to me, ③my enthusiasm had gone down so much that ④I kept my four hundred dollars - ⑤and stole a dime from the plate. ⑥So, you see,

⑦time sometimes leads to crime.
- ①그 헌금접시가 너무 늦게 왔어요. ②마침내 그것이 내가 왔을 때, ③제 열정은 너무나 사라져서, ④전 400달러를 간직할 수 있었죠. - ⑤그리고 접시에서 1개의 동전도 몰래 훔쳤죠.. ⑥그래서, 여러분도 알듯이 ⑦시간은 때때로 범죄를 일으키죠.

①Oh, many a time ②have I thought of that and ③regretted it, and ⑤I adjure you all to give ④ while the fever is on you. ⑥Referring to woman's sphere in life, ⑦I'll say that woman is always right. ⑧For twenty-five years ⑨I've been a woman's rights man. ⑪I ⑭have always believed, ⑩ long before my mother died, that, ⑫with her gray hairs and admirable intellect, ⑬perhaps she knew as much as I did. ⑮Perhaps she knew as much about voting as I.
- ①오, 너무나 많은 시간 ②저는 그것에 고민했고 ③후회했고, ④그 열정이 여러분에게 있는 동안 ⑤여러분 모두가 베푸는 것을 간청합니다. ⑥사는 동안 그 여자의 상황을 언급하면서, ⑦저는 그 여자가 늘 옳다고 전 말할 것입니다. ⑧25년 동안 ⑨저는 여성 권리를 위해 일해 왔습니다. ⑩저희 어머니가 돌아가시기 오래 전부터, ⑪전, ⑫백발이 된 흰 머리카락과 감동스런 지성으로, ⑬아마도 그녀는 제가 아는 것만큼 알았을 것이라 ⑭늘 믿어 왔습니다. ⑮아마도 그녀는 저만큼 투표에 관해 알고 있으셨죠.

①I ③should like to see the time come ②when women shall help to make the laws. ④I ⑦should like to see ⑤that, whiplash, the ballot, ⑥in the hands of women. ⑧As for this city's government, ⑩I don't want to say much, ⑨except that it is a shame - a shame; ⑪but if I should live twenty-five years longer - and ⑫there is no reason why I shouldn't. ⑬I think I'll see women handle the ballot. ⑭If women had the ballot to-day, ⑮the state of things in this town would not exist.
- ①전 ②여성들이 입법을 하는데 도움이 될 때가 ③오기를 기대합니다. ④전 ⑤그런 자극과 투표용지를 ⑥손에 든 여성들을 ⑦보고 싶습니다. ⑧이 시정부에 관해, ⑨그것은 부끄러움이라는 것 외에는 ⑩많은 것을 말하고 싶진 않습니다.; ⑪혹시 제가 25년 더 오래 산다면 - ⑫제가 바라는 이유가 있습니다. - ⑬그것 여성들이 투표하는 것을 보는 것이라 생각합니다. ⑭만일 여성들이 오늘 투표를 할 권리를 갖는다면, ⑮이 마을에서 많은 것들이 바뀔 것입니다.

①If all the women in this town had a vote today ②they ④would elect a mayor ③at the next election, and ⑤they ⑥would rise in their might and ⑧change the awful state of things ⑦now existing here.
- ①만일 이 마을에 사는 모든 여성들이 오늘 투표한다면, ②그들은 ③다음 선거에서 ④한 시장을 뽑을 것이고, ⑤그들은 ⑥자신들의 힘으로 일어설 것이고 ⑦지금 이곳에 존재하는 ⑧끔찍한 상황들은 바뀔 것입니다.

🖎 단어분석
- **afford** [əfɔ́ːrd] vt. ~의 여유가 있다. / **on [upon] the spot** (1) (바로) 그 자리에서, 즉석에서. (2) 현장에서[의] / **impulse** [impʌls] n. U,C (마음의) 충동, 일시적 충격. / **swelter** [swéltər] vi. 무더위에 지치다; 더위 먹다; 땀투성이가 되다. / **pant** [pænt] vi. 헐떡거리다, 숨차다. / **missionary** [míʃ-ənèri] n. ① 선교사, 전도사. / **telling** [téliŋ] a. 효력이 있는, 현저한. / **cellar** [sélər] n. 지하실 / **loft** [lɔːft] n. (교회·강당 따위의) 위층, 위층의 관람석(gallery) / **widow** [wídou] n. 미망인; 홀어미, 과부 / **mite** [mait] n. 적으나마 갸륵한 기부, 조금. / **appeal** [əpíːl] n. U,C (여론 따위에의) 호소, 호소하여 동의를 구함. 매력, 사람의 마음을 움직이는 힘. / fever-heat 열광, 이상 흥분 / **beneficence** [bənéfəsəns] n. U 선행, 은혜; 자선; 덕행. / **adjure** [ədʒúər] vt. ~에게 엄명하다; ~에게 간원하다, 탄원하다(entreat) (to) / whiplash 자극 / **ballot** [bǽlət] n. C (무기명) 투표용지; U 비밀(무기명) 투표, U (the ~) 투표[선거]권.

독해 The Votes for Women Speech

by Mark Twain

동영상 강좌 http://youtu.be/HZEOmIUS_Lo

✸ 다음 글을 읽고 물음에 답하시오. [1~5]

Ladies and Gentlemen - It is a small help that I can afford, but Ⓐ it is just such help that one can give as coming from the heart through the mouth. The report of Mr. Meyer was admirable, and I was as interested in it as you have been. Why, I'm twice as old as he, and I've had so much experience that I would say to him, when he makes his appeal for help: Ⓑ "Don't make it for today or tomorrow, but collect the money on the spot."

We are all creatures of sudden impulse. We must be worked up by steam, as it were. Get them to write their wills now, or it may be too late by-and-by. Fifteen or twenty years ago I had an experience I shall never forget. I got into a church which was crowded by a sweltering and panting multitude. The city missionary of our town - Hartford - made a telling appeal for help. He told of personal experiences among the poor in cellars and top lofts requiring instances of devotion and help. Ⓒ **The poor are always good to the poor.** When a person with his millions gives a hundred thousand dollars it makes a great noise in the world, but he does not miss it; it's the widow's mite that makes no noise but does the best work.

1. 위 글로 보아, 작가가 강조하는 것은?

① today　　　　② tomorrow
③ right now　　④ the past
⑤ the future

2. 위 글의 밑줄 친 Ⓐ가 의미하는 것은?

① common help　　② special support
③ extraordinary aid　④ sincere assistance
⑤ unique service

3. 위 글의 밑줄 친 Ⓑ가 의미하는 것은?

① Think carefully before you go a step forward.
② Be careful when you want to succeed in your target.
③ Today or tomorrow won't be believable.
④ Money is everything.
⑤ Don't delay what you really have to do.

4. 위 글 Ⓒ와 어울리는 속담은?

① Sweet after bitter
② Birds of a feather flock together.
③ Lay up for a rainy day.
④ A light before the wind
⑤ Bear in mind all the time

5. 위 글과 일치하지 않은 것은?

① 제 도움은 큰 것은 아닐지라도, 정성어린 도움이다.
② 인간은 충동에 의해서가 아닌, 정렬로 깨어나야만 한다.
③ 작가는 영원히 잊지 못할 경험을 했다.
④ 무더운 여름 한 선교사는 헌금을 호소하고 있었다.
⑤ 한 미망인의 헌금은 요란하지도 효과도 없다.

✸ 다음 글을 읽고 물음에 답하시오. [6~10]

I remember on that occasion in the Hartford church the collection was being taken up. The appeal had so stirred me that I could hardly wait for the hat or plate to come my way. I had four hundred dollars in my pocket, and I was anxious to drop it in the plate and wanted to borrow more. But the plate was so long in coming my way that the fever-heat of beneficence was going down lower and lower - going down at the rate of a hundred dollars a minute. Ⓐ**The plate was passed too late.** When it finally came to me, my enthusiasm had gone down so much that I kept my four hundred dollars - and stole a dime from the plate. So, you see, time sometimes leads to crime. Oh, many a time have I thought of that and regretted it, and I adjure _____.

Referring to woman's sphere in life, I'll say that woman is always right. For twenty-five years I've been a woman's rights man. I have always believed, long before my mother died, that, with her gray hairs and admirable intellect, perhaps she knew as much as I did. Perhaps she knew as much about voting as I.

I should like to see the time come Ⓑ **when women shall help to make the laws.** I should like to see that whiplash, the ballot, in the hands of women. As for this city's government, I don't want to say much, except that it is a shame - a shame; but if I should live twenty-five years longer - and there is no reason why I shouldn't - I think I'll see women handle the ballot. If women had the ballot to-day, the state of things in this town would not exist.

If all the women in this town had a vote today they would elect a mayor at the next election, and they would rise in their might and change the awful state of things now existing here.

6. 위 글에서 Ⓐ가 암시하는 것은?

① The weather was so sultry that it might delay the circulation of the plates.
② The church was too small to get good enough plates.
③ Church-goers were so impressed that they might give more contribution.
④ There were no plates big enough to be collected more money.
⑤ It was just the author's feeling that was in hurry to give donation.

7. 위 글 밑줄 친 Ⓑ와 관련된 사항과 거리가 먼 것은?

① They would appear at the voting office with ballots in their hands.
② It would take more time to be pass on the woman suffrage.
③ The situations in the town would change, no longer existing like before.
④ They would elect a new mayor at the next election.
⑤ After 25 years, there will be no day women vote.

8. 위 글 빈칸에 적절한 표현은?

① you don't wait for the time to come
② you all to give while the fever is on you
③ you should think of the bright future
④ you ought to save some for the donation
⑤ you return back whatever you've got for free

9. 위 글의 첫 문단에서의 작가의 심정의 변화는?

① indifferent   impressed

② motivated   discouraged

③ impressed   cool

④ inspired   indifferent

⑤ interested   excited

10. 위 글과 일치하지 <u>않은</u> 것은?

① The clergy addressed a good sermon to inspire most of the present people.

② As being spent the time, man doesn't intend to keep his previous resolution.

③ The writer felt his mind change, but he wasn't shaken up like ordinary people.

④ For the feminism the author tried his best.

⑤ On the memory of his mother, he could bring about the importance of women's right.

1. ③	2. ④	3. ⑤	4. ②	5. ⑤
6. ③	7. ⑤	8. ②	9. ③	10. ③

UNIT 10 The American Equal Rights

by Elizabeth Cady Stanton

[난이도 ★★☆☆☆]

동영상 강좌 http://youtu.be/wt6S2t9waSk

In considering the question of suffrage, there are two starting points: one, that this right is a gift of society, in which certain men, having inherited this privilege from some abstract body and abstract place, have now the right to secure it for themselves and their privileged order to the end of time. This principle leads logically to governing races, classes, families; and, in direct antagonism to our idea of self-government, takes us back to monarchies despotisms, to a experiment that has been tried over and over again, 6,000 years, and uniformly failed. "I do not hold my liberties," says Gratz Brown in the Senate of the United States, "by any such tenure. On the contrary, I believe, whenever you establish that doctrine, whenever you crystallize that idea in the public mind of this country, you ring the death-knell of American liberties."

Ignoring this point of view as untenable and anti-republican, and taking the opposite, that suffrage is a natural right—as necessary to man under government, for the protection of person and property, as are air and motion to life—we hold talisman by which to show the right of all classes to the ballot, to remove every obstacle, to answer every objection, to point out the tyranny of every qualification to the free exercise of this sacred right.

🔖 **본문해석**

①**In considering the question of suffrage,** ②**there are two starting points:** ③**one, that** ④**this right is** ⑩**a gift of society, in which** ⑥**certain men, having inherited this privilege** ⑤**from some abstract body and abstract place,** ⑨**have now the right to secure it** ⑧**for themselves and their privileged order** ⑦**to the end of time.**

- ①참정권의 문제를 고찰해 볼 때, ②2개의 출발점이 있습니다. ③하나는 ④이 권리는 ⑤어떤 추상적인 조직과 추상적인 장소로부터 ⑥이 특권을 부여받은 특정한 남성들이 ⑦죽을 때까지 ⑧자신들과 특권의 질서를 위해 ⑨그것을 보호할 권리를 지금 갖는 ⑩사회의 선물입니다.

- In considering[부사구=When we consider] / [도치문] there are[동사] two starting points[주어]: one 과 that[절]은 동격절 / society in which[관계대명사: 그 사회에서 ~을 부여받은 특정한 남성들은], (who have=having) inherited / have now the right to secure it[=this right] / to the end of time[끝까지, 죽을 때까지]

---

①**This principle** ④**leads** ②**logically** to ③**governing races, classes, families; and,** ⑤**in direct antagonism to our idea of self-government,** ⑩**takes us back** ⑨**to monarchies despotisms,** ⑧**to a experiment that** ⑥ **has been tried over and over again, 6,000 years, and** ⑦**uniformly failed.** "④**I do not hold my liberties**," ⑤**says** ①**Gratz Brown** ②**in the Senate of the United States,** "③**by any such tenure.** ①**On the contrary,** ⑧**I believe,** ②**whenever you establish that doctrine, whenever** ③**you** ⑤**crystallize that idea** ④ **in the public mind of this country,** ⑥**you** ⑦**ring the death-knell of American liberties.**"

- ①이 원리는 ②논리적으로 ③인종, 계급, 가족을 통치하는 것을 ④이끌고 있습니다.; 그리고 ⑤우리 생

The American Equal Rights

by Elizabeth Cady Stanton

각의 절제에 직접적인 반감이 일어날 때, ⑥6,000년 동안 반복해서 시도 되었지만, ⑦한결같이 실패한 ⑧실험, ⑨즉 군주제로 ⑩우리를 도로 끌고 갑니다. ①Gratz Brown은 ②미 상원 연설에서 "③임기 내에서 조차 ④저는 제 자유를 갖고 있지 않습니다."⑤라고 말했죠. ①반대로, ②여러분이 그런 정책을 세울 땐 늘, ③여러분이 ④이 나라의 대중들의 마음속에 ⑤그런 생각을 구체화시킬 땐 늘, ⑥여러분은 ⑦미국인의 자유의 종말의 종을 울리고 있다고 ⑧저는 믿습니다.

- lead to[전치사: ~을 이끌다] / in direct ~[부사구: ~할 때] / (This principle) takes us back to[우리를 도로 ~으로 데려가다] / (takes us back to) to a experiment 문장으로 연결됨] / whenever[복합관계부사: ~언제나] / ring the death-knell[종말의 종을 울리다]

---

③**Ignoring** ①**this point of view as untenable and** ②**anti-republican, and** ⑧**taking the opposite,** ⑦ **that suffrage is a natural right** — ⑥**as necessary to man under government,** ④**for the protection of person and property,** ⑤**as are air and motion to life** — ③**we hold talisman by which** ⑨**to show the right of all classes to the ballot,** ⑩**to remove every obstacle,** ⑪**to answer every objection,** ⑫**to point out the tyranny of every qualification to the free exercise of this sacred right.**

- ①이런 견해를 옹호할 수도 없고 ②반공화적인 것으로 ③무시하면서, ④개인과 재산을 보호하기 위한 ⑤생명에 필요한 공기와 활동과 같이 ⑥정부 하에서 사람에 필요한 것으로써, ⑦참정권은 타고난 권리라는 것을 ⑧반대하면서, ⑨모든 계층의 권리를 투표로 보여주기 위한, ⑩모든 장애를 제거하기 위한, ⑪모든 반대에 답하기 위한, ⑫이 신성한 권리의 자유로운 행사에 대한 모든 자격을 학대를 지적하기 위해, ⑬우리는 부적의 힘을 주장합니다.

- [분사구문] (Though they ignore=Ignoring ~ 그들이 무시할지라도) / (though they take=taking ~을 반대할지라도) / [동급비교] as A[necessary] as B[are air and motion to life 생명에 절대적인 공기와 활동같이 필요한] / [주절] we ~ / to show[보여주기 위해서], to remove[제거하기 위해서], (and) to point out[지적하기 위해서]

🖉 단어분석

- **suffrage** [sʌ́fridʒ] n. C 투표; U 참정권 / **inherit** [inhérit] vt. (재산·권리 따위를) 상속하다. / **abstract** [æbstrǽkt, -´-] a. 추상적인, 관념상의. [opp.] concrete. / **secure** [sikjúə:r] vt. 안전하게 하다, 굳게 지키다, 굳게 하다(against). / **principle** [prínsəpəl] n. 원리, 원칙, (물리·자연의) 법칙 / **logical** [ládʒikəl] a. 논리적인; / **govern** [gʌ́vərn] vt. (국가·국민 등을) 통치하다, 다스리다(rule) / **antagonism** [æntǽgənìzəm] n. U 적대(관계), 대립(against: to: between), 적의(hostility) / **monarchy** [mánərk] n. U 군주제, 군주 정치[정체]. / **despotism** [déspətìzəm] n. U 독재, 전제; 전제 정치; 폭정. / **uniform** [júːnəfɔ̀ːrm] a. 한결같은, 균일한, 같은(형상·빛깔 따위). [opp.] multiform. / **doctrine** [dáktrin] n. 주의, 학설; 공식(외교)정책. / **tenure** [ténjuə:r]n. 재직기간, 임기; / **crystallize** v. vt. (사상·계획 등을) 구체화하다(into). / **death knell** (종말·죽음·파멸) 조짐; =PASSING BELL. / **untenable** [ʌnténəbəl] a. 유지[지지, 옹호]할 수 없는 / **talisman** [tǽlismən, -iz-] n. (pl. ~s) 호부(護符), 부적 / **ballot** [bǽlət] n. 비밀[무기명] 투표 / **obstacle** [ábstəkəl] n. 장애(물)(to). / **objection** [əbdʒékʃən] n. C,U 반대; 이의, 반론 / **tyranny** [tírəni] n. U 폭정, 전제 정치. / **qualification** [kwàləfikéiʃən / kwɔ̀l-] n. C 자격, 권한; U 자격 부여(for). 수정, 완화(modification). / **sacred** [séikrid] a. ① 신성한(holy); 신에게 바쳐진, 신을 모신. [SYN.] ⇨ HOLY. ② 종교적인, 성전(聖典)의. [opp.] profane, secular.

✳ 다음 글을 읽고 물음에 답하시오. [1~5]

In considering the question of suffrage, there are two starting points: one, that Ⓐ **this right** is a gift of society, in which certain men, having inherited this privilege from some abstract body and abstract place, ① **has** now the right to secure it for themselves and their privileged order to the end of time. This principle leads logically to ② **governing** races, classes, families; and, in direct antagonism to our idea of self-government, takes us back to monarchies despotisms, ③ **to** a experiment that has been tried over and over again, 6,000 years, and uniformly failed. "I do not hold my liberties," says Gratz Brown in the Senate of the United States, "by any such tenure. On the contrary, I believe, whenever you establish that doctrine, whenever you crystallize that idea in the public mind of this country, you ring the death-knell of American liberties."

Ignoring this point of view as untenable and anti-republican, and ④ **taking** the opposite, that suffrage is a natural right—as necessary to man under government, for the protection of person and property, ⑤**as** are air and motion to life—we hold talisman by which to show the right of all classes to the ballot, to remove every obstacle, to answer every objection, to point out the tyranny of every qualification to the free exercise of this sacred right.

1. 위 글의 주제로 가장 적절한 것은?

① The privileged classes have their own right.
② There are lots of reasons why suffrage has come true.
③ Equal right, suffrage, is far from practical execution.
④ Talisman tolls well when governments don't listen to the public opinion.
⑤ Americans should rise up with the equal right.

2. 위 글에 나타난 분위기로 가장 적절한 것은?

① affirmative ② critical
③ arrogant ④ disappointing
⑤ acceptable

3. 위 글에서 밑줄 친 Ⓐ가 의미하는 것이 아닌 것은?

① suffrage
② inherited privilege
③ abstract body and place
④ this sacred right
⑤ a natural right

4. 위 글의 밑줄 친 ①~⑤ 중, 어법상 어색한 것은?

① ② ③ ④ ⑤

5. 위 글과 일치하지 않은 것은?

① 참정권은 타고난 권리이다.
② 참정권의 오랫동안 시행되어 왔으나, 늘 실패했다.

③ 상원의원들은 여성의 참정권을 반대한다.

④ 부적의 힘을 주장한다는 것은 실천의 의지가 없다는 것을 의미한다.

⑤ 특권으로 받은 참정권을 죽을 때까지 지키고자 한다.

TOEIC형 문제

6. 빈칸에 공통으로 적절한 것은?

> In considering the question of suffrage, there are two starting points: one, that this _____ is a gift of society, in which certain men, having inherited this privilege from some abstract body and abstract place, have now the _____ to secure it for themselves and their privileged order to the end of time.

① event
② right
③ answer
④ warranty

7. 빈칸 Ⓐ, Ⓑ에 적절한 단어는?

> This principle leads ___Ⓐ___ to governing races, classes, families; and, in direct antagonism to our idea of self-government, takes us back to monarchies despotisms, to a experiment that has been tried over and over again, 6,000 years, and ___Ⓑ___ failed.

① theoretically   variously
② practically   unfortunately
③ logically   uniformly
④ really   terrifyingly

8. 빈칸에 가장 적절한 것은?

> "I do not hold my liberties," says Gratz Brown in the Senate of the United States, "by any such tenure. _____, I believe, whenever you establish that doctrine, whenever you crystallize that idea in the public mind of this country, you ring the death-knell of American liberties."

① On the contrary   ② Therefore
③ As a result   ④ Moreover

❋ **다음을 읽고 물음에 답하시오. [9~10]**

> Ignoring this point of view as ___Ⓐ___ and anti-republican, and taking the opposite, that suffrage is a natural right—as necessary to man under government, for the protection of person and property, as are air and motion to life—we hold talisman by which to show the right of all classes to the ballot, to ___Ⓑ___ every obstacle, to answer every objection, to point out the tyranny of every qualification to the free exercise of this sacred right.

9. 빈칸 Ⓐ에 적절한 단어는?

① abiding   ② complying
③ untenable   ④ understanding

10. 빈칸 Ⓑ에 적절한 단어는?

① install   ② shed
③ remove   ④ pay attention to

1. ③	2. ②	3. ③	4. ①has → have	
5. ②	6. ②	7. ③	8. ①	9. ③
10. ③				

To discuss the question of suffrage for women and negroes, as women and negroes, and not as citizens of a republic, implies that there are some reasons for demanding this right for these classes that do not apply to "white males."

The obstinate persistence with which fallacious and absurd objections are pressed against their enfranchisement—as if they were anomalous beings, outside all human laws and necessities—is most humiliating and insulting to every black man and woman who has one particle of healthy, high-toned self-respect. There are no special claims to propose for women and negroes, no new arguments to make in their behalf. The same already made to extend suffrage to all the white men in this country, the same John Bright makes for the working men of England, the same made for the enfranchisement of 22,000,000 Russian serfs, are all we have to make for black me and women. As the greater includes the less, an argument for universal suffrage covers the whole question, the rights of all citizens. In thus relaying the foundations of government, we settle all these side issues of race, color and sex, end all class legislation, and remove forever the fruitful cause of all the jealousies, dissensions and revolution of the past. This is the platform of the American Equal Rights Association. "We are masters of the situation." Here black men and women are buried in the citizen. As in the war, freedom was the keynote of victory, so now is universal suffrage the keynote of reconstruction.

📖 본문해석

④**To discuss the question of suffrage** ③**for women and negroes,** ①**as women and negroes, and** ② **not as citizens of a republic,** ⑧**implies that** ⑦**there are some reasons** ⑥**for demanding this right** ⑤ **for these classes that do not apply to "white males."**

- ①여성들과 흑인으로서 그리고 ②공화국의 시민으로서가 아닌, ③여성들과 흑인들을 위한 ④참정권 문제를 토론하는 것은 ⑤백인남성들에게 적용되지 않는 이러한 계층들을 위한 ⑥이 권리를 요구하는 ⑦여러 이유가 있다는 것을 ⑧암시합니다.

③**The obstinate persistence with which** ①**fallacious and absurd objections** ②**are pressed against their enfranchisement** — ④**as if** ⑥**they were anomalous beings,** ⑤**outside all human laws and necessities** — ⑨**is most humiliating and insulting** ⑧**to every black man and woman who** ⑦**has one particle of healthy, high-toned self-respect.**

- ①잘못되고 불합리한 반대가 ②그들의 참정권에 반하여 억압하는 ③완고한 고집은 - ④마치 ⑤모든 인간의 법과 필요성에 소외된, ⑥그들이 이상한 존재인 것처럼 - ⑦건전하고 고결한 자존심의 한 티끌을 갖고 있는 ⑧모든 흑인과 여성에겐 ⑨가장 모욕적이고 멸시하는 것입니다.

The American Equal Rights

There ②are no special claims ①to propose for women and negroes, ④no new arguments ③to make in their behalf.

- ①여성들과 흑인들을 위해 제안되는 ②어떤 특별한 요구도 없습니다. ③그들을 옹호하여 만들어지는 ④어떤 새로운 논쟁도 없습니다.

③The same already made to extend suffrage ②to all the white men ①in this country, ⑤the same ④ John Bright makes for the working men of England, ⑦the same made ⑥for the enfranchisement of 22,000,000 Russian serfs, are ⑧all we ⑨have to make ⑨for black me and women.

- ①이 나라에서 ②모든 백인남성들에게 ③참정권을 확대하기 위해 이미 만들어진 것과 같은 것, ④John Bright가 영국 노동자들을 위해 만든 것과 ⑤같은 것, ⑥2천2백만 러시아 농노의 참정권을 위해 ⑦만들어진 것과 같은 것을, ⑧우리 모두가 ⑨흑인남성들과 여성을 위해 ⑩만들어야만 하는 것입니다.

①As the greater includes the less, ②an argument for universal suffrage ⑤covers ③the whole question, ④the rights of all citizens.

- ①더 큰 것이 더 작은 것을 포함하듯, ②보편적 참정권을 위한 논쟁은 ③전체의 문제, ④즉 모든 시민들의 권리를 ⑤포함합니다.

①In thus relaying the foundations of government, ②we ④settle ③all these side issues of race, color and sex, ⑤end all class legislation, and ⑧remove forever ⑧the fruitful cause ⑦of all the jealousies, dissensions and revolution ⑥of the past.

- ①그리하여 정부의 기초를 다시 고칠 때, ②우리는 ③인종, 색깔, 성의 모든 이러한 부차적인 문제들을 ④해결하고, ⑤모든 계층을 차별화하는 입법을 종식시키며, ⑥과거의 ⑦모든 질투, 알력, 그리고 혁명의 ⑧풍부한 가능성의 원인들을 ⑧영원히 제거할 수 있습니다.

This is the platform of the American Equal Rights Association. "We are masters of the situation." Here black men and women are buried in the citizen. ①As in the war, ②freedom was the keynote of victory, so ③now is ④universal suffrage ⑤the keynote of reconstruction.

- 이것이 미국평등권리협회의 강령입니다. "우리는 상황의 대가입니다." 이곳에 흑인남성들과 여성들은 시민들 속에 묻혀 있습니다. ①전쟁 때와 같이, ②자유는 승리의 기본인 것처럼, ③지금 ④보편적 참정권은 ⑤재건의 기본입니다.

🔖 단어분석

- **imply** [implái] vt. 암시하다(suggest). / **obstinate** [ábstənit / ɔ́b-] a. 완고한, 억지센, 강팍한, 끈질긴; 완강한(저항 따위). / **persistence** [pəːrsístəns] n. U 끈덕짐, 고집. / **fallacious** [fəléiʃəs] a. 불합리한, 틀린, 그른; 거짓의; / **absurd** [æbsə́ːrd, -zə́ːrd] a. 불합리한; 부조리한; 엉터리없는, 터무니없는, 우스꽝스런. / **enfranchise** [enfræntʃaiz] vt. 선거권[공민권]을 주다. 석방하다. / **anomalous** [ənámələs a. 변칙의, 파격의, 이례의; 이상한. / **humiliating** [hjuːmílièitiŋ] a. 면목없는, 치욕이 되는, 굴욕적인. / **insulting** [insʌ́ltiŋ] a. 모욕적인, 무례한. / **particle** [páːrtikl] n. 극소(량(量)), 극히 작음. / **high-toned** [háitóund] a. 고상한; 고결한; 멋부리는; / **self-respect** [sélfrispékt] n. U 자존(심), 자중(自重). ㉞〜ful, 〜ing ―a. 자존심 있는. / **extend** [iksténd] vt. 〜의 기한을 연장하다, 연기하다. / **John Bright**(1811~1889) British politician and noted orator who was a founder of the Anti-Com law league / **serf** [sə: rf] n. 농노(農奴)(토지와 함께 매매된 봉건 시대의 최하위 계급의 농민); (비유) 노예 (같은 사람); 고역을 치르는 사람. / **re-lay** [ri: léi]vt. (p., pp. -laid [-léid]) 다시 놓다; (철도 따위를) 다시 부설하다; 고쳐 칠하다. / **legislation** [lèdʒisléiʃ-ən] n. U 입법, 법률제정. / **jealousy** [dʒéləsi] n. U,C ① 질투, 투기, 시샘. / **dissension**[disénʃən] n. U 의견 차이; C 불화(의 씨); (pl.) 알력, 분쟁. / **revolution** [rèvəlú: ʃ-ən] n. C 혁명; 변혁. / **platform** [plǽtfɔ: rm] n (정당의) 강령, 정강(그 각 조항을 plank라 함); / **keynote** [kí: nòut] n. 바탕음; (연설 등의) 요지 / **keynote** [kí: nòut] n. (연설 등의) 요지, 주지(主旨), (행동·정책·성격 따위의) 기조, 기본 방침. / **universal** [jù: nəvə́: rsəl] a. 보편적인, 일반적인. / **reconstruction** [rì: kənstrʌ́kʃ-ən] n. ① 재건, 개축; 개조; 부흥.

동영상 강좌 http://youtu.be/WAi5XL4xUw0

✸ **다음 글을 읽고 물음에 답하시오. [11~15]**

To discuss the question of suffrage for women and negroes, as women and negroes, and not as citizens of a republic, implies that there are some reasons for demanding (a)**this right** for these classes that do not ① **apply** to "white males."

The obstinate persistence with which fallacious and absurd objections are pressed against their enfranchisement—as if they were ② **ordinary** beings, outside all human laws and necessities—is most humiliating and insulting to every black man and woman who has one ③ **particle** of healthy, high-toned self-respect. There are no special claims to propose for women and negroes, no new arguments to make in their behalf. The same already made to extend suffrage to all the white men in this country, (b)**the same** John Bright makes for the working men of England, the same made for the enfranchisement of 22,000,000 Russian serfs, are all we have to make for black me and women. As the greater includes the less, an argument for universal suffrage covers the whole question, (c)**the rights** of all citizens. In thus relaying (d)**the foundations** of government, we settle all these side issues of race, color and sex, end all class legislation, and remove ④ **forever** the fruitful cause of all the jealousies, dissensions and revolution of the past. This is the platform of the American Equal Rights Association. "We are masters of the situation." Here black men and women are buried in the citizen. As in the war, ⑤ **freedom** was the keynote of victory, so now is universal suffrage (e)**the keynote** of reconstruction.

11. 위 글의 주제로 가장 적절한 것은?

① Each class has its privilege.
② We should follow the good examples in the world.
③ There are many causes to block the suffrage.
④ The time to discuss the problem is little left.
⑤ Universal suffrage has to extend now.

12. 위 글의 분위기로 가장 어울리는 것은?

① sympathetic   ② appealing
③ humiliating   ④ encouraging
⑤ humorous

13. 위 글에서 밑줄 친 ①~⑤ 중, 문맥상 단어의 뜻이 <u>어색한</u> 것은?

①   ②   ③   ④   ⑤

14. 위 글에서 밑줄 친 (a)~(e) 중, 가리키는 대상이 나머지 넷과 <u>다른</u> 것은?

① (a)   ② (b)   ③ (c)   ④ (d)   ⑤ (e)

15. 위 글의 내용과 일치하지 <u>않은</u> 것은?

① 잘못되고 불합리한 반대가 그들의 참정권을 반하여 억압하는 완고한 고집이 가장 모욕적이다.
② 여성들과 흑인들을 위해 제안되는 요구는 없는 실정이다.
③ 영국 노동자들은 투표권을 얻었다.
④ 미국평등권리협회의 강령은 전 세계의 모든 여성과 흑인을 위한 보편적 권리를 받게 하는 것이다.
⑤ 다수가 소수를 포함하듯, 참정권을 위한

논쟁은 전체 문제인 모든 시민의 권리를
포괄할 수 있다.

16. 아래의 빈칸에 가장 적절한 것은?

> To discuss the question of suffrage for
> women and negroes, as women and
> negroes, and not as citizens of a republic,
> implies that there are some reasons for
> demanding this right for these classes that
> do not _____ "white males."

① contribute to   ② attribute to
③ devote to   ④ apply to

17. 아래의 빈칸에 가장 적절한 것은?

> The obstinate persistence with which
> _____ and absurd objections are
> pressed against their enfranchisement—as
> if they were anomalous beings, outside
> all human laws and necessities—is most
> humiliating and insulting to every black
> man and woman who has one particle of
> healthy, high-toned self-respect.

① correct   ② fallacious
③ observatory   ④ obsessive

18. 아래의 빈칸에 가장 적절한 것은?

> There are no special claims to propose for
> women and negroes, no new arguments to
> make in their behalf. The same already made
> to _____ suffrage to all the white
> men in this country, the same John Bright
> makes for the working men of England, the
> same made for the enfranchisement of
> 22,000,000 Russian serfs, are all we have to
> make for black me and women.

① possess   ② eradicate
③ threaten   ④ extend

19. 아래의 빈칸에 가장 적절한 것은?

> As the greater includes the less, an
> argument for _____ suffrage
> covers the whole question, the rights of
> all citizens. In thus relaying the
> foundations of government, we settle all
> these side issues of race, color and sex,
> end all class legislation, and remove
> forever the fruitful cause of all the
> jealousies, dissensions and revolution of
> the past.

① privileged   ② ordinary
③ suffocating   ④ universal

20. 아래의 빈칸에 가장 적절한 것은?

> This is the platform of the American
> Equal Rights Association. "We are
> masters of the situation." Here black
> men and women are buried in the
> citizen. As in the war, freedom was the
> _____ of victory, so now is universal
> suffrage the _____ of
> reconstruction.

① keynote   ② ressentiment
③ restoration   ④ resurgence

11. ⑤   12. ②   13. ②ordinary → anomalous
14. ⑤   15. ④   16. ④   17. ②   18. ④
19. ④   20. ①

The American Equal Rights

by Elizabeth Cady Stanton

동영상 강좌 http://youtu.be/8SFbiKb-OSE

"Negro suffrage" may answer as a party cry for an effete political organization through another Presidential campaign; but the people of this country have a broader work on hand to-day than to save the Republican party, or, with some abolitionists, to settle the rights of races. The battles of the ages have been fought for races, classes, parties, over and over again, and force always carried the day, and will until we settle the higher, the holier question of individual rights. This is our American idea, and on a wise settlement of this question rests the problem whether our nation shall live or perish.

The principle of inequality in government has been thoroughly tried, and every nation based on that idea that has not already perished, clearly shows the seeds of death in its dissensions and decline. Though it has never been tried, we know an experiment on the basis of equality would be safe; for the laws in the world of morals are as immutable as in the world of matter. As the Astronomer Le Verrier discovered the planet that bears his name by a process of reason and calculation through the variations of other planets from known laws, so can the true statesman, through the telescope of justice, see the genuine republic of the future amid the ruins of the mighty nations that have passed away. The opportunity now given us to make the experiment of self-government should be regarded by every American citizen as a solemn and a sacred trust. When we remember that a nation's life and growth and immortality depend on its legislation, can we exalt too highly the dignity and responsibility of the ballot, the science of political economy, the sphere of government? Statesmanship is, of all sciences, the most exalted and comprehensive, for it includes all others. Among men we find those who study the laws of national life more liberal and enlightened on all subjects than those who confine their researchers in special directions. When we base nations on justice and equality, we lift government out of the mists of speculation into the dignity of a fixed science. Everything short of this is trick, legerdemain, sleight of hand. Magicians may make nations seem to live, but they do not. The Newtons of our day who should try to make apples stand in the air or men walk on the wall, would be no more puerile in their experiments than are they who build nations outside of law, on the basis of inequality.

동영상 강좌 http://youtu.be/8SFbiKb-OSE

✎ 본문해석

"①Negro suffrage" ④may answer ③as a party cry for an effete political organization ② through another Presidential campaign; but ⑤the people of this country ⑥have a broader work on hand today than ⑥to save the Republican party, or ⑦with some abolitionists, ⑧to settle the rights of races.

- ①흑인 참정권은 ②다른 대통령 선거를 통한 ③맥빠진 정치조직을 위한 한 당의 하소연으로서 ④답할지 모릅니다.; 그러나 ⑤이 나라 국민들은, ⑥공화당을 구하는 것 보다, 또는 ⑦노예제도 폐지론자와 함께 ⑧인종 권리를 해결하는 것 보다, ⑨오늘날 할 일을 더욱 많이 갖고 있습니다.

①The battles of the ages ④have been fought ②for races, classes, parties, ③over and over again, and ⑥force always carried ⑤the day, and ⑩will until ⑦we ⑨settle the higher, the holier question ⑧of individual rights.

- ①여러 시대에 걸친 그 전쟁은 ②인종, 계층, 정파를 위해 ③계속해서 ④싸워왔고, 그리고 ⑤오늘날까지 ⑥힘은 늘 이어져오고 있고. 그리고 ⑦우리가 ⑧개개인의 권리를 ⑨더 높이 더 신성한 문제로 해결할 ⑩때까지 계속될 것입니다.

①This is our American idea, and ④on a wise settlement of this question ⑤rests ③the problem ② whether our nation shall live or perish.

- ①이것이 우리 미국의 사고이고, ②우리 국가가 생존하거나 멸망하는지는 ③그 문제가 ④이 질문의 현명한 해결에 ⑤달려 있다는 것입니다.

①The principle of inequality in government ②has been thoroughly tried, and ④every nation ③based on that idea that has not already perished, ⑥clearly shows the seeds of death ⑤in its dissensions and decline.

- ①정부 내에서 불평등의 원리가 ②철저히 시도되고, ③아직 사라지지 않은 있는 그 사고에 근거한 ④모든 국가들은 ⑤불화와 쇠퇴 속에서 ⑥죽음의 씨앗을 분명 보고 있습니다.

①Though it has never been tried, ④we know ②an experiment on the basis of equality ③would be safe; ⑤for the laws in the world of morals ⑦are as immutable ⑥as in the world of matter.

- ①비록 그것이 결코 시도된 적은 없을지라도, ②평등에 입각한 실험은 ③안전할 것이라는 것을 ④우리는 압니다.; ⑤왜냐하면 도덕의 세계 속에 있는 법은 ⑥문제의 세계 속에서와 같이 ⑦불변하기 때문입니다.

As ①the Astronomer Le Verrier ⑤discovered the planet that bears his name ④by a process of reason and calculation ③through the variations of other planets ②from known laws, so can ⑥the true statesman, ⑦through the telescope of justice, ⑨see the genuine republic of the future ⑧amid the ruins of the mighty nations that have passed away.

- ①우주비행사인 Le Verrier가 ②알려진 법칙으로 ③다른 행성들의 변화를 통한 ④이성과 계산의 과정에 의해 ⑤자신의 이름을 가진 행성을 발견했던 것처럼, ⑥정직한 정치인도 ⑦정의의 망원경을 통해, ⑧멸망한 강력한 국가들의 파괴에서 ⑨미래의 진정한 공화국을 봅니다.

The American Equal Rights

by Elizabeth Cady Stanton

②The opportunity now given us ①to make the experiment of self-government ⑤should be regarded ③by every American citizen ④as a solemn and a sacred trust.

- ①자기통제의 실험을 하기 위해 ②우리에게 주어진 기회는 ③모든 미국 시민들에 의해 ④엄숙하고 신성한 믿음으로 ⑤간주되어야만 합니다.

③When we remember that ①a nation's life and growth and immortality ②depend on its legislation, can ④we ⑧exalt too highly ⑤the dignity and responsibility of the ballot, ⑥the science of political economy, ⑦the sphere of government?

- ①한 국가의 생존과 성장 그리고 불멸은 ②자국의 법에 달려있다는 것을 ③우리가 기억할 때, ④우리는 ⑤투표의 고결성과 책임감, ⑥정치경제의 과학 그리고 ⑦정부의 영역을 ⑧드높이 고양시킬 수 있겠습니까?

②Statesmanship ④is, ①of all sciences, ③the most exalted and comprehensive, ④for it ⑥includes ⑤all others.

- ①모든 과학 분야에서 ②정치가의 수완은 ③가장 드높고 포괄적인 것④입니다. ④왜냐하면 그것은 ⑤다른 모든 것을 포괄하기 때문입니다.

①Among men ②we ⑥find ③those who study the laws of national life ⑧more liberal and enlightened ⑦on all subjects ⑥than those who confine ④their researchers ⑤in special directions.

- ①사람들 중에 ②우리는 ③국가의 생존법칙 연구하는 사람들이 ④자신들의 연구를 ⑤특별한 방향에 ⑥한정 시키는 사람들 보다 더, ⑦모든 문제에서 ⑧더욱 자유롭고 사리를 잘 판단하는 것을 ⑨입니다.

When ①we ④base ②nations on justice and equality, ⑤we ⑨lift ⑥government ⑦out of the mists of speculation ⑧into the dignity of a fixed science.

- ①우리가 ②국가들을 ③정의와 평등에 ④근거할 때, ⑤우리는 ⑥정부를 ⑦억측의 희미한 안개 속에서 끌어내 어 ⑧고정된 과학의 고결성 안으로 ⑨끌어올릴 수 있습니다.

②Everything ①short of this ④is ③trick, legerdemain, sleight of hand.

- ①이것이 부족한 ②모든 것은 ③기교, 궤변이자 요술의 속임수④입니다.

Magicians may make nations seem to live, but they do not.

- 마술가들은 국가를 생존하게 할 것 같습니다만은 그들은 그렇게 할 수 없습니다.

③The Newtons of our day who should try ①to make apples stand in the air or ②men walk on the wall, would ④be no more puerile in their experiments than ⑥are they who build nations outside of law, ⑤on the basis of inequality.

- ①사과를 공중에 서게 하려고 하는 또는 ②사람이 벽 위를 걷게 하려는 ③우리시대의 뉴톤과 같은 사람들 은 ④그들의 실험에서 철없는 것처럼, ⑤불평등을 근거로 ⑥법 밖에서 국가를 건설하는 사람과 같습니다.

🔖 단어분석

- **effete** [efíːt] a. 활력을 잃은, 약해진, 시대에 뒤진(제도·조직). / **abolitionize** [æ̀bəlíʃənàiz] vt. (사람·지역·주(州) 따위를) 노예 제도 폐지론에 전향(轉向)시키다. / **on hand** = available 이용 가능한 / **dissension** [disénʃən] n. U 의견 차이; C 불화(의 씨) / **immutable** [imjúːtəbəl] a. 변경 할 수 없는 / **variation** [vὲəriéiʃən] n. U,C 변화(change), 변동, 변이(變異). / **pass away** 멸망하다 / **solemn** [sáləm]a. 엄숙한, 장엄한 / **exalt** [igzɔ́ːlt] vt. (명예·품위 따위를) 높이다. / **statemanship** 정치가의 능력 / **enlightened** [enláitnd] a. 사리를 잘 아는. / **speculation** [spὲkjəléiʃ-ən] n. U 숙고 / **mist** [mist]n. C,U (a ~) (판단 따위를) 흐리게 하는 것. / **legerdemain** [lὲdʒəːrdəméin] n. 눈속임; 속임수 (deception); 궤변, 억지. / **sleight** [slait]n. U,C 능숙한 솜씨, 속임수(trick). / **puerile** [pjúːəril] a. 철 없는, 미숙한. / **no more A than B** : A가 아닌 것은 B가 아닌 것과 같은

10 The American Equal Rights
by Elizabeth Cady Stanton

동영상 강좌 http://youtu.be/g2oAN5ufiUY

✽ 다음 글을 읽고 물음에 답하시오. [21~25]

"Negro suffrage" may answer as a party cry for an effete political organization through another Presidential campaign; but the people of this country have ① **a broader work on hand to-day** than to save the Republican party, or, with some abolitionists, to settle the rights of races. The battles of the ages have been fought for races, classes, parties, over and over again, and force always carried the day, and will until we settle ② **the higher, the holier question of individual rights**. This is our American idea, and on a wise settlement of this question rests the problem whether our nation shall live or perish.

The principle of inequality in government has been thoroughly tried, and every nation based on that idea that has not already perished, clearly shows the seeds of death in its dissensions and decline. Though it has never been tried, _____; for the laws in the world of morals are as immutable as in the world of matter. As the Astronomer Le Verrier discovered the planet that bears his name by ③ **a process of reason and calculation** through the variations of other planets from known laws, so can the true statesman, through ④ **the telescope of justice**, see the genuine republic of the future amid the ruins of the mighty nations that have passed away. The opportunity now given us to make the experiment of self-government should be regarded by every American citizen as a solemn and a sacred trust. When we remember that a nation's life and growth and immortality depend on its legislation, can we exalt too highly the dignity and responsibility of the ballot, the science of political economy, the sphere of government? Statesmanship is, of all sciences, the most exalted and comprehensive, for it includes all others. Among men we find those who study the laws of national life more liberal and enlightened on all subjects than ⑤ **those who confine their researchers in special directions**. When we base nations on justice and equality, we lift government out of the mists of speculation into the dignity of a fixed science. Everything short of this is trick, legerdemain, sleight of hand. Magicians may make nations seem to live, but they do not. The Newtons of our day who should try to make apples stand in the air or men walk on the wall, would be no more puerile in their experiments than are they who build nations outside of law, on the basis of inequality.

21. 위 글에서 지은이가 강조하는 것과 거리가 먼 것은?

① Presidential campaign
② a process of reason and calculation
③ the genuine republic of the future
④ a solemn and a sacred trust
⑤ nation's legislation

22. 위 글의 밑줄 친 ①~⑤ 중, 성격이 다른 하나는?

①   ②   ③   ④   ⑤

23. 위 글 빈칸에 적절한 표현은?

① the endless experiments may be fallible or successful
② we should gather more enlightened scholars to research
③ we know an experiment on the basis of equality would be safe
④ the nations' safety will be accomplished through inequalities.
⑤ we should learn more experiences from the past dissensions and decline

24. 위 글이 성격은?

① Many examples help readers understand easily.
② The historical backgrounds makes feel terrifying.
③ Many trials and errors must be unavoidable.
④ The author's requirements are too overwhelming to accept comfortably.
⑤ It hopes that the powerful man should be born to handle these problems.

25. 위 글과 일치하는 것은?

① 흑인의 참정권은 대통령선거 기간 중, 화두가 될 것이다.
② 여러 시대에 걸쳐 인종, 계층, 정파를 위해 많은 전쟁이 있어 왔다.
③ 개인의 권리의 더 높고 고결한 문제는 시간이 지남에 따라 해결될 것이다.
④ 정직한 정치인도 우주비행사로 부터 그들의 경험을 배워야만 할 것이다.
⑤ 자신의 연구를 특별한 방향에 한정시키는 사람들이 더 자유롭고 사리 판단이 더 빠르다.

TOEIC형 문제

26. 아래의 빈칸에 가장 적절한 것은?

"Negro suffrage" may answer as a party cry for an _____ political organization through another Presidential campaign; but the people of this country have a broader work on hand to-day than to save the Republican party, or, with some abolitionists, to settle the rights of races.

① effete
② energetic
③ structural
④ reserved

27. 아래의 빈칸에 가장 적절한 것은?

The battles of the ages have been fought for races, classes, parties, over and over again, and force always carried the day, and will until we settle the higher, the holier question of individual rights. This is our American idea, and on a wise settlement of this question rests the problem whether our nation shall _____.

① develop or underdevelop
② stop its effects
③ live or perish
④ be prosperous or recessional

28. 아래의 빈칸에 가장 적절한 것은?

The principle of inequality in government has been _____ tried, and every nation based on that idea that has not already perished, clearly shows the seeds of death in its dissensions and decline.

① lazily
② thoroughly
③ honestly
④ reasonably

29. 아래의 빈칸에 가장 적절한 것은?

> _____ it has never been tried, we know an experiment on the basis of equality would be safe; for the laws in the world of morals are as immutable as in the world of matter.

① Whether   ② Though
③ Unfortunately   ④ Because

30. 아래의 빈칸에 가장 적절한 것은?

> As the Astronomer Le Verrier discovered the planet that bears his name by a process of reason and calculation through the _____ of other planets from known laws, so can the true statesman, through the telescope of justice, see the genuine republic of the future amid the ruins of the mighty nations that have passed away.

① tactics   ② variations
③ environments   ④ exterminations

31. 아래의 빈칸에 가장 적절한 것은?

> The _____ now given us to make the experiment of self-government should be regarded by every American citizen as a solemn and a sacred trust.

① education   ② research
③ opportunity   ④ consummation

32. 아래의 빈칸에 가장 적절한 것은?

> When we remember that a nation's life and growth and immortality depend on its legislation, can we _____ too highly the dignity and responsibility of the ballot, the science of political economy, the sphere of government?

① exalt   ② rise
③ arise   ④ carry

33. 아래의 빈칸에 가장 적절한 것은?

> Statesmanship is, of all sciences, the most exalted and comprehensive, for it includes all others. Among men we find those who study the laws of national life more liberal and enlightened on all subjects than those who _____ their researches in special directions.

① share   ② provide
③ confine   ④ extend

34. 아래의 빈칸에 가장 적절한 것은?

> When we base nations on justice and equality, we lift government out of the mists of speculation into the _____ of a fixed science.

① corruption   ② unprecedented
③ principle   ④ dignity

35. 아래의 빈칸에 가장 적절한 것은?

> Everything short of this is trick, legerdemain, sleight of hand. Magicians may make nations seem to live, but they do not. The Newtons of our day who should try to make apples stand in the air or men walk on the wall, would be ________ puerile in their experiments ___ are they who build nations outside of law, on the basis of inequality.

① so　as　② more　than
③ no more　than　④ not more　than

21. ①	22. ⑤	23. ③	24. ①	25. ②
26. ①	27. ③	28. ②	29. ②	30. ②
31. ③	32. ①	33. ③	34. ④	35. ③

The American Equal Rights

by Elizabeth Cady Stanton

What thinking man can talk of coming down into the arena of politics? If we need purity, honor, self-sacrifice and devotion anywhere, we need them in those who have in their keeping the life and prosperity of a nation. In the enfranchisement of woman, in lifting her up into this broader sphere, we see for her new honor and dignity, more liberal, exalted and enlightened views of life, its objects, ends and aims, and an entire revolution in the new world of interest and action where she is soon to play her part. And in saying this, I do not claim that woman is better than man, but that the sexes have a civilizing power on each other. The distinguished historian, Henry Thomas Buckle, says:

"The turn of thought of woman, their habits of mind, their conversation, invariably extending over the whole surface of society, and frequently penetrating its intimate structure, have, more than all other things put together, tended to rise us into an ideal world, and lift us from the dust into which we are too prone to grovel.

And this will be her influence in exalting and purifying the world of politics. When woman understands the momentous interests that depend on the ballot, she will make it her first duty to educate every American boy and girl into the idea that to vote is the most sacred act of citizenship—a religious duty not to be discharged thoughtlessly, selfishly or corruptly; but conscientiously, remembering that, in a republican government, to every citizen is entrusted the interests of the nation. "Would you fully estimate the responsibility of the ballot, think of it as the great regulation power of a continent, of all our interests, political, commercial, religious, educational, social and sanitary!"

🖎 본문해석

①**What thinking man** ③**can talk of** ②**coming down into the arena of politics?** ①**If we** ④**need** ③**purity,** **honor, self-sacrifice and devotion** ②**anywhere,** ⑤**we** ⑨**need them** ⑧**in those who have** ⑥**in their** **keeping** ⑦**the life and prosperity of a nation.**

- ①어떠한 생각 있는 사람이 ②정계에 들어오는 것에 ③말할 수 있나요? ①만일 우리가 ②어디에서든 ③순수함, 명예, 자기희생과 헌신을 ④필요로 한다면, ⑤우리는 ⑥그들의 책임 하에 ⑦국가의 생존과 번영을 ⑧위하는 사람에서 ⑨그것들을 필요로 합니다.

①**In the enfranchisement of woman,** ②**in lifting her up into this broader sphere,** ④**we** ⑩**see** ③**for her** **new honor and dignity,** ⑦**more liberal, exalted and enlightened views of life,** ⑧**its objects, ends and** **aims,** ⑨**and an entire revolution** ⑥**in the new world of interest and action** ⑤**where she is soon to play** **her part.**

- ①여성의 투표로 인해, ②그녀가 이 넓은 영역으로 상승될 때, ③그녀의 새로운 명예와 품위로 인해, ④우리는 ⑤그녀가 곧 자신의 역할을 발휘할 ⑥흥미와 행동의 새로운 세계에서 ⑦더욱 자유롭고 고양되고 분별력 있는 삶의 견해, ⑧그 목표, 목적 ⑨그리고 전반적인 혁명을 ⑩볼 수 있습니다.

①**And in saying this,** ②**I** ④**do not claim that** ③**woman is better than man,** but that ⑤**the sexes** ⑥**have** ⑦**a civilizing power** ⑥**on each other.** The distinguished historian, Henry Thomas Buckle, says(저명한

역사학자 Henry Thomas Buckle은 말합니다):

- ①그리하여 이것을 말할 때, ②저는 ③남성보다 여성이 더 우월하다는 것을 ④주장하는 것이 아닌, ⑤성은 ⑥ 서로에 대해 ⑦같은 문명화된 힘을 ⑧갖는다는 것을 주장하는 바입니다.

①**'The turn of thought of woman,** ②**their habits of mind, their conversation,** ③**invariably extending over the whole surface of society,** ④**and frequently penetrating its intimate structure, have,** ⑤**more than all other things put together,** ⑦**tended to rise us** ⑥**into an ideal world, and** ⑨**lift us** ⑧**from the dust into** ⑨**which we are too prone to grovel.**

- ①여성의 사고의 변화인, ②마음의 습관과, 그들의 대화는, ③사회 전반에 걸쳐 다양하게 확장되어, ④그리고 사회의 친밀한 구조를 빈번히 스며들어, ⑤다른 모든 것을 합친 것보다 더, ⑥이상적인 세계 안으로 ⑦ 우리를 상승시키는 경향이 있어왔고, ⑧하찮은(먼지) 것으로부터 ⑨비굴하게 엎드릴필요가 없는 곳으로 ⑩ 우리를 상승시켜 줍니다.

①**And this** ③**will be her influence** ②**in exalting and purifying the world of politics.** ④**When woman understands the momentous interests that depend on the ballot,** ⑤**she will make it** ⑥**her first duty to educate every American boy and girl into the idea that** ⑦**to vote is the most sacred act of citizenship** — ⑨**a religious duty** ⑧**not to be discharged thoughtlessly, selfishly or corruptly; but** ⑩ **conscientiously, remembering that,** ⑪**in a republican government,** ⑫**to every citizen is entrusted the interests of the nation.**

- ①그리고 이것은 ②정치세계를 고양시키고 정화시킬 때 ③여성의 영향력이 될 것이다. ④여성들이 투표에 관한 중대한 흥미를 이해할 때, ⑤여성은 ⑥모든 미국 소년 소녀들을 교육시킬 첫 임무를 띠어 ⑦투표하는 것이 시민정신 가장 신성한 행위라는 생각을 갖도록 할 것이다. — ⑧분별없이, 이기적으로 또는 타락하여 면제 것이 아닌 ⑨종교적 의무입니다.; 그러나 ⑩양심적으로 ⑪한 공화국 정부 하에서 ⑫모든 시민들에게 국가의 이익을 위임하는 것을 기억하는 것이 ⑬또한 종교적 의무입니다.

"①**Would you fully estimate the responsibility of the ballot?, think of** ②**it** ③**as the great regulation power of a continent,** ⑥**of all our interests,** ⑤**political, commercial, religious, educational, social and sanitary!**"

- "①여러분은 투표의 책임을 완전히 평가하시죠? ②그것을 ③한 대륙의 위대한 법규의 힘으로 ④생각하시고, ⑤정치적, 상업적, 종교적, 교육적, 사회적 그리고 위생적인 ⑥우리 모두의 흥미를 생각하시길 바랍니다!"

📖 단어분석

- **arena** [ərí: nə] n. 투기장(고대 로마의 원형 경기장 중앙에 모래를 깐); 경기장; 투쟁·활동의 장소 / **keeping** [kí: piŋ] n. U 보관; 보존, 저장(성). / **sphere** [sfiə: r] n. 구체(球體), 구(球), 구형, 구면. / **dignity** [dígnəti] n. U 존엄, 위엄; 기품; 체면, 긍지. / **exalted** [igzɔ́: ltid] a. 고귀한, 지위가[신분이] 높은, 고위의; 고상한, 숭고한; 우쭐한, / **object** [ábdʒikt] n. 물건, 물체, 사물. / **penetrate** [pénətrèit] vt. 꿰뚫다, 관통하다, 침입하다. / **prone** [proun] a. ~하기 쉬운, ~의 경향이 있는; ~에 걸리기 쉬운(to). / **grovel** [grávəl] vi.굴복하다, 비굴한 태도를 취하다, 비하하다(before; to); 천박한 환락에 빠지다. / **momentous** [mouméntəs] a. 중대한, 중요한, 쉽지 않은. / **discharge** [distʃá: rdʒ] vt. (차량의 짐·승객을) 내리다. (책임·의무를 아무로부터) 면제하다. 「~ oneself of의 꼴로」 (자기의 책임·약속 따위를) 이행[실행]하다. / **entrust** [entrást] vt. 맡기다, 기탁[위탁]하다, 위임하다. / **sanitary** [sǽnətèri] a. ① (공중) 위생의, 보건상의. ② 위생적인, 깨끗한; 균 없는.

The American Equal Rights

※ 다음 글을 읽고 물음에 답하시오. [36~40]

What thinking man can talk of coming down into the arena of politics? If we need purity, honor, self-sacrifice and devotion anywhere, we need them in those who have in their keeping the life and prosperity of a nation. _____, in lifting her up into this broader sphere, we see for her new honor and dignity, more liberal, exalted and enlightened views of life, its objects, ends and aims, and an entire revolution in the new world of interest and action where she is soon to play her part. And in saying this, I do not claim that woman is better than man, but that the sexes have a civilizing power on each other. The distinguished historian, Henry Thomas Buckle, says:

"The turn of thought of woman, their habits of mind, their conversation, invariably extending over the whole surface of society, and frequently penetrating its intimate structure, have, more than all other things put together, tended to rise us into an ideal world, and lift us from the dust into which we are too prone to grovel.

And this will be her influence in exalting and purifying the world of politics. When woman understands the momentous interests that depend on the ballot, she will make it her first duty to educate every American boy and girl into the idea that to vote is the most sacred act of citizenship—a religious duty not to be discharged thoughtlessly, selfishly or corruptly; but conscientiously, remembering that, in a republican government, to every citizen is entrusted the interests of the nation. "Would you fully estimate the responsibility of the ballot, think of it as the great regulation power of a continent, of all our interests, political, commercial, religious, educational, social and sanitary!"

36. 위 글의 분위기로 가장 옳지 <u>않은</u> 것은?

① emphasizing   ② influential

③ persuasive   ④ discouraging

⑤ energetic

37. '여성의 투표권 갖고서 일어나는 상황'이 <u>아닌</u> 것은?

① They will lift themselves up into the broader sphere.

② They will have more priority than men.

③ They will soon play their part.

④ They will extend their abilities over the whole surface of society.

⑤ They will educate all American youngsters for better citizenship.

38. 위 글의 주제로 가장 적절한 것은?

① The women's power sometimes causes side effects.

② The long way to go doesn't seem to come soon.

③ The positive effect after woman's enfranchisement spreads all over the world of society.

④ Woman's enfranchisement has two different sides.

⑤ For the social unity women's right should rise up immediately.

39. 위 글의 빈칸에 가장 적절한 표현은?

① In the time of unequality between men and women

② In the enfranchisement of woman

③ In the difficult situation without women's democratic right

④ When women try to go into social lives

⑤ In the confrontation with social changes

40. 위 글과 일치하지 <u>않은</u> 것은?

① 여성의 영향력은 정치세계를 고향시키고 정화시킬 것이다.

② 여성의 사고의 변화는 모든 것을 합친 것보다 더 강력하다.

③ 남녀 서로 문명화된 힘을 갖게 될 것이다.

④ 여성들의 새로운 명예와 품으로 인해 사회 전반의 변혁이 일어날 것이다.

⑤ 종교적 혜택으로 인해 분별없고 이기적인 삶은 면제를 받게 될 것이다.

The American Equal Rights

by Elizabeth Cady Stanton

To many minds, this claim for the ballot suggests nothing more than a rough polling-booth where coarse, drunken men, elbowing each other, wade knee-deep in mud to drop a little piece of paper two inches long into a box—simply this and nothing more. The poet Wordsworth, showing the blank materialism of those who see only with their outward eyes, says of his Peter Bell:

"A primrose on the river's brink A yellow primrose was to him, And it was nothing more."

So our political Peter Bells see the rough polling-booth, in this great right of citizenship, and nothing more. In this act, so lightly esteemed by the mere materialist, behold the realization of that great idea struggled for in the ages and proclaimed by the Fathers, the right of self-government. That little piece of paper dropped into a box is the symbol of equality, of citizenship, of wealth, virtue, education, self-protection, dignity, independence and power—the mightiest engine yet placed in the hand of man for the uprooting of ignorance, tyranny, superstition, the overturning of thrones, altars, kings, popes, despotisms, monarchies and empires. What phantom can the sons of the Pilgrims, be chasing, when they make merchandise of a power like this? Judas Iscariot, selling his Master for thirty pieces of silver, is a fit type of those American citizens who sell their votes, and thus betray the right of self-government. Talk not of the "muddy pool of politics," as if such things must need be. Behold, with the coming of woman into this higher sphere of influence, the dawn of the new day, when politics, so called, are to be lifted into the world of morals and religion; when the polling-booth shall be a beautiful temple, surrounded by fountains and flowers and triumphal arches, through which young men and maidens shall go up in joyful procession to ballot for justice and freedom; and when our elections shall be like the holy feasts of the Jews at Jerusalem. Through the trials of this second revolution shall not our nation rise up, with new virtue and strength, to fulfill her mission in leading all the peoples of the earth to the only solid foundation of government, "equal rights to all?"

🔖 **본문해석**

①To many minds, ②this claim for the ballot ⑧suggests nothing more than a rough polling-booth ⑦ where ④coarse, drunken men, ③elbowing each other, ⑥wade knee-deep in mud ⑤to drop a little piece of paper two inches long into a box — ⑨simply this and nothing more.

- ①많은 사람들에게, ②투표를 주장하는 것은 ③서로를 밀치는 ④거칠고 술 취한 사람들이 ⑤2인치 길이의 한 장의 작은 용지를 상자 안에 넣기 위해 ⑥무릎까지 빠지는 진흙탕을 걸어오는 ⑦곳인 ⑧삭막한 투표소를 암시하는 것에 불과합니다. — ⑨단지 이것뿐입니다.

①The poet Wordsworth, ③showing the blank materialism of those who see ②only with their outward eyes, ④says of his Peter Bell:
"⑤A primrose on the river's brink ⑥A yellow primrose was to him, And ⑦it was nothing more."

- ①시인 Wordsworth는 ②단지 관심 없는 눈으로 ③보는 사람들의 공허한 물질 만능주의를 보여주고자 ④자

신의 Peter Bel에 관해 다음과 같이 말합니다. : "⑤강가의 금달맞이 꽃은 ⑥그에겐 노란색을 불과하죠. ⑦ 그 이상도 아니었죠."

①**So our political Peter Bells** ③**see the rough polling-booth,** ②**in this great right of citizenship, and** ④**nothing more.**
- ①그래서 우리의 정치적 Peter Bells는 ②시민정신의 이 위대한 권리를 ③시끄러운 기표소로 보며 ④그 이상은 보질 못합니다.

②**In this act,** ①**so lightly esteemed by the mere materialist,** ⑦**behold** ⑤**the realization of that great idea** ③**struggled for in the ages and** ④**proclaimed by the Fathers,** ⑥**the right of self-government.**
- ①단지 물질만능주의자의해 너무 경박하게 간주되어온, ②이런 행위에서, ③오랫동안 투쟁되고 ④대부들을 위해 선언된 ⑤그 위대한 사고의 실현을 ⑥자기통제의 권리로 ⑦보세요.

①**That little piece of paper dropped into a box** ③**is the symbol of** ②**equality, of citizenship, of wealth, virtue, education, self-protection, dignity, independence and power** — ⑦**the mightiest engine** ⑥**yet placed in the hand of man** ④**for the uprooting of ignorance, tyranny, superstition,** ⑤**the overturning of thrones, altars, kings, popes, despotisms, monarchies and empire**s.
- ①한 상자 안으로 떨어진 그 작은 종이 한 장은 ②평등, 시민권리, 부, 덕망, 교육, 자기보호, 고결성, 독립성 그리고 힘의 ③상징입니다. ― ④무지, 독재, 미신을 근절시키기 위한, ⑤왕관, 제단, 왕, 교황, 독재, 군주, 제국의 전복을 위해 ⑥사람의 손 안에 쥐어져 있는 ⑦가장 강력한 동력입니다.

④**What phantom can** ②**the sons of the Pilgrims,** ③**be chasing),** ①**when they make merchandise of a power like this?**
- ①순례자들의 아들들이 이와 같은 힘의 상품을 만들 때, ②그들이 ③쫓을 수 있는 것은 ④무슨 환영일까요?

②**Judas Iscariot,** ①**selling his Master for thirty pieces of silver,** ⑤**is a fit type of those American citizens** ③**who sell their votes,** ④**and thus betray the right of self-government.**
- ①은 30량 때문에 자신의 주인을 팔려는, ②Judas Iscariot ③그들의 투표권을 팔고 ④그리하여 자신의 정부의 권리를 배반하는 ⑤그런 미국 시민들의 정형입니다.

③**Talk not of** ②**the "muddy pool of politics,"** ①**as if such things must need be.**
- ①마치 그러한 것들이 필요해야만 하는 것처럼, ②"진흙탕 정치"라 ③말하지 마세요.

⑦**Behold,** ⑤**with the coming of woman into this higher sphere of influence,** ⑥**the dawn of the new day,** ①**when politics, so called, are to be lifted into the world of morals and religion; when the polling-booth shall be a beautiful temple**(기표소가 아름다운 사원이 되게 될 때)**,** ②**surrounded by fountains and flowers and triumphal arches,** ③**through which young men and maidens shall go up in joyful procession to ballot for justice and freedom; and** ④**when our elections shall be like the holy feasts of the Jews at Jerusalem.**
- ①이른바 정치가 도덕성과 종교의 세계 안으로 들어올 때를; ②분수대와 꽃 그리고 승리의 아치에 둘러싸여, ③이곳을 통해 젊은 남녀들이 정의와 자유를 위해 투표하는 기쁨에 찬 행렬 속에서; ④그리고 우리의

The American Equal Rights

by Elizabeth Cady Stanton

선거가 예루살렘에서 유대인들의 신성한 축제처럼 되게 될 때, ⑤이 더 높은 영향력 안으로 들어오고 있는 여성들의 출현과 더불어, ⑥새로운 시대의 여명 ⑦보세요.

①**Through the trials of this second revolution shall not** ⑤**our nation** ⑦**rise up,** ②**with new virtue and strength,** ④**to fulfill her mission** ③**in leading all the peoples of the earth to the only solid foundation of government,** "⑥**equal rights to all**?"

- ①이 두 번째 혁명의 시험을 통해 ②새로운 덕망과 강인함을 갖고 ③지구상의 모든 사람들을 정부의 유일하게 단단한 기초로 이끌 때, ④조국의 임무를 수행하기 위해 ⑤우리나라는 ⑥"모든 사람들에게 동등한 권리"를 ⑦끌어 올리지 않을까요?

🛡️ 단어분석

- **mind** [maind] n.(마음·지성을 지닌) 사람, 인물. / **pólling bòoth** 【영국】 (투표장의) 기표소(voting booth). / **rough** [rʌf] a. (속어) 시끄러운, 떠들썩한. / **coarse** [kɔːrs] a. 조잡한, 조악(粗惡)한, 열등한. 야비한, 상스러운 / **elbow** [élbou] vt. 팔꿈치로 밀다[찌르다], 팔꿈치로 밀어제치고 나아가다; (몸을) 들이밀다. vi. 팔꿈치로 밀어제치고 나아가다. / **wade** [weid] vi. (진창·눈길·모래밭·풀숲 따위를) 힘들여 걷다, 간신히 지나다(across; into; through). / **blank** [blæŋk] a. 공백의, 백지의, 기입하지 않은. / **materialism** 물질 만능주의 / **primrose** [prímròuz] n.그 꽃; 금달맞이꽃(evening primrose); U 앵초색, 연노랑색. / **brink** [briŋk] n. (벼랑 따위의) 가장자리 / **esteem** [istíːm] vt. 존경하다(respect), 존중하다. ~으로 간주하다. / **behold** [bihóuld] vt. 보다(look at). / **proclaim** [proukléim] vt. 포고[선언]하다, 공포하다; 성명하다. / **uproot** [ʌprúːt] vt. 뿌리째 뽑다(root up). (비유) (악습을) 근절[절멸]시키다. / **tyranny** [tírəni] n. ① C,U 포학, 학대; 포학행위. ② U 폭정, 전제 정치. / **superstition** [sùːpərstíʃən] n. U,C 미신; 미신적 관습[행위] / **overturn** [òuvərtɔ́ːrn] vt., vi. 뒤집어 엎다, 뒤집히다, 전복시키다[하다]; 멸망시키다. / **throne** [θroun]n. 왕좌, 옥좌. / **altar** [ɔ́ːltər] n. 제단; 제대(祭臺); (교회의) 성찬대. / **despotism** [déspətìzəm] n. U 독재, 전제; 전제 정치; 폭정. / **empire** [émpaiər] n. 제국(帝國). / **phantom** [fǽntəm] n. 환영(幻影), 유령. / **pilgrim** [pílgrim] n. 순례자, 성지 참배자. / **chase** [tʃeis] vt. 쫓다, 추적하다; 추격하다. (away; off); 몰아내다(from; out of); 몰아넣다(into; to). / **merchandise** [mə́ːrtʃəndàiz] vt., vi. 거래하다; (상품을) 취급하다. ~의 판매를 촉진하다(광고 선전으로). / **fit** [fit] a. (-tt-) ① (꼭)맞는, 알맞은, 적당한(suitable); 어울리는, 마침가락[안성맞춤]의. / **betray** [bitréi] vt. 배반[배신]하다; (조국·친구 등을) 팔다(in; into); (남편·아내·여자 등을) 속이다. / **arch** [ɑːrtʃ]n. 아치 문. ② 호(弧), 궁형(弓形); / **procession** [prəséʃən] n. 행진, 행렬. / **ballot** [bǽlət] vi. (무기명으로) 투표하다(for; against) vt. 투표하다; 투표로 정하다, 추첨하다. / **feast** [fiːst] n. ① 축제(일) (주로 종교상의).

※ 다음 글을 읽고 물음에 답하시오. [41~45]

To many minds, this claim for the ballot suggests nothing more than a rough polling-booth where coarse, drunken men, elbowing each other, wade knee-deep in mud to drop a little piece of paper two inches long into a box—simply this and nothing more. The poet Wordsworth, showing the blank materialism of those who see only with their outward eyes, says of his Peter Bell:

Ⓐ **"A primrose on the river's brink A yellow primrose was to him, And it was nothing more."**

Ⓑ **So our political Peter Bells see the rough polling-booth, in this great right of citizenship, and nothing more. In this act, so lightly esteemed by the mere materialist, behold the realization of that great idea struggled for in the ages and proclaimed by the Fathers, the right of self-government.** _____Ⓒ_____ is the symbol of equality, of citizenship, of wealth, virtue, education, self-protection, dignity, independence and power—the mightiest engine yet placed in the hand of man for the uprooting of ignorance, tyranny, superstition, the overturning of thrones, altars, kings, popes, despotisms, monarchies and empires. What phantom can the sons of the Pilgrims, be chasing, when they make merchandise of a power like this? Judas Iscariot, selling his Master for thirty pieces of silver, is a fit type of those American citizens who sell their votes, and thus betray the right of self-government. Talk not of the "muddy pool of politics," as if such things must need be. Behold, with the coming of woman into this higher sphere of influence, the dawn of the new day, when politics, so called, are to be lifted into the world of morals and religion; when the polling-booth shall be a beautiful temple, surrounded by fountains and flowers and triumphal arches, through which young men and maidens shall go up in joyful procession to ballot for justice and freedom; and when our elections shall be like the holy feasts of the Jews at Jerusalem. Through the trials of this second revolution shall not our nation rise up, with new virtue and strength, to fulfill her mission in leading all the peoples of the earth to the only solid foundation of government, "equal rights to all?"

1. 위 글의 주제로 가장 어울리는 것은?

① The path of people wading to the ballot booths isn't easy.
② The stronger government will be need for people.
③ More beautiful the ballot rooms are, more people will take part in voting.
④ Women's ballot will make the nation new and solid.
⑤ Ballot by women is necessary but a long way to go.

2. 위 글에서 밑줄 친 Ⓐ가 의미하는 것은?

① The ballot isn't necessary and important.
② The flower isn't beautiful.
③ River flower should be taken care of.
④ There are few flowers in the river brink.
⑤ People don't look at the flowers.

3. 위 글의 밑줄 친 Ⓑ의 분위기는?

① impressing   ② admiring
③ sarcastic   ④ encouraging

⑤ enlightening

4. 위 글에서 빈칸 ⓒ에 가장 적절한 표현은?

① The power of people
② The strongest government
③ The people who are willing to go into the polling booths
④ Women who finished voting now
⑤ That little piece of paper dropped into a box

5. 위 글과 일치하지 <u>않은</u> 것은?

① 많은 사람들은 투표를 주장하는 것은 번거롭게 생각한다.
② 자기 정부의 권리를 주장하는 대부들은 단지 물질만능주의자들에 의해 경박하게 간주되었다.
③ 한 상자 안으로 떨어진 그 작은 종이 한 장은 가장 강력한 동력이다.
④ Judas Iscariot는 올바른 정부의 권리를 위한 전형적인 미국인을 말한다.
⑤ 모든 사람들에게 동등한 권리가 바로 투표이다.

TOEIC형 문제

6. 아래의 빈칸에 가장 적절한 것은?

> To many minds, this claim for the ballot suggests nothing more than a rough polling-booth _____ coarse, drunken men, elbowing each other, wade knee-deep in mud to drop a little piece of paper two inches long into a box— simply this and nothing more.

① when
② which
③ that
④ where

7. 아래의 빈칸에 가장 적절한 것은?

> The poet Wordsworth, showing the blank materialism of those who see only _____, says of his Peter Bell: "A primrose on the river's brink A yellow primrose was to him, And it was nothing more."

① with sincere mind
② with their outward eyes
③ without masked face
④ without saying a lie

8. 아래의 빈칸에 가장 적절한 것은?

> So our political Peter Bells see the rough polling-booth, in this great right of citizenship, and nothing more. In this act, so _____ esteemed by the mere materialist, behold the realization of that great idea struggled for in the ages and proclaimed by the Fathers, the right of self-government.

① really
② lightly
③ strongly
④ honestly

9. 아래의 빈칸에 가장 적절한 것은?

> That little piece of paper dropped into a box is the symbol of equality, of citizenship, of wealth, virtue, education, self-protection, dignity, independence and

power—the mightiest engine yet placed in the hand of man for the uprooting of ignorance, tyranny, superstition, the _____ of thrones, altars, kings, popes, despotisms, monarchies and empires.

① overturning   ② alternation
③ protection   ④ initiation

10. 아래의 빈칸에 가장 적절한 것은?

What phantom can the sons of the Pilgrims, be chasing, when they make merchandise of a power like this? Judas Iscariot, selling his Master for thirty pieces of silver, is a fit type of those American citizens who sell their votes, and thus _____ the right of self-government.

① betray   ② protect
③ announce   ④ make

11. 아래의 빈칸에 가장 적절한 것은?

Talk not of the "muddy pool of politics," _____ such things must need be. Behold, with the coming of woman into this higher sphere of influence, the dawn of the new day, when politics, so called, are to be lifted into the world of morals and religion;

① because   ② as if
③ when   ④ therefore

12. 아래의 빈칸에 가장 적절한 것은?

when the polling-booth shall be a beautiful temple, surrounded by fountains and flowers and triumphal arches, _____ young men and maidens shall go up in joyful procession to ballot for justice and freedom; and when our elections shall be like the holy feasts of the Jews at Jerusalem.

① through which   ② which
③ in that   ④ that

13. 아래의 빈칸에 가장 적절한 것은?

Through the trials of this second revolution shall not our nation rise up, with new virtue and strength, to _____ her mission in leading all the peoples of the earth to the only solid foundation of government, "equal rights to all?"

① exercise   ② spread
③ fulfill   ④ raise

41. ④	42. ①	43. ④	44. ⑤	45. ④
46. ④	47. ②	48. ②	49. ①	50. ①
51. ②	52. ①	53. ③		

The Nobel Lecture Speech

by Mother Teresa

[난이도 ★★★☆☆]

①As we have gathered here together to thank God for the Nobel Peace Prize I think ②it will be beautiful that we pray the prayer of St. Francis of Assisi ③ which always surprises me very much - we pray this prayer every day after Holy Communion, ④because it is very fitting for each one of us, and I always ⑤wonder that 4-500 years ago ⑥as St. Francis of Assisi composed this prayer that they had the same difficulties that we have today, as we compose this prayer that fits very nicely for us also. I think some of you already have got ⑦it- so we will pray together.

Let us thank God for ⑧the opportunity that we all have together today, ⑨for this gift of peace that reminds us that we have been created to live that peace, and Jesus became man to ⑩bring that good news to the poor. He being God became man in all things like us except sin, and he proclaimed very clearly that he had come to give the good news. The news was peace to all of good will and this is something that we all want - the peace of heart - and God loved the world ⑪so much that he gave his son - it was a giving - it is ⑫as much as if to say it hurt God to give, because he loved the world so much that he gave his son, and he gave him to Virgin Mary, and what did she do with him?

⑬As soon as he came in her life - immediately she went in haste to give that good news, and ⑭as she came into the house of her cousin, the child- the unborn child- the child in the womb of Elizabeth, ⑮leapt with joy. He was ⑯that little unborn child, was the first messenger of peace. He recognized the Prince of Peace, he recognized that Christ has come to bring the good news for you and for me. And ⑰as if that was not enough- it was not enough to become a man - he died on the cross to show that greater love, and he died ⑱for you and for me and for that leper and for that man dying of hunger and that naked person lying in the street not only of Calcutta, but of Africa, and New York, and London, and Oslo - and ⑲ insisted that we love one another ⑳as he loves each one of us. And we read that in the Gospel very clearly- love as I have loved you- as I love you- as the Father has loved me, I love you- and the harder the Father loved him, he gave him to us, and how much we love one another, we, too, must give each other ㉑until it hurts. It is not enough for us to say: I love God, but I do not love my neighbour. St. John says you are a liar ㉒if you say you love God, and you don't love your neighbour.

🔖 문법 분석

① As[접속사 ∼하는 동안, 때] While[When] we have gathered[현재완료, 결과] 우리가 모여 있는 이때에

② it[가주어] will be beautiful that[진주어] ∼: ∼는 아름다운 일이 될 것입니다.

③ the prayer which[관계 대명사, the prayer를 수식] 저를 크게 놀라게 하는 기도

④ because[접속사]: ','가 있으므로 '계속적인 용법'으로 해석, ～이기 때문입니다.

⑤ wonder that[목적어, 명사절] ～: ～가 궁금해 왔습니다.

⑥ as A, as B: A인 것처럼 B한

⑦ it = this prayer: 이 기도

⑧ the opportunity that we all have: have의 목적어 the opportunity, ～우리 모두가 가진 기회

⑨ for[전치사, 계속적인 용법으로] ～that reminds A[us] that B[we have ～], and (for) Jesus ～.

⑩ bring A to B: A를 B에게 가져다주다.

⑪ so A that B: 너무 A해서 B이다.

⑫ as much as (if it say 말하자면) it hurt God to give: 하느님에게 아픔과도 같은 / he gave Virgin Mary him[4형식 문장]

⑬ [접속사] ～하자마자 곧

⑭ [접속사, when] ～때

⑮ leap의 과거, 기뻐서 껑충 뛰었다.

⑯ that[지시대명사] 그(저) 어린 태어나지 않은 아이.

⑰ [접속사] 마치 ～인 것처럼

⑱ 계속해서 for로 연결되는 문장임.

⑲ insisted that[명사절] we (should) love 우리가 ～하라고 을 강조하셨다.

⑳ as[접속사] ～처럼

㉑ [접속사, 계속의 용법] ～일 때까지, 사랑이 상처를 받을 때까지

㉒ [접속사, 조건절] 만일 ～라면

🔖 본문해석

As we have gathered here together to thank God for the Nobel Peace Prize(우리가 하나님에게 노벨 평화상 수상에 감사를 드리고자 이곳에 함께 모여 있으므로), **I think it will be beautiful that we pray the prayer of St. Francis of Assisi which always surprises me very much**(늘 저를 너무나 많이 놀라게 하는 프란시스 성자에게 기도를 올리니 오늘은 아름다운 날이 될 것 같습니다) - **we pray this prayer every day after Holy Communion**(성찬식 후, 우리는 매일 이 기도를 합니다), **because it is very fitting for each one of us**(왜냐하면 그것은 우리 개개인에 아주 잘 어울리고), **and I always wonder**(저는 ～늘 궁금해 하기 때문입니다.) **that 4-500 years ago as St. Francis of Assisi composed this prayer that they had the same difficulties that we have today**(4～500년 전 프란시스 성자가 우리가 오늘날 갖고 있는 것과 같은 시험에서 이 기도를 하였을까), **as we compose this prayer that fits very nicely for us also**(우리도 또한 우리에게 아주 잘 어울리는 기도를 하고 있는 걸까). **I think some of you already have got it- so we will pray together**(여러분 중 누군가는 이 기도를 이미 하고 있습니다. - 그래서 우리는 함께 기도할 것입니다).

Let us thank God for the opportunity that we all have together today(우리 모두가 오늘 함께 모일 기회를 갖게 된 것을 하나님께 감사를 드립시다), **for this gift of peace that reminds us that we have been created to live that peace**(우리는 그런 평화로 살 수 있도록 창조되었다는 것을 상기 시켜주는 평화의 선물을 위해), **and Jesus became man to bring that good news to the poor**(예수님이 그 좋은 소식을 가난한 자들에게 내려주시고자 인간이 되었음을). **He being God became man in all things like us except sin**(하나님이 되신 그는 죄를 제외하곤 우리와 모든 면에서 같은 사람이었습니다), **and he proclaimed very clearly that he had come to give the good news**(그리고 그는 그 좋은 소식을 전하려 오셨던 것을 아주

분명히 증명하셨습니다). **The news was peace to all of good will and this is something that we all want - the peace of heart**(그 소식은 모든 선의의 평화이고 이것은 우리 모두가 바라는 마음의 평화입니다) **- and God loved the world so much that he gave his son**(그리고 하나님은 세상을 너무나 사랑하셔서 그의 아들을 주셨습니다) **- it was a giving**(그것은 선물이었습니다) **- it is as much as if to say it hurt God to give**(말하자면, 그것은 주는 하나님의 아픔과 마찬가지입니다), **because he loved the world so much that he gave his son**(왜냐하면 그는 세상을 너무 사랑하셔서 그의 아들을 주셨습니다), **and he gave him to Virgin Mary**(그리고 그는 그에게 동정녀 마리아를 주셨습니다), **and what did she do with him**(그리고 그녀가 그와 함께 무엇을 했나요)?

As soon as he came in her life(그가 그녀의 생명 안으로 들어가자마자) **- immediately she went in haste to give that good news**(즉시 그녀는 급히 그 좋은 소식을 주고자 갔습니다), **and as she came into the house of her cousin**(그리고 그녀가 그녀의 사촌집 안으로 들어갔을 때), **the child - the unborn child - the child in the womb of Elizabeth, leapt with joy**(그 아이, 태어나지 않은 아이, 엘리자베스의 배 속에 있는 아이는 기뻐서 껑충 뛰었습니다). **He was that little unborn child, was the first messenger of peace**(그는 저 작은 태어나지 않은 아이였고 평화의 첫 번째 전도사였습니다). **He recognized the Prince of Peace, he recognized that Christ has come to bring the good news for you and for me**(그는 평화의 왕자를 알아챘고 그는 예수님이 좋은 소식을 당신과 나에게 가져 온 것을 알았습니다). **And as if that was not enough - it was not enough to become a man**(그리고 그것이 충분하지 않은 것처럼 - 인간이 되기에 충분하지 않은 것처럼) **- he died on the cross to show that greater love**(그는 그렇게 더 큰 사랑을 보여주고자 십자가 위에서 승하하셨습니다), **and he died for you and for me and for that leper and for that man dying of hunger and that naked person lying in the street not only of Calcutta, but of Africa, and New York, and London, and Oslo**(그리고 그는 당신과 나와 그 나병환자와 굶주림으로 죽어가는 저 사람과 캘커타, 아프리카, 뉴욕, 런던, 그리고 오슬로의 거리에 누워 저 벌거벗은 사람을 위해 돌아가셨습니다) **- and insisted that we love one another as he loves each one of us**(그가 우리 서로를 사랑하는 것처럼 우리가 서로를 사랑하도록 강조하셨습니다). **And we read that in the Gospel very clearly**(성서에서 아주 분명히 ∼우리는 읽고 있습니다) **- love as I have loved you**(내가 당신을 사랑한 것 같은 사랑) **- as I love you**(내가 당신을 사랑하고 있는 것 같은 사랑) **- as the Father has loved me**(하느님이 나를 사랑한 것 같은 사랑), **I love you**(내가 당신을 사랑하고 있는 것 같은 사랑) **- and the harder the Father loved him**(하느님이 그를 더 열심히 사랑한 것 같은 사랑), **he gave him to us**(그가 그를 우리에게 준 것 같은 사랑), **and how much we love one another**(얼마만큼 우리가 서로를 사랑하는지에), **we, too, must give each other until it hurts**(우리가 또한 상처를 받을 때까지의 서로에게 주어야만 하는 사랑). **It is not enough for us to say**(우리가 다음과 같이 말하는 것으론 충분하지 않습니다): **I love God, but I do not love my neighbour**(나는 하느님을 사랑하지만 나는 내 이웃을 사랑하지 않습니다). **St. John says you are a liar if you say you love God, and you don't love your neighbour**(성자 존은 만일 당신이 하느님을 사랑하고 이웃을 사랑하지 않으면 당신은 거짓말쟁이라고 말합니다).

🔖 **단어분석**

- ✝ **pray** [prei] v. —vi. ① 『∼ / +전+명』 간원(懇願)하다(for); 빌다(to). ② 『+전+명』 희구하다(for). —vt. ① 『∼+목/ +목+전+명/ +목+to do/ +목+that절』 (신(神)에게) 기원하다, 기도하다; (사람에게) 간원하다, 탄원하다. ② 『∼+목/ +that절』 희구하다, 기구(祈求)하다. ③ (기도를) 올리다. / **Holy Communion**: 성찬식 / ✝ **fitting** [fítiŋ] a. 적당한, 어울리는, 꼭 맞는. ㉺∼ly / -ad. 적당하게, 어울리게. / **∗∗wonder** [wʌ́ndə: r]v. —vi. ① 『∼ / +전+명/ +to do』 놀라다, 경탄하다(at). ② 『+전+명』 의

아하게 여기다, 의심하다(about); 호기심을 갖다, 알고 싶어 하다. —vt. ① 『+(that)절』 ～을 이상하게 여기다, ～이라니 놀랍다. ② 『+wh.절 / +wh. to do』 ～나 아닐까 생각하다, ～인가 하고 생각하다. / ⁑ **compose** [kəmpóuz] v. —vt. ① 『～+목/ +목+전+명』 「보통 수동태」 조립하다, 조직하다, 구성하다. ② (시·글을) 만들다, 작문하다; 작곡하다; (그림을) 구도(構圖)하다. ③ 〖인쇄〗 식자[조판]하다; (활자를) 짜다(SET up). ④ 수습하다, 가라앉히다, 정돈하다; (논쟁·쟁의 따위를) 진정시키다, 조정하다, 수습하다. / *⁑**fit** [fit] v. (-tt-) —vt. ① ～에 맞다, ～에 적합하다, ～에 어울리다(suit), 꼭 맞다. ② 『～+목/ +목+전+명/ +목+to do』 맞추다, 적합하게 하다(adapt)(to). / ⁑ **proclaim** [proukléim, prə-] v. —vt. ① 『～+목/ +목+(to be) 보/ +that절』 포고[선언]하다, 공포하다; 성명하다. [SYN.] ⇨ DECLARE. ② 『～+목/ +목+(to be) 보/ +that절』 ～을 증명하다, 분명히 나타내다. ③ (일부 지역 등에) 금지령을 내리다. / ⁑ **recognize** [rékəgnàiz] v. —vt. ① 『～+목/ +목+as보』 알아보다, 보고 곧 알다, 알아[생각해]내다; 인지하다. ② (공로 따위를) 인정하다, 감사하다, 표창하다. / ⁑ **insist** [insíst] vi., vt. ～+전+명 / +that절』 ① 우기다 (maintain), (끝까지) 주장하다, 고집하다, 단언하다; 역설[강조]하다(on, upon). ② 강요하다; 조르다(on, upon). / *⁑**father** [fáːðər] n. ① 아버지, 부친; 의붓아버지, 양아버지, 시아버지, 장인. ② (보통 pl.) 선조, 조상(forefather). ③ (아버지와 같은) 옹호자. ④ (the F-) 하느님 아버지, 신.

The Nobel Lecture Speech

by Mother Teresa

동영상 강좌 http://youtu.be/t_Xgr2-OhNg

✹ 다음 글을 읽고 물음에 답하시오. [1~6]

As we have gathered here together to thank God for the Nobel Peace Prize I think it will be beautiful that we pray the prayer of St. Francis of Assisi which always surprises me very much- we pray this prayer every day after Holy Communion, because it is very **fitted/fitting** for each one of us, and I always wonder that 4-500 years ago as St. Francis of Assisi composed this prayer that they had the same difficulties that we have today, ① **as** we compose this prayer that fits very **nice/nicely** for us also. I think some of you already have got Ⓐ **it** - so we will pray together.

Let us thank God for the opportunity that we all have together today, for this gift of peace that reminds us that we have ② **created** to live that peace, and Jesus became man to bring that good news to the poor. He ③ **being** God became man in all things like us **except/with** sin, and he proclaimed very clearly that he had come to give the good news. The news was peace to all of good will and this is something that we all want - the peace of heart- and God loved the world so ④ **much** that he gave his son - it was a giving - it is as much as if to say it hurt God to give, because he loved the world so much that he gave his son, and he gave him to Virgin Mary, and what did she do with him?

As soon as he came in her life - immediately she went in ⑤ **haste** to give that good news, and as she came into the house of her cousin, the child- the unborn child- the child in the womb of Elizabeth, leapt with joy. He was that little unborn child, was the first messenger of peace. He recognized the Prince of Peace, he recognized that Christ has come to bring the good news for you and for me. And as if that was not enough- it was not enough to become a man - he died on the cross to show that greater love, and he died for you and for me and for that leper and for that man dying of hunger and that naked person lying in the street not only of Calcutta, but of Africa, and New York, and London, and Oslo- and insisted that we love one another as he loves each one of us. And we read that in the Gospel very clearly- love as I have loved you- as I love you- as the Father has loved me, I love you- and the harder the Father loved him, he gave him to us, and how much we love one another, we, too, must give each other _____.

It is not enough for us to say: I love God, but I do not love my neighbour. St. John says you are a liar if you say you love God, and you don't love your neighbour.

1. 위 글의 주제로 가장 적절한 것은?

① The position I am standing on is thankful for you.

② The way I've worked is too hard to say a word.

③ The giving is God's gift and his hurt.

④ The Nobel Peace Price is very important for the world peace.

⑤ We should follow the same that God gave us.

2. 위 글에서 밑줄 친 Ⓐ가 가리키는 것은?

① God
② the Nobel Peace Prize
③ Holy Communion
④ Some of you
⑤ the prayer

3. 위 글에서 밑줄 친 ①~⑤ 중, 어법상 <u>어색</u>한 것은?

①   ②   ③   ④   ⑤

4. 위 글에서 밑줄 친 빈 칸에 가장 적절한 표현은?

① until it hurts
② until it is given the reward
③ though it doesn't matter that it doesn't fall down to us
④ though we are sometimes faced with the trials
⑤ though others blame us

5. 위 글에서 네모상자 안의 적절한 단어는?

① fitted   nice   except
② fitting   nice   with
③ fitted   nicely   except
④ fitting   nicely   with
⑤ fitting   nicely   except

6. 위 글과 일치하지 <u>않은</u> 것은?

① 노벨평화상 수상에 대해 우리 모두 하나님께 감사를 드린다.
② 프란시스 성자의 가르침대로 오늘날 우리도 같은 기도를 드린다.
③ 하나님은 세상을 너무나 사랑하셔서 그

의 아들을 주셨다.
④ 엘리자베스의 갓 태어난 아이는 평화의 메신저가 되었다.
⑤ 예수님은 전 세계의 모든 고통 받는 사람들을 위해 돌아가셨다.

1. ⑤   2. ⑤   3. ② been created
4. ①   5. ⑤   6. ④

The Nobel Lecture Speech

by Mother Teresa

How can you love God ① <u>whom</u> you do not see, if you do not love your neighbour <u>whom you see</u>, whom you touch, with <u>whom</u> you live? And so this is very important for us to ② <u>realize that love, to be true, has to hurt</u>. It hurt Jesus to love us, it hurt him. And ③ <u>to make sure</u> we remember his great love ④ <u>he made himself the bread of life to satisfy</u> our hunger for his love. Our hunger for God, ⑤ <u>because</u> we have been created for that love. We have been created in his image. We have been created ⑥ <u>to love and be loved</u>, and then he has become man to <u>make it possible for us to love</u> as he loved us. <u>He makes himself the hungry one</u>- the naked one - the homeless one- the sick one- the one in prison- the lonely one - the unwanted one- and he says: ⑦ <u>You did it to me</u>. Hungry for our love, and this is the hunger of our poor people. This is ⑧ <u>the hunger that you and I must find</u>, it may be in our own home.

I never forget ⑨ <u>an opportunity I had</u> in visiting a home where they had all these old parents of sons and daughters ⑩ <u>who</u> had just put <u>them</u> in an institution and forgotten maybe. And I went there, and I saw ⑪ <u>in that home they had everything, beautiful things</u>, but everybody was looking towards the door. And I did not see ⑫ <u>a single one with their smile on their face</u>. And I turned to the Sister and I asked: How is that? How is it that ⑬ <u>the people they have everything here</u>, why are they all looking towards the door, why are they not smiling? I ⑭ <u>am so used to seeing</u> the smile on our people, even the dying one smile, and she said: ⑮ <u>This</u> is nearly every day, they are expecting, they are hoping that a son or daughter will come to visit them. ⑯ <u>They are hurt because they are forgotten</u>, and <u>see - this is where love comes</u>. That poverty comes right there in our own home, even neglect of love. Maybe in our own family we have somebody who is feeling lonely, who is feeling sick, who is feeling worried, and these are difficult days for everybody. ⑰ <u>Are we there, are we there to receive them, is the mother there to receive the child?</u>

I was surprised in the West to see so many young boys and ⑱ <u>girls given into drugs</u>, and I tried to find out why- ⑲ <u>why it is like that</u>, and the answer was: Because there is no one in the family to receive them. Father and mother are ⑳ <u>so busy they have no time</u>. Young parents are in some institution and the child takes back to the street and gets ㉑ <u>involved in something</u>. We are talking of peace. These are things that break peace, but I feel the greatest destroyer of peace today is ㉒ <u>abortion, because it is a direct war, a direct killing- direct murder by the mother herself</u>.

📎 문법 분석

① whom[목적격 관계대명사] you do not see God / you see neighbour / you live with your neighbour.

② realize that[명사절 접속사] love[주어], to be true[부사구], has to hurt[동사].

③ to make sure (that) ∼: 반드시 ∼하도록 하기 위해.

④ make A B to satisfy: 만족하도록 A로 B를 만들었다. / hunger: 갈망

⑤ because[이유, 목적 부사절] ',' 뒤에서 계속적인 용법 ～때문이다.

⑥ [목적의 부사절] to love(사랑하는 것) and be loved(수동태, 사랑 받는 것) / make it[가목적어] possible[형용사] for us[의미상의 주어] to love[진 목적어] 우리가 사랑하는 것을 가능하게 하기 위해 / makes himself[목적어] + the hungry one[목적격 보어, 배고픈 사람]: 5형식 문장

⑦ 너희가 그것(사랑)을 나에게 해주었느니라.

⑧ the hunger [that, which 목적격 관계대명사로 생략가능] find의 목적어는 the hunger이므로 선행사가 됨.

⑨ an opportunity (that, which) I had in visiting[when I visited] a home where[at which] ～.

⑩ sons and daughters who ～them(=these old parents)

⑪ 넉넉한 집안 분위기

⑫ 단 한 사람 조차도 얼굴에 미소를 짓는

⑬ the people과 they는 동격: 무슨 일일까?

⑭ be used to ～ing: ～에 익숙하다.

⑮ This(I am so used to seeing the smile) is nearly every day(이것은 일상적인 일이다), (but) they are expecting,

⑯ 그들이 잊힌 사람이라는 것 때문에 상처를 받다. see - this is ～. 그리고 알게 되었다. 가정의 소중함을. there = home

⑰ 우리는 그곳에 있나요, 우리는 그들을 받아들일 준비가 됐나요? 어머니는 아이를 가정에서 받아줄 준비가 됐나요? be to용법: ～할 예정이다.

⑱ 마약에 빠지다.

⑲ 이유가 뭘까?

⑳ so busy (that) they have no time: 너무 바빠 그들은 시간이 없다.

㉑ 무언가에 몰입하다. 빠져들다.

㉒ abortion(낙태), a direct war(직접적인 전쟁), direct killing(직접살인)

💊 **본문해석**

How can you love God whom you do not see, if you do not love your neighbour whom you see, whom you touch, with whom you live(당신이 만나는 여러분의 이웃, 당신이 교감을 갖는 이웃, 함께 사는 이웃을 사랑하지 않으면, 당신이 볼 수 없는 하느님을 어떻게 사랑할 수 있나요)? **And so this is very important for us to realize that love, to be true, has to hurt**(그리하여 우리가 사랑하는 것은, 진정으로, 상처를 받아야 하는 것을 깨닫는 것이 아주 중요합니다). **It hurt Jesus to love us, it hurt him**(사랑은 우리를 사랑하시는 예수님에게 상처를 주고 그를 아프게 합니다). **And to make sure we remember his great love**(그리하여 우리가 그의 위대한 사랑을 반드시 기억하도록 하기 위해) **he made himself the bread of life to satisfy our hunger for his love**(그는 자신의 몸으로 생명의 빵을 만들어 자신의 사랑을 위한 우리의 배고픔을 만족시켜 주었습니다). **Our hunger for God, because we have been created for that love**(우리는 그 사랑으로 창조되었기에 우리의 배고픔은 하나님을 위한 것입니다). **We have been created in his image**(우리는 그의 모습에 비추어 만들어졌습니다). **We have been created to love and be loved**(우리는 사랑하고 사랑받기 위해 만들어졌습니다), **and then he has become man to make it possible for us to love as he loved us**(그리하여 그는 우리로 하여금 그가 우리를 사랑하는 것과 같이 우리도 사랑이 가능하도록 인간이 되셨습니다). **He makes himself the hungry one - the naked one - the homeless one- the sick one - the one in prison - the lonely one - the unwanted one**(그는 스스로 배고픈 사람 - 벌거벗은

The Nobel Lecture Speech

by Mother Teresa

사람 - 집 없는 사람 - 아픈 사람 - 죄인 - 외로운 사람 - 버림받은 사람이 되셨습니다) - **and he says: You did it to me**(그리하여 그는 말씀하십니다. 당신은 그것을 나에게 해주었느니). **Hungry for our love, and this is the hunger of our poor people**(사랑의 굶주림 그리고 이것은 우리 가난한 사람들의 갈망입니다). **This is the hunger that you and I must find, it may be in our own home**(이것은 당신과 제가 찾아야 하는 갈망이자 우리 가정에 있어야 하는 것입니다).

  I never forget an opportunity I had in visiting a home(저는 한 가정을 방문한 기회를 결코 잊을 수가 없습니다) **where they had all these old parents of sons and daughters who had just put them in an institution and forgotten maybe**(집에서 그들은 자녀들 모두 늙은 부모님들을 보호 시설에 맡기고 아마 잊어버린 것 같았습니다). **And I went there**(그리고 제가 그곳을 방문했고), **and I saw in that home they had everything, beautiful things**(그 집에는 모든 것을 갖추고 있었습니다), **but everybody was looking towards the door**(그러나 모든 가족들은 문만 바라다보고 있었습니다). **And I did not see a single one with their smile on their face**(그리고 저는 그들의 얼굴에 어느 한 사람도 미소가 없다는 것을 알았죠). **And I turned to the Sister and I asked: How is that?**(그래서 그 자매에게 고개를 돌려 무슨 일 있나요? 라고 물어 보았습니다) **How is it that the people they have everything here**(모든 것을 소유한 사람들은 어떤가요)?, **why are they all looking towards the door**(왜 그들은 문만 쳐다보고 있는가요)?, **why are they not smiling**(왜 그들은 미소를 잃었나요)? **I am so used to seeing the smile on our people, even the dying one smile**(저는 임종을 앞둔 사람을 비롯하여 사람의 미소에 너무나 익숙해져 있습니다), **and she said**(그랬더니 그녀는 말을 했습니다): **This is nearly every day, they are expecting**(이런 일은 거의 매일 반복되고 무언가를 바라고 있다고), **they are hoping that a son or daughter will come to visit them**(그들은 자녀들이 방문할 것을 기대하고 있었습니다). **They are hurt because they are forgotten**(그들은 자신들이 잊혀 있기 때문에 상처를 받고 있습니다), **and see**(그리고 그들은 압니다) - **this is where love comes**(가정은 사랑이 시작되는 곳이라는 것을). **That poverty comes right there in our own home, even neglect of love**(사랑의 결핍은 바로 우리의 자신의 가정에 있고 사랑의 결핍입니다). **Maybe in our own family we have somebody who is feeling lonely, who is feeling sick, who is feeling worried**(아마도 우린 가족 중에 외롭고, 아프고, 걱정하는 가족을 갖고 있습니다), **and these are difficult days for everybody**(그리고 이런 일들은 모두에게 힘든 날들입니다). **Are we there, are we there to receive them, is the mother there to receive the child**(우리가 그곳에 있나요, 우리가 그들을 받아들일 준비는 되었나요, 어머니는 자녀를 받아들일 준비가 되었나요)?

  I was surprised in the West to see so many young boys and girls given into drugs(저는 서방세계에서 많은 어린 아이들이 마약에 빠져있다는 사실에 놀랐습니다), **and I tried to find out why- why it is like that**(그리고 이유는 무언지를 찾고자 했습니다), **and the answer was**(그리고 그 답변): **Because there is no one in the family to receive them**(바로 가족에서 그들을 받아줄 사람이 전혀 없었기 때문입니다). **Father and mother are so busy they have no time**(부모는 너무 바빠 시간이 전혀 없죠). **Young parents are in some institution and the child takes back to the street and gets involved in something**(젊은 부모는 일터에 있고 자녀는 도로나 거리로 나가 무언가에 빠져들죠). **We are talking of peace**(우리는 평화에 관해 이야기를 하고 있습니다). **These are things that break peace**(이런 것들이 평화를 해치는 것들입니다), **but I feel the greatest destroyer of peace today is abortion**(그러나 오늘날 평화의 진정한 파괴자는 다름 아닌 낙태입니다), **because it is a direct war, a direct killing- direct murder by the mother herself**(왜냐하면 그것은 직접적인 전쟁이자, 직접적인 살인행위입니다. 어머니 스스로가 하는 직접살인입니다).

📝 단어분석

- ****touch** [tʌtʃ] v. —vt. ① (무엇이) ~에 닿다, 접촉하다. ②『~+목/ +목+전+명』(사람이) ~에 (손·손가락 따위를) 대다, ~을 만지다. ③『+목+전+명』어루만지다, (특히) 치료를 위해 손으로 만지다 ([cf.] king's evil); 〖의학〗촉진(觸診)하다. ④ ~에 인접하다; ~와 경계를 접하다, ~에 연하다. / ****realize** [ríː əlàiz] v. —vt. ① (소망·계획 따위를) 실현하다, 현실화하다. ② 여실히 보이다; ~에게 현실감을 주다. ③ 실감하다, (생생하게) 깨닫다. ④ (재산·이익을) 얻다, 벌다. ⑤ 현금으로 바꾸다. ⑥ (얼마에) 팔리다. / ****hurt** [həː rt] v. (p., pp. ~) —vt. ① 상처 내다, ~을 다치게 하다(wound). ② ~에 아픔을 느끼게 하다[주다]. ③ (감정을) 상하게 하다(offend); (아무를) 불쾌하게 하다. ④ (비유) 상하게 하다, 해치다. —vi. ① 고통을 주다. ② 아프다. / **♯ satisfy** [sǽtisfài]v. —vt. ①『~+목/ +목+전+명/ +목+to do』만족시키다; (희망 등을) 충족시키다, 채우다. ②『~+목/ +목+전+명/ +목+that절』(의심 따위를) 풀다, (아무를) 안심[확신]시키다, 납득시키다(convince)(of). ③『~+목/ +목+전+명』(채권자에게) 변제하다; (빚 등을) 갚다; (배상 요구 등에) 응하다; (의무를) 이행하다. ④〖수학〗~의 조건을 충족시키다. —vi. 만족을 주다; / ****create** [kriéit] v. —vt. ① 창조하다; 창시[창작]하다; 〖컴퓨터〗만들다. ② 안출[고안]하다; (유행형 등을) 디자인하다. / ****image** [ímidʒ] n. ① (시각·거울 따위에 비친) 상(像), 모습, 모양, 꼴. ② (조형된) 비슷한 모습; 화상(畵像), 초상; 조상(彫像). 성상(聖像), 우상. / **hunger** [hʌ́ŋgər] n. ① U 공복, 배고픔; 굶주림, 기아; C 기근. ② (a ~) (비유) 갈망, 열망(for; after). / **♯ institution** [instətjúː ʃən] n. ① (학술·사회적) 회, 학회, 협회, (공공) 시설, (공공) 기관[단체]; 그 건물. (노인, 정신 질환자 등을 위한) 보호 시설 / **♯ opportunity** [ùpərtjúː nəti / ɔ̀pər-] n. C,U 기회, 호기; 행운; 가망(of; to; for). / **♯ poverty** [pávərti / pɔ́v-] n. U ① 가난, 빈곤([opp.] wealth). ② 결핍, 부족(of; in). ③ 열등, 빈약. / **♯ neglect** [niglékt] n. U ① 태만, 부주의

※ 다음 글을 읽고 물음에 답하시오. [7~12]

How can you love ⒜ **God** whom you do not see, if you do not love your neighbour whom you see, whom you touch, with whom you live. And so this is very important for us to realize that love, to be true, has to hurt. It hurt Jesus to love us, it hurt him. And to make sure we remember his great love he made himself the bread of life to satisfy our hunger for his love. Our hunger for God, because we have been created for that love. We have been created in his image. We have been created to love and be loved, and then he has become man to make it possible for us to love as he loved us. He makes himself the hungry one- the naked one - the homeless one- the sick one- the one in prison- the lonely one - the unwanted one- and he says: You did it to me. Hungry for our love, and this is the hunger of our poor people. This is the hunger that you and I must find, it may be in our own home.

I never forget an opportunity I had in visiting ⒝ **a home** where they had all these old parents of sons and daughters who had just put them in an institution and forgotten maybe. And I went there, and I saw in that home they had everything, beautiful things, but everybody was looking towards the door. And I did not see a single one with their smile on their face. And I turned to the Sister and I asked: How is that? How is it that the people they have everything here, why are they all looking towards the door, why are they not smiling? ⒞ **I** am so used to see/seeing the smile on our people, even the dying one smile, and she said: This is nearly every day, they are expecting, they

are hoping that a son or daughter will come to visit them. They are hurt _____, and see- this is where love comes. That poverty comes right there in our own home, even neglect of love. Maybe in our own family we have somebody who is feeling lonely, who is feeling sick, who is feeling worried, and these are difficult days for everybody. Are we there, are we there to receive them, is the mother there to receive the child?

I was surprised in the West to see so many young boys and girls given by/into drugs, and I tried to find out why - why it is like that, and the answer was: Because there is no one in the family to receive them. Father and mother are so busy they have no time. Young parents are in some institution and the child takes back to the street and gets involved/involving in something. We are talking of peace. These are things that break peace, but I feel the greatest destroyer of peace today is abortion, because it is a direct war, a direct killing- direct murder by the mother herself.

7. 위 글의 주제로 가장 적절한 것은?

① Love is to give and to take.
② Life is to love and to be loved.
③ The love given by God should be taken care of by us at home first.
④ We should devote ourselves to saving many poor people in need of help.
⑤ Man should be trained more in order to be like a saint.

8. 위 글에서 밑줄 친 Ⓐ와 관계가 <u>없는</u> 것은?

① We can't see him.

② He made his great love for us.

③ Because we have been created for God's love, we are always hungry for God.

④ He makes himself the hungry man.

⑤ He is the hunger that you and I must find.

9. 위 글에서 밑줄 친 Ⓑ가 의미하는 것은?

① a home without love

② a home without parents

③ a place with much love

④ a place with many members of a family

⑤ a home with much wealth

10. 위 글에서 밑줄 친 Ⓒ의 품행으로 가장 적절한 것은?

① narrow-mined   ② unthoughtful

③ arrogant   ④ obedient

⑤ benevolent

11. 위 글에서 빈칸에 가장 적절한 표현은?

① because they have no enough support to the children

② because they have got the love from others

③ because they live alone

④ because they are forgotten

⑤ because they have no children

12. 위 글에서 네모상자 안의 적절한 단어는?

① see   by   involved

② see   into   involved

③ seeing   by   involving

④ seeing   into   involved

⑤ seeing   by   involved

And ① we read in the Scripture, for God says very clearly: ② Even if a mother could forget her child- I will not forget you - I have ③ carved you in the palm of my hand. We ④ are carved in the palm of His hand, so close to Him that unborn child ⑤ has been carved in the hand of God. And that is ⑥ what strikes me most, the beginning of that sentence, that even if a mother could forget something impossible - but even if she could forget - I will not forget you. And today ⑦ the greatest means - the greatest destroyer of peace is abortion. And ⑧ we who are standing here - our parents wanted us. ⑨ We would not be here if our parents would do that to us. Our children, we want them, we love them, but ⑩ what of the millions. Many people ⑪ are very, very concerned with the children in India, with the children in Africa where ⑫ quite a number ⑬ die, maybe of malnutrition, of hunger and so on, but millions ⑭ are dying deliberately by the will of the mother. And ⑮ this is what is the greatest destroyer of peace today. Because if a mother can kill her own child- ⑯ what is left for me to kill you and you kill me - there is nothing between. And this I appeal in India, I appeal everywhere: Let us bring the child back, and this year being the child's year: ⑰ What have we done for the child? At the beginning of the year I told, I spoke everywhere and I said: Let us make this year that ⑱ we make every single child born, and unborn, wanted. And today is the end of the year, have we really made the children wanted? I will give you ⑲ something terrifying. We are fighting abortion by adoption, we have saved thousands of lives, we have ⑳ sent words to all the clinics, to the hospitals, police stations - please don't destroy the child, we will take the child. So ㉑ every hour of the day and night it is always somebody, we have quite a number of ㉒ unwedded mothers- tell them come, we will take care of you, we will take the child from you, and ㉓ we will get a home for the child. And we have ㉔ a tremendous demand from families who have no children. that is the blessing of God for us. And also, we are ㉕ doing another thing which is very beautiful- we are ㉖ teaching our beggars, our leprosy patients, our slum dwellers, our people of the street, natural family planning.

And in Calcutta alone in six years- it is all in Calcutta- we have had ㉗ 61,273 babies less from the families who would have had, but because they practise this natural way of abstaining, of self-control, out of love for each other. We teach them the temperature meter ㉘ which is very beautiful, very simple, and our poor people understand.

📎 문법 분석

① 성결 구절에서 뜻을 파악하다 / for = because ② [양보절] 비록 ~일지라도 / could: can의 과거형 조동사 ③ carve A in B: A를 B 안에 새겨 넣다. ④ [수동태] ~안에 새겨져 있다. / so ~that ~: 너무 ~ 해도 …한 / Him = God. ⑤ [현재완료] 이미 새겨져 있다. ⑥ [보어] 나에게 가능 큰 감동을 주는 것 ⑦ 가장 큰 수단 ⑧ 우리들의 부모님이 우리를 원했기 때문에, 우린 이곳에 서 있습니다. ⑨ [가정법 과거, 현재 사실의 반대] 만일 우리의 부모님이 그렇게 했다면, 우린 이곳에 없을 것입니다. that = abortion ⑩ what about the millions? 수백만의 아이들은 어떤가요? ⑪ ~에 관계하다 / be concerned about ~에 걱정하다. ⑫ 아주

많은 수 ⑬ die of ~: ~로 죽다. ⑭ [현재완료 진행형] ~에 의해 고의적으로 죽어가고 있다. ⑮ this = abortion(낙태) ⑯ 나에게 남겨진 일(해야 할 일). ⑰ [반어법] 우리가 아이들을 위해 무엇을 해 주었나요? ⑱ make + 목적어 + 목적격보어: every single child와 born and wanted은 수동형 관계: 한 아이라도 태어나게, 태어나지 않은, 원했던 아이도 태어나게 하다의 의미. ⑲ [문맥상] 놀라운 소식을 말함 / 입양을 통해 낙태와 싸운다. ⑳ send A to B: A를 B에게 보내다. 서신을 보내다. ㉑ 매 시간마다 ㉒ 미혼모 ㉓ 아이들을 입양시키다. ㉔ 많은 가족들이 입양을 원한다. ㉕ 여러 가지 일 중 다른 것. ㉖ teach A[our ~the street] B[natural family planning]: A에게 B를 가르치다. ㉗ 약 61,273명의 아기들 ㉘ [관계 대명사] which의 선행사는 the temperature meter

---

📖 본문해석

And we read in the Scripture(그리고 우리가 성경구절을 읽음으로써 알 수 있습니다), **for God says very clearly**(왜냐하면 하느님이 분명히 말씀하시기 때문입니다): **Even if a mother could forget her child**(비록 어머니가 그녀의 자녀를 잊을지 모르나) - **I will not forget you**(저는 당신을 잊지 않을 것입니다) - **I have carved you in the palm of my hand**(저는 당신을 내 손바닥에 새겨 놓았습니다). **We are carved in the palm of His hand**(우리는 하느님의 손바닥에 새겨져 있습니다), **so close to Him that unborn child has been carved in the hand of God**(너무나 그와 가깝게 있어 태어나지 않은 아이조차도 하느님의 손바닥에 새겨져 있습니다). **And that is what strikes me most**(그리고 그것은 저에게 가장 큰 감명을 주는 구절입니다), **the beginning of that sentence**(문장의 시작부터), **that even if a mother could forget something impossible**(비록 어머니가 불가능한 무언가를 잊을지 모르나) - **but even if she could forget**(그러나 그녀가 잊을 지라도) - **I will not forget you**(저는 당신을 잊지 않겠습니다). **And today the greatest means**(그리하여 오늘날 가장 심각한 수단) - **the greatest destroyer of peace is abortion**(그 평화의 가장 큰 파괴자는 낙태입니다). **And we who are standing here - our parents wanted us**(그리고 우리들의 부모님은 우릴 원하셨기에 우린 여기에 서있습니다). **We would not be here if our parents would do that to us**(만일 우리들의 부모님이 우리에게 그것을 하려한다면, 우리는 여기에 있지 못할 것입니다). **Our children, we want them, we love them**(우리의 자녀들 우리는 그들을 원하고 그들을 사랑합니다), **but what of the millions**(그러나 수백만의 아이들은 어떤가요). **Many people are very, very concerned with the children in India, with the children in Africa where quite a number die**(많은 사람들이 인도의 아이들, 너무나 많은 아이들이 죽어가는 아프리카에 많은 관심을 기울입니다), **maybe of malnutrition, of hunger and so on**(영양실조, 굶주림 기타 등등으로), **but millions are dying deliberately by the will of the mother**(그러나 수백만의 아이들은 그 어머니가 뜻에 따라 고의적으로 죽어가고 있습니다). **And this is what is the greatest destroyer of peace today**(그리고 이것이 오늘날 평화의 가장 큰 파괴자인 것입니다). **Because if a mother can kill her own child - what is left for me to kill you and you kill me**(만일 한 어머니가 자신의 자녀를 죽일 수 있다면 - 제가 당신을 죽이고 당신이 나를 죽이는 일이라면) - **there is nothing between**(그 사이엔 아무것도 없습니다). **And this I appeal in India, I appeal everywhere**(그리고 이것이 제가 인도에서 호소하고 모든 곳에서 간청하는 것입니다): **Let us bring the child back, and this year being the child's year**(그 아이들에게 생명을 줍시다, 그리고 올해는 아동의 해입니다): **What have we done for the child**(우리가 아이들에게 해준 것이 무엇입니까)? **At the beginning of the year I told, I spoke everywhere and I said**(올 초에 모든 곳에서 말했습니다. 그리고 말했습니다): **Let us make this year that we make every single child born, and unborn, wanted**(올해에 우리는 단 한명의 아이도. 아직 태어나지 않은 아이도, 원했던 아이도 갖는 해로 만듭시다). **And today is the end of the year, have we really made the children wanted**(그리고 오늘이 올해의 마지막 날입니다. 우린 진정 원했던 아이를 가졌나

The Nobel Lecture Speech

by Mother Teresa

요)? **I will give you something terrifying**(저는 여러분들에게 끔찍한 얘기를 하려 합니다). **We are fighting abortion by adoption**(우리는 입양을 통해 낙태와 싸우고 있습니다), **we have saved thousands of lives**(우리는 수천 명의 생명을 구했습니다), **we have sent words to all the clinics, to the hospitals, police stations**(우리는 모든 진료소로, 병원으로, 경찰서로 호소문을 보냈습니다) - **please don't destroy the child, we will take the child**(제발 아이들을 파괴하지 마세요. 우리가 그 아이들을 데려가겠습니다). **So every hour of the day and night it is always somebody**(그래서 24시간마다 늘 누군가가 있습니다), **we have quite a number of unwedded mothers**(우리는 너무나 많은 미혼모들을 갖고 있습니다) - **tell them come**(그들에게 이곳으로 오라 말합니다), **we will take care of you**(우리가 당신을 돌봐줄 겁니다), **we will take the child from you**(우리가 당신으로부터 그 자녀를 보살필 것입니다), **and we will get a home for the child**(그리고 우리가 그 아이들을 위해 가정을 만들어 줄 것입니다). **And we have a tremendous demand from families who have no children**(그리고 우리는 자녀들이 없는 가족으로부터 엄청난 요청을 받고 있습니다), **that is the blessing of God for us**(그것은 우리를 위한 신의 축복입니다). **And also, we are doing another thing which is very beautiful**(그리고 또한 우리는 아주 아름다운 또 다른 일을 하고 있습니다) - **we are teaching our beggars, our leprosy patients, our slum dwellers, our people of the street, natural family planning**(우리는 우리의 거지들, 나병환자들, 빈민가 거주자들, 거리의 노숙자들에게 자연스런 가족계획을 가르치고 있습니다).

And in Calcutta alone in six years(그리고 6년 동안 캘커타에서만) - **it is all in Calcutta**(캘커타에서 모두 합쳐) - **we have had 61,273 babies less from the families who would have had**(우리는 그럴 수 없었던 가족으로부터 61,273명 정도의 아이들 데려왔습니다), **but because they practise this natural way of abstaining, of self-control, out of love for each other**(그러나 그들은 절제하고, 통제하고 서로를 사랑하는 것으로 자연스런 방식을 실행에 옮기고 있습니다). **We teach them the temperature meter which is very beautiful, very simple, and our poor people understand**(우리는 그들에게 아주 아름답고 아주 간편한 온도측정기를 가르치고 있습니다. 그리고 우리의 가엾은 사람들은 이해하고 있습니다).

🖎 단어분석

- †**scripture** [skríptʃəːr]n. (the S-(s)) 성서(Holy Scripture). 성서의 한 절, 성구(聖句). / ‡**carve** [kɑːrv] v. —vt.『+목+전+명』새겨 넣다[새겨 만들다]. (식탁에서 고기 등을) 베다, 저미다. / ‡**palm** [pɑːm] n. ① 손바닥 / **strike** 『~+목/ +목+전+명』~의 마음을 울리다[찌르다], ~에 감명을 주다. / **forget** [fərgét] v. (-got [-gát / -gɔ́t]; -gotten [-gátn / -gɔ́tn], -got; -getting) —vt. ①『~+목/ +wh. to do/ +that 절/ +wh.절』잊다, 망각하다, 생각이 안 나다. / **abortion** [əbɔ́ːrʃən] n. ① U,C 유산(miscarriage); 임신 중절, 낙태. / ‡**concern** [kənsɔ́ːrn] vt.『+목+전+명』「수동태 또는 재귀용법」관계하다, 관여하다, 종사하다(in; with; about). [cf.] concerned. ③『~+목/ 목+전+명』「수동태 또는 재귀용법」관심을 갖다, 염려하다, 걱정하다(about; for; over). / **malnutrition** [mæ̀lnjuːtríʃ-ən] n. U 영양실조[장애], 영양 부족. / ‡**deliberately** [dilíbəritli] ad.신중히; 유유히; 일부러. / ‡**appeal** [əpíːl] v. —vi.『+전+명』① (법률·양심·무력 등에) 호소하다. ②『+전+명+to do』(~에게 도움·조력 등을 간청[간원]하다. / **single** [síŋg-əl] a. ① 단 하나의, 단 한 개의, 단지 홀로의. / †**adoption** [ədápʃən, ədɔ́p-] n. U,C 채용, 채택; 양자결연; (입후보자의) 공천; (외래어의) 차용. / ‡**tremendous** [triméndəs]a. ① 무서운, 굉장한, 무시무시한. ② (차이 따위가) 엄청난, 어이없는. ③ (구어) 거대한; 굉장한 양의. ④ (구어) 멋진, 대단한, 비범한. / ‡**beggar** [bégər] n. ① 거지; 가난뱅이; / **leprosy** [léprəsi] n. U 〖의학〗나병, 한센병; / †**dweller** [dwélər] n. ① 거주자, 주민. / **temperature**: 온도

※ 다음을 읽고 물음에 답하시오. [13~18]

And we read in the Scripture, for God says very clearly: **Because/Even if** a mother could forget her child - I will not forget you - I have carved you in the palm of my hand. We are carved in the palm of His hand, so close to Him that unborn child has been carved in the hand of God. And ① **that** is what strikes me most, the beginning of that sentence, that even if a mother could forget something impossible - but even if she could forget - I will not forget you. And today ② **the greatest means** - the greatest destroyer of peace is abortion. And we who are standing here - our parents wanted us. We would not be here **though/if** our parents would do ③ **that** to us. Our children, we want them, we love them, but what of the millions. Many people are very, very concerned with the children in India, with the children in Africa where quite a number die, maybe of malnutrition, of hunger and so on, but millions are dying deliberately by the will of the mother. And ④ **this** is **how/what** is the greatest destroyer of peace today. Because if a mother can kill her own child - what is left for me to kill you and you kill me - there is nothing between. And this I appeal in India, I appeal everywhere: Let us bring the child back, and this year being the child's year: ⑤ **What have we done for the child?** At the beginning of the year I told, I spoke everywhere and I said: Let us make this year that we make every single child born, and unborn, wanted. And today is the end of the year, have we really made the children wanted? I will give you something terrifying. We are fighting abortion by adoption, we have saved thousands of lives, we have sent words to all the clinics, to the hospitals, police stations - please don't destroy the child, we will take the child. So every hour of the day and night it is always somebody, we have quite a number of unwedded mothers - tell them come, we will take care of you, we will take the child from you, and we will get a home for the child. And we have a tremendous demand from families who have no children, _____. And also, we are doing another thing which is very beautiful - we are teaching our beggars, our leprosy patients, our slum dwellers, our people of the street, natural family planning.

And in Calcutta alone in six years- it is all in Calcutta- we have had 61,273 babies less from the families who would have had, but because they practise this natural way of abstaining, of self-control, out of love for each other. We teach them the temperature meter which is very beautiful, very simple, and our poor people understand.

13. 위글의 주제로 가장 적절한 것은?

① Because there are many poor children, we should adopt them all.

② More educational systems need to get rid of poverty.

③ We should all get together for saving children.

④ The campaign such as adoption for saving children is the greatest way.

⑤ Some international institutions must be established for the children in need.

14. 위 글에서 밑줄 친 ①~⑤ 중, 가리키는 것이 **다른** 것은?

① Unborn child has been carved in the hand of God.

② abortion

③ abortion

④ millions are dying deliberately by the will of the mother.

⑤ We had done much thing for children.

15. 위 글의 분위기에 어울리지 **않는** 것은?

① impressive   ② admirable

③ respectable   ④ surprising

⑤ despairing

16. 위 글에서 빈칸에 적절한 표현은?

① that is the reasonable choice for them

② which isn't easy to adopt

③ which is good for themselves

④ which will be supported by government agencies

⑤ that is the blessing of God for us

17. 위 글에서 네모상자 안의 적절한 단어는?

① Because   though   how
② Because   if   what
③ Even if   though   how
④ Even if   if   what
⑤ Even if   if   how

18. 위 글과 일치하지 **않은** 것은?

① 태어나지 않은 아이도 이미 하느님의 손에 적혀져 있다.

② 전쟁은 평화의 가장 큰 파괴자이다.

③ 많은 사람들이 아이들을 위해 힘쓰고 있다.

④ 작가는 과연 우리가 아이들에게 해준 것이 무언지를 반문하고 있다.

⑤ 낙태를 물리치는 놀라운 방법은 바로 입양이다.

13. ④   14. ⑤   15. ⑤   16. ⑤   17. ④
18. ②

And you know what they have told me? Our family is healthy, our family is united, and we can have a baby ① whenever we want. ② So clear - those people in the street, those beggars- and I think that if our people can do like that how much more you and all the others who can know the ways and means without destroying ③ the life that God has created in us.

The poor people are very great people. They can ④ teach us so many beautiful things. The other day one of them came to thank and said: ⑤ You people who have vowed chastity you are the best people to teach us family planning. Because it is ⑥ nothing more than self-control out of love for each other. And I think they said a beautiful sentence. And ⑦ these are people who maybe have nothing to eat, maybe they have not a home where to live, but they are great people. ⑧ The poor are very wonderful people. One evening we went out and we picked up four people from the street. And ⑨ one of them was in a most terrible condition- and I told the Sisters: You take care of ⑩ the other three, I take of this one that looked worse. So ⑪ I did for her all that my love can do. I put her in bed, and there was such a beautiful smile on her face. She took hold of my hand, ⑫ as she said one word only: Thank you - and she died.

I ⑬ could not help but examine my conscience before her, and I asked ⑭ what would I say if I was in her place. And my answer was very simple. I ⑮ would have tried to draw a little attention to myself, I would have said I am hungry, that I am dying, I am cold, I am in pain, or something, but she gave me much more - she gave me her grateful love. And she died with a smile on her face. ⑯ As that man whom we picked up from the drain, half eaten with worms, and we brought him to the home. I have lived like an animal in the street, but I am going to die like an angel, loved and cared for. And ⑰ it was so wonderful to see the greatness of that man who could speak like that, who could die like ⑱ that ⑲ without blaming anybody, without cursing anybody, without comparing anything. Like an angel - this is the greatness of our people. And that is why we believe what Jesus had said: I was hungry - I was naked - I was homeless - I was unwanted, unloved, uncared for - and ⑳ you did it to me.

I believe that we are not real social workers. We may be doing social work in the eyes of the people, but ㉑ we are really contemplatives in the heart of the world. For we are touching the Body Of Christ 24 hours. ㉒ We have 24 hours in this presence, and so you and I. You too try to bring that presence of God in your family, ㉔ for the family that prays together stays together.

🖉 문법 분석
① [복합 관계부사] ~언제든지
② (They are) so clear that how much more ~(can help them) 의미상 생략된 구문임.

③ the life that[관계대명사] God created (the life) in us 하느님이 우리 안에 생명을 주신.

④ [4형식 문장] teach[동사] + us[간접 목적어] + so many beautiful things[직접 목적어] ~에게 …을 가르쳐 주다.

⑤ You people who[관계 대명사] have ~, you[동격]: 수녀들을 말함. 순결을 약속한 사람들.

⑥ only의 뜻. self-control를 강조.

⑦ [양보절] Though these are ~, they are great people.

⑧ the + 형용사: 복수 보통명사(가난한 사람들)

⑨ one of 복수명사: 그들 중 한 사람.

⑩ 거리에서 데려온 4명 중, 3명.

⑪ I did (for her) all that[관계 대명사] my love can do. did의 목적어는 all. 최선을 대해 보살펴 주었다.

⑫ while[as, ~하는 동안]

⑬ can[could] not help + 동사의 원형[~하지 않을 수 없다] 그녀 앞에서 양심에 가책을 받다.

⑭ 그녀의 입장이었다면 난 무슨 얘기를 했을까? would[가정법 과거 표현]

⑮ [가정법 과거완료] would have tried ~하고자 했을 것이다 / would have said ~말했었을 것이다.

⑯ As that man whom[목적격 관계대명사] we picked up (that man) from the drain, ~그 사람도 똑같은 말을 했음을 의미.

⑰ it[가주어] ~to see[진주어] ~that man who[주격 관계대명사] 그처럼 말할 수 있는 그 사람의 위대함을 보는 것은 참으로 경이로운 것 이었다.

⑱ that 위에서 언급한 '여자'처럼 고마움을 전하면서 죽어갔다는 것을 의미함.

⑲ without blaming ~, without cursing ~, (and) without comparing 남을 탓하지도, 남을 저주하지도, 비교하지도 않으면서.

⑳ 그러기에 당신이(Jesus) me(저희에게) it(사랑)을 베풀어 주셨다.

㉑ '우리는 세상 사람들의 마음을 헤아리려 하다'의 의미.

㉒ 모든 사람이 동일한 24시간을 가족에게 사랑을 베풀자.

㉔ [결론] 왜냐하면 함께 기도하는 가족은 함께 오랫동안 머무르기 때문이다.

📖 **본문해석**

  And you know what they have told me(그리고 그들이 저에게 한 말을 당신은 아시나요)**? Our family is healthy, our family is united, and we can have a baby whenever we want**(우리 가족은 건강하고, 우리 가족은 단합되어 있고 우리는 원할 땐 언제든 아이를 가질 수 있어요)**. So clear - those people in the street, those beggars**(거리에 있는 사람들, 거지들도 너무나 분명합니다) **- and I think that if our people can do like that**(만일 우리가 그것처럼 할 수만 있다면) **how much more you and all the others who can know the ways and means without destroying the life that God has created in us**(하느님이 우리 안에서 창조해 주신 삶을 파괴하는 것 없이 방법과 수단을 알고 있는 당신과 모든 다른 사람들은 더 많은 것을 할 수가 있습니다)**. The poor people are very great people**(가난한 사람들은 아주 위대한 사람들입니다)**. They can teach us so many beautiful things**(그들은 우리에게 너무나 많은 아름다운 일들을 가르쳐 줍니다)**. The other day one of them came to thank and said**(그 어느 날 그들 중 한 분이 감사를 표하기 위해 와서 말했습니다)**: You people who have vowed chastity you are the best people to teach us family planning**(순결을 신께 맹세한 당신네 사람들은 우리에게 가족계획을 가르쳐 주는 최고의 사람들입니다)**. Because it is nothing more than self-control out of love for each other**(서로를 위해 사랑으로 자제를 한다는 것이 최고의 것이기 때문입니다)**. And I think they said a beautiful sentence**(그리고 그들은 아름다운

한 구절을 말했습니다). **And these are people who maybe have nothing to eat**(그리고 이런 사람들은 아마도 먹을 것이 전혀 없는 사람일지 모릅니다), **maybe they have not a home where to live**(그들은 살 집도 없을지도 모릅니다), **but they are great people**(하지만 그들은 위대한 사람들입니다). **The poor are very wonderful people**(가난한 사람들은 아주 경이로운 사람들입니다). **One evening we went out and we picked up four people from the street**(어느 날 아침 우리는 외출을 해서 거리의 4명을 선택했습니다). **And one of them was in a most terrible condition**(그리고 그들 중 한 명은 상태는 아주 나빴습니다) - **and I told the Sisters**(그리고 저는 자매들에게 말했습니다): **You take care of the other three**(당신은 다른 세 명을 돌봐 주세요), **I take of this one that looked worse**(제가 더 나빠 보이는 이 사람을 돌보겠습니다). **So I did for her all that my love can do**(그래서 그녀를 위해 최선을 다했습니다). **I put her in bed, and there was such a beautiful smile on her face**(제가 그녀를 침대에 눕히고 나니 그녀의 얼굴에 그런 아름다운 미소가 흘렀습니다). **She took hold of my hand, as she said one word only: Thank you - and she died**(그녀가 감사하다는 한 마디를 하면서 내 손을 꽉 잡았고 그녀는 죽었습니다). **I could not help but examine my conscience before her**(저는 그녀 앞에서 제 양심의 가책을 받지 않을 수 없었습니다), **and I asked what would I say if I was in her place**(그리고 만일 내가 그녀의 입장이었다면 난 무슨 말을 하고 싶었을까). **And my answer was very simple**(그리고 저의 답변은 아주 간단했습니다). **I would have tried to draw a little attention to myself**(저는 내 자신에 조금 더 집중하려고 했을 거야), **I would have said I am hungry**(나는 배가 고파요), **that I am dying, I am cold**(나는 죽어가고 있고, 춥다고), **I am in pain, or something**(나는 아프고 그리고), **but she gave me much more**(그러나 그녀는 저에게 더욱더 많은 것을 주었습니다) - **she gave me her grateful love**(그녀는 저에게 그녀의 감사하는 사랑을 주었습니다). **And she died with a smile on her face**(그리고 그녀는 미소를 머금고 죽었습니다). **As that man whom we picked up from the drain, half eaten with worms**(반쯤 벌레에 먹힌, 하수구에서 건져 올린 그 남자처럼), **and we brought him to the home**(그리고 우리는 그를 집으로 데려 왔습니다). **I have lived like an animal in the street**(저는 거리의 동물처럼 살아 왔습니다), **but I am going to die like an angel, loved and cared for**(그러나 저는 사랑받고 보살핌을 받는 천사처럼 죽고 싶습니다). **And it was so wonderful to see the greatness of that man who could speak like that**(그처럼 말할 수 있는 그 남자의 위대함을 보는 것은 정말로 경이로운 것 이었습니다), **who could die like that without blaming anybody**(다른 이를 탓하지 않고 그처럼 죽을 수 있는), **without cursing anybody**(어느 누구도 저주하지 않고), **without comparing anything**(어떠한 것과도 비교하지 않고). **Like an angel - this is the greatness of our people**(천사처럼 이 사람은 우리들의 위대한 표상입니다). **And that is why we believe what Jesus had said**(그리고 그것이 왜 우리가 예수님이 말씀했던 것을 믿는 이유입니다): **I was hungry - I was naked - I was homeless - I was unwanted, unloved, uncared for - and you did it to me**(저는 배고프고 - 저는 벌거벗고 - 저는 집이 없고 - 저는 버림받았고, 사랑받지 못했고, 보살핌도 받지 못했습니다 - 그래서 당신은 이것을 제에게 해 주었습니다). **I believe that we are not real social workers**(우리는 진정한 사회 복지사들이 아니라고 저는 믿고 있습니다). **We may be doing social work in the eyes of the people**(우리는 사람들의 눈에 특별한 일을 하고 있는 것입니다), **but we are really contemplatives in the heart of the world**(그러나 우리는 세상 사람들의 가슴속에서 진정한 명상을 합니다). **For we are touching the Body Of Christ 24 hours**(왜냐하면 우리는 온종일 예수님의 육신을 만지기 때문입니다). **We have 24 hours in this presence, and so you and I**(우리는 사는 동안 24시간을 갖고 있고 당신과 저도 같습니다). **You too try to bring that presence of God in your family**(당신도 또한 하느님의 존재를 당신의 가족으로 가져오고자 노력합니다), **for the family that prays together stays together**(함께 기도하는 가족은 함께 머무는 것이기 때문입니다).

The Nobel Lecture Speech

by Mother Teresa

🍃 **단어분석**

- ‡ **vow** [vau] v. —vt. ① 『～+목/ +that 절/ +to do』 맹세하다, 서약하다. ② 『+목+전+명』 신에 맹세하고 바치다, 헌신하다. / **chastity** [tʃǽstəti] n. U 정숙; 순결; 고상; 순정; 간소. / † **self-control** [sélfkəntróul] n. U 자제(심), 극기. / ***terrible** [térəb-əl] a. ① 무서운, 가공할, 소름끼치는, 굉장한. [cf.] fearful. ② (구어) 심한, 대단한. ③ (구어) 지독한, 터무니없는, 서투른. / ‡ **examine** [igzǽmin] v. -vt ① 『～+목/ +목+전+명』 시험하다(in; on, upon). [SYN.] ⇨ TEST. ② 『～+목/ +wh.절』 검사하다, 조사[심사]하다(inspect, investigate); 고찰[검토, 음미]하다. / ‡ **conscience** [kánʃəns / kɔ́n-] n. U,C ① 양심, 도의심, 도덕 관념. ② 의식, 자각. / ‡ **grateful** [gréitfəl] a. ① 감사하고 있는, 고마워하는. ② 「한정적」 감사를 나타내는, 감사의. / ‡ **drain** [drein] n. ① 배수, 방수(放水); 유출. ② 배수관; 배수 도랑, 하수구(sewer); (pl.) 하수 (시설); / ‡ **blame** [bleim]vt. 『～+목/ +목+전+명』 ① (아무를) 나무라다, 비난하다(for). ② ～의 책임[원인]으로 돌리다(on ; for). / ‡ **curse** [kəː rs] v. (p., pp. ～d [-t], (고어) curst [-t]) —vt.① 저주하다, 악담[모독]하다.[opp.] bless. ② 욕설을 퍼붓다, ～의 욕을 하다. / **contemplative** [kəntémplətiv, kántəmplèi- / kɔ́ntemplèi-] a. 명상적인, 정관적인, 관조적인; 응시하는, 명상에 잠기는(of). / ‡ **presence** [prézəns] n. U ① 존재, 현존, 실재. ② 출석, 임석; 참석;

And you know what they have told me? Our family is healthy, our family is united, and we can have a baby whenever we want. So clear - those people in the street, those beggars - and I think that if our people can do like that Ⓐ **how much more you and all the others** who can know the ways and means without destroying the life that God has created in us.

The poor people are very great people. ① **They** can teach us so many beautiful things. The other day one of ② **them** came to thank and said: You ③ **people** who have vowed chastity you are the best people to teach ④ **us** family planning. Because it is nothing more than self-control out of love for each other. And I think ⑤ **they** said a beautiful sentence. And these are people who maybe have nothing to eat, maybe they have not a home where to live, but they are great people. The poor are very wonderful people. One evening we went out and we picked up four people from the street. And one of them was in a most terrible condition - and I told the Sisters: You take care of the other three, I take of Ⓑ **this one** that looked worse. So I did for her all that my love can do. I put her in bed, and there was such a beautiful smile on her face. She took hold of my hand, as she said one word only: Thank you - and she died.

I could not help but examine my conscience before her, and I asked what would I say if I was in her place. And my answer was very simple. I would have tried to draw a little attention to myself, I would have said I am hungry, that I am dying, I am cold, I am in pain, or something, but

she gave me much more - she gave me her grateful love. And she died with a smile on her face. As that man whom we picked up from the drain, half eaten with worms, and we brought him to the home. I have lived like an animal in the street, but I am going to die like an angel, loved and cared for. And it was so wonderful to see the greatness of that man who could speak like that, who could die like that without blaming anybody, without cursing anybody, without comparing anything. Like an angel- this is the greatness of our people. And that is why we believe what Jesus had said: I was hungry- I was naked- I was homeless - I was unwanted, unloved, uncared for - and you did it to me.

I believe that we are not real social workers. We may be doing social work in the eyes of the people, but we are really contemplatives in the heart of the world. For we are touching the Body Of Christ 24 hours. We have 24 hours in this presence, and so you and I. You too try to bring that presence of God in your family, for

_____.

19. 위 글의 주제로 가장 적절한 것은?

① The spirit of the career is nothing more than important.
② The pure love sprung up in the deep mind is the cleanest in the world.
③ More institutions will be needed to accompany people in the street.
④ We should do the volunteering work for the poor.
⑤ To examine one's conscience is sometimes necessary.

20. 위 글에서 밑줄 친 Ⓐ가 뜻하는 것은?

① You and all the others keep the words of God.

② The social workers should be sacrificed for the poor.

③ Though many need some love, there are no people enough to help them.

④ We had better be taught more lessons from the people in destitution.

⑤ If we pay a little more attention to them, we can help them in many ways.

21. 위 글에서 밑줄 친 ①~⑤ 중, 가리키는 대상이 <u>다른</u> 하나는?

①   ②   ③   ④   ⑤

22. 위 글에서 밑줄 친 Ⓑ에 해당되지 <u>않는</u> 것은?

① one who was in the street

② one who was brought into the home

③ one who was in the worse condition

④ one who was taken care of by much affection from the writer

⑤ one who got better after sometime

23. 위 글에 밑줄 친 빈칸에 가장 적절한 어구는?

① Your family is always with you.

② You should work harder for your family.

③ the family sometimes gives you some burdensome.

④ the family that prays together stays together

⑤ the family should unit each other.

24. 위 글과 일치하지 <u>않은</u> 것은?

① 한 교육프로그램에 참여한 가족은 행복하게 살고 있다.

② 작가는 가장 상태가 나쁜 노숙자를 보살폈다.

③ 작가는 노숙자에게서 강한 감동을 받았다.

④ 그들의 죽음에 이르러 남을 탓하거나 책망하지 않았다.

⑤ 주어진 하루 24시간을 가족을 위해 더 열심히 일해야만 한다.

19. ② 20. ⑤ 21. ③ 22. ⑤ 23. ④
24. ⑤

What Libraries Mean To The Nation

by Eleanor Roosevelt

[난이도 ★★☆☆☆]

동영상 강좌 http://youtu.be/IDDEWak6vuc

It has been a great pleasure to be here this evening and to hear all the things that have been said about libraries in the district and in general, and the librarians, without whom the libraries would be of little use, I am afraid. But as I sat here I fear that I have thought a good deal about the fact that there are so many places in the United States that have no libraries and that have no way of getting books.

What the libraries mean to the nation is fairly obvious to all of us, especially to those who are here this evening. We know that without libraries, without education, which is based largely on libraries, we cannot have an educated people who will carry on successfully our form of government, and it seems to me that what we really are interested in is how we can make this country more conscious of what it has not got, because we do pat ourselves on the back for the things that we have and that we do. I was looking over some maps which were sent to me and I longed to have these maps very much enlarged and put up in many, many places throughout this country, because I do not think that many people know how many states do not spend more than ten cents per capita for library books a year, and how many states have large areas, particularly rural areas, where one cannot get books.

📖 **본문해석**

It has been a great pleasure(큰 기쁨이 되었습니다) **to be here this evening and to hear all the things**(오늘 저녁 이곳에서 모든 것을 들을 수 있어) **that have been said about libraries in the district**(이 지역의 도서관들에 대해 들리는) **and in general**(일반적으로), **and the librarians, without whom the libraries would be of little use, I am afraid**(도서관들이 거의 사서들 없어, 거의 이용되지 않아왔던 것이 안타깝습니다). **But as I sat here**(제가 여기 앉았을 때) **I fear that I have thought a good deal**(저는 ~많은 생각을 하고 있다는 것이 걱정스럽습니다) **about the fact that there are so many places in the United States**(미국에서 너무나 많은 곳이 있다는 사실에) **that have no libraries and that have no way of getting books**(도서관도 전혀 없고 책을 빌릴 방법이 전혀 없다는 곳).

What the libraries mean to the nation(도서관들이 국가에 의미하는 것은) **is fairly obvious to all of us**(우리 모두에게 아주 분명합니다), **especially to those who are here this evening**(특히 오늘 저녁 이곳에 계신 분들에게). **We know**(우리는 ~알고 있습니다) **that without libraries, without education, which is based largely on libraries**(도서관에 아주 큰 기초를 둔 도서관과 교육이 없다면), **we cannot have an educated people who will carry on successfully our form of government**(우리는 정부형태를 성공적으로 수행할 지식 있는 사람들을 갖지 못할 수 있습니다), **and it seems to me**(저에게 ~인 것 같습니다) **that what we really are interested in**(우리가 진정 관심을 두는 것은) **is how we can make this country more conscious of what it has not got**(어떻게 우리가 이 나라로 하여금 이 나라가 갖고 있지 않은 것을 깨닫도록 할 수 있느냐), **because we do pat ourselves on the back**(왜냐하면 우리는 진정 우리 자신을 ~위로하기 때문입니다) **for the things that we have and that we do**(우리가 진정 갖고 있는 것에). **I was looking over some maps which were sent to me**(저는 제게 보내온 몇몇 지도들을 훑어보고 있으면서) **and I longed to have these maps very much enlarged**(이 지도들이 훨씬 더 확대되기를 열

What Libraries Mean To The Nation

by Eleanor Roosevelt

망했습니다) **and put up in many, many places throughout this country**(그리고 전국에 걸쳐 많고 많은 지역들에 도서관들을 세울 것을), **because I do not think**(저는 ~생각하지 않기 때문입니다) **that many people know how many states do not spend more than ten cents per capita for library books a year**(많은 국민들이 몇 개의 주들이 1년에 도서관을 위해 개인당 10센트 이상을 지출하지 않는다는 것을 알고 있다고), **and how many states have large areas, particularly rural areas, where one cannot get books**(그리고 몇 개의 주들이 사람이 책을 빌릴 수 없는 큰 지역들, 특히 시골 지역들을 갖고 있는지).

📖 **단어분석**

⚕ **district** [dístrikt] n. ① 지역; 지구(행정·사법·선거·교육 등을 위해 나눈); 【미국】 선거구; 【영국】 분교구(큰 교구(parish)를 나눈 한 구역); / ⚕ **librarian** [laibrέ-əriən] n. 도서관 직원; 사서(司書). / ⚕ **obvious** [ábviəs / ɔ́b-] a. ① 명백한, 명확한, 명료한. [SYN.] ⇨ CLEAR, EVIDENT. ② (감정·농담 따위가) 속이 들여다뵈는, 빤한. ③ 알기[이해하기] 쉬운. ④ 눈에 잘 띄는. / ⚕ **largely** [láːrdʒli] ad. ① 크게, 충분히(much). ② 대부분, 주로(mainly). ③ 대규모로, 광범위하게. ④ 풍부하게, 활수(滑手)하게, 아낌없이(generously). / † **educate** [édʒukèit] vt. ①『~+목/ +목+to do/ +목+전+명』(사람을) 교육하다, 훈육하다; 육성하다. [SYN.] ⇨ TEACH. ②『+목+전+명』학교에 보내다, ~에게 교육을 받게 하다. ③『+목+전+명』견문을 넓히다; (예술적 능력·취미 등을) 기르다, 훈련하다(in; to). / ⚕ **pat** [pæt] v. (-tt-) — vt. ①『+목+전+명』똑똑 두드리다, 가볍게 치다(손바닥·손가락 따위로), 쳐서 모양을 만들다. ②『~+목/ +목+전+명』(애정·찬의 따위를 나타내어) ~을 가볍게 치다. / ⚕ **conscious** [kánʃəs / kɔ́n-] a. ① 의식[자각]하고 있는, 알고 있는(of; that). [opp.] unconscious. ② 의식적인. ③ 지각[의식] 있는, 제정신의. ④ 자의식이 강한, 사람 앞임을 의식하는. / ♣ **look over** (1) (~을) 대충 훑어보다; (~을) 조사하다, (~을) 음미하다. (2) (~을) 눈감아 주다, 봐 주다 / ⚕ **enlarge** [enláːrdʒ] v. —vt. ① 크게 하다, 확대[증대]하다; (건물 등을) 넓히다, (책을) 증보하다. [SYN.] ⇨ INCREASE. ② ~의 범위를 넓히다; (마음·견해 따위를) 넓게 하다; (사업 따위를) 확장하다. / **capita** [kǽpitə] n. 【L.】 CAPUT의 복수. ♣ **per** ~1인당 (per head). / ⚕ **rural** [rúərəl] a. ① 시골의, 지방의, 시골풍의, 전원(田園)의. [opp.] urban. ② 농업의, 농사의.

✳ 다음 글을 읽고 물음에 답하시오. [01~05]

It has been a great pleasure to be here this evening and to hear 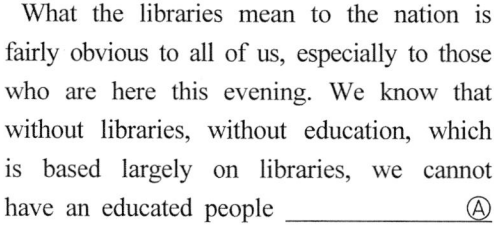 all the things that have been said about libraries in the district and in general, and the librarians, without whom the libraries would be of little use, I am afraid. But as I sat here I fear that I have thought a good deal about the fact that there are so many places in the United States that have no libraries and that have no way of getting books.

What the libraries mean to the nation is fairly obvious to all of us, especially to those who are here this evening. We know that without libraries, without education, which is based largely on libraries, we cannot have an educated people _____ Ⓐ _____, and it seems to me that what we really are interested in is how we can make this country more conscious of what Ⓑit has not got, because we do pat ourselves on the back for the things that we have and that we do. I was looking over some maps which were sent to me and I longed to have these maps very much enlarged and put up in many, many places throughout this country, because I do not think that many people know how many states do not spend more than ten cents per capita for library books a year, and how many states have large areas, particularly rural areas, where one cannot get books.

1. 위 글의 주제로 가장 적절한 것은?

① We need much funding from states to build up more libraries.

② To recruit more educated people for the country is important.

③ The lack of the libraries throughout the country is so big problems.

④ The flexible use of libraries is based on how many times people get books from library in a year.

⑤ The libraries will contribute to the future of the country.

2. 위 글에서 빈칸 Ⓐ에 가장 적절한 표현은?

① who will carry on successfully our form of government

② who have built more libraries throughout the country

③ who will become teachers to teach many rural people

④ who will borrow more books than ever

⑤ who will use libraries more often for their research

3. 위 글에서 밑줄 친 Ⓑ가 가리키는 것은?

① a library

② a book

③ this country

④ our government

⑤ an educated person

4. 위 글에 나타난 지은이의 심경은?

① excited   ② worried

③ hopeful   ④ bored

⑤ indifferent

5. 위 글과 일치하지 <u>않은</u> 것은?

① The addressor is pleased to hear the real situation.

② There are few librarians, which I am really afraid of.

③ The libraries are significant for the nation.

④ We, our adults, should teach youngsters how to get books.

⑤ Many people don't know how many states don't invest in library books.

동영상 강좌 http://youtu.be/8cX6mkJnPw4

6. Select the best answer to complete the sentence?

> It has been a great pleasure to be here this evening and to hear all the things that have been said about libraries in the district and in general, and the librarians, _____ the libraries would be of little use, I am afraid.

① without whom   ② without who

③ with who   ④ with who

7. Select the best answer to complete the sentence?

> But as I sat here I fear that I have thought a good deal about the fact there are so many places in the United States that have no libraries and that have no way of getting books.

① which   ② in which

③ that   ④ in that

8. Select the best answer to complete the sentence?

> What the libraries mean to the nation is fairly obvious to all of us, _____ to those who are here this evening.

① fortunately   ② universally

③ totally   ④ especially

9. Select the best answer to complete the sentence?

> We know that without libraries, without education, which is based largely on libraries, we cannot have an educated people who will carry on _____ our form of government, and it seems to me that what we really are interested in is how we can make this country more conscious of what it has not got, because we do pat ourselves on the back for the things that we have and that we do.

① potentially   ② futuristically

③ successfully   ④ successively

10. Select the best answer to complete the sentence?

I was looking over some maps which were sent to me and I _____ have these maps very much enlarged and put up in many, many places throughout this country, because I do not think that many people know how many states do not spend more than ten cents per capita for library books a year, and how many states have large areas, particularly rural areas, where one cannot get books.

① longed to
② looked forward to
③ anticipated
④ responded to

What Libraries Mean To The Nation

by Eleanor Roosevelt

동영상 강좌 http://youtu.be/4Y8P06-EoeU

One of the things that I have been particularly grateful for in the years of the depression--and, of course, I think, sad as it has been, we have some things to be grateful for--is that we have discovered so many things that we had not known before. These facts have come to the knowledge of a great many people who had simply passed them by before, because they did not happen to think about them, and one of these things, that we used to be able to hide, is the areas of the country which are not served in any way by libraries. I have seen photographs, for instance, of girls going out on horseback with libraries strapped on behind them, taking books to children and grown people in places that have been without libraries. We know a good deal about Mrs. Breckinridge's nursing service in Kentucky, but we know very little about the libraries that go out in the same way that her nurses do, on horseback.

I have lived a great deal in the country, in a state which prides itself in spending much money on education, and I am quite sure that some people think there is no lack of education and no lack of library facilities, and sometimes I long to take people and let them see some of the back country districts that I know, in New York State. I know one place in the northern part of the state where I camped for a while in the summer, and I went to the school and talked to the teachers. They are using school books which have been passed down from one child to another. They have practically no books outside of the textbooks. The children in the district are so poor and some of them so pathetic that I suppose the struggle to live has been so great you could not think much about what you fed the mind, but I came away feeling that right there, in one of the biggest and richest states in the country, we had a big area that needed books and needed libraries to help these schools in the education of the children, and, even more, to help the whole community to learn to live through their minds.

🔖 **본문해석**

One of the things that I have been particularly grateful for in the years of the depression(제가 몇 년간의 불경기 속에서 특히 감사하는 것 중 하나는) - **and, of course**(물론), **I think, sad as it has been** (그것이 안타까울지라도), **we have some things to be grateful for**(우리가 감사하는 몇 가지를 갖고 있습니다) - **is that we have discovered so many things that we had not known before**(우리가 전에 알지 못했던 너무나 많은 것을 발견했다는 것입니다). **These facts have come to the knowledge of a great many people**(이러한 사실들은 ～너무나 많은 사람들이 알게 되었습니다) **who had simply passed them by before**(전엔 그런 사실들을 그냥 지나쳤던), **because they did not happen to think about them**(왜냐 하면 그들은 그것들에 관해 우연히 생각하지 못했고), **and one of these things**(이것들 중 하나는), **that we used to be able to hide**(우리가 숨기곤 했던), **is the areas of the country which are not served in any way by libraries**(도서관에 의해 어떻게든 도움을 받지 못한 국가의 여러 지역들이 있다는 것입니다).

I have seen photographs, for instance, of girls going out on horseback with libraries strapped on behind them(예를 들어 그들 뒤로 묶여있는 책들과 함께 말을 타고 가고 있는 여러 소녀들의 사진을 보았습니다), taking books to children and grown people in places that have been without libraries(도서관이 없는 지역에 있는 아이들과 어른들에게 책을 가져다주고 있는).

We know a good deal about Mrs. Breckinridge's nursing service in Kentucky(우리는 켄터키에서 Breckinrideg(브렉킨리데그)씨의 보육봉사에 관해 많은 것을 알고 있습니다), but we know very little about(그러나 우리는 ～관해 거의 알지 못합니다) the libraries that go out in the same way that her nurses do, on horseback(말을 타고 그녀의 간호업무가 책과 똑같이 이루어진다는 것에).

I have lived a great deal in the country(저는 오랜 기간 이 나라에 살고 있습니다), in a state which prides itself in spending much money on education(많은 돈을 교육에 지출하는 데 자부심을 느끼는 국가), and I am quite sure(저는 아주 확신합니다) that some people think there is no lack of education and no lack of library facilities(어떤 사람들은 교육과 도서관 시설은 전혀 부족하지 않다고 생각한다는 것을), and sometimes I long to take people and let them see some of the back country districts that I know(때때로 저는 사람들을 데리고 가서 뉴욕에 있는 제가 아는 몇몇 후미진 시골지역들을 보여주기를 열망합니다), in New York State. I know one place in the northern part of the state(저는 그 주 북쪽 지역의 한 곳을 알고 있습니다) where I camped for a while in the summer(제가 여름기간 동안 잠시 야영했던 곳), and I went to the school and talked to the teachers(저는 그 학교로 가서 선생님들과 얘기를 나누었습니다). They are using school books which have been passed down from one child to another(그들은 아이들로부터 물려지고 있는 교과서를 사용하고 있습니다). They have practically no books outside of the textbooks(그들은 교과서 이외의 어떠한 책도 실제로 갖고 있지 않습니다). The children in the district are so poor and some of them so pathetic(그 지역의 아이들은 너무 가난하고 그들 중 몇몇은 너무 애처로워) that I suppose(저는 생각합니다) the struggle to live has been so great(생존의 투쟁이 너무 심각해서) you could not think much about what you fed the mind(당신이 마음의 양식을 쌓는 것에 관해 생각할 수 없었다고), but I came away feeling(저는 ～기분으로 떠났습니다) that right there, in one of the biggest and richest states in the country(우리나라의 가장 크고 가장 부유한 주 중 한 곳인 바로 그곳에서), we had a big area that needed books and needed libraries to help these schools in the education of the children(우리는 그 아이들의 교육에서 이런 학교들을 돕기 위해 책과 도서관들이 필요한 큰 지역을 갖고 있었습니다), and, even more(그리고 더더욱), to help the whole community to learn to live through their minds(전 공동체가 그들의 양식을 쌓으면서 살고 배우는 것을 돕기 위해).

📖 단어분석

✝ grateful [gréitfəl] a. ① 감사하고 있는, 고마워하는. ②「한정적」감사를 나타내는, 감사의. ③ 기분 좋은, 쾌적한(pleasant). / ✝ depression [dipréʃən] n. ① U 의기 소침, 침울, 우울;〖의학〗울병(鬱病), 우울증. ② C 불경기, 불황; (the D-) =GREAT DEPRESSION. ③ U 내리누름[눌림], 하강, 침하(沈下). / ✝ strap [stræp] vt. (-pp-) ① 끈으로 매다[묶다]. ② 가죽끈으로 때리다. / ✝ nursing [nə́ː rsiŋ] a. 수유(授乳)[포유]하는, 양육[보육]하는; 간호하는. / ✝ long vi. 『+전+명/ +전+명+to do/ +to do』간절히 바라다, 열망하다(for; to do); 동경하다, 그리워하다, 사모하다. / pass down 전해 내려오다 / ✝ practically [præktikəli] ad. ① 실제적으로, 실용적으로, 실지로. ② 사실상, 거의 ～나 다름없이(almost). / ✝ pathetic, -ical [pəθétik], [-əl] a. ① a) 애처로운, 애수에 찬. b) 감동적인. / ♣ come away (1) (어느 곳에서) (～와) 떠나가다(from; with);「종종 보어를 수반하여」(～한 기분을 안고) 떠나가다(with; doing). /

137

What Libraries Mean To The Nation

by Eleanor Roosevelt

동영상 강좌 http://youtu.be/SfWzge8qcVQ

＊ 다음 글을 읽고 물음에 답하시오. [11~15]

One of the things that I have been particularly grateful for in the years of the depression--and, of course, I think, sad as it has been, we have some things to be grateful for--is that we have discovered so many things that we had not known before. These facts have come to the knowledge of a great many people who had simply passed them by before, because they did not happen to think about them, and one of Ⓐthese things, that we used to be able to hide, is the areas of the country which are not served in any way by libraries. I have seen photographs, for instance, of girls going out on horseback with libraries strapped on behind them, taking books to children and grown people in places that have been without libraries. We know a good deal about Ⓑ Mrs. Breckinridge's nursing service in Kentucky, but we know very little about the libraries that go out in the same way that her nurses do, on horseback.

I have lived a great deal in the country, in a state which prides itself in spending much money on education, and I am quite sure that some people think there is no lack of education and no lack of library facilities, and sometimes I long to take people and let them see some of the back country districts that I know, in New York State. I know one place in the northern part of the state where I camped for a while in the summer, and I went to the school and talked to the teachers. They are using school books which have been passed down from one child to another. They have practically no books outside of the textbooks. The children in the district are so poor and some of them so pathetic that I suppose the struggle to live has been so great Ⓒyou could not think much about what you fed the mind, but I came away feeling that right there, in one of the biggest and richest states in the country, we had a big area that needed books and needed libraries to help these schools in the education of the children, and, even more, to help the whole community to learn to live through their minds.

11. 위 글의 주제로 가장 적절한 것은?

① We've done to analyze the educational problems thoroughly.
② The more libraries we have, the more people will be educated.
③ Education is to see the prospect of 100 years later.
④ Educational benefits should equally give all of areas.
⑤ People should recognize that there are so many places which don't have educational facilities, such as libraries and other books.

12. 위 글에서 밑줄 친 Ⓐ가 가리키는 것은?

① these facts
② the areas of the country
③ we used to be able to hide
④ libraries
⑤ many grateful things

13. 위 글에서 밑줄 친 ⓑ가 의미하는 것은?

① riding on horseback
② extensive medical service
③ direct service by people's visit
④ the expansion of libraries
⑤ many laboring employees

14. 위 글에서 밑줄 친 ⓒ가 의미하는 것은?

① they were so busy studying hard.
② there were no enough teachers.
③ much equipment need to fix some problems.
④ much reading books is necessary.
⑤ they didn't have the time to read books leisurely.

15. 위 글과 일치하지 <u>않은</u> 것은?

① 지은이는 어려운 환경에서도 현실을 깨달았다는 것에 감사한다.
② 사람들은 과거에 무심코 지나쳤던 사실을 알게 되었다.
③ 작가는 도서를 배달하고 있는 소녀들의 사진에 감동을 받았다.
④ 이 나라는 많은 교육예산을 들여 도서관 시설에 투자하려 한다.
⑤ 작가는 우연한 기회에 시골지역의 교육현실을 알게 되었다.

TOEIC형 문제 http://youtu.be/G2lJUw3ctN0

16. Select the best answer to complete the sentence?

One of the things that I have been particularly _____ for in the years of the depression -- and, of course, I think, sad as it has been, we have some things to be _____ for -- is that we have discovered so many things that we had not known before.

① depressed
② grateful
③ enthusiastic
④ exciting

17. Select the best answer to complete the sentence?

These facts have come to the _____ of a great many people who had simply passed them by before, because they did not happen to think about them, and one of these things, that we used to be able to hide, is the areas of the country which are not served in any way by libraries.

① knowledge
② information
③ education
④ understandings

18. Select the best answer to complete the sentence?

I have seen photographs, for instance, of girls going out on horseback with libraries _____ on behind them, taking books to children and grown people in places that have been without libraries.

① chasing
② riding
③ reading
④ strapped

19. Select the best answer to complete the sentence?

> We know a good deal about Mrs. Breckinridge's nursing service in Kentucky, but we know very _____ about the libraries that go out in the same way that her nurses do, on horseback.

① few   ② little
③ much   ④ ever

20. Select the best answer to complete the sentence?

> I have lived a great deal in the country, in a state which prides _____ in spending much money on education, and I am quite sure that some people think there is no lack of education and no lack of library facilities, and sometimes I long to take people and let them see some of the back country districts that I know, in New York State.

① myself   ② oneself
③ itself   ④ ourselves

21. Select the best answer to complete the sentence?

> I know one place in the northern part of the state where I camped for a while in the summer, and I went to the school and talked to the teachers. They are using school books which have been _____ from one child to another.

① passed down   ② inherited
③ disconnected   ④ successful

22. Select the best answer to complete the sentence?

> They have _____ no books outside of the textbooks.

① earnestly   ② hardly
③ practically   ④ sincerely

23. Select the best answer to complete the sentence?

> The children in the district are so poor and some of them so _____ that I suppose the struggle to live has been so great you could not think much about what you fed the mind, but I came away feeling that right there, in one of the biggest and richest states in the country, we had a big area that needed books and needed libraries to help these schools in the education of the children, and, even more, to help the whole community to learn to live through their minds.

① pleased   ② indeterminable
③ fortunate   ④ pathetic

11. ⑤	12. ③	13. ③	14. ⑤	15. ④
16. ②	17. ①	18. ④	19. ②	20. ③
21. ①	22. ③	23. ④		

Fact and Fiction

by Bertrand Russell

[난이도 ★☆☆☆☆]

동영상 강좌 http://youtu.be/sqc5Jg3aOmg

Is it possible to induce mankind to live without war? War is an ancient institution which has existed for at least six thousand years. It was always wicked and unusually foolish, but in the past the human race managed to live with it. Modern ingenuity has changed this. Either Man will abolish war, or war will abolish Man. For the present, it is nuclear weapons that cause the greatest danger, but bacteriological or chemical weapons may, before long, offer an even greater threat.

🔖 본문해석

Is it possible to induce mankind to live without war(인류가 전쟁 없이 살도록 설득하는 것이 가능할까?)**? War is an ancient institution**(전쟁은 고대 제도이다) **which has existed for at least six thousand years**(적어도 6천 년 동안 존재해온). **It was always wicked and unusually foolish**(그것(전쟁)은 늘 사악하고 아주 어리석었다), **but in the past**(그러나 과거에) **the human race managed to live with it**(인간은 그것(전쟁)과 더불어 살지 않을 수 없었다). **Modern ingenuity has changed this**(오늘날의 정교함(기술발달)은 이것을 바꾸어 놓았다). **Either Man will abolish war, or war will abolish Man**(인간이 전쟁을 없애든, 아니면 전쟁이 인간을 말살시키든 둘 중 하나이다). **For the present**(오늘날), **it is nuclear weapons**(핵무기가 바로 그것이다) **that cause the greatest danger**(가장 큰 위험을 낳는), **but bacteriological or chemical weapons**(그러나 세균과 화학무기는) **may, before long, offer an even greater threat**(머지않아(곧) 아주 더 큰 위협을 줄 것 같다).

🔖 단어분석

- **induce** [indjúːs] v. —vt. ① 『~+목+to do / +목+전+명』 꾀다, 권유하다, 설득[권유]하여 ~하게 하다. [SYN.] ⇨ URGE. / **ancient** [éinʃənt] a. ① 옛날의, 고대의(중세·근대에 대해). / **institution** [ìnstətjúːʃən] n. ① (학술·사회적) 회, 학회, 협회, (공공) 시설, (공공) 기관[단체]; 그 건물. ② C (확립된) 제도, 관례, 관습, 법령. / **exist** [igzíst] vi. ① 존재하다, 실재하다, 현존하다. / **wicked** [wíkid] a. ① 악한, 사악한; 부정(不正)의, 불의(不義)의; 악의 있는. / **ingenuity** [ìndʒənjúːəti] n. ① U 발명의 재주, 현명함, 재간. ② 교묘[정교]함. / **abolish** [əbáliʃ / əbɔ̀l-] vt. (관례·제도 등을) 폐지[철폐]하다; 완전히 파괴하다. / **present** [prézənt] a. ① 「보통 서술적」 있는, 출석하고 있는. [opp.] absent. / **bacteriological** 세균 / **chemical** [kémikəl] a. 화학의, 화학상의; 화학용의; 화학 약품에 의한; 화학적인. / **offer** [ɔ́(ː)fər, áf-] v. —vt. ① 『~+목/ +목+목/ +목+전+명』 ~을 권하다, 제공하다. ② 제안하다; 신청하다. [SYN.] ⇨ PROPOSE. / **threat** [θret] n. ① 으름장, 위협, 협박. ② (~의) 우려(of), 징조.

Fact and Fiction

by Bertrand Russell

동영상 강좌 http://youtu.be/w_Ts78NMbal

I have always wondered at the passion many people have to meet the celebrated. The prestige you acquire by being able to tell your friends that you know famous men proves only that you are yourself of small account. The celebrated develop a technique to deal with the persons they come across. They show the world a mask, often an impressive one, but take care to conceal their real selves.

📖 본문해석

I have always wondered at the passion(나는 늘 ∼에 열중하는 것을 의아해 한다) **many people have to meet the celebrated**(많은 사람들이 유명인들을 만나야만 한다는 것). **The prestige you acquire by being able to tell you friends**(당신이 친구들에게 ∼을 말할 수 있는 것으로 얻는 위신은) **that you know famous men**(유명한 사람들을 안다) **proves only that you are yourself of small account**(당신이 스스로 하찮은 사람이라는 것만을 입증할 뿐이다). **The celebrated develop**(유명인들은 ∼개발한다) **a technique to deal with the persons they come across**(그들이 만나는 사람들을 다루는 기술을). **They show the world a mask, often an impressive one**(그들은 세상 사람들에게 가면을 쓰고, 종종 감동적인 가면을 보여 준다), **but take care to conceal their real selves**(그러나 자신들의 진정한 자아를 숨기고자 안간힘을 쓴다).

📖 단어분석

- **wonder** [wʌ́ndəːr] v. —vi. ① 의아하게 여기다, 의심하다(about); 호기심을 갖다, 알고 싶어하다. —vt. ①『+(that)절』 ∼을 이상하게 여기다, ∼이라니 놀랍다. / ⫶ **passion** [pǽʃən] n. ① U,C 열정(熱情); 격정(激情); (어떤 일에 대한) 열, 열심, 열중(for). / † **celebrated** [séləbrèitid] a. ① 고명한, 유명한. ② 세상에 알려진(for). [SYN.] ⇨ FAMOUS. / † **prestige** [prestíːdʒ, préstidʒ] n. U 명성, 신망, 세력. / ⫶ **acquire** [əkwáiər] vt. ① 손에 넣다, 획득하다; (버릇·기호·학력 따위를) 몸에 익히다, 습득하다. [SYN.] ⇨ GET. / ⫶ **prove** [pruːv] v. (∼d; ∼d, proven [prúːvən]) —vt. ①『∼+목/ +목+보/ +목+(to be) 보/ +that절』 증명하다, 입증(立證)하다; 「재귀용법으로」 자기가 ∼임을 증명하다. / ⁂**account** [əkáunt] n. ① 계산, 셈; 계산서, 청구서. ② 계정(略: A/C); 예금 계좌; 외상셈(charge ∼); 신용 거래: ⇨ CURRENT ACCOUNT. / ⁂**develop** [divéləp] v. —vt. ①『∼+목/ +목+전+명』 발전시키다, 발달시키다(from; into); / ⫶ **technique** [tekníːk] n. ① C (예술상의) 수법, 기법, 기교, 테크닉, 예풍(藝風), 화풍; (음악의) 연주법 / ⫶ **impressive** [imprésiv] a. 인상에 남는, 인상적인, 감동을 주는. / ⫶ **conceal** [kənsíːl] vt. ∼+목/ 목+전+명』 숨기다, 비밀로 하다. [SYN.] ⇨ HIDE.

✳ 다음 글을 읽고 물음에 답하시오. [1~5]

Is it possible to induce mankind **living/to live** without war? War is an ancient institution which **has existed/has been existed** for at least six thousand years. ⒶIt was always wicked and unusually foolish, but in the past the human race managed to live with it. Modern ingenuity has changed Ⓑthis. Either Man will abolish war, or war will abolish Man. For the present, Ⓒit is nuclear weapons that **cause/is caused** the greatest danger, but bacteriological or chemical weapons may, before long, offer an even greater threat.

1. 위 글의 제목으로 가장 적절한 것은?

① Human's fatality: To live with Wars
② The Technology: Necessary to develop for Wars
③ Wars: No more than Serious
④ Nuclear Weapons: Human's Masterpiece
⑤ Many ways to prevent Wars

2. 위 글의 네모상자 안의 적절한 단어는?

① living　　　has existed　　　cause
② living　　　has existed　　　is caused
③ to live　　 has been existed　cause
④ to live　　 has been existed　is caused
⑤ to live　　 has existed　　　cause

3. 위 글의 밑줄 친 Ⓐ가 가리키는 것은?

① mankind
② war
③ an ancient tribe
④ modern ingenuity
⑤ danger

4. 위 글에서 밑줄 친 Ⓑ가 가리키는 것을 우리말로 표현한 것으로 적절한 것은?

① 인류가 전쟁과 더불어 살 수 밖에 없었던 것
② 전쟁은 인류의 문명 발달에 기여해 왔다는 것
③ 전쟁은 잔인하고 아주 어리석은 행위라는 것
④ 전쟁의 고대 제도였다는 것
⑤ 전쟁으로 더 심각한 무기가 계속 개발되고 있는 것

5. 위 글의 밑줄 친 Ⓒ의 문법적 용도는?

① 도치문　　　　② 강조문
③ 감탄문　　　　④ 선택문
⑤ 유도문

동영상 강좌 http://youtu.be/gJHkdoEq5Uo

※ 다음 글을 읽고 물음에 답하시오. [6~10]

I have always wondered at the passion many people have to meet the celebrated. The prestige ⒜**you** acquire by being able to tell your friends that you know famous men proves only that you are yourself of small account. The celebrated ⒝**develop a technique** to deal with the persons they come across. They show the world a mask, often an impressive one, but take care to conceal their real selves.

6. 위 글의 제목으로 적절한 것은?

① Let's learn the technique to make a mask.
② Your passion: the endless challenge
③ Who are the famous?
④ To have an impression on others
⑤ To conceal is more important than any others.

7. 위 글에 나타난 작가의 심정은?

① disappointed   ② encouraged
③ indifferent   ④ excited
⑤ gloomy

8. 위 글의 밑줄 친 ⒜와 관계가 없는 것은?

① looking forward to some prestige
② eager to meet the celebrated
③ having small mind
④ developing some technique to learn more
⑤ wandering to come across the famous

9. 위 글에서 밑줄 친 ⒝와 관계되는 단어는?

① wonder   ② acquire
③ prove   ④ celebrate
⑤ conceal

10. 위 글의 내용과 일치하지 <u>않은</u> 것은?

① 사람들은 유명인들에 열광한다.
② 유명인들에게 열망함으로서 얻는 것은 자신의 미천한 존재일 뿐이다.
③ 유명인들은 사람들을 다루는 기법에 능숙한 사람들이다.
④ 우리 모두 사람들과의 만남의 기술을 습득하다.
⑤ 자신에 대한 존중을 할 필요가 있다.

1. ①   2. ⑤   3. ②   4. ①   5. ②
6. ③   7. ①   8. ④   9. ⑤   10. ④

Spanish Armada Speech

by Queen Elizabeth I

[난이도 ★★★☆☆]

동영상 강좌 http://youtu.be/HK6gTvXxhkE

My loving people, we have been persuaded by ①some, that are careful of our safety, <u>to take heed</u> how we commit ourselves to armed multitudes, for fear of treachery; but I assure you, I do not desire to live to distrust my faithful and loving people.

②<u>Let tyrants fear</u>; <u>I have always so behaved myself</u> that, <u>under God</u>, I have <u>placed</u> my chiefest strength and safeguard <u>in</u> the loyal hearts and good will of my subjects. And therefore I am come amongst you at this time, not as for my recreation or sport, but being resolved, in the midst and heat of the battle, to live or die amongst you all; to lay down, for my God, and for my kingdom, and for my people, my honour and my blood, even the dust.

I know I have ③<u>but</u> the body of a weak and feeble woman; but I have the heart of a king, and of a king of England, too; and think foul scorn that Parma or Spain, or any prince of Europe, ④<u>should dare to</u> invade the borders of my realms: ⑤<u>to which</u>, rather than any dishonour should grow by me, <u>I myself will take up arms</u>; I myself will be your general, judge, and rewarder of every one of your virtues in the field.

I know already, by your forwardness, that ⑥<u>you have deserved rewards and crowns</u>; and we <u>do</u> assure you, on the word of a prince, ⑦<u>they shall be duly paid you</u>. In the mean my lieutenant general shall be in my stead, ⑧<u>than whom never prince commanded a more noble and worthy subject</u>; not doubting by your obedience to my general, by your concord in the camp, and by your valour in the field, ⑨<u>we shall shortly have a famous victory over the enemies of my God, of my kingdom, and of my people.</u>

🖎 **문법분석**

① some, that are careful of our safety: some은 that관계대명사의 수식을 받음 / to take heed ∼: [부사구, 이유] ∼을 신뢰하면

② Let[사역동사] tyrants[목적어] fear[원형동사]: 폭군을 두렵게 만들다. / 저는 ∼를 늘 절제해왔습니다. [현재완료 계속] / under God: 신에 맹세코 / place A in B: A를 B에 놓다 / I have place A[my chiefest strength and safeguard B[in the loyal hearts and good ∼my subjects.: 저의 가장 강한 국력과 안위는 충실한 국민과 확고한 백성들 속에 있다는 것을

③ but = only

④ 감히 ∼하다.

⑤ I myself will take up arms to any prince of Europe. 제 스스로 어떤 유럽의 왕자에 대항하여 무기를 들 것입니다.

⑥ have deserved: ∼할 자격이 있어왔다. do[강조용법]

⑦ 그들은 정식으로 대가를 치르게 될 것입니다.

⑧ 왕자가 한 명 이상 고상하고 가치 있는 신하에게 조차도 명령을 내릴 수 없는 것보다는

⑨ ∼을 단숨에 무찌르게 될 것입니다.

동영상 강좌 http://youtu.be/HK6gTvXxhkE

📗 **본문해석**

My loving people(사랑하는 국민여러분), **we have been persuaded by some**(~ 우리는 확신하게 되었습니다.), **that are careful of our safety**(우리의 안녕을 염려하는), **to take heed how we commit ourselves to armed multitudes**(우리 군대에 전적으로 신뢰를 하면서), **for fear of treachery**(반역 행위에 염려하기 때문에); **but I assure you**(그러나 저는 여러분을 확신합니다.), **I do not desire to live to distrust my faithful and loving people**(저의 충실하고 사랑하는 국민을 불신하면서는 살고 싶지 않다는 것을).

Let tyrants fear(폭군을 두렵게 합시다); **I have always so behaved myself that**(저는 늘 몸서 실천해 왔습니다), **under God**(신에 맹세코), **I have placed my chiefest strength and safeguard**(저의 가장 강한 국력과 안위는) **in the loyal hearts and good will of my subjects**(충실한 국민과 확고한 백성들에게 속에 있는 것을). **And therefore**(그러므로) **I am come amongst you at this time**(저는 지금 여러분과 함께 이 곳에 왔습니다), **not as for my recreation or sport**(휴가를 보내기 위해서도 운동을 즐기기 위해서도 아닌), **but being resolved**(그러나 결단코), **in the midst and heat of the battle**(한창 진행 중인 전투의 중앙에서), **to live or die amongst you all**(여러분 모두와 함께 살거나 죽기 위해서); **to lay down, for my God**(신에게 맹세하면서 ~내려놓기 위해), **and for my kingdom, and for my people, my honour and my blood, even the dust**(그리고 저의 왕국과 국민들을 위해 저의 영예와 제 피와 육신조차도).

I know I have but the body of a weak and feeble woman(저는 연약하고 나약한 여성에 불과하다는 것을 알고 있습니다); **but I have the heart of a king, and of a king of England, too**(그러나 저는 왕의 심장과 영국 왕의 심장을 또한 갖고 있습니다); **and think foul scorn**(더러운 멸시라 생각합니다) **that Parma or Spain, or any prince of Europe, should dare to invade the borders of my realms**(팔마, 또는 스페인, 또는 유럽의 어느 왕자도 나의 왕국의 국경을 감히 침범하는 것을): **to which, rather than any dishonour should grow by me**(어떠한 불명예가 내 옆에 있는 것보다는), **I myself will take up arms**(제 스스로 무기를 들 것입니다); **I myself will be your general, judge, and rewarder of every one of your virtues in the field**(제 스스로 여러분의 장군, 심판관, 그리고 전장에서의 여러분의 덕망의 각각의 보상자가 될 것입니다).

I know already, by your forwardness(저는 이미 여러분의 용맹함으로 ~알고 있습니다), **that you have deserved rewards and crowns**(여러분은 보상을 받을 자격과 왕관을 지킬 자격이 있다는 것을); **and we do assure you**(저는 진정 확신합니다), **on the word of a prince**(한 왕자의 언행에 대해), **they shall be duly paid you**(그들은 여러분에 정식으로 대가를 치르게 된다는 것을). **In the mean my lieutenant general shall be in my stead**(중앙에 제 장군이 저를 대신할 것입니다), **than whom never prince commanded a more noble and worthy subject**(왕자가 한 명 이상 고상하고 가치 있는 신하에게 조차도 명령을 내릴 수 없는 것보다는); **not doubting by your obedience to my general**(장군에 대한 여러분의 충성심은 확고하면), **by your concord in the camp**(진형이 일치단결 되어), **and by your valor in the field**(전장에서 여러분의 용맹성에 의해), **we shall shortly have a famous victory over the enemies of my God, of my kingdom, and of my people**(우린 나의 신, 나의 왕국, 저의 국긴의 적을 단숨에 무찌를 것입니다).

📗 **단어분석**

- ♣**take heed** [no ～] of ～에 조심[유념]하다[하지 않다] / **commit**『～+목/ +목+전+명/ +목+to do』「재귀용법 또는 수동태」(약속·단언 따위를 하여) 약속하다, (명예·체면을) 위태롭게 하다; 전념하다. / ‡**multitude** [mʌ́ltitjùː d] n. ① C,U 다수; 수가 많음. ② C 군중, 군집(群集); (the ～) 대중. / ‡**treachery** [trétʃ-əri]n. U 배반, 반역; 변절; C 반역[불신] 행위. / ‡**tyrant** [tái-ərənt]n. ① 폭군 / **behave oneself** 절제하다 / ⁑**subject** [sʌ́bdʒikt] n. ① 국민; 주제, 문제 / ♣**as for** =as to ～은 어떠냐 하면, ～로 말한다면, ～에 관해서는 / ⁑**recreation** [rèkriéiʃ-ən] n. U ① 휴양 ② 기분전환, 오락 / **lay down** 내려놓다 / ‡**dust** [dʌst] n. U ① 먼지, 티끌: (a ～) (일어나는) 먼지, 사진(沙塵) / **foul scorn** 모욕적인 경멸(멸시) / ‡**invade** [invéid] v. —vt. ① ～에 침입하다 / **rewarder** 보상자 / ‡**virtue** [vɔ́ː rtʃuː] n. ① U 미덕, 덕, 덕행, 선행. [opp.] vice. ⇨ CARDINAL VIRTUES. / **forwardness** 스스럼없는 행동, 용맹성 / ‡**duly** [djúː li] ad. ① 정식으로 ② 충분히(sufficiently). 때에 알맞게. / **on the word of** ～말에 책임을 져 / **in the mean** 중앙에 / **lieutenant general** 육군중장 / **in my stead** 나를 대신하여 / ‡**concord** [kʌ́ŋkɔː rd] n. ① U (의견·이해의) 일치; (사물간의) 화합, 조화(harmony). [opp.] discord. / **valor** (전쟁터에서) 용기 /

동영상 강좌 http://youtu.be/Q7LqjsdtYMY

✳ **다음 글을 읽고 물음에 답하시오. [1~5]**

My loving people, we have been persuaded by some, that are careful of our safety, to take heed how/what we commit ourselves to armed multitudes, for fear of treachery; but ⒶI assure you, I do not desire to live to distrust my faithful and loving people.

Let tyrants fear; I have always so behaved myself that, under God, I have placed my chiefest strength and safeguard in the loyal hearts and good will of my subjects. And therefore I am come amongst you at this time, not as for my recreation or sport, but being resolved, in the midst and heat of the battle, to live or die amongst you all; to lay down, for my God, and for my kingdom, and for my people, my honour and my blood, even the dust.

I know I have but the body of a weak and feeble woman; but I have the heart of a king, and of a king of England, too; and think foul scorn that Parma or Spain, or any prince of Europe, should dare to invade the borders of my realms: to which, rather than any dishonour should grow by me, I myself will take up arms; I myself will be your general, judge, and rewarder of every one of your virtues in the field.

I know already, by your forwardness, that you have deserved rewards and crowns; and we do assure you, on the word of a prince, _____. In the mean my lieutenant general shall be in my stead, than whom never prince commanded a more noble and worthy subject; not doubting by your obedience to my general, by your concord in the camp, and by your valour in the field, Ⓑwe shall shortly have a famous victory over the enemies of my God, of my kingdom, and of my people.

1. 위 글에 나타난 분위기는?

① urgent
② catastrophic
③ relaxed
④ unbelievable
⑤ bloody

2. 위 글의 밑줄 친 Ⓐ의 심정으로 적절하지 않은 것은?

① affirmative
② royal
③ negative
④ optimistic
⑤ serious

3. 위 글의 밑줄 친 빈칸에 적절한 표현은?

① they will fight against the England
② he will apologize what he said
③ they shall be duly paid you
④ we don't know whose army would win yet
⑤ let's take time more to think deeply

4. 위 글의 밑줄 친 ⑧가 의미하는 것은?

① Our kingdom would not be damaged by any invaders.
② By the blessing of my God, we shall defeat the enemy.
③ Our victory depends upon how well you can fight.
④ Our triumph is just before us, so don't run away.
⑤ I assure you that as long as we can stand against the enemy, we can keep our camp.

5. 위 글과 일치하지 <u>않은</u> 것은?

① The king of England is a woman, but takes part in the battle herself.
② As long as the soldiers win, the rewards must be given.
③ The king is rhetoric in the battle field.
④ The king's address is to encourage the army's fighting spirit.

1. ①　2. ③　3. ③　4. ②　5. ①

[난이도 ★★★☆☆]

동영상 강좌 http://youtu.be/0rhdlsV0bTk

[01~05]

The idea of the Belly Button Rule was initially discovered in a study by W. T. James in the 1930s. Through a series of tests that had respondents identifying almost 350 different meanings for various poses from a series of photographs, James was able to determine that the direction of the torso plays a key role in determining a person's level of interest. James separated belly button directionality into four key groups: approach (interest), withdrawal (disinterest), expansion (heightened interest and confidence), and contraction (nervousness and slightly reduced interest). About thirty years later, Dr. Albert Mehrabian further refined James's studies, noting that belly button direction was the most important aspect of reading a person's intention. Numerous studies have appeared since that time, confirming that the Belly Button Rule is one of the most accurate ways of gauging a person's interest and intent. The direction our belly button faces reflects our attitude and reveals our emotional state. When we suddenly turn our belly button toward a door or an exit or simply away from someone, we subconsciously send the signal that we want out of the conversation and perhaps even out of the interaction.

📝 본문해석

The idea of the Belly Button Rule(배꼽 법칙에 관한 생각은) **was initially discovered in a study by W. T. James in the 1930s**(1930년대 W. T. James가 연구하는 중 처음 발견되었다). **Through a series of tests**(계속된 실험에) **that had respondents identifying almost 350 different meanings for various poses from a series of photographs**(피 실험자들에게 연속된 사진으로부터 다양한 위치를 갖는 거의 350개의 다른 의미 차이점을 확인해 보는), **James was able to determine**(James는 ~을 확인할 수 있었다) **that the direction of the torso plays a key role**(몸통의 방향이 결정적 역할을 한다) **in determining a person's level of interest**(한 사람의 흥미수준을 결정할 때). **James separated belly button directionality into four key groups**(James는 배꼽법칙 방향성을 4개의 주요 집단으로 분리했다): **approach (interest), withdrawal (disinterest), expansion (heightened interest and confidence)**(접근(흥미), 움추림(흥미 없음), 확장(고조된 흥미와 자신감)), **and contraction (nervousness and slightly reduced interest)**(그리고 수축(긴장감과 약간의 흥미감소)). **About thirty years later**(약 30년이 지나), **Dr. Albert Mehrabian further refined James's studies**(Albert Mehrabian박사는 James연구를 더 세밀하게 구분 지었다), **noting that belly button direction was the most important aspect of reading a person's intention**(belly button의 방향은 사람의 의도를 파악하는데 가장 중요한 요소였다). **Numerous studies have appeared since that time**(수많은 연구가 그 이후로 계속 되었다), **confirming that the Belly Button Rule is one of**(배꼽규칙은 ~라 입증하면서) **the most accurate ways of gauging a person's interest and intent**(사람의 흥미와 의도를 측정하는데 가장 정교한 방법 중 하나라고). **The direction our belly button faces reflects our attitude**(우리의 배꼽이 위치하는 방향은 우리의 태도를 반영하고) **and reveals our emotional state**(우리의 감정의 상태를 보여준다). **When we suddenly turn our belly button toward a door or an exit or simply away from someone**(우리가 갑자기 우리의 배꼽을 문 쪽으로 또는 출구 쪽으로 방향을 바꾸거나

누군가와 단순히 떨어질 때), we subconsciously send the signal(우리는 무의식적으로 ~의 신호를 보낸다) that we want out of the conversation and perhaps even out of the interaction(우리는 그 대화에서 벗어나고 싶어 하거나 아마 그 반응에서 벗어나고픈).

🖎 **단어분석**

- ⵐ **initial** [iníʃəl] a. ① 처음의 ② 머리글자의 / **series** [sí-əriː z] n. (pl. ~) ① 일련, 한 계열, 연속. ② 연속물[프로]; 연속 강의; 연속 시합 / **respondent** [rispándənt] a. 대답[응답]하는; 감응하는 / ⵐ **identify** [aidéntəfài] v. —vt. ① (본인·동일물임을) 확인하다; (사람의 성명·신원, 물건의 명칭·분류·소속 따위를) 인지[판정]하다 ② 『+목+전+명』(~와) 동일시하다, 동일한 것으로 간주하다(~ A with B, ~A and B) / **torso** [tɔ́ː rsou] n. (pl. ~s, -si [-siː]) (인체의) 몸통(trunk) / ⵐ **approach** [əpróutʃ] n. ① U 가까워짐, 접근(of; to); 가까이함 ② (문제 따위의) 다루는 방법, 접근법, 해결 방법. / † **withdrawal** [wiðdrɔ́ː -əl, wiθ-] n. U,C ① 움츠려들임 ② (예금·출자금 등의) 회수. ③ 철수 / ⵐ **expansion** [ikspǽnʃən] n. U,C ① 신장 ② 확장 / † **contraction** [kəntrǽkʃən] n. U ① 수축, 수렴 ② (말이나 글의) 단축 / † **refine** [rifáin] v. —vt. ① 세련하다, 품위 있게 하다 / ⵐ **aspect** [ǽspekt] n. ① C,U 외관, (사람의) 얼굴 생김새(appearance). ② 정세(phase). [SYN.] ⇨ PHASE / ⵐ **intention** [inténʃən] n. ① 목적; 의도(of). [SYN.] ⇨ PURPOSE. / **confirm** [kənfɔ́ː rm] vt. ① 확실히 하다, 확증하다. ② 확인하다. / † **gauge** vt. (p., pp. ~d; gauging) ① 측정하다; 평가[판단]하다. / ⵐ **reflect** [riflékt]v. —vt. ① (빛·소리·열 따위를) 반사하다, 되튀기다. ② (비유) 반영하다, 나타내다. / ⵐ **attitude** [ǽtitjùː d] n. ① (사람·물건 등에 대한) 태도, 마음가짐. ② 자세(posture) / **subconscious** [sʌbkánʃəs / -kɔ́n-] a., n. U 잠재의식(의) / **interaction** [ìntərǽkʃən] n. U,C 상호 작용[영향], 교호(交互) 작용;

동영상 강좌 http://youtu.be/0YHDUgdXKD0

[06~10]

In one classic experiment, divers learned lists of words in two environments, on dry land and underwater. They were later asked to recall the words in one of the two environments: either in the original environment in which the words were leaned or in the alternative environment. Lists learned underwater had higher recall underwater, and lists learned on dry land had higher recall on dry land. The experimenters later proved that this effect was one of context-dependent memory and not related to the disruption of moving environments. Some companies have used this effect to their advantage. In The Experience Economy, Pine and Gilmore quote the example of Standard Parking of Chicago, which had a parking garage at O'Hare Airport. To help customers remember on which floor they parked their car, they played a different signature tune at each level of the garage, and decorated the walls with the icons of different local sports franchises, so the Bulls were on one floor and the Blackhawks on another. They quote one local resident saying, 'You never forget where you parked!'

본문해석

In one classic experiment(한 고전적인 실험에서), divers learned lists of words in two environment(다이버들은 두 서로 다른 환경에서 단어로 된 목록을 배웠다), on dry land and underwater(건조한 땅위에서와 수중에서). They were later asked to recall the words(그들은 그 터득한 단어들을 기억해 보라고 나중에 요청받았다) in one of the two environment(두 다른 환경 중 한 상황에서): either in the original environment(본래의 환경이나) in which the words were learned(단어들을 터득했던) or in the alternative environment(대안이 되는 다른 환경에서). Lists learned underwater(수중에서 터득한 목록들은) had higher recall underwater(수중에서 더 높은 기억을 발휘했다), and lists learned on dry land had higher recall on dry land(그리고 지상에서 터득한 목록들은 지상에서 더 높은 기억력을 발휘했다). The experiments later proved(그 실험은 차후 ~을 증명했다) that this effect was one of context-dependent memory(이런 효과는 배경에 근거한 기억력 중 하나였다고) and not related to the disruption of moving environments(변화는 환경의 혼란과 관련이 없는). Some companies(일부 기업들은) have used this effect to their advantage(이런 효과를 자신들의 이점으로 이용하고 있다). In The Experience Economy(경험경제라는 것에서), Pine and Gilmore(파인과 길모어는), which had a parking garage at O'Hare Airport(오헤어 공항에서 주차장이 있었던). To help customers remember on which floor they parked their car(고객들이 그들이 주차한 차가 몇 층에 있는지를 기억하는데 도움을 주기 위해), they played a different signature tune(그들은 다른 특징의 분위기를 연출했다) at each level of the garage(주차장의 각 층에), and decorated the walls with the icons of different local sports franchises (다른 지역의 스포츠 체인점의 상징마크를 벽에 그려 넣었다), so the Bulls were on one floor(황소는 일층에) and the Blackhawks on another(블랙호크는 다른 층에 그렸다). They quote one local resident saying(그들은 지역 주민이 ~말하는 것을 인용한다), 'You never forget where you parked(‘당신의 주차한 곳을 잊을 일 없어요’라고)!"

단어분석

- ‡ **recall** [rikɔ́ː l] vt. ① 『+목+전+명』 (일이 사람에게 의무감 등을) 상기시키다; (마음·주의를 현실 등으로) 되부르다(to) / **alternative** [ɔː ltə́ː rnətiv, æl-] n. ① (보통 the ~) (둘 중, 때로는 셋 이상에서) 하나를 택할 여지. ② 대안 ③ (pl.) (하나를) 선택해야 할 양자, 양자[삼자] 택일 / † **context** [kántekst / kɔ́n-] n. (글의) 전후 관계, 문맥; (사건 등에 대한) 배경 / † **disruption** [disrʌ́pʃən] n. U 분열; (특히 국가·제도의) 붕괴, 방해; 환경 파괴(environmental ~); / ‡ **effect** [ifékt] n. ① C,U 결과(consequence). [SYN.] ⇨ RESULT. / ‡ **relate** [riléit] v. —vt. ① 관계시키다, 관련시켜서 설명하다(to; with). ② 『+목+전+명』 「수동태」 ~와 이어져 있다(to). ③ 이야기하다, 말하다. [SYN.] / ‡ **signature** [sígnətʃəː r] n. ① 서명(하기). ② 징후 / ‡ **decorate** [dékərèit] vt. ① 『~+목/ +목+전+명』 꾸미다, 장식하다(with). / ‡ **quote** [kwout] v. —vt. ① 『~+목/ +목+전+명』 (남의 말·문장 따위를) 인용하다, 따다 쓰다.

[11~15]

Certain key position in your company may have revolving-door loyalty. Just when you have a treasured employee fully trained, he hits the road. If you see this pattern repeat itself, you may need to redesign the position. UPS found that when they redesigned their drivers' position so that it no longer included the thankless job of loading the trucks, they were able to dramatically increase the length of driver employment. UPS made a strategic decision. They determined that the drivers were the face of the company and that their customers didn't appreciate meeting a new driver every six months. Alternatively, the company figured that the loading jobs were lower-skilled and likely always to be high-turnover jobs. This didn't concern them, because the training period for the loading jobs were much shorter than for the driver jobs and the customer contact was minimal. Sometimes employee retention is just a matter of strategic thinking.

🔖 본문해석

Certain key position in your company may have revolving-door loyalty(당신의 회사에서의 특정한 중요 직책은 자주 바뀌는 충성도를 갖고 있는 것 같다). Just when you have a treasured employee fully trained(당신의 중요한 직원을 완벽히 훈련시켰을 바로 그때), he hits the road(그는 직장을 떠난다). If you see this pattern repeat itself(당신이 이러한 추세가 반복됨을 안다면), you may need to redesign the position(당신은 그 직책에 수정을 가할 필요성을 느낄 것이다). UPS found that(UPS회사는 알아냈다) when they redesigned their drivers' position(그들이 자신들의 운전자들의 직책을 다시 수정했을 때) so that it no longer included the thankless job of loading the trucks(그것(운전 직책)이 더 이상 짐을 싣는 달갑지 않은 일을 포함하지 않도록), they were able to dramatically increase the length of driver employment(그들은 운전자의 고용 기간을 상당히 연장할 수 있었다). UPS made a strategic decision(UPS는 전략적 결정을 내렸다). They determined(그들은 결정을 했다) that the drivers were the face of the company(운전자들은 회사의 이미지이고) and that their customers didn't appreciate meeting a new driver every six months(그들 고객들은 6개월 마다 새로운 운전자를 만나는 것을 달갑지 않는다는 것을). Alternatively(대안으로), the company figured(회사는 인식했다) that the loading jobs were lower-skilled(짐을 싣는 일은 큰 기술을 요하지 않는다는 것과) and likely always to be high-turnover jobs(늘 이직률이 높다는 것을). This didn't concern them(이것은 큰 관심사는 아니었다), because the training period for the loading jobs were much shorter than for the driver jobs(왜냐하면 짐을 싣는 훈련기간은 운전직업 보다 더 짧기 때문이고) and the customer contact was minimal(고객과의 만남의 시간은 길지 않기 때문에). Sometimes employee retention is just a matter of strategic thinking(때때로 직원유지는 단지 전략적인 사고의 문제이다).

🔖 단어분석

- **revolving-door loyalty** 자주 바뀌는 충성도 / **hit the road** 직장을 떠난다 / † **thankless** [θǽŋklis] a. ① 감사하지 않는 / **turnover** [tɔ́ː rnòuvə: r] n. U,C ① TURN over 회전, 반전, 전복, 재편성. ② 반대쪽으로의 이동, 방향 전환 / **retention** [riténʃ-ən] n. U ① 보유, 보존; 보류; 유지. ② 기억력 /

동영상 강좌 http://youtu.be/kD6Wa4pgU6M

[16~20]

  Off in the distance General Longstreet picked up a conversation between two men. It was an argument. One man must have found out that the other had some sort of sympathy for the Union Army across the way. He became very angry and very violent, and he said bad things about the Union Army. The other man responded to his friend's comments by explaining that he was not siding with them, and that he would never side with them. He was only making a point that he had three cousins across the field, and he hoped that they were still alive and well. The angry man settled down, apologized, and told his friend that, after all, he and his cousins had chosen their sides of that fight, and that it would be God's way to decide which of them would be able to go home. The Union "sympathizer" held his head low. The other man came over to him, rubbed his head, and told the man, "I sure hope that you are the one going home."

📝 **본문해석**

Off in the distance(멀리 떨어져) General Longstreet picked up a conversation between two men(롱스트리트 장군은 두 남자의 얘기를 엿들었다.). It was an argument(그것은 말다툼이었다). One(한 남자는) man must have found out(알아 챈게 분명했다) that the other had some sort of sympathy for the Union Army across the way(다른 남자는 길 건너편에 있는 연방(북부)군에게 약간의 동정심을 갖았다). He became very angry(그는 아주 화를 내며) and very violent(아주 폭력적이었다), and he said bad things about the Union Army(그리고 그는 연방군에 관해 험담을 했다). The other man responded to his friend's comments(다른 남자는 그의 친구의 말에 응수했다) by explaining that he was not siding with them(자신은 그들 편은 아니라 설명하면서), and that he would never side with them(그리고 그들 편이 되지도 않을 거라면서). He was only making a point(그는 단지 한가지의 요점을 말하고 있었다) that he had three cousins across the field(그는 전장에 세 명의 조카가 있다), and he hoped that they were still alive and well(그는 그들이 아직 살아있고 무사하기를 바란다고). The angry man settled down, apologized(그 화를 낸 남자는 진정하며 사과했다), and told his friend(그리고 친구에게 말했다) that, after all(결국), he and his cousins had chosen their sides of that fight(그와 조카들은 그 전쟁하는 쪽을 선택했다고), and that it would be God's way(신만이 안다고) to decide which of them would be able to go home(그들 중 누가 살아서 집으로 갈 것인지는). The Union "sympathizer" held his head low(연방군 동조자는 머리를 떨구었다). The other man came over to him(그 다른 남자는 그의 마음이 이해가되), rubbed his head, and told the man(그의 머리를 쓰다듬으며(미안해하면서) 말하기를), "I sure hope that you are the one going home(너희들 모두가 살아서 집으로 갈길 바랄께)."

📝 **단어분석**

- ‡ **argument** [άːrgjəmənt] n. C ① U,C 논의, 논증; 논거; 논법(against; for; in favor of; with; on; over). ② (각본·소설 따위의) 줄거리. / ‡ **sympathy** [símpəθi] n. U ① U,C 동정, 헤아림; (종종 pl.) 조위(弔慰), [opp] antipathy. / ‡ **violent** [váiələnt] a. ① (자연 현상·사람의 행동·감정 따위가) 격렬한, 맹렬한. [SYN.] ⇨ WILD. ② 극단적인, 비상한, 폭력적인. / ‡ **apologize** [əpálədʒàiz] vi. ①『~/ +전+명』 사죄하다, 사과하다. ② 변명[해명]하다. / ‡ **rub** [rʌb] v. (-bb-) —vt. ①『~+목/ +목+부/ +목+전+명』 문지르다, 비비다; 마찰하다.

[21~25]

Our delusion that happiness comes from the things that we desire, and that therefore by desiring and acquiring more things we will become more happy, is a vicious circle. Because we desire something, we feel happy when we obtain it, and because we feel happy when we obtain it, we desire more of it. In this way our desires are always continuously increasing and multiplying. The raging fire of our desires can never be extinguished by the objects of our desire. The more we acquire those objects, the more intensely our desire for them and for other such objects will rage. Trying to extinguish the fire of our desires by fulfilling them is like trying to extinguish a fire by pouring petrol upon it. The objects of our desire are the fuel that keeps the fire of our desires burning. The only way we can extinguish this fire of our desires is by knowing the truth that all the happiness that we seem to derive from the objects of our desire do not actually come from those objects but only from within ourself.

🔖 **본문해석**

Our delusion that happiness comes from the things that we desire(행복은 우리가 바라는 것으로부터 온다는 것과 ~라는 망상은), and that therefore by desiring and acquiring more things(그리하여 더 많은 것을 바라고 얻는 것으로) we will become more happy(우리는 더욱 행복해질 것이다), is a vicious circle(잘못되게 반복된다). Because we desire something(우리는 무언가를 바라기 때문에), we feel happy when we obtain it(우리가 그것을 얻을 때 우린 행복을 느낀다), and because we feel happy when we obtain it(우리가 그것을 얻을 때 행복하기 때문에), we desire more of it(우린 더 많은 그것을 얻기를 바란다). In this way(이와 같이) our desires are always continuously increasing and multiplying(우리의 욕망은 늘 계속 증가하며 배가 되고 있다). The raging fire of our desires(우리의 욕망의 맹렬한 불꽃은) can never be extinguished by the objects of our desire(결코 우리의 욕망 목적에 의해 꺼질 수가 없다). The more we acquire those objects(우리가 더 많은 그러한 목적을 얻으면 얻을수록), the more intensely our desire for them and for other such objects will rage(그것들과 다른 그러한 것들을 위한 우리의 욕망은 더더욱 맹렬히 타오를 것이다). Trying to extinguish the fire of our desires by fulfilling them(그것들은 채우기 위해 우리의 욕망의 불꽃을 끄고자 노력하는 것은) is like trying to extinguish a fire by pouring petrol upon it(기름을 그 위에 붓고 불을 끄고자하는 것과 다를 봐 없다). The objects of our desire(우리의 욕망의 목표는) are the fuel that keeps the fire of our desires burning(우리의 욕망의 불꽃을 타오르게 하는 연료이다). The only way we can extinguish this fire of our desires(우리가 우리의 욕망의 이런 불꽃을 끌 수 있는 유일한 길은) is by knowing the truth that all the happiness that we seem to derive from the objects of our desire(우리가 우리의 욕망의 목표로부터 오는 것 같다고 느끼는 모든 행복은 ~라는 진실을 아는 것 이다.) do not actually come from those objects but only from within ourself(실제로 그러한 목표에서 오는 것이 아닌, 단지 우리들 내면에서 온다는 것이).

🔖 **단어분석**

- † **delusion** [dilú: ʒən] n. ① U 미혹, 기만. ② U,C 망상. / ‡ **vicious** [víʃəs] a. ① 사악한, 악덕한; 타락한. ② 악의 있는, 심술궂은. / **raging** [réidʒiŋ] a. 격노한; 거칠어지는, 쑤시고 아픈; 터무니없는. / ‡ **extinguish** [ikstíŋgwiʃ] vt. ① (빛·불 따위를) 끄다; (화재를) 소화시키다, 진화하다. ② (희망·정열 따위를) 소멸시키다, 잃게 하다. / ‡ **object** [ábdʒikt] n. ① 물건, 물체, 사물. ② (동작·감정 등의) 대상. ③ 목적, 목표(goal); 동기. [SYN.] ⇨ PURPOSE. /

동영상 강좌 http://youtu.be/pADEd-cYM8g

[26~30]

If we attempt to specify the ways in which human beings are unique and different from other animal species, we must quickly conclude that most, if not all, differences are in degree, not in kind. That is, other animals may possess a particular trait similar to humans, but not to the same extent. For example, if we say that a distinctive characteristic of humankind is language, it is possible to point to communication among dolphins or the sign language learned by apes in certain experiments as simple and basic forms of the same behavior. Or, if we say that social organizations are a human trait, a parallel might be found in the behaviors of bees or ants. We have elaborate rituals connected with death, but elephants have been observed engaging in what might be called a burial ceremony. Music may even have its animal counterpart in whalesong or birdsong - to a degree. However, it is the degree of human involvement in such behaviors as language, social organizations, rituals, and music that separate us from other animals.

🖉 **본문해석**

If we attempt to specify the ways(만일 우리가 그 방법들을 상세히 기술하고자 한다면) in which human beings are unique and different from other animal species(인간은 유일하고 다른 동물들과 다르다는 점에서), we must quickly conclude that most(우린 빨리 ~결론을 내야만 한다), if not all(전부는 아닐지 몰라도), differences are in degree, not in kind(대부분의 차이점은 본질적인 것이 아닌 정도의 차이이다). That is(다시 말해), other animals may possess a particular trait similar to humans(다른 동물들은 인간과 유사한 특별한 특징을 소유하고 있다), but not to the same extent(그러나 같은 정도는 아닌). For example(예를 들어), if we say that a distinctive characteristic of humankind is language(만일 우리가 인간의 뚜렷한 특징은 언어라 말한다면), it is possible to point to(~ 지적하는 것은 가능하다) communication among dolphins or the sign language learned by apes in certain experiments(특정한 실험에서 돌고래나 원숭이들이 터득한 신호언어들 사이에서 의사소통하는 것을) as simple and basic forms of the same behavior(같은 행동의 단순하고 기본적인 형태로서). Or, if we say that social organizations are a human trait(만일 사회적 조직체는 인간의 특성이다 라고 우리가 말한다면), a parallel might be found in the behaviors of bees or ants(꿀벌이나 개미의 행동에서도 동일한 것을 찾을 수 있다). We have elaborate rituals connected with death(우리는 죽음과 정교한 의식을 갖고 있다), but elephants have been observed engaging in what might be called a burial ceremony(그러나 코끼

리들은 매장의식이라 불리는 것과 연관되어 관찰되어 왔다). Music may even have its animal counterpart in whalesong or birdsong(음악도 고래나 새들의 노래에서 동물의 같은 점을 갖게 된다) - to a degree(어느 정도). However, it is the degree of human involvement in such behaviors(그러나 ~과 같은 행동은 인간과 관련된 정도이다) as language, social organizations, rituals, and music that separate us from other animals(우리를 다른 동물 구별시키는 언어, 사회적인 조직체, 의식들 그리고 음악).

🔖 단어분석

- †**specify** [spésəfài] vt. ① 일일이 이름을 들어 말하다 ② 상술하다 ③ 명세서에 기입하다. / **in degree** 정도의 / **in kind** 본질적인 / **to the same extent** 같은 정도 / ‡**parallel** [pǽrəlèl] n. ① 평행선[면], 평행물. ② 필적하는 것[사람] ③ 비교(comparison). / ‡**elaborate** [ilǽbərit] a. 공들인, 정교한. / †**counterpart** [káuntərpàːrt] n. ① 짝의 한 쪽. 상대물[인], 대응물[자] / †**involvement** [inválvmənt / -vólv-] n. ① U 연루, 연좌(in). ② 포함. ③ C 어려움; (재정) 곤란.

동영상 강좌 http://youtu.be/9tm7qDrR0_c

[31~35]

It is sometimes (A)easy/difficult to get knocked off your target by the other party during a negotiation. It therefore pays to carry your goals with you and, if you feel yourself getting swept away, take a break and review them before going forward. The point is not to lose sight of your goals in the confusion of a actual negotiation. Barry Diller, the successful television executive and entrepreneur, learned his lesson the hard way when he got caught up in bidding for the rights to the first television showing of the movie The Poseidon Adventure in the early 1970s. Representing ABC, Diller ended up bidding $3.3 million - by far the highest amount ever paid for such a property at the time - and (B)losing/making money for his network. The reason Diller paid so much? He agreed to participate in the first open-bid auction for TV rights to a movie. In the frantic bidding that followed. he (C)forgot/remembered about his primary goal - making a profit - and got caught up in what one CBS executive who bid against him called the "fever" of winning a competition.

🔖 본문해석

It is sometimes (A)easy/difficult(때때로 쉽다/어렵다) to get knocked off your target(당신의 목표가 중단되는 것은) by the other party during a negotiation(협상 중에 상대에 의해). It therefore pays to carry your goals with you(그러므로 그것이 당신의 목표를 진행하는데 어려움을 준다) and, if you feel yourself getting swept away(만일 당신이 이끌려 간다고 느낀다면), take a break and review them(잠시 멈춰서 그것(목표)들을 검토하라) before going forward(진척시키기 전에). The point is not to lose sight of your goals(그 핵심은 당신의 목표 잃는 것은 아니다) in the confusion of a actual negotiation(실제 협상의 혼돈 속에서). Barry Diller, the successful television executive and entrepreneur(성공한 텔레비젼 방송국의

157

중역이자 사업가인 바리 딜러는), learned his lesson the hard way(힘들게 자신의 교훈을 터득했다) when he got caught up in bidding for the rights(그가 ~권리 입찰에서 몰두했을 때) to the first television showing of the movie The Poseidon Adventure in the early 1970s(1970년대 초에 첫 텔레비젼에 방영될 영화인 'The Poseidon Adventure'). Representing ABC, Diller ended up bidding $3.3 million(ABC 방송국을 대표하는 딜러는 결국 33억 달러 입찰로 끝을 냈다) - by far the highest amount ever paid for such a property at the time(지금까지 당시로서는 그러한 자산에 투자된 적이 없는 가장 높은 액수) - and (B)losing/making money for his network(자신의 방송국의 돈을 잃게 되는/벌게 되는). The reason Diller paid so much?(딜러가 그러한 천문학적인 돈을 투자한 이유는?) He agreed to participate in the first open-bid auction for TV rights to a movie(그는 영화방영권을 위한 첫 번째 공개 경매에 참여하기로 했다). In the frantic bidding that followed(뒤따르는 광적인 입찰 속에서). he (C)forgot/remembered about his primary goal(그는 자신의 일차적인 목표를 잃었다/기억했다) - making a profit(수익을 내는 것) - and got caught up(몰두했다) in what one CBS executive who bid against him called the "fever" of winning a competition(자신과 경쟁하는 한 CBS 방송국 임원이 경재에서 이기고자하는 열병이라 칭한).

🔖 단어분석

- ♣**knock off** (—vt.) (1) 두드려 떨어버리다. (2) (구어) (일을) 그만하다, 중단하다. / **pay to carry** 수행하는 어려움을 격다. / ♣**sweep away** (1) 일소하다, 휩쓸어 가다. (2) 멀리 퍼지다. get swept away 이끌려 가다 / †**frantic** [fræntik] a. 미친 듯 날뛰는, 광란의; 필사적인; / †**bidding** [bídiŋ] n. U 명령; 입찰; 입후보; 초대. / †**primary** [práimeri, -məri] a. ① 첫째의, 제1의, 수위의, 주요한. [cf.] secondary. ② 최초의, 처음의, 본래의. /

동영상 강좌 http://youtu.be/yvy1O7ltbOw

[36~40]

A basis of influence with special relevance to personal relationships and groups is referent power. This exists when we admire or identify with a person or group and want to be like them. In such cases, we may ①**voluntarily** copy their behavior or do what they ask because we want to become similar to them. In everyday life we may not think of ②**identification** as a type of influence, but it can be very effective. A young child who looks up to an older brother, tries to ③**avoid** his mannerisms, and adopts his interest is one illusion. A young man who drinks a particular brand of beer because he identifies with the "macho" image of the sportsmen promoting the product in TV commercials is also being ④ **influenced** by referent power. Recently, Raven has discussed the possibility of "negative referent power," which occurs when we want to ⑤**separate** ourselves from a disliked or unappealing person or group. To avoid being identified with the unattractive other, we may deliberately avoid copying their behavior.

* referent power 준거적 권력 ** macho남성적

A basis of influence(~ 영향력의 기본을) with special relevance to personal relationships and groups (개인적 관계와 집단과의 특별한 관계를 갖는) is referent power(준거적 권력이라 한다). This exists(이것은 발생한다) when we admire or identify with a person or group(우리가 어/떤 사람이나 집단에 감동하거나 동일시하고) and want to be like them(그들과 같이 되고 싶어 할 때). In such cases(그러한 경우에), we may ①voluntarily copy their behavior(우리는 그들의 행동을 자발적으로 흉내 내거나) or do what they ask(그들이 요구하는 것을 할 것 같다) because we want to become similar to them(우리는 그들과 비슷하게 되기를 원하기 때문이다). In everyday life(일상에서) we may not think of ②identification(우리는 동일한 것을 생각지 않는다) as a type of influence(영향을 끼치는 형태로서), but it can be very effective(그러나 그것은 아주 효과를 끼친다). A young child who looks up to an older brother(자기의 형을 우러러보는 어린 동생은), tries to ③avoid his mannerisms(그의 버릇을 피하려고 한다), and adopts his interest is one illusion(그리하여 그의 관심은 한 환상이라는 것을 받아들인다). A young man who drinks a particular brand of beer(특별한 맥주 제품을 마시는 한 젊은이는) because he identifies with the "macho" image of the sportsmen(그가 ~운동선수의 강인한 이미지와 동일시하기 때문에) promoting the product in TV commercials(TV광고의 제품을 홍보하고 있는) is also being ④influenced by referent power(또한 준거적 권력에 의해 영향을 받고 있는 것이다). Recently(최근에), Raven has discussed the possibility of "negative referent power,"(레이번은 부정적인 준거적 권력의 가능성을 주장했다) which occurs(발생하는) when we want to ⑤separate ourselves from a disliked or unappealing person or group(우리가 우리 자신을 싫어하거나 혐오하는 사람이나 집단으로 분리시키고 싶어 할 때). To avoid being identified with the unattractive other(매력적이지 않은 다른 사람과의 동일시되는 것을 피하기 위해), we may deliberately avoid copying their behavior(우리는 그들의 행동을 모방하는 것을 고의적으로 피하는 것 같다).

* referent power 준거적 권력 ** macho남성적

- **relevance**, —**cy** [réləvəns], [-si] n. U ① 관련; 적당, 적절(성). / ǂ **admire** [ædmáiər, əd-] v. ① ~에 감복[찬탄]하다, 칭찬하다, 사모하다. [SYN.] ⇨ REGARD. / ǂ **identify** [aidéntəfài] v. —vt. ①『~+목 / +목+as 보』(본인·동일물임을) 확인하다; (사람의 성명·신원, 물건의 명칭·분류·소속 따위를) 인지[판정]하다; 동일한 것으로 간주하다(~ A with B, ~A and B); (~와) 제휴시키다; (~에) 관계[공명]하게 하다(with); / **mannerism** [mǽnərìz-əm] n. 매너리즘(특히 문학·예술의 표현 수단이 틀에 박힌 것); 버릇 (태도·언행 따위의). / ǂ **adopt** [ədɑ́pt] vt. ①『~+목 / +목+as 보 / +목+전+명』양자[양녀]로 삼다 ② (의견·방침·조처 따위를) 채용[채택]하다, 골라잡다. / ǂ **illusion** [ilúː ʒən] U,C ① 환영(幻影), 환각. ② 〖심리학〗 착각; C 환상, 망상

동영상 강좌 http://youtu.be/KEkdweGar-8

[41~45]

Before developing invention designs, inventors likely first identify the intended function of the invention. When the inventor then generates initial invention designs, he often (A)constrains/disregards the form of the invention through implicit analogies to components of nature or existing products whose function matches or approximates that of the intended invention. For example, early airplane inventors frequently (B)imitated/eliminated the form of animals capable of flight, modeling their flying craft after albatrosses, bats, and various insects such as beetles. Similarly, architects have made structural innovations through analogies to our actions toward objects and to the forces, tensions, and interactions within our skeletomuscular system. Such analogies seem a (C)plausible/groundless basis for invention in the mechanical realm as well. For example, joysticks, such as those found on many video games, may well have evolved through an analogy to human ball-and-socket joints, such as the shoulder joint.

* skeletomuscular system 근·골격계 ** ball-and-socket joint 구관절

📎 본문해석

Before developing invention designs(발명 디자인을 개발하기 전), inventors likely first identify the intended function of the invention(발명가들은 그 발명품의 의도된 기능을 우선 확인하는 것 같다). When the inventor then generates initial invention designs(그리고 나서 그 발명가가 초기 발명 디자인을 만들 때), he often (A)constrains/disregards the form of the invention(그는 그 발명품의 형태를 종종 고집을 부린다/무시한다) through implicit analogies to components of nature or existing products(자연의 요소나 존재하는 제품의 ～암시적 유사성을 통해) whose function matches or approximates that of the intended invention(그 기능이 의도된 발명품의 것과 어울리거나 근접하는). For example(예를 들어), early airplane inventors frequently (B)imitated/eliminated the form of animals capable of flight(초기 비행기 발명가들은 비행 능력이 있는 동물의 형태를 종종 모방하였다/줄였다), modeling their flying craft after albatrosses, bats, and various insects such as beetles(신천옹, 박쥐 그리고 풍뎅이와 같은 다양한 곤충들을 닮은 그들의 비행체 설계했다). Similarly(이와 유사하게), architects have made structural innovations(건축가들은 구조적인 혁신을 이루었다) through analogies to our actions toward objects(물체에 대한 우리의 행동과 유사하고) and to the forces, tensions, and interactions within our skeletomuscular system(우리의 근골격계 내에서 힘, 긴장 그리고 상호반응과 유한 것을 통하여). Such analogies seem a (C)plausible/groundless basis for invention(그러한 유사성은 발명을 위한 그럴듯한/근거 없는 기초인 것 같다) in the mechanical realm as well(또한 기계적인 분야에서). For example(예를 들어), joysticks, such as those found on many video games(많은 비디오 게임에서 발견되어진 것과 같은 조이스틱은), may well have evolved(발전되어지고 있는 것 같다) through an analogy to human ball-and-socket joints, such as the shoulder joint(어깨관절과 같은 인간의 구관절과 유사한 것으로).

* skeletomuscular system 근·골격계 ** ball-and-socket joint구관절

📎 단어분석

- ⚕ **identify** [aidéntəfai] v. —vt. ① 『～+목 / +목+as 보』 (본인·동일물임을) 확인하다; (사람의 성명·신원, 물건의 명칭·분류·소속 따위를) 인지[판정]하다; ～의 신원을 밝히다; 감정하다. / ⚕ **constrain** [kənstréin] vt. ① 『～+목/ +목+to do』 강제하다, 강요하다, 무리하게 ～시키다(to). / † **implicit** [implísit] a. ① 은연중의, 함축적인, 암시적인, 암묵의. [opp.] explicit. 내재[잠재]하는(potential)(in). / ⚕ **analogy** [ənǽlədʒi] n. ① C,U 유사, 비슷함, 닮음(between; to; with). / † **approximate** [əpráksəmèit / -rɔ́k-] v. —vi. 『+전+명』 (위치·성질·수량 등이) ～에 가까워지다. —vt. ① (수량 따위가) ～에 가까워지다[가깝다];

〜와 비슷하다. / $**$model [mád]v. —vt. ① 『〜+목/ +목+전+명』 〜의 모양[모형]을 만들다; ② 설계하다. ③ 〜의 모형을 만들다. ④ (〜을) 따라 만들다, 본뜨다(after; on, upon)./ $⸸$ imitate [ímitèit] vt. ① 모방하다, 흉내내다; 따르다, 본받다. ② 모조[위조]하다. / albatross [ǽlbətrɔ̀(ː)s / -tràs] n. 골칫거리, 걱정거리, 제약. / $⸸$ tension [ténʃ-ən] n. U ① 팽팽함; 켕김, 긴장; 신장(伸長). ② (정신적인) 긴장, 흥분; 노력. / $⸸$ plausible [plɔ́ː zəbəl] a. ① (이유·구실 따위가) 그럴듯한, 정말 같은. ② 그럴 듯한 말을 하는, 말 재주가 좋은. / $⸸$ realm [relm] n. ① 범위, 영역; (학문의) 부문. / $⸸$ evolve [iválv / ivɔ́lv] v. —vt. ① 발전시키다; 전개하다; 진화[발달]시키다.

동영상 강좌 http://youtu.be/TyrkUuG6fYl

[46~50]

The Massachusetts-based company Advanced Cell Technology is planning to clone certain dead creatures to bring them back to life. There's talk of trying to bring back the Tasmanian tiger, a wolflike animal that lost its last grip on survival in the 1930s. Even the prehistoric mammoth is being considered for a possible comeback. It's a fascinating scientific gimmick, a perfect example of doing something because we can. We should leave it at that. But we won't. There's excited talk of cloning and genetic engineering offering a marvelous boost to wildlife conservation, a high-tech solution to our tendency to drive plant and animal species to extinction. This is nonsense, for the cloning of endangered species completely contradicts the spirit and practice of conservation. Conservation isn't just about saving a particular species; it's about reducing our destructive impact on natural systems that are in increasing danger of being unable to sustain themselves.

🔖 본문해석

The Massachusetts-based company Advanced Cell Technology(매사츄세츠에 본사를 둔 Advanced Cell Technology는) is planning to clone certain dead creatures(어떤 죽은 생명체를 복제할 계획이다) to bring them back to life(그들을 다시 살려내는). There's talk of trying to bring back the Tasmanian tiger, a wolflike animal(늑대와 같은 동물인 태스매니언 호랑이를 되 살리고자하는 노력의 이야기가 있다) that lost its last grip on survival in the 1930s(1930년대에 마지막 생존력을 잃어버린(사라진)). Even the prehistoric mammoth is being considered for a possible comeback(선사시대 매머드 조차도 가능성 있는 복귀로 고려되어지고 있다). It's a fascinating scientific gimmick(그것은 호기심을 자극하는 과학적 비법이다), a perfect example of doing something because we can(우리가 할 수 있는 무언가를 하는 완벽한 예). We should leave it at that(우리는 그것을 지켜보아야만 한다). But we won't(그렇지는 않다). There's excited talk(과열된 이야기가 있다) of cloning and genetic engineering offering a marvelous boost to wildlife conservation(야생동물 보존 엄청난 후원을 하는 유전자복제와 유전자 공학에 관한), a high-tech solution to our tendency to drive plant and animal species to extinction(식물과 동물종들을 멸종으로 몰아넣는 우리의 경향에 대한 고도의 기술). This is nonsense(이것은 쓸모없는 일이다), for the cloning of endangered species(왜냐하면 멸종위기의 종의 복제는) completely contradicts(완전한 모순이

다) the spirit and practice of conservation(보존 정신과 관행에). Conservation isn't just about saving a particular species(보존이란 특별한 종을 단지 보존하는 것은 아니다); it's about reducing our destructive impact on natural systems(그것은 자연적 체계에 대한 우리의 파괴적인 충격을 줄이는 것이다) that are in increasing danger of being unable to sustain themselves(그들 스스로 유지할 수 없는 증가하는 위험에 처했을 때).

📎 단어분석

- **clon(e)** [kloun] vt., vi. 〖생물〗 무성 생식을 하다[시키다]; 꼭 닮게 만들다. ♣lose one's grip 능력이[열의가] 없어지다, 통제력을 잃다. / **gimmick** [gímik] n. 「일반적」 장치, 고안; 새 고안물; 마약 주사를 위한 기구. ㉿gimmicky —a. (구어) 속임수가 있는; 겉만 번드르르한. / ‡**marvelous** [máːrv-ələs] a. ① 불가사의한, 이상한, 놀라운. [SYN.] ⇨ WONDER. ② 기적적인, 믿기 어려운(improbable). / **offer A to B**: A에게 B를 제공하다 / ‡**tendency** [téndənsi] n. ① 경향, 풍조, 추세(to; towards; to do). ② 성향(to; toward; to do). / †**contradict** [kàntrədíkt / kɔ̀n-] v. —vt. ① (진술·보도 따위를) 부정[부인]하다, 반박하다; ② ~와 모순되다. / **conservation** [kànsəːrvéiʃən / kɔ̀n-] n. U (자연·자원의) 보호, 관리; 보존, 유지. / **impact** [ímpækt] n. U,C 충돌(collusion); 충격, 영향(력)(on, upon; against). / **sustain** [səstéin] vt. ① (아래서) 떠받치다. ② 유지하다, 계속하다. ③ 부양하다, 양육하다, 기르다. ④ (손해 따위를) 받다, 입다.

동영상 강좌 http://youtu.be/PrFL0194Grw

[51~55]

At the Christmas season I'd expected a modest office party, dinners with Jack's clients, maybe a simple reception at Matt and Claire's, but none of those happened. Instead Jack brought home extravagantly wrapped presents and a tree that had to be topped in order to fit under the high ceiling of our living room. When I asked what he wanted me to fix for our holiday dinner, he said he'd arranged to have it catered - hors d'oeuvres, standing-rib roast, horseradish sauce, Yorkshire pudding, assorted vegetables, everything down to the plum pudding, which I had never imagined. And champagne and expensive wines, of course. He'd invited Matt and Claire, and selected appropriate presents for them. A design firm was coming to trim the tree. Meanwhile, I found myself rather discouraged by his preparation and mourning the loss of our previous simple Christmas in Los Angeles.

📎 본문해석

At the Christmas season(크리스마스 휴가 동안) I'd expected a modest office party(나는 검소한 사무실 파티를 기대했었다), dinners with Jack's clients(잭의 고객들과 저녁식사를), maybe a simple reception at Matt and Claire's(아마 Matt and Claire's에서의 간단한 만찬), but none of those happened(그러나 그러한 아무 일도 일어나지 않았다). Instead Jack brought home extravagantly wrapped presents(대신 잭은 값 비싼게 포장된 선물들 ~을 집으로 가져왔다) and a tree that had to be topped in order to fit under the high ceiling of our living room(우리의 거실에 높은 천장에 맞도록 가지를 쳐야만 하는 나무

와). When I asked what he wanted me to fix for our holiday dinner(내가 그에게 우리의 휴가 저녁 메뉴를 무엇으로 할까 물어봤을 때), he said he'd arranged to have it catered(그는 음식제공업체에 주문했다고 말했다) - hors d'oeuvres, standing-rib roast, horseradish sauce(hors d'oeuvres와 늘 나오는 갈비구이, 양고추냉이 소스), Yorkshire pudding(Yorkshire 푸딩), assorted vegetables(다채로운 야채들), everything down to the plum pudding(모든 것이 자두 푸딩에 아래 놓여), which I had never imagined(내가 상상해 본적이 없는). And champagne and expensive wines, of course(그리고 샴페인과 비싼 포도주도 물론). He'd invited Matt and Claire(그는 Matt와 Claire도 초대했었다), and selected appropriate presents for them(그리고 그들을 위한 적당한 선물도 선택했다). A design firm was coming to trim the tree(한 디자인 회사가 나무 가지를 치기위해 올 예정이었다). Meanwhile(그러는 동안에), I found myself rather discouraged by his preparation(나는 그의 (거창한)준비에 오히려 낙심했다) and mourning the loss of our previous simple Christmas in Los Angeles(로스앤젤레스에서의 우리의 이전 소박한 크리스마스가 아닌 것이 슬펐다).

🔖 **단어분석**

- ⍭ **modest** [mάdist / mɔ́d-]a. ① 겸손한, 얌전한, 온당한. / ⍭ **extravagant** [ikstrǽvəgənt] a. 돈을 함부로 쓰는, 낭비벽이 있는. / **top** (식물 따위의) 꼭대기를 자르다, 순을 치다. / **cater** [kéitər] v. —vi. 『+전+명』 ① 음식물을 조달[장만]하다(for). ② 영합하다(to; for). / **standing** 고정된, 일시적이 아닌, 정해진(주문 따위); 일정한, 늘 나오는(요리) / ⍭ **mourn** [mɔːrn] v. —vi. 『+전+명』 ① 슬퍼하다, 한탄하다(for; over). / **horseradish** [-rædiʃ] n. 식물』 양고추냉이. / ⍭ **assorted** [əsɔ́ːrtid] a. 유별한, 여러 종류로 된, 다채로운, 조화를 이룬.

동영상 강좌 http://youtu.be/jMpa67p3akw

[56~60]

"The greatest room for music and opera in the world - bar none" was Frank Lloyd Wright's assessment of the Auditorium Theatre of Roosevelt University. Designed by Louis Sullivan and Dankmar Adler in 1886, the Auditorium remains one of the most acoustically perfect theatres of the era. Located inside the Auditorium Building with a hotel and restaurant, the Auditorium Theatre survived the decades partly because it would have been too expensive to demolish. A move to destroy it failed in 1923, but another setback came in 1929 when the Chicago Opera Company found a newer home. The theatre closed in 1941, then reopened as a recreation center for soldiers during World War II, with a bowling alley installed on the stage. Roosevelt College (later Roosevelt University) acquired the Auditorium Building in 1946 and used the hotel floors for classes and offices while the theatre stood empty. In the 1960s, Beatrice T. Spachner led a drive to restore the Auditorium Theatre. It reopened in 1967, yet restoration work continued for two decades.   * bar none: 단연코, 예외 없이

🔖 **본문해석**

"The greatest room for music and opera in the world - bar none(단연코, 세계에서 음악과 오페라 공연을 위한 가장 큰 곳은)" was Frank Lloyd Wright's assessment of the Auditorium Theatre of Roosevelt University(프랭크 로이드 라이트가 평가한 루즈벨트 대학의 대강당이다). Designed by Louis Sullivan and Dankmar Adler in 1886(1886년에 루이스 설리번과 댄크마르 아드러에의해 설계된), the Auditorium remains one of the most acoustically perfect theatres of the era(그 시대의 가장 음향적으로 완벽한 공연장 중 하나로 남아 있다.). Located inside the Auditorium Building with a hotel and restaurant(그 공연장 내부에 호텔과 식당을 갖춘), the Auditorium Theatre survived the decades(그 공연장은 수 십 년을 버텨왔다) partly because it would have been too expensive to demolish(철거하는데 드는 엄청난 비용 부분적인 이유인 것 같다). A move to destroy it failed in 1923(1923년에 철거할 움직임이 중단되었다), but another setback came in 1929(그러나 1929년 또 다른 차질이 빚어졌다) when the Chicago Opera Company found a newer home(시카고 오페라 회사가 더욱 새로운 공연장을 찾았을 때). The theatre closed in 1941(그 공연장은 1941년에 폐쇄되었다), then reopened as a recreation center for soldiers during World War II(그리고 나서 2차 세계대전 당시 군인들을 위한 오락장소로 다시 문을 열었다), with a bowling alley installed on the stage(무대 위에 설치된 볼링대를 포함하여). Roosevelt College (later Roosevelt University) acquired the Auditorium Building in 1946(루즈벨트 전문대학이(이후 루즈벨트 대학) 1946년에 그 공연장을 인수했고) and used the hotel floors for classes and offices(교실과 사무실로 그 호텔층을 사용했다) while the theatre stood empty(공연장은 여전히 비워둔 채로). In the 1960s, Beatrice T. Spachner led a drive to restore the Auditorium Theatre(1960년대에 비트리스 T. 스패츠너는 그 공연장을 복원하는 운동을 벌였다). It reopened in 1967(1967년에 다시 문을 열었다), yet restoration work continued for two decades(그러나 복원공사는 20년 동안 지속되었다).

* bar none: 단연코, 예외 없이

📎 **단어분석**

- †**assessment** [əsésmənt] n. U ① (과세를 위한) 사정, 평가; 부과; C 세액, 평가액, 사정액 / **acoustic, -tical** [əkúː stik], [-əl] a. 음향(학)상의. / †**demolish** [dimáliʃ / -mɔ́l-] vt. ① 부수다, 폭파[분쇄]하다; (계획·제도·지론 따위를) 뒤엎다. / **setback** [sétbæk] n. ① 방해; 좌절, 차질. ② 역류, 역수(逆水). / **alley** [æli] n. ① 【미국】 뒷골목(back-lane); (정원·숲 속 등의) 오솔길(shady walk) ⇨ ROAD

동영상 강좌 http://youtu.be/VMG7hh6WHkw

[61~65]

The Katsura Palace is located near the Katsura River, to the southwest of the imperial city of Kyoto in Japan. The palace and gardens provided a place for the Imperial family in the cultural ear of the late 16th century. The main palace is an open, timber-framed construction with simple tatami (rice-straw) matted rooms and elevated verandas from which to contemplate the changing seasons. The garden arbors and pavilions surrounding the main palace are approached from a sequence of carefully staged routes. The buildings have an understated simplicity, and the landscape has been subtly manipulated to blur the distinction between artificial and natural environments. Artificial objects, such as fences and paving stones, have been subjected to the forces of nature, such as weathering, while natural features have been clipped, aligned and polished to emphasize their eccentricity and "unnaturalness." The effect is discreet and fascinating, contributing to a heightened aesthetic awareness of the architecture and the landscape.

* arbor 정자

🔖 본문해석

The Katsura Palace is located near the Katsura River(카트수마 궁전은 카트수마 강 근처에 위치해 있다), to the southwest of the imperial city of Kyoto in Japan(일본 교토의 군국도시의 남서쪽 방향에). The palace and gardens provided a place for the Imperial family(그 궁전과 정원들은 제국 황실의 거처를 제공했다) in the cultural ear of the late 16th century(16세기 후반 문화시대에). The main palace is an open, timber-framed construction(그 궁전의 중심부는 개방된 통나무 틀의 구조이다) with simple tatami (rice-straw) matted rooms(소박한 타태미(짚)으로 엮은 돗자리가 있는 방과) and elevated verandas(그리고 베란다를 갖춘) from which to contemplate the changing seasons(그곳으로부터 계절을 변화를 느낄 수 있도록). The garden arbors and pavilions surrounding the main palace(궁전 중심부를 둘러쌓고 있는 정원 정자와 누각은) are approached from a sequence of carefully staged routes(연속된 세심하게 계획된 오솔길로부터 접근 가능하다). The buildings have an understated simplicity(그 건물은 겸손한 단순함을 갖고 있고), and the landscape has been subtly manipulated(배경은 섬세하고 처리되었다) to blur the distinction between artificial and natural environments(인공적이고 자연적인 환경 차이를 줄이고자). Artificial objects, such as fences and paving stones(울타리와 보도와 같은 인위적인 물체들은), have been subjected to the forces of nature, such as weathering(풍화작용), while natural features have been clipped, aligned and polished(반면 자연적 특징은 다듬어지고 정렬되고 윤기가 흐리게 되어졌다) to emphasize their eccentricity and "unnaturalness."(그것들의 괴상함과 비자연적인 것을 강조하기 위해서) The effect is discreet and fascinating(그 효과는 은근하고 환상적이어서), contributing to a heightened aesthetic awareness of the architecture and the landscape(그 건축물과 배경의 고조된 심미안적인 인식에 기여하고 있다). * arbor 정자

🔖 단어분석

- ⚕ **imperial** [impíəriəl] a. ① 제국(帝國)의 ② 황제(皇帝)[황후]의, 제위(帝位)의(sovereign), 지상(至上)의 (supreme). / ⚕ **contemplate** [kántəmplèit] v. —vt. ① 관찰하다. ② 심사 숙고하다 / ⚕ **pavilion** [pəvíljən] n. (공원·정원의) 누각, 정자; (본관에서 내단) 별관 / ⚕ **stage** [steidʒ] v. —vt. ① 무대에 올리다, 상연하다. ③ (파업·정치 운동·군사 작전 등을) 계획하다, 해내다, 행하다. / ⚕ **sequence** [síː kwəns] n. ① U 연달아 일어남, 속발. ② U 연속, 계속. [SYN.] ⇨ SERIES. ③ U 전후 관련. / **understate** [ʌ̀ndərstéit] vt. 삼가서 말하다, (수 따위를) 적게 말하다. / † **manipulate** [mənípjəlèit]v. —vt. ① (사람·여론 등을) (부정하게) 조종하다. ② (문제를) 솜씨있게 처리하다. / **subtly** 은은하게, 섬세하게 / † **blur** [bləː r] v. (-rr-) —vi. ① (눈·시력·시야·경치가) 희미해지다, 부예지다. / ****subject** [səbdʒékt] vt. 『+목+전+명』 ① 복종[종속]시키다 (to). ② (좋지 않은 일을) 당하게[받게] 하다, 입히다(to) / ****weather** [wéðə: r] v. —vt. ① 비바람에 맞히다;. ② 「과거분사」 (외기에 쐬어) 풍화[탈색]시키다. / † **eccentricity** [è ksentrísəti] n. U ① (복장·행동 따위의) 엉뚱함; C 기행(奇行), 기이한 버릇. / † **discreet** [diskríː t] a. 생각이 깊은; 신중한 [SYN.] ⇨ CAREFUL. /

동영상 강좌 http://youtu.be/8xkYef9GAUs

[66~70]

The use of motion in movie composition can be positive. For example, movement along a definite line can tend to carry the audience's eye with it or even ahead of it, acting as a sort of _____. Imagine a New England landscape nicely framed in foreground foliage, with a white ribbon of road curving across the picture and leading toward a village. Ordinarily, the white line of the road itself would probably be the strongest factor in the composition. But suppose we have a car driver along the road in the direction of the village. The movement will tend strongly to send the audience's eyes racing along the road ahead of the car to focus on the village, logically setting the mental stage for following scenes made in the village itself. This, by the way is true even if you only show the car moving along the road., without taking the time to have it completely cross the frame and reach the village in that one shot.

📄 본문해석

The use of motion in movie composition can be positive(영화구성에서 움직임 활용은 긍정적인 것 같다). For example(예들 들어), movement along a definite line(분명한 직선을 따른 이동은) can tend to carry the audience's eye with it(시청자의 눈이 그것에 따라가게 하거나) or even ahead of it(그것에 미리 앞서 가게 할 수 있다), acting as a sort of(일종의 ~로서) _____. Imagine a New England landscape nicely framed in foreground foliage(나뭇잎 전경의 멋진 영상의 뉴잉글랜드 풍경을 상상해 보아라), with a white ribbon of road(~ 도로의 흰색 리본 같은 길이 있는) curving across the picture and leading toward a village(그림을 가로지는 굴곡지고 마을로 뻗어 있는). Ordinarily(보통), the white line of the road itself(도로 그 자체의 흰색선은) would probably be the strongest factor in the composition(아마도 그 구성에서 가장 강력한 요소일 것이다). But suppose we have a car driver along the road in the direction of the village(그러나 우리가 마을 방향으로 나있는 도로를 따를 운전하는 운전자를 보고 있다고 가정해 보자). The movement will tend strongly to send the audience's eyes(그 움직임은 시청자의 시선을 ~하도록 강렬하게 보낼 것이다) racing along the road ahead of the car to focus on the village(마을에 초점을 맞추기 위해 그 자동차에 앞서 도로를 달리게), logically setting the mental stage for following scenes made in the village itself(마을 그 자체에 만들어진 다음 장면을 위한 정신적 무대를 논리적으로 설정한다). This, by the way is true(어쨌든 이것은 사실이다) even if you only show the car moving along the road(비록 당신이 도로를 따라 이동하는 자동차만 볼지라도), without taking the time(시간적 여유도 없이도) to have it completely cross the frame(그 자동차가 완전히 그 영상을 가로질러 가게 할) and reach the village in that one shot(그리고 그 한 화면에서의 마을에 도달할).

📄 단어분석

- ‡ **definite** [défənit] a. ① (윤곽·한계가) 뚜렷한. ② (태도 따위가) 명확한. [opp] indefinite. / † **foliage** [fóuliidʒ] n. ① 「집합적」 잎; 잎의 무성함, 군엽(群葉). / ‡ **composition** [kàmpəzíʃən / kɔm-]

n. ① U 구성, 성분. ② U (타고난) 기질, 성질, 배합(arrangement). / **suppose [səpóuz] v. —vt. ①『~+목/ +(that)절』가정하다(assume), 상상하다. 생각하다. [SYN.] ⇨ THINK. / † logical [ládʒikəl / lɔ́dʒ-] a. 논리적인; (논리상) 필연의; 논리(학)상의; 분석적인 / † complete [kəmplíːt] a. ① 완전한, 완벽한; 흠잡을 데 없는, 완비된. ② 전부의, 전부 갖춘(with)

동영상 강좌 http://youtu.be/L_tLK8fH19k

[71~75]

Physicians are too rarely aware of their patients' need for _____, so they often don't know how to account for dramatic improvements in their patients' conditions. Recently, I received a letter from a doctor telling me that a woman with extensive breast cancer, whom we had both cared for, had returned to his office five months after he had sent her to a nursing home - and that he had "never seen her looking so well!" No further comment by the doctor was made. I told the medical student who was walking with me to call the woman and find out her story, because I was sure there would be one. The woman told the student that when she got to the nursing home, she found conditions there so unbearable and depressing that she led a revolution among the other "inmates" to insist that they receive better treatment. She spent time talking with the staff about the tenderness and love the patients needed, and she transformed the place. Then she felt so good that she went home and bought herself a new car!

🖎 본문해석

Physicians are too rarely aware of their patients' need for _____(내과의사들은 ~한 그들 환자의 필요성을 거의 인식하지 못하고 있다), so they often don't know how to account(그래서 그들은 ~ 관해 설명할 방법을 종종 모른다) for dramatic improvements in their patients' conditions(그들 환자들의 상태가 아주 호전되는 것). Recently(최근에), I received a letter from a doctor telling me(나는 나에게 ~것에 관한 얘기를 하는 한통의 편지를 받았다) that a woman with extensive breast cancer(몸 전체로 전이된 유방암 여성 환자), whom we had both cared for(우리 둘다 치료한적 있는), had returned to his office(그의 사무실로 찾아온 적이 있었다는) five months after he had sent her to a nursing home(그가 그녀를 요양원으로 보낸 후 5개월이 지나) - and that he had "never seen her looking so well!"(그리고 그는 그녀가 그렇게 회복되리라고는 기대한 적이 없었다는) No further comment by the doctor was made(그 의사에 의한 더 이상의 자세한 설명은 없었다). I told the medical student who was walking with me(나는 나와 함께 걷고 있었던 의과학생에게 ~하라고 말했다) to call the woman and find out her story(그녀에게 전화를 해서 그녀의 상황을 알아보라고), because I was sure there would be one(나는 분명 무언가가 있을 것이라 확신했기 때문이다). The woman told the student(그 여자는 그 학생에게 ~라 말했다) that when she got to the nursing home(그녀가 요양원에 도착했을 때), she found conditions there so unbearable and depressing(그녀는 자신의 상태가 너무나 참을 수 없고 우울해서) that she led a revolution among the other "inmates" to insist(그녀는 다른 입원자들 사이에 ~을 주장

하는 혁명을 이끌었다) that they receive better treatment(그들은 더 좋은 치료를 받아야만 한다는 것). She spent time talking with the staff about the tenderness and love the patients needed(그녀는 환자들이 필요한 애정과 사랑에 관해 직원들과 얘기를 나누며 시간을 보냈다), and she transformed the place(그리하여 그녀는 그곳을 바꿔 놓았다). Then she felt so good that she went home and bought herself a new car(그리고 나서 그녀는 너무 호전이 된 기분이 들어 집으로 가 새 차를 구입했다고)!

🖊 단어분석

- **too rarely** 너무나 ～않는 / **account for** ～설명하다 / **so unbearable and depressing that**…: 너무 ～해서 …한 / † **improvement** [imprúːvmənt] n. ① U,C 개량, 개선(in). ② C 개량한 곳, 개선점; 개량[개선]한 것. / † **unbearable** [ʌnbɛ́ərəbəl] a. 참을 수 없는, 견딜 수 없는. / **depressing** [diprésiŋ] a. 침울한. / † **revolution** [rèvəlúːʃən] n. ① C 혁명; 변혁; ② U,C 회전(운동), 1회전. / † **insist** [insíst] vi., vt. ～+전+명 / +that절』① 우기다 (maintain), 단언하다; 역설[강조]하다(on, upon). ② 강요하다; 조르다(on, upon). / † **inmate** [ínmèit] n. ① (병원·교도소 따위의) 입원자, 재감자(在監者), 피수용자. / † **transform** [trænsfɔ́ːrm] vt. —vt. 『～+목/ +목+전+명』① (외형) 변형시키다(into).

동영상 강좌 http://youtu.be/zw58a1DSiuw

[76～80]

As video became part of the day-to-day production and promotion of popular music during the 1980s, the initial response of many performers, fans and commentators was to argue that it was trivializing music. The construction of an image had become more important than the production of sound and the ability of the listener to imagine their own images had been colonized and replaced by the promotional mechanism of the industry. Many writers were quick to take issue with such an argument by pointing out that for centuries music _____. Sean Cubitt and Jody Berland both argued that the sounds and visuals of musical performance had actually become temporarily separated with the introduction of the technologies of the gramophone, radio, photography and silent film. But even then the visual had not disappeared completely. As Andrew Goodwin has pointed out, the 'image' was signified in the surrounding texts of popular music, such as album sleeves, newspapers and magazine articles, publicity photographs and descriptions of performers given on radio and even by the stereo 'positioning' of instruments.

🖊 본문해석

As video became part of the day-to-day production and promotion of popular music during the 1980s(비디오가 1980년대 동안 대중음악의 일상적 작곡과 홍보의 일부가 됨에 따라), the initial response of many performers, fans and commentators(많은 음악가들과 팬들 그리고 비평가들의 초기 반응은) was to argue that it was trivializing music(그것은 음악의 가치를 떨어 떨어트리고 있다고 주장하는 것이었다). The construction of an image(이미지의 제작이) had become more important than the production of sound and the ability of the listener(음악작곡과 청취자의 능력 보다 더 중요하게 되었다) to imagine(가정하면서) their own images had been colonized and replaced by the promotional mechanism of the industry(그들 자신들의 이미지는 기업의 홍보도구로 식민지가 되고 대체되었다고). Many writers were quick to take issue(많은 비평가들은 빠르게 문제를 이슈화했다) with such an argument by pointing out(~ 라 지적하는 그러한 논쟁으로) that for centuries music _____(수 세기동안 음악은 ~이다). Sean Cubitt and Jody Berland both argued(신 큐비트와 죠디 버랜드는 둘다 ~을 주장했다) that the sounds and visuals of musical performance(음악적 연주의 소리와 영상은) had actually become temporarily separated(일시적인 단절이 실제로 되었다고) with the introduction of the technologies of the gramophone, radio, photography and silent film(축음기, 라디오, 사진 그리고 무성영화의 기술 도입과 더불어). But even then(그러나 그때 이후조차도) the visual had not disappeared completely(그 음악적 시각적 효과(영상)는 완전히 사라진 적은 없었다). As Andrew Goodwin has pointed out(앤드류 구드윈이 지적한 봐와 같이), the 'image' was signified in the surrounding texts of popular music(그 음악적 이미지는 ~대중음악의 배경 가사들 속에서 나타났다), such as album sleeves, newspapers and magazine articles, publicity photographs and descriptions of performers(앨범 케이스, 신문 그리고 잡지기사, 음악가들의 광고 사진들과 설명과 같은) given on radio (라디오에서 제공되는) and even by the stereo 'positioning' of instruments(그리고 심지어 입체음양의 도구에 의해).

🦪 단어분석

- **trivialize** [trívivilàiz] vt. 하찮게 하다, 평범화하다. / **colonize** [kálənàiz] vt., vi. 식민지로 만들다; 식민시키다; 입식(入植)하다; 이식하다; / ✝ **gramophone** [grǽməfòun] n. 축음기 / † **signify** [sígnəfài]v. — vt. ① 의미하다,(mean). ② 『~+목/ +that절』 표시하다; 나타내다(represent). ③ 알리다. **album sleeve** 앨범 케이스 / ✝ **publicity** [pʌblísəti] n. U ① 널리 알려짐. [opp.] privacy. ② 명성, 평판. /

동영상 강좌 http://youtu.be/uYncBrVflAc

[81~85]

For two reasons, there will be a modest return towards making goods which _____. First, environmental considerations will put pressure on manufacturers to take back products at the end of their life. It is - and will continue to be - expensive to take a car, or a washing machine, to bits, and there will therefore be a market for products which have a long service life. Second, a combination of a relatively affluent population and concern about waste will create a market for products which are durable. This trend will be reinforced by the combination of low inflation and low interest rates, for that will remove the need to get the most rapid payback possible. Not only will there be a greater demand for quality, rather than quantity, but it will be economic to meet that demand - rather in the way that the best-built homes in Europe were built at the end of the nineteenth century, after a long period of stable prices.

📎 **본문해석**

For two reasons(두 가지 이유로 인해), there will be a modest return(온건한 복귀가 있을 것이다) towards making goods which _____(~한 제품을 생산하는 것에). First(첫째로), environmental considerations will put pressure on manufacturers(환경적인 고려는 제조업자들로 하여금 ~하도록 압력을 가할 것이다) to take back products at the end of their life(제품 수명이 다할 때 제품을 수거). It is - and will continue to be - expensive to take a car, or a washing machine, to bits(자동차나 세탁기를 분해하는 것은 비용이 많이 들고 계속해서 비용이 많이 들 것이다), and there will therefore be a market(그러므로 ~시장이 생겨날 것이다) for products which have a long service life(장기적인 서비스 수명을 갖는 제품을 위한). Second(두 번째로), a combination of a relatively affluent population and concern about waste(쓰레기에 관한 비교적 풍부한 인구와 걱정의 결합은) will create a market for products which are durable(내구성이 강한 제품을 위한 시장을 만들 것이다). This trend will be reinforced by the combination of low inflation and low interest rates(이러한 경향은 낮은 물가와 낮은 이자율의 결합의해 강화될 것이다), for that will remove the need to get the most rapid payback possible(왜냐하면 그것은 가장 빠른 원금회수를 가능하게 하는 필요성을 제거할 것이기 때문이다). Not only will there be a greater demand for quality, rather than quantity(양보다는 질적인 더 큰 수요가 있을 뿐만 아니라), but it will be economic to meet that demand(그 수요를 충적시키는 것이 경제적이 될 것이다) - rather in the way(오히려 ~한 방식에서) that the best-built homes in Europe were built at the end of the nineteenth century(유럽에서 최고의 주택들이 19세기 말에 지어졌다), after a long period of stable prices(안정된 가격의 오랜 기간 후에).

📎 **단어분석**

- ✝ **modest** [mάdist / mɔ́d-]a. ① 겸손한, 조심성 있는, 삼가는. ② 정숙한 ③ 알맞은 ④ 간소한 / **take A to bits**: A를 분해하다 / **payback** [péibæ̀k] n., a. 환불(의); 원금 회수(의); 보복(의).

동영상 강좌 http://youtu.be/tdfoLn2W8pk

[86~90]

The mind sees its job as _____ in order to bring about a better future. Its logic is that if we are happy now, we won't do anything to make things better. So it looks for what's wrong with the way things are so that it can figure out what to do to fix or improve things. This keeps the mind very busy and leaves us with an ongoing sense of incompleteness and lack. Because there is always something going on that could be labeled bad, there is always something to fix or improve upon. As a result, we have an ever-expanding to-do list in our minds. We may feel the need to improve our diet, our appearance, our finances, our health, our relationships, and our career. More immediately, we may feel the need to change how we feel wherever a strong feeling or sensation occurs.

📎 **본문해석**

The mind sees its job as _____(마음은 직장을 ～로서 본다) in order to bring about a better future(너 좋은 미래를 가져오기 위해). Its logic is(이런 논리는 ～이다) that if we are happy now(만일 우리가 지금 행복하다면), we won't do anything to make things better(우린 무언가를 더 좋게 만들려 어떤 것도 하지 않을 것이다). So it looks for what's wrong with the way things are(그것은 어떤 것들이 있는 방식에 잘못이 무언지를 찾는 것이다) so that it can figure out what to do to fix or improve things(그것은 어떤 것들을 고치거나 개선하기 위해 무엇을 이해할 수 있는지를 위해). This keeps the mind very busy(이것은 마음을 아주 분주하게 하며) and leaves us with an ongoing sense of incompleteness and lack(우리에게 불완전함과 부족한 계속적인 느낌을 남겨 놓는다). Because there is always something going on that could be labeled bad(나쁘다고 명명될 수 있는 계속되는 뭔가가 늘 있기 때문에), there is always something to fix or improve upon(고치거나 개선할 무언가가 늘 있다). As a result(결과적으로), we have an ever-expanding to-do list in our minds(우리는 마음속에 계속 확장되는 해야 할 명단을 가지고 있다). We may feel the need to improve(우리는 ～을 개선할 필요성을 느끼는 것 같다) our diet, our appearance, our finances, our health, our relationships, and our career(우리의 식생활, 외모, 재정, 건강, 관계 또는 직업). More immediately(더욱 더), we may feel the need(우리는 ～필요성을 느끼는 것 같다) to change how we feel(우리가 느끼는 방법을 변화할) wherever a strong feeling or sensation occurs(강한 느낌이나 동요가 일어날 땐 늘).

🔖 단어분석

- **figure out** 이해하다 / ⁜ **label** [léibəl] vt. (-l-, 【영국】 -ll-) ① ～에 레테르[딱지]를 붙이다. ② ～에 명칭을 붙이다, 분류하다. / ⁜ **sensation** [senséiʃən] n. ① U 감각, 지각(知覺). [SYN.] ⇨ SENSE. ② U,C 감동, 흥분. ③ C 대사건.

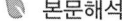
동영상 강좌 http://youtu.be/CGMv-Fh2bVM

[91~95]

On the screen, seeing an action and hearing its accompanying sounds adds little but a characteristic "realism" to the import of a scene. When the sound is easily recognizable, we do not have to see the action or object to know what produced the noise. The viewer mentally supplies the thing or kind of action associated with it. If, for example, a person hears a bell toll, he will associate its sound with a church, even though the church is not seen. If a barking dog is heard while a child is seen looking down at the ground, the viewer assumes that the child is starting down at the animal. Paul Rotha, the British film director and historian, noted this fact when he wrote that sound separated from its source "will not only become a symbol of that source, but also a symbol of what that source represents." This association of ideas has been used by filmmakers to good advantage to _____.

*import 의지, 취미

🔖 본문해석

On the screen(화면상에서), seeing an action and hearing its accompanying sounds(행위를 보고 그 행위에 따르는 소리를 듣는 것은) adds little but a characteristic "realism" to the import of a scene(단지 특징적 사실감을 한 장면 부가할 뿐이다). When the sound is easily recognizable(소리가 쉽게 인식될 때), we do not have to see the action or object(우리는 그 행위와 물체를 볼 필요가 없다) to know what produced the noise(그 소리를 만들어 낸 것을 알기 위해). The viewer mentally supplies the thing or kind of action associated with it(시청자는 그것(소음)과 연관된 행위의 물체나 종류를 정신적으로 제공한다(마음속에 상상한다)). If, for example, a person hears a bell toll(예를 들어, 만일 사람이 벨이 울리는 소리를 듣는다면), he will associate its sound with a church(그는 그 소리를 교회와 연관시킬 것이다), even though the church is not seen(비록 교회가 보이질 않아도). If a barking dog is heard(개 짖는 소리를 듣는다면) while a child is seen looking down at the ground(한 아이가 땅을 내려다보는 것으로 보이는 동안), the viewer assumes(시청자는 ～추측한다) that the child is starting down at the animal(그 아이가 그 동물이 있는 곳으로 내려가고 있다고). Paul Rotha, the British film director and historian, noted this fact(영국의 영화감독이자 역사학자인 폴 로타는 이런 사실을 직감했다) when he wrote(그가 대본을 썼을 때) that sound separated from its source(그 음원으로부터 분리된 소리는) "will not only become a symbol of that source(그 음원의 상징일 뿐 아니라), but also a symbol of what that source represents(그 음원을 대표하는 상징이라고)." This association of ideas has been used(사고의 연상의 ～사용되어지고 있다) by filmmakers to good advantage to _____(～의 좋은 이점을 이용하기 위해서 영화제작자들에 의해). *import 의지, 취미

🖋 **단어분석**

- **accompanying** [əkʌ́mpəniiŋ] a. 수반하는(징후 따위); 동봉[첨부]한 (편지 따위). / **add A to B**: A를 B에 더하다 / **little but** ～이외엔 거의 …않는 / ✝ **characteristic** [kæ̀riktərístik] a. 특색을 이루는, 특질의, 독자적인. / **realism** [ríː əlìz-əm] n. ① 현실주의. / **not have to** ～할 필요가 없다 / ✝ **toll** [toul] v. — vt. ① (만종·조종 등을) 울리다(천천히 규칙적으로). ② (시계·종 따위를) 울려서 알리다[불러모으다]. —vi. 종을 울리다; (종이) 느린 가락으로 울리다. / ✝ **association** [əsòusiéiʃən, -ʃi-] n. U ① 연합, 관련, 제휴(with). ② 교제, 친밀(한 관계). ③ C 협회, 조합, ～회. ④ (종종 pl.) 연상(聯想). /

동영상 강좌 http://youtu.be/_s_to35kQx0

[96~100]

It is much easier and much more effective to switch the standards of comparison. Win by comparing apples to orange and the _____. If you are in a selling situation where there is head-on competition, even competitive bidding, this technique can still be used. Recently I was consulting with a manufacturing company in direct competitive bid warfare with a lower-price opponent. My client was losing bid after bid. I said, "Something has to change here." They said, "If we can't come in with the lower bid, we might as well come in with an even higher bid - but let's change the rules of the game when we do it." They began changing the specifications for the bids, adding value, bundling goods and services together, extending warranties, and including delivery and completion guarantees. Then we built a "How to Compare Our Bid with Others Checklist." When it was all said and done, my client started getting projects the company had been losing to low bidders before.

* specifications 설명서

📖 본문해석

It is much easier and much more effective(더욱 더 쉽고 더욱 효과적이다) to switch the standards of comparison(비교표준을 바꾸는 것은). Win by comparing apples to orange and the _____(사과를 오랜지로 바꾸는 것으로 이겨라). If you are in a selling situation(만일 당신이 판매상황에 놓여 있다면) where there is head-on competition, even competitive bidding(정면 대결, 심지어 경쟁 입찰 상황에 있다면), this technique can still be used(이 기술은 여전히 사용될 수 있다). Recently I was consulting with a manufacturing company(최근에 나는 한 제조회사에 고문 역할을 하고 있었다) in direct competitive bid warfare with a lower-price opponent(저가 경쟁업체와의 직접적인 경쟁 입찰에 대해). My client was losing bid after bid(나의 고객은 계속해서 입찰에 떨어지고 있었다). I said, "Something has to change here."(이 시점에서 무언가를 바꿔야한다고 말했다) They said, "If we can't come in with the lower bid(만일 우리가 더 낮은 입찰을 제시할 수 없다면), we might as well come in with an even higher bid(우리는 더욱 더 높은 입찰가를 제시하는 것이 당연하다 라고 그들은 말했다) - but let's change the rules of the game(그러나 그 경쟁 입찰 규칙을 바꿔보자) when we do it(우리가 입찰을 할 때)." They began changing the specifications for the bids(그들은 입찰을 위한 설명서를 바꾸기 시작했다), adding value, bundling goods and services together(가격과 끼워주는 상품과 서비스를 함께 추가 시키며), extending warranties, and including delivery and completion guarantees(품질보증기간을 늘리고 배송과 완제품 보증서를 포함시켰다). Then we built a "How to Compare Our Bid with Others Checklist."(그때 우리는 우리의 입찰을 다른 대조표와 비교하는 방법을 만들었다) When it was all said and done(모든 것이 협의되어 끝났을 때), my client started getting projects(나의 고객은 프로젝트를 따내기 시작했다) the company had been losing to low bidders before(그 회사가 전에 너 낮은 입찰자들에게 지고 있었다는).   * specifications 설명서

📖 단어분석

- ✝ **switch** [switʃ] n. 『+목+전+명』 (생각·화제 따위를) 바꾸다, 전환하다. / **head-on** [hédán / -ɔ́n] a. 정면의. / ✝ **bidding** [bídiŋ] n. U 명령; 입찰, 초대. / ✝ **consult** [kənsʌ́lt] v. —vt. ① ~의 의견을 듣다, ~의 충고를 구하다; ~의 진찰을 받다. ② (사전·서적 등을) 참고하다, 찾다, 보다. —vi. ① 의논하다, 협의하다; (변호사 등에게) 조언을 구하다(with a person about a matter). ② (회사 등의) 고문[컨설턴트] 노릇을 하다(for). / ✝ **warfare** [wɔ́ːrfɛ̀əːr] n. U 전투(행위), 교전(상태); 전쟁(war); 싸움. / **come in with** ~제안[제시]하다 / **might[may] as well** ~하는 것은 당연하다 / ✝ **extend** [iksténd] v. —vt. ① (손·발 따위를) 뻗다, 펴다. ② (선·거리·기간 따위를) 연장하다, 늘이다; 연기하다. / **warranty** [wɔ́(ː)rənti, wɑ́r-] n. C 『법률』 담보; 보증(서); 영장, 명령서; / **completion guarantees** 완제품 보증서 / **chéck lìst** 【미국】 대조표, 점검표; 선거인 명부. /

동영상 강좌 http://youtu.be/mCTp3gMJ7zE

다음 글을 읽고 물음에 답하시오. [1~5]

The idea of the Belly Button Rule was initially discovered in a study by ⒶW. T. James in the 1930s. Through a series of tests that had respondents identifying almost 350 different meanings for various poses from a series of photographs, James was able to determine that the direction of the torso plays a key role in determining a person's level of interest. James separated belly button directionality into four key groups: approach (interest), withdrawal (disinterest), expansion (heightened interest and confidence), and contraction (nervousness and slightly reduced interest). About thirty years later, ⒷDr. Albert Mehrabian further refined James's studies, noting that belly button direction was _____. Numerous studies have appeared since that time, confirming that the Belly Button Rule is one of the most accurate ways of gauging a person's interest and intent. The direction our belly button faces reflects our attitude and reveals our emotional state. When we suddenly turn our belly button toward a door or an exit or simply away from someone, we subconsciously send the signal that we want out of the conversation and perhaps even out of the interaction.

1. 위 글의 주제로 가장 적절한 것은?

① In spite of the long experiments, their results proved unrealistic.
② The continuation of some research is necessary for the development.
③ A part of one's body is useful to understand his or her intention.
④ To escape from an unfavorable conversation is important.
⑤ The Belly Button Rule is adapted to our social environment.

2. 위 글의 밑줄 친 Ⓐ, Ⓑ 연구원의 공통점은?

① same subject
② each different research
③ same topic, but different result
④ different subject, and different result
⑤ contemporary researcher

3. 위 글로부터 다음과 같이 요약할 때 빈칸 Ⓐ, Ⓑ에 적절한 것은?

> The Belly Button Rule is ___Ⓐ___ to ___Ⓑ___.

① Ⓐ a reliable indication
　 Ⓑ reject the favor
② Ⓐ a realistic adaption
　 Ⓑ apply for any social lives
③ Ⓐ a exaggerated gesture
　 Ⓑ cause misunderstanding
④ Ⓐ a believable method
　 Ⓑ read someone's mind
⑤ Ⓐ an untruthful theory
　 Ⓑ turn out to be unnecessary

4. 위 글의 빈칸에 적절한 표현으로 올바른 것은?

① the implication on someone's physical attitude

② the most important aspect of reading a person's intention

③ applicable to the relationship between men

④ needed further experiments later

⑤ to inspire more researcher to do more jobs

5. 위 글의 내용과 일치하지 <u>않은</u> 것은?

① James' samples were a series of photographs to indicate the physical way by the mentality.

② James made five catalogues separately.

③ James' divided sections was made according to the change of emotions.

④ Dr. Albert made James' theory more developed and accurate.

⑤ Two researchers had the same opinion about how torso reacts

동영상 강좌 http://youtu.be/436P2Lwfgdo

※ 다음 글을 읽고 물음에 답하시오. [6~10]

In one classic experiment, divers learned lists of words in two environments, on dry land and underwater. They were later asked to recall the words in one of the two environments: either in the ①**original** environment in which the words were leaned or in the ②**alternative** environment. Lists learned underwater had higher recall underwater, and lists learned on dry land had higher recall on dry land. The experimenters later proved that this effect was _____ and not related to the ③**disruption** of moving environments. Some companies have used this effect to their advantage. In The Experience Economy, Pine and Gilmore quote the example of Standard Parking of Chicago, which had a parking garage at O'Hare Airport. To help customers remember on which floor they parked their car, they played a ④**same** signature tune at each level of the garage, and decorated the walls with the icons of different local sports franchises, so the Bulls were on one floor and the Blackhawks on ⑤**another**. They quote one local resident saying, 'You never forget where you parked!'

6. 위 글의 요지로 가장 적절한 것은?

① The concentration is going to be higher in the familiar environment.

② Every person has a different sensitivity to the world.

③ To think back is efficient to improve the memory.

④ The past experience takes a great influence on the forecast of the future.

⑤ The environmental clues help to memorize in data putting into.

7. 위 글의 빈칸에 가장 적절한 표현은?

① by means of the divers' long experiences
② surprisingly unbelievable
③ no reasons
④ one of context-dependent memory
⑤ the importance for divers' survival

8. 위 글에서 밑줄 친 ①~⑤ 중, 문맥상 단어의 쓰임이 어색한 것은?

①   ②   ③   ④   ⑤

9. 위 글을 아래와 같이 요약할 때, Ⓐ, Ⓑ에 적절한 단어는?

> The marks people have been ___Ⓐ___ with is one of the ___Ⓑ___ to improve their memory.

	Ⓐ	Ⓑ
①	satisfied	excitements
②	familiar	benefits
③	pleased	tools
④	experienced	damages
⑤	playing	powers

10. 위 글과 일치하지 <u>않은</u> 것은?

① The experiments have two different examples.
② The result from the participants was always same.
③ Some industries have applied its effects to their works.
④ The association is to help drivers' parking their cars.
⑤ The symbols of local sports chains help people come to improve their memory.

동영상 강좌 http://youtu.be/KMBOh9gLEIc

※ 다음 글을 읽고 물음에 답하시오. [11~15]

Certain key position in your company may have Ⓐ**revolving-door loyalty**. Just when you have a treasured employee fully trained, he hits the road. If you see this pattern repeat itself, you may need to redesign the position. UPS found that when they redesigned their drivers' position so that it no longer included the thankless job of loading the trucks, they were able to dramatically increase the length of driver employment. UPS made a strategic decision.

They determined that the drivers were the face of the company and that their customers didn't appreciate meeting a new driver every six months. ___Ⓑ___, the company figured that the loading jobs were lower-skilled and likely always to be high-turnover jobs. This didn't concern them, because the training period for the loading jobs were much shorter than for the driver jobs and the customer contact was minimal. Sometimes ___Ⓒ___ _____.

11. 위 글의 요지로 가장 적절한 것은?

① To improve the company's image, it is necessary to communicate with each position flexibly.

② To designate the adequate job for the position, it is essential to refer to employees' opinion.

③ To reduce the turnover jobs, it's important to redesign the job of the position.

④ The workers leaving their company volunteerly knows of the company's problem well.

⑤ Before sharing the work, there must be ready for the justifiable standard.

12. 위 글에서 밑줄 친 Ⓐ에 뜻하는 단어는?

① treasured employee
② turnover jobs
③ redesign the position
④ increase the length of driver employment
⑤ retention

13. 위 글의 밑줄 친 Ⓑ에 적절한 단어는?

① Additionally   ② However
③ Alternatively   ④ Moreover
⑤ Therefore

14. 위 글의 빈칸 Ⓒ에 적절한 표현 어구는?

① More payroll would satisfy leaving workers to change their minds.

② More and more workers have to be employed.

③ More sufficient training is necessary for workers not to leave out the company.

④ employee retention is just a matter of strategic thinking

⑤ The new management is needed for solving this problem.

15. 위 글과 일치하지 <u>않은</u> 것은?

① 직원들이 자주 바뀌는 것은 회사의 이미지에 타격을 준다.

② 자신에 맞는 직책은 직원들의 회사에 대한 충성도를 높인다.

③ UPS회사의 문제는 간단히 해결되었다.

④ 이직률은 직업만족도와 비례한다.

⑤ 직원유지는 단지 전략적인 사고의 문제이다.

동영상 강좌 http://youtu.be/rlboOzN1svA

❊ 다음 글을 읽고 물음에 답하시오. [16~20]

Off in the distance General Longstreet picked up a conversation between two men. It was an argument. One man must find/have found out that Ⓐthe other had some sort of sympathy for the Union Army across the way. He became very angry and very violent, and he said bad things about the Union Army. The other man responded/responded to his friend's comments by explaining that he was not siding with them, and that he would never side with them. He was only making a point that he had three cousins across the field, and he hoped that they were still alive and well. The angry man _____ Ⓑ _____ and told his friend that, after all, he and his cousins had chosen their sides of that fight, and that it would be God's way to decide which/whom of them would be able to go home. The Union "sympathizer" held his head low. The other man came over to him, rubbed his head, and told the man, "I sure hope that you are the one going home."

16. 위 글의 분위기의 변화는?

① nervous → disappointing
② argumental → disputable
③ colliding → harmonious
④ worried → comfortable
⑤ gloomy → misunderstanding

17. 위 글에서 네모상자 안의 적절한 단어는?

① find	responded	which
② have found	responded to	which
③ find	responded	whom
④ have found	responded to	whom
⑤ find	responded to	which

18. 위 글에서 밑줄 친 Ⓐ에 관계되지 <u>않은</u> 것은?

① He was not siding with the Union Army.
② He had three cousins fighting in the field.
③ He had chosen his side of that fight.
④ He finally got alive from the war.
⑤ He was given the comfort from his friend.

19. 위 글에서 빈칸 Ⓑ의 적절한 표현으로 옳은 것은?

① got more and more angry
② got disappointed
③ had to join the Union Army for his friends
④ didn't accept the apology from his friend
⑤ settled down, apologized,

20. 위 글과 일치하지 <u>않은</u> 것은?

① The two men had an argument, but they understood each other later.
② The General heard of his subordinate fighting in words.
③ The two men had a different view on the Union Army.
④ The sympathizer had his relatives in the battle field.
⑤ The respondent to his friend's sympathy apologized to his friend at last.

✻ 다음 글을 읽고 물음에 답하시오. [21~25]

Ⓐ**Our delusion** that happiness comes from the things that we desire, and ①**that** therefore by desiring and acquiring more things we will become more happy, is a vicious circle. Because we desire something, we feel happy when we obtain it, and because we feel happy when we obtain it, we desire more of it. In this way our desires are always ② **continuously** increasing and multiplying. The raging fire of our desires can never be extinguished by the objects of our desire. The more we acquire those objects, the more intensely our desire for them and for other such objects will rage. ③**Trying** to extinguish the fire of our desires by fulfilling them is like trying to extinguish a fire by pouring petrol upon it. The objects of our desire are the fuel that keeps the fire of our desires ④ **burning**. The only way we can extinguish this fire of our desires is by knowing the truth that all the happiness that we seem to derive from the objects of our desire ⑤**do** not actually come from those objects _____ Ⓑ _____.

21. 위 글의 주제로 가장 적절한 것은?

① Man in the pursuit of happiness is beautiful when he conquers his goals.

② The fire of our desires should be put out by external help.

③ Man's desires are endless, but there is a way to control.

④ The desires by men are no ways to go forward.

⑤ The educational system should be ready for the men's right dreams.

22. 위 글의 밑줄 친 Ⓐ에 해당하는 것은?

① One has a plan to go abroad for studying.

② One who has made some money is trying to earn it more.

③ All the happiness comes from the desires we obtain more and more.

④ Happiness is a dream never to reach.

⑤ The fire of desires is roaring in the happiness.

23. 위 글의 밑줄 친 ①~⑤에서 문법상 어색한 것은?

① ② ③ ④ ⑤

24. 위 글의 밑줄 친 Ⓑ에 적절한 표현은?

① but only from emotional complaints

② but only from our happiness

③ and our realization of the truth

④ but only from within ourself

⑤ and from how much we have knowledge and power

25. 위 글과 일치하지 않은 것은?

① 우리의 망상은 계속해서 반복되는 주기이다.

② 인간의 욕망은 끝이 없는 터널이다.

③ 우리의 욕망은 결코 꺼질 수가 없다.

④ 욕망의 불꽃을 끄고자하는 것은 그 위에 기름을 붓는 일과도 같다.

⑤ 끝없는 욕망은 인간의 문명의 발달에 기여한다.

동영상 강좌 http://youtu.be/7skXLMXMZDo

❈ 다음 글을 읽고 물음에 답하시오. [26~30]

If we attempt to specify the ways ①**in which** human beings are unique and different from other animal species, we must quickly conclude that most, if not all, differences are _____Ⓐ_____. That is, other animals may possess a particular trait similar to humans, but not to the same extent. _____Ⓑ_____, if we say that a distinctive characteristic of humankind is language, it is possible to point to communication among dolphins or the sign language ②**learned** by apes in certain experiments as simple and basic forms of the same behavior. Or, if we say ③**that** social organizations are a human trait, a parallel might be found in the behaviors of bees or ants. We have elaborate rituals connected with death, but elephants have been ④**observed** engaging in what might be called a burial ceremony. Music may even have its animal counterpart in whalesong or birdsong - to a degree. Ⓒ_____, it is the degree of human involvement in such behaviors as language, social organizations, rituals, and music that ⑤**separate** us from other animals.

26. 위 글의 빈칸 Ⓑ, Ⓒ의 적절한 단어는?

① For example   However
② For instance   Therefore
③ However   For example
④ Therefore   For example
⑤ On the other hand   Therefore

27. 위 글의 밑줄 친 ①~⑤ 중, 어법상 어색한 것은?

①   ②   ③   ④   ⑤

28. 위 글의 밑줄 친 Ⓐ에 적절한 표현은?

① in kind, not in degree
② in degree, not in kind
③ in kind and degree
④ the same
⑤ no measurement

29. 위 글의 분위기로 가장 적절한 것은?

① complex and misunderstanding
② persuasive and encouraging
③ confusing, but analytic
④ instructive, but useless
⑤ unreasonable and irrational

30. 위 글과 일치하지 않은 것은?

① 정도와 같은 것과는 분명한 차이가 있다.
② 여러 동물들은 인간과 같은 특성들을 갖고 있다.
③ 죽음 의식을 갖는 동물도 존재한다.
④ 인간과 동물의 비교는 정보의 차이에 불과하다.
⑤ 사회적 조직을 갖는 동물은 인간이 유일하다.

✳ 다음 글을 읽고 물음에 답하시오. [31~35]

It is sometimes (A)easy/difficult to get knocked off your target by the ①other party during a negotiation. It therefore pays to carry your goals with you and, _____, take a break and review them before going forward. The point is not to lose sight of your goals in the confusion of a actual negotiation. Barry Diller, the successful television executive and entrepreneur, learned his lesson the hard way when he got ②caught up in bidding for the rights to the first television showing of the movie The Poseidon Adventure in the early 1970s. Representing ABC, Diller ended up bidding $3.3 million - by far the highest amount ever ③payment for such a property at the time - and (B)losing/making money for his network. The reason Diller paid so much? He agreed to participate in the first open-bid auction for TV rights to a movie. In the frantic bidding that ④followed. he (C)forgot/remembered about his primary goal - making a profit - and got caught up in ⑤what one CBS executive who bid against him called the "fever" of winning a competition.

31. 위 글의 주제로 가장 적절한 것은?

① At any time the only thing is to believe oneself.
② Overflowing fever sometimes leads to mistaken judgement.
③ The cooperation with enemies is important in the bidding.
④ The right of broadcasting shows is not easy.
⑤ The spirit of challenge should be spread out.

32. 위 글의 네모상자안의 적절한 단어는?

① easy	losing	forgot
② easy	losing	remembered
③ difficult	making	remembered
④ difficult	making	forgot
⑤ difficult	losing	forgot

33. 위 글의 빈칸에 적절한 표현은?

① though you have enough idea
② even if they are almost near to your dream
③ if you feel yourself getting swept away
④ if you think that you will lose your money
⑤ if there is much possibility to win

34. 위 글에서 밑줄 친 ①~⑤ 중, 어법상 어색한 것은?

①　　②　　③　　④　　⑤

35. 위 글과 일치하지 않은 것은?

① A negotiation doesn't depend upon one's intention.
② It's necessary to think back and take something into consideration sometimes.
③ Diller experienced one of the most important lessons before losing much money.
④ Above all don't get out of the primary goal of his own.
⑤ Man would be more matured through his suffering loss.

동영상 강좌 http://youtu.be/phAWEFZnkpo

※ 다음 글을 읽고 물음에 답하시오. [36~40]

A basis of influence with special relevance to personal relationships and groups is Ⓐ**referent power**. This exists when we admire or identify with a person or group and want to be like them. In such cases, we may ①**voluntarily** copy their behavior or do what they ask _____.

In everyday life we may not think of ② **identification** as a type of influence, but it can be very effective. A young child who looks up to an older brother, tries to ③**avoid** his mannerisms, and adopts his interest is one illusion. A young man who drinks a particular brand of beer because he identifies with the "macho" image of the sportsmen promoting the product in TV commercials is also being ④ **influenced** by referent power. Recently, Raven has discussed the possibility of "negative referent power," which occurs when we want to ⑤**separate** ourselves from a disliked or unappealing person or group. To avoid being identified with the unattractive other, we may deliberately avoid copying their behavior.

36. What is the main idea of the above paragraph?

① Referent power is called substitutive satisfaction.
② Referent power is a bad behaviour.
③ Through referent power, one should get into his goal.
④ As referent power is illusion, it's unnecessary.
⑤ When there exists referent power in one's mind, that will be treated with professional medication.

37. What is probably adequate in the underlined blank?

① because we want to go over them in competition
② because we never follow them
③ because they mask themselves with fake.
④ because we want to become similar to them
⑤ because they are always good enough to live happily

38. 위 글에서 문맥상 밑줄 친 ①~⑤ 중, 단어의 쓰임이 어색한 것은?

①   ②   ③   ④   ⑤

39. 위 글의 밑줄 친 Ⓐ에 관련이 적은 것은?

① to imitate other's behavior
② to be identified with others
③ to be a kind of illusion
④ to follow an appealing or unappealing person or group
⑤ to accept purposely unfavorable man

40. 위 글과 일치하지 않은 것은?

① We imitate other's behaviour or image.
② Referent power always has an affirmative influence.
③ Referent power is that we don't know of itself.
④ Referent power is called illusion.
⑤ Referent power has each of opposite faces.

✳ 다음 글을 읽고 물음에 답하시오. [41~45]

Before developing invention designs, Ⓐ**inventors** likely first identify the intended function of the invention. When the inventor then generates initial invention designs, he often (A)constrains/disregards the form of the invention through implicit analogies to components of nature or existing products whose function matches or approximates that of the intended invention. For example, early airplane inventors frequently (B)imitated/eliminated the form of animals capable of flight, modeling their flying craft after albatrosses, bats, and various insects such as beetles. Ⓑ_____, architects have made structural innovations through analogies to our actions toward objects and to the forces, tensions, and interactions within our skeletomuscular system. Such analogies seem a (C)plausible/groundless basis for invention in the mechanical realm as well. Ⓒ_____, joysticks, such as those found on many video games, may well have evolved through an analogy to human ball-and-socket joints, such as the shoulder joint.

* skeletomuscular system 근.골격계
** ball-and-socket joint 구관절

41. 위 글의 제목으로 가장 적절한 것은?

① Inventors: Who are they?
② The Nature: Tremendous Power
③ Creativity: We should follow endlessly.
④ Human beings: No existence without Nature
⑤ Invention: Not easy to go forward

42. 위 글 (A), (B), (C)의 각 네모 안에서 문맥에 맞는 낱말로 가장 적절한 것은?

① constrains	imitated	plausible
② constrains	imitated	groundless
③ disregards	eliminated	plausible
④ disregards	imitated	plausible
⑤ disregards	eliminated	groundless

43. 위 글의 밑줄 친 Ⓐ의 특성으로 어울리지 **않는** 것은?

① They try to confirm that their potential functions would be identified with their intention.
② The form of their invention has implicity of analogies to nature or existing products.
③ They get ideals from their creativity, not from the nature.
④ Their invention help people live comfortably.
⑤ The objects around them give them ideas for innovation.

44. 위 글의 밑줄 친 Ⓑ, Ⓒ에 적절한 단어는?

① On the other hand	Therefore
② However	For example
③ Similarly	For example
④ Similarly	Therefore
⑤ Therefore	On the other hand

45. 위 글의 내용과 일치하지 <u>않은</u> 것은?

① 발명가들은 자신들의 의도된 기능을 먼저 확인하는 경향이 있다.

② 자연의 존재는 암시적 유사성을 내포하고 있다.

③ 초기 비행발명가들은 자연으로부터 아이디어를 얻었다.

④ 건축가들은 자연과 인간의 상호반응과 유사한 기능을 포함시킨다.

⑤ 인간의 신체구조의 연구는 의학발전에 기여했다.

동영상 강좌 http://youtu.be/Nn4lj0dHyzg

※ 다음 글을 읽고 물음에 답하시오. [46~50]

The Massachusetts-based company Advanced Cell Technology is planning to clone certain dead creatures to bring them back to life. There's talk of trying to bring back the Tasmanian tiger, a wolflike animal that Ⓐ<u>lost its last grip on survival</u> in the 1930s. Even the prehistoric mammoth is being considered for a possible comeback. It's a fascinating scientific gimmick, a perfect example of doing something because we can. We should leave it at that. But we won't. There's excited talk of cloning and genetic engineering offering a marvelous boost to wildlife conservation, a high-tech solution to our tendency to drive plant and animal species to extinction. _____ Ⓑ _____, for the cloning of endangered species completely contradicts the spirit and practice of conservation. Conservation isn't just about saving a particular species; it's about reducing our destructive impact on natural systems that are in increasing danger of being unable to sustain themselves.

46. 위 글에 나타난 필자의 어조로 가장 적절한 것은?

① admiring ② critical

③ sympathetic ④ optimistic

⑤ humorous

47. 위 글의 주제로 가장 적절한 것은?

① The cloning of animals in danger is necessary for their future extinction.

② We should make a sense of what the conversation is.

③ The cloning needs the agreement to the public.

④ The marvelous research in the cloning is supported by a level of governments.

⑤ The company will be able to succeed in the cloning.

48. 위 글의 밑줄 친 Ⓐ와 가장 밀접한 단어는?

① endanger   ② contradict

③ extinguish   ④ gimmick

⑤ comeback

49. 위 글의 빈칸 Ⓑ에 적절한 표현은?

① This is nonsense

② This is the right of human beings'

③ This is the justifiable measures

④ We need more time to think of

⑤ We invest much money in the researches.

50. 위 글과 일치하지 <u>않은</u> 것은?

① 한 회사는 죽은 생명체를 복제를 통한 복원을 꿈꾸고 있다.

② 멸종위기의 복제는 미래의 인류의 자연 환경에 획기적 도움을 가져다준다.

③ 독자는 유전자 복제에 반대의견을 갖고 있다.

④ 인간의 보존정신과 관행을 다시 짚어 새겨야만 한다.

⑤ 본존이란 인간이 자연에 충격을 줄이는 것이다.

동영상 강좌 http://youtu.be/03NpgCNLpYU

✳ 다음 글을 읽고 물음에 답하시오. [51~55]

At the Christmas season I'd expected a modest office party, dinners with Jack's clients, maybe a simple reception at Matt and Claire's, but none of those happened. Instead Ⓐ**Jack** brought home extravagantly wrapped presents and a tree that had to be topped in order to fit under the high ceiling of our living room. When I asked what he wanted me to fix for our holiday dinner, he said he'd arranged to have it cater/**catered** - hors d'oeuvres, standing-rib roast, horseradish sauce, Yorkshire pudding, **assorted**/assorting vegetables, everything down to the plum pudding, which I had never imagined. And champagne and expensive wines, of course. He'd invited Matt and Claire, and selected appropriate presents for them. A design firm was coming to trim the tree. Meanwhile, I found myself rather **discouraged**/discouraging by his preparation and mourning the loss of our previous simple Christmas in Los Angeles.

51. 위 글의 제목으로 적절한 것은?

① The Pretty wonderful party

② What presents would be nice for the holiday

③ The importance in deciding the party

④ Party: Simple, but memorable

⑤ The longing previous holiday

52. 위 글에 나타난 필자의 어조로 가장 적절한 것은?

① jealous   ② touched

③ satisfied   ④ nervous

⑤ disappointed

53. 위 글에 네모상자 안의 적절한 단어는?

① cater   assorted   discouraged

② catered   assorted   discouraged

③ cater   assorted   discouraging

④ catered   assorting   discouraging

⑤ catered   assorting   discouraged

54. 위 글의 밑줄 친 Ⓐ의 성격은?

① ostentatious   ② frugal

③ affectionate   ④ economical

⑤ industrious

55. 위 글과 일치하지 <u>않은</u> 것은?

① Jack은 처음 검소한 파티를 준비했다.

② Jack은 큰 나무를 집으로 가져왔다.

③ 나는 휴가 저녁준비를 도왔다.

④ 많은 음식이 준비되었다.

⑤ 지난 추억의 크리스마스가 떠올랐다.

동영상 강좌 http://youtu.be/142pmjyUzeY

❋ 다음 글을 읽고 물음에 답하시오. [56~60]

"The greatest room for music and opera in the world - bar none" was Frank Lloyd Wright's assessment of the Auditorium Theatre of Roosevelt University. Designed by Louis Sullivan and Dankmar Adler in 1886, the Auditorium remains one of the most acoustical/acoustically ①**perfect** theatres of the era. Located/Locating inside the Auditorium Building with a hotel and restaurant, the Auditorium Theatre survived the decades ②**partly** because it have been /would have been too expensive to demolish. A move to destroy it failed in 1923, but _____ in 1929 when the Chicago Opera Company found a ③**newer** home. The theatre closed in 1941, then reopened as a recreation center for soldiers during World War II, with a bowling alley installed on the stage. Roosevelt College(later Roosevelt University) ④**sold** the Auditorium Building in 1946 and used the hotel floors for classes and offices while the theatre stood empty. In the 1960s, Beatrice T. Spachner led a drive to restore the Auditorium Theatre. It reopened in 1967, yet restoration work ⑤ **continued** for two decades.

     * bar none: 단연코, 예외 없이

56. 위 글의 제목으로 적절한 것은?

① Still famous theatre in the world

② Acoustic equipment: the most important in the performance

③ Who had used the theatre, the most famous one?

④ The theatre: to have coped with much adversities

⑤ How about the fate of the theatre?

57. 위 글의 네모상자 안의 적절한 단어는?

① acoustical located have been
② acoustical locating would have been
③ acoustically located have been
④ acoustically locating would have been
⑤ acoustically located would have been

58. Auditorium Theatre of Roosevelt University 에 관한 다음 글의 내용과 일치하지 <u>않은</u> 것은?

① It proved the most wonderful place for music and opera in the world.
② Its facilities had a hotel and a restaurant inside.
③ It reopened for recreation by soldiers in the World War II.
④ It was used for lecture rooms by Roosevelt College.
⑤ After its reopening, it continued to restore for 20 years.

59. 위 글의 밑줄 친 빈칸에 적절한 표현은?

① demolition began
② another setback came
③ it reopened
④ it was being renovated
⑤ it held many events

60. 위 글의 밑줄 친 ①~⑤ 중, 문맥상 단어의 쓰임이 <u>어색한</u> 것은?

①   ②   ③   ④   ⑤

동영상 강좌 http://youtu.be/MKOv9LXM9TQ

✻ 다음 글을 읽고 물음에 답하시오. [61~65]

The Katsura Palace is located near the Katsura River, to the southwest of the imperial city of Kyoto in Japan. The palace and gardens provided a place for the Imperial family in the cultural ear of the late 16th century. The main palace is an open, timber-framed construction with simple tatami (rice-straw) matted rooms and elevated/elevates verandas from which/of which to contemplate the changing seasons. The garden arbors and pavilions surrounding the main palace are approached from a sequence of carefully staged routes. The buildings have an understated simplicity, and the landscape has been subtly manipulated to blur the distinction between artificial and natural environments. Artificial objects, such as fences and paving stones, have been subjected to the forces of nature, such as weathering, while natural features have been clipped, aligned and polished to emphasize their eccentricity and "unnaturalness." The effect is discreet and fascinating, contributed/contributing to a heightened aesthetic awareness of the architecture and the landscape.

* arbor 정자

61. 위 글의 분위기로 적절한 것은?

① marvelous　　② harmonious
③ majestic　　④ trivial
⑤ terrifying

62. Katsura Palace에 관한 다음 글의 내용과 일치하는 것은?

① It's located near Katsura river to the southwest.
② It provided the room for Imperial family in the beginning of 16th.
③ Its main palace is the construction with rice-straw matted rooms.
④ The building is the modest appearance and its surroundings are natural environment.
⑤ The man-made objects are far from the influences of nature.

63. 위 글의 네모상자 안의 적절한 단어는?

① elevated　　from which　　contributed
② elevated　　of which　　contributed
③ elevated　　from which　　contributing
④ elevates　　of which　　contributing
⑤ elevates　　from which　　contributing

64. 위 글에서 언급된 단어의 영영풀이가 <u>어색한</u> 것은?

① contemplate: to look at attentively and thoughtfully
② approach: to come near or nearer
③ understate: to express with restraint
④ manipulate: to operate or control by unskilled use of the hands
⑤ aesthetic: concerning the appreciation of beauty or good taste

65. 위 글의 제목으로 가장 적절한 것은?

① A symbol of the imperialism in Japan
② A palace to influence tourism
③ The Features of the Katsura river
④ Artificial and natural harmony
⑤ The specifications of Japan's construction

동영상 강좌 http://youtu.be/8ca7nX3RH3g

✳ 다음 글을 읽고 물음에 답하시오. [66~70]

The use of motion in movie composition can be positive. For example, movement along a ① **definite** line can tend to carry the audience's eye with it or even ②**ahead of** it, acting as a sort of _____. Imagine a New England landscape nicely framed in foreground foliage, with a white ribbon of road curving across the picture and leading toward a village. Ordinarily, the white line of the road itself would probably be the ③**strongest** factor in the composition. But suppose we have a car driver along the road in the direction of the village. The movement will tend strongly to send the audience's eyes racing along the road ahead of the car to focus on the village, logically setting the ④**practical** stage for following scenes made in the village itself. Ⓐ**This**, by the way is true even if you only show the car moving along the road., ⑤**without** taking the time to have it completely cross the frame and reach the village in that one shot.

66. 위 글의 주제로 가정 적절한 것은?

① The movement in the films gives audiences more exciting sensation.

② To produce impressive shots is to attract more movie-goers.

③ The background and foreground in the movement are important factors above all.

④ The audience's eyes make the following happening situation.

⑤ The audience's eyes are easy to make something distorted.

67. 위 글의 밑줄 친 ①~⑤ 중, 문맥상 단어의 쓰임이 <u>어색한</u> 것은?

①   ②   ③   ④   ⑤

68. 위 글의 빈칸에 들어갈 말로 가장 적절한 것은?

① probable ending

② mainstream storyline

③ compositional pointer

④ equivalent counterpart

⑤ unexpected background

69. 위 글의 밑줄 친 Ⓐ가 가리키는 것은?

① logical stage for next scenes

② the direction of the village

③ ahead of the car

④ the audience's eyes

⑤ the movement

70. 위 글과 일치하지 <u>않은</u> 것은?

① 영화 구성에서 동작의 사용은 긍정적인 영향을 끼칠 수 있다.

② 영화 속의 움직임은 관객의 시선을 잡는다.

③ 관객은 시선은 주어진 물체에 앞선다.

④ 관객의 상상력은 이동하는 물체에 앞선 가상의 세계를 창조한다.

⑤ 어떤 마을에 시선을 집중시키기 위해서 자동차 보다는 오솔길이 더 효율적이다.

동영상 강좌 http://youtu.be/SS5BuhcDtZw

✳ 다음 글을 읽고 물음에 답하시오. [71~75]

Physicians are too **quite/rarely** aware of their patients' need for _____, so they often don't know how to account for dramatic improvements in their patients' conditions. Recently, I received a letter from a doctor telling me that Ⓐ**a woman** with extensive breast cancer, whom we had ①**both** cared for, had returned to his office five months after he had sent her to a nursing home - and that he had "never seen her ②**looking** so well!" No further comment by the doctor was made. I told the medical student who was walking with me to call the woman and find out her story, because I was sure there ③**would** be **one/ones**. The woman told the student that when she got to the nursing home, she found conditions there so **unbearable and depressing/unbearably and depressingly** that she led a revolution among the other "inmates" to insist that they ④ **received** better treatment. She spent time talking with the staff about the tenderness and love the patients needed, and she transformed the place. Then she felt so ⑤ **good** that she went home and bought herself a new car!

71. 위 글의 네모상자 안의 문맥상 올바른 것은?

① quite   one   unbearable and depressing
② quite   ones   unbearable and depressing
③ rarely   one   unbearable and depressing
④ rarely   one   unbearably and depressingly
⑤ rarely   ones   unbearably and depressingly

72. 위 글에서 밑줄 친 ①~⑤ 중, 어법상 어색한 것은?

①   ②   ③   ④   ⑤

73. 위 글의 빈칸에 들어갈 말로 가장 적절한 것은?

① peace of mind
② external support networks
③ information on their disease
④ purpose and meaning in life
⑤ confidence in their doctor's therapy

74. 위 글의 밑줄 친 Ⓐa woman과 관계가 없는 것은?

① no further comment
② dramatic improvements
③ extensive breast cancer
④ a revolution
⑤ a new car

75. 위 글과 일치하지 않은 것은?

① The main character got the terminal breast cancer.
② I was curious about how the patient got over her disease.
③ I finally found out that the patient spent her time at the nursing home positively.
④ I asked the patient about how she could get better in private.
⑤ What the patient really needed was affection and love.

동영상 강좌 http://youtu.be/Li5Bpt5Z7Nk

✹ 다음 글을 읽고 물음에 답하시오. [76~80]

As video became part of the day-to-day production and promotion of popular music during the 1980s, the initial response of many performers, fans and commentators was to argue that it was trivializing music. ① The construction of an image had become more important than the production of sound and the ability of the listener to imagine their own images had been colonized and replaced by the promotional mechanism of the industry. ② Many writers were quick to take issue with such an argument by pointing out that for centuries music _____. ③ Sean Cubitt and Jody Berland both argued that the sounds and visuals of musical performance had actually become temporarily separated with the introduction of the technologies of the gramophone, radio, photography and silent film. ④ As Andrew Goodwin has pointed out, the 'image' was signified in the surrounding texts of popular music, such as album sleeves, newspapers and magazine articles, publicity photographs and descriptions of performers given on radio and even by the stereo 'positioning' of instruments. ⑤

76. 위 글의 제목으로 적절한 것은?

① The collision between music and video
② The arrogant acceptance of video
③ The visuals once as an element of popular music
④ The popular music as a tool of everyday life
⑤ The development of music industry

77. 위 글의 분위기의 변천은?

① optimistic → pessimistic
② pessimistic → optimistic
③ pleasant → gloomy
④ argumental → disputable
⑤ critical → negotiable

78. 위 글의 빈칸에 들어갈 말로 가장 적절한 것은?

① has been reflecting the tastes of audiences
② has contributed to improving our imagination
③ has been the pastime of people of high status
④ has focused more on its sound than on its function
⑤ has been associated with performance and spectacle

79. 위 글에서 아래의 문장이 들어갈 적절한 위치는?

But even then the visual had not disappeared completely.

①   ②   ③   ④   ⑤

80. 위 글과 일치하지 <u>않은</u> 것은?

① the first response to video was affirmative.

② The image was considered more serious than music itself.

③ Sean Cubitt and Jody Berland thought that music was separated with the new technologies.

④ Andrew Goodwin pointed out that music was assisted by other popular medias.

⑤ The visual in music won't disappear.

동영상 강좌 http://youtu.be/I1XoyBh0Dwk

✳ 다음 글을 읽고 물음에 답하시오. [81~85]

For two reasons, there will be a ①**modest** return towards making goods which _____. First, environmental considerations will put pressure on manufacturers to take back products at the end of their life. It is - and will continue to be - ②**inexpensive** to take a car, or a washing machine, to bits, and there will therefore be a market for products which have a ③**long** service life. Second, a combination of a relatively affluent population and concern about waste will create a market for products which are ④**durable**. This trend will be reinforced by the combination of low inflation and low interest rates, for that will remove the need to get the most ⑤**rapid** payback possible. Not only will there be a greater demand for quality, rather than quantity, but it will be economic to meet that demand - rather in the way that the best-built homes in Europe were built at the end of the nineteenth century, after a long period of stable prices.

81. 위 글의 제목으로 가장 적절한 것은?

① The prospect by the change of social environment

② The payback: too expensive to take an action

③ The durable products: necessary and easy

④ The low inflation and modest product prices

⑤ The consumers' desire: the endless pursuit

82. 위 글의 밑줄 친 ①~⑤ 중, 문맥상 단어의 쓰임이 <u>어색한</u> 것은?

①   ②   ③   ④   ⑤

83. 위 글 빈칸에 들어가 말로 가장 적절한 것은?

① can be used for multiple purposes
② are both disposable and recyclable
③ can be repaired, rather than replaced
④ are mostly made of natural materials
⑤ work manually, rather than automatically

84. 아래의 빈칸에 가장 적절한 단어는?

> Manufacturers and consumers are all concerned about the _____.

① social pressure   ② waste
③ interest rates   ④ loan
⑤ quantity

85. 위 글과 일치하지 <u>않은</u> 것은?

① The two reasons are environmental considerations and many consumers about waste
② The companies are in the pursuit of quick payback.
③ The best-built homes in Europe was economic.
④ The demand tends to create durable products.
⑤ The industries' revenue will reduce as a result.

동영상 강좌 http://youtu.be/jIT7HEz_SE8

✺ 다음 글을 읽고 물음에 답하시오. [86~90]

The mind sees its job as _____ in order to bring about a better future. Its logic is that if we are ①**happy** now, we won't do anything to make things better. So it looks for what's ②**wrong** with the way things are so that it can figure out what to do to fix or improve things. This keeps the mind very ③**busy** and leaves us with an ongoing sense of incompleteness and lack. Because there is always something going on that could be labeled ④**good**, there is always something to fix or improve upon. _____Ⓐ_____, we have an ever-expanding to-do list in our minds. We may feel the need to improve our diet, our appearance, our finances, our health, our relationships, and our career. _____Ⓑ_____, we may feel the need to change how we feel wherever a ⑤**strong** feeling or sensation occurs.

86. 위 글의 제목으로 적절한 것은?

① Always a lack of relation
② The way of seeing the present situation
③ Mind's role
④ To improve how we feel
⑤ Mind: too deep to understand

87. 위 글에서 밑줄 친 빈칸 Ⓐ, Ⓑ에 적절한 단어는?

  ① Moreover   However
  ② As a result   More immediately
  ③ Therefore   For example
  ④ On the other hand   Nevertheless
  ⑤ Additionally   Accordingly

88. 위 글의 빈칸에 들어갈 가장 적절한 것은?

  ① making situations obscure
  ② accepting the world as it is
  ③ emphasizing the current happiness
  ④ rejecting what is presently going on
  ⑤ complementing social relationships

89. 위 글의 밑줄 친 ①~⑤의 단어 중, 문맥상 어색한 것은?

  ①   ②   ③   ④   ⑤

90. 위 글과 일치하지 않은 것은?

  ① The mind wants to bring about a better future.
  ② Owing to our unsatisfaction at present, we will do anything to make things better.
  ③ To fix or improve things in life is our desire.
  ④ If the lack would be filled with something, that would be enough.
  ⑤ That we feel the need to change how we feel is almost everything.

동영상 강좌 http://youtu.be/My2WSIDBei0

※ 다음 글을 읽고 물음에 답하시오. [91~95]

On the screen, seeing an action and hearing its accompanied/accompanying sounds adds little but a characteristic "realism" to the import of a scene. When the sound is easily recognizable, we do not have to see the action or object to know what produced the noise. The viewer mentally supplies the thing or kind of action associated/associating with it. If, for example, a person hears a bell toll, he will associate its sound with a church, even though the church is not seen. If a barked/barking dog is heard while a child is seen looking down at the ground, the viewer assumes that the child is starting down at the animal. Ⓐ**Paul Rotha**, the British film director and historian, noted this fact when he wrote that sound separated from its source "will not only become a symbol of that source, but also a symbol of what that source represents." This association of ideas has been used by filmmakers to good advantage to _____.

  *import 의지, 취미

91. 위 글의 제목으로 적절한 것은?

  ① Popular movies produced with sounds in secrete
  ② Unchangeable rule in movie-making
  ③ Why is sound different from action?
  ④ The way of watching movies more interestingly
  ⑤ The role of sound by letting more than a seen scene guessed

92. 위 글의 네모상자 안의 올바른 단어는?

① accompanied   associated   barked
② accompanied   associating   backed
③ accompanied   associated   barking
④ accompanying   associating   barking
⑤ accompanying   associated   barking

93. 위 글의 빈칸에 들어갈 말로 가장 적절한 것은?

① tell the viewer how to guess how the movie is created
② lead the viewer to be unwittingly absorbed in the movie
③ inform the viewer of the production process of the movie
④ create an illusion that tells the viewer more than he sees
⑤ make a suggestion that the viewer judge the movie on his own

94. 위 글의 밑줄 친 Ⓐ의 핵심은 무엇인가?

① the creativity of sound
② the independent of sound
③ the absolute of sound
④ the association of sound
⑤ the scarcity of sound

95. 위 글과 일치하지 <u>않은</u> 것은?

① Sound inspires viewers with illusion in mind.
② Film-makers apply sound to movie productions.
③ Mental association with sound can be possible to guess the next scene.
④ The separation between action and sound is important secrete in move-making.
⑤ When a sound tolls, viewers think that it might be what they judge.

동영상 강좌 http://youtu.be/Xz_LLevD1NM

❋ 다음 글을 읽고 물음에 답하시오. [96~100]

It is much easier and much more effective to switch the standards of comparison. Win by comparing apples to orange and the _____. If you are in a selling situation where there is head-on competition, even competitive bidding, this technique can still be used. Recently Ⓐ**I** was consulting with ①**a manufacturing company** in direct competitive bid warfare with a lower-price opponent. ②**My client** was losing bid after bid. I said, "Something has to change here." ③**They** said, "If we can't come in with the lower bid, we might as well come in with an even higher bid - but let's change the rules of the game when we do it." ④**They** began changing the specifications for the bids, adding value, bundling goods and services together, extending warranties, and including delivery and completion guarantees. Then we built a "How to Compare Our Bid with Others Checklist." When it was all said and done, my client started getting projects the company had been losing to ⑤**low bidders** before.   * specifications 설명서

96. 위 글의 제목으로 가장 적절한 것은?

① Who is the best consultant to win the bidding?
② The way of developing newer and more unprecedented strategy.
③ The rule of bidding to make itself distinctive
④ More and more higher bid than opponents
⑤ More often to change specifications

97. 위 글의 분위기로 적절한 것은?

① frustrating   ② disappointing
③ arrogant   ④ nervous
⑤ analysing

98. 위 글의 빈칸에 들어갈 말로 가장 적절한 것은?

① try to keep in touch with your customers
② throw in the superior quality at no extra cost
③ analyze the specifications for your presentation
④ explain your new project with a traditional view
⑤ check our again all purposes of the bid you are in

99. 위 글에서 밑줄 친 ①~⑤ 중, 가리키는 대상이 다른 것은?

①   ②   ③   ④   ⑤

100. 위 글의 밑줄 친 ⓐ'I'와 관련이 없는 것은?

① I was a consultant for a company.
② My client lost bid all the time.
③ Before my consultation, my client had only two options; lower bid or higher bid.
④ I was rewarded for it to get more projects.
⑤ My analysis proved out winning the bids.

1. ③	2. ①	3. ④	4. ②	5. ②
6. ⑤	7. ④	8. ④	9. ②	10. ②
11. ③	12. ②	13. ③	14. ④	15. ③
16. ③	17. ②	18. ④	19. ⑤	20. ②
21. ③	22. ③	23. ⑤	24. ④	25. ⑤
26. ①	27. ⑤	28. ②	29. ③	30. ⑤
31. ②	32. ①	33. ③	34. ③	35. ③
36. ①	37. ③	38. ③	39. ⑤	40. ②
41. ①	42. ①	43. ④	44. ③	45. ⑤
46. ②	47. ②	48. ③	49. ①	50. ②
51. ⑤	52. ⑤	53. ②	54. ①	55. ③
56. ④	57. ⑤	58. ④	59. ②	60. ④
61. ②	62. ①③	63. ③	64. ④	65. ①
66. ④	67. ④	68. ③	69. ①	70. ⑤
71. ③	72. ④	73. ④	74. ①	75. ④
76. ③	77. ②	78. ⑤	79. ④	80. ①
81. ①	82. ②	83. ③	84. ②	85. ⑤
86. ③	87. ②	88. ④	89. ④	90. ④
91. ⑤	92. ⑤	93. ④	94. ④	95. 모두정답
96. ③	97. ⑤	98. ②	99. ⑤	100. ④

[난이도 ★★★☆☆]

동영상 강좌 http://youtu.be/OtDgoKocPmY

On Friday evening last I received from His Majesty the mission to form a new administration. It was the evident will of Parliament and the nation that this should be conceived on the broadest possible basis and that it should include all parties.
I have already completed the most important part of this task.

A war cabinet has been formed of five members, representing, with the Labour, Opposition, and Liberals, the unity of the nation. It was necessary that this should be done in one single day on account of the extreme urgency and rigor of events. Other key positions were filled yesterday. I am submitting a further list to the king tonight. I hope to complete the appointment of principal ministers during tomorrow.

The appointment of other ministers usually takes a little longer. I trust when Parliament meets again this part of my task will be completed and that the administration will be complete in all respects. I considered it in the public interest to suggest to the Speaker that the House should be summoned today. At the end of today's proceedings, the adjournment of the House will be proposed until May 21 with provision for earlier meeting if need be. Business for that will be notified to MPs at the earliest opportunity.

I now invite the House by a resolution to record its approval of the steps taken and declare its confidence in the new government.

The resolution:

"That this House welcomes the formation of a government representing the united and inflexible resolve of the nation to prosecute the war with Germany to a victorious conclusion."

To form an administration of this scale and complexity is a serious undertaking in itself. But we are in the preliminary phase of one of the greatest battles in history. We are in action at many other points-in Norway and in Holland-and we have to be prepared in the Mediterranean. The air battle is continuing, and many preparations have to be made here at home.

In this crisis I think I may be pardoned if 1 do not address the House at any length today, and I hope that any of my friends and colleagues or former colleagues who are affected by the political reconstruction will make all allowances for any lack of ceremony with which it has been necessary to act.

I say to the House as I said to ministers who have joined this government, I have nothing to offer but blood, toil, tears, and sweat. We have before us an ordeal of the most grievous kind. We have before us many, many months of struggle and suffering.

You ask, what is our policy? I say it is to wage war by land, sea, and air. War with all our might and with all the strength God has given us, and to wage war against a monstrous tyranny never surpassed in the dark and lamentable catalogue of human crime. That is our policy.

You ask, what is our aim? I can answer in one word. It is victory. Victory at all costs - Victory in spite of all terrors - Victory, however long and hard the road may be, for without victory there is no survival.

Let that be realized. No survival for the British Empire, no survival for all that the British Empire has stood for, no survival for the urge, the impulse of the ages, that mankind shall move forward toward his goal.

I take up my task in buoyancy and hope. I feel sure that our cause will not be suffered to fail among men. I feel entitled at this juncture, at this time, to claim the aid of all and to say, "Come then, let us go forward together with our united strength."

📝 본문해석

On Friday evening last I received from His Majesty the mission to form a new administration(지난 금요일 저녁 전 여왕폐하로부터 새로운 정부를 구성하라는 임무를 받았습니다). It was the evident will of Parliament and the nation(그것은 의회와 국가의 분명한 의지였습니다) that this should be conceived on the broadest possible basis(이것은 가장 폭넓은 가능한 토대 위에서 생각되어져야 하고) and that it should include all parties(그것은 모든 정당들을 아우어야만 한다는).

I have already completed the most important part of this task(저는 이 업무의 가장 중요한 핵심을 이미 완성해 놓았습니다).

A war cabinet has been formed of five members, representing, with the Labour, Opposition, and Liberals, the unity of the nation(전쟁각료는 5인으로 구성되어 있고, 노동당, 오코지션당, 그리고 자유당과 함께 국민당으로 구성되어 있습니다). It was necessary that this should be done in one single day(이 각료는 단 하루 만에 구성되어야 할 필요성이 있었습니다) on account of the extreme urgency and rigor of events(아주 급박하고 어려운 상황 때문에). Other key positions were filled yesterday(다른 중요 직책들은 어제 임명되었습니다). I am submitting a further list to the king tonight(저는 더 상세한 명단을 오늘밤 폐하께 제출할 것입니다.). I hope to complete the appointment of principal ministers during tomorrow(저는 오늘 중으로 중요 장관들 임명을 끝마치기를 바랍니다).

The appointment of other ministers usually takes a little longer(다른 각료들의 임명은 보통 약간 더 시간이 걸립니다). I trust(확신합니다) when Parliament meets again(의원들이 다시 소집될 때) this part of my task will be completed and that the administration will be complete in all respects(저의 임무 중 이 분야는 완성될 것이고 관리는 모든 면에서 끝날 것을). I considered it in the public interest(국민들은 이것에 많은 관심이 있으시리라 생각합니다) to suggest to the Speaker that the House should be summoned today(하원을 오늘 소집해야 한다는 것을 하원의장님에게 제안하는 것에 관해). At the end of today's proceedings(오늘 절차를 마무리하면서), the adjournment of the House will be proposed until May 21(하원 휴회가 5월 21일까지 제안될 것입니다) with provision for earlier meeting if need be(필요하다면 더 빠른 소집의 조항을 달아서). Business for that will be notified to MPs at the earliest opportunity(그것에 관한 것은 가능한 빨리 의원 여러분께 통보될 것입니다).

I now invite the House by a resolution(저는 지금 단호히 하원에게 요청 합니다) to record its approval of the steps taken(필요한 조치에 관한 승인을 기록하여) and declare its confidence in the new government(새 정부에 신임을 줄 것을).

The resolution(다음은 결의문입니다):

"That this House welcomes the formation of a government representing the united and inflexible resolve of the nation(이 하원은~ 국가의 통합되고 확고한 결의를 대표하는 정부 구성을 지지한다) to prosecute the war with Germany to a victorious conclusion(독일과의 전쟁에서 승리를 쟁취하기 위한)." To form an administration of this scale and complexity(이러한 규모의 복잡한 행정부를 구성하는 것은) is a serious undertaking in itself(그 자체가 중대한 책임이다). But we are in the preliminary phase of one of the greatest battles in history(그러나 우리는 역사에서 가장 큰 전쟁 중 하나의 초기단계에 있습니다). We are in action at many other points-in Norway and in Holland-and(우린 많은 노르웨이와 폴란드에서 선봉의 전투를 치루고 있고) we have to be prepared in the Mediterranean(지중해에서도 준비를 해야만 합니다). The air battle is continuing(공중전이 계속되며), and many preparations have to be made here at home(많은 준비가 이곳 국내에서 완성되어야만 합니다).

In this crisis(이 위기 상황 하에서) I think I may be pardoned if I do not address the House at any length today(제가 하원 여러분들에게 오늘 장황하게 긴 연설을 하지 않음을 양해를 구합니다), and I hope that any of my friends and colleagues or former colleagues who are affected by the political reconstruction(정치적 재건에 영향을 받아온 모든 분들에게) will make all allowances(참작해 주실 것을) for any lack of ceremony with which it has been necessary to act(이러한 행위에 필요한 부족한 행사에 대해).

I say to the House as I said to ministers who have joined this government(제가 이 정부를 구성하는 각료들에게 말씀드린 것처럼 하원여러분에게도 말합니다), I have nothing to offer but blood, toil, tears, and sweat(제게 피와 수고, 눈물 그리고 땀 이외에 줄 것은 아무것도 없다는 것을). We have before us an ordeal of the most grievous kind(우리들 앞에 놓여 있는 가장 가혹한 시련을 격고 있습니다). We have before us many, many months of struggle and suffering(우리 앞에는 너무나 오래 계속될 투쟁과 고통이 놓여 있습니다).

You ask, what is our policy?(우리의 정책은 무엇이냐고 묻고 싶습니다) I say it is to wage war by land, sea, and air(그것은 육지, 바다 그리고 공중에서 전투를 벌이는 것이라고 저는 말합니다). War with all our might and with all the strength God has given us(우리의 강력한 힘과 강인함 신의 도움 하에 전쟁은 우리에게 승리를 주고 있고), and to wage war against a monstrous tyranny never surpassed in the dark and lamentable catalogue of human crime(어둡고 비참한 인간범죄의 슬픈 것도 결코 괴물스런 독재자에 대항하는 전쟁에 굴복하지 않는 것). That is our policy(이것이 우리의 정책입니다).

You ask, what is our aim?(우리의 목표가 무엇인가를 저는 묻습니다) I can answer in one word(저는 한 단어로 답할 수 있습니다). It is victory(그것은 승리입니다). Victory at all costs - Victory in spite of all terrors(모든 희생을 치른 승리 - 모든 공포를 이겨낸 승리) - Victory, however long and hard the road may be(비록 길고 험난한 길일 지라도), for without victory there is no survival(승리 없이는 생존도 없기 때문입니다).

Let that be realized(이런 사실을 직시합시다). No survival for the British Empire(영국제국을 위한 어떠한 생존도), no survival for all that the British Empire has stood for(영국제국이 버텨왔던 어떠한 생존도), no survival for the urge, the impulse of the ages(강인한 힘과 시대의 추진력을 위한 어떠한 생존도), that mankind shall move forward toward his goal(인류가 목표를 향해 앞으로 전진하지 못할 것입니다). I take up my task in buoyancy and hope(저는 낙천적인 기질과 희망을 갖고 제 임무를 수락합니다). I feel sure that our cause will not be suffered to fail among men(우리의 대의는 사람들 사이에서의 패배로 고통받지 않을 것임을 확신합니다). I feel entitled at this juncture, at this time, to claim the aid of all and to say(이 중대한 때에, 바로 이 시점에 여러분 모두의 지지를 요청하고 ~말하는 것이 저의 책임이라 느낍니다.), "Come then, let us go forward together with our united strength(이제 우리 함께 우

리의 단결된 힘으로 함께 전진합시다)."

🗨 단어분석

- ‡**majesty** [mǽdʒisti, -dʒəs-]n. U ① 위엄(dignity); 장엄. ② 「집합적」 왕족; (M-) 폐하. / †**conceive** [kənsíːv] v. —vt. ① (감정·의견 따위를) 마음에 품다. ② 이해하다. / †**urgency** [ə́ːrdʒənsi] n. U ① 긴급, 절박, 화급. / †**rigor** [rígəːr] n. U ① 엄함, 엄격, 엄숙. / ‡speaker [spíːkəːr] n. ① 강연자 ② (보통 S-) (영·미 등 하원의) 의장. / ‡**summon** [sʌ́mən] vt. ① 소환하다, 호출하다(call) (to); / ‡**proceeding** [prousíːdiŋ] n. 진행; 행동; 조처; (pl.) 소송 절차; 변론; / ‡**adjourn** [ədʒə́ːrn] v. —vt. ① ~을 휴회[산회, 폐회]하다. / ‡**provision** [prəvíʒən] n. U ① 예비, 준비, 설비 (for; against). ② 조항(clause). / ‡notify [nóutəfài] vt. ~에게 통지하다, ~에 신고하다(of). / **at the earliest opportunity** 가능한 빨리 / **MPs members of Parliament** 의원 여러분 / ⁂**invite** [inváit] vt. ① 초청하다 ②『+목+to do』권유하다. / ‡**confidence** [kánfidəns / kɔ́n-] n. U ① (남에 대한) 신용, 신뢰. [SYN.] ⇨ BELIEF. ② C 비밀. ③ (자기에 대한) 확신. [opp.] diffidence. / ‡**resolution** [rèzəlúːʃən] n. ① U,C 결심, 결의. ② U 확고한 정신. / †**formation** [fɔːrméiʃ-ən] n. ① U 형성; 성립; 설립. / **inflexible** [infléksəbəl] a. 불굴의; 강직한, 완고한; 불변의. / †**prosecute** [prásəkjùːt / prɔ́-] v. —vt. ① 수행하다. ② (장사 따위에) 종사하다. / ‡**undertaking** [ʌndərtéikiŋ] n. ① 사업, 기업 (enterprise). / **in itself** 본질적으로, 그것 자체가 / ‡**preliminary** [prilímənèri / -nəri] a. ① 예비의, 시초의. / ‡**phase** [feiz] n. ① (발달·변화의) 단계, 국면. / **points-in**『군사』 첨병(尖兵), 선봉; / ‡**pardon** [páːrdn] vt. ① 용서하다(forgive). / ♣**at any[great] length** 길게 장황하게. / ♣**make [make no] ~(s) for** ~을 참작하다[참작하지 않다] / †**ordeal** [ɔːrdíːəl, ɔ́ːrdiːl] n. ① 호된 시련, 고된 체험. / †**grievous** [gríːvəs] a. ① 슬픈, 통탄할, 비통한 / ‡**surpass** [sərpǽs, -páːs] vt. ~보다 낫다, ~을 능가하다, 뛰어나다; ~을 넘다[초월하다]. [SYN.] ⇨ EXCEL. / †**lamentable** [lǽməntəb-əl] a. 슬퍼할 / ‡**urge** [əːrdʒ] n. (강한) 충동. / ‡**impulse** [impʌls] n. ① C 추진(력); 충격; 자극. / **buoyancy, -ance** [bɔ́iənsi, búːjən-], [-əns] n. U ① 부력; 뜨는 성질. / ⁂**cause** [kɔːz] n. U,C ① 원인([opp.] effect); 이유(reason); 대의, 큰 목적/ ♣**at this juncture** 이 중대한 때에

✱ 다음 글을 읽고 물음에 답하시오. [1~5]

On Friday evening last I received from His Majesty the mission to form a new administration. It was the evident will of Parliament and the nation that Ⓐ<u>this</u> should be conceived on the broadest possible basis and that it should include all parties.

I have already completed the most important part of this task.

Ⓑ<u>**A war cabinet**</u> has been formed of five members, representing, with the Labour, Opposition, and Liberals, the unity of the nation. It was necessary that this should be done in one single day on account of the extreme urgency and rigor of events. Other key positions were filled yesterday. I am submitting a further list to the king tonight. I hope to complete the appointment of principal ministers during tomorrow.

Ⓒ<u>**The appointment of other ministers usually takes a little longer**</u>. I trust when Parliament meets again this part of my task will be completed and that the administration will be complete in all respects. I considered it in the public interest to suggest to the Speaker that the House should be summoned today. At the end of today's proceedings, the adjournment of the House will be proposed until May 21 with provision for earlier meeting if need be. Business for that will be notified to MPs at the earliest opportunity.

I now invite the House by a resolution to record its approval of the steps taken and declare its confidence in the new government.

1. 위 글의 제목으로 가장 적절한 것은?

① Respectable Members of the House
② The Majesty of the England
③ A New Government
④ the Importance of Unity
⑤ Parliament and Prime Minister

2. 위 글의 밑줄 친 Ⓐ와 관계가 <u>없는</u> 것은?

① a new adminstration
② the most important par of this task
③ A war cabinet
④ the extreme urgency and rigor of events
⑤ Parliament

3. 위 글의 밑줄 친 Ⓑ의 구성요건과 관계가 <u>없는</u> 것은?

① 5명으로 구성되었다.
② 다른 야당과 협력하여 구성되었다.
③ 어렵고 힘든 시기에 협력을 기대한다.
④ 의회의 협력이 끌어들이기에 아직 역부족이다.
⑤ 작가는 의회의 지지를 호소하고 있다.

4. 위 글에서 밑줄 친 Ⓒ의 원인은 무엇인가?

① Because of the approval by the House
② No proposal from the Majesty
③ The House being adjourned now
④ The public not wanting to wage the war
⑤ No enough reasons in the political system

5. 위 글과 일치하지 <u>않은</u> 것은?

① A new adminstration will be planned on the basis of widest inclusion.
② It is very seriously urgent and rigorous.
③ The addressor hopes to complete all appointment for today.
④ The House representatives will be summoned at any time.
⑤ The support by the House is absolutely necessary.

✳ 다음 글을 읽고 물음에 답하시오. [6~10]

Ⓐ**The resolution:**

"That this House welcomes the formation of a government representing the united and inflexible resolve of the nation to prosecute the war with Germany to a victorious conclusion."

To form an administration of this scale and complexity is a serious undertaking in itself. But we are in the preliminary phase of one of the greatest battles in history. We are in action at many other points-in Norway and in Holland-and we have to be prepared in the Mediterranean. The air battle is continuing, and many preparations have to be made here at home.

In this crisis I think I may be pardoned if I do not address the House at any length today, and I hope that any of my friends and colleagues or former colleagues who are affected by the political reconstruction will make all allowances _____ with which it has been necessary to act.

I say to the House as I said to ministers who have joined this government, I have nothing to offer but blood, toil, tears, and sweat. We have before us an ordeal of the most grievous kind. We have before us many, many months of struggle and suffering.

You ask, what is our policy? I say it is to wage war by land, sea, and air. War with all our might and with all the strength God has given us, and to wage war against a monstrous tyranny never surpassed in the dark and lamentable catalogue of human crime. That is our policy.

You ask, what is our aim? I can answer in one word. It is victory. Victory at all costs - Victory in spite of all terrors - Victory, however long and hard the road may be, for without victory there is no survival.

Let that be realized. No survival for the British Empire, no survival for all that the British Empire has stood for, no survival for the urge, the impulse of the ages, that mankind shall move forward toward his goal.

I take up my task in buoyancy and hope. I feel sure that our cause will not be suffered to fail among men. I feel entitled at this juncture, at this time, to claim the aid of all and to say, "Come then, let us go forward together with our united strength."

6. 위 글의 분위기로 가장 적절한 것은?

① decisive   ② feeble
③ skeptical   ④ depressed
⑤ unfeasible

7. 위 글의 밑줄 친 Ⓐ에 포함되지 <u>않은</u> 것은?

① It is to execute the war.
② It is to consist of an adminstration.
③ It is to make all allowances to all people.
④ It is to show the strong determination.
⑤ It is to suggest there might be an alternative to compromise with the enemy.

8. 위 글 빈칸에 적절한 표현은?

① for the confrontation with the war
② for any lack of ceremony
③ for any welcoming hospitality
④ for the delay of my address
⑤ for the coming great victory

9. 위 글에 따르면 영국의 정책과 목표는 무엇인가?

① to fight against the enemy and contribute to the world peace
② to guarantee the security and support the House
③ to obtain a victory and form a new government
④ to wage war and win a victory
⑤ to survive from the war and punish the war criminals

10. 위 글과 일치하지 <u>않은</u> 것은?

① 독일과의 전쟁에서 승리를 쟁취하기 위한 것이다.
② 우리는 여러 지역에서 전쟁을 치르고 있다.
③ 하원 의원들에게 양해를 구하고 있다.
④ 비록 길고 험난한 전쟁일지라고, 곧 끝날 것을 확신한다.
⑤ 영국제국의 생존은 영원할 것을 확신한다.

1. ③	2. ⑤	3. ④	4. ①	5. ③
6. ①	7. ⑤	8. ②	9. ④	10. ④

The Black Man's History

by Malcolm X

[난이도 ★★★☆☆]

동영상 강좌 http://youtu.be/8JZF1YSepDw

I want to thank Allah for coming and giving to us ①our leader and teacher here in America, The Honorable Elijah Muhammad. I want to thank Brother Benjamin at the outset ②for doing a wonderful job of opening up our eyes and giving us ③a good preliminary basic understanding of ④the means and the objectives of The Honorable Elijah Muhammad, and also I am thankful to Allah for ⑤bringing so many people out here tonight, especially just before Christmas. You know, it's next to a miracle when you get this many of our people together ⑥so close to Christmas ⑦interested in anything whatsoever that's serious. And actually ⑧what this shows is the change that's taking place among the so-called Negroes ⑨not only here in New York but throughout the entire world. Today dark mankind is waking up and is undertaking a new type of thinking, and ⑩it is this new type of thinking that is creating new approaches and new reactions that ⑪make it almost impossible to figure out what the black man is going to do next, and by black man we mean, as we are taught by The Honorable Elijah Muhammad, we include all those who are nonwhite. He teaches us ⑫that black is the basic color, that black is the foundation or the basis of all colors. And all of our people who ⑬have not yet become white are still black, or at least part of the Black Nation, and here at Muhammad's Mosque when you hear us using the term "black" we mean everybody who's here, regardless of your complexion.

🖎 문법분석

① our leader and teacher와 The Honorable Elijah Muhammad는 동격.
② for doing ~and giving ~: and로 연결됨.
③ 훌륭한 예비 기본 지식
④ 수단과 방법
⑤ bring A out B: A를 B로 모이게 하다.
⑥ (when it is so) ~: 시간이 가까워짐에 따라
⑦ out people (who are) interested in ~으로 구성된 문장.
⑧ what this shows[주어, 명사절]: 이런 현상의 보여주는 것.
⑨ not only A but (also) B: A뿐만 아니라 B인
⑩ [강조용법] it is A that B: B라 하는 것은 바로 A이다.
⑪ make A[가목적어] B to [진목적어] ~[5형식]: 이해하는 것을 거의 불가능하게 만들다.
⑫ He teaches us A, B, or C: 그는 우리에게 검정은 기본이 되는 색상, 검은색이 모든 색의 기초이자 근본이라는 것을 가리킨다.
⑬ 아직 ~가 아닌

📖 본문해석

I want to thank Allah for coming and giving to us our leader and teacher here in America, The Honorable Elijah Muhammad(저는 알라신께 미국인 이곳에서 우리의 지도자이자 스승인, 엘리자흐 모하메드공을 보내주신 것에 감사드리고 싶습니다). I want to thank Brother Benjamin at the outset for doing a wonderful job of opening up our eyes(저는 우리의 눈을 뜨게 위대한 일을 하신 벤자민 형제에게 처음 감사드리고 싶습니다) and giving us a good preliminary basic understanding of the means and the objectives of The Honorable Elijah Muhammad(그리고 우리에게 영예로운 엘리자흐 모하메드공의 수단과 방법의 예비 근본 지식을 주신데 대해서도 감사드리고 싶습니다), and also I am thankful to Allah for bringing so many people out here tonight, especially just before Christmas(그리고 또한 특히 크리스마스 전야에 너무나 많은 사람들을 이곳에 모이게 한 것에 대해서도 알라신께 감사드립니다). You know(여러분도 알듯이), it's next to a miracle(그것은 기적을 일으킵니다.) when you get this many of our people together so close to Christmas interested in anything whatsoever that's serious(여러분이 이렇게 많은 우리 동포들을 신중한 무언가에 흥미를 주는 크리스마스에 가까운 시점에 모이게 할 때). And actually what this shows is the change that's taking place among the so-called Negroes not only here in New York but throughout the entire world(그리고 실제로 이런 현상이 보여주는 것은 이곳 뉴욕 여기뿐만 아니라 전 세계에 이른바 검둥이(흑인)들 사이에 일어나는 변화입니다). Today dark mankind is waking up and is undertaking a new type of thinking(오늘날 검은 인종은 잠에서 깨어나 새로운 유형의 사고를 받아드리고 있습니다), and it is this new type of thinking that is creating new approaches and new reactions that make it almost impossible to figure out what the black man is going to do next(그리고 이것은 바로 흑인들이 옆에서 할 것을 이해할 수 없게 하는 새로운 해법과 반응을 창조하는 새로운 유형의 사고를 말합니다), and by black man we mean, as we are taught by The Honorable Elijah Muhammad(우리가 의미하는 흑인에 의해, 이른바 엘리자흐 모하메드공에 의해, 우리가 이곳에서 배워오듯), we include all those who are nonwhite(우리는 백인이 아닌 모든 사람들을 포함합니다). He teaches us that black is the basic color, that black is the foundation or the basis of all colors(그는 우리에게 검은색은 기본색상이고 모든 색상의 기본이자 기초라는 사실을 가리켜 줍니다). And all of our people who have not yet become white are still black(그리고 아직 흰색이 되지 않은 우리 모두는 여전히 검은색이거나), or at least part of the Black Nation(적어도 검은색 국가의 일부이거나), and here at Muhammad's Mosque(이곳 사원에서) when you hear us using the term "black"(당신이 우리가 검은색이란 용어를 사용하는 것을 들을 때) we mean everybody who's here, regardless of your complexion(우리는 여러분의 외모와 무관하게 여기에 모든 사람들을 의미합니다).

📖 단어분석

† **outset** [áutsèt] n. (the ~) 착수; 시작, 최초. / ‡ **preliminary** [prilímənèri / -nəri] a. ① 예비의, 준비의; 임시의; 시초의. ② 서문의. / ‡ **honorable** [ánərəbəl / ɔ́n-] a. ① 명예 있는, 명예로운; 명예를 손상치 않는. / ‡ **means** [miːnz] n. pl. ①「단·복수취급」수단, 방법; 기관. ②「복수취급」자력(資力), 재산, 수입. / † **objective** [əbdʒéktiv] n. ① 목적, 목표. [SYN.] ⇨ PURPOSE. / † **whatsoever** [hwàtsouévər] pron., a.「강의어(한자어)」= WHATEVER. / ‡ **miracle** [mírəkəl] n. ① 기적. / ‡ **serious** [síəriəs] a. ① 진지한, 정색을 한 (사람·표정 따위). ② 중대한, 심상치 않은(important) / take place: 일어나다, 발생하다. / ‡ **throughout** [θruːáut] prep. ①「시간」~을 통하여 ②「장소」~의 전체에 걸쳐서 / **type** [taip] n. ① a) 형(型), 타입, 유형. b) C,U 전형 모범, 견본, 표본. c)「생물」형, 유형 / ‡ **entire** [entáiər] a. ① 전체[전부]의. ② 완전한. [SYN.] ⇨ COMPLETE. ③ 흠 없는, 온전한. / ‡

undertake [ʌ̀ndərtéik] v. (-took [-túk]; -taken [-téikən]) —vt. ① 떠맡다, ~의 책임을 지다. ② 『~+목/ +to do/ +that 절』 (~할) 의무를 지다, 약속하다; 보증하다, 책임지고 말하다, 장담(壯談)하다, 단언하다 (affirm). / ǂ **approach** [əpróutʃ] n. ① U 가까워짐, 접근(of; to); 가까이함. ② 해결 방법. / ǂ **reaction** [riː ǽkʃ-ən] n. U,C ① 반응 ② 반항 ③ (정치상의) 반동, 복고(운동) / ǂ **foundation** [faundéiʃ-ən] n. ① U 창설, 설립. ② C (종종 pl.) 기초, 토대. [SYN.] ⇨ BASE. ③ U 근거. ④ C (재단 등의) 기본금, 유지 기금. / † **complexion** [kəmplékʃən] n. ① 피부색, 얼굴의 윤기 ② (사태의) 외관, 모양; 양상, 국면. ③ 기질; 성격; (중세(中世) 생리학에서 hot, cold, moist, dry의 조합에 의해 정해지는) 체질.

✻ 다음을 읽고 물음에 답하시오. [1~5]

I want to thank Allah for coming and giving to us our leader and teacher here in America, The Honorable Elijah Muhammad. I want to thank Brother Benjamin at the outset for doing a wonderful job of opening up our eyes and giving us a good preliminary basic understanding of the means and the objection/objectives of The Honorable Elijah Muhammad, and also I am thankful to Allah for bringing so many people out here tonight, especially just before Christmas. You know, Ⓐit's next to a miracle when you get this many of our people together so close to Christmas interested in anything whatsoever that's serious. And actually what this shows is the change that's taking place among the so-called Negroes not only here in New York but throughout the entire world. Today dark mankind _____ a new type of thinking, and it is this new type of thinking that is creating new approaches and new reactions that make it/them almost impossible to figure out what the black man is going to do next, and by black man we mean, as we are taught by The Honorable Elijah Muhammad, we include all those who are nonwhite. He teaches us that black is the basic color, that black is the foundation or the basis of all colors. And all of our people who have not yet become white are still black, or at least part of the Black Nation, and here at Muhammad's Mosque

when you hear us using the term "black" we mean everybody who's here, in regard to/regardless of your complexion.

1. 위 글의 주제로 가장 적절한 것은?

① The black should thank all of the teachers and mentors.
② It's necessary for the black to get together.
③ A new type of thinking will give the black waking-up from their complex.
④ The miracle will occur whenever we try to find out it.
⑤ Don't forget the day like Christmas.

2. 위 글에서 밑줄 친 Ⓐit가 가리키는 것은?

① the means and the objectives
② Allah
③ the black man
④ a good preliminary basic understanding
⑤ a wonderful job

3. 위 글에서 밑줄 친 빈칸에 가장 적절한 표현은?

① excludes and modifies
② is creating and spreading
③ is trying to understand, but is unconscious of
④ is memorizing
⑤ is waking up and is undertaking

4. 위 글에서 네모상자 안의 적절한 단어는?

① objection　　it　　　in regard to
② objection　　them　　regardless of
③ objectives　　it　　　regardless of
④ objectives　　them　　in regard to
⑤ objectives　　it　　　in regard to

5. 위 글과 일치하지 <u>않은</u> 것은?

① 작가는 엘리자흐 모하메드공과 벤자민 형제에게 감사를 전하고 있다.
② 작가는 수단과 방법의 예비 근본 지식을 배우게 되었다.
③ 기적은 우리 바로 곁에서 일어난다.
④ 새로운 해법과 반응은 흑인들이 다음에 할 일을 이해하는 것을 가능하게 하는 것이다.
⑤ 검은색은 기본색상이고 모든 색상의 기본이다.

동영상 강좌 http://youtu.be/H−GQ−tRHqbQ

6.

> I want to thank Allah for _____ to us our leader and teacher here in America, The Honorable Elijah Muhammad.

① coming and inviting
② addressing and making
③ speaking and teaching
④ coming and giving

7.

> I want to thank Brother Benjamin at the _____ for doing a wonderful job of opening up our eyes and giving us a good preliminary basic understanding of the means and the objectives of The Honorable Elijah Muhammad, and also I am thankful to Allah for bringing so many people out here tonight, especially just before Christmas.

① place　　　　② final
③ time　　　　④ outset

8.

> You know, it's next to a miracle when you get this many of our people together so close to Christmas _____ in anything whatsoever that's serious.

① interested　　　② interesting
③ being interested　④ be interesting

9.

> And actually what this shows is the _____ that's taking place among the so-called Negroes not only here in New York but throughout the entire world.

① collision　　　② change
③ recession　　　④ discrimination

10.

Today dark mankind is waking up and is undertaking a new type of thinking, and it is this new type of thinking that is creating new _____ and new reactions that make it almost impossible to figure out what the black man is going to do next, and by black man we mean, as we are taught by The Honorable Elijah Muhammad, we include all those who are nonwhite.

① revolution   ② success

③ approaches   ④ inventiveness

11.

He teaches us that black is the basic color, that black is the _____ or the basis of all colors.

① spectrum   ② foundation

③ configuration   ④ combination

12.

And all of our people who _____ become white are still black, or at least part of the Black Nation, and here at Muhammad's Mosque when you hear us using the term "black" we mean everybody who's here, regardless of your complexion.

① have   ② have had

③ have not yet   ④ would have

1. ③	2. ②	3. ⑤	4. ③	5. ④
6. ④	7. ④	8. ①	9. ②	10. ③
11. ②	12. ③			

동영상 강좌 http://youtu.be/g9il3C_RLUY

If you're here at the Mosque you're black, because ①the only ticket you need to get into Muhammad's Mosque is to be black. So if you got in you know you're black. You ②may not have known that you were black before you came here. In fact, ③very few of our people really look upon themselves as being black. ④They think of themselves as practically everything else on the color spectrum except black. And ⑤no matter how dark one of our people may be, you rarely hear him call himself black. But ⑥now that The Honorable Elijah Muhammad has been teaching among the so-called Negroes, ⑦you find our people of all complexions going around bragging that "I'm a black man." This shows you that a new teaching is taking place and there is new thinking among the so-called Negroes. ⑧Yet just yesterday you would have to admit that it was very difficult to get our people to ⑨refer to themselves as black. Now all of a sudden our people of all complexions ⑩are not apologizing for being black but bragging about being black. So there's a new thinking all over America among the so-called Negroes. And ⑪the one who is actually the author of this new thinking is The Honorable Elijah Muhammad. ⑫It is what he is teaching that is making our people, for the first time, proud to be black, and what's most important of all, for the first time ⑬it makes our people want to know more about black, want to know why black is good, or what there is about black that is good.

I ⑭might stop right here to point out that some of you may say, "I came up here to listen to some religion about Islam, but now all I hear you talk about is black." We don't ⑮separate our color from our religion. The white man doesn't. The white man never has separated Christianity from white, ⑯nor has he separated the white man from Christianity. When you hear the white man bragging, "I'm a Christian," he's bragging about being a white man. ⑰Then you have the Negro. When he is bragging about being a Christian, he's bragging that he's a white man, or he wants to be white, and usually ⑱those Negroes who brag like that, I think you have to agree, in their songs and the things the sing in church, they show that they have a greater desire to be white than anything else. My mother was a Christian and my father was a Christian and I ⑲used to hear them when I was a little child sing the song "Wash Me White As Snow." My father was a black man and my mother was a black woman, ⑳but yet the songs that they sang in their church were designed to fill their hearts with the desire to be white. So may people, especially our people, get resentful when they hear me say something like this. But ㉑rather than get resentful ㉒all they have to do is think back on many of the songs and much of the teachings and the doctrines that they were taught while they were going to church and they'll have to agree that ㉓it was all designed to make us look down on black and up at white.

📎 문법분석

① the only ticket (you need): need의 목적어인 the only ticket / is to be black: be to의 용법 의무, 강제

② may have + 과거분사: (과거추측) 몰랐을 것이다.

③ [부분부정] 거의 ～하지 않은

④ think of A as B: A를 B로 생각하다.

⑤ [양보절] 비록 ～일지라도: 비록 우리 사람들(여러분)이 검은 피부를 갖고 있을지라도.

⑥ [접속사] ～이니깐

⑦ [5형식문장] find A(our people of all complexions) B(going around bragging): 모든 얼굴모습의 여러분이 ～을 자랑하며 돌아다니는 것을 알게 됩니다.

⑧ 그러나 어제만 하더라도. / [가정법 과거] would ～였을 것이다.

⑨ refer to A as B: A를 B로서 언급하다.

⑩ not A but B: A가 아닌 B인

⑪ the one[그 사람] who[주격관계대명사] is ～: 이 새로운 사고의 실적인 창시자는 바로 ～이다.

⑫ [강조용법] It is what he is teaching[강조] that ～: ～은 바로 'he is teaching(그의 가르침이다)'.

⑬ it makes our people A(want to know ～), B(want to know ～), or (want to know) what there ～.

⑭ ～하려하다.

⑮ separate A from B: A를 B로부터 분리시키다.

⑯ [도치문] nor = or he has not separated

⑰ 그러므로 당신은 검둥이인 것입니다.

⑱ those Negroes와 they는 동격임.

⑲ (과거에) ～하곤 했다.

⑳ 하지만 이제 ～라는 사실을 알게 되었다 것을 암시함.

㉑ ～라기 보다는

㉒ all (they have to do): 그들이 할 의무는.

㉓ 그 모든 것은 ～로 고안된 것이다.

📎 본문해석

If you're here at the Mosque you're black(만일 여러분이 이곳 사원에 있으면, 당신은 흑인입니다), because the only ticket you need to get into Muhammad's Mosque is to be black(왜냐하면 당신이 이 사원으로 들어오기 위해 필요한 유일한 티켓은 흑인을 위한 것이기 때문입니다). So if you got in you know you're black(그래서 당신이 들어왔다면, 당신은 흑인입니다). You may not have known that you were black before you came here(당신은 이곳에 오기 전, 당신이 흑인이라는 것을 몰랐을 것입니다). In fact, very few of our people really look upon themselves as being black(사실, 우리들 중 누구도 자신을 거의 흑인으로 바라보진 않습니다). They think of themselves as practically everything else on the color spectrum except black(그들은 검은색을 제외한 색상 범위에서 실제로 다른 색으로서 자신들을 생각합니다). And no matter how dark one of our people may be(그리고 우리들 중 한분이 비록 검은색이라 하더라도), you rarely hear him call himself black(당신은 그가 자신을 검은색으로 부르는 것을 거의 듣지 못합니다). But now that The Honorable Elijah Muhammad has been teaching among the so-called Negroes(그러나 엘리자흐 모하메드공 이른바 검둥이들 사이에서 가르침을 내리고 있으므로), you find our people of all complexions going around bragging that "I'm a black man."(여러분은 이

211

제야 다양한 피부색의 우리 사람들이 "나는 흑인이야"라고 외쳐대며 다닌다는 것을 알았을 겁니다). This shows you that a new teaching is taking place and there is new thinking among the so-called Negroes(이것은 당신에게 새로운 방식의 교육이 이루어지고 흑인들 사이에서 새로운 사상이 일어나고 있다는 것을 보여 줍니다). Yet just yesterday you would have to admit that it was very difficult to get our people to refer to themselves as black(그러나 어제만 해도 당신은 우리 사람들이 자신을 검은색으로 언급하도록 하는 것이 참 힘들었다고 인정해야만 했을 것입니다). Now all of a sudden(지금 갑자기) our people of all complexions are not apologizing for being black but bragging about being black(모든 피부색의 우리 사람들이 검은색을 변명하지 않고 오히려 자랑하고 있습니다). So there's a new thinking all over America among the so-called Negroes(그리하여 미전역에서 이른바 검둥이들 사이에 새로운 생각이 도래했습니다). And the one who is actually the author of this new thinking is The Honorable Elijah Muhammad(이 새로운 사상의 창시자는 바로 엘리자흐 모하메드공이십니다). It is what he is teaching that is making our people, for the first time, proud to be black(처음으로 우리 흑인들이 검은색에 자부심을 느끼게 하는 것은 바로 그의 가르침입니다), and what's most important of all(가장 중요한 것은), for the first time(처음) it makes our people want to know more about black(그것은 우리 흑인들이 검은색에 관해 더 많은 것을 알고 싶어 하도록 만드는 것이고), want to know why black is good(검은색이 좋은 이유를 알고 싶어 하는 것이고), or what there is about black that is good(또한 검은색에 관한 것은 좋은 것이다 라는 것을).

I might stop right here to point out (저는 ~을 정리하면서 이만 마치겠습니다)that some of you may say(여러분 중 몇몇은 말합니다), "I came up here to listen to some religion about Islam(내가 이곳에 온 것은 이슬람종교에 관한 것을 들으러 왔지), but now all I hear you talk about is black."(당신 얘기는 오로지 검은색에 관한 것입니다). We don't separate our color from our religion(저는 우리의 피부색을 우리의 종교와 분리하지 않습니다). The white man doesn't(백인도 그렇습니다). The white man never has separated Christianity from white(백인도 기독교를 흰색과 분리하지 않습니다), nor has he separated the white man from Christianity(또한 백인은 백인을 기독교와도 분리하지 않습니다). When you hear the white man bragging, "I'm a Christian,"(당신이 백인이 "난 기독교인이다."라고 자랑하는 것을 들을 때), he's bragging about being a white man(그는 백인이라는 것을 자랑하고 있는 것입니다). Then you have the Negro(그때 당신은 검둥이를 갖고 있을 뿐입니다). When he is bragging about being a Christian(그가 기독교인이라는 것에 관해 자랑하고 있을 때), he's bragging that he's a white man(그는 자신이 백인이라는 것을 자랑하고 있거나), or he wants to be white(그가 백인이 되고 싶어 한다는 것과), and usually those Negroes who brag like that, I think you have to agree, in their songs and the things the sing in church(제 생각에 당신이 동의 해야만 하는, 그들의 노래와 교회의 찬송가 속에서, 보통 그것과 같은 것을 자랑하는 검둥이인), they show(그들은 보여주고 있는 것입니다) that they have a greater desire to be white than anything else(그들은 다른 것 보단 백인이 되기 위한 더 큰 욕심을 갖고 있다는 것을). My mother was a Christian and my father was a Christian(저희 부모님은 두 분 모두 기독교인입니다) and I used to hear them when I was a little child sing the song "Wash Me White As Snow."(제가 어린 시절에 그들이 "저를 눈처럼 하야케 나를 씻어 달라"는 노랠 듣곤 했습니다) My father was a black man and my mother was a black woman(두 분 다 흑인이십니다), but yet the songs that they sang in their church were designed to fill their hearts with the desire to be white(그러나 이제 그분들이 교회에서 불렀던 노래들은 자신들의 가슴을 백인이 되고자하는 욕심으로 가득 채우고자 고안된 것이었음을 이제 알았습니다). So may people, especially our people, get resentful when they hear me say something like this(그리하여 특히 우리와 같은 흑인들은 제가 이것과 같은 것을 말하

는 것을 듣는다면 분개할 것 같습니다). But rather than get resentful(그러나 화를 내기 보다는) all they have to do(그들이 해야만 하는 모든 일은) is think back on many of the songs and much of the teachings and the doctrines that they were taught(그들이 배웠던 많은 그 노래들과 많은 가르침과 교리를 되돌아보는 것입니다) while they were going to church(교회에 다니는 동안) and they'll have to agree that it was all designed to make us look down on black and up at white(그리고 그것은 모두다 우리로 하여금 흑인을 깔보게 하고 백인을 우러러 보게 하는 것으로 교묘히 고안되었다는 사실을 그들은 알아야만 할 것입니다).

🐟 단어분석

- **mosque** [mɑsk / mɔsk] n. 이슬람교 성원(聖院), 회교 사원(回敎寺院). / †**practical** [prǽktikəl] a. ① 실제의, 실제상의; 실리상의. [cf.] speculative, theoretical. 실질적인. [SYN.] ⇨ REAL. / †**spectrum** [spéktrəm]n. (pl. -tra [-trə], ～s) 〖물리〗 스펙트럼, 분광; (눈의) 잔상(殘像); (변동이 있는 것의) 범위, 연속체; / †**brag** [bræg] v. (-gg-) ―vi. 『～/ +전+명』 자랑하다, 허풍떨다(of; about). ―vt. ～을 자랑하다. / ‡**refer** [rifə́ː r]v. (-rr-) ―vi. ① 관계하다, 관련하다(to); (규칙 따위가) 적용되다. ②『+전+명』 조회[문의]하다, 참고로 하다(to). / ‡**apologize** [əpálədʒàiz / əpɔ́l-] vi. ①『～/ +전+명』 사죄하다, 사과하다. ② 변명[해명]하다. / ‡**author** [ɔ́ː θər] n. ① 저자, 작가, 저술가(보통 여성도 포함). ② (저자의) 저작(물), 작품. / point ―vi. ①『+전+명』 가리키다(at; to). ②『+전+명』 지시하다, 시사하다(to). / ‡**separate** [sépərèit] v. ―vt. ① 잘라서 떼어 놓다, 분리하다, 가르다. ② 식별하다, 구별하다. / **Christian** [krístʃən] n. ① 기독교도; 그리스도의 가르침을 지키는 사람. / **resentful** [rizéntfəl] a. 분개한, 성 마른; 성 잘 내는. / ‡**doctrine** [dáktrin / dɔ́k-] n. ① 교의, 교리. ② 주의, (정치·종교·학문상의) 신조, 학설; 공식(외교)정책. / **look down on**: 멸시하다

동영상 강좌 http://youtu.be/1YuILkyG0g0

❋ 다음을 읽고 물음에 답하시오. [13~17]

If you're here at the Mosque you're black, because the only ticket you need to get into Muhammad's Mosque is to be black. So if you got in you know you're black. You may not have known that you were black before you came here. Ⓐ , very few of our people really look upon themselves as being black. They think of themselves as practically everything else on the color spectrum except black. And no matter how/what dark one of our people may be, you rarely hear him call himself black. But _____ Ⓑ _____ The Honorable Elijah Muhammad has been teaching among the so-called Negroes, you find our people of all complexions going/gone around bragging that "I'm a black man." This shows you that a new teaching is taking place and there is new thinking among the so-called Negroes. Yet just yesterday you would have to admit that it was very difficult to get our people to refer to themselves as black. Now all of a sudden our people of all complexions are not apologizing for being black but bragging about being black. So there's a new thinking all over America among the so-called Negroes. And the one who is actually the author of this new thinking is The Honorable Elijah Muhammad. It is what he is teaching that is making our people, for the first time, _____, and what's most important of all, for the first time it makes our people want to know more about black, want to know why black is good, or how/what there is about black that is good.

I might stop right here to point out that some of you may say, "I came up here to listen to some religion about Islam, but now all I hear you talk about is black." We don't separate our color from our religion. The white man doesn't. The white man never has separated Christianity from white, nor has he separated the white man from Christianity. When you hear the white man bragging, "I'm a Christian," he's bragging about being a white man. Then you have the Negro. When he is bragging about being a Christian, he's bragging that he's a white man, or he wants to be white, and usually those Negroes who brag like that, I think you have to agree, in their songs and the things the sing in church, they show that they have a greater desire to be white than anything else. My mother was a Christian and my father was a Christian and I used to hear them when I was a little child sing the song "Wash Me White As Snow." My father was a black man and my mother was a black woman, but yet the songs that they sang in their church were designed to fill their hearts with the desire to be white. So may people, especially our people, get resentful when they hear me say something like this. But rather than get resentful all they have to do is think back on many of the songs and much of the teachings and the doctrines that they were taught while they were going to church and they'll have to agree that it was all designed to make us look down on black and up at white.

13. 위 글의 주제로 가장 적절한 것은?

① The black should recognize their complexions as black, which gives them self-confidence.

② Let's try to find out what the songs in church mean.

③ If someone calls you black, you should get resentful.

④ The new thinking should happen in the white.

⑤ There are many ways to separate colors from our skin.

14. 위 글에서 네모상자 안의 적절한 단어는?

① how   going   how

② how   gone   what

③ what   gone   how

④ what   going   what

⑤ how   going   what

15. 위 글에서 빈칸에 가장 적절한 표현은?

① understandable to their selves

② afraid of being black

③ realize what they have to do

④ demonstrate their complexions

⑤ proud to be black

16. 위 글에서 빈칸 Ⓐ, Ⓑ에 적절한 것은?

① In fact   now that

② As a matter of fact   although

③ However   while

④ Meanwhile   because

⑤ On the other hand   as if

17. 위 글과 일치하지 <u>않은</u> 것은?

① 사원에 들어오기 전, 흑인들은 자신들의 실체를 깨닫는다.

② 엘리자흐 모하메드공은 새로운 사고의 가르침을 창시했다.

③ 흑인들 사이에 새로운 방식의 교육이 이루어지고 있다.

④ 검은색에 대한 자부심을 가져야만 한다.

⑤ 부모님들이 배운 노래에는 흑인들을 업신여기는 교활한 술책이 숨어있었다.

18.

If you're here at the Mosque you're black, because the only ticket you need to get into Muhammad's Mosque is to be black. So if you got in you know you're black. You _____ that you were black before you came here.

① should not have known

② may not have known

③ have not known

④ might have known

19.

In fact, very few of our people really look upon themselves as being black. They think of themselves as practically everything else on the color spectrum except black. And no matter how dark one of our people may be, you _____ hear him call himself black.

① hard   ② really

③ do   ④ rarely

The Black Man's History

by Malcolm X

20.

But now that The Honorable Elijah Muhammad has been teaching among the so-called Negroes, you find our people of all complexions going around _____ that "I'm a black man."

① bragging   ② hiding
③ confessing   ④ covering

21.

This shows you that a new teaching is taking place and there is new thinking among the so-called Negroes. Yet just yesterday you would have to _____ that it was very difficult to get our people to refer to themselves as black.

① reject   ② admit
③ demonstrate   ④ remind

22.

Now all of a sudden our people of all complexions are not _____ for being black but bragging about being black. So there's a new thinking all over America among the so-called Negroes.

① revealing   ② announcing
③ apologizing   ④ remembering

23.

And the one who is actually the author of this new thinking is The Honorable Elijah Muhammad. It is what he is teaching that is making our people, for the first time, proud to be black, and what's most important of all, for the first time it makes our people want to know more about black, want to know _____ black is good, or what there is about black that is good.

① what   ② how
③ because   ④ why

24.

I might stop right here to point out that some of you may say, "I came up here to listen to some religion about Islam, but now all I hear you talk about is black." We don't _____ our color from our religion. The white man doesn't.

① mix   ② separate
③ assemble   ④ look at

25.

The white man never has separated Christianity from white, _____ has he separated the white man from Christianity. When you hear the white man bragging, "I'm a Christian," he's bragging about being a white man.

① or   ② but
③ nor   ④ which

26.

Then you have the Negro. When he is bragging about being a Christian, he's bragging that he's a white man, or he wants to be white, and usually those Negroes who brag like that, I think you have to agree, in their songs and the things the sing in church, _____ show that they have a greater desire to be white than anything else.

① they   ② theirs

③ their   ④ themselves

27.

My mother was a Christian and my father was a Christian and I used to hear them when I was a little child sing the song "Wash Me White As Snow." My father was a black man and my mother was a black woman, but yet the songs that they sang in their church _____ to fill their hearts with the desire to be white.

① were designed   ② designed

③ had designed   ④ are designed

동영상 강좌 http://youtu.be/QNBGnvT0dlg

So ①the religion that we have, the religion of Islam, the religion that makes us Muslims, the religion that The Honorable Elijah Muhammad is teaching us here in America today, is designed to ②undo in our minds what the white man has done to us. It's designed to undo the type of brainwashing that we ③have had to undergo for four hundred years at the hands of the white man ④in order to bring us down to the level that we're at today. So when you hear us often refer to black in almost a boastful way, ⑤actually we're not boasting, we're speaking of it in a factual sense. All we're doing is telling the truth about our people. Whenever you exalt black, that's not propaganda; when you exalt white, that's propaganda. Yet ⑥no one can give biological evidence to show that black actually is the stronger or superior of ⑦the two ⑧if you want to make that kind of comparison. So never think ill of the person ⑨whom you hear representing The Honorable Elijah Muhammad ⑩if an overemphasis seems to be placed on the word black, but rather sit and analyze and try to get an understanding.

The Honorable Elijah Muhammad ⑪teaches us that of all the things that the black man, or any man for that matter, can study history is the best qualified to reward all research. You have to have a knowledge of history ⑫no matter what you are going to do; ⑬anything that you undertake you have to have a knowledge of history in order to be successful in ⑭it. ⑮The thing that has made the so-called Negro in America fail, more than any other thing, is your, my, lack of knowledge concerning history. We know ⑯less about history than anything else. There are black people in America ⑰who have mastered the mathematical sciences, have become professors and experts in physics, are able to toss sputniks out there in the atmosphere, out in space. They are masters in that field. We have black men who have mastered the field of medicine, we have black men who have mastered other fields, but ⑱very seldom do we have black men in America who have mastered the knowledge of the history of the black man himself. We have among our people those who are experts in every field, but ⑲seldom can you find one among us who is an expert on the history of the black man. And because of his lack of knowledge ⑳concerning the history of the black man, ㉑no matter how much he excels in the other sciences, he's always confined, he's always relegated to ㉒the same low rung of the ladder that the dumbest of our people are relegated to. And all of this stems from his lack of knowledge concerning history.

📎 문법분석

① [동격]

② undo (in our minds) what ~: undo의 목적어 what ~to us

③ [현재완료 계속] 4백 년 동안 감당해야만 했다.

④ in order to ~하기 위해서 / bring us down to ~으로 끌어 내리다. / the level that we're at today 현재 우리의 수준

⑤ actually we're not boasting, (but) we're ~. 사실 우리는 자랑하는 것이 아닌 사실에 입각하여 그것의 진실을 말하고 있는 것이다. it = the truth

⑥ no one = nobody(아무도 ~못하는)

⑦ the two = black and white

⑧ if[though] ~[양보절] 만일 당신의 비교를 하더라도

⑨ you hear the person[whom] representing ~: 목적어[the person]이 목적격 관계대명사가 됨.

⑩ if ~한다면[조건] / ~할지라도[양보]: 두 가지 경우 가능

⑪ teaches A[us] B[that절]: A에게 B를 가르치다 / of all the things ~can study[부사구] / history[주어]

⑫ [양보절] 당신이 무슨 일을 하든지.

⑬ [양보절] anything(no matter what you undertake) 용법.

⑭ it = anything

⑮ The thing[fail의 목적어] that ~fail, more than any other thing[다름 아닌], ~

⑯ less A than B: B보다 A가 덜한(못한).

⑰ who have mastered ~, (who) have become ~, (who) are able to ~.

⑱ [부분부정, 도치문] 우리는 거의 흑인을 배출하지 못하고 있습니다.

⑲ [부분부정, 도치문]

⑳ concerning = about

㉑ [양보절] 그가 과학분야에 뛰어나더라도.

㉒ the same A as[that절] B: B와 같은 A

📖 본문해석

So the religion that we have, the religion of Islam, the religion that makes us Muslims(그래서 우리가 갖고 있는 종교인 이슬람교이자 우리를 이슬람교도로 만드는 그 종교), the religion that The Honorable Elijah Muhammad is teaching us here in America today(오늘 엘리자흐 모하메드경이 이곳 미국에서 우리들에게 가르치는 종교는), is designed to undo in our minds what the white man has done to us(우리들 마음속에 백인들이 그동안 해왔던 것을 일깨워 줍니다). It's designed to undo the type of brainwashing that we have had to undergo for four hundred years(그것은 우리가 4백 년 동안 감당해야만 했던 세뇌를 회복시켜 주고자 창시된 것입니다.) at the hands of the white man in order to bring us down to the level that we're at today(오늘날 우리가 처해있는 수준으로 강등시키기 위해 백인들 손에서 놀아난). So when you hear us often refer to black in almost a boastful way(그래서 당신이 우리가 거의 자랑스럽게 흑인을 종종 언급하는 것을 들을 때), actually we're not boasting, we're speaking of it in a factual sense(사실 우리는 자랑하는 것이 아닌 사실에 입각하여 그것의 진실을 말하고 있는 것이다). All we're doing is telling the truth about our people(우리가 하는 것은 흑인에 관한 진실을 말하는 것이다). Whenever you exalt black, that's not propaganda; when you exalt white, that's propaganda(당신이 흑인을 칭찬할 때는 언제나, 과대선전은 아닙니다.; 백인을 외칠 때만이 그 과대선전인 것이다). Yet no one can give biological evidence to show that black actually is the stronger or superior of the two(그러나 아무도 흑인이 실제로 그 둘 중 더 강하다거나 우월하다는 것을 보여줄 생물학적 증거를 제시할 수는 없습니다.) if you want to make that kind of comparison(만일 당신이 비교하고 싶더라도). So never think ill of the person whom you hear representing The Honorable Elijah

Muhammad(당신이 누군가가 엘리자흐 모하메드경을 험담하는 소릴 듣더라도 그를 욕하지 마세요) if an overemphasis seems to be placed on the word black(흑인에 대한 지나친 험담이 있더라도), but rather sit and analyze and try to get an understanding(그럴 땐 차라리 앉아 분석하고 이해를 하도록 노력하세요).

The Honorable Elijah Muhammad teaches us (엘리자흐 모하메드경이 우리에게 가르침을 주고자하는 것은) that of all the things that the black man, or any man for that matter, can study(그 문제로 인해 흑인 또는 다른 인종이 연구할 수 있는 모든 것 중에) history is the best qualified to reward all research(역사가 모든 연구에 대한 보상을 주는 가장 적합한 분야입니다). You have to have a knowledge of history(당신은 역사에 관한 지식을 쌓아야만 합니다) no matter what you are going to do(당신이 무엇을 하든); anything that you undertake you have to have a knowledge of history in order to be successful in it(당신이 하는 일이 어떤 것이든, 당신이 하는 일에 성공하기 위해서는 역사에 관한 지식이 필수입니다). The thing that has made the so-called Negro in America fail(미국에서 이른바 검둥이를 실패 하도록 만든 것은), more than any other thing(다름 아닌), is your, my, lack of knowledge concerning history(당신과 나의 역사에 대한 지식부족 때문입니다). We know less about history than anything else(우리는 다른 무엇보다 역사에 관해 덜 알고 있습니다). There are black people in America who have mastered the mathematical sciences(수학의 대가인 흑인들), have become professors and experts in physics(물리학 교수와 전문가들), are able to toss sputniks out there in the atmosphere, out in space(대기 밖의 우주로 인공위성을 쏘아 올릴 수 있는). They are masters in that field(그들은 그 분야의 대가들 입니다). We have black men who have mastered the field of medicine(우리는 의학 분야의 대가를 갖고 있으며), we have black men who have mastered other fields(우리는 다른 분야의 흑인도 배출했습니다), but very seldom do we have black men in America who have mastered the knowledge of the history of the black man himself(그러나 바로 흑인 자신의 역사에 정통한 흑은 거의 갖지 못하고 있습니다). We have among our people those who are experts in every field(우리는 모든 분야의 전문가들을 갖고 있습니다), but seldom can you find one among us who is an expert on the history of the black man(그러나 흑인 역사 전문가는 우리 중에 찾기가 아주 어렵습니다). And because of his lack of knowledge concerning the history of the black man(그리고 흑인 역사의 지식부족으로 인해), no matter how much he excels in the other sciences(다른 분야에서 우월 할지라도), he's always confined(그는 늘 한계에 봉착합니다), he's always relegated to the same low rung of the ladder that the dumbest of our people are relegated to(가장 멍청한 흑인이 쫓겨난 것과 같은 승진의 낮은 단계에 늘 머물게 됩니다). And all of this stems from his lack of knowledge concerning history(그리고 이 모든 것은 역사인식 부족이 원인입니다).

🦪 단어분석

† **undo** [ʌndúː] v. (-did [-díd]; -done [-dʌ́n]) ─vt. ① (일단 해버린 것을) 원상태로 돌리다, 원상태로 하다, 취소하다. / **brainwash** [bréinwɑ̀ʃ, -wɔ̀(ː)ʃ] n., vt. 세뇌(하다), ∼을 강제로 사상 전향시키다. ㉒∼ing ─n. 세뇌, (강제적인) 사상 전향. / † **boastful** [bóustfəl] a. ① 자랑하는(of). ② 과장된(말 따위). / † **factual** [fǽktʃuəl] a. 사실의(actual). / **exalt** [igzɔ́ː lt] v. ─vt. 『∼+목/ +목+전+명』 (명예·품위 따위를) 높이다; (관직·신분 따위를) 올리다, 승진시키다. ─vi. 마음을 고양시키다. / ‡ **propaganda** [prɑ̀pəgǽndə / prɔ̀p-] n. ① U,C 「보통 무관사」 (주의·신념의) 선전; 주장. ② C 선전 기관[단체]. / **biological** 생물학의, 생물학적인. / ‡ **evidence** [évidəns] n. ① C 증거(of; for); U 〖법률〗증언. ② 형적, 흔적(sign)(of; for). / ‡ **comparison** [kəmpǽrisən] n. ① U,C 비교, 대조(of A with B). ② 필적하

는 것. / † **represent** [rèprizént] vt. ① 묘사하다, 그리다. ② 마음에 그리다, 상상하다. ③『+목+as보/ +목+(to be) 보/ +that절』말하다, 기술하다, 말로 표현하다, 주장[단언]하다. / **overemphasis** [òuvərémfəsis] n. 지나친 강조. / † **analyze**, 【영국】 -lyse [ǽnəlàiz] vt. 『〜+목 / +목+전+명』① 분석하다, 분해하다. ② (분석적으로) 검토하다. / **qualified** [kwáləfàid / kwɔ́l-] a. ① 자격 있는; 적임의, 적당한 (fitted)(for; to do); 면허의, 검정을 거친. [SYN.] ⇨ ABLE. / **sputnik** [spú: tnik, spʌ́t-] n. 【Russ.】 (=traveling companion) (종종 S-) 스푸트니크(옛소련의 인공 위성; 1호는 1957년 발사); 「일반적」 인공 위성. / † **toss** [tɔ: s, tɑs / tɔs] v. (p., pp. 〜ed [-t], (고어·시어) tost [-t]) —vt. ① (가볍게·아무렇게나) 던지다, (공을) 토스하다; 급히 던져 올리다. [SYN.] ⇨ THROW. ②『〜+목/ +목+부』(머리 따위를) 갑자기 쳐들다, 뒤로 젖히다(up)(경멸·초조 따위로). / † **atmosphere** [ǽtməsfiər] n. ① (the 〜) 대기; 천체를 둘러싼 가스체. ② C 분위기, 기분, 주위의 상황. / † **confine** [kənfáin] v. —vt. ①『+목+전+명』제한하다, 한하다(to; within). ② 들어박히게 하다(to). / **relegate** [réləgèit] vt. +목+전+명』① 퇴거를 명하다, 추방하다(out of); 지위를 떨어뜨리다, 좌천시키다(to; into). / **rung** [rʌŋ] n. (사닥다리의) 발을 딛는 가로장; (의자 따위의) 가로대; (수레의) 바퀴살(spoke); (사회적 지위 등의) 단계. / **dumbest**: 가장 멍청한 /

동영상 강좌 http://youtu.be/5XTNShmHTrU

※ 다음 글을 읽고 물음에 답하시오. [28~34]

So the religion that we have, the religion of Islam, the religion that makes us Muslims, the religion that The Honorable Elijah Muhammad is teaching us here in America today, is designed to undo in our minds what the white man has done to us. Ⓐ**It**'s designed to undo the type of brainwashing that we have had to undergo for four hundred years at the hands of Ⓑ**the white man** in order to bring us down to the level that we're at today. So when you hear us often refer to black in almost a boastful way, actually we're not boasting, we're speaking of it in a factual sense. All we're doing is telling the truth about our people. Whenever you exalt black, that's not propaganda; when you exalt white, that's propaganda. Yet no one can give biological evidence to show that black actually is the stronger or superior of the two if you want to make that kind of comparison. So never think ill of the person who/whom you hear representing The Honorable Elijah Muhammad if an overemphasis seems to be placed on the word black, but rather sit and analyze and try to get an understanding.

The Honorable Elijah Muhammad teaches us that of all the things that the black man, or any man for that matter, can study history is the best qualified to reward all research. You have to have a knowledge of history no matter how/what you are going to do; anything that you undertake you have to have a knowledge of history in order to be successful in Ⓒ**it**. The thing that has made the so-called Negro in America fail, more than any other thing, is your, my, lack of knowledge concerning history. We know less about history than anything else. There are black people in America who have mastered the mathematical sciences, have become professors and experts in physics, are able to toss sputniks out there in the atmosphere, out in space. They are masters in that field. We have black men who have mastered the field of medicine, we have black men who have mastered other fields, but very seldom do we have black men in America who have mastered the knowledge of the history of the black man himself. We have among our people those who are experts in every field, but seldom can you find one among us who is an expert on the history of the black man. And because of his lack of knowledge concerning the history of the black man, no matter how/what much he excels in the other sciences, he's always confined, he's always relegated to the same low rung of the ladder that the dumbest of our people are relegated to. And all of this stems form his lack of knowledge concerning history.

28. 위 글의 주제로 가장 적절한 것은?

① Every field has to be occupied by the black before the white.
② Sometimes overemphasis is necessary for overcoming our shortcomings.
③ The white should go far away from the black.
④ The unity between the black and the white is essential.
⑤ A lack of knowledge in history should be filled with.

29. 위 글에서 밑줄 친 Ⓐ가 가리키는 것은?

① Muslims
② Islam
③ Honorable Elijah Muhammad
④ America
⑤ what the white man has done to us

30. 위 글에서 밑줄 친 Ⓑ와 일치하는 것은?

① brainwashing　　② look up to
③ exalt black　　　④ propaganda
⑤ boasting

31. 위 글에서 작가의 심정은?

① resentful　　　② ignoring
③ disappointing　④ cool
⑤ indifferent

32. 위 글에서 밑줄 친 Ⓒ가 가리키는 것은?

① a knowledge　　② history
③ research　　　　④ matter
⑤ anything

33. 위 글에서 네모상자 안의 적절한 단어는?

① who　　　how　　　how
② whom　　what　　　what
③ who　　　how　　　how
④ whom　　what　　　how
⑤ who　　　how　　　what

34. 위 글과 일치하지 <u>않은</u> 것은?

① 우리의 종교인 이슬람교는 백인들이 해 왔던 세뇌교육에서 벗어나게 해준다.
② 사실에 입각하여 진실을 말하는 것이 중요하다.
③ 백인과 비교하여 볼 때, 흑인이 좀 더 우월하다.
④ 누군가가 흑인을 험담할 때, 냉정해져야만 한다.
⑤ 역사인식은 무엇보다 중요하다.

동영상 강좌 http://youtu.be/9aRgYbedW8Q

35.

So the religion that we have, the religion of Islam, the religion that makes us Muslims, the religion that The Honorable Elijah Muhammad is teaching us here in America today, _____ undo in our minds what the white man has done to us.

① designed to　　② is designed to
③ is designed　　 ④ designs

36.

It's designed to undo the type of brainwashing that we _____ undergo for four hundred years at the hands of the white man in order to bring us down to the level that we're at today.

① had to　　　　② have had to
③ had been to　　④ had had to

37.

So when you hear us often refer to black in almost a boastful way, _____ we're not boasting, we're speaking of it in a factual sense.

① actually　　　② barely
③ seldom　　　　④ fortunately

38.

All we're doing is telling the truth about our people. _____ you exalt black, that's not propaganda; when you exalt white, that's propaganda.

① Whatever　　　② Whenever
③ However　　　　④ Whatsoever

39.

Yet no one can give biological evidence to show that black actually is the stronger or superior of the two _____ you want to make that kind of comparison.

① if　　　　② as if
③ until　　④ because

40.

So never _____ the person whom you hear representing The Honorable Elijah Muhammad if an overemphasis seems to be placed on the word black, but rather sit and analyze and try to get an understanding.

① think well of
② think ill of
③ think bad of
④ think good of

41.

The Honorable Elijah Muhammad teaches us that of all the things that the black man, or any man for that matter, can study history _____ the best qualified to reward all research.

① are　　　　② having
③ being　　　④ is

42.

You have to have a knowledge of history _____ you are going to do; anything that you undertake you have to have a knowledge of history in order to be successful in it.

① no matter how
② no matter when
③ no matter what
④ no matter where

43.

The thing that has made the so-called Negro in America _____, more than any other thing, is your, my, lack of knowledge concerning history. We know less about history than anything else.

  ① succeed   ② develops
  ③ fail   ④ do

44.

There are black people in America who have mastered the mathematical sciences, have become professors and experts in physics, _____ sputniks out there in the atmosphere, out in space. They are masters in that field.

  ① able to toss
  ② is able to toss
  ③ being able to toss
  ④ are able to toss

45.

We have black men who have mastered the field of medicine, we have black men who have mastered other fields, but very _____ we have black men in America who have mastered the knowledge of the history of the black man himself.

  ① seldom   ② seldom do
  ③ seldom does   ④ seldom not

28. ⑤ 29. ② 30. ① 31. ④ 32. ⑤
33. ④ 34. ③ 35. ② 36. ② 37. ①
38. ② 39. ① 40. ② 41. ④ 42. ③
43. ③ 44. ④ 45. ②

동영상 강좌 http://youtu.be/SP2t7zbr6NY

①What made Dr. George Washington Carver a Negro scientist instead of a scientist? What made Paul Robeson a Negro actor instead of an actor? What made, or makes, Ralph Bunche a Negro statesman instead of a statesman? ②The only difference between Bunche and Carver and these others I just mentioned is they don't know the history of the black man. Bunche is an expert, and international politician, but he doesn't know himself, he doesn't know the history of the black people. He can be sent all over the world by America ③to solve problems for America, or to solve problems for other nations, but he can't solve problems for his own people in this country. Why? ④What is it that ties our people up in this way? The Honorable Elijah Muhammad says that it ⑤boils down to just one word - history.

When you study the history of Bunche, his history is different from the history of the black man who just came here from Africa. And ⑥if you notice, when Bunche was in Atlanta, Georgia, during the summer NAACP Convention, he was Jim Crowed, he was segregated, he ⑦ was not allowed to go in a hotel down there. Yet there are Africans who come here, ⑧black as night, who can go into those cracker hotels. Well, what is the difference between Bunche and one of them? The difference is Bunche doesn't know his history, and they, the Africans, ⑨ do know their history. They may come here out of the jungles, but they know their history. They may come here wearing sheets ⑩with their heads all wrapped up, but they know their history. You and I can come our of Harvard but we don't know our history. There's a basic difference in why we are treated ⑪as we are: one knows his history and one doesn't know his history! The American so-called Negro is a soldier who doesn't know his history; he's a servant who doesn't know his history; he's a graduate of Columbia, or Yale, or Harvard, or Tuskeegee, who doesn't know his history. ⑫He's confined, he's limited, he's held under the control and the jurisdiction of the white man who knows more about the history of the Negro than the Negro knows about himself. But when you and I wake up, as we're taught by The Honorable Elijah Muhammad, and ⑬learn our history, learn the history of our kind, and the history of the white kind, then the white man will be at a disadvantage and we'll be at an advantage, ⑭ the only thing that puts you and me at a disadvantage is our lack of knowledge concerning history. So one of the reasons, one of the missions, one of the objectives of The Honorable Elijah Muhammad here in America is ⑮not only to teach you and me the right religions but to teach you and me history.

🔖 문법분석

① [의문사, 주어]What + [동사]made + [목적어] Dr. ～[목적격보어]a Negro scientist [부사구, 멸시받는 과학자]instead of a scientist(일반 과학자)?

② [주어] The only different(그 유일한 차이점) ～these others (that) I just mentioned [동사]is [주격보

어] they don't ~.

③ [부사구, 목적] ~문제를 풀도록 하기 위해.

④ it = that은 동격 / tie A up: A를 속박[구속]하다.

⑤ boil down to: 요약하다.

⑥ if[as] you notice: 당신도 알아 차렸듯이.

⑦ be allowed to do: ~하도록 허락받다.

⑧ 밤처럼 새깜한 피부색의 흑인

⑨ [강조용법] do = really , very: 자신들의 역사를 진정 안다.

⑩ with + 신체의 일부 + 과거분사: 머리를 온통 싸매고.

⑪ 이처럼, 현재와 같이

⑫ confined(감금된), ~limited(제한된), ~held under(~아래에 놓여있는)

⑬ (as we) learn ~, (as we) learn ~,

⑭ 당신과 저를 곤경에 빠트리는 유일한 것은 바로

⑮ not only A, but (also) B: A뿐만 아니라 B도

📎 **본문해석**

What made Dr. George Washington Carver a Negro scientist instead of a scientist?(무엇이 조지 워싱턴 카버박사를 일반 과학자가 아닌 검둥이 박사로 만들었나? What made Paul Robeson a Negro actor instead of an actor?(무엇이 폴 로베슨을 일반 배우가 아닌 검둥이 배우로 만들었나?) What made, or makes, Ralph Bunche a Negro statesman instead of a statesman?(무엇이 라프 번치를 일반 정치인이 아닌 검둥이 정치인으로 만들었나?) The only difference between Bunche and Carver and these others I just mentioned(제가 언급한 번치, 카버 그리고 이 다른 분들의 유일한 차이점은) is they don't know the history of the black man(그들은 흑인 역사를 모른다는 것입니다). Bunche is an expert, and international politician, but he doesn't know himself(번치는 전문가이자 국제 정치인이지만, 그는 자신을 모른다는 것입니다), he doesn't know the history of the black people(그는 흑인 역사를 모릅니다). He can be sent all over the world by America to solve problems for America(그는 미국을 위한 문제를 해결하도록 전 세계로 파견됩니다), or to solve problems for other nations(다른 국가들의 문제를 해결하도록), but he can't solve problems for his own people in this country(그러나 그는 이 나라에서 자신의 동족인 흑인 문제를 풀 수 없습니다). Why(이유가 뭘까요)? What is it that ties our people up in this way(우리 흑인들을 이런 방식으로 속박하는 것은 무엇일까요)? The Honorable Elijah Muhammad says that it boils down to just one word - history(엘리자흐 모하매드경은 단지 한 개의 단어, 즉 역사로 요약합니다). When you study the history of Bunche(당신이 번치의 이력을 살펴보면), his history is different from the history of the black man who just came here from Africa(그의 이력은 아프리카에서 이곳으로 온 흑인들의 역사와 다릅니다). And if you notice(그리고 당신도 알아차렸듯이), when Bunche was in Atlanta, Georgia, during the summer NAACP Convention(번치가 하계 NAACP 총회기간동안 아틀란타 조지아에 있을 때), he was Jim Crowed, he was segregated, he was not allowed to go in a hotel down there(그는 짐 크로우드였고, 인종차별을 받았고 그곳 호텔에 숙박을 제지당했습니다). Yet there are Africans who come here, black as night, who can go into those cracker hotels(그러나 이곳에 오는 밤처럼 새까만 피부색의 아프리카인들이 있습니다. 그들은 그런 고급호텔에 들어갈 수 있습니다). Well, what is the difference between Bunche and one of them(음, 번치와 그들 중 한 사람과의 차이점은 무엇인가요)? The difference is Bunche doesn't know his history, and they, the Africans, do know their history(그 차이

점은 번치는 자신의 역사를 모른다는 것이고 아프리카에서 온 그들은 자신들의 역사를 안다는 것입니다). They may come here out of the jungles, but they know their history(그들은 밀림을 빠져나와 이곳에 오는 것 같지만 자신들의 역사는 알고 있습니다). They may come here wearing sheets with their heads all wrapped up(그들은 흰 천으로 머리를 온통 싸매고 이곳으로 옵니다), but they know their history(그러나 자신들의 역사를 알고 있습니다). You and I can come our of Harvard but we don't know our history(당신과 저는 하버드대학을 나올 수 있지만, 우리의 역사는 모릅니다). There's a basic difference in why we are treated as we are(왜 우리가 이처럼 취급받고 있는 이유엔 근본적인 차이점이 있기 때문입니다): one knows his history and one doesn't know his history!(자신의 역사를 아는 것과 모르는 차이점입니다) The American so-called Negro is a soldier who doesn't know his history(이른바 검둥이인 미국인은 자신의 역사를 모르는 병사입니다); he's a servant who doesn't know his history(그는 자신의 역사를 모르는 하인입니다); he's a graduate of Columbia, or Yale, or Harvard, or Tuskeegee, who doesn't know his history(그는 자신의 역사를 모르는 콜롬비아대, 예일대, 하버드대, 또는 터스키지대의 졸업생입니다). He's confined, he's limited(그는 감금되고 금지되고), he's held under the control and the jurisdiction of the white man who knows more about the history of the Negro than the Negro knows about himself(그는 그 검둥이가 자신에 관해 아는 것보다 검둥이의 역사를 더 많이 아는 백인의 통제와 사법권 아래에 억눌려 있습니다). But when you and I wake up(그러나 당신과 제가 깨어날 때), as we're taught by The Honorable Elijah Muhammad(엘리자흐 모하마드경에게 배우듯이), and learn our history(역사를 배우듯이), learn the history of our kind(우리 흑인의 역사를 배우듯이), and the history of the white kind(백인의 역사를 배우듯이), then the white man will be at a disadvantage(그때 백인은 곤경에 처할 것이고) and we'll be at an advantage(우리는 강점을 갖게 될 것입니다), the only thing that puts you and me at a disadvantage is our lack of knowledge concerning history(당신과 저를 곤경에 빠트리는 유일한 것은 바로 역사에 관한 부족함입니다). So one of the reasons, one of the missions, one of the objectives of The Honorable Elijah Muhammad here in America(그리하여 한 가지 이유, 한 가지 임무, 엘리자gm 모하마드경의 목표 중 하나는) is not only to teach you and me the right religions but to teach you and me history(단지 당신과 저에게 올바른 종교뿐만 아니라 역사를 가르치는 것입니다).

🔖 단어분석

- ⊹ **mention** [ménʃən] vt. 『~+목/ +목+전+명/ +that절』 말하다, ~에 언급하다, 얘기로 꺼내다, (~의 이름을) 들다(흔히 수동태로 쓰임). / ⊹ **statesman** [stéitsmən] n. (pl. -men [-mən]) 정치가 / ⊹ **expert** [ékspə: rt] n. ① 숙달자, 전문가, 숙련가, 달인, 명인(at; in; on). / ****tie** [tai] v. (p., pp. ~d; tying) —vt. ① 『~+목/ +목+부/ +목+전+명』 (끈·새끼로) 묶다, 매다, 잇다; 매어서[묶어서] 만들다. / boil down to 요약하다 / ⊹ **notice** [nóutis]vt. ① ~을 알아채다(perceive), ~을 인지하다; ~에 주의하다, ~을 유의하다. ② 『~+목/ +목+to do』【미국】 (아무에게) 통지[예고]하다; 통고하다. / **segregate** [ségrigèit]v. —vt. 분리[격리]하다(separate, isolate)(A from B); (어떤 인종·사회층)에 대하여 차별 대우를 하다; / ⊹ **cracker** [krǽkər] n. (영국구어) 대단한 것, 매우 기분 좋은 인물[물건] / ⊹ **sheet** [ʃi: t] n. ① 시트, (서적·인쇄물·편지·신문 따위의) 한 장. / ⊹ **wrap** [rǽp] v. (p., pp. ~ped [rǽpt], ~t [rǽpt]; ″ ~ping) —vt. ① 감싸다, 싸다; 포장하다(up; in). ② 『+목+전+명』 둘러싸다, 감다, 얽다 (about; around; round). / ⊹ **confine** [kənfáin] v. —vt. ① 『+목+전+명』 제한하다, 한하다(to; within). / ⊹ **jurisdiction** [dʒùərisdíkʃən] n. U ① 재판권, 사법권; 재판곤·할. ② 지배. / ⊹ **disadvantage** [dìsədvǽntidʒ, -vá: n-] n. ① C 불리, 불이익 ② U 손해, 손실, 불명예(to). /

❇ 다음 글을 읽고 물음에 답하시오. [46~52]

What made Dr. George Washington Carver a Negro scientist instead of a scientist? What made Paul Robeson a Negro actor instead of an actor? What made, or makes, Ⓐ **Ralph Bunche** a Negro statesman instead of a statesman? The only difference between Bunche and Carver and these others I just mentioned is they don't know the history of the black man. Bunche is an expert, and international politician, but he doesn't know himself, he doesn't know the history of the black people. He can ①**be sent** all over the world by America to solve problems for America, or to solve problems for other nations, but he can't solve problems for his own people in this country. Why? What is it that ties our people up in this way? The Honorable Elijah Muhammad says that it boils down to just one word-history.

When you study the history of Bunche, his history is different from the history of the black man who just came here from Africa. And if you notice, when Bunche was in Atlanta, Georgia, during the summer NAACP Convention, he was Jim Crowed, he was segregated, he was not allowed to go in a hotel down there. Yet there are Africans who come here, Ⓑ**black as night**, who can go into those cracker hotels. Well, what is the difference between Bunche and one of them? The difference is Bunche doesn't know his history, and they, the Africans, do know their history. They may come here ②**out of** the jungles, but they know their history. They may come here wearing sheets with their heads all wrapped up, but they know their history. You and I can come our of Harvard but we don't know our history. There's a ③ **basic** difference in why we are treated as we are: one knows his history and one doesn't know his history! The American so-called Negro is a Ⓒ**soldier** who doesn't know his history; he's a servant who doesn't know his history; he's a graduate of Columbia, or Yale, or Harvard, or Tuskeegee, who doesn't know his history. He's confined, he's limited, he's ④**held** under the control and the jurisdiction of the white man who knows more about the history of the Negro than the Negro knows about himself. But when you and I wake up, as we're taught by The Honorable Elijah Muhammad, and learn our history, learn the history of our kind, and the history of the white kind, then the white man will be at a disadvantage and we'll be at an advantage, the only thing that puts you and me at ⑤**an advantage** is our lack of knowledge concerning history. So one of the reasons, one of the missions, one of the objectives of The Honorable Elijah Muhammad here in America is only to teach you and me the right religions but to teach you and me history.

46. 위 글에서 제목으로 가장 적절한 것은?
① The history: we should know
② Some foolish Negros
③ Good educational background to be treated right
④ Solutions to American
⑤ Importance in School education

229

47. 위 글의 분위기로 가장 적절한 것은?

① theoretical
② contradictory
③ admirable
④ misunderstandable
⑤ unsolvable

48. 위 글에서 밑줄 친 Ⓐ와 일치하지 않은 것은?

① He was a Negro politician.
② He doesn't know of his own history of the black.
③ He is busy traveling around the world.
④ Not only can he solve his country's problems, but other countries.
⑤ He used to be segregated in other cities.

49. 위 글에 밑줄 친 Ⓑ가 의미하는 것은?

① as many black people as night stars
② unclear as much as night
③ dark skin as much as night
④ dark as much as night
⑤ as many as Africans

50. 위 글에 밑줄 친 Ⓒ가 의미하는 것은?

① who is tough and strong
② who fights well and defeats enemies
③ who is as a hero
④ who is indicated as a common person
⑤ who is just brave, not intelligent

51. 위 글에서 밑줄 친 ①~⑤ 중, 문맥상 어색한 것은?

①　　②　　③　　④　　⑤

52. 위 글과 일치하지 않은 것은?

① 예를 들어 독자의 이해를 쉽게 하였다.
② 정치인 벤치는 자신의 흑인 역사를 모르므로, 차별을 당한다.
③ 아프리카에서 온 사람들도 미국 흑인들과 같은 차별을 받는다.
④ 유수한 대학을 졸업한 흑인들 조차도 자신들의 역사를 모른다.
⑤ 흑인 역사를 배우는 순간, 백인보다 강점에 설 수 있다.

53.

What made Dr. George Washington Carver a Negro scientist instead of a scientist? What made Paul Robeson a Negro actor instead of an actor? What made, or makes, Ralph Bunche a Negro statesman instead of a statesman? The _____ between Bunche and Carver and these others I just mentioned is they don't know the history of the black man.

① only difference
② unique similarity
③ friendly companionship
④ knowledge

54.

Bunche is an expert, and international politician, but he doesn't know himself, he doesn't know the history of the black people. He can be sent all over the world by America to solve problems for America, or to solve problems for other nations, but he can't solve problems _____ in this country.

① for other country
② for his country
③ for his own people
④ for his organization

55.

Why? What is it that ties our people up in this way? The Honorable Elijah Muhammad says that it _____ just one word - history.

① exaggerates   ② boils down to
③ lengthens   ④ mentions

56.

_____ you study the history of Bunche, his history is different from the history of the black man who just came here from Africa. And if you notice, when Bunche was in Atlanta, Georgia, during the summer NAACP Convention, he was Jim Crowed, he was segregated, he was not allowed to go in a hotel down there.

① Though   ② However
③ When   ④ Because

57.

Yet there are Africans who come here, black as night, who can go into those cracker hotels. Well, what is the _____ between Bunche and one of them?

① expression   ② reputation
③ difference   ④ recognition

58.

They may come here out of the jungles, but they know their history. They may come here _____ sheets with their heads all wrapped up, but they know their history. You and I can come our of Harvard but we don't know our history.

① wear   ② be worn
③ wearing   ④ to wear

46. ① 47. ② 48. ④ 49. ③ 50. ⑤
51. ⑤ a disadvantage 52. ③ 53. ①
54. ③ 55. ② 56. ③ 57. ③ 58. ③

[난이도 ★★★☆☆]

동영상 강좌 http://youtu.be/RXAVeMjHoQ0

①Five score years ago, a great American, in whose symbolic shadow we stand signed the Emancipation Proclamation. This momentous decree ②came as a great beacon light of hope to millions of Negro slaves who had been seared in the flames of withering injustice. ③It came as a joyous daybreak to end the long night of captivity.

But one hundred years later, we must face ④the tragic fact that the Negro is still not free. One hundred years later, the life of the Negro is still sadly crippled by the manacles of segregation and the chains of discrimination. One hundred years later, the Negro ⑤lives on a lonely island of poverty in the midst of a vast ocean of material prosperity.

One hundred years later, the Negro is still languishing in the corners of American society and ⑥finds himself an exile in his own land. So we have come here today to dramatize an appalling condition.

In a sense we have come to our nation's capital ⑦to cash a check. When the architects of our republic wrote the magnificent words of the Constitution and the declaration of Independence, they were signing a promissory note to which every American was ⑧to fall heir. This note was ⑨a promise that all men would be guaranteed the inalienable rights of life, liberty, and the pursuit of happiness.

It is obvious today that America has defaulted on this promissory note insofar as her citizens of colour are concerned. Instead of honoring this sacred obligation, America has given the Negro people a bad check which has come back ⑩marked "insufficient funds." But we refuse to believe that the bank of justice is bankrupt. ⑪We refuse to believe that there are insufficient funds in the great vaults of opportunity of this nation. So we have come to cash this check -- a check that will give us upon demand the riches of freedom and the security of justice. We have also come to this hallowed spot to remind America of the fierce urgency of now. ⑫This is no time to engage in the luxury of cooling off or to take the tranquillising drug of gradualism. ⑬Now is the time to rise from the dark and desolate valley of segregation to the sunlit path of racial justice. Now is the time to open the doors of opportunity to all of God's children. ⑭Now is the time to lift our nation from the quick-sands of racial injustice to the solid rock of brotherhood.

🔖 문법분석

① score: 20년 - 5 scores: 100년 전 / whose = a great American's(한 위대한 미국인의: 소유격 관계대명사)

② came[과거] ～who had been seared[과거완료, 먼저 일어난 상황]

③ It = a great beacon light of hope[희망의 위대한 햇불] / came as: ～처럼 다가왔다.

④ [동격] the tragic fact that[동격의 접속사] + 절(～): ～라는 비극적인 사실

⑤ lives on island: 섬 위에서 살다.

⑥ find A B[5형식]: 스스로 유랑자임을 알다.

⑦ 빚을 받으러 오다.

⑧ fall heir to a promissory note: 약속어음을 받을 상속인이 되다.

⑨ [동격] a promise that ∼라는 약속

⑩ "지급불능"이라 적힌.

⑪ [강한 어조] 반드시 믿고 있다.

⑫ [긴박함] ∼할 시간이 없다.

⑬ [기회를 나타냄] 바로 지금이 기회이다.

⑭ [국가의 도약을 강조함]

📖 본문해석

Five score years ago(100년 전), **a great American**(한 위대한 미국인은), **in whose symbolic shadow we stand**(지금 우리가 서 있는 그의 상징적 그늘 아래에서) **signed the Emancipation Proclamation**(노예해방에 서명했습니다). **This momentous decree came as a great beacon light of hope to millions of Negro slaves**(이 중대한 선언은 ∼수백만 흑인노예들에게 희망의 위대한 횃불로 다가왔습니다) **who had been seared in the flames of withering injustice**(압도적인 불평등의 불꽃에 그을려왔던). **It came as a joyous daybreak to end the long night of captivity**(그것은 마치 구금상태의 긴 밤의 종말을 알리는 환희에 찬 새벽녘으로 다가 왔습니다).

But one hundred years later(그러나 100년이 지난 지금), **we must face the tragic fact that the Negro is still not free**(우리는 흑인은 여전히 자유롭지 못하다는 사실에 직면해야만 합니다). **One hundred years later**(백년이 지나 지금), **the life of the Negro is still sadly crippled by the manacles of segregation and the chains of discrimination**(흑인들의 삶은 인종차별의 속박과 차별의 쇠사슬로 여전히 슬프게 절름발이가 되고 있습니다). **One hundred years later**(백년이나 지난 지금), **the Negro lives on a lonely island of poverty in the midst of a vast ocean of material prosperity**(흑인들은 물질적 번영의 거대한 대양의 한 가운데에서 가난으로 찌든 고립된 섬에서 살고 있습니다). **One hundred years later, the Negro is still languishing in the corners of American society and finds himself an exile in his own land**(흑인들은 미국사회의 구석에서 아직도 시들어가고 있고 자신의 땅에서 스스로 유랑자가 됨을 압니다). **So we have come here today to dramatize an appalling condition**(그래서 우리는 섬뜩한 상황을 극적으로 표현하기 위해 오늘 이곳에 왔습니다).

In a sense we have come to our nation's capital to cash a check(어떤 의미에서 우리는 수표를 현찰로 바꾸기(빚을 받으러) 위해 이곳 워싱턴에 왔습니다). **When the architects of our republic wrote the magnificent words of the Constitution and the declaration of Independence**(우리 공화국의 개척자들은 헌법과 독립선언서의 위대한 글을 작성할 때), **they were signing a promissory note to which every American was to fall heir**(그들은 모든 미국은 약속어음을 받을 상속자임을 서명했습니다). **This note was a promise that all men would be guaranteed the inalienable rights of life, liberty, and the pursuit of happiness**(이 증서는 모든 사람은 생명, 자유, 그리고 행복추구의 빼앗을 수 없는 권리를 보장할 것이라는 약속이었습니다).

It is obvious today that America has defaulted on this promissory note insofar as her citizens of colour are concerned(미국의 유색시민들이 연루되는 한 이 약속어음은 채무불이행이 되고 있다는 것은 오늘날 분명합니다). **Instead of honoring this sacred obligation**(이 신성한 의무를 이해하는 것 대신), **America has given the Negro people a bad check which has come back marked "insufficient funds."**(미국은 흑인들에게 "지급불능"이라 적힌 부도난 수표를 되돌려 주었습니다). **But we refuse to believe that the bank of justice is bankrupt**(그러나 우리는 법 정의의 은행이 파산되었다고 믿지는 않습

니다). **We refuse to believe that there are insufficient funds in the great vaults of opportunity of this nation**(우리는 이 나라의 기회의 큰 금고가 자금이 부족하다는 사실을 믿지 않습니다). **So we have come to cash this check**(그래서 우리는 현찰로 바꾸기 위해 온 것입니다) - **a check that will give us upon demand the riches of freedom and the security of justice**(우리가 요구할 땐 풍요로운 자유와 정의의 안전을 보장하는 수표입니다). **We have also come to this hallowed spot to remind America of the fierce urgency of now**(우리는 미국에게 지금의 아주 급박한 심정을 알리려 이 신성한 곳에 와 있습니다). **This is no time to engage in the luxury of cooling off or to take the tranquillizing drug of gradualism**(마음을 진정시킬 사치스런 일에 관여하거나 점진적 해결을 위한 신정안정제를 복용할 시간이 없습니다). **Now is the time to rise from the dark and desolate valley of segregation to the sunlit path of racial justice**(지금은 어둡고 황량한 인종차별의 계곡으로부터 인종의 정의가 있는 햇볕이 드는 길로 나올 때입니다). **Now is the time to open the doors of opportunity to all of God's children**(지금은 모든 신의 자녀들에게 균등한 기회의 문을 열어줄 때입니다). **Now is the time to lift our nation from the quick-sands of racial injustice to the solid rock of brotherhood**(지금은 인종적 부정으로 모래와 같은 위험한 상태로부터 형제애의 단단한 바위로 국가를 도약시킬 때입니다).

📎 단어분석

- ‡ **score** [skɔː r] n. ① a) (pl. ~) 20, 스무 사람[개]. b) (pl.) 다수, 다대. ② (경기 등에서) 득점(표), (시험의) 득점, 성적 / † **symbolic, —ical** [simbálik / -ból-], [-əl] a. 상징하는(cf); / † **emancipation** [imænsəpéiʃən] n. U,C (노예) 해방; 이탈; / † **proclamation** [pràkləméiʃən / pròk-] n. ① U 선언, 포고, 발포. ② 선언[성명]서. / † **momentous** [mouméntəs] a. 중대한, 중요한, 쉽지 않은 / ‡ **decree** [dikrí ː] n. ① 법령, 포고, 명령. / † **beacon** [bíː kən] n. ① 횃불, 봉화; 봉화대[탑]; 등대; 신호소. / **sear** [siə ː r] v. —vt. 태우다, 그을리다; 낙인을 찍다; 무감각하게 하다, (양심 따위를) 마비시키다; 시들게[마르게] 하다. / **wither** [wíðə ː r] v. —vi. ①『~ / +부』시들다(up; away). ② 쇠퇴하다, 쇠약해지다, 희박해지다(away). —vt. ①『~+목 / +목+부』시들게 하다. / ‡ **injustice** [indʒʌ́stis] n. U,C ① (도의적인) 부정, 불의, 불공평. [cf.] unjustice. / ‡ **joyful** [dʒɔ́ifəl] a. ① 즐거운(happy), 기쁜. ② (마음을) 기쁘게 하는. / ‡ **daybreak** [déibrèik] n. U 새벽녘. / † **captivity** [kæptívəti] n. U 사로잡힌 몸[기간], 감금; 속박. / **cripple** [krípəl] v. —vt. 불구[절름발이]가 되게 하다; 무능케 하다. / **manacle** [mǽnəkl] n. (보통 pl.) 속박, 구속. / **segregation** [sègrigéiʃ-ən] n. U 분리, 격리, 차단; 인종 차별(대우) / † **discrimination** [diskrìmənéiʃən] n. U ① 구별, 안식(in). ② 차별, 차별 대우. / **prosperity** [prɑspérəti / prɔs-] n. ① U 번영, 행운, 부유 / † **languish** [lǽŋgwiʃ] vi. ① 기운이 없어지다, (쇠)약해지다, 시들다. ② 초췌해지다, 괴로워하다. ③ 동경하다, 그리워하다(for), 간절히 바라다. / † **exile** [égzail, éks-] n. U ① (자의에 의한) 망명, 국외 생활[유랑], 타향살이. ② (자국·마을·집으로부터의) 추방, 유형, 유배. / † **dramatize** [drǽmətàiz] v. —vt. 극화[각색]하다; 과장하다. / † **appalling** [əpɔ́ː liŋ] a. 섬뜩하게 하는, 질색인; (구어) 지독한, 형편없는. / ‡ **magnificent** [mægnífəsənt] a. ① 장대한(grand), 장엄한, 장려한. ② 당당한, 훌륭한, (생각 따위가) 고상한, 격조 높은. / **promissory** [práməsɔ̀ː ri / prɔ-] a. 약속하는, 약속의;『상업』지급을 약속하는. ------•a ~note『상업』약속 어음(略: p.n.). / **inalienable** [inéiljənəbəl] a. ① (권리 등이) 양도할[넘겨 줄] 수 없는. ② (아무에게서) 빼앗을 수 없는. / **default** [difɔ́ː lt] v. —vt. ① (약속·채무 따위를) 이행하지 않다, 태만히[게을리]하다. / **insofar as** ~하는 한 / **honor** 『상업』 (어음을) 인수하다, (기일에) 지급하다. / **vault** [vɔː lt] n. ① 둥근 천장, 아치형 천장. 지하 감옥. / † **hallow** [hǽlou] vt. ① 신성하게 하다, 깨끗하게 하다, 신에게 바치다. ② (신성한 것으로서) 숭배하다. / ‡ **fierce** [fiərs] a. (fiercer; -est) ① 흉포한, 몹시 사나운(savage). ② (구어) 지독한, 고약한. / † **urgency** [ə́ ː rdʒənsi] n. U ① 긴급, 절박, 화급. ② (pl.) 긴급한 일[필요]. / **cool off**: 진정시키다 / **tranquilizing drug**: 안정제 / **gradualism**: 점진주의 / ‡ **desolate** [désəlit] a. ① 황폐한; 황량한. ② 쓸쓸한, 외로운, 고독한

※ 다음을 읽고 물음에 답하시오. [1~7]

(1)Five score years ago, a great American, in whose symbolic shadow we stand signed the Emancipation Proclamation. This momentous decree came as a great beacon light of hope to millions of ⓐ**Negro** slaves who had been seared in the flames of withering injustice. It came as a joyous daybreak to ①**start** the long night of captivity.

(2)But one hundred years later, we must face the tragic fact that/which the Negro is still not ②**free**. One hundred years later, the life of the Negro is still sadly crippled by the manacles of segregation and the chains of discrimination. One hundred years later, the Negro lives on a lonely island of poverty in the midst of a vast ocean of material prosperity.

(3)One hundred years later, the Negro is still languished/languishing in the corners of American society and finds ③**himself** an exile in his own land. So we have come here today to dramatize an appalling condition. In a sense we have come to our nation's capital to cash a check. When the architects of our republic wrote the magnificent words of the Constitution and the declaration of Independence, they were signing a promissory note to which every American was to fall heir. This note was a promise that all men would be guaranteed the inalienable rights of life, liberty, and the pursuit of happiness.

(4)It is obvious today that America has defaulted on this promissory note insofar as her citizens of colour are concerned. Instead of honoring this sacred obligation, America has given the Negro people a ④**bad** check which has come back marked "insufficient funds." But we refuse to believe that the bank of justice is bankrupt. We refuse to believe that there are insufficient funds in the great vaults of opportunity of this nation.

(5)So we have come to cash this check -- a check that will give us upon demand the riches of freedom and the security of justice. We have also come to this ⑤**hallowed** spot to remind America of the fierce urgency of now. This is no time to engage in the luxury of cooling off or to take the tranquillizing drug of gradualism. Now is the time to rise from the dark and desolate valley of segregation to the sunlighted/sunlit path of racial justice. Now is the time to open the doors of opportunity to all of God's children. _____ from the quick-sands of racial injustice to the solid rock of brotherhood.

1. 위 글의 (1)~(5)중, 주제로 가장 적절한 문단은?

① (1) ② (2) ③ (3) ④ (4) ⑤ (5)

2. 위 글의 밑줄 친 ⓐ와 관계가 <u>없는</u> 것은?

① They had looked forward to opening the equal doors according to the Emancipation Proclamation.
② They haven't been changed in their situations.
③ Their promissory note would be paid out soon.
④ The liberty guaranteed by the law should be observed.
⑤ There is little time enough to wait and see.

235

3. 위 글에서 밑줄 친 ①~⑤ 중, 문맥상 단어의 쓰임이 <u>어색한</u> 것은?

①   ②   ③   ④   ⑤

4. 위 글에서 네모상자 안의 적절한 단어는?

① that   languished   sunlighted
② which   languishing   sunlighted
③ that   languishing   sunlit
④ which   languished   sunlit
⑤ that   languished   sunlit

5. 위 글에서 밑줄 친 빈칸에 적절한 표현은?

① Now is the time to make more prosperous
② Now is the time to solve segregation
③ Now is the time to enlighten our children
④ Now is the time to pay cash for the note
⑤ Now is the time to lift our nation

6. 위 글의 분위기와 어울리지 <u>않는</u> 단어는?

① withering   ② crippling
③ languishing   ④ dramatizing
⑤ appalling

7. 위 글과 일치하지 <u>않은</u> 것은?

① 100년 전, 노예해방선언은 흑인들에게 희망의 큰 횃불이 되었다.
② 100년이 지난 지금, 흑인들은 여전히 자유롭지 못하다.
③ 흑인들은 번영의 거대한 대양 속에서 찐든 삶을 산다.
④ 자유와 정의 안전을 보장하는 수표는 부도가 난지 오래다.
⑤ 점진적 해결책만이 유일한 해결책이 될 수 있다.

1. ⑤   2. ③   3. ① end   4. ③
5. ⑤   6. ④   7. ⑤

①It would be fatal for the nation to overlook the urgency of the moment and to underestimate the determination of the Negro. This sweltering summer of the Negro's legitimate discontent ②will not pass until there is an invigorating autumn of freedom and equality. ③Nineteen sixty-three is not an end, but a beginning. ④Those who hope that the Negro needed to blow off steam and will now be content will have a rude awakening if the nation returns to business as usual. ⑤There will be neither rest nor tranquillity in America until the Negro is granted his citizenship rights. ⑥The whirlwinds of revolt will continue to shake the foundations of our nation until the bright day of justice emerges.

But ⑦there is something that I must say to my people who stand on the warm threshold which leads into the palace of justice. In the process of gaining our rightful place we must not be guilty of wrongful deeds. ⑧Let us not seek to satisfy our thirst for freedom by drinking from the cup of bitterness and hatred.

We must forever conduct our struggle on the high plane of dignity and discipline. ⑨We must not allow our creative protest to degenerate into physical violence. Again and again we must rise to the majestic heights of meeting physical force with soul force. The marvellous new militancy which has engulfed the Negro community must not lead us to distrust of all white people, for many of our white brothers, ⑩as evidenced by their presence here today, have come to realize that their destiny is tied up with our destiny and their freedom is inextricably bound to our freedom. We cannot walk alone.

And as we walk, ⑪we must make the pledge that we shall march ahead. We cannot turn back. There are those who are asking the devotees of civil rights, "When will you be satisfied?" ⑫We can never be satisfied as long as our bodies, heavy with the fatigue of travel, cannot gain lodging in the motels of the highways and the hotels of the cities. We cannot be satisfied as long as the Negro's basic mobility is from a smaller ghetto to a larger one. We can never be satisfied as long as a Negro in Mississippi cannot vote and a Negro in New York believes ⑬he has nothing for which to vote. No, no, we are not satisfied, and we will not be satisfied until justice rolls down like waters and ⑭righteousness like a mighty stream.

📝 문법분석

① It[가주어]+would be[가정법]+for the nation[의미상의 주어]+to overlook[진주어] ~and to underestimate ~.

② will not A until B: B해서야 비로소 A하다.

③ not A, but B: A가 아닌 B인

④ Those who[~ 하는 사람들] ~that the Negro A and B will have[본동사] ~if[조건절] ~.

⑤ neither A nor B until C: C가 되서야 비로소 A 또는 B인

⑥ continue to shake: 계속해서 흔들다 / until 정의의 밝은 그날이 올 때까지

⑦ something that I must say[목적어인 something을 수식] to my people[내 형제들] who stand on the warm threshold[열망하는] which[관계대명사] leads into ～.

⑧ 만족했다고 생각지 마세요.

⑨ allow+our creative protest[목적어]+to degenerate[부정사]+into physical violence[전치사 into의 목적어] 우리의 창의적인 항의가 물리적 폭력으로 변질되게 하다.

⑩ 그들의 존재로 입증되었듯이.

⑪ 평화롭게 행진한다는 것을 약속하다.

⑫ can never A as long as B: B를 하는 한 A를 할 수 없다.

⑬ 투표권을 갖고 있지 않다.

⑭ righteousness (rolls down) like a mighty stream.

📎 본문해석

It would be fatal for the nation to overlook the urgency of the moment and to underestimate the determination of the Negro(현재의 위기감을 간과하거나 흑인의 결단을 과소평가하는 국가는 치명적이 될 것입니다). **This sweltering summer of the Negro's legitimate discontent will not pass until there is an invigorating autumn of freedom and equality**(흑인의 정당한 불만이 가득한 이 무더운 여름은 자유와 평등의 상쾌한 가을이 오고서야 물러날 것입니다). **Nineteen sixty-three is not an end, but a beginning**(1963년은 끝이 아닌 시작입니다). **Those who hope that the Negro needed to blow off steam and will now be content will have a rude awakening if the nation returns to business as usual**(흑인들이 잠시 울분을 달랬고 앞으로 만족할 거라고 바라는 사람들은, 만일 국가가 그래왔듯 일상으로 돌아간다면, 잔인한 아침을 맞게 될 것입니다). **There will be neither rest nor tranquillity in America until the Negro is granted his citizenship rights**(흑인들이 자신들의 시민의 권리를 인정받을 때만이 미국에 휴식이나 평온이 올 것입니다). **The whirlwinds of revolt will continue to shake the foundations of our nation until the bright day of justice emerges**(반감의 거센 회오리는 정의의 밝은 그날이 올 때까지 계속해서 우리나라의 근간을 흔들 것입니다).

But there is something that I must say to my people who stand on the warm threshold which leads into the palace of justice(정의의 궁궐로 나있는 따스한 문지방 위에 서있는 제 형제들에게 제가 말해야만 하는 것이 있습니다). **In the process of gaining our rightful place we must not be guilty of wrongful deeds**(우리의 정당한 터전을 얻기 위한 과정에서, 잘못된 행동에 대해 죄책감을 느껴서는 안 됩니다). **Let us not seek to satisfy our thirst for freedom by drinking from the cup of bitterness and hatred**(괴로움과 증오로 가득 찬 한 모금의 물로 자유의 열망을 만족 시켰다고 생각지 마세요).

We must forever conduct our struggle on the high plane of dignity and discipline(우리는 품위와 규율의 높은 수준에서 우리의 투쟁을 영원히 해야만 합니다). **We must not allow our creative protest to degenerate into physical violence**(우리의 창의적인 항의가 물리적 폭력으로 변질되게 해서는 안 됩니다). **Again and again we must rise to the majestic heights of meeting physical force with soul force**(다시금 말해, 우리는 물리적 힘이 영혼의 힘을 만나는 장엄한 곳을 향해 일어서만 합니다). **The marvellous new militancy which has engulfed the Negro community must not lead us to distrust of all white people**(흑인사회를 삼켜버리는 굉장한 새로운 호전성이 우리로 하여금 모든 백인들의 불신을 야기 시키게 해서는 안 됩니다), **for many of our white brothers, as evidenced by their presence here today**(오늘날

이곳에서 그들의 존재에 의해 드러나듯 많은 우리 백인형제들은), **have come to realize that their destiny is tied up with our destiny**(자신들의 운명은 우리의 것과 묶여 있고) **and their freedom is inextricably bound to our freedom**(그들이 자유는 우리의 것과 완전히 결박되어 있다는 것을 깨닫게 되었습니다). **We cannot walk alone**(우리는 홀로 나가갈 수 없습니다).

And as we walk, we must make the pledge that we shall march ahead(우리가 걸어갈 땐, 앞으로 평화롭게 행진한다는 것을 맹세해야만 합니다). **We cannot turn back**(우리는 되돌아 설 수 없습니다). **There are those who are asking the devotees of civil rights**(열성가들에게 시민 권리를 물어보는 사람들이 있습니다.), **"When will you be satisfied?**(당신은 언제쯤 만족하실 건가요?)" **We can never be satisfied**(우리는 만족할 수 없습니다) **as long as our bodies, heavy with the fatigue of travel**(긴 여행의 피로로 지친 우리 몸이), **cannot gain lodging in the motels of the highways and the hotels of the cities**(고속도로 모텔이나 도시 호텔에서 정당히 묵을 수 있을 때까지). **We cannot be satisfied as long as the Negro's basic mobility is from a smaller ghetto to a larger one**(흑인이 더 작은 빈민가에서 더 큰 빈민가로 제한되어 있는 동안 만족할 수 없습니다). **We can never be satisfied as long as a Negro in Mississippi cannot vote and a Negro in New York believes he has nothing for which to vote**(미시시피에 사는 한 흑인이 투표할 수 없는 한, 뉴욕에 사는 한 흑인이 투표권이 없는 한, 우린 결코 만족할 수 없습니다). **No, no, we are not satisfied**(절대로, 우린 만족하지 않으며), **and we will not be satisfied until justice rolls down like waters and righteousness like a mighty stream**(정의가 물처럼 흐르고 정의가 강력한 시냇물처럼 흐를 때 비로소 우린 만족할 것입니다).

📖 단어분석

- ‡ **fatal** [féitl] a. ① 치명적인(to), 생명에 관계되는; 사활을 결단하는(to). [SYN.] ⇨ DEADLY. ② 파멸적인(destructive), 몸을 망치는; 돌이킬 수 없는(잘못 따위), 중대한, 엄청난. ③ 운명의[에 관한]; 숙명적인(fateful), 피할 수 없는(inevitable). ④ 불길한, 섬뜩한. ⑤ 흉악한, 악질의. / ‡ **overlook** [òuvərlúk] vt. ① 바라보다, 내려다보다; (건물·언덕 따위가) ~을 내려다보는 위치에 있다. ② 감독[감시]하다, 돌보다, 검열[시찰]하다; 훑어보다. ③ (나무·봉우리 따위가) ~보다 높이 솟다. ④ 빠뜨리고 보다; (결점 따위를) 눈감아 주다, 너그럽게 보아주다. [SYN.] ⇨ NEGLECT. / † **underestimate** [ʌndəréstəmèit] vt., vi. 싸게 어림하다, 실제보다 낮게[적게] 어림하다, 과소 평가[판단]하다; 얕보다. / **sweltering** [swéltəriŋ] a. 찌는 듯이 더운; 땀투성이의, 더위에 허덕이는. / † **legitimate** [lidʒítəmit] a. ① 합법의, 적법의; 옳은, 정당한. [opp.] illegitimate. [SYN.] ⇨ LAWFUL. ② 본격적인, 정통의, 정계(正系)의; 적출의. / † **discontent** [dìskəntént] n. U (욕구) 불만(의 근원), 불평; / **invigorating** [invígərèitiŋ] a. 기운을 돋구는, (공기·산들바람 등이) 상쾌한. / **blow off steam**: 울분을 달래다. / ‡ **rude** [ru: d]a. ① 버릇없는, 무례한 (impolite), 실례의(to). ② 교양이 없는, 야만의; 무무한, 조야한, ③ 무뚝뚝한; 거친. ④ 미발달의; 미가공의. ⑤ 미숙한, 조잡한; 대강의. ⑥ 튼튼한, 건강한. [opp.] delicate. ⑦ 귀에 거슬리는; (음식이) 맛없는, 소홀한. ⑧ 격심한; 돌연한. / **awakening** [əwéikəniŋ] n. U,C 눈뜸, 깸, 각성; 자각, 인식; (종교에 대한 관심의) 부활. / † **tranquil(l)ity** [træŋkwíləti] n. U 평정, 평온, 평안, 침착. / **grant** [grænt, gra: nt] v. —vt. ① 『~+목/ +목+목/ +목+전+명』 주다, 수여하다, 부여하다(bestow); (면허 등을) 교부하다; (허가를) 주다(to). [SYN.] ⇨ GIVE. ② 『~+목/ +목+목/ +that절/ +목+to do)) 승인하다, 허가하다(allow). / † **whirlwind** [hwɔ́: rlwìnd] n. ① 회오리 바람, 선풍. ② 급격한 행동, 격렬한 감정. / ‡ **revolt** [rivóult] n. ① 반란, 반역; 폭동. ② U 반항(심), 반항적인 태도.③ U 혐오감, 불쾌, 반감(against; at; from). / † **emerge** [imə́: rdʒ] vi. ① 『~ / +전+명』 (물 속·어둠 속 따위에서) 나오다, 나타나다(appear)(from). [opp] submerge. ② 『+전+명』 (빈곤, 낮은 신분 등에서) 벗어[헤어]나다, 빠져나오다(come out)(from). /

⁺18 I Have a Dream

by Martin Luther King

✝**threshold** [θréʃhould] n. ① 문지방, 문간, 입구. ② (비유) 발단, 시초, 출발점. ③ 한계, 경계, (특히) 활주로의 맨 끝; / ✝**rightful** [ráitfəl] a. 올바른, 정의에 근거를 둔; 정당한; 당연한; 적법의, 합법의 / ✝**bitterness** [bítərnis] n. 쓴맛, 씀; 신랄함, 빈정댐; 슬픔, 괴로움. / ✝**thirst** [θəː rst]n. U (또는 a ~) ① 갈증, 목마름. ② (구어) 갈망, 열망(after; for; of; to do). / **conduct** [kəndʌkt] v. —vt. ①『~+목/ +목+전+명/ +목+부』인도하다, 안내하다, 호송하다. [SYN.] ⇨ GUIDE. ② 지도하다, 지휘하다. ③ (업무 등을) 집행하다, 처리 [경영, 관리]하다. ④「재귀용법」행동하다, 거동하다, 처신하다. / ✝**dignity** [dígnəti] n. ① U 존엄, 위엄; 존엄성; 품위, 기품; 체면, 긍지. ② U (태도 따위가) 무게 있음, 장중함, 위풍. / ✝**discipline** [dísəplin] n. U ① U,C 훈련, 훈육; 단련, 수양. ② 규율, 풍기, 자제(自制), 버릇들이기. / ✝**degenerate** [didʒénərèit] vi. ①『~ / +전+명』나빠지다, 퇴보하다 (from); 타락하다(into). ②『생물』퇴화하다(to); 『의학』변질하다. / ✝**majestic, -tical** [mədʒéstik], [--əl] a. 장엄한, 위엄 있는(dignified), 웅대한, 당당한. / **height** [hait] n. ① U 높음. ② 높이, 키; 고도, 표고. ③ C (보통 pl.) 고지, 산, 언덕. / ✝**marvelous**, 【영국】 -vellous [máː rv-ələs] a. ① 불가사의한, 이상한, 놀라운. [SYN.] ⇨ WONDER. ② 기적적인, 믿기 어려운(improbable). ③ (구어) 훌륭한, 최고의, 굉장한. / **militancy** [mílitənsi] n. U 교전 상태; 호전성, 투쟁 정신. / **engulf** [engʌlf] vt. (늪·깊은 속·파도 등의 속으로) 삼켜버리다; (~을 물속으로) 가라앉히다(in; into); 몰두케 하다(in; into). / ✝**evidence** [évidəns] vt. ① 증언하다. ② 입증하다; ~의 증거가 되다. ③ 명시하다; (감정 등을) 겉으로 나타내다. / **inextricable** [inékstrikəbəl] a. ① 탈출할[헤어날] 수 없는. ② 풀 수 없는(문제 따위), 뒤엉킨; 해결할 수 없는. / **devotee** [dèvoutíː] n. 열애가(熱愛家); 열성가(of); / ✝**mobility** [moubíləti] n. U ① 가동성, 이동성, 변동성. ② 변덕. ③『사회학』(주민의 주소·직업 따위의) 유동성, 이동. / **ghetto** [gétou] n. (pl. ~(e)s) 【It.】 유대인 강제 거주 구역; (특정 사회 집단의) 거주지; 【미국】 (흑인 등 소수 민족) 빈민굴; 슬럼(slum)가, 고립 집단(지구). /

❋ 다음 글을 읽고 물음에 답하시오. [8~13]

It would be ①**fatal** for the nation to overlook the urgency of the moment and to underestimate the determination of the Negro.

This sweltering summer of the Negro's legitimate discontent will not pass until there is an invigorated/invigorating autumn of freedom and equality. Nineteen sixty-three is not an end, but a beginning. ⒶThose who hope that the Negro needed to blow off steam and will now be content will have a rude awakening if the nation returns to business as usual. There will be neither rest nor tranquillity in America until the Negro is granted his citizenship rights. The whirlwinds of revolt will continue to shake the foundations of our nation until the bright day of justice emerges.

But there is something that I must say to my people who stand on the ②**warm** threshold which leads into the palace of justice. In the process of gaining our rightful place we must not be guilty of wrongful deeds. Let us not seek to satisfy our thirst for freedom by drinking from the cup of bitterness and hatred.

We must forever conduct our struggle on the high plane of dignity and discipline. We must not allow our creative protest to ③ **degenerate** into physical violence. Again and again we must raise/rise to the majestic heights of meeting physical force with soul force. The marvellous new militancy which has engulfed the Negro community must not lead us to distrust of all white people, for many of our white brothers, as evidenced by their presence here today, have come to realize that their destiny is tied up with our destiny and their freedom is inextricably bound to our freedom. We cannot walk ④**together**.

And as we walk, we must make the pledge that we shall march ahead. We cannot turn back. There are those who are asking the devotees of civil rights, "When will you be satisfied?" We can never be satisfied as long as our bodies, ⑤**heavy** with the fatigue of travel, cannot gain lodging in the motels of the highways and the hotels of the cities. We cannot be satisfied as long as the Negro's basic/free mobility is from a smaller ghetto to a larger one. We can never be satisfied as long as a Negro in Mississippi cannot vote and a Negro in New York believes he has nothing for which to vote. No, no, we are not satisfied, and we will not be satisfied until justice rolls down like waters and righteousness like a mighty stream.

8. 위 글의 주제로 가장 적절한 것은?

① Please demonstrate peacefully and march ahead.

② Don't stop until the Negro's civil right is complete.

③ We should understand our given environment.

④ Intimidate the nation until we are accepted as a citizen.

⑤ Long way to go for liberty needs some rest and comfort.

9. 위 글의 네모상자 안의 적절한 단어는?

① invigorated   raise   basic
② invigorating   rise   basic
③ invigorated   rise   basic
④ invigorating   rise   free
⑤ invigorated   raise   free

10. 위 글에서 밑줄 친 Ⓐ가 가리키는 것은?

① recommendation   ② invitation
③ warning   ④ consolation
⑤ affirmation

11. 위 글에서 밑줄 친 ①~⑤ 중, 문맥상 단어의 쓰임이 <u>어색한</u> 것은?

①   ②   ③   ④   ⑤

12. 위 글의 표현 방식은?

① metaphorical   ② indicative
③ descriptive   ④ illustrative
⑤ exaggerative

13. 위 글과 일치하지 <u>않은</u> 것은?

① 현재의 위기감을 무시하거나 흑인의 결단을 과소 평가하는 국가는 멸망할 수 있다.
② 흑인들이 잠시 울분을 달래는 것이므로 잠시 시간이 지나면 일상으로 돌아갈 것이라 믿는다.
③ 반감의 거센 회오리는 정의의 밝은 그날이 올 때까지 계속해서 우리의 근간을 흔들 것이다.
④ 정당한 터전을 얻기 위한 과정에서 죄책감을 느껴서는 안 된다.
⑤ 괴로움과 증오로 가득 찬 한 모금의 물로 만족하지 말자.

8. ②   9. ②   10. ③
11. ④ together → alone   12. ①   13. ②

I am not unmindful that some of you have come here ①out of great trials and tribulations. Some of you have come fresh from ②narrow cells. Some of you have come from ③areas where your quest for freedom ④left you battered by the storms of persecution and staggered by the winds of police brutality. You have been ⑤the veterans of creative suffering. Continue to work ⑥with the faith that unearned suffering is redemptive.

Go back to Mississippi, go back to Alabama, go back to Georgia, go back to Louisiana, go back to the slums and ghettos of our northern cities, ⑦knowing that somehow this situation can and will be changed. Let us not wallow in the valley of despair.

⑧I say to you today, my friends, that in spite of the difficulties and frustrations of the moment, I still have a dream. It is a dream deeply rooted in the American dream.

I have ⑨a dream that one day this nation will rise up and live out the true meaning of its creed: "We hold these truths to be self-evident: that all men are created equal."

I have a dream that one day on the red hills of Georgia the sons of former slaves and the sons of former slave-owners will be able to sit down together at a table of brotherhood.

I have a dream that one day even ⑩the state of Mississippi, a desert state, sweltering with the heat of injustice and oppression, will be transformed into an oasis of freedom and justice.

I have a dream that my four children will one day live in a nation where they will not be judged by the colour of their skin but by the content of their character.

I have a dream today.

I have a dream that one day the state of Alabama, ⑪whose governor's lips are presently dripping with the words of interposition and nullification, will be transformed into a situation where little black boys and black girls will be able to join hands with little white boys and white girls and walk together as sisters and brothers.

I have a dream today.

I have a dream that one day every valley ⑫shall be exalted, every hill and mountain shall be made low, the rough places will be made plain, and the crooked places will be made straight, and the glory of the Lord shall be revealed, and all flesh shall see it together.

🔖 문법분석

① 벗어나

② 좁은 감방

③ areas where + A[절]: A라는 곳 지역

④ left[본동사]+you[목적어]+battered[목적격 보어] ~and staggered[목적격 보어] ~. 당신의 ~되게 하다.

243

⑤ 이골이 나 있다.(풍부한 경험이 쌓였다).
⑥ 뜻하지 않은 고통을 속죄한다는 신념.
⑦ 명령문, + and know[=knowing]: 돌아가면, 알게 될 것이다.
⑧ I say to you today, my friends[동격], that[목적어인 명사절], in spite of the difficulties[부사구] 주어 + 동사.
⑨ a dream that: 동격절
⑩ the state of Mississippi[주어], a desert state[동격], (which is) swelltering with ～, will be transformed into[동사]
⑪ [소유격 관계대명사] 주지사의 법안 방해와 폐기로 가득 찬 알라바마 주
⑫ 문어적 문맥에서 운명적인 필연·예언을 나타냄」 ～하리라, ～이리라.

📖 **본문해석**

I am not unmindful that some of you have come here out of great trials and tribulations(저는 여러분 중에는 큰 시련과 억압에서 벗어나 이곳에 오셨다는 것을 압니다). **Some of you have come fresh from narrow cells**(여러분 중에는 좁은 교도서의 독방에서 막 출감한 분이 있을 겁니다). **Some of you have come from areas where your quest for freedom left you battered by the storms of persecution and staggered by the winds of police brutality**(여러분 중에는 자유의 외침이 거대한 폭풍 같은 박해로 강탈당하고 경찰관의 잔인함으로 인해 머뭇거렸던 분이 있을 겁니다). **You have been the veterans of creative suffering**(여러분은 독창적인 고난을 참아내는 대가가 되었습니다). **Continue to work with the faith that unearned suffering is redemptive**(갑자기 생긴 고통을 속죄한다는 마음으로 계속 일을 하세요). **Go back to Mississippi**(미시시피로 돌아가), **go back to Alabama**(알라바마로 돌아가), **go back to Georgia**(조오지아로 돌아가), **go back to Louisiana**(루지애나로 돌아가), **go back to the slums and ghettos of our northern cities**(빈민가와 북부 빈민촌으로 들어가), **knowing that somehow this situation can and will be changed**(조금 이런 상황이 바뀔 수 있고 바뀔 것이라는 것을 알게 될 것입니다). **Let us not wallow in the valley of despair**(절망의 계곡 속에서 방황하지 마세요).
I say to you today, my friends,(제 친구인 여러분에게 말하려 합니다) **that in spite of the difficulties and frustrations of the moment**(지금의 고난과 좌절에도 불구하고), **I still have a dream**(저는 여전히 꿈을 갖고 있습니다). **It is a dream deeply rooted in the American dream**(그것은 미국인의 꿈 깊은 곳에 자리 잡은 꿈입니다).
I have a dream that one day this nation will rise up and live out the true meaning of its creed(어느 날 이 나라는 도약할 것이고 ～신조의 진정한 의미가 이루어지는 것이 제 꿈입니다): **"We hold these truths to be self-evident: that all men are created equal**(우리는 모든 사람은 동등하게 창조되었다는 자명한 진리를 간직하고 있습니다)."
I have a dream that one day on the red hills of Georgia the sons of former slaves and the sons of former slave-owners will be able to sit down together at a table of brotherhood(어느 날 조오지아의 붉은 언덕 위에서 노예의 후예의 아들들과 노예 주인이었던 자식들이 형제의 식탁에 함께 앉는 것이 제 꿈입니다).
I have a dream that one day even the state of Mississippi, a desert state, sweltering with the heat of injustice and oppression, will be transformed into an oasis of freedom and justice(어느 날 불의와 억압의 열기로 무더운 황폐한 주인 미시시피주에서 조차도 자유와 정의의 오아시스로 바뀌는 것을 보는 것이 제 꿈입니다).

I have a dream that my four children will one day live in a nation where they will not be judged by the colour of their skin but by the content of their character(어느 날 저의 4자녀가 피부색이 아닌 그들의 품성으로 판단되는 그런 나라에서 살게 되는 것이 제 꿈입니다).

I have a dream today(저는 오늘 꿈을 갖고 있습니다).

I have a dream that one day the state of Alabama, whose governor's lips are presently dripping with the words of interposition and nullification, will be transformed into a situation where little black boys and black girls will be able to join hands with little white boys and white girls and walk together as sisters and brothers(어느 날 주지사의 입술에서 오늘날 방해와 폐기 법안으로 가득 찬 알라바마 주가 바뀌어 어린 흑인 백인 소년소녀가 함께 손잡고 누이와 형제로서 함께 거니는 것이 저의 꿈입니다).

I have a dream today(저는 오늘 꿈을 갖고 왔습니다).

I have a dream that one day every valley shall be exalted, every hill and mountain shall be made low, the rough places will be made plain, and the crooked places will be made straight, and the glory of the Lord shall be revealed, and all flesh shall see it together(어느 날 모든 계곡이 강하게 찬양되고, 모든 언덕과 산이 낮아지고, 거친 곳은 평탄하게 되며 굽은 곳은 곧게 펴지고 신의 찬사가 나타나 모든 인간들이 함께 볼 수 있게 되는 것이 제 꿈입니다).

🖋 단어분석

- **unmindful** [ʌnmáindfəl] a. 무심한, 부주의한, 무관심한(regardless)(of; that). / **ǂ trial** [tráiəl] n. C,U ① 〘법률〙 공판, 재판, 심리. ② 시도, 시험; 시용, 시운전. ③ 시련, 고난, 재난. ④ 골칫거리, 귀찮은 사람. / **tribulation** [trìbjəléiʃ-ən] n. U,C 고난, 고생, 시련; 재난 / **ǂ cell** [sel] n. ① 작은 방; (수도원 따위의) 독방, 작은 수도원〔수녀원〕. ② (교도소의) 독방, 〘군사〙 영창. / **ǂ quest** [kwest] n. ① 탐색(search), 탐구(hunt), 추구(pursuit)(for). ② 탐색여행, 원정(특히 중세 기사의 모험을 찾아서의). / **ǂ batter** v. —vt. ① 『~+목/ +목+전+명』 연타[난타]하다. ② 『+목+부』 쳐[때려]부수다(down). ③ (모자·문 따위를) 쳐서 쭈그러뜨리다(in). ④ 난폭하게 다루어 상하게 하다; / **† persecution** [pə̀ː rsikjúː ʃən] n. U,C ① (특히 종교상의) 박해. ② 성가시게[끈질기게] 졸라댐, 괴롭힘. / **ǂ stagger** [stǽgə r] v. —vi. ① 『~/ +부/+전+명』 비틀거리다, 비틀거리며 나아가다(totter) (to). ② 『~/ +전+명』 망설이다, 주저하다(hesitate), 마음이 흔들리다. / **brutality** [bruː tǽləti] n. U 잔인, 무자비; C 야만적 행위. / **unearned** [ʌnə́ː rnd] a. 노력하지 않고 얻은, 저절로 굴러 들어온(수입 따위); 상대팀의 에러에 의한; 미수(未收)의; 부(적)당한. / **redemptive** [ridémptiv] a. 되찾는, 되사는; 속전을 내어 몸을 구해 내는; 상각의; 구조[구제]의, 속죄의. / **wallow** [wálou / wɔ́l-] vi. ① 『~/+전+명』 뒹굴다(진창·모래·물 속에서). ② 『+전+명』 탐닉하다, (주색 따위에) 빠지다(in). ③ 허위적거리며 나아가다, 간신히 나아가다. / **self-evident** [sélfévədənt] a. 자명한. / **† brotherhood** [brʌ́ðərhùd] n. U ① 형제의 관계; 형제애. ② 단체, 협회, 조합; 동료, 「집합적」 동업자. / **ǂ desert** [dézərt] a. ① 사막의; 불모의(barren); 황량한. ② 사람이 살지 않는. ③ 사막에 사는. ------●a ～island 무인도.② 파~ed [-id] —a. ① 사람이 살지 않는, 황폐한: a ～ed street 사람의 왕래가 없는 거리. ② 버림받은. / **ǂ drip** [drip] v. (p., pp. dripped, dript:[-t]; dripping) —vi. ① (액체가) 듣다, 똑똑 떨어지다(from). ② 『~ / +전+명』 (젖어) 물방울이 떨어지다, 흠뻑 젖다, 넘칠 정도이다(with). ③ (비유) (음악 등이) 조용히 흐르다. / **interposition** [ìntərpəzíʃən] n. U 개재(의 위치); 삽입; 중재, 개입; 간섭; 방해; / **nullification** [nʌ̀ləfikéiʃ-ən] n. U 무효로 함[됨], 폐기, 취소;

by Martin Luther King

동영상 강좌 http://youtu.be/srsp74hiUxl

❋ 다음을 읽고 물음에 답하시오. [14~21]

I am not unmindful that Ⓐ<u>some of you</u> have come here out of great trials and tribulations. Some of you have come fresh from narrow cells. Some of you have come from areas where your quest for freedom left you battered by the storms of persecution and staggered by the winds of police brutality. You have been the veterans of Ⓑ**creative suffering**. Continue to work with the faith that unearned suffering is redemptive.

Go back to Mississippi, go back to Alabama, go back to Georgia, go back to Louisiana, go back to the slums and ghettos of our northern cities, knowing that somehow this situation can and will be changed. Let us not ①**wallow** in the valley of despair.

I say to you today, my friends, that in spite of the difficulties and frustrations of the moment, I still have a dream. It is a dream deeply rooted in the American dream.

I have a dream that one day this nation will rise up and live out the true meaning of its creed: "We hold these truths to be ②**self-evident**: that all men are created equal." I have a dream that one day on the red hills of Georgia the sons of former slaves and the sons of former slave-owners will be able to sit down together at a table of brotherhood.

I have a dream that one day even the state of Mississippi, a desert state, ③**sweltering** with the heat of injustice and oppression, will be transformed into an oasis of freedom and justice.

I have a dream that my four children will one day live in a nation where they will not be judged by the colour of their skin but by the ④**content** of their character.

I have a dream today.

I have a dream that one day the state of Alabama, Ⓒ<u>**whose governor's lips are presently dripping with the words of interposition and nullification**</u>, will be transformed into a situation where little black boys and black girls will be able to join hands with little white boys and white girls and walk together as sisters and brothers.

I have a dream today.

I have a dream that one day every valley shall be exalted, every hill and mountain shall be made ⑤**high**, the rough places will be made plain, and the crooked places will be made straight, and the glory of the Lord shall be revealed, and all flesh shall see it together.

14. 위 글의 제목으로 가장 적절한 것은?

① I have a dream.
② Many things suffered by the white
③ Why the black have to be persecuted until now
④ Very big gathering
⑤ Many ways to come out of the unequal treatments

15. 위 글에서 밑줄 친 Ⓐ에 포함되지 <u>않은</u> 것은?

① some suffering from ordeal or under affliction

② some set free from prisons

③ some hit by abuse or harassment

④ some veterans from wars

⑤ some longing for freedom

16. 위 글에서 밑줄 친 Ⓑ가 가리키는 것은?

① intolerant suffering

② understandable suffering

③ mental suffering

④ a newly variety of suffering

⑤ well-known suffering

17. 위 글에서 밑줄 친 ①~⑤ 중, 문맥상 단어의 쓰임이 <u>어색한</u> 것은?

①　　　②　　　③　　　④　　　⑤

18. 위 글에서 지은이가 강조하는 것과 거리가 <u>먼</u> 것은?

① The nation will be changed.

② Don't stay in the valley of despair.

③ The difficulties and frustration make him stronger.

④ All men will be created equal.

⑤ The glory of the Lord shall toll.

19. 위 글의 분위기는?

① worrying → discouraging

② sunlit → darkening

③ gloomy → frustrating

④ suffering → hopeful

⑤ energetic → hesitant

20. 위 글에서 밑줄 친 Ⓒ가 의미하는 것은?

① interference　　② cooperation

③ harmony　　　④ unity

⑤ campaign

21. 위 글과 일치하지 <u>않은</u> 것은?

① 이곳에 온 많은 사람들은 저마다의 학대와 멸시를 받았다.

② 고난을 속죄로 생각하며, 더 열심히 일하자.

③ 고난과 좌절 속에서도 꿈을 갖자.

④ 백인과의 상황이 반전될 날을 기다리자.

⑤ 저의 꿈의 이뤄질 것입니다.

14. ① 　15. ④ 　16. ④ 　17. ⑤ high → low 　18. ④ 　19. ④ 　20. ① 　21. ④

동영상 강좌 http://youtu.be/mx8y0DByuW4

This is our hope. This is ①the faith with which I return to the South. With this faith we will be able to ②hew out of the mountain of despair a stone of hope. With this faith we will be able to ③transform the jangling discords of our nation into a beautiful symphony of brotherhood. With this faith we will be able to work together, to pray together, to struggle together, to go to jail together, to stand up for freedom together, ④ knowing that we will be free one day.

This will be ⑤the day when all of God's children will be able to sing with a new meaning, "My country, 'tis of thee, sweet land of liberty, of thee I sing. ⑥Land where my fathers died, land of the pilgrim's pride, from every mountainside, let freedom ring."

And ⑦if America is to be a great nation this must become true. So let freedom ring from the prodigious hilltops of New Hampshire. Let freedom ring from the mighty mountains of New York. Let freedom ring from the heightening Alleghenies of Pennsylvania!

Let freedom ring from the snow-capped Rockies of Colorado!

Let freedom ring from the curvaceous peaks of California!

⑧But not only that; let freedom ring from Stone Mountain of Georgia!

Let freedom ring from Lookout Mountain of Tennessee!

Let freedom ring from every hill and every molehill of Mississippi. From every mountainside, let freedom ring.

When we let freedom ring, when we let it ring from every village and every hamlet, from every state and every city, ⑨we will be able to speed up that day when all of God's children, black men and white men, Jews and Gentiles, Protestants and Catholics, will be able to join hands and sing in the words of the old Negro spiritual, "Free at last! free at last! thank God Almighty, we are free at last!"

🔖 **문법분석**

① I return to the South with the faith. / which의 선행사는 the faith임.

② hew out of ~despair a stone of hope: hew의 목적어는 'a stone of hope - 절망의 거대한 산에서 희망의 보석을 깎아 내다.

③ transform A into B: A를 B로 바꾸다.

④ knowing[and know]

⑤ the day (when [부사절 생략가능]) ~하는 날.

⑥ Land (where [부사절 생략가능]) ~한 땅.

⑦ if[조건절, 만일 ~한다면] is to[목적, ~하고 싶다면] this must become true(이것이 틀림없이 사실이 되어야만 한다).

⑧ 그러나 그것이 전무가 아닙니다.

⑨ 그날을 빨리 볼 수 있을 것입니다.

📖 **본문해석**

This is our hope(이것이 우리의 희망입니다). **This is the faith with which I return to the South**(저는 이 믿음을 갖고 남부로 돌아갑니다). **With this faith**(이 신념을 갖고) **we will be able to hew out of the mountain of despair a stone of hope**(우리는 절망의 거대한 산에서 희망의 단단한 돌을 깎아 새길 수 있을 것입니다). **With this faith**(이 신념으로) **we will be able to transform the jangling discords of our nation into a beautiful symphony of brotherhood**(우리는 우리 국가의 거슬리는 불협화음을 형제애의 아름다운 하모니로 바꿀 수 있을 것입니다). **With this faith**(이 믿음으로) **we will be able to work together, to pray together, to struggle together, to go to jail together, to stand up for freedom together, knowing that we will be free one day**(우리는 함께 일하고, 함께 기도하고, 함께 투쟁하고, 함께 감옥에도 가고, 자유를 위해 함께 일어서서 어느 날 우리가 자유인이 되었다는 것을 알게 될 것입니다).

This will be the day when all of God's children will be able to sing with a new meaning, "My country, 'tis of thee, sweet land of liberty, of thee I sing(이것은 모든 신의 사제들이 새로운 의미를 갖는 자유로운 달콤한 이 땅, 내 나라의 노래를 부를 수 있게 되는 날이 될 것입니다). **Land where my fathers died, land of the pilgrim's pride, from every mountainside, let freedom ring**(그 땅은 우리 부모님이 돌아가신 땅, 순교자의 자부심이 새겨 있는 땅, 모든 산기슭으로부터 자유의 종소리가 울리게 합시다)."

And if America is to be a great nation this must become true(그리고 만일 미국이 위대한 나라가 되고 싶다면, 이것은 틀림없는 사실이 되어야만 합니다). **So let freedom ring from the prodigious hilltops of New Hampshire**(그래서 뉴햄프셔의 거대한 언덕으로부터 자유의 종소리가 울리게 합시다). **Let freedom ring from the mighty mountains of New York**(뉴욕의 강력한 산으로부터 자유의 종소리가 울리게 합시다). **Let freedom ring from the heightening Alleghenies of Pennsylvania**(펜실배니아의 드높은 알레헤니로부터 자유의 종소리가 울리게 합시다)!

Let freedom ring from the snow-capped Rockies of Colorado(콜로라도의 눈으로 덮여 있는 로키산맥으로부터 자유의 종소리가 울리게 합시다)!

Let freedom ring from the curvaceous peaks of California(캘리포니아의 부드러운 곡선미의 정상으로부터 자유의 종소리가 울리게 합시다)!

But not only that; let freedom ring from Stone Mountain of Georgia(그러나 그것 뿐만은 아닙니다. 조지아의 스톤마운틴에서부터 자유의 종소리가 울리게 합시다)!

Let freedom ring from Lookout Mountain of Tennessee(테네시의 룩아웃 마운틴으로부터 자유의 종소리가 울리게 합시다)!

Let freedom ring from every hill and every molehill of Mississippi(미시시피의 모든 언덕과 모든 두더지 언덕에서도 자유의 종소리가 울리게 합시다). **From every mountainside, let freedom ring**(모든 산기슭으로부터 자유의 종소리가 울리게 합시다).

When we let freedom ring(우리가 자유의 종을 울릴 때), **when we let it ring from every village and every hamlet, from every state and every city**(우리가 모든 주와 모든 도시에서 모든 마을과 모든 부락에서 자유의 종을 울릴 때), **we will be able to speed up that day**(우리는 그날을 더 빨리 기대할 수 있을 것입니다) **when all of God's children, black men and white men, Jews and Gentiles, Protestants and Catholics, will be able to join hands and sing in the words of the old Negro spiritual, "Free at last! free at last! thank God Almighty**(모든 신의 사제들인 흑인과 백인, 유태인과 비 유태인, 신교도와 구교도는 손을 맞잡고 옛 흑인 영가인 "드디어 자유야, 드디어 자유야!"의 노래를 부를 수 있을 때), **we**

are free at last!(우리 비로소 자유를 얻게 되는 것입니다)"

📎 **단어분석**

- †**hew** [hjuː] v. (~ed; hewn [hjuː n], ~ed) —vt. 『~+목 / + 목+전+명 / + 목+부』 ① (도끼·칼 따위로) 자르다(cut), 마구 베다, 토막내다; 베어 넘기다(down); 베어[잘라] 내다(down; off; out; from). ② 만들다, 깎아 새기다. [cf.] cut, carve. / **jangle** [dʒǽŋgəl] vt., vi. (방울 소리를) 딸랑딸랑 울리다; 귀에 거슬리는 소리를 내다; 시끄럽게 다투다; (신경을) 괴롭히다. / †**transform** [trænsfɔ́ː rm] vt. —vt. 『~+목/ +목+전+명』 ① (외형) 변형시키다(into). ② 바꾸다(성질·기능·구조 등을); ~을 다른 물질로 바꾸다. [SYN.] ⇨ CHANGE. / ‡**pilgrim** [pílgrim] n. ① 순례자, 성지 참배자. ② 나그네, 방랑자(wanderer). / †**prodigious** [prədídʒəs] a. ① 거대한, 막대한(vast, enormous). ② 비범한, 이상한, 놀라운. / ‡**mighty** [máiti] a. (mightier; -iest) ① 강력한. [SYN.] ⇨ STRONG. ② 위대한, 거대한. / †**heighten** [háitn] v. —vt. ① 높게 하다, 높이다; 고상하게 하다. [opp.] lower. ② 더하다, 강화시키다, 증대[증가]시키다. ③ (묘사 따위를) 과장하다. / **curvaceous, —cious** [kəː rvéiʃəs] a. (구어) 곡선미의, 육체미의(여성에 대한 말). / **hamlet** [hǽmlit] n. 작은 마을, 부락, (특히) 교회 없는 작은 마을. /

❋ 다음 글을 읽고 물음에 답하시오. [22~29]

Ⓐ**This is our hope**. This is the faith with which I return to the South. With this faith we will be able to ①**hew** out of the mountain of despair a stone of hope. With this faith we will be able to ②**transform** the jangling discords of our nation into a beautiful symphony of brotherhood. With this faith we will be able to work together, to pray together, to struggle together, to go to jail together, to stand up for freedom together, ③**know** that we will be free one day.

This will be the day when all of God's children will be able to ④**sing** with a new meaning, "My country, 'tis of thee, sweet land of liberty, of thee I sing. Land where my fathers died, land of the pilgrim's pride, from every mountainside, let freedom ring."

And if America is to be a great nation this must ⑤**become** true. So let freedom ring from the (1)**prodigious** hilltops of New Hampshire. Let freedom ring from the (2)**mighty** mountains of New York. Let freedom ring from the (3)**lowing** Alleghenies of Pennsylvania!

Let freedom ring from the (4)**snow-capped** Rockies of Colorado!

Let freedom ring from the (5)**curvaceous** peaks of California!

But not only that; let freedom ring from Stone Mountain of Georgia!

Let freedom ring from Lookout Mountain of Tennessee!

Let freedom ring from every hill and every molehill of Mississippi. From every mountainside, let freedom ring.

When we let freedom ring, when we let it ring from every village and every hamlet, from every state and every city, _____ when all of God's children, black men and white men, Jews and Gentiles, Protestants and Catholics, will be able to join hands and sing in the words of the old Negro spiritual, "Free at last! free at last! thank God Almighty, we are free at last!"

22. 위 글의 주제로 가장 적절한 것은?

① The Absolute already decided the nation must be happy.
② Let's freedom ring until the nation understand our position.
③ We should go forward to the future for the nation.
④ We often have to get together to show our strength.
⑤ From now on, little black and white should meet and learn how to catch their hands.

23. 위 글에서 밑줄 친 Ⓐ에 속하지 <u>않은</u> 것은?

① To pick up a value of hope from the gigantic despair.
② To change the disparity into the be beautiful symphony.
③ To live in the same communities in the spirit of coexistence.
④ To sing with a new meaning, "For the land of liberty."
⑤ To commemorate the Emancipation Proclamation.

24. 위 글에 나타난 분위기는?

① sentimental   ② pragmatistic
③ pessimistic   ④ futuristic
⑤ realistic

25. 위 글에서 밑줄 친 ①~⑤ 중, 어법상 어색한 것은?

①   ②   ③   ④   ⑤

26. 위 글에서 밑줄 친 빈칸에 가장 적절한 표현은?

① we will not forget how hard ancestors worked for the national unity.
② we start inviting all neighbors for that day
③ we should try to find where the rings are installed
④ we will be able to speed up that day
⑤ we will understand how valuable today is

27. 위 글에서 밑줄 친 (1)~(5)중, 문맥상 단어의 쓰임이 어색한 것은?

① (1)   ② (2)   ③ (3)   ④ (4)   ⑤ (5)

28. 위 글을 요약하였다. 빈칸 Ⓐ, Ⓑ에 적절한 표현은?

> The freedom we have sought for should be scattered to not only _____Ⓐ_____, but ___Ⓑ___.

① our neighbors   the world
② our nearness   the whole country
③ our communities   the universe
④ our homes   our cities
⑤ our rural areas   our urban areas

29. 위 글과 일치하지 <u>않은</u> 것은?

① 희망의 자유의 종은 함께 울릴 때만 가능하다.
② 오늘 우리의 희망은 남부로 전해질 것이다.
③ 흑백의 갈등은 종을 울림으로서 해결할 수 있다.
④ 우리의 자유의 종은 전국적으로 울려 퍼져야만 한다.
⑤ 함께 흑인영가를 부를 때, 그날이 바로 자유를 얻는 날이다.

22. ③   23. ⑤   24. ②④   25. ③ knowing
26. ④   27. ③ lowering → heightening
28.   29. ③

The Obituary to Diana Princess of Wales

by the Earl of Spencer

[난이도 ★★★★☆]

동영상 강좌 http://youtu.be/emIRU7IZmPA

I stand ①before you today, the representative of a family in grief, in a country in mourning, before a world in shock.

We are all united, ②not only in our desire to pay our respects to Diana, but rather in our need to do so, because ③such was her extraordinary appeal that the tens of millions of people taking part in this service all over the world via television and radio who never actually met her feel that they too lost someone close to them in the early hours of Sunday morning.

④It is a more remarkable tribute to Diana that I can ever hope to offer to her today.

Diana was the very essence of compassion, of duty, of style, of beauty.

All over the world she was the symbol of selfless humanity. ⑤A standard bearer for the rights of the truly downtrodden. A very British girl who transcended nationality. Someone with a natural nobility who was classless and who proved in the last year that she needed no royal title to continue to generate her particular brand of magic.

Today is our chance to say 'thank you' for ⑥the way you brightened our lives, ⑦even though God granted you but half a life. We will all ⑧feel cheated always that you were taken from us so young and yet we must learn to be grateful that you came at all.

⑨Only now you are gone do we truly appreciate what we are without, and we want you to know that life without you is very, very difficult.

We ⑩have all despaired for our loss over the past week and ⑪only the strength of the message you gave us through your years of giving has afforded us the strength to move forward.

There is a temptation to rush, to canonize your memory. There is no need to do ⑫so. You stand tall enough as a human being of unique qualities, and do not need to be seen as a saint.

Indeed, to sanctify your memory would be to miss out on ⑬the very core of your being— your wonderfully mischievous sense of humor with a laugh that bent you double, your joy for life transmitted wherever you took your smile and the sparkle in those unforgettable eyes, your boundless energy which you could barely contain.

But your greatest gift was your intuition and it was a gift you used wisely. This is what underpinned all your other wonderful attributes.

📝 문법분석

① before(~앞에) you today, (the representative[동격] of a family in grief[슬픔에 잠긴]), in a country in mourning[애도하는 국가], (and) before a world in shock[충격에 빠진 세상 앞에]
- 저는 오늘 여러분, 슬픔에 잠긴 가족 친지 여러분, 애도하는 이 나라에서, 충격에 빠진 세상 앞에 섰습니다.

② not only A, but rather B: A뿐만 아니라 오히려 B한 / so = pay our respects to Diana.

③ such was her extraordinary appeal that ~: 그것은 ~할 만큼 그녀의 놀라운 매력이었습니다. / ~ people[주어] (who are) taking part in ~her feel[본동사] that /

④ it is a more remarkable tribute to Diana[강조어구] that A: A하는 것은 바로 다이애나에 대한 아주 훌륭한 존경심입니다. / offer의 목적어는 tribute /

⑤ (She was) A standard ~. (She was) A very British ~. (She was) Someone ~. /

⑥ the way (that) you brightened our lives: 우리의 삶에 빛을 준 방식.

⑦ 짧은 생을 마감하다.

⑧ 늘 죄책감을 느끼다.

⑨ only[문장의 도치를 유도함] ~do / what we are without (you): 당신이 없는 현실 /

⑩ [현재완료 계속] /

⑪ 많은 것 중에서 '메시지만으로'도 힘을 얻게 됨을 의미함.

⑫ so = to canonize your memory

⑬ the very core를 자세히 나열하여 설명함.

📎 **본문해석**

I stand before you today, the representative of a family in grief, in a country in mourning, before a world in shock(저는 오늘 여러분, 슬픔에 잠긴 가족 친지 여러분, 애도하는 이 나라에서, 충격에 빠진 세상 앞에 섰습니다).

We are all united, not only in our desire to pay our respects to Diana(우리 모두는 다이애나에 존경을 표하고자 하나가 되었습니다), **but rather in our need to do so**(뿐만 아니라 오히려 그렇게 해야 할 필요성을 절감하고 있습니다), **because such was her extraordinary appeal**(그러한 것은 바로 그녀의 놀라운 매력은 ~입니다) **that the tens of millions of people taking part in this service all over the world via television and radio who never actually met her**(왜냐하면 전 세계에서 텔레비전과 라디오로 이 장례식에 참여하고 그녀를 만난 적이 없는 수 천만 사람들은) **feel that they too lost someone close to them in the early hours of Sunday morning**(그들이 일요일 이른 아침에 그들과 너무나 가까운 누군가를 또한 잃었다는 것을 느끼고 있습니다).

It is a more remarkable tribute to Diana that I can ever hope to offer to her today(그것은 제가 오늘 지금껏 그녀에게 주고 싶어 했던 다이애나에 대한 아주 훌륭한 존경심입니다).

Diana was the very essence of compassion, of duty, of style, of beauty(다이애나는 동정심, 의무, 품격 그리고 미의 진정한 실체였습니다).

All over the world she was the symbol of selfless humanity(세계적으로 그녀는 헌신적인 인간애의 상징이었습니다). **A standard bearer for the rights of the truly downtrodden**(아주 짓밟힌 사람들의 권리를 전해주는 모범이었습니다). **A very British girl who transcended nationality**(국적을 초월한 진정한 영국의 소녀였습니다). **Someone with a natural nobility who was classless and who proved in the last year that she needed no royal title to continue to generate her particular brand of magic**(계급차별이 없는 한 국가의 고결함을 갖고 있고 그녀의 신비로운 특별한 장점을 계속 살리고자 왕실자격이 필요 없다는 것을 작년에 입증한 여자였습니다).

Today is our chance to say 'thank you' for the way you brightened our lives(오늘은 그녀가 우리의 삶을 환하게 비추어진 길에 감사를 드리는 기회입니다), **even though God granted you but half a life**(비록 신께서 그녀를 일찍 내려갔을지라도). **We will all feel cheated always that you were taken from us so young and yet we must learn to be grateful that you came at all**(우리는 당신이 너무나 젊은 나이

에 우리를 떠났고 이제야 우리는 당신이 이곳에 온 것에 대해 감사를 해야 하는 우리들 자신을 앞으로도 계속 속일 것 같습니다).

Only now you are gone do we truly appreciate what we are without(이제 당신이 우리 곁을 떠나니, 우린 당신이 없는 우리 자신을 진정 절감합니다), **and we want you to know that life without you is very, very difficult**(그리고 우린 당신이 없는 삶이 얼마나, 얼마나 힘들지를 당신이 알아주기를 원합니다).

We have all despaired for our loss over the past week and only the strength of the message you gave us through your years of giving has afforded us the strength to move forward(우리 모두는 지난 주내내 우리의 크나큰 손실에 절망하고 있고 당신이 우리에게 평생 베풀어 준 그 메시지만으로도 강인함은 우리로 하여금 앞으로 전진 할 힘을 주고 있습니다).

There is a temptation to rush, to canonize your memory(성급히 당신의 추억을 추앙하는 유혹도 있습니다). **There is no need to do so**(그럴 필요성은 없습니다). **You stand tall enough as a human being of unique qualities, and do not need to be seen as a saint**(당신은 유일한 품성의 존재로 이미 우뚝 서 있고 성인으로서 보여 질 필요는 없습니다).

Indeed, to sanctify your memory would be to miss out on the very core of your being(실제로, 당신의 추억을 신성시하는 것은 당신의 존재의 핵심을 잊어버리는 것이 될 것입니다)— **your wonderfully mischievous sense of humor with a laugh that bent you double**(당신을 배로 웃게 한 미소를 품은 멋진 개구쟁이 같은 유머감각), **your joy for life transmitted wherever you took your smile**(당신이 미소를 품은 곳 어디나 전달되는 삶의 기쁨) **and the sparkle in those unforgettable eyes**(그런 잊지 못할 눈망울 속에 반짝이는 광채), **your boundless energy which you could barely contain**(당신의 넘쳐나는 무한한 에너지).

But your greatest gift was your intuition and it was a gift you used wisely(그러나 당신의 가장 큰 재능은 직관력이고 그것은 당신이 슬기롭게 활용한 것입니다). **This is what underpinned all your other wonderful attributes**(이것이 모든 당신의 훌륭한 품성의 바탕입니다).

📝 단어분석

- † **representative** [rèprizéntətiv] n. ① 대표자, 대행자, 대리인(of; from; on; at); 재외(在外) 사절; 후계자, 상속자. ② 대의원; (R-) 【미국】 하원 의원. / ‡ **grief** [griː f] n. ① U (깊은) 슬픔, 비탄, 비통. [SYN.] ⇨ SORROW. ② C 슬픔의 씨앗, 비탄의 원인, 통탄지사. / ‡ **mourning** [mɔ́ː riŋ] n. U ① 비탄(sorrowing), 슬픔; 애도(lamentation). ② 상(喪), 거상(기간); 기중(忌中). ③ 상복, 상장(喪章), 조기(弔旗). / ‡ **unite** [juː náit] v. —vt. ① 『~+목/ +목+전+명』 결합하다, 하나로 묶다, 합하다, 접합하다(with); 합병하다, 합동시키다. [SYN.] ⇨ JOIN. ② 『~+목/ +목+전+명』 (사회적·가족적 관계로) 맺다, 결혼시키다; (정신적으로) 결합하다. / ‡ **extraordinary** [ikstrɔ́ː rdənèri, èkstrɔ́ː rdənəri] a. ① 대단한, 비상한, 보통이 아닌, 비범한, 엄청난. ② 터무니없는, 놀라운, 의외의. ③ 특별한, 임시의. / ‡ **tribute** [tríbjuː t]n. ① U,C 공물, 조세; 과도한 세[관세, 부과금, 임대료], 터무니 없는 징수금; 납공[납세] 의무. ② C,U 찬사, 칭찬[감사, 존경]을 나타내는 말[행위, 선물, 표시]. / ‡ **remarkable** [rimáː rkəb-əl] a. 주목할 만한, 현저한, 남다른, 훌륭한, 놀랄 만한. [SYN.] ⇨ EXTRAORDINARY. / ‡ **essence** [ésəns] n. ① U 본질, 진수, 정수; 핵심, 요체. ② U,C 에센스, 엑스. ③ C 『철학』 실재, 실체; (특히) 영적인 실재. / † **compassion** [kəmpǽʃən] n. U 불쌍히 여김, (깊은) 동정(심). / **selfless** [sélflis] a. 사심[이기심] 없는, 무욕[무사]의(unselfish); 헌신적인. / ‡ **humanity** [hjuː mǽnəti] n. ① U 인류. ② U 인간성, 인도; (pl.) 인간의 속성, 인간다움. ③ U 인간애, 박애, 자애, 인정. / † **bearer** [béərər] n. ① 나르는 사람; 짐꾼, 인부; 상여꾼 / **downtrodden** [-tràdn / -trɔ̀dn] a. 짓밟힌 / **transcend** [trænsénd] vt., vi. (경험·이해력 등의

범위·한계를) 넘다; (우주·물질적 존재 따위를) 초월[초절(超絶)]하다. / ⧾ **nobility** [noubíləti] n. ① U 고귀(성), 숭고, 고결함, 기품; 고귀한 태생[신분]. / **canonize** [kǽnənàiz] vt. 시성(諡聖)하다; 성인(聖人)으로 추앙하다 / ⧾ **temptation** [temptéiʃ-ən] n. ① U 유혹, 유혹함[됨]. ② 유혹물, 마음을 끄는 것. / ⧾ **sanctify** [sǽŋktəfài] vt. ① 신성하게 하다, 축성(祝聖)하다, 신에게 바치다; 숭배하다. / ⧾ **intuition** [ìntjuíʃən] n. U 직각(直覺), 직관(력); 직관적 통찰; 직관적 지식[사실]. / **underpin** [ʌndərpín] vt. (-nn-) (건물 등의) 약한 토대를 갈다[보강하다], ~의 밑에 버팀을 대다; 지지하다(support), 응원하다.

✳ 다음 글을 읽고 물음에 답하시오. [1~7]

I stand before you today, the representative of a family in grief, in a country in mourning, before a world in shock.

We are all united, not only in our desire to pay our respects to Diana, but rather in our need to do Ⓐ**so**, because such was her extraordinary appeal that the tens of millions of people ①**taking** part in this service all over the world via television and radio who never actually met her ②**feeling** that they too lost someone close to them in the early hours of Sunday morning.

It is a more remarkable tribute to Diana ③**that** I can ever hope to offer to her today.

Diana was the very essence of compassion, of duty, of style, of beauty.

All over the world she was the symbol of selfless humanity. A standard bearer for the rights of the truly downtrodden. A very British girl who transcended nationality. Someone with a natural nobility who was classless and who ④**proved** in the last year that she needed no royal title to continue to generate her particular brand of magic.

Today is our chance to say 'thank you' for the way you brightened our lives, even though Ⓑ**God granted you but half a life**. Ⓒ**We will all feel cheated always that you were taken from us so young and yet we must learn to be grateful that you came at all**.

Only now you are gone ⑤**do** we truly appreciate what we are without, and we want you to know that life without you is very, very difficult.

Ⓓ**We have all despaired for our loss over the past week and only the strength of the message you gave us through your years of giving has afforded us the strength to move forward**.

Ⓔ**There is a temptation to rush, to canonize your memory. There is no need to do so. You stand tall enough as a human being of unique qualities, and do not need to be seen as a saint**.

Indeed, to sanctify your memory would be to miss out on the very core of your being —your wonderfully mischievous sense of humor with a laugh that bent you double, your joy for life transmitted wherever you took your smile and the sparkle in those unforgettable eyes, your boundless energy which you could barely contain.

But your greatest gift was your intuition and it was a gift you used wisely. This is what underpinned all your other wonderful attributes.

1. 위 글의 주제로 가장 적절한 것은?

① You will be long engraved on our mind.

② The saddest things must be avoided.

③ We, mourners, should be in pursuit of the details of her accident.

④ As soon as we should forget the sad things, we have to rise up for the future.

⑤ In order not to forget her, we should build a memorial center.

2. 위 글에서 밑줄 친 Ⓐ가 가리키는 것은?

① commemorating the mourning event
② standing before all the world
③ falling into the grief
④ all being united
⑤ paying our respects to Diana

3. 위 글에서 밑줄 친 ①~⑤ 중, 어법상 <u>어색</u>한 것은?

①   ②   ③   ④   ⑤

4. 위 글에서 밑줄 친 Ⓑ가 의미하는 것은?

① Everybody has a short lifespan.
② God takes anyone who is sacrificed earlier.
③ God has an equality to everybody.
④ Diana's unfortune was foreseen before.
⑤ Diana should have lived longer.

5. 위 글에서 밑줄 친 Ⓒ에 대한 지은이의 심정은?

① inappreciative   ② respective
③ admirable   ④ indifferent
⑤ regretful

6. 위 글에서 밑줄 친 Ⓓ에 대한 지은이의 심정은?

① in retrospect   ② disappointed
③ thankful   ④ pessimistic
⑤ frustrated

7. 위 글에서 밑줄 친 Ⓔ에 나타난 'You'에 대한 지은이의 심정은?

① To hope you will stay with us as a valuable friend.
② To wish you would stand up with more qualities.
③ To anticipate that you should be respected as a saint.
④ To expect that you might as well be a supernatural woman.
⑤ To memorize your achievement should be kept in the museum.

1. ①   2. ⑤   3. ② feel   4. ⑤
5. ⑤   6. ③   7. ①

And if we ①look to analyse what it was about you that had such a wide appeal we find ②it in your instinctive feel <u>for</u> what was really important in all our lives.

②<u>Without</u> your God-given sensitivity, we would <u>be immersed in greater ignorance</u> at the anguish of Aids and HIV sufferers, the plight of the homeless, the isolation of lepers, the random destruction of land mines.

Diana explained to me once that ③<u>it was her innermost feelings of suffering that made it possible for her to connect with her constituency of the rejected.</u>

And here we <u>come to another truth</u> about her. ④<u>For all the status, the glamour, the applause</u>, Diana remained throughout a very insecure person at heart, almost childlike in her desire to do good for others so she could ⑤<u>release herself from</u> deep feelings of ⑥ <u>unworthiness of which her eating disorders were merely a symptom.</u>

<u>The world sensed this part of her character and cherished her vulnerability.</u>

⑦<u>The last time I saw Diana</u> was on July 1st, her birthday, in London when typically she was <u>not</u> taking time to <u>celebrate her special day with</u> friends <u>but</u> was guest of honour at a fund-raising charity evening. <u>She sparkled</u>, of course.

But I ⑧<u>would rather cherish the days I spent with her</u> in March when she came to visit me and my children at our home in South Africa. I am proud of ⑨<u>the fact that</u>, <u>apart from when</u> she was on public display meeting President Mandela, we <u>managed to contrive to stop</u> the <u>ever-present paparazzi</u> from getting a single picture of her. That meant a lot to her.

These are days I will always treasure. ⑩<u>It was as if</u> we ⑪<u>were transported back to</u> our childhood when we spent ⑫<u>such</u> an enormous amount of time together <u>as</u> the two youngest in the family.

Fundamentally she hadn't changed at all from the big ⑬<u>sister who</u> mothered me as a baby, fought with me at school, who endured ⑭<u>those long journeys between our parents' home</u> with me at weekends.

It is a tribute to <u>her level-headedness and strength</u> that despite the most bizarre life after her childhood, she ⑮<u>remained intact, true to herself.</u>

⑯<u>There is no doubt</u> she was <u>looking for</u> a new direction in her life <u>at this time</u>.

🖎 문법분석

① 살펴 볼 것을 기대하다.

② it = a wide appeal / for[because] 무언가가 우리 모두의 인생에서 정말로 중요했던 것이기 때문

② [가정법 과거완료] without = if it were not for ~이 없었다면, if it were not for your God-given sensitivity / be immersed in greater ignorance ~을 모르다.

③ [강조용법] it is[was] + [강조어구] that ~/ made it[가목적어] + 형용사 + for her[의미상의 주어]

259

to[진주어] 그녀가 버림받은 사람들의 후원과 연계를 가능하게 하다. / com to[become aware of] another truth 또 다른 진실을 알게 되다.

④ For[~에도 불구하고], Diana는 평생 마음이 허전했다 /

⑤ release A from B: A가 B로부터 자유롭게 되다.

⑥ a symptom of unworthiness: 하찮은 증세 / which의 선행사는 unworthiness
The world[세상 사람들] sensed[이해했다] this part of her character[그녀의 품성의 이 단면을] and cherished her vulnerability[그리하여 그녀의 약점을 소중하게 하였다.]

⑦ The las time[주어] (when) I saw Diana was[동사] / not A but B: A가 아닌 B인 / celebrate[spend ~을 보내다] 지인들과 자신의 생일을 보내다. / She sparked 행사를 밝혀 주다.

⑧ 아주 ~하고 싶다[그녀와 함께 보낸 날들을 소중히 간직하다].
the days (that, which) I spent with her

⑨ [동격] ~라는 사실. / [전치사 절] apart from when ~: ~을 할 때를 제외하고 / managed to[겨우 ~하다] contrive[궁리하다]
ever-presetn paparazzi 늘 쫓아 다니는 파파라치 / stop A from ~ing: A가 ~하는 것을 멈추게 하다.

⑩ It was as if: 그날은 마치 ~인 것 같았다.

⑪ 황홀한 과거로 돌아가다.

⑫ such + A[명사] as B[구]: A와 같은[로써] B인

⑬ sister who mothered ~, (who) fought with ~, and who

⑭ 부모와 떨어 삼. / 그녀의 분별력과 강인함.

⑮ remain + 형용사: 그녀 자신에게 완벽하고 솔직하게 살다.

⑯ There is no doubt that ~: ~는 분명하다. / looking for ~을 찾고 있었다. / at this time 이때에

📎 본문해석

And if we look to analyse what it was about you that had such a wide appeal(그리고 만일 우리가 그런 다방면의 매력이 무엇인지를 살펴본다면) **we find it in your instinctive feel for what was really important in all our lives**(우리는 우리의 모든 인생에서 정말로 중요했던 것이 당신의 본능적인 감정 안에서 그것을 찾게 됩니다).

Without your God-given sensitivity(당신의 신이 내린 감각이 없었다면), **we would be immersed in greater ignorance at the anguish of Aids and HIV sufferers, the plight of the homeless, the isolation of lepers, the random destruction of land mines**(우리는 에이즈 환자의 고통과 집이 없는 사람들의 재앙, 나환자들의 고립감, 그리고 지뢰에 의한 무자비한 파괴 전혀 몰랐을 것입니다).

Diana explained to me once(다이애나는 한 때 저에게 설명해 주었습니다) **that it was her innermost feelings of suffering that made it possible for her to connect with her constituency of the rejected**(그것은 그녀가 버림받은 사람의 후원과 연계를 가능하게 하는 것은 바로 그녀의 내면 깊은 곳에 있는 고통의 느낌이라고).

And here we come to another truth about her(그리고 여기서 우린 그녀에 관한 또 다른 진실을 알게 됩니다). **For all the status, the glamour, the applause, Diana remained throughout a very insecure person at heart, almost childlike in her desire to do good for others so she could release herself from deep feelings of unworthiness of which her eating disorders were merely a symptom**(모든 지위, 매력, 찬사에도 불구하고, 다이애나는 언제나 실제론 아주 불안한 사람이었고 다른 사람들을 위해 선행을 할 땐 거의 아이와도 같았습니다. 그래서 그녀는 식이장애를 단지 가벼운 증세라는 느낌으로부터 스스로

해방될 수 있었습니다).

The world sensed this part of her character and cherished her vulnerability(세상 사람들은 그녀의 이런 성격도 이해하며 그녀의 약점도 소중히 생각했습니다).

The last time I saw Diana was on July 1st, her birthday, in London(지난번 제가 다이애나를 그녀의 생일인 7월 1일에 보았습니다) **when typically she was not taking time to celebrate her special day with friends**(그때 늘 그랬듯 지인들과 특별한 날을 보낼 시간이 없었습니다) **but was guest of honour at a fund-raising charity evening**(그러나 그녀는 모금행사 저녁식사에 특별 손님으로 참석 중이었습니다). **She sparkled, of course**(그녀는 물론 환하게 빛나고 있었습니다).

But I would rather cherish the days I spent with her in March when she came to visit me and my children at our home in South Africa(그러나 저는 그녀가 남아프리카에 있는 제 집을 방문했던 때인 3월 그와 함께 지낸 몇 칠이 아주 소중하게 간직하고 싶습니다). **I am proud of the fact**(~한 사실이 자랑스럽습니다) **that, apart from when she was on public display meeting President Mandela**(그녀가 만델라 대통령과의 공식적 회동과 별개로), **we managed to contrive to stop the ever-present paparazzi from getting a single picture of her**(우리는 늘 따라 다니는 파파라치가 그녀의 사진 한 장도 찍지 못하게 할 것을 가까스로 궁리해 냈습니다). **That meant a lot to her**(그것은 그녀에게 아주 중요했습니다).

These are days I will always treasure(이런 날들을 저는 늘 소중히 간직할 것입니다). **It was as if we were transported back to our childhood**(그날은 마치 우리가 어린 시절로 황홀하게 돌아갔던 것 같았습니다) **when we spent such an enormous amount of time together as the two youngest in the family**(우리가 한 가정의 두 어린아이로서 수많은 시간을 함께했던 때).

Fundamentally she hadn't changed at all from the big sister who mothered me as a baby(근본적으로 그녀는 저를 애기로서 엄마 역할을 해준 큰 누나로서 전혀 바뀌지 않았습니다), **fought with me at school**(학교에서 저와 싸웠던), **who endured those long journeys between our parents' home with me at weekends**(주말엔 나를 데리고 저희 부모님을 방문하는 그 긴긴 여행을 참아냈던).

It is a tribute to her level-headedness and strength that despite the most bizarre life after her childhood, she remained intact, true to herself(그것은 어린 시절 후 가장 끔찍한 삶일지라도, 그녀는 자신에게 완벽하고 솔직했던 그녀의 완벽함과 강인함에 대한 존경입니다).

There is no doubt she was looking for a new direction in her life at this time(이때에 그녀는 새로운 길을 찾고 있었던 것이 분명합니다).

🖎 단어분석

- ****wide** [waid] a. ① 폭넓은; [opp.] narrow. [SYN.] ⇨ BROAD. 다방면의. / † **instinctive** [instíŋktiv] a. 본능적인, 천성의. / ‡ **immerse** [imə́ː rs] vt. 몰두시키다(in). / ‡ **ignorance** [ígnərəns] n. U 무지, 무학; (어떤 일을) 모름. / † **anguish** [ǽŋgwiʃ] n. U (심신의) 고통, 번민. / ‡ **plight** [plait] n. 곤경, 어려운 입장[처지, 상태]. / † **homeless** [hóumlis] a. 집 없는 · ‡ **isolation** [àisəléiʃən, ìsə-] n. U,C ① 고립(화), 격리, 교통 차단; / **leper** [lépəː r] n. ① 나(병)환자, 문둥이. / ‡ **random** [rǽndəm] a. ① 닥치는 대로의, 되는 대로의, 임의의. / ‡ **destruction** [distrʌ́kʃən] n. U ① 파괴; 분쇄. [opp] construction./ † **innermost** [ínərmòust] n. 가장 깊숙한 / **constituency** [kənstítʃuənsi] n. ① (한 지구의) 선거인, 유권자. ② 단골, 고객/ † **status** [stéitəs, stǽtəs] n. U,C ① 상태; 지위; 자격 / † **glamour, -or** [glǽmər] n. U,C ① (마음을 홀릴 정도의) 매력, 황홀하게 만드는 매력; / ‡ **applause** [əplɔ́ː z] n. U 박수 갈채; 칭찬. / **insecure** [insikjúər] a. (-curer; -est) ① 불안정[불안전]한 ② 불안한, 불확실한 / ♣ **at heart** 마음속은, 실제로는: / ‡ **merely** [míərli] ad. 단지, 전혀. / † **symptom** [símptəm] n. 징후, 조짐,

전조(of). / ****sense** [sens] vt. ① 느껴 알다, 지각하다. ② 알아채다; 깨닫다. / **vulnerability** 취약점, 약점 / ③ (미국구어) 알다, 납득[이해]하다; / **guest of honor** 초대손님 / †**typical** [típik-əl] a. ① 전형적인, 대표적인. ② 특유의, 특징적(of). ③ 상징적인. / **fund-raising charity** 자선모금 행사 / †**sparkle** [spá: rk-əl] v. —vi. ① 불꽃을 튀기다. ② 번생기[활기]가 있다. / **manage to** ～: ～+목/ +to do』 어떻게든 해서 ～하다. / **contrive** [kəntráiv] v. —vt. ① 연구하다; 고안[발명]하다; 설계하다. [SYN.] ⇨ INVENT. / ****treasure** [tréʒə: r] vt. ①『～+목/ +목+부』 ① (안전·장래를 위하여) 비축해 두다 (귀중품을) 비장하다(up); 소중히 하다. / †**transport** [trænspó: rt] vt. ① 수송하다, 운반하다. [SYN.] ⇨ CARRY. / **level-headed** [lév: -əlhédid] a. 온건한, 분별 있는. / bizarre [bizá: r] a. 【F.】 기괴한 (grotesque), 좀 별난, 별스러운. / **intact** [intǽkt] a. 본래대로의, 손대지 않은 (untouched), 완전한([SYN.] ⇨ COMPLETE); /

☀ 다음 글을 읽고 물음에 답하시오. [8~13]

And if we look to analyse what it was about you that had such a wide appeal we find Ⓐ**it** in your instinctive feel for what was really important in all our lives.

Without your God-given sensitivity, we would be/have been immersed in greater ignorance at the anguish of Aids and HIV sufferers, the plight of the homeless, the isolation of lepers, the random destruction of land mines.

Diana explained to me once that it was her innermost feelings of suffering that made it/that possible for her to connect with her constituency of the rejected.

And here we come to another truth about her. For all the status, the glamour, the applause, Diana remained throughout a very insecure person at heart, almost childlike in her desire to do good for others so she could release herself for/from deep feelings of unworthiness of which her eating disorders were merely a symptom.

The world sensed this part of her character and cherished her vulnerability.

The last time I saw Diana was on July 1st, her birthday, in London when typically she was not taking time to celebrate her special day with friends but was guest of honour at a fund-raising charity evening. She sparkled, of course.

But I would rather cherish the days I spent with her in March when she came to visit me and my children at our home in South Africa. I am proud of the fact that, apart from when she was on public display meeting President Mandela, we managed to contrive to stop the ever-present paparazzi from getting a single picture of her. That meant a lot to her.

These are days I will always treasure. _____ _____ when we spent such an enormous amount of time together as the two youngest in the family.

Fundamentally she hadn't changed at all from the big sister who mothered me as a baby, fought with me at school, who endured those long journeys between our parents' home with me at weekends.

It is a tribute to her level-headedness and strength that despite the most bizarre life after her childhood, she remained intact, true to herself.

There is no doubt she was looking for a new direction in her life at this time.

8. 위 글의 주제가 가장 적절한 것은?

① Diana's hardship was to escape from royal background

② Diana's eating disorder made her more devotional.

③ Many lessons we should learn from her are forgettable.

④ Diana's sacred spirit would be memorized.

⑤ Diana's long struggling is so sad we cannot help bear her in heart.

9. 위 글에서 밑줄 친 Ⓐ가 가리키는 것은?

① a wide appeal
② your instinctive feel
③ all our lives
④ death
⑤ our feeling

10. 위 글에서 알 수 있는 'Diana'의 품성과 거리가 먼 것은?

① humanitarian   ② responsible
③ devotional   ④ royal proud
⑤ altruism

11. 위 글에서 네모상자 안의 적절한 단어는?

① be   it   for
② have been   that   from
③ be   that   from
④ have been   that   for
⑤ be   it   from

12. 위 글의 빈 칸에 가장 적절한 표현은?

① It was as if we were transported back to our childhood
② It was as if we dreamed a dream for the future
③ It was as if we though of our bad family background
④ It was as if we regretted of not going back to the good days
⑤ It was as if we couldn't live together

13. 위 글로 보아 지은이와 Diana와의 관계는?

① in a family
② in a neighbor
③ in a royal family
④ in a friend
⑤ in a social contact

8. ④   9. ①   10. ④   11. ⑤   12. ①
13. ①

She talked endlessly of getting away from England, ①mainly because of the treatment that she received at the hands of the newspapers.

I don't think she ever understood ②why her genuinely good intentions were sneered at by the media, ③why there appeared to be a permanent quest on their behalf to bring her down. It is baffling.

④My own and only explanation is that genuine goodness is threatening to ⑤those at the opposite end of the moral spectrum.

It is a point to remember that of all the ironies about Diana, perhaps ⑥the greatest was this: a girl given the name of the ancient goddess of hunting was, in the end, the most hunted person of the modern age.

She would want us today to pledge ourselves to protecting her beloved boys, William and Harry, from a similar fate, and I ⑦do this here, Diana, on your behalf.

We will ⑧not allow them to suffer the anguish that used regularly to drive you to tearful despair. And beyond that, on behalf of your mother and sisters, ⑨I pledge that we, your blood family, will do all we can to continue the imaginative and loving way in which you were steering these two exceptional young men so that their souls are not simply immersed by duty and tradition but can sing openly as you planned.

We fully respect the heritage ⑩into which they have both been born and will always respect and encourage them in their royal role. But we, like you, recognize the need for them to experience ⑪as many different aspects of life as possible to arm them spiritually and emotionally for the years ahead. I know you ⑫would have expected nothing less from us.

⑬William and Harry, we all care desperately for you today. We are all chewed up with sadness at the loss of a woman who wasn't even our mother. ⑭How great your suffering is we cannot even imagine.

⑮I would like to end by thanking God for the small mercies he has shown us at this dreadful time, for taking Diana at her most beautiful and radiant and when she had joy in her private life.

Above all, we give thanks for the life of a woman I'm so proud to be able to ⑯call my sister the unique, the complex, the extraordinary and irreplaceable Diana whose beauty, both internal and external, will never be extinguished from our minds.

🖋 문법분석

① 주로 ~때문에 the treatment (that) she received

② [문장 안에서] why[의문사] her ~[주어] were[동사]

③ why [도치문] there appeared to be a permanent quest[주어] ~on their behalf[전치사구, ~을 대신

하여] to bring her down[부정사의 부사적용법, 그녀를 끌어 내리기 위해서]

baffling = frustrating[좌절 시키는]

④ 제가 진정 드리고자 하는 제 소견은 ～이다.

⑤ 도덕적 범위 반대 끝에 있는 사람들(선의를 왜곡하는 사람들) / It is ～that A: A는 ～기억할 핵심입니다.

⑥ [부가적인 설명] a girl (who was given) ～was, in the end(결국에), ～(현대판 사냥감이었습니다). / protect A from B: A를 B로부터 보호하다.

⑦ do = protect

⑧ allow them[목적어] to suffer[to 부정사] the anguish that[관계대명사] used to[～하곤했다] regularly[늘] to drive you[목적어] to[전치사] tearful despair.

⑨ I pledge(약속합니다) that[명사절] we, your blood family[동격], will do all (that) we can(최선을 다할 것이다) to continue the imaginative and loving way in which[선행사는 the imaginative and loving way] you were ～young men so that[접속사, ～하기 위해서, 목적] their souls are not simply ～(～가 아닌) but(～ 인) ～ as you planned.

⑩ they have both been born into the heritage: which의 선행사는 the heritage. / for the years ahead 앞으로.

⑪ as many ～as possible: 가능한 많은 ～.

⑫ [가정법 과거완료 표현, 과거사실의 반대] 기대하였을 것입니다(즉, 기대하지 않았다) / nothing less: 단지

⑬ [도치문] we all care William and Harry ～.

[강조, 반어법]a woman ～our mother: 우리의 어머니와 같았던 어머니

⑭ [도치문] How great your suffering [명사절, 목적] is (that) we ～. We cannot even imagine how great your suffering.

at this dreadful time and when ～: 이 끔찍한 때에 그리고 그녀가 그녀의 사생활을 즐겼던 때에.

⑮ thanking God for A, for B, at C and D.: A에 대한 감사와 C와 D한 때 B에 대해 신께 감사드리다.

⑯ call A[a woman] B[my sister] the unique, the complex, the extraordinary and irreplaceable Diana[my sister와 동격] whose[소유격 관계대명사, 그녀의]

🔖 **본문해석**

She talked endlessly of getting away from England(그녀는 영국을 벗어나는 것을 끝없이 말했습니다), **mainly because of the treatment that she received at the hands of the newspapers**(주로 언론에 통제되어 그녀가 받았던 대접 때문에).

I don't think she ever understood why her genuinely good intentions were sneered at by the media(그녀는 왜 그녀의 진정한 선의가 언론에 의해 조롱당하는 것을 지금껏 이해했는지 저는 이해가 되지 않습니다), **why there appeared to be a permanent quest on their behalf to bring her down**(그녀를 끌어 내리기 위해 그들을 대신하여 왜 영원한 질문이 있어 왔는지). **It is baffling**(그것은 좌절감입니다).

My own and only explanation is that genuine goodness is threatening to those at the opposite end of the moral spectrum(제 자신의 유일한 설명은 진심어린 선의는 도덕적 범위 반대 끝에 있는 사람들에게 위협이 된다는 것입니다).

It is a point to remember that of all the ironies about Diana, perhaps the greatest was this(다이애나에 관한 모든 모순 중에, 아마도 가장 큰 모순은 바로 이것이라고 기억하는 것이 저의 요지입니다): **a girl**

given the name of the ancient goddess of hunting was, in the end, the most hunted person of the modern age(고대 사냥의 여신의 이름을 갖진 한 여인은 현대판의 최고의 사냥감이었습니다).

She would want us today to pledge ourselves to protecting her beloved boys, William and Harry, from a similar fate, and I do this here, Diana, on your behalf(그녀는 오늘 우리에게 그녀가 사랑하는 두 아들인 윌리엄과 해리가 비슷한 운명으로부터 보호되기를 원할 것입니다. 그리고 저는 이곳에서 약속합니다. 그녀를 대신하여 그들을 보호한다고).

We will not allow them to suffer the anguish that used regularly to drive you to tearful despair(우리는 당신을 늘 슬픈 절망으로 몰아 넣곤 했던 그 고통을 그들이 당하게 해서는 안 될 것입니다). **And beyond that, on behalf of your mother and sisters**(그리고 그것을 넘어, 당신의 어머니와 누이들을 대신하여), **I pledge**(저는 약속합니다) that we, your blood family, will do all we can to continue the imaginative and loving way(우리, 피를 나눈 가족은 그 상상력이 풍부하고 애정 어린 길로 계속 나아갈 모든 힘을 쏟을 것입니다) in which you were steering these two exceptional young men(당신이 이 두 뛰어난 젊은 두 아들을 나아가게 했던) so that their souls are not simply immersed by duty and tradition but can sing openly as you planned(그들의 영혼이 의무와 전통에 단순히 빠져드는 것이 아닌 당신이 계획한대로 활짝 노래할 수 있도록 하기 위해서).

We fully respect the heritage into which they have both been born and will always respect and encourage them in their royal role(우리는 그들 둘이 태어난 유산을 아주 존경하고 그들의 왕실 역할을 잘하도록 늘 존경하고 용기를 줄 것입니다). But we, like you, recognize the need for them to experience as many different aspects of life as possible to arm them spiritually and emotionally for the years ahead(그러나 우리는 당신처럼 그들이 정신적으로나 감정적으로 수년 동안 무장하기 위해 가능한 많은 인생의 다른 여러 환경을 경험할 필요성이 있다는 것을 깨닫고 있습니다). I know you would have expected nothing less from us(저는 당신이 우리로부터 이상은 기대하지 않았을 것을 압니다).

William and Harry, we all care desperately for you today(윌리엄과 해리를 우리 모두는 당신을 위해 오늘부터 필사적으로 보호합니다). We are all chewed up with sadness at the loss of a woman who wasn't even our mother(우리 모두는 우리의 어머니가 아닌 한 여성의 희생에 슬픔으로 잠겨 있습니다). How great your suffering is we cannot even imagine(당신의 고통이 얼마나 큰 것이었는지 우린 전혀 상상할 수 없습니다).

I would like to end by thanking God for the small mercies he has shown us at this dreadful time, for taking Diana at her most beautiful and radiant and when she had joy in her private life(저는 이 모진 시간에 저희에게 보여 준신 자비와 다이애나가 가장 아름답고 빛날 때 그리고 그녀가 자신이 개인 삶을 즐겼을 때 데려가신 신께 감사드리며 고별사를 맺고 싶습니다).

Above all(무엇보다도), we give thanks for the life of a woman I'm so proud to be able to call my sister the unique, the complex, the extraordinary and irreplaceable Diana whose beauty, both internal and external, will never be extinguished from our minds(우리는 제가 유일하고 복잡하고 비범하고 둘도 없는 다이애나를 그리고 내외적으로 그녀의 아름다움이 결코 우리들 마음속에서 꺼지지 않을 여인을 누이라 부를 수 있는 자부심에 감사드립니다).

📖 단어분석

✝ **treatment** [trí: tmənt] n. U,C ① 취급; 대우. ② 처리(법). / ✝ **genuine** [dʒénjuin] a. ① 진짜의, 정짜의. [SYN.] ⇨ REAL. ② 진심에서 우러난, 성실한(sincere, real). / ✝ **intention** [inténʃən] n. ① 의향, 의지, 목적; 의도(of). [SYN.] ⇨ PURPOSE. ② 의미, 취지. / ✝ **sneer** [sniə: r] v.—vi. 냉소[조소]

하다(at); 비웃다, 비꼬다(at). / ‡ **permanent** [pə́ːrmənənt] a. ① 영구한, 영속ㅎ·는; 불변의, 내구성의. [SYN.] ⇨ EVERLASTING. / **on one'e behalf**: ～을 대신하여 / **bring down**: 을 무시하다 / † **baffle** [bǽfəl] v. —vt. ① 좌절시키다, 곤란케 하다, 당황케 하다. / ‡ **goodness** [gúdnis] n. U ① 선량, 미덕, 친절, 우애, 자애. / † **spectrum** [spéktrəm]n. (pl. -tra [-trə], ～s) (눈의) 잔상(殘像); (변동이 있는 것의) 범위, 연속체 / ‡ **irony** [áirəni] n. ① a) U 풍자, 비꼬기, 빈정댐, 빗댐. / ‡ **regular** [régjələːr] a. ① 규칙적인, 정연한, 균형 잡힌, 규칙적인. ② 일상의, 불변의. / † **imaginative** [imǽdʒənətiv, -nèitiv] a. ① 상상의 ② 상상력[창작력, 구상력]이 풍부한 / ‡ **steer** [stiəːr] v. —vt. ① 조종하다; (어떤 방향으로) 돌리다. / † **exceptional** [iksépʃənəl] a. 예외적인, 이례의, 특별한, 비범한 † **immerse** [imə́ːrs] vt. ① 빠져들게 하다, 몰두시키다(in). / ‡ **desperate** [déspərit] a. ① 자포자기의. ② 필사적인; 혈안이 된, 열중한; ～하고 싶어 못 견디다(for). / ‡ **chew** [tʃuː] vt.,vi. ① (심사) 숙고하다(over; upon). / ‡ **mercy** [mə́ːrsi] n. ① U 자비, 연민, 인정. / ‡ **dreadful** [drédfəl] a. ① 무서운, 두려운. ② (구어) 몹시 불쾌한. / ‡ **radiant** [réidiənt] a. ① 빛나는; 밝은. ② (행복·희망 따위로) 빛나는, 밝은. / † **unique** [juːníːk] a. ① 유일(무이)한, 하나밖에 없는(sole). [SYN.] ⇨ ONLY, SINGLE. / ‡ **complex** [kəmpléks] a. ① 복잡한, 착잡한; (문제가) 어려운. [opp.] simple. / ‡ **extraordinary** [ikstrɔ́ːrdənèri, èkstrɔ́ːrdənəri] a. ① 대단한, 엄청난. ② 터무니없는. / **irreplaceable** [ìripléisəbəl] a. 바꿔 놓을[대체할] 수 없는; 둘도 없는.

✹ 다음 글을 읽고 물음에 답하시오. [14~19]

She talked endlessly of getting away from England, mainly because of the treatment that she received at the hands of the newspapers.
ⒶI don't think she ever understood why her genuinely good intentions were sneered at by the media, why there appeared to be a permanent quest on their behalf to bring her down. It is baffling.

My own and only explanation is that genuine goodness is threatening to Ⓑthose at the opposite end of the moral spectrum.

It is a point to remember that of all the ironies about Diana, perhaps the greatest was this: Ⓒa girl given the name of the ancient goddess of hunting was, in the end, the most hunted person of the modern age.

She would want us today to pledge ourselves to protecting her beloved boys, William and Harry, from ①a similar fate, and I do this here, Diana, on your behalf.

We will not allow them to suffer the anguish that used regularly to drive you to tearful despair. And beyond that, on behalf of your mother and sisters, I pledge that we, your blood family, will do all we can to continue the imaginative and loving way in which you were steering these two exceptional young men so that their souls are not simply immersed by duty and tradition but can sing openly ②as you planned.

We fully respect the heritage into which they have both been born and will always respect and encourage ③them in their royal role. But we, like you, recognize the need for them to experience as many different aspects of life as possible to arm them spiritually and emotionally for the years ahead. I know you would have expected nothing less from us.

William and Harry, we all care desperately for you today. We are all chewed up with sadness at the loss of a woman who wasn't even our mother. How great your suffering is we cannot even imagine.

I would like to end by thanking God for the small mercies he has shown us at this dreadful time, for taking Diana ④at her most beautiful and radiant and when she had joy in her private life.

Above all, we give thanks for the life of a woman I'm so proud to be able to call my sister the unique, the complex, the extraordinary and ⑤irreplaceable Diana whose beauty, both internal and external, will never be extinguished from our minds.

14. 위 글로 미루어 Diana의 삶을 조명하는 단어로 어울리지 <u>않은</u> 것은?

① genuine   ② irony

③ tearful despair   ④ extraordinary

⑤ unique

15. 위 글에서 밑줄 친 Ⓐ에 나타난 '작가'와 'she'의 성격은?

① baffling   disappointed

② complex   indifferent

③ serious   gloomy

④ blaming   encouraged

⑤ confusing   generous

16. 위 글에서 밑줄 친 ⑧에 해당하는 사람들은?

① people in need
② people in suffering
③ people in the media
④ people in a family
⑤ people in a social relation

17. 위 글에서 밑줄 친 ⓒ의 분위기와 일치하지 <u>않은</u> 것은?

① contractional
② discrepancy
③ irony
④ consistency
⑤ ridiculous

18. 위 글에서 밑줄 친 ①~⑤ 중, 각각이 의미하는 것이 <u>다른</u> 것은?

① the most hunted person of the modern age
② you were steering young men in the imaginative and loving way
③ William and Harry
④ very young age
⑤ a sister who died

19. 위 글과 일치하지 <u>않은</u> 것은?

① Diana는 언론의 통제 아주 민감했다.
② 진심어린 선의는 도덕적 범위 반대 끝에 있는 사람에게 베풀어 져서는 안 된다.
③ 윌리엄과 해리에 대해 많은 걱정을 한다.
④ Diana는 윌리엄과 해리에 대한 보호 이외는 바라는 것이 없을 것이다.
⑤ Diana는 가장 아름다운 나이에 이 세상을 떠났다.

14. ② 15. ⑤ 16. ③ 17. ④ 18. ⑤
19. ①

20 The Quit India

by Mahatma Ganhdi

[난이도 ★★★☆☆]

동영상 강좌 http://youtu.be/JCGhJMC2xIE

Before you ①discuss the resolution, let me place before you one or two things, I want you to understand two things very clearly and to consider them from the same point of view ②from which I am placing them before you. I ask you to consider ③ it from my point of view, ④because if you approve of it, you will be enjoined to carry out ⑤ all I say. ⑥It will be a great responsibility. There are people who ⑦ask me whether I am the same man that I was in 1920, or whether there has been any change in me. You are right in asking that question.

Let me, however, hasten to assure that I am the same Gandhi as I was in 1920. I have not changed in any fundamental respect. I ⑧attach the same importance to non-violence that I did then. ⑨If at all, my emphasis on it has grown stronger. There is no real contradiction between the present resolution and my previous writings and utterances.

⑩Occasions like the present do not occur in everybody's and but rarely in anybody's life. I want you to know and feel that there is ⑪nothing but purest Ahimsa in all that I am saying and doing today. The draft resolution of ⑫the Working Committee is based on Ahimsa, the contemplated struggle similarly ⑬has its roots in Ahimsa. If, therefore, there is ⑭ any among you who has lost faith in Ahimsa or is wearied of it, ⑮let him not vote for this resolution.

Let me explain my position clearly. God has ⑯vouchsafed to me a priceless gift in the weapon of Ahimsa. I and my Ahimsa are ⑰on our trail today. ⑱If in the present crisis, when the earth is being scorched by the flames of Himsa and crying for deliverance, I failed to make use of the God given talent, God will not forgive me and I shall be judged un-wrongly of the great gift. I must act now. ⑲I may not hesitate and merely look on, when Russia and China are threatened.

📃 문법분석

① discuss(타동사)로 about/over와 같은 전치사를 수반해서는 안됨. / place의 목적어는 one or two things = let me place one or two things before you.

② I am placing them(one or two things) from the same point of view before you. which의 선행사 는 the same point of view(같은 견해)

③ it = the same point of view를 가리킴

④ , because: 앞 ','로 인해 계속적인 용법으로 해석

⑤ all (that/which) I say: say의 목적어 all을 수식하여 관계대명사(that 또는 which)가 생략됨.

⑥ It = you will ∼all I say(제가 말하는 것을 이행하지 않을 수 없는 것)

⑦ ask me whether A or B: 나에게 A인지 B인지를 물어보다.

⑧ attach A to B: A를 B에 첨가하다: 비폭력을 똑같이 강조하다. / did = attached

⑨ if at all = at least적어도

⑩ 결코 변화는 없을 것을 강조함. but rarely 단지 ～않는

⑪ nothing but = only / Ahimsa: 비폭력주의를 일컬음 = non-violence

⑫ 운영위원회

⑬ ～에 뿌리를 두다

⑭ ～한 사람이 혹시라도 있으시면,

⑮ let[사역동사]+him[목적어]+not vote[원형동사]: 그가 이 결의안에 투표를 하게해서는 안 된다.

⑯ vouchsafe to A B: A에게 B를 주다

⑰ 진행 중인

⑱ If[가정법현재] in ～crisis[부사구], when ～deliverance[부사절], I failed ～. [종속절], God will ～[주절].

⑲ may(～하고 싶다): 머뭇거리거나 단지 방관하고 싶지 않다.

🔖 **본문해석**

Before you discuss the resolution(여러분이 해결안을 토론하기 전), **let me place before you one or two things**(제가 여러분 앞에 한두 가지를 제안하겠습니다), I want you to understand two things very clearly and to consider them(저는 여러분이 그 두 가지를 아주 명확하게 이해하여 숙고하시길 바랍니다) from the same point of view(같은 견해로) from which I am placing them before you(제가 여러분 앞에 2가지 제시하고 있는). I ask you to consider it from my point of view(저의 견해로 여러분이 그것에 숙고하시길 요청 드립니다), because if you approve of it(만일 여러분이 그것을 승인하신다면), you will be enjoined to carry out all I say(여러분은 제가 말하는 것을 이행하지 않을 수 없기 때문입니다). It will be a great responsibility(그것은 큰 책임입니다). There are people who ask me(저에게 물어보는 사람들이 있습니다) whether I am the same man that I was in 1920(제가 1920년과 같은 사람인지), or whether there has been any change in me(제가 변했는지 아닌지를). You are right in asking that question(그 질문을 하시는 여러분은 정당합니다).

Let me, however, hasten to assure that I am the same Gandhi as I was in 1920(그러나 저는 1920년과 같은 똑같은 사람임을 강조하려 합니다). I have not changed in any fundamental respect(저는 근본적으로 전혀 변하지 않았습니다). I attach the same importance to non-violence that I did then(제가 그 당시 강조한 비폭력에 중요성을 두고 있습니다). If at all(적어도), my emphasis on it has grown stronger(그에 대한 저의 확신은 더욱 강해졌습니다). There is no real contradiction(전혀 모순은 없습니다) between the present resolution and my previous writings and utterances(현재의 결단과 이전 글과 언행사이에).

Occasions like the present do not occur in everybody's and but rarely in anybody's life(현재와 같은 상황은 모든 사람의 인생에서 일어나지도 않고 어떤 이의 인생에서도 거의 일어나지 않습니다). I want you to know and feel that there is nothing but purest Ahimsa1 in all that I am saying and doing today(제가 오늘 말씀드리고자하는 것은 단지 가장 순수한 비폭력주의를 여러분이 알고 느끼고자하는 것입니다). The draft resolution of the Working Committee is based on Ahimsa(운영위원회의 결의안 초안은 비폭력주의에 기초를 둡니다), the contemplated struggle similarly has its roots in Ahimsa(숙고한 투쟁은 이와 유사하게 비폭력주의에 뿌리를 두고 있습니다). If, therefore, there is any among you who has lost faith in Ahimsa or is wearied of it(그러므로, 혹시, 여러분 중 비폭력주의의 신념을 잃었거나 그것에 지쳐있는 사람이 있으시다면), let him not vote for this resolution(그분이 이 결의안을 위한 투표

를 하시면 안 됩니다).

Let me explain my position clearly(제가 제 입장을 명확히 밝혀두겠습니다). God has vouchsafed to me a priceless gift in the weapon of Ahimsa(신은 비폭력주의 무기의 값진 선물을 저에게 내려 주셨습니다). I and my Ahimsa are on our trail today(저와 비폭력주의는 지금 진행 중입니다). If in the present crisis, when the earth is being scorched by the flames of Himsa and crying for deliverance(만일 현재의 위기상황에서, 지상이 비폭력주의 불꽃에 그슬리고 해방을 울부짖어), I failed to make use of the God given talent(제가 신이 주신 재능을 최대한 발휘하지 못한다면), God will not forgive me(신은 저를 용서하지 않을 것이며) and I shall be judged un-wrongly of the great gift(저는 단연코 그 재능에 대한 벌을 받게 될 것입니다). I must act now(저는 행동으로 보여야만 합니다). I may not hesitate and merely look on(머뭇거리거나 단지 방관도하고 싶지 않습니다), when Russia and China are threatened(러시아와 중국이 위협을 하는 이때에).

📎 **단어분석**

- ‡quit [kwit] a. 용서되어; 면제되어. / ‡resolution [rèzəlú: ʃ-ən] n. ① U,C 결심, 결의. ② U 확고한 정신, 과단. ③ C 결의, 결의안[문]. ④ U 해결, 해답(of). ⑤ U 분해, 분석(into). / **Place [pleis] v. —vt. ①『~+목/ 목+전+명』 두다, 놓다; 명중시키다; 배치[배열]하다, 정돈하다; (광고를) 신문[잡지]에 싣다; (심의 따위를 하기 위해) (계획 따위를) 제출하다, 의제로서 내놓다. [SYN.] ⇨ PUT. ②『+목+전+명』 직위에 앉히다; 임명하다; (아무에) 일[집]을 찾아 주다. ③『+목/ +목+전+명』 (주문을) 내다, ~을 주문하다. / †enjoin [endʒɔ́in] vt. ①『+목+전+명/ +목+to do/ +that절』 ~에게 명령하다, (침묵·순종 따위를) 요구하다(demand); (행동 따위를) 강요하다(on, upon). ②『+목+전+명』『법률』 ~을 금하다, ~에게 —하는 것을 금하다(prohibit)(from). / ‡hasten [héisn] v. —vt.『~+목 / +목+부』 서두르다, 죄어치다, 재촉하다; 빠르게 하다, 촉진하다. —vi.『~ / +부 / +to do / +전+명』 서둘러 가다(to); 서두르다. [cf.] hurry. / ‡fundamental [fʌndəméntl] a. ① 기초의, 기본의, 근본적인, 중요[주요]한, 필수의. / †contradiction [kàntrədíkʃən / kɔ̀n-] n. U,C ① 부인, 부정; 반박, 반대. ② 모순, 당착; 모순된 행위 / †utterance1 [ʌ́tərəns] n. U ① 말함, 발언, 발성; 말하는 능력, 발표력; / Working Committee 운영위원회 / draft resolution 결의안 초안 / ‡contemplate [kántəmplèit / kɔ́ntem-] v.—vt. ① 찬찬히 보다, 정관하다, 관찰하다. ② 잘 생각하다, 심사 숙고하다. [SYN.] ⇨ CONSIDER. / vouchsafe [vautʃséif] vt. ~+목/ +목+목/ +to do』 허용하다, 주다, 내리다; ~해주시다. / ‡scorch [skɔː rtʃ]v.—vt. ① ~을 눕게 하다, 그슬리다. ② (햇볕이 살갗을) 태우다, (초목을 열로) 시들게 하다, 말라죽게 하다. ③ 호되게 헐뜯다, 몹시 꾸짖다, ~에게 욕지거리하다. / deliverance [dilívərəns] n. ① U 구출, 구조; 석방, 해방(from). ② (공식) 의견; 진술; 발표; (배심의) 평결(verdict).

동영상 강좌 http://youtu.be/5BGh_uzKC6g

❋ 다음 글을 읽고 물음에 답하시오. [1~5]

Before you discuss the resolution, let me place before you one or two things, I want you to understand two things very clearly and consider/to consider them from the same point of view from which I am placing them before you. I ask you to consider it from my point of view, because if you approve of it, you will be enjoined/enjoin to carry out all I say. It will be a great responsibility. There are people who ask me when/whether I am the same man that I was in 1920, or whether there has been any change in me. You are right in asking that question.

Let me, however, hasten to assure that I am the same Gandhi as I was in 1920. I have not changed in any fundamental respect. I attach the same importance to non-violence that I did then. If at all, _____. There is no real contradiction between the present resolution and my previous writings and utterances.

Occasions like the present do not occur in everybody's and but rarely in anybody's life. I want you to know and feel that there is nothing but purest Ahimsa1 in all that I am saying and doing today. The draft resolution of the Working Committee is based on Ahimsa, the contemplated struggle similarly has its roots in Ahimsa. If, therefore, there is any among you who has lost faith in Ahimsa or is wearied of it, let him not vote for this resolution.

Let me explain my position clearly. God has vouchsafed to me a priceless gift in the weapon of Ahimsa. I and my Ahimsa are on our trail today. If in the present crisis, when the earth is being scorched by the flames of Himsa2 and crying for deliverance, I failed to make use of the God given talent, God will not forgive me and I shall be judged un-wrongly of the great gift. I must act now. I may not hesitate and merely look on, when Russia and China are threatened.

1. What's is the main topic?

① India under the tremendous threat
② India's independence
③ Non-violence; Ahimsa
④ Many people have many minds.
⑤ Who will lead India?

2. What is the addressor's mood?

① resolved   ② resonant
③ resourceful   ④ respectful
⑤ resolvable

3. What is the proper expression in the underlined blank?

① my emphasis on it has grown stronger.
② I'm very sorry to change my mind.
③ my expression makes you a little confused.
④ you should all understand my emphasis.
⑤ Who will give us the freedom of speech?

4. 위 글의 네모상자 안의 적절한 단어는?

① consider   be enjoined   when
② to consider   enjoin   when
③ consider   enjoin   whether
④ to consider   be enjoined   whether
⑤ consider   be enjoined   whether

5. 위 글과 일치하지 <u>않은</u> 것은?

① 작가는 2가지 제안을 명확히 숙고할 것을 부탁하고 있다.
② 여러분의 책임은 결정을 순순히 따르는 것이다.
③ 제가 과거와 약간의 변화를 말씀드리지 않을 수 없다.
④ 작가의 주장은 비폭력주의가 원칙이다.
⑤ 비폭력주의의 신념에 흔들리는 사람은 결의안에 투표해서는 안 된다.

TOEIC 문제

6.

> Before you discuss the resolution, let me place before you one or two things, I want you to understand two things very clearly and to consider them from the same point of view _____ I am placing them before you.

① from which   ② which
③ at which   ④ of which

7.

> I ask you to consider it from my point of view, because if you approve of it, you will be enjoined to carry out all I say. It will be a great _____.

① possibility   ② opportunity
③ consideration   ④ responsibility

8.

> _____ people who ask me whether I am the same man that I was in 1920, or whether there has been any change in me. You are right in asking that question.

① It has   ② There are
③ When   ④ If

9.

> Let me, however, hasten to assure that I am the same Gandhi as I was in 1920. I have not changed in any fundamental respect. I _____ the same importance to non-violence that I did then.

① attach   ② detach
③ reserve   ④ ignore

10.

If at all, my emphasis on it has grown stronger. There is no real _____ between the present resolution and my previous writings and utterances.

① satisfaction   ② theory
③ contradiction   ④ equality

11.

Occasions like the present do not occur in everybody's and _____ in anybody's life. I want you to know and feel that there is nothing but purest Ahimsa in all that I am saying and doing today.

① make   ② hard
③ does   ④ but rarely

12.

The draft resolution of the Working Committee is based on Ahimsa, the contemplated struggle similarly has its roots in Ahimsa. _____, therefore, there is any among you who has lost faith in Ahimsa or is wearied of it, let him not vote for this resolution.

① Because   ② Because of
③ If   ④ Though

13.

Let me explain my position _____. God has vouchsafed to me a priceless gift in the weapon of Ahimsa. I and my Ahimsa are on our trail today.

① vaguely   ② tightly
③ clearly   ④ monotonously

14.

If in the present crisis, when the earth is being scorched by the flames of Himsa and crying for _____, I failed to make use of the God given talent, God will not forgive me and I shall be judged un-wrongly of the great gift.

① deliverance   ② restraint
③ benevolence   ④ death

15.

I must act now. I may not hesitate and _____ look on, when Russia and China are threatened.

① extraordinary   ② infamously
③ surprisingly   ④ merely

1. ③	2. ①	3. ①	4. ④	5. ③
6. ①	7. ④	8. ②	9. ①	10. ③
11. ④	12. ③	13. ③	14. ①	15. ④

①Ours is not a drive for power, but purely a non-violent fight for India's independence. In a violent struggle, a successful general has been often known to effect a military coup and to set up a dictatorship. But under the Congress scheme of things, ②essentially non-violent as it is, there can be no room for dictatorship. A non-violent soldier of freedom ③will covet nothing for himself, he fights only for the freedom of his country. The Congress ④is unconcerned as to who will rule, when freedom is attained. The power, ⑤when it comes, will belong to the people of India, and ⑥it will be for them to ⑦ decide to whom it placed in the entrusted. May be that the reins will be placed in the hands of the Parsis, for instance - ⑧as I would love to see happen - or they may be handed to some others whose names are not heard in the Congress today. It will not be for you then to object saying, "This community is microscopic. That party did not play its due part in the freedom's struggle; why ⑨should it have all the power?" ⑩Ever since its inception the Congress has kept itself meticulously free of the communal taint. ⑪It has thought always in terms of the whole nation and has acted accordingly. . .

I know ⑫how imperfect our Ahimsa is and how far away we are still from the ideal, but in Ahimsa there is no final failure or defeat. I have faith, therefore, that if, in spite of our shortcomings, the big thing does happen, ⑬it will be because God wanted to help us by crowning with success our silent, unremitting Sadhana for the last twenty-two years.

I believe that in the history of the world, ⑭there has not been a more genuinely democratic struggle for freedom than ours. I read Carlyle's French Resolution while I was in prison, and Pandit Jawaharlal has told me something about the Russian revolution. But ⑮it is my conviction that ⑯inasmuch as these struggles were fought with the weapon of violence they failed to realize the democratic ideal. In the democracy which I have envisaged, a democracy established by non-violence, there will be equal freedom for all. Everybody will be his own master. ⑰It is to join a struggle for such democracy that I invite you today. ⑱ Once you realize this you will forget the differences between the Hindus and Muslims, and think of yourselves as Indians only, engaged in the common struggle for independence.

📝 문법분석

① Ours = our drive / not A, but B: A가 아닌 B인
② the Congress scheme of things, (which is) essentially non-violent as it is(현재와 같이)
③ will[의지, 고집의 용법]: 자신을 위한 어떠한 것도 탐하지 않으려 하다.
④ ～무관심하다
⑤ 도래하여, 기회가 되어
⑥ it = the power

⑦ decide to A(whom) B(it placed[과거분사]) in the entrusted: A에게 B를 주는 것을 결정하다.

⑧ as I would love to see happen(제가 원하듯이) - or they(the reins) may be handed to some others(권력이 이행되다) whose names are not heard in the Congress today(의회에서 낯설은 인물)

⑨ 후회, 유감, it=the party: 왜 그들이 모든 권력을 가져야 하지?

⑩ has kept(현재완료 계속): 초기부터 의회는 자치단체의 오점으로부터 아주 자유로운 상태로 유지되어 왔다.

⑪ It[the Congress] / in terms of[관점에서] / accordingly 따라서

⑫ how+형용사+주어+동사 and how+형용사+주어+동사: 우리의 비폭력주의가 참으로 불안전하고 우리는 그 이상과는 아주 멀리 떨어져 있다는 것

⑬ it will be because ～: 그것은 ～이기 때문이다.

⑭ not more A than B: B를 강조함: B보다 더한 A는 없는 / ours = our genuinely democratic struggle

⑮ [강조용법] it is my conviction that ～: ～은 바로 제 양심입니다. /

⑯ because의 뜻

⑰ [강조용법] It is to join a struggle ～that …: 저는 오늘 여러분들을 초대하여 이 민주적인 투쟁에 함께하고자 합니다.

⑱ [접속사] 일단 ～한다면

📖 본문해석

Ours is not a drive for power, but purely a non-violent fight for India's independence(우리의 운동은 힘을 내세운 운동이 아닌 인도독립을 위한 순수한 비폭력 저항입니다). **In a violent struggle**(폭력적인 투쟁에서), **a successful general has been often known to effect a military coup and to set up a dictatorship**(성공한 장군은 군사반란의 빌미 제공하며 독재정권을 세우는 것으로 잘 알려져 있습니다). **But under the Congress scheme of things**(그러나 의회제도 하에서), **essentially non-violent as it is**(지금과 같은 근본적인 비폭력적인), **there can be no room for dictatorship**(독재정권의 여지는 전혀 없습니다). **A non-violent soldier of freedom will covet nothing for himself**(자유를 염원하는 비폭력 군인은 자신을 위해 어떠한 보답을 탐하지도 않고), **he fights only for the freedom of his country**(자신의 조국을 위한 자유의 일념으로 투쟁합니다). **The Congress is unconcerned as to who will rule, when freedom is attained**(자유가 쟁취될 때, 의회는 누가 국가를 통치하든 관심이 없습니다). **The power, when it comes, will belong to the people of India**(때가 되면, 권력은 인도 국민들 것이 될 것이고), **and it will be for them to decide to whom it placed in the entrusted**(국민들로 하여금 신임 하에 있는 사람에게 권력을 주 결정하는 것이 권력입니다). **May be that the reins will be placed in the hands of the Parsis**(권력이 파시교도(인도 사람들)의 손에 놓이게 해 주소서), **for instance**(예를 들어) - **as I would love to see happen**(제가 원하듯) - **or they may be handed to some others whose names are not heard in the Congress today**(권력이 오늘날 의회에서 거론된 적이 없는 사람에게 권력이 양도되도록). **It will not be for you then to object saying**(다음과 같은 말을 반대하는 것은 여러분에 이롭지 않을 것입니다), **"This community is microscopic. That party did not play its due part in the freedom's struggle; why should it have all the power?**(이 사회는 참으로 하찮아. 그 당은 독립투쟁에서 제 역할을 하지 않았잖아; 왜 그 당이 모든 권력을 가져야 하지?" **Ever since its inception**(권력이 시작부터) **the Congress has kept itself meticulously free of the communal taint**(의회는 자치단체의 오점으로부터 아주 자유로운 상태로 유지되고 있습니다). **It has thought always in terms of the whole nation and has acted accordingly**(의회는 국가라는 관점에서 늘 고려되어져 왔고 그에 따라 행동해 왔습니다).

I know how imperfect our Ahimsa is and how far away we are still from the ideal(우리의 비폭력주의가 참으로 불안전하고 우리는 그 이상과는 아주 멀리 떨어져 있다는 것을 저는 압니다), **but in Ahimsa there is no final failure or defeat**(그러나 비폭력주의에선 어떠한 궁극적인 실패나 패배는 없습니다). **I have faith, therefore**(그러므로 저는 믿음을 갖고 있습니다), **that if, in spite of our shortcomings**(우리의 부족함에도 불구하고), **the big thing does happen**(큰 일이 일어난다면), **it will be because God wanted to help us by crowning with success our silent, unremitting Sadhana for the last twenty-two years**(그것은 신이 지난 22년 동안 성공적으로 우리의 침묵하고 꾸준한 성취의 노력에 보답을 주고자 우리를 도운 것이기 때문일 것입니다).

I believe that in the history of the world, there has not been a more genuinely democratic struggle for freedom than ours(세계의 역사에서 우리의 역사보다 더 아주 진정한 민주적인 자유 투쟁은 없었습니다). **I read Carlyle's French Resolution while I was in prison, and Pandit Jawaharlal has told me something about the Russian revolution**(저는 감옥에 있는 동안 Carlyle의 프랑스인의 결단에 관한 책을 읽었고 Pandit은 저에게 러시아혁명에 관한 것을 들려주었습니다). **But it is my conviction**(바로 저의 인식입니다) **that inasmuch as these struggles were fought with the weapon of violence**(이러한 투쟁은 폭력을 위한 무기를 들고 싸웠기 때문에) **they failed to realize the democratic ideal**(그들은 민주적인 이상을 실현하지는 못했습니다). **In the democracy which I have envisaged**(제가 마음속에 그린 민주주의는), **a democracy established by non-violence**(비폭력에 의해 구성된 민주주의이며), **there will be equal freedom for all**(모든 국민들에게 동등한 자유를 주는 것입니다). **Everybody will be his own master**(모든 사람이 자신의 주인이 될 것입니다). **It is to join a struggle for such democracy that I invite you today**(저는 오늘 여러분들을 초대하여 이 민주적인 투쟁에 함께하고자 합니다). **Once you realize this**(일단 여러분이 이 사실을 깨달으면) **you will forget the differences between the Hindus and Muslims**(힌두교와 이슬람교의 차이점을 잊게 될 것이고), **and think of yourselves as Indians only**(오로지 인도 국민으로서 자신을 생각할 것입니다), **engaged in the common struggle for independence**(독립을 위한 공통의 투쟁에 참여하는).

🔖 단어분석

coup [kuː] n. (pl. ~s [kuːz]) 【F.】 타격; 멋진[불의의] 일격; (사업 등의) 대히트, 대성공; 명안; 쿠데타. / †effect [ifékt] vt. ① (변화 등을) 가져오다, 초래하다. ② 실행하다; (목적 따위를) 성취하다, 완수하다. / ‡scheme [skiːm] n. ① 계획, 기획, 설계. [SYN.] ⇨ PLAN. ② 획책, 책략, 음모; 비현실적인 계획. ③ 짬, 조직, 기구. / †covet [kʌ́vit] v. —vt. ① (남의 것을) 몹시 탐내다, 바라다, 선망하다. ② 갈망하다, 절망[열망]하다. —vi. 『+전+명』 몹시 바라다. / unconcerned [ʌ̀nkənsə́ːrnd] a. ① 걱정하지 않는; 태연한, 무사 태평한(about). ② 관계치 않는, 상관없는(in); 관심을 가지지 않는, 개의치 않는(with; at). / ‡attain [ətéin] v. —vt. ① (장소·위치 등에) 이르다, 도달하다. ② (목적·소원을) 달성하다, ~에 달하다; (명성·부귀 따위를) 획득하다, 손에 넣다. / belong to ~에 속하다 / †rein [rein] n. ① (종종 pl.) 고삐. ② U,C 통어하는 수단; 구속(력). ③ (pl.) 지배권, 지휘권. / Parsis: 파시교도(회교도의 박해로 8세기에 인도로 피신한 조로아스터 교도의 자손들) / **object [əbdʒékt] v. —vi. 『~/ +전+명』 ① 반대하다, 이의를 말하다, 항의하다(to; against). ② 불평을 품다, 반감을 가지다, 싫어하다, 불만이다(to). / †microscopic, -ical [màikrəskápik / -skɔ́p-], [-əl] a. 현미경의[에 의한]; 현미경적인; 현미경 관찰의; 극히 작은, 극미의; / ‡saying [séiiŋ] n. ① 말하기, 말, 진술. ② 속담, 격언; 전해 오는 말. / inception [insépʃən] n. 처음, 시작, 개시, 발단; / meticulous [mətíkjələs] a. (구어) (주의 따위가) 지나치게 세심한; 매우 신중한; 소심한; 엄밀한(about). ㉙~ly —ad. 너무 세심하게, 지나치게 소심하여. / communal [kəmjúː nl, kámjə- / kɔ́m-] a. 자치단체의, 시읍면(市邑面)의; 공공의; / †taint [teint]n. ① C 더럼; 얼룩, 오점. [cf.] soil, stain. ② C 오명; 치욕(of). ③ U 감염; 병독, 해독; 부패, 타락; 폐해; 결함. ④ C 기미, 흔적. / †shortcoming [ʃɔ́ː rtkʌ̀miŋ] n. ① 결점, 단점, 모자라는 점. ② 결핍, 부족. ③ 흉작. / ✲✲ crown [kraun] vt. ① 『～+목/ +목+보』 ～에게 왕관을 씌우다; 왕위에 앉히다. ② 『+목+전+명』 ～의 꼭대기에 얹다[올려놓다](with), (치아에 금관 따위를) 씌우다. ③ 『～+목/ +목+전+명』 ～에게 영관(榮冠)을 주다; (종국에 가서) 갚다, 보답하다; ～의 최후를 장식하다, 마무르다, 성취하다. / unremitted [ʌ̀nrimítid] a. 사면[경감]되지 않는(죄·부채); 부단한, 꾸준한. / Sadhana: 성취의 수단 / †genuine [ʤénjuin] a. ① 진짜의, 정짜의. [SYN.] ⇨ REAL. ② (원고·서명 등이) 저자 친필의. ③ 진심에서 우러난, 성실한 (sincere, real). / †conviction [kənvíkʃən] n. ① U,C 신념, 확신. [SYN.] ⇨ CONFIDENCE. ② U 설득(력), 설득행위. ③ U 죄의 자각, 양심의 가책. / pandit [pʌ́ndit, pǽn-] n. 【Ind.】 학자, 교사; (P-) (존칭으로서) ～선생; 관리. / inasmúch às [ìnəzmʌ́tʃ-] ～이므로, ～하므로, ～인 까닭에 (because, since, seeing that～); / envisage [invízidʒ] vt. (상황을) 마음 속에 그리다, 상상하다. /

동영상 강좌 http://youtu.be/tOIJxUXWHXc

❋ 다음 글을 읽고 물음에 답하시오. [16~20]

Ours is not a drive for power, but purely a non-violent fight for India's independence. In a violent struggle, a successful general has been often known to effect a military coup and to set up a dictatorship. But under the Congress scheme of things, essentially non-violent as it is, there can be no room/rooms for dictatorship. A non-violent soldier of freedom will covet nothing for himself, he fights only for the freedom of his country. The Congress is unconcerned as to who will rule, when freedom is attained. The power, when it comes, will belong to the people of India, and it will be for them to decide to whom it placed/is placed in the entrusted. May be that the reins will be placed in the hands of the Parsis, for instance-as I would love to see happen-or they may be handed to some others whose names are not heard in the Congress today. It will not be for you then to object saying, "This community is microscopic. That party did not play its due part in the freedom's struggle; why should it have all the power?" Ever since its inception the Congress has kept itself meticulously free of the communal taint. It has thought always in terms of the whole nation and has acted accordingly. . .

I know how imperfect our Ahimsa is and how far away we are still from the ideal, but in Ahimsa there is no final failure or defeat. I have faith, therefore, that if, in spite of our shortcomings, the big thing does happen, it will be because God wanted to help us by crowning with success our silent, unremitting Sadhana for the last twenty-two years.

I believe that in the history of the world, there has not been a more genuinely democratic struggle for freedom than ours. I read Carlyle's French Resolution while I was in prison, and Pandit Jawaharlal has told me something about the Russian revolution. But it is my conviction that/which inasmuch as these struggles were fought with the weapon of violence they failed to realize the democratic ideal. In the democracy which I have envisaged, a democracy established by non-violence, there will be equal freedom for all. Everybody will be his own master. It is to join a struggle for such democracy that I invite you today. Once you realize this you will forget the differences between the Hindus and Muslims, and think of yourselves as Indians only, engaged in the common struggle for independence.

16. 위 글의 주제가 가장 적절한 것은?

① In retrospect, sometimes the means and ends is necessary.
② Indians should rise up for the strong congress.
③ Our priority is to seek for non-violent struggle.
④ The unity of peoples is a starting step for democracy.
⑤ The prosperity for India is far away from now.

17. 위 글에서 지은이가 강조하는 것과 거리가 먼 것은?

① Congress scheme
② communal taint
③ no final failure or defeat
④ our silent, unremitting Sadhana
⑤ our history

18. What is not related to the Congress?

① based on non-violent essentially
② secretly concerned about who will rule the country
③ free of communal corruption
④ acting in terms of the whole nation
⑤ the place on which the author places the emphasis

19. 위 글에서 네모상자 안의 적절한 단어는?

① room   it placed   that
② room   is placed   that
③ rooms   it placed   that
④ rooms   is placed   which
⑤ rooms   it placed   which

20. 위 글과 일치하지 <u>않은</u> 것은?

① 우리의 독립운동은 순수한 비폭력 저항이다.
② 성공한 장군은 군사반란의 빌미를 제공한다.
③ 의회제도 하에서는 독재정권의 여지는 전혀 없다.
④ 비폭력적인 병사는 의회 제도를 위해 헌신한다.
⑤ 권력은 국민에 의한 선택된 자에게 부여된다.

TOEIC 문제

21.

> Ours is not a drive for power, but purely a non-violent fight for India's independence. In a violent struggle, a successful general has been often known to _____ a military coup and to set up a dictatorship.

① do   ② avoid
③ defeat   ④ effect

22.

> But under the Congress scheme of things, essentially non-violent as it is, there can be no room for dictatorship. A non-violent soldier of freedom will _____ nothing for himself, he fights only for the freedom of his country.

① regain   ② covet
③ earn   ④ expect

23.

The Congress is _____ as to who will rule, when freedom is attained. The power, when it comes, will belong to the people of India, and it will be for them to decide to whom it placed in the entrusted.

① unconcerned   ② enthusiastic

③ struggling   ④ predominant

24.

May be that the reins will be placed in the hands of the Parsis, for instance - as I would love to see happen - or they may be handed to some others _____ names are not heard in the Congress today.

① their   ② whom

③ of   ④ whose

25.

It will not be for you then to object saying, "This community is microscopic. That party did not play its _____ part in the freedom's struggle; why should it have all the power?"

① improper   ② due

③ small   ④ irresponsible

26.

Ever since its inception the Congress has kept itself meticulously free of the communal taint. It has thought always _____ the whole nation and has acted accordingly.

① in terms of   ② in order for

③ in addition to   ④ regardless of

27.

I know how _____ our Ahimsa is and how far away we are still from the ideal, but in Ahimsa there is no final failure or defeat.

① accomplished   ② reasonable

③ imperfect   ④ successful

28.

I have faith, therefore, that if, in spite of our shortcomings, the big thing does happen, it will be _____ God wanted to help us by crowning with success our silent, unremitting Sadhana for the last twenty-two years.

① why   ② where

③ when   ④ because

29.

I believe that in the history of the world, there has not been a more genuinely democratic struggle for freedom than _____. I read Carlyle's French Resolution while I was in prison, and Pandit Jawaharlal has told me something about the Russian revolution.

① our freedom   ② ours

③ our resolution   ④ theirs

30.

> But it is my _____ that inasmuch as these struggles were fought with the weapon of violence they failed to realize the democratic ideal.

① memory   ② conviction

③ background   ④ knowledge

31.

> In the democracy _____ I have envisaged, a democracy established by non-violence, there will be equal freedom for all. Everybody will be his own master.

① which   ② in which

③ of which   ④ from which

16. ③   17. ②   18. ②   19. ①   20. ④
21. ④   22. ②   23. ①   24. ④   25. ②
26. ①   27. ③   28. ④   29. ②   30. ②
31. ①

Then, there is the question of your attitude towards the British. I have noticed that there is hatred towards the British among the people. ①The people say they are disgusted with their behaviour. The people make no distinction between British imperialism and the British people. To them, ②the two are one. This hatred would even make them welcome the Japanese. It is most dangerous. It means that they will ③exchange one slavery for another. We must get rid of this feeling. Our quarrel is not with the British people, we fight their imperialism. The proposal for the withdrawal of British power did not come out of anger. ④It came to enable India to play its due part at the present critical juncture ⑤It is not a happy position for a big country like India to be merely helping with money and material obtained willy-nilly from ⑥her while the United Nations are conducting the war. We cannot evoke the true spirit of sacrifice and valor, ⑦so long as we are not free. I know the British Government will not be able to ⑧withhold freedom from us, when we have made enough self-sacrifice. We must, therefore, purge ourselves of hatred. ⑨Speaking for myself, I can say that I have never felt any hatred. As a matter of fact, I feel myself to be a greater friend of the British ⑩now than ever before. One reason is that they are today in distress. My very friendship, therefore, demands that I should try to save them from their mistakes. As I view the situation, they are ⑪on the brink of an abyss. ⑫It, therefore, becomes my duty to warn them of their danger even though ⑬it may, for the time being, anger them to the point of cutting off ⑭the friendly hand that is stretched out to help them. People may laugh, nevertheless that is my claim. ⑮At a time when I may have to launch the biggest struggle of my life, I may not harbour hatred against anybody.

🖎 문법분석

① The people(인도 국민들) say ~with their behaviour(영국 사람들의 행위).

② the two = the British imperialism and the British people

③ exchange A for B: A를 B로 바꾸다.

④ It = the withdrawal of British power

⑤ It 가주어 / for a big country 진주어

⑥ her = British

⑦ as[so] long as ~하는 한

⑧ withhold A from B: B로부터 A를 억누르다.

⑨ 솔직히

⑩ 과거와 지금을 비교하는[비교급]

⑪ 나락에 떨어지기 직전

⑫ It[가주어] becomes my duty[진주어]

⑬ it = warning

⑭ 구원의 손길
⑮ At a time (when) ~: ~할 시점에

📖 본문해석

Then, there is the question of your attitude towards the British(그렇다면, 영국 사람들에 대한 여러분의 태도에 관한 문제가 있습니다). **I have noticed that there is hatred towards the British among the people**(저는 국민들 사이에 영국 사람들에 대한 증오가 있다는 것을 인지해 왔습니다). **The people say they are disgusted with their behaviour**(인도 국민들은 영국인들의 행위에 분개한다고 말합니다). **The people make no distinction between British imperialism and the British people**(인도 국민들은 영국제 국주의와 영국민을 구별하지 못합니다). **To them, the two are one. This hatred would even make them welcome the Japanese**(그들에게 있어서, 그 두 가지는 이 증오가 심지어 일본인들을 환영한다는 것이 하나입니다). **It is most dangerous**(그것은 지극히 위험합니다). **It means that they will exchange one slavery for another**(한 노예상태를 또 다른 노예상태로 바꾸는 것을 의미합니다). **We must get rid of this feeling**(우리는 이러한 느낌을 제거해야만 합니다). **Our quarrel is not with the British people, we fight their imperialism**(우리의 투쟁은 영국인들이 아닌 그들의 제국주의입니다). **The proposal for the withdrawal of British power did not come out of anger**(영국군의 철수 제안은 분노로부터 오지 않았습니다). **It came to enable India to play its due part at the present critical juncture**(그것은 인도가 현재의 중요한 전환기에서 충실한 역할을 할 수 있었기 때문입니다). **It is not a happy position for a big country like India to be merely helping with money and material obtained willy-nilly from her**(인도와 같은 대국이 영국으로부터 좋든 싫든 얻은 자금과 물질로 겨우 도움이 되는 것은 좋은 상황이 안입니다) **while the United Nations are conducting the war**(유엔이 전쟁을 치르고 있는 동안). **We cannot evoke the true spirit of sacrifice and valor, so long as we are not free**(우리가 자유롭지 않으면 진정한 희생과 용기를 일으킬 수 없습니다). **I know the British Government will not be able to withhold freedom from us, when we have made enough self-sacrifice**(우리가 충분한 자기희생정신을 갖고 있을 때, 영국 정부는 우리로부터 자유를 억압할 수 없을 거라는 것을 알고 있습니다). **We must, therefore, purge ourselves of hatred**(그러므로 우리는 우리 자신의 증오를 일소해야만 합니다). **Speaking for myself**(제 자신에게), **I can say that I have never felt any hatred**(저는 어떠한 증오도 느껴본 적이 없다고 말할 수 있습니다). **As a matter of fact, I feel myself to be a greater friend of the British now than ever before**(사실, 과거보다 지금이 영국의 더 우호적인 친구라 생각합니다). **One reason is that they are today in distress**(한 가지 이유는 영국은 지금 곤란한 상태에 빠져 있습니다). **My very friendship, therefore, demands that I should try to save them from their mistakes**(그러므로, 저의 진정한 우정은 그들이 실수를 범하지 않기를 바랄뿐입니다). **As I view the situation**(제가 상황을 파악하자면), **they are on the brink of an abyss**(그들은 나락에 떨어질 직전입니다). **It, therefore, becomes my duty to warn them of their danger**(그러므로 제 의무가 그들로 하여금 분노케 합니다) **even though it may, for the time being, anger them to the point of cutting off the friendly hand that is stretched out to help them**(비록 그것이 당분간 도움의 손길을 자를 시점에까지 분노케 할지라도). **People may laugh, nevertheless that is my claim**(그럼에도 불구하고, 사람들은 그것은 제 주장일 뿐이라고 비웃습니다). **At a time when I may have to launch the biggest struggle of my life**(제가 제 인생의 가장 큰 투쟁을 시작해야만 할 시점에), **I may not harbour hatred against anybody**(저는 어느 누구에게도 증오를 품지 않으려 합니다).

---

disgusted [disgʌ́stid] a. 정떨어진, 욕지기나는, 싫증난; 화나는, 분개한(at; with; by). / † distinction [distíŋkʃən] n. U ① 구별, 차별; C 구별 짓기. ② 대조, 대비; (TV의) 선명도; 품등, 등급. ③ U,C 상위, 다름; 차이(점)(difference). ④ (차이를 나타내는) 특성, 특질, 특징. ⑤ 탁월(성), 우수(성); 고귀, 저명. ⑥ (문체의) 특징, 개성, 기품이 높음; 기품 있는 풍채[태도]; 눈에 띄는 외관. / imperialism [impíəriəlìzəm] n. U 제국주의, 영토 확장주의; 제정(帝政). / get rid of ~을 제거하다 / † quarrel [kwɔ́: rəl / kwɑ́r-] n. ① 싸움, 말다툼, 티격남, 불화. ② 싸움[말다툼]의 원인, 불평(against; with); 싸움의 구실. / juncture [dʒʌ́ŋktʃər] n. ① U 접합, 접속, 연결; C 이음매, 접합점, 관절. ② U (중대한) 때, 경우, 정세, 전기(轉機); 위기(crisis). / † withdrawal [wiðdrɔ́: -əl, wiθ-] n. U,C ① 움츠려들임; 움츠림; 물러남; 퇴학, 탈퇴. ② (예금·출자금 등의) 되찾기, 회수. ③ 철수, 철퇴, 철병. ④ 취소, 철회 / willy-nilly [wíliníli] ad. 싫든 좋든 간에, 좋아 하든 말든, 다짜고짜로([cf.] nill); 닥치는 대로, 마구잡이로; 난잡하게. / † conduct [kəndʌ́kt] v. —vt. ①『~+목/ +목+전+명/ +목+부』인도하다, 안내하다, 호송하다. [SYN.] ⇨ GUIDE. ② 지도하다, 지휘하다. ③ (업무 등을) 집행하다, 처리 [경영, 관리]하다. ④「재귀용법」행동하다, 거동하다, 처신하다. / † evoke [ivóuk] vt. ① (기억·감정을) 불러일으키다, 환기하다; (웃음·갈채 따위를) 자아내다; (영혼 따위를) 불러내다. / † sacrifice [sǽkrəfàis] n. ① 희생, 산 제물, 제물. ② 희생적인 행위, 헌신 / withhold [wiðhóuld, wiθ-] vt. (p., pp. -held [-héld])『~+목 / +목+전+명』① 주지「허락하지」않고 두다, (승낙 등을) 보류하다. ② 억누르다, 억제하다, 말리다. / † purge [pə: rdʒ] v. —vt. ①『~+목/ +목+전+명』(몸·마음을) 깨끗이 하다(of; from). ②『~+목/ +목+부/ +목+전+명』(죄(罪)·더러움을) 제거하다, 일소하다(away; off; out). / † distress [distrés] n. U ① 심통(心痛), 비탄(grief), 고민, 걱정(worry); C 걱정거리. [SYN.] ⇨ SORROW. ② 고통(pain); C 피로. [SYN.] ⇨ SUFFERING. ③ 가난, 곤궁; 고난, 재난, 불행; (배·비행기의) 조난. / † brink [briŋk] n. ① (벼랑 따위의) 가장자리; (산 따위의) 정상. ② 물가. ③ (~하기) 직전, (아슬아슬한) 고비. [cf.] edge, verge. ♣ on [at] the ~ of (멸망·죽음 등)에 임하여, ~의 직전에: / † abyss [əbís] n. 심연(深淵); 끝없이 깊은 구렁; 나락; (천지 창조 전의) 혼돈; / † stretch [stretʃ] v. —vt. ①『~+목/ +목+전+명/ +목+보』뻗치다, 늘이다, 펴다, 잡아당기다. ② (시트 따위를) 깔다. ③『~+목/ +목+부/ +목+전+명』(손 따위를) 내밀다, 내뻗다(out). ④ (입·두 눈 등을) 크게 벌리다[뜨다]. ⑤ (신경 등을) 극도로 긴장시키다, 과로시키다. ⑥ (구어) (법·주의·진실 따위를) 왜곡하다, 확대 해석하다; 남용[악용]하다; (구어) 과장하다. ⑦ (음식물·마약·그림 물감 등을) (~로) 묽게 하여 양을 늘리다(with; by). / † launch1 [lɔ: ntʃ, lɑ: ntʃ] v. —vt. ① (새로 만든 배를) 진수시키다. ② 발진(發進)시키다; (보트를) 물 위에 띄우다; (비행기를) 날리다; (로켓·수뢰 등을) 발사하다; (글라이더를) 활공[이륙]시키다. ③『+목+전+명』(세상에) 내보내다, 진출[독립]시키다, (상품 따위를) 시장에 내다; (책을) 발행하다. ④ (사업 등을) 시작[착수]하다, 일으키다. / † harbor, 【영국】 -bour [hɑ́: rbər] v. —vt. ① 피난[은신]처를 제공하다; 감추다, (죄인 등을) 숨기다. ②『~+목 / +목+전+명』(악의 따위를) 품다.

동영상 강좌 http://youtu.be/qlCgjJZFK94

※ 다음 글을 읽고 물음에 답하시오. [32~36]

Then, there is the question of your attitude towards the British. I have noticed that there is hatred towards the British among the people. The people say ①**they** are disgusted with their behaviour. The people make no distinction between British imperialism and the British people. To ②**them**, the two are one This hatred would even make ③**them** welcome the Japanese. It is most dangerous. It means that ④**they** will exchange one slavery for another. We must get rid of this feeling. Our quarrel is not with the British people, we fight ⑤**their** imperialism. The proposal for the withdrawal of British power did not come out of anger. It came to enable India to play its due part at the present critical juncture It is not a happy position for a big country like India to be merely helping with money and material obtained willy-nilly from her while the United Nations are conducting the war. We cannot evoke the true spirit of sacrifice and valor, so long as we are not free. I know the British Government will not be able to withhold freedom from us, when we have made enough self-sacrifice. We must, therefore, purge ourselves of hatred. Speaking for myself, I can say that I have never felt any hatred. ____ⒶA____, I feel myself to be a greater friend of the British now than ever before. One reason is that they are today in distress. My very friendship, therefore, demands that I should try to save them from their mistakes. As I view the situation, they are on the brink of an abyss. It, ____ⒷB____, becomes my duty to warn them of their danger even though it may, for the time being, anger them to the point of cutting off the friendly hand that is stretched out to help them. People may laugh, nevertheless that is my claim. At a time when I may have to launch the biggest struggle of my life, I may not harbour hatred against anybody.

32. 위 글의 분위기로 어울리지 <u>않은</u> 것은?

① persuasive   ② affirmative
③ patient   ④ gloomy
⑤ unshaken

33. 위 글에서 밑줄 친 ①~⑤ 중, 가리키는 것이 나머지 넷과 <u>다른</u> 것은?

①   ②   ③   ④   ⑤

34. 위 글에서 'British'에 상황과 일치하지 <u>않은</u> 것은?

① The British is an imperialism.
② It makes Indian disgusted by its behaviour.
③ It is at the present critical juncture.
④ It can't withhold freedom from us if we have enough self-sacrifice.
⑤ It may cut off the helpful hands because of anger.

35. 위 글에서 밑줄 친 빈칸 Ⓐ, Ⓑ에 적절한 단어는?

① For example   nevertheless
② On the other hand   therefore
③ As a matter of fact   however
④ As a matter of fact   therefore
⑤ However   nevertheless

36. 위 글과 일치하지 <u>않은</u> 것은?

① 영국 사람들에 대한 인도 국민의 태도를 바꿔야 한다.
② 인도 국민들은 제국주의와 영국민을 구별하지 못한다.
③ 일본제국주의를 받아들이는 것은 또 다른 노예상태를 의미한다.
④ 영국군의 철수는 인도 국민의 분노가 시발점이 되었다.
⑤ 작가는 영국 국민에겐 우호적이다.

TOEIC 문제

37.

> Then, there is the question of your _____ towards the British. I have noticed that there is hatred towards the British among the people.

① situation   ② mood
③ career   ④ attitude

38.

> The people say they are disgusted with their behaviour. The people make no _____ between British imperialism and the British people.

① contradiction   ② use
③ distinction   ④ consideration

39.

> To them, the two are one. This hatred would even make them welcome the Japanese. It is most dangerous. It means

> that they will _____ one slavery for another.

① devote   ② work
③ exchange   ④ share

40.

> We must _____ this feeling. Our quarrel is not with the British people, we fight their imperialism. The proposal for the withdrawal of British power did not come out of anger.

① laugh at   ② get rid of
③ lift up   ④ bear in mind

41.

> It came to enable India to play its due part at the present critical juncture It is not a happy position for a big country like India to be merely helping with money and material obtained _____ from her while the United Nations are conducting the war.

① willy-nilly
② willingly
③ with pleasure
④ with a good grace

42.

We cannot evoke the true spirit of sacrifice and valor, _____ we are not free. I know the British Government will not be able to withhold freedom from us, when we have made enough self-sacrifice.

① though
② so long as
③ because of
④ as if

43.

We must, therefore, _____ ourselves of hatred. Speaking for myself, I can say that I have never felt any hatred. As a matter of fact, I feel myself to be a greater friend of the British now than ever before.

① purge
② evoke
③ melt
④ pour

44.

One reason is that they are today in distress. My very friendship, therefore, demands that I should try to save them from their mistakes. As I view the situation, they are _____ an abyss.

① for the sake
② on the way of
③ on the brink of
④ on the mercy of

45.

It, therefore, becomes my duty to warn them of their danger _____ it may, for the time being, anger them to the point of cutting off the friendly hand that is stretched out to help them.

① because
② once
③ therefore
④ even though

46.

People may laugh, nevertheless that is my claim. At a time when I may have to launch the biggest struggle of my life, I may not _____ hatred against anybody.

① remember
② harbour
③ forget
④ cherish

32. ④ 33. ⑤ 34. ③ 35. ④ 36. ④
37. ④ 38. ③ 39. ③ 40. ② 41. ①
42. ② 43. ① 44. ③ 45. ④ 46. ②

장문독해 A History of Freedom of Thought

by John B. Bury

[난이도 ★★★☆☆]

동영상 강좌 http://youtu.be/wZ2g-rsJyBE

It is a common saying that thought is free. A man can never be hindered from thinking whatever he chooses as long as he conceals what he thinks. The working of his mind is limited only by the bounds of his experience and the power of his imagination. But this natural liberty of private thinking is of little value. It is unsatisfactory and even painful to the thinker himself, if he is not permitted to communicate his thoughts to others, and it is obviously of no value to his neighbors. Moreover it is extremely difficult to hide thoughts that have any power over the mind. If a man's thinking leads him to call in question ideas and customs which regulate the behavior of those about him, to reject beliefs which they hold, to see better ways of life than those they follow, it is almost impossible for him, if he is convinced of the truth of his own reasoning, not to betray by silence, chance words, or general attitude that he is different from them and does not share their opinions. Some have preferred, like Socrates, some would prefer today, to face death rather than conceal their thoughts. Thus freedom of thought, in any valuable sense, includes freedom of speech.

📝 문법분석

[강조용법]It is a common saying[강조] that thought is free. A man[일반인] can never be hindered[수동태: 방해받지 않는다] from thinking whatever[복합관계대명사: 무엇이든] he chooses as long as[접속사: ~하는 한] he conceals what he thinks[목적어: 그가 생각하는 것]. The working of his mind[마음의 작용] is limited only by[단지~에 의해서만] the bounds of his experience and the power of his imagination. But this natural liberty of private thinking is of little value[of+명사: 형용사구 = little valuable 거의 가치가 없는]. It[지시대명사: 그것=private thinking] is unsatisfactory and even painful to[전치사: ~에게] the thinker himself, if[조건절: 만일 ~라면] he is not permitted to[수동태: 금지되다] communicate his thoughts to[전치사: ~에게] others, and it is obviously[부사: 형용사를 수식] of no value[little valuable] to his neighbors. Moreover[부사: 더욱이] it[가주어] is extremely difficult to hide thoughts[진주어: 사고를 숨기는 것] that[관계대명사] have any power over the mind[마음을 통제하는 어떤 힘]. If a man's thinking leads[lead A + to부정사: A가 B하도록 이끌다] him to call in question ideas and customs which[관계대명사: 선행사는 ideas and customs] regulate the behavior of those about him, to reject beliefs which[관계대명사] they hold[목적어는 beliefs: 그들이 갖고 있는 믿음], to see better[비교급] ways of life than those[=beliefs] (that[관계대명사 생략]) they follow, it[가주어] is almost impossible for him[의미상의 주어], [삽입된 조건절]if he is convinced of the truth of his own reasoning, not to betray[진주어: 배반하지 않는 것은] by silence, chance words, or general attitude that[접속사: 동격, 그가 그들과 다르다는 일반적인 태도] he is different from them and does not share their opinions. Some[=some people] have preferred, [삽입 전치사구: 소크라테스처럼]like Socrates, some would prefer today, to face death rather than[비교급: ~라기 보다는] conceal their thoughts. Thus freedom of thought, [삽입 전치사구: ~어떤 귀중한 의미에서]in any valuable sense, includes freedom of speech.

📖 본문해석

It is a common saying(~라는 것은 흔한 얘기이다) that thought is free(생각은 자유다). A man can never be hindered from thinking whatever he chooses(사람은 자신이 선택한 무엇이든 생각하는 것으로부터 자유로울 수 없다) as long as he conceals what he thinks(자신의 생각하는 것을 숨기는 한). The working of his mind(마음의 작용은) is limited(제한된다) only by the bounds of his experience and the power of his imagination(자신의 경험의 한계와 상상력으로 만). But this natural liberty of private thinking(그러나 개인적인 사고의 이 타고난 자유는) is of little value(거의 쓸모가 없다). It is unsatisfactory and even painful to the thinker himself(그것은 생각하는 자 스스로에게 만족스럽지 못하고 아주 고통스럽다), if he is not permitted to communicate his thoughts to others(만일 자신의 생각을 다른 사람들에게 전달이 금지된다면), and it is obviously of no value to his neighbors(그리고 그것은 자신의 이웃사람들에게도 아주 쓸모가 없다). Moreover(더욱이) it is extremely difficult to hide thoughts(~ 생각을 숨기기는 아주 어렵다) that have any power over the mind(그 마음을 능가하는 어떠한 힘을 갖는). If a man's thinking leads him to(만일 한 사람의 생각이 자신을 ~로 이끈다면) call in question ideas and customs(~ 생각과 관습을 의문시하는 것) which regulate the behavior of those about him(자신 주위의 사람들의 행동을 조절하는), to reject beliefs which they hold(그들이 갖고 있는 믿음을 거부하는 것으로), to see better ways of life than those they follow(자신이 따르는 믿음 보다 삶의 더 낳은 방식을 보는 것으로), it is almost impossible for him(그가 ~것은 거의 불가능하다), if he is convinced of the truth of his own reasoning(만일 그가 자기 자신의 이성적인 진실을 납득한다면), not to betray by silence, chance words, or general attitude(침묵, 우연한 말 또는 일반적인 태도에 의해 배신당하지 않는) that he is different from them and does not share their opinions(자신이 그들과 다르고 그들의 의견을 공유할 수 없다는). Some have preferred(누군가는 ~것 을 선호한다), like Socrates(소크라테스처럼), some would prefer today(누군가는 오늘날 선호할 ~것이다), to face death rather than conceal their thoughts(자신의 생각을 숨기기보다는 죽음을 택하는). Thus freedom of thought(그리하여 사고의 자유는), in any valuable sense(어떤 귀중한 의미에선), includes freedom of speech(표현(말)의 자유를 포함한다).

📖 단어분석

- ‡ **saying**[séiiŋ] n. ① 말하기, 말, 진술. ② 속담, 격언; 전해 오는 말. n. adage[ǽdidʒ], aphorism[ǽfərìzəm], epigram[épigræm], expression[ikspréʃən], maxim[mæksim], motto[mɔ́to] proverbprάvəːrb] / ‡ **hinder**[híndər] v. —vt. 『~+목 / +목+전+명』 ① 방해하다, 훼방하다(in). ② ~의 방해를 하다; 지체케 하다, 늦게 하다. —vi. 방해가 되다, 행동을 방해하다. v. foil[fɔil], frustrate[frʌ́streit], hamper[hǽmpər], impede[impíːd], obstruct[əbstrʌ́kt], thwart[θwɔːrt], circumscribe[sə́ːrkəmskráib], curb[kəːrb], inhibit[inhíbit], limit[límit], ant. facilitate[fəsílətèit]용이하게 하다 / ‡ **conceal**[kənsíː l] vt. ~+목/ 목+전+명』 숨기다, 비밀로 하다. [SYN.] ⇨ HIDE.v. cloak[klouk], hide[haid], screen[skriː n], secrete[sikríː t], camouflagekǽmuflὰː ʒ] disguise[disgáiz], mask[mæsk], obscure[əbskjúər] ant. expose[ikspóuz] reveal[rivíː l] / ＊＊**imagination**[imæ̀dʒənéiʃən] n. U,C ① 상상(력), 창작력, 구상력(構想力); (종종 one's ~) 마음. ② 임기응변의 지혜, 기략, 기지(機智). ③ 상상[공상]의 산물, 심상; 공상, 망상. n. fancy[fǽnsi], inspiration[ìnspəréiʃən], vision[víʒən], ingenuity[ìndʒənjúː əti], originality[ərìdʒənǽləti] / ‡ **extremely**[ikstríː mli] ad. ① 극단(적)으로, 극도로. ② 아주, 대단히, 몹시. / ＊＊**hide**[haid] v. (hid [hid]; hidden [hídn], hid) —vt.① 숨기다. ② 덮어 가리다, 덮다. ③『~+목 / +목+전+명』 감추다, 비밀로 하다 / ‡ **regulate**[régjəlèit] vt. ① 규정하다; 통제[단속]하

다. ② 조절하다, 정리하다. ──•~ the traffic 교통을 정리하다.② ㉤-lative, -latory [-lèitiv, -lə-], [-lətɔ̀ː ri / -təri] ──a. 규정하는; 단속의; 정리하는. [관련어] regulation ──n. v. adjust[ədʒʌ́st], direct[dirékt], govern[gʌ́vərn], manage[mǽnidʒ], monitor[mɑ́nitər], confine[kənfáin], control[kəntróul], limit[límit], restrict[ristríkt] ant. neglect[niglékt] free[friː] / ╂ **reject**[ridʒékt]vt. ① a) (요구·제의 등을) 거절하다, 사절하다, 각하하다. b) (무효·불량품으로서) 물리치다, 버리다; 퇴짜놓다, 무시하다. [SYN.] ⇨ REFUSE. ② a) (위가 음식을) 받지 않다, 게우다;〚생리〛 (이식된 장기(臟器) 따위에) 거부반응을 나타내다. b) (record changer가 세트한 판을) 연주하지 않고 건너뛰다. v. decline[dikláin], rebuff[ribʌ́f], refuse[rifjúː z], repel[ripél], repudiate[ripjúː dièit], repulse[ripʌ́ls], spurn[spəː rn] ant. accept[æksépt] / ╂ **convince**[kənvíns] vt. +목+전+명/ +목+that절』 ~에게 납득시키다, ~에게 깨닫게 하다, ~에게 확신시키다; (폐어) 논박하다, 압도하다(of; that). v. induce[indjúː s], influence[ínfluː əns], persuade[pəː rswéid], sway[swei], assure[əʃúər], reassure[riː əʃúəː r], satisfy[sǽtisfài] ant. dissuade[diswéid] discourage[diskʌ́ː ridʒ] / ╂ **betray**[bitréi] v. ──vt. ①『~+목/ +목+전+명』 배반[배신]하다; (조국·친구 등을) 팔다(in; into); (남편·아내·여자 등을) 속이다. ② (신뢰·기대·희망 따위를) 저버리다, 어기다. ③『+목(+전+명)』 (비밀을) 누설하다, 밀고하다(to).④『~+목』 (감정·무지·약점 등을) 무심코 드러내다. ⑤『+that 절/ +목+(to be) 보』 ~임을 나타내다; ~이 ~임을 알다. v. deceive[disíː v], delude[dilúː d], trick[trik], disclose[disklóuz], divulge[divʌ́ldʒ], expose[ikspóuz], report[ripɔ́ː rt], reveal[rivíː l], abandon[əbǽndən] / ╂ **attitude**[ǽtitjùː d] n. ① (사람·물건 등에 대한) 태도, 마음가짐. ② 자세(posture), 몸가짐, 거동. ③〚항공·우주〛 (비행) 자세(지평선이나 특정 별과 기체의 축과의 관계로 정해지는 항공기나 우주선의 위치[방향]). ④ (사물에 대한) 의견, 심정(to, toward).

동영상 강좌 http://youtu.be/t5r-NWo0IYg

While it is true that there is no law that compels us to say "Please," there is a social practice much older and more sacred than any law which enjoins us to be civil. And the first requirement of civility is that we should acknowledge a service. "Please" and "Thank you" are the small change with which we pay our way as social beings. They are the little courtesies by which we keep the machine of life oiled and running sweetly. They put our intercourse upon the basis of a friendly cooperation, an easy give and take, instead of on the basis of superiors dictating to inferiors. It is a very vulgar mind that would wish to command where he can have the service for the asking, and have it with willingness and good feeling instead of resentment.

🖉 문법분석

[접속사(부사절) ~하는 동안]While it[가주어] is true that[진주어] there is no law that[관계대명사] compels[compel A to B: A가 B하도록 재촉하다] us to say "Please," there is a social practice (which is 생략됨) much[비교급 수식: 훨씬 더 오래된] older and more[비교급 수식: 더욱 신성한] sacred than[비교급] any law which[관계대명사] enjoins[enjoin A to B: A가 B하라고 명령하다] us to be civil. And the first requirement of civility is that[접속사: 명사절(보어임)] we should[조동사(권고,

충고, 후회): ～해야만 하다] acknowledge a service. "Please" and "Thank you" are the small change with which[관계대명사: 선행사는 the small change] we pay our way as[전치사: ～로써] social beings. They[=please and thank you] are the little courtesies by which[관계대명사: 선행사는 the little courtesies] we keep[keep A B: A가 B되도록 유지하다(5형식)] A(the machine of life) B(oiled and running sweetly). They put[put A 전치사(upon) B: A를 B에 놓다] our intercourse upon the basis of a friendly cooperation, an easy give and take, instead of[전치사구: ～대신에] on the basis of[전치사구: ～에 기반하여] superiors dictating to inferiors. [강조용법]It is a very vulgar mind[강조] that would wish to command where[부사절: ～곳에] he can have the service for the asking, and have it with willingness and good feeling instead of resentment.\

📖 본문해석

While it is true that there is no law that compels us to say "Please,"(어떠한 법도 우리를 "Please"라고 말하도록 강제하는 것이 없다는 것은 사실일지라도,) there is a social practice much older and more sacred(～보다 더 오래되고 신성한 사회적 통념이 있다) than any law which enjoins us to be civil(우리를 예의 바르게 강요하는 어떠한 법). And the first requirement of civility is(그리하여 정중함의 첫 번째 요구는 ～이다) that we should acknowledge a service(우리는 봉사를 인식해야만 한다는 것). "Please" and "Thank you" are the small change("Please"와 "Thank you"는 작은 변화이다) with which we pay our way as social beings(우리가 사회적 존재로서 떳떳이 살아가는). They are the little courtesies(그것들은 작은 예의이다) by which we keep the machine of life oiled and running sweetly(우리가 삶이라는 기계에 기름을 치고 부드럽게 돌아가도록 하는 것으로). They put our intercourse upon the basis of a friendly cooperation(그것들은 우리의 대화를 우호적인 협력의 토대 위에 올려놓는다), an easy give and take(쉽게 주고받는), instead of on the basis of superiors dictating to inferiors(아랫사람에게 명령하는 웃사람의 토대 대신에). It is a very vulgar mind(～저속한 사람이다) that would wish to command(명령하고 싶어 하는) where he can have the service for the asking(그가 요청하면 봉사를 받을 수 있는 곳을), and have it with willingness and good feeling instead of resentment(화를 내는 것 대신에 의지와 선의로 봉사를 가질 수 있는).

📖 단어분석

- ⴕcompel [kəmpél] v. (-ll-) —vt. ① 『+목+전+명/ +목+to do』 강제하다, 억지로 ～시키다. ② 『+목+to do』 「수동태」 ～하지 않을 수 없다, 할 수 없이 ～하다. v. coerce[kouə́ːrs], constrain[kənstréin], force[fɔːrs], necessitate[nisésətèit], oblige[əbláidʒ], require[rikwáiəːr] ant. coax[kouks]감언으로 설득하다 / ⴕsacred [séikrid] a. ① 신성한(holy); 신에게 바쳐진, 신을 모신. [SYN.] ⇨ HOLY. ② 종교적인, 성전(聖典)의. [opp.] profane, secular. ③ 신성 불가침의; 신성시되는. ④ (사람·사물·목적 등에) 바쳐진(dedicated)(to). / enjoin [endʒɔ́in] vt. ① 『+목+전+명/ +목+to do/ +that절』 ～에게 명령하다, (침묵·순종 따위를) 요구하다(demand); (행동 따위를) 강요하다(on, upon). ② 『+목—전+명』 『법률』 ～을 금하다, ～에게 —하는 것을 금하다(prohibit)(from). ------•～ obedience[silence] 순종[침묵]을 명하다.① v. advise[ædváiz, əd-], command[kəmǽnd], counsel[káunsəl], direct[dirékt], urge[əːrdʒ], warn[wɔːrn], ban[bæn], forbid[fəːrbíd], hinder[híndər], prohibit [prouhíbit] ant. permit / civil [sívəl] a. ① 시민[공민(公民)]의, 공민으로서의, 공민적인. ② 문명(사회)의(civilized); 집단활동을 하는. ③ 정중한, 예의 바른, 친절한. [SYN.] ⇨ POLITE. ④ (무관에 대하여) 문관의: (군에 대하여) 민간의, 일반인의. ⑤ 국가의, 국내의, 사회의, 내정의. / pay one's way 자활하다, 빚지지 않고 살아가다, 수지가 맞다 / ⴕ courtesy [kɔ́ːrtəsi] n. U ① 예의바름, 공손[정중]함. ② C 정중[친절]한 말[행위]. ③ 호의(favor), 우대, 특별 취급. / ╪intercourse [íntərkɔ̀ːrs] n. U ① (인간의) 교제, 교섭, 왕래. ② (국가 간의) 교통, 거래. ③ (신과 사람과의) 영적 교통. / ╪superior [səpíəriər , su-] n. ① 윗사람, 좌상, 상관, 선배. ② 뛰어난 사람, 상수, 우월한 사람 (in; as). / ╪dictate [díkteit , -́-́] v. —vt.『~+목/ +목+전+명』① 구술하다, (말하여) 받아쓰게 하다(to). ② 명령하다, 지시하다(to). —vi.『+전+명』① 받아쓰기를 시키다, 구술하여 필기케 하다(to). ② 지시[명령]하다(to). / vulgar [vʌ́lgər] a. ① 저속한, (교양·취미 따위가) 야비한, 속된, 비천한; 대중의, 서민의. ② 통속적인, 세속의, 일반적으로 유포된. / for the asking 부탁하는 / 청구하는 대로, 거저, 무상으로(for nothing): / ╪resentment [rizéntmənt] n. U 노함, 분개; 원한.

동영상 강좌 http://youtu.be/v8V9dOw_MP0

✳ 다음 글을 읽고 물음에 답하시오. [1~5]

It is a common saying that ①**thought is free**. A man can never be hindered from thinking whatever he chooses as long as he conceals ② **what he thinks**. The working of his mind is limited only by the bounds of his experience and the power of his imagination. But this natural liberty of ③**private thinking** is of little value. It is unsatisfactory and even painful to the thinker himself, if he is not permitted to communicate his thoughts to others, and it is obviously of no value to his neighbors. Moreover it is extremely difficult to hide thoughts that have any power over the mind. If a man's thinking leads him to call in question ideas and customs which regulate the behavior of those about him, to reject ④**beliefs** which they hold, to see better ways of life than those they follow, it is almost impossible for him, _____, not to betray by silence, chance words, or general attitude that he is different from them and does not share their opinions. Some have preferred, like Socrates, some would prefer today, to face death rather than conceal their thoughts. Thus ⑤**freedom of thought**, in any valuable sense, includes freedom of speech.

1. 위 글에 나타난 지은의 심정은?

① critical   ② confirmatory
③ admonishing   ④ thinking
⑤ unpersuasive

2. 위 글의 밑줄 친 ①~⑤ 중, 나머지 넷과 가리키는 것이 <u>다른</u> 것은?

①   ②   ③   ④   ⑤

3. 위 글의 주제로 가장 적절한 것은?

① To believe is to be more important than any other thinking.
② The death of Socrates is the good example to many people.
③ The thought is not to be concealed, but to be shared with others.
④ The thinking pain is made by the concealment of communication.
⑤ The private thinking always contributes to good relationship among others.

4. 위 글의 빈칸에 적절한 표현 어구는?

① if he is convinced of the truth of his own reasoning
② though he always believes whatever he chooses
③ when he gets a chance to communicate with others
④ because the lump of words should be sent to others
⑤ if he runs the risk of death after speaking of his reasoning.

5. 위 글과 일치하지 <u>않은</u> 것은?

① 생각은 자신만의 우일한 자유의 영역이다.
② 경험의 한계와 상상력만으로 생각의 한계가 있다.
③ 자신의 사고가 전달되지 않는 경우엔 고통이 따른다.
④ 생각의 자유는 연설의 자유와 일맥상통한다.
⑤ 소크라테스와 같은 사상을 지지하는 사람들은 자신의 생각을 숨기려 죽음을 불사한다.

✳ 다음 글을 읽고 물음에 답하시오. [6~10]

While it is true that there is no law that compels us to say "Please," there is a social practice much older and more sacred than any law which enjoins us to be civil. And the first requirement of civility is that we should acknowledge a service. "Please" and "Thank you" are the small change with which we pay our way as social beings. ⒶThey are the little courtesies by which we keep the machine of life oiled and running sweetly. They put our intercourse upon the basis of a friendly cooperation, an easy give and take, instead of on the basis of superiors dictating to inferiors. It is Ⓑa very vulgar mind that would wish to command where he can have the service for the asking, and have it with willingness and good feeling instead of resentment.

6. 위 글의 주제로 가장 적절한 것은?

① the law for civility should be passed on soon.

② The adequate education would be necessary for superiors.

③ We should keep the word, "Give and Take".

④ A little friendliness makes a society more abundant.

⑤ Our communication should be on the basis of a service.

7. 위 글의 밑줄 친 Ⓐ가 가리키는 것은?

① services

② "Please" and "Thank you"

③ social beings

④ small changes

⑤ social practices

8. 위 글의 밑줄 친 Ⓑ에 밀접한 관계가 있는 것은?

① one whose mind isn't good for others tries to be kind.

② one whom he wants to talk to doesn't want accept his favor.

③ one feels angry at unjustice or unkindness.

④ one has good terms with others.

⑤ one who wants to get something without courtesies

9. 위 글의 주제와 관련이 가장 적은 단어는?

① civility   ② service

③ courtesy   ④ cooperation

⑤ command

10. 위 글과 일치하지 않은 것은?

① 사회적 관행을 중요시하고 있다.

② 정중한 예의는 봉사에 대한 인식이다.

③ 사회의 일원으로서 지켜야 할 도리를 말하고 있다.

④ 원활한 사회의 순환은 같은 작은 배려로 시작된다.

⑤ 아랫사람에게의 작은 봉사는 더 좋은 유대관계를 만든다.

1. ②	2. ④	3. ③	4. ①	5. ⑤
6. ④	7. ②	8. ⑤	9. ⑤	10. ⑤

[난이도 ★★★★★]

동영상 강좌 http://youtu.be/YjglZZXNdb0

Inaugural Address

Fellow-Citizens of the Senate and of the House of Representatives:

Among the vicissitudes incident to life no event ①could have filled me with greater anxieties than ②that of which the notification was transmitted by your order, and ③ received on the 14th day of the present month. On the one hand, I was summoned ④by my country, whose voice I can never hear but with veneration and love, from a retreat which I had chosen with the fondest predilection, and, in my flattering hopes, with an immutable decision, as the asylum of my declining years— a retreat which was rendered every day more necessary as well as more dear to me ⑤by the addition of habit to inclination, and of frequent interruptions in my health to the gradual waste committed on it by time. On the other hand, ⑥the magnitude and difficulty of the trust to which the voice of my country called me, being sufficient ⑦to awaken in the wisest and most experienced of her citizens a distrustful scrutiny into his qualifications, could not but overwhelm with despondence one who ⑧(inheriting inferior endowments from nature and unpracticed in the duties of civil administration) ought to be peculiarly conscious of his own deficiencies. In this conflict of emotions ⑨all I dare aver is that it has been my faithful study to collect my duty from a just appreciation of every circumstance ⑩by which it might be affected. All I dare hope is that ⑪if, in executing this task, I have been too much swayed by a grateful remembrance of former instances, or by an affectionate sensibility to this transcendent proof of the confidence of my fellow-citizens, and have thence too little consulted my incapacity as well as disinclination for the weighty and untried cares before me, ⑫my error will be palliated by the motives which mislead me, and its consequences be judged by my country with some share of the partiality in which they originated.

📎 **문법분석**

① no event could have filled: ~을 채운 적이 없었던 것 같다

② that of which 국민 여러분의 명령에 의해 전달된 통지서의 사건 / that은 event를 가리킴

③ and (the notification was) received

④ whose voice = my country's voice(소유격 관계대명사): 제가 존경심과 사랑으로 밖엔 들을 수 없는 제 조국의 부름의 목소리의 의해 / I was summoned by my country, from a retreat, and with an immutable decision: and로 연결된 구문임 - 조국의 부름과 은둔지로부터 그리고 확고한 결심으로 저는 소환되었습니다. /

⑤ by the addition of habit to inclination, and (by the addition) of frequent interruptions in my health to the gradual waste: 습관화되는 경향과 제 건강에서 종종 중단되는 쇠약, add A to B: A를 B에 더하다 / committed on it by time: 시간이 흐름에 따라 건강에 억매인(구속된) /

⑥ the voice of my country called me to the magnitude and difficulty of the trust: call A to B: A

를 B로 소환하다 - 내 조국의 부름의 목소리가 나를 불러 맡긴 신뢰의 중대함과 어려움은 ∼/

⑦ to awaken (in the wisest and most experienced of her citizens) a distrustful scrutiny into his qualifications: awaken의 목적어는 a distrustful scrutiny - 가장 현명하고 가장 경험 있는 조국의 시민들 속에서 불신의 의미를 깨우쳐 자신의 자격을 부여하리 / can not but: ∼하지 않을 수는 / with despondence = despondently (부사구) 낙담하여 /

⑧ one who (was) inheriting and unpracticed: inherit(타) 물려받다, unpracticed(형) 경험이 부족한 /

⑨ all I dare aver is that 명사절: 제가 감히 주장하는 것은

⑩ it might be affected by a just appreciation of every circumstance: 그것은 모든 상황의 정확한 인식에 의해 영향을 받을 것 같다 /

⑪ if I have been too much swayed by a grateful remembrance of former instances or (if I have been too much swayed) by an affectionate sensibility to this transcendent proof of the confidence of my fellow-citizens, and (if I) have thence too little consulted my in capacity

⑫ 주절이 시작됨 / its consequences (will) be judged by

📖 본문해석

Fellow-Citizens of the Senate and of the House of Representatives:(상하의원 그리고 동포시민 여러분) **Among the vicissitudes incident to life**(인생의 흥망성쇠의 사건들 중에) **no event could have filled me with greater anxieties**(어떠한 사건도 ∼보다 더 큰 걱정으로 나를 채운 적이 없었습니다.**) than that of which**(∼ 그것보다) **the notification was transmitted by your order**(그 통지서가 여러분의 명령에 의해 발송되었고), **and received on the 14th day of the present month**(이번 달 14일에 수취된). **On the one hand**(한편으론), **I was summoned by my country**(∼ 로부터 ∼국가의 의해 부름을 받았습니다), **whose voice I can never hear but with veneration and love**(국가의 부름의 목소리를 전 존경심과 사랑을 제외하곤 결코 들을 수 없는), **from a retreat which I had chosen with the fondest predilection**(제가 가장 좋아하는 편협한 마음을 가지고 선택했던 은둔지로부터), **and, in my flattering hopes**(아첨하는 바람에서), **with an immutable decision**(되돌릴 수 없는 결정으로), **as the asylum of my declining years**(나의 쇠약해지는 노년의 피난처처럼) ― **a retreat which was rendered every day more necessary as well as more dear to me**(일상에서 나에게 더욱 귀중하고 필요하게 된 운둔지) **by the addition of habit to inclination**(한쪽으로 기우는 습관의 경향에 의해), **and of frequent interruptions in my health to the gradual waste committed on it by time**(저의 건강에 종종 방해가 되어 그리고 시간에 의해 나에게 맡겨진 점차적인 쇠약에 익숙한(경향에 의해)).

On the other hand(다른 한편으로), **the magnitude and difficulty of the trust to which the voice of my country called me**(내 조국의 부름의 목소리가 나를 불러 맡긴 신뢰의 중대함과 어려움은 ∼), **being sufficient to awaken in the wisest and most experienced of her citizens a distrustful scrutiny into his qualifications**(가장 현명하고 가장 경험 있는 조국의 시민들 속에서 불신의 의미를 깨우쳐 자신의 자격을 부여할 만큼 충분하게 되어), **could not but overwhelm with despondence one who**(낙심하여 ∼한 사람을 압도하지 않을 수 없었습니다.) **(inheriting inferior endowments from nature**(처음부터 타고난 열등한 재능 갖고 있는) **and unpracticed in the duties of civil administration**(공직의 의무를 수행한적 없는) **ought to be peculiarly conscious of his own deficiencies**(자신의 부족함을 특히 의식해야만 하는).

In this conflict of emotions(이런 감정의 갈등 속에서) **all I dare aver**(제가 감히 확언하는 것은) **is that it has been my faithful study**(그것은 ∼저의 충실한 노력이 되어왔다는 것입니다). **to collect my duty from a just appreciation of every circumstance**(모든 환경의 정확한 인식으로부터 제 의무에 집중하기

위해) **by which it might be affected**(그것(저의 충실한 노력)이 영향을 받을 것 같은).

All I dare hope(제가 감히 바라는 것은) **is that if, in executing this task**(이 직무를 수행할 때), **I have been too much swayed by a grateful remembrance of former instances**(만일 제가 이전의 선례의 감사의 추억에 너무나 흔들려 왔거나), **or by an affectionate sensibility to this transcendent proof of the confidence of my fellow-citizens**(또는 저의 동료 시민 여러분의 자신감의 탁월한 증거에 대한 다정한 감각에 의해), **and have thence too little consulted my incapacity as well as disinclination for the weighty and untried cares before me**(그리하여 제 앞에 놓인 무겁고 시도되지 않은 관심을 싫어하거나 저의 무능함을 거의 염두에 두지 않아 왔다면), **my error will be palliated by the motives which mislead me**(제 잘못은 저를 잘못 이끄는 동기에 의해 변명되어질 것입니다.), **and its consequences be judged by my country**(그 결과는 ～을 갖고 제 조국에 의해 판단될 것입니다.) **with some share of the partiality in which they originated**(그들(그 결과)에서 비롯된 어떠한 편견 몫).

🖋 단어분석

- **vicissitude** [visísətjùː d] n. C 변화, 변천; U (고어·시어) 순환, 교체; (pl.) 흥망, 성쇠. ──● the ～s of life 인생의 부침(浮沈). ⑭ vicissitudinary, -tudinous [-dənèri / -nəri], [-nəs] ──a. 변천하는, 변화무쌍한; 성쇠가 있는. / **notification** [nòutəfikéiʃ-ən] n. U 통지, 통고, 고시; 최고(催告); C 신고서, 통지서; 공고문(notice); 출생 신고; 사망 신고. / **transmit** [trænsmít, trænz-]v. (-tt-) ──vt. ① (화물 등을) 보내다, 발송하다. ② (지식·보도 따위를) 전하다, 전파[보급]시키다. / **summon** [sʌ́mən] vt. ① 『～+목/ +목+전+명/ +목+to do』 소환하다, 호출하다(call) (to); (피고 등에게) 출두를 명하다. / **veneration** [vènəréiʃən] n. U 존경, 숭앙; 숭배; 존경심, 경의(敬意). / **retreat** [ritríː t] n. U 은퇴, 은둔. / **predilection** [prìː dəlékʃən, prèd-] n. 선입(先入)적 애호, 편애(偏愛) / **flattering** [flǽtəriŋ] a. 빌붙는, 아부[아첨]하는 / **immutable** [imjúː təbəl] a. 변경할 수 없는, 불변의, 변치[바뀌지] 않는. / **asylum** [əsáiləm] n. 일반적」은신처, 피난처. / **inclination** [ìnklənéiʃən] n. ① U 기울기, 기욺. ② C,U 경향, 성향, 성벽. / **waste** [weist] n. 쇠퇴, 쇠약, 소모. / **magnitude** [mǽgnətjùː d] n. U ① (길이·규모·수량) 크기, 양. ② 중대(성), 중요함; 위대함, 고결. / **qualification** [kwὰləfikéiʃən / kwɔ̀l-] n. ① C 자격, 권한; U 자격 부여(for). / **despondence, -ency** [dispάndəns / -spɔ́nd-], [-ənsi] n. U 낙담, 의기소침. / **endowment** [endάumənt] n. (보통 pl.) 천부의 재주, 타고난 재능. / **study** [stʌ́di]n. U (끊임없는) 노력; 배려[노력]의 대상. / **aver** [əvə́ː r] vt. (-rr-) 확인하다, 단언[주장]하다. / **collect** [kəlékt] v. (생각을) 집중[정리]하다, (마음을) 가라앉히다; (용기를) 불러일으키다; (기력 따위를) 회복하다. / **affectionate** [əfékʃnit] a. ① 애정 깊은, 사랑에 넘친. ② 다정한, 인정 많은. / **transcendent** [trænséndənt] a. 뛰어난, 탁월한; / **disinclination** [dìsinklinéiʃən, ──--] n. U 기분이 내키지 않음, 싫음(for; to do). / **palliate** [pǽlièit] vt. ① (병세 따위를) 누그러지게 하다, 편하게 하다, 완화하다. ② (과실·죄 따위를) 가볍게 하다, 참작하다. ③ 변명하다; (허물 따위를) 가볍게 보이게 하다. / **partiality** [pὰː rʃiǽləti] n. U 편파, 불공평, 치우침; / **originate** [ərídʒənèit] v. ──vi. 『+전+명』 ① 비롯하다, 일어나다, 생기다, 시작하다(from; in; with). - that of which the notification ⋯ your order = that(지시대명사, which의 선행사) which(관계대명사) the notification ⋯ your order of /

Fellow-Citizens of the Senate and of the House of Representatives:

Among the vicissitudes incident to life Ⓐ **no event could have filled me with greater anxieties than that of which the notification was transmitted by your order**, and received on the 14th day of the present month. On the one hand, I was summoned by my country, whose voice I can never hear but with veneration and love, from a retreat which I had chosen with the fondest predilection, and, in my flattering hopes, with an immutable decision, as the asylum of my declining years—a retreat which was rendered every day more necessary as well as more dear to me by Ⓑ**the addition of habit to inclination, and of frequent interruptions in my health to the gradual waste committed on it by time**. On the other hand, the magnitude and difficulty of the trust to which the voice of my country called me, being sufficient to awaken in the wisest and most experienced of her citizens a distrustful scrutiny into his qualifications, could not but overwhelm with despondence one who Ⓒ(**inheriting inferior endowments from nature and unpracticed in the duties of civil administration**) ought to be peculiarly conscious of his own deficiencies. In this conflict of emotions all I dare aver is that it has been my faithful study to collect my duty from a just appreciation of every circumstance by which it might be affected. All I dare hope is that if, in executing this task, I have been too much swayed by a grateful remembrance of former instances, or by an affectionate sensibility to this transcendent proof of the confidence of my fellow-citizens, and have thence too little consulted my incapacity as well as disinclination for the weighty and untried cares before me, Ⓓ**my error will be palliated by the motives which mislead me**, and its consequences be judged by my country with some share of the partiality in which they originated.

1. 위 글의 제목으로 가정 적절한 것은?

① The Greatest Happiness never seen before
② Modest Acceptance of Your Order
③ The Unwillingness under the Forceful Duty
④ Transcendant Addressing Ability
⑤ Congratulations to Your Presidency

2. 위 글에서 밑줄 친 Ⓐ가 뜻하는 것은?

① I'd glad to get this position, so I appreciate greatly your kindness.
② I feel burdensome heavily, accepting my duty.
③ Greater anxieties press on me, so I don't want to do this.
④ The command you order to me is less important than any other events.
⑤ I'm willing to embrace your notification.

3. 위 글에서 밑줄 친 Ⓑ의 심정은?

① unavoidable   ② corruptive
③ obligatory   ④ aging
⑤ hopeful

4. 위 글의 밑줄 친 ⓒ를 우리말로 옳게 옮긴 것은?

① 태어날 때부터 타고난 열등한 재능과 공직을 경험하지 못한

② 타고난 열등한 재능에도 불구하고 공직에 타고난

③ 자연으로부터 물려받은 타고난 재능과 공직에 대한 감사

④ 자연의 우월한 재능을 받아 공직에 수행하지 못한

⑤ 태어날 때부터 탁월하여 공직을 수행할 기회가 없었던

5. 위 글의 밑줄 친 ⓓ가 가리키는 것은?

① 분수를 모름

② 자신을 앎으로써 경지에 오른

③ 실수를 본보기로 삼기

④ 실수는 병가지상사

⑤ 실수는 내 탓이 아님

1. ② 2. ② 3. ④ 4. ① 5. ①

Such being the impressions ①under which I have, in obedience to the public summons, repaired to the present station, it would be peculiarly improper to omit in this first official act my fervent supplications to that Almighty Being who ②rules over the universe, who presides in the councils of nations, and whose providential aids can supply every human defect, ③that His benediction may consecrate to the liberties and happiness of the people of the United States a Government instituted by themselves for these essential purposes, and may enable every instrument employed in its administration to execute with success the functions allotted to his charge. In tendering this homage to the Great Author of every public and private good, I assure myself that it expresses your sentiments ④not less than my own, nor those of my fellow-citizens at large less than either. ⑤No people can be bound to acknowledge and adore the Invisible Hand which conducts the affairs of men more than those of the United States. ⑥Every step by which they have advanced to the character of an independent nation seems to have been distinguished by some token of providential agency; and in the important revolution just accomplished in the system of their united government the tranquil deliberations and voluntary consent of ⑦so many distinct communities from which the event has resulted can not be compared with the means by which most governments have been established without some return of pious gratitude, ⑧ along with an humble anticipation of the future blessings which the past seem to presage. These reflections, arising out of the present crisis, have forced themselves ⑨too strongly on my mind to be suppressed. You will join with me, I trust, in thinking that there are none under the influence ⑩of which the proceedings of a new and free government can more auspiciously commence.

🖐 문법분석

① I have repaired to the present station under the impression in obedience to the public summons: 국민의 소환의 순응할 때 받은 감동 하에 저는 현재의 위치로 향했습니다. / (As I am) such being the impressions: 제가 그러한 감동을 받을 때 / to omit (in this first official act) my fervent supplications to that Almighty Being: omit('생략하다'의 목적어는 my fervent…) - 전능하신 하나님의 ~하신 저의 열렬한 탄원을 (제 첫 번째 공직생활에서) 생략한다는 것 /

② rules over(통치하고), presides in(관장하고), and whose providential aids(신의 전능하신 도움~): and(등위 접속사로) 연결된 구문

③ my fervent supplications to that Almighty Being ~, that His benediction may ~, and may ~ 로 연결되는 구문임

  • consecrate a Government to the liberties and happiness: 연방정부가 미국국민의 자유와 행복에 헌신하도록 /

  • enable + (every instrument employed in its administration 목적어) + to execute(부정사) with

success(부사구) the functions allotted to his charge.: 정부의 행정에 고용된 모든 관리들이 자신의 임무에 할당된 기능을 성공적으로 수행하도록 하기 위해서

④ not less, nor ~at large less than either: 그것은 저 자신의 것에 못지않게 여러분의 소회를 피력하는 것이고 어느 쪽에 못지않게 소회를 피력하는 것

⑤ No people ~more than those(affairs) of the United States(어떠한 국민도 미국국민 보다 ~하지 않다)

⑥ they have advanced to the character of an independent nation by every step 그 합중국 국민이 독립국의 지위로의 한 걸음 한 걸음 전진할 때 / seems to have been distinguished by(완료형 부정사): ~의해 구별되었던 것 같다 /

⑦ the event has resulted from so many distinct communities 혁명을 가능케 했던 많은 각각의 공동체들 / most governments have been established by the means 대부분의 정부들이 그 수단에 의해 수립되었던 /

⑧ along with(~와 더불어) an humble anticipation of the future blessings which the past seem to presage(presage의 목적어는 the future blessings): 과거에 예시된 듯한 미래의 축복에 대한 겸허한 기대와 더불어

⑨ too strongly on my mind to be suppressed(too~to…의 용법: 너무 ~해서 …못하는) 제 마음에 이러한 생각이 억누를 수 없을 만큼 거세게

⑩ the proceedings ~can more auspiciously commence(자동사, 시작되다) of the influence 새로운 자유정부의 본보기가 더욱 상서로이 시작할 수 있는 영향력을 갖춘 정부는 없다

동영상 강좌 http://youtu.be/_-fjnvS2W7Y

🦪 본문해석

Such being the impressions(이러한 감회로) **under which I have, in obedience to the public summons**(조국의 소환에 복종하여), **repaired to the present station**(현재의 위치로 향했을 때), **it would be peculiarly improper to omit in this first official act my fervent supplications** (이 첫 번째 공직에서 나의 뜨거운 탄원을 생략하는 것은 더욱이 부당한 것입니다) **to that Almighty Being who rules over the universe**(우주를 관장하는 하느님에 대해), **who presides in the councils of nations**(국가들의 회의를 관장하시고), **and whose providential aids can supply every human defect**(그리고 신의 섭리에 의한 도움으로 모든 인간의 결함을 보완해 주시고), **that His benediction may consecrate to the liberties and happiness of the people of the United States a Government instituted by themselves for these essential purposes**(그의 축복이 본질적인 목적으로 그들 스스로 세운 미 정부의 국민의 자유와 행복에 헌신해 주시고)), **and may enable every instrument employed in its administration to execute with success the functions allotted to his charge**(시정을 위한 모든 기관이 자신의 책임으로 할당된 직분을 성공적으로 수행하도록). **In tendering this homage to the Great Author of every public and private good**(모든 공익과 사익의 창조주께 이렇게 경의를 표할 때), **I assure myself**(저는 ~을 확신합니다) **that it expresses your sentiments not less than my own, nor those of my fellow-citizens at large less than either**(그것은 저 자신의 것에 못지않게 여러분의 소회를 피력하는 것이고 어느 쪽에 못지않게 소회를 피력하는 것). **No people can be bound to acknowledge and adore the Invisible Hand which conducts the affairs of men more than those of the United States**(어떠한 국민도 보이지 않은 손을 인정하고 경배할 의무를 합중국의 국민보다 더 많이 진 국민은 없

습니다). **Every step by which they have advanced to the character of an independent nation**(합중국 국민이 독립국의 지위로의 한 걸음 한 걸음) **seems to have been distinguished by some token of providential agency**(신의 섭리를 보여주는 어떠한 징표로 구별되었던 것 같습니다); **and in the important revolution just accomplished in the system of their united government**(그리고 통일된 정부의 체제로 막 성취한 혁명을 두고 볼 때), **the tranquil deliberations and voluntary consent of so many distinct communities**(많은 개별 공동체들의 차분한 숙고와 자발적인 동의는) **from which the event has resulted** (혁명을 가능케 했던) **can not be compared with the means**(~그 수단과 비교될 수 없습니다) **by which most governments have been established without some return of pious gratitude**(경건한 감사와 같은 답례 없이 대부분의 정부들이 수립되었던), **along with an humble anticipation of the future blessings which the past seem to presage**(과거에 예시된 듯 미래의 축복에 대한 겸허한 기대와 더불어). **These reflections, arising out of the present crisis**(작금의 위기에서 연유하는 반향은), **have forced themselves too strongly on my mind to be suppressed**(제 마음에 이러한 생각이 억누를 수 없을 만큼 거세게 밀려 들게 하고 있습니다). **You will join with me, I trust, in thinking**(제 생각에 여러분이 동의하리라고 믿습 니다) **that there are none under the influence of which the proceedings of a new and free government can more auspiciously commence**(새로운 자유정부의 본보기가 더욱 상서로이 시작할 수 있는 영향력을 갖춘 정부는 없습니다).

📓 **단어분석**

- **repair** vi. ① 『~ / +전+명』 가다, 다니다, 종종 가다(to); 여럿이 가다(to). ② 『+전+명』 구하러[의지하 러] 가다, 의지하다(to; for). / **fervent** [fə́ːrvənt] a. 뜨거운; 타는 듯한; 열심인, 열렬한, 격심한, 백열의. / **peculiarly** [pikjúːljərli] ad. ① 특(별)히. ② 개인적으로. ③ 기묘하게. / **supplication** [sʌ̀pləkéiʃən] n. U 탄원, 애원(to; for); U,C 〘종교〙 기원. / **providential** [prɑ̀vədénʃəl / prɔ̀-] a. 섭리의, 신의 뜻에 의한; 천우의, 행운의. / **benediction** [bènədíkʃən] n. ① (예배 따위의 끝) 기도, (식전·식후의) 감사기도. ② 축 복. / **consecrate** [kɑ́nsəkrèit / kɔ́n-] vt. ① 『~+목/ +목+전+명』 신성하게 하다, 성화(聖化)하다; 〘가톨 릭〙 (미사에서 빵과 포도주를) 성별(聖別)하다; 봉헌하다(to); 성직에 임명하다. ② 『+목+전+명』 (어떤 목 적에) 바치다, 전념하다. / **tender** [téndəːr] v. —vt. ① 『~+목/ +목+목/ +목+전+명』 제출하다; 제공하 다, 신청하다. / **homage** [hɑ́midʒ / hɔ́m-] n. U 존경; (봉건시대의) 충성(의 맹세), 신하로서의 예 / **sentiment** [séntəmənt] n. (종종 pl.) 소감, 감상, 생각; 취지; (말 자체에 대해 그 이면의) 뜻, 생각, 기분. / **bound** [baund] a. 『~+to do』 ~하지 않을 수 없는, ~할 의무가[책임이] 있는; 꼭[필연적으로] ~하게 되어 있는. / **character** [kǽriktər] n. U 특성, 특질, 성질. 신분, 자격, 지위. / **distinguish** [distíŋgwiʃ] v. —vt. 『~+목/ +목+전+명』 ① 구별하다, 분별[식별]하다(from; by); 분류하다(into). ② ~을 특징 지우 다; ~의 차이를 나타내다(from). / **presage** [présidʒ, priséidʒ] vt., vi. ① ~의 전조가 되다, 예시(豫示) 하다; 예언하다. ② 예지[예감]하다. / **proceeding** [prousíːdiŋ] n. 진행; 행동; 조처; (pl.) 소송 절차; 변 론; (pl.) 의사(議事), 의사록, 회의록, (학회의) 회보. / **auspicious** [ɔːspíʃəs] a. 길조의, 경사스런, 상서로 운; 행운의. /

동영상 강좌 http://youtu.be/_-fjnvS2W7Y

❋ 다음 글을 읽고 물음에 답하시오. [6~10]

Such being the impressions under which I have, in obedience to the public summons, repaired to the present station, it would be peculiarly improper to omit in this first official act my fervent supplications to that Ⓐ**Almighty Being** who rules over the universe, who presides in the councils of nations, and whose providential aids can ① **supply** every human defect, that His benediction may consecrate to the liberties and happiness of the people of the United States a Government instituted by themselves for these essential purposes, and may enable every instrument employed in its administration to execute with success the functions allotted to his charge. In ② **tendering** this homage to the Great Author of every public and private good, I assure myself that it expresses your sentiments not less than my own, nor Ⓑ**those** of my fellow-citizens at large less than either. No people can ③**be bound to** acknowledge and adore the Invisible Hand which conducts the affairs of men more than Ⓒ**those** of the United States. Every step by which they have advanced to the character of an independent nation seems to have been distinguished by some token of providential agency; and in the important revolution just accomplished in the system of their united government the tranquil deliberations and voluntary consent of so many distinct communities from which the event has ④ **resulted** can not be compared with the

means by which most governments have been established without some return of pious gratitude, along with an humble anticipation of the future blessings which the past seem to presage. These reflections, ⑤**disappearing** out of the present crisis, have forced themselves too strongly on my mind to be suppressed. You will join with me, I trust, in thinking that there are none under the influence of which the proceedings of a new and free government can more auspiciously commence.

6. 위 글의 분위기로 가장 적절하지 <u>않은</u> 것은?

① auspicious   ② pious

③ fervent   ④ providential

⑤ objective

7. 위 글의 밑줄 친 Ⓐ와 관련이 <u>적은</u> 것은?

① 모든 우주를 지배한다.

② 모든 국가 위원회를 주관한다.

③ 인간의 부족함을 채워준다.

④ 미국 독립에 기여했다.

⑤ 미 국민들의 자유와 행복을 봉헌한다.

8. 위 글의 밑줄 친 ①~⑤ 중, 문맥상 쓰임이 <u>어색한</u> 것은?

①   ②   ③   ④   ⑤

9. 위 글과 일치하지 <u>않은</u> 것은?

① 나는 조국의 부름으로 감명에 젖어 이곳에 왔다.
② 우주를 주관하시는 하느님만이 인간의 부족함을 채워줄 수 있다.
③ 자신의 책임 하에 맡겨진 행정기관은 스스로 반드시 성공을 거둬야만 한다.
④ 미국 국민만이 보이지 않은 절대적인 손에 인식하고 경배할 줄 안다.
⑤ 통합된 정부체계 아래서 경건한 숙고와 자발적인 동의는 대부분의 정부와 비교될 수 없다.

10. 위 글의 밑줄 친 ⑧, ⓒ가 각각 가리키는 것은?

① sentiments   the Invisible hands
② sentiments   affairs
③ public and private   affairs
④ public and private   conducts
⑤ sentiments   conducts

6. ⑤   7. ④   8. ⑤ disappearing → arising   9. ③   10. ②

동영상 강좌 http://youtu.be/LgVesscX6x8

①By the article establishing the executive department it is made the duty of the President "to recommend to your consideration such measures as he shall judge necessary and expedient." The circumstances ②under which I now meet you will acquit me from entering into that subject further than to refer to the great constitutional charter under which you are assembled, and which, in defining your powers, designates the objects to which your attention is to be given. It will be ③more consistent with those circumstances, and far more congenial with the feelings which actuate me, to substitute, in place of a recommendation of particular measures, the tribute that is due to the talents, the rectitude, and the patriotism which adorn the characters selected to devise and adopt them. In these honorable qualifications I behold the surest pledges that as on one side no local prejudices or attachments, no separate views nor party animosities, will misdirect the comprehensive and equal eye which ought to watch over this great assemblage of communities and interests, so, on another, that the foundation of our national policy will be laid in the pure and immutable principles of private morality, and the preeminence of free government be exemplified by all the attributes which can win the affections of its citizens and command the respect of the world. I ④dwell on this prospect with every satisfaction which an ardent love for my country can inspire, since there is no truth more thoroughly established than that there exists in the economy and course of nature an indissoluble union between virtue and happiness; between duty and advantage; between the genuine maxims of an honest and magnanimous policy and the solid rewards of public prosperity and felicity; since we ought to be ⑤no less persuaded that the propitious smiles of Heaven can never be expected on a nation that disregards the eternal rules of order and right which Heaven itself has ordained; and since the preservation of the sacred fire of liberty and the destiny of the republican model of government are justly considered, perhaps, as deeply, as finally, staked on the experiment entrusted to the hands of the American people.

📝 문법분석

① 행정부 설립조항에 따르면, article과 the executive department는 능동형관계 / it(가주어) is made the duty to recommend(진주어) ~는 의무로 정해져 있다 / such measures as he shall judge: shall은 주어의 의지, 필요하고 합당하다고 판단하는 법안들을 /

② I now meet you under the circumstances 제가 지금 여러분과 마주한 상황에서 / entering into 착수하다 / acquit A further than B: A를 피하고 B를 하는 것이 / the great constitutional charter which, (in defining your powers), designates the objects to which your attention is: which의 선행사는 charter임: 여러분의 주의를 기울여야 할 대상을 명시한 위대한 헌법 /

③ more consistent with 더욱 일치하는 / far more congenial with 훨씬 더 설득력이 있는 /
  • in place of ~을 대신하여 / to substitute, A(in place of ~), B(the tribute that ~): A를 대신하여

B를 가름하는 것(대체시키는 것) / selected 과거분사 / 그 법안을 창안하고 채택하기 위해 선발된 인물들의

- as A so B: A인 것처럼 B한, 어떠한 지방적 편견이나 애착, 개별적 소신이나 당파적 적대감 때문에 감시해야 할 포괄적이고 공정한 눈이 오도되지 않을 것처럼 / on another (side) / free government (will) be exemplified by 자유정부는 모든 특성에 의해 좋은 예가 될 것이라는 /

④ dwell on A(this prospect) 부사구(with every satisfaction) which 주어(an ardent love for my country) 동사(can inspire)의 목적어는 this prospect임: 조국에 대한 열렬한 사랑을 불러일으킬 수 있는 이런 관점에 아주 만족하여 숙고하다 /

- no truth than that A: A라는 것보다 더한 진실은 없다 /

⑤ no less A that B: B 못지않게 B한, 하늘의 자애로운 미소를 기대할 수 없다는 것을 그 진리에 못지않게 확신하기 때문이며 /

- 그만큼 깊게, 결정적으로

본문해석

By the article establishing the executive department(행정부 설립에 관한 조항에 따르면) **it is made the duty of the President**(대통령의 의무로 되어 있습니다.) **"to recommend to your consideration**(여러분의 심의에 붙이는 것) **such measures as he shall judge necessary and expedient**(필요하고 합당하다고 판단하는 법안들을)." **The circumstances under which I now meet you**(제가 지금 여러분과 마주한 상황에서) **will acquit me from entering into that subject**(그 문제에 대한 상세한 논의는 피하고) **further than to refer to the great constitutional charter**(위대한 헌법을 언급하는 것이) **under which you are assembled**(여러분을 이곳에 소집하여), **and which, in defining your powers**(여러분의 권한을 규정함과), **designates the objects to which your attention is to be given**(여러분의 주의를 기울여야 할 대상을 명시한). **It will be more consistent with those circumstances**(그러한 상황이보다 합치할 것입니다), **and far more congenial with the feelings which actuate me**(그리고 나의 가슴을 휩싸는 느낌에도 훨씬 걸맞을 것), **to substitute, in place of a recommendation of particular measures**(특별한 법안 심의를 요청하는 것 대신에), **the tribute that is due to the talents, the rectitude, and the patriotism which adorn**(더 돋보이게 하는 재능, 성실성 및 애국심에 마땅히 돌아가야 하는 찬사로 가름하는 것이) **the characters selected to devise and adopt them**(그 법안을 창안하고 채택하기 위해 선발된 인물들의). **In these honorable qualifications**(이러한 영예로운 자질들 속에서) **I behold the surest pledges**(저는 가장 확실한 징표를 목격한 바입니다) **that as on one side**(한편으로는) **no local prejudices or attachments, no separate views nor party animosities**(어떠한 지방적 편견이나 애착, 개별적 소신이나 당파적 적대감이), **will misdirect the comprehensive and equal eye which ought to watch over**(감시해야 할 포괄적이고 공정한 눈이 오도되지 않을 것처럼) **this great assemblage of communities and interests**(다양한 공동체들과 이해 집단들이 모인 이 위대한 의회를), **so, on another**(또 한편으로는), **that the foundation of our national policy**(우리나라의 정책의 기본이) **will be laid in the pure and immutable principles of private morality**(개인의 도덕성의 순수하고 변치 않는 원리 안에 놓여 있을 것이고), **and the preeminence of free government**(자유정부의 탁월성이) **be exemplified by all the attributes**(모든 특성에 의해 좋은 예가 될 것이라는) **which can win the affections of its citizens**(국민들의 애정을 듬뿍 받고) **and command the respect of the world**(세계의 존경을 모을 수 있는). **I dwell on this prospect with every satisfaction**(저는 이러한 전망에서 ～온갖 만족감을 누립니다) **which an ardent love for my country can inspire**(조국에 대한 열렬한 사랑을 불러일으킬 수 있는), **since**(왜냐하면) **there is no truth more thoroughly established than**(～보다 더 완벽하게 확증된 진리는 없기 때문이고) **that there exists in the economy**

and course of nature(자연의 경제와 이치로 보건대) **an indissoluble union**(떼려야 뗄 수 없는 연관이 있다는 것) **between virtue and happiness**(미덕과 행복 사이에); **between duty and advantage**(의무와 편의 사이에); **between the genuine maxims of an honest and magnanimous policy and**(정직하고 관대한 정책이라는 참된 금언과) **the solid rewards of public prosperity and felicity**(공공의 번영과 행복이란 알찬 보상 사이에); **since we ought to be no less persuaded**(~ 것을 그 진리에 못지않게 확신하기 때문이며) **that the propitious smiles of Heaven can never be expected**(하늘의 자애로운 미소를 기대할 수 없다는) **on a nation that disregards the eternal rules of order and right which Heaven itself has ordained**(하늘이 스스로 정한 질서와 정의의 영원한 법칙을 경시하는 나라); **and since the preservation of the sacred fire of liberty and the destiny of the republican model of government**(그리고 자유의 성스러운 불길의 보존과 모범적인 공화 정부의 운명이) **are justly considered, perhaps, as deeply, as finally**(그만큼 깊게, 결정적으로 달려 있다고 정당하게 간주되기 때문입니다), **staked on the experiment entrusted to the hands of the American people**(미국 국민의 손에 맡겨진 이 실험에).

📖 **단어분석**

- **consideration** [kənsìdəréiʃən] n. ① U 고려, 숙려(熟廬), 고찰. ② U (남에 대한) 동정, 참작, 헤아림 (for). ③ C 행하, 보수, 팁; 〖법률〗 (계약상의) 약인(約因), 대가(對價). ④ C 고려의 대상, (고려할) 사정, 항목; 동기, 이유. ⑤ U 중요시, 경의, 존경. / **expedient** [ikspíːdiənt] a. ① 편리한, 편의의; 마땅한, 유리한, 상책인. ② 편의주의의, 방편적인, 정략적인(politic); 사리(私利)를 추구하는. / **acquit** [əkwít] vt. (-tt-) ① 『~+목 / +목+전+명』 석방하다, 무죄로 하다(of). ② 『+목+전+명』 ~에게 면제해 주다(of). / **consistent** [kənsístənt] a. ① (의견·행동·신념 등이) (~와) 일치 [조화·양립]하는(with). ② (주의·방침·언행 등이) 불변한, 견지하는, 시종일관된, 견실한(in). / **congenial** [kəndʒíːnjəl] a. ① 같은 성질의, 마음이 맞는, 같은 정신의, 같은 취미의(with; to). ② (건강·취미 따위에) 적합한(to), 기분 좋은, 쾌적한(to). ③ 붙임성 있는, 인상이 좋은. / **actuate** [ǽktʃuèit] vt. (동력원이 기계를) 움직이다; (장치 등을) 발동[시동, 작동]시키다; (아무를) 자극하여 ~하게 하다(to do); 격려하다. / **substitute** [sʌ́bstitjùːt] v. —vt. ① 『~+목 / +목+전+명』 대용(代用)하다, 바꾸다(for); ~을 대리케 하다(for). / **tribute** [tríbjuːt]n. ① U,C 공물, 조세; 과도한 세[관세, 부과금, 임대료], 터무니없는 징수금; 납공[납세] 의무. ② C,U 찬사, 칭찬[감사, 존경]을 나타내는 말[행위, 선물, 표시]. / **rectitude** [réktətjùːd] n. U ① 정직, 실직(實直), 청렴. ② (판단·방법의) 올바름, 정확(correctness). / **adorn** [ədɔ́ːrn] vt. ① 『~+목 / +목+전+명』 꾸미다, 장식하다 (with). [cf.] decorate, ornament. ② ~에 광채를[아름다움을] 더하다; 보다 매력적[인상적]으로 하다. / **behold** [bihóuld] v. (p., pp. beheld [-héld]) —vt. 보다(look at). / **pledge** [pledʒ] n. ① U 서약(vow), 언질. [SYN.] ⇨ PROMISE. ② U 저당, 담보, 전당; C 저당[담보]물. ③ C 보증, (우정 따위의) 증거 (token). / **preeminence** [priémənəns] n. U 걸출, 탁월, 발군(in; of). / **command** [kəmǽnd, -máːnd] v. —vt. ① 『~+목/ +목+to do/ + (that)절』 ~에게 명(령)하다, ~에게 호령[구령]하다, 요구하다. [opp.] obey. ② 지휘하다, ~의 지휘권을 갖다; 통솔하다. ③ (감정 따위를) 지배하다, 누르다, 제어하다. ④ (남의 존경·동의 따위를) 모으다, 일으키게 하다; (사물이) ~을 강요하다; ~할 만하다, ~의 값어치가 있다. / **indissoluble** [ìndisáljəbəl / -sɔ́l-] a. 용해[분해, 분리]시킬 수 없는; 해소[파기]할 수 없는, 확고한; 불변의, 영속성 있는(계약 따위). / **magnanimous** [mægnǽniməs] a. 도량이 넓은, 관대한, 아량 있는; 고결(高潔)한. / **felicity** [filísəti] n. C 경사; U 더없는 행복(bliss); U (표현의) 교묘함; C 적절한 표현. / no less ~(1) ~보다 적지 않은(것), 그 정도의 (것): We expected no ~. 그 정도는 각오하고 있었다. (2) 「부가적; 종종 반어적」 바로, 확실히 / **propitious** [prəpíʃəs] a. ① 순조로운, (형편) 좋은(favorable)(for; to); 상서로운, 길조의. ② (신이) 호의를 가진, 자비로운; 행운의 / **ordain** [ɔːrdéin] vt. ① (신·운명 등이) 정하다; (법률 등이) 규정하다, 제정하다, 명하다. / **stake** [steik] vt. ① 『~+목/ +목+전+명』 (생명·돈 따위를) 걸

다(wager) (on). ② 위험에 내맡기다. /

동영상 강좌 http://youtu.be/DwBemiQnUgk

❊ 다음 글을 읽고 물음에 답하시오. [11~18]

By the article **being established/establishing** the executive department it is made the duty of the President "to recommend to your consideration **as/such measures** as he shall judge **necessary and expedient/necessarily and expediently**." The circumstances under which I now meet you will acquit me from **enter/entering into** that subject further than to refer to the great constitutional charter under which you are assembled, and which, in defining your powers, designates the objects **to which/which** your attention is to be given. It will be more consistent with those circumstances, and ①**far** more congenial with the feelings which actuate me, to substitute, in place of a recommendation of particular measures, the tribute that is due to the talents, the rectitude, and the patriotism which adorn the characters selected to devise and ② **adapt** Ⓐ**them**. In these honorable qualifications I behold the surest pledges that as on one side no local prejudices or attachments, no separate views nor party animosities, will misdirect the comprehensive and equal eye which ought to watch over this great assemblage of communities and interests, so, on another, that the ③**foundation** of our national policy will be laid in the pure and ④**immutable** principles of private morality, and the preeminence of free government be exemplified by all the attributes which can win the affections of its citizens and

command/commanded by the respect of the world. I dwell on this prospect with every satisfaction which an ardent love for my country can inspire, since there is no truth more thoroughly established than that there **exist/exists** in the economy and course of nature _____ between virtue and happiness; between duty and advantage; between the genuine maxims of an honest and magnanimous policy and the solid rewards of public prosperity and felicity; since we ought to be no less ⑤ **persuaded** that the propitious smiles of Heaven can never be expected on a nation that disregards the eternal rules of order and right which Heaven itself **has ordained/has been ordained**; and since the preservation of the sacred fire of liberty and the destiny of the republican model of government are justly considered, perhaps, as deeply, as finally, staked on the experiment entrusted to the hands of Ⓑ**the American people**.

11. 위 글의 주제로 가장 적절한 것은?

① 의원 여러분의 재능, 성실성 그리고 애국심은 타의 추종을 불허합니다.

② 대통령의 막강한 권한을 인정해야 합니다.

③ 때론 여러 공동체와 이익집단을 대표할 필요가 있습니다.

④ 모든 것을 초월한 미국의 이익을 위해 단결합시다.

⑤ 민주주의의 근간이 되는 원리는 자유와 평등입니다.

12. 위 글의 밑줄 친 ①~⑤ 중, 문맥상 쓰임이 <u>어색한</u> 것은?

① ② ③ ④ ⑤

13. 위 글의 네모상자 안의 적절한 단어를 골라 쓰시오.

_____

_____

_____

_____

_____

_____

14. 위 글의 밑줄 친 빈칸에 적절한 표현은?

① one beyond the other
② an indissoluble union
③ unsolvable complexity
④ unnecessary comparison
⑤ pure emotion

15. 위 글의 분위기는?

① forceful   ② encouraging
③ pessimistic   ④ indifferent
⑤ gloomy

16. 위 글의 밑줄 친 ⒜가 가리키는 것은?

① characters   ② measures
③ qualifications ④ circumstances
⑤ talents

17. 위 글과 일치하지 <u>않은</u> 것은?

① 대통령은 필요하고 합당하다면, 법안을 상정할 수 있다.
② 연설자는 문제를 상세히 다루기보다는 위대한 헌법을 강조하고 있다.
③ 국가의 정책은 개인의 도덕성의 근간이 된다.
④ 모범적인 공화정부는 유능한 인재 선발을 게을리 해서는 안 된다.
⑤ 신이 부여한 질서와 권리의 영원한 법칙을 무시하는 국가는 신의 은총을 받을 권리가 없다.

18. 위 글 밑줄 친 ⒝의 의무로 적절치 <u>않은</u> 것은?

① supervision   ② experiment
③ submission   ④ morality
⑤ affection

11. ④   12. ② adapt → adopt
13. establishing / such measures / necessary and expedient / enter into / to which / command / exists / has ordained   14. ②   15. ②   16. ②
17. ④   18. ③

①Besides the ordinary objects submitted to your care, it will remain with your judgment to decide how far an exercise of the occasional power delegated by the fifth article of the Constitution is rendered expedient at the present juncture ②by the nature of objections which have been urged against the system, or by the degree of inquietude which has given birth to them. Instead of undertaking particular recommendations on this subject, ③in which I could be guided by no lights derived from official opportunities, I shall again ④ give way to my entire confidence in your discernment and pursuit of the public good; ⑤for I assure myself that whilst you carefully avoid ⑥every alteration which might endanger the benefits of an united and effective government, or which ought to await the future lessons of experience, ⑦a reverence for the characteristic rights of freemen and a regard for the public harmony will sufficiently influence your deliberations on the question how far ⑧the former can be impregnably fortified or the latter be safely and advantageously promoted.

📋 문법분석

① Besides(이외에) / submitted to(~에게 제출된(과거분사)): 여러분이 살펴야 할 통상적인 대상들 이외에 / it(가주어) ~to decide(진주어) / delegated by(~의해 위임된, 과거분사) / is rendered expedient(적절히 되어지다) /

② by A or by B: A또는 B에 의해, 그러한 제도에 대해 강력하게 제기되어 온 이의의 성격과 그런 이의의 바탕에 깔린 불안감의 정도로 보아 /

③ in which(where) / I could be guided in particular recommendations / by no lights derived from official opportunities 공직의 경험에서 생기는 식견을 갖추지 못했기에 나로서는 /

④ 전적으로 신뢰하다

⑤ because / whilst = while

⑥ every alternation which might endanger ~, or which ought to await 위태롭게 할지모르고 기다려야만 하는 일체의 개정 /

⑦ a reverence(주어) ~will sufficiently influence(동사): 주절을 이끔 /

⑧ the former(a reverence) ~or the latter(a regard): 전자에 대한 존중과 후자에 대한 배려

📋 본문해석

①**Besides the ordinary objects submitted to your care**(여러분이 살펴야 할 통상적인 대상들 이외에), ⑦**it will remain with your judgment to decide**(~ 결정하는 것도 여러분의 판단에 달려 있을 것입니다.) **how far** ②**an exercise of the occasional power delegated by the fifth article of the Constitution**(헌법 제5조에 의해 위임된 임시 권한의 행사가) ⑥**is rendered expedient**(얼마나 합리화될 수 있는가를) ⑤ **at the present juncture**(현재의 중대한 고비에서) **by the** ③**nature of objections which have been urged against the system**(그러한 제도에 대해 강력하게 제기되어 온 이의의 성격과), **or** ④**by the degree of inquietude which has given birth to them**(그런 이의의 바탕에 깔린 불안감의 정도로 보아). /②**Instead of undertaking particular recommendations on this subject**(이 문제에 대해 특별한 권고를 하는 대신에), ①**in which I could be guided by no lights derived from official opportunities**(공직의 경험에서 생기는 식견을 갖추지 못했기에 나로서는), ③**I shall again give way to my entire confidence in your**

discernment and pursuit of the public good(다시 한 번 공익에 대한 여러분의 분별력과 추진력을 전적으로 신뢰할 것입니다.); ⑫**for I assure myself that**(확신하기 때문입니다.) ④**whilst you carefully avoid every alteration**(일체의 개정을 세심하게 피하는 한편으로) ①**which might endanger the benefits of an united and effective government**(왜냐하면 여러분이 통일된 효율적인 정부의 이점을 위태롭게 할지도 모르는), ③**or which ought to await the future lessons of experience**(또는 경험을 통한 장래의 교훈을 기다려야만 할), **a reverence** ④**for the characteristic rights of freemen**(자유인 특유의 권리가) **and a regard for** ⑥**the public harmony**(공공의 화합이) ⑪**will sufficiently influence**(충분히 반영될 것으로) ⑧**your deliberations on the question**(문제를 숙고함에 있어) ⑨**how far the former**(여러분이 지닌 전자에 대한 존중과) **can** ⑤**be impregnably fortified**(얼마나 확고하게 강화되고) ⑩**or the latter**(후자에 대한 배려가) ⑦**be safely and advantageously promoted**(얼마나 안전하고 유익하게 증진될 수 있는가 하는).

🖋 **단어분석**

- ****besides** [bisáidz] prep. ① ～외에(도), ～에다가 또. ② 「부정·의문문에서」 외에(는), ～을 제외하고(는)(except). / **delegate** [déligèit] vt. ① 『+목+to do/ +목+전+명』 대리[대표]로 보내다[파견하다], 대리로 내세우다. ② 『+목+전+명』 (권한 등을) 위임하다. / **expedient** [ikspíːdiənt] a. ① 편리한, 편의의; 마땅한, 유리한, 상책인. ② 편의주의의, 방편적인, 정략적인(politic); 사리(私利)를 추구하는 / **junction** [dʒʌ́ŋkʃən] n. ① U 연합, 접합, 연접, 연락, 합체. ② C 접합점, 교차점; (강의) 합류점; 연락역, 갈아타는 역; / **inquietude** [inkwáiətjùːd] n. U 불안, 동요(restlessness); (pl.) 불안한 생각, 근심. / **derive** [diráiv] v. —vt. ① 『+목+전+명』 끌어내다(from); 손에 넣다, 획득하다(from). ② 『+목+전+명』 ～의 기원을[유래를] 찾다(from); 「종종 수동태」 ～에서 나와 있다, ～에서 시작하다(from). / **discernment** —n. U 식별(력), 안식, 통찰(력), 명민. / **alternation** [ɔ̀ːltərnéiʃən, æ̀l-] n. U,C 교호, 교대, 교체; 하나 거름; / **deliberation** [dilìbəréiʃən] n. U 숙고; U,C 협의, 심의, 토의; U 신중, 세심; 유장(悠長), 침착. / **impregnable** [imprégnəbəl] a. 난공불락의, 견고한; 움직일 수 없는; (신념 따위가) 확고부동한. / **fortify** [fɔ́ːrtəfài] v. —vt. ① 『～+목/ +목+전+명』 요새화[방어 공사를] 하다. ② 『～+목/ +목+전+명』 강하게 하다, (육체적·정신적으로) 튼튼히 하다. / **advantageous** [æ̀dvəntéidʒəs] a. 유리한; 형편이 좋은.

✻ 다음 글을 읽고 물음에 답하시오. [19~25]

Beside/Besides the ordinary objects submitted to your care, it will remain with your judgment to decide how far an exercise of the occasional power delegated by the fifth article of the Constitution is rendered expedient/expediently at the present juncture by the nature of objections which have been urged against the system, or by the degree of inquietude which has given birth to Ⓐthem. Instead of undertaking particular recommendations on this subject, in which ⒷI could be guided by no lights derived from official opportunities, I shall again give way to my entire confidence in your discernment and pursuit of the public good; for I assure myself that whilst you carefully avoid every alteration which might endanger the benefits of an united and effective government, or which ought to await /wait the future lessons of experience, a reverence for the characteristic rights of freemen and a regard for the public harmony will sufficiently influence your deliberations on the question how far Ⓒthe former can be impregnably fortified or Ⓓ the latter be safely and advantageously promoted.

19. 위 글의 주제로 가장 적절한 것은?

① the unconditional objections
② the systematical analysis
③ the importance of expedient consideration
④ You confidence
⑤ alterative reverence

20. 위 글에서 네모상자 안의 적절한 단어를 고르시오.

① Beside   expedient   await
② Beside   expediently   await
③ Besides   expedient   wait
④ Besides   expediently   wait
⑤ Besides   expedient   wait

21. 위 글의 밑줄 친 Ⓐ가 가리키는 것은?

① measures   ② systems
③ objections   ④ recommendations
⑤ delegations

22. 위 글의 밑줄 친 Ⓑ의 분위기는?

① condescendence   ② abjectness
③ conceit   ④ futility
⑤ frustration

23. 위 글의 Ⓒ, Ⓓ가 각각 가리키는 것은?

① rights   harmony
② rights   deliberations
③ a reverence   harmony
④ a reverence   a regard
⑤ rights   a regard

24. 위 글의 내용과 일치하지 않은 것은?

① 현재의 위기는 체제에 대한 반대와 불안한 정도에 의해 야기될 수 있다.
② 작가는 공직에 대한 경험이 풍부하다.
③ 작가는 공인의 분별과 추구를 신뢰한다.
④ 존중과 배려가 무엇보다 중요하다고 강조한다.
⑤ 현재를 중대한 고비로 생각한다.

25. 위 글에 나타난 단어들의 올바른 우리말 표현으로 어색한 것은?

① ordinary objects: 통상적인 대상

② occasional power: 임시권한

③ every alternation: 일체의 개정

④ characteristic rights: 특유의 권리

⑤ impregnably fortified: 불안하게 강화된

19. ③ 20. ⑤ 21. ③ 22. ① 23. ④
24. ② 25. ⑤

George Washington 독해

동영상 강좌 http://youtu.be/QZ1t5mmpCbo

①To the foregoing observations I have one to add, which will be <u>most properly addressed to</u> the House of Representatives. It concerns myself, and will therefore be ②<u>as brief as possible</u>. When I <u>was first honored with a call into</u> the service of my country, then <u>on the eve of</u> an arduous struggle for its liberties, ③<u>the light in which</u> I contemplated my duty <u>required</u> that I should renounce every pecuniary compensation. From ④<u>this resolution I have in no instance departed</u>; and ⑤<u>being still under the impressions which produced it</u>, I must ⑥<u>decline as inapplicable to myself any share</u> in the personal emoluments which may be indispensably included in a permanent provision for the executive department, and must accordingly pray that the pecuniary estimates for the station ⑦ <u>in which</u> I am placed may during my continuance in ⑧<u>it</u> be limited to ⑨<u>such</u> actual expenditures <u>as</u> the public good may be thought to require.

📎 **문법분석**

① add A to B: I have A(one) to add to the foregoing observation - 나는 이상의 소견에 한 가지를 덧붙이고자 하는데 / most properly 가장 적절한 / be addressed to ~에게 말하다 /

② as B(형/부사) as A: A만큼 B한, be동사의 보어가 와야 하므로 brief(형용사) / be honored with ~로 명예를 부여 받으므로(영광스럽게) / on the eve of ~의 전야에 /

③ I contemplated my duty in the light: which의 선행사는 the light(주어, 전야의 불빛) - 그 불빛 속에서 내게 주어진 의무를 곰곰 생각해 보니, / the light required that 구문 / ④ this resolution은 I should renounce every pecuniary compensation(나에게 어떠한 금전적 보상도 단념해야만 하는 것) / in no instance은 never의 뜻 / I have in no instance departed에서 departed의 목적어는 this resolution - 나는 결코 이 결심을 저버린 적이 없습니다. /

⑤ 분사구문절 As(Because) I am still under ~, / which produced it에서 it은 this resolution를 가르킴 /

⑥ as(전치사) inapplicable to myself(나에겐 적용되지 않은 것으로서) / decline의 목적어는 any share(어떠한 몫도 거절하다) /

⑦ I am place in the station(내 직책을 위임받아), which의 선행사는 the station /

⑧ it는 the station을 가리킴 /

다음 같이 요약할 수 있다.

the pecuniary estimates may be limited to

⑨such A as ~: ~하는 것 같은 A

동영상 강좌 http://youtu.be/QZ1t5mmpCbo

📎 **본문해석**

To the foregoing observations I have one to add(나는 이상의 소견에 한 가지를 덧붙이고자 하는데), **which will be most properly addressed to the House of Representatives**(그것은 하원을 상대로 하여 말하는 것이 마땅할 것입니다). **It concerns myself, and will therefore be as brief as possible**(그것은 나

자신에 관계된 것이기에 가능한 한 간략히 하도록 하겠습니다.). **When I was first honored with a call into the service of my country**(영광스럽게도 조국에 대한 봉사의 부름을 처음 받았을 때), **then on the eve of an arduous struggle for its liberties**(이 나라의 자유를 위한 험난한 투쟁의 전야에), **the light in which I contemplated my duty**(그 불빛 속에서 내게 주어진 의무를 곰곰이 생각해 보니) **required that I should renounce every pecuniary compensation**(그 빛은 마치 나에게 어떠한 금전적 보상도 단념할 것을 명하는 것 같았습니다). **From this resolution I have in no instance departed**(나는 결코 이 결심을 저버린 적이 없습니다.); **and being still under the impressions which produced it**(그리고 지금도 그렇게 결심했을 때의 감회를 간직하고 있기에), **I must decline as inapplicable to myself**(나 자신에게는 해당되지 않는 것으로 나는 사절하며) **any share in the personal emoluments which may be indispensably included in a permanent provision for the executive department**(행정부에 관한 영구적 규정 속에 필수적으로 포함될 개인적 보수의 어떠한 몫도), **and must accordingly pray**(회구하는 바입니다.) **that the pecuniary estimates for the station in which I am placed**(그런 까닭에 내가 차지한 지위에 대한 금전적 계상도) **may during my continuance**(재직 기간 동안) **in it be limited to such actual expenditures as the public good may be thought to require**(공익을 위해 필요하다고 생각되는 실질 경비로 한정되기를).

🐚 단어분석

- **observation** [àbzərvéiʃən / ɔb-] n. U 관찰, 주목, 주시. (on). [SYN.] ⇨ REMARK. / **arduous** [áːrdʒuəs / -dju-] a. 힘드는, 곤란한; 분투적인, 끈기 있는, 끈질긴; (미국·영국고어) 오르기 힘든, (길이) 험한. / **contemplate** [kántəmplèit / kóntem-] v. —vt. ① 찬찬히 보다, 정관하다, 관찰하다. / ② 잘 생각하다, 심사 숙고하다. [SYN.] ⇨ CONSIDER. / **renounce** [rináuns] v. —vt. ① (권리 등을 정식으로) 포기하다(surrender), 단념하다. / **pecuniary** [pikjúːnièri / -njəri] a. ① 금전(상)의, 재정상의. ② 벌금을 물려야 할. / **compensation** [kàmpənséiʃən / kòm-] n. C,U ① U 배상, 변상, 벌충(for). / **emolument** [imáljəmənt / imɔ́l-] n. (보통 pl.) 급료, 봉급 이득(profit)(of) / **indispensable** [ìndispénsəbəl] a. ① 불가결의, 긴요한(to; for). [SYN.] ⇨ NECESSARY. ② (의무·약속 등을) 게을리[기피] 할 수 없는. / **continuance** [kəntínjuəns] n. U,C 계속, 연속; 체류(in a place); (이야기의) 계속, 속편; 〖계속[체류]기간. / **expenditure** [ikspénditʃər] n. U,C 지출; 소비;

동영상 강좌 http://youtu.be/MMTWhaNY7DA

❋ 다음 글을 읽고 물음에 답하시오. [26~30]

To the ①**foregoing** observations I have one to add, which will be most properly ②**addressed** to the House of Representatives. It concerns myself, and will therefore be as **brief/briefly** as possible. When I was first honored with a call into the service of my country, then on the eve of an arduous struggle for its liberties, the light in which I contemplated my duty required that I should renounce every ③**pecuniary** compensation. From this resolution I have in no instance departed; and being still under the impressions which produced Ⓐ**it**, I must decline as ④**applicable** to myself any share in the personal emoluments which may be indispensably included in a permanent provision for the executive department, and must accordingly pray that the pecuniary estimates for the station in which I am placed may during my continuance in Ⓑ**it** **be limited/limit** to such actual expenditures as the public ⑤**good** may be thought to **be required/require**.

26. 위 글의 'I'의 심경은?

① determined　　② sad

③ bored　　④ uncertain

⑤ hopeful

27. 위 글의 밑줄 친 ①~⑤ 중, 문맥상 단어의 쓰임이 어색한 것은?

①　　②　　③　　④　　⑤

28. 위 글의 네모상자 안의 적절한 단어를 고르시오.

① brief	be limited	be required
② brief	limit	require
③ brief	be limited	require
④ briefly	limit	be required
⑤ briefly	be limited	require

29. 위 글의 밑줄 친 Ⓐ, Ⓑ가 각각 가리키는 것은?

① compensation	my continuance
② instance	the executive department
③ this resolution	my continuance
④ this resolution	the station
⑤ compensation	the station

30. 위 글과 일치하지 않은 것은?

① 그는 하원의원에게 간략한 마무리 인사를 하였다.

② 첫 번째 공직을 시작할 때, 자유를 위한 투쟁을 시작하는 전야에 명상하였다.

③ 그는 급여를 받지 않을 것이다.

④ 그의 급여수령은 가끔 그에게 혼돈을 주었다.

⑤ 공무원의 급여는 영구적인 조항에 포함되어 있다.

26. ①　27. ④ applicable → inapplicable

28. ③　29. ④　30. ④

①<u>Having thus imparted to</u> you my sentiments as they have been awakened by ② <u>the occasion which brings us together</u>, I shall take my present leave; but not without ③<u>resorting</u> once more <u>to</u> the benign Parent of the Human Race in humble supplication that, since He has been pleased to favor the American people ④<u>with opportunities for</u> deliberating in perfect tranquillity, <u>and dispositions for</u> deciding with unparalleled unanimity on a form of government for the security of their union and the advancement of their happiness, so His divine blessing may be equally conspicuous in ⑤<u>the enlarged views</u>, <u>the temperate consultations</u>, and <u>the wise measures on which</u> the success of this Government must depend.

🔖 **문법분석**

① After I have thus imparted ~분사구문절임 / impart A to B: A에게 B를 전하다 /
② which의 선행사 the occasion: 우리를 함께 모이게 하는 계제(의식)
③ resort to ~에 의지하다
④ with opportunities for ~, and with dispositions for~: ~한 기회와 ~한 심성을 갖고
⑤ 등위 접속사 and로 연결된 구문임(드넓은 전망, 절도 있는 협의 및 현명한 법안들에도)
   the success of this Government must depend on the wise measures: which의 선행사는 the wise measures(이 정부의 성공을 가름할)

🔖 **본문해석**

Having thus imparted to you my sentiments as they have been awakened by the occasion which brings us together(우리는 이 자리에 한데 모은 계제에 의해 촉발되었던 제 감회를 이렇게 여러분에게 전하였으니), **I shall take my present leave**(이제 작별 인사를 드리고자 합니다); **but not without resorting once more to the benign Parent of the Human Race**(그러나 한 번 더 인류의 자애로운 부모님께 다음과 같은) **in humble supplication**(겸허한 기원을 올리는 일을) **that, since He has been pleased to favor**(즐거이 허락하셨기에) **the American people**(미국 국민에게) **with opportunities for deliberating in perfect tranquillity**(완벽한 평온의 상태에서 숙고할 기회와), **and dispositions for deciding with unparalleled unanimity**(유례없는 만장일치로 결정할 수 있는 심성을) **on a form of government for the security of their union and the advancement of their happiness**(연방의 안전과 국민의 행복 증진을 위한 정부의 형태에 관하여), **so His divine blessing may be equally conspicuous**(신성한 축복이 똑같이 뚜렷하기를 빕니다) **in the enlarged views, the temperate consultations, and the wise measures**(드넓은 전망, 절도 있는 협의 및 현명한 법안들에도) **on which the success of this Government must depend**(이 정부의 성공을 가름할).

🔖 **단어분석**

- **impart** [impάːrt] vt. 『+목+전+명』 ① 나누어주다, 주다 (give)(to). ② (지식·비밀 따위를) 전하다 (communicate), 알리다(tell) (to). / **occasion** [əkéiʒən] n. ① (특정한) 경우, 때(on), 시(時); 일. ② (~할) 기회, 호기(好機) (for), 알맞은 때. [SYN.] ⇨ OPPORTUNITY. ③ 중요한 때, 경사스러운 때; 축전

(祝典), 행사. ④ U 이유, 근거; 유인(誘因), 원인. / **resort** [rizɔ́ːrt] vi. ① 『+전+명』 가다; 잘 가다[다니다](to). ② 『+전+명』 의지하다, 도움을 청하다, 호소하다(to). / **supplication** [sʌ̀pləkéiʃən] n. U 탄원, 애원(to; for); U,C 〚종교〛 기원. / **deliberate** [dilíbərèit] v. —vt. 『~+목/ wh. to do/ + wh. 절』 잘 생각하다, 숙고하다; ~을 심의하다. [SYN.] ⇨ THINK. —vi. 『~ / +전+명』 ① 숙고하다(on; over). ② 심의하다, 협의하다(on; over). / **tranquil(l)ity** [træŋkwíləti] n. U 평정, 평온, 평안, 침착. / **disposition** [dìspəzíʃən] n. ① U,C 성벽(性癖), 성질, 기질; 경향; U 의향. [SYN.] ⇨ MOOD. ② U,C 배열, 배치; (pl.) 작전계획. / **unparalleled** 비할 데 없는, 유례없는 / **unanimity** [jùːnəníməti] n. U 전원 이의 없음, 동의, 합의, 만장일치. / **conspicuous** [kənspíkjuəs] a. ① 눈에 띄는, 똑똑히 보이는. [SYN.] ⇨ EVIDENT. ② 특징적인, 사람 눈에 띄는. / **temperate** [témp-ərit] a. ① (기후·계절 등이) 온화한; (지역 따위) 온대성의. ② 삼가는, 알맞은, 중용의, 온건한, 적당한. ③ 절제하는; 금주의. /

❋ 다음 글을 읽고 물음에 답하시오. [31~35]

Having thus imparted to you my sentiments as Ⓐ**they** have ① **awakened** by the occasion which brings us together, _____; but not without ②**resorting** once more to the benign Parent of the Human Race in humble supplication that, since Ⓑ **He** has been pleased to ③**favor** the American people with opportunities for deliberating in perfect tranquillity, and dispositions for ④**deciding** with unparalleled unanimity on a form of government for the security of their union and the advancement of their happiness, so His divine blessing may be equally conspicuous in the enlarged views, the temperate consultations, and the wise measures ⑤**for which** the success of this Government must depend.

31. 위 글에 나타난 지은이의 심경은?

① to desire the bright future

② to leave for the long journey

③ to compromise the dispute

④ to ask a favor of the public to support him

⑤ to resign from the position

32. 위 글의 밑줄 친 Ⓐ가 가리키는 것은?

① the members of the Senate and the House of Representatives

② the American people

③ sentiments

④ the world people

⑤ a pile of measures

33. 위 글의 밑줄 친 Ⓑ와 관련이 적은 것은?

① 자비롭다.

② 미국 국민들에게 기회를 베푼다.

③ 만장일치의 기회를 준다.

④ 연방의 안정과 행복의 증진을 허락한다.

⑤ 세계의 안정과 평화를 축복을 내린다.

34. 위 글의 밑줄 친 빈칸에 가장 적절한 표현은?

① I will start my address right now.

② all of you should take steps for the world.

③ I shall take my present leave

④ let's recommend to your consideration the measures

⑤ May God bless all, the Americans, and the world!

35. 위 글의 밑줄 친 ①~⑤ 중, 어법상 어색한 것은?

①   ②   ③   ④   ⑤

31. ①   32. ③   33. ⑤   34. ③   35. ①⑤

[난이도 ★★★★★]

동영상 강좌 http://youtu.be/NKYjVtMexsl

September 19,

Friends and Citizens:

①The period for a new election of a citizen to administer the executive government of the United States being not far distant, and ②the time actually arrived when your thoughts must be employed in designating the person who is to be clothed with that important trust, ③it appears to me proper, especially as it may conduce to a more distinct expression of the public voice, ④that I should now ⑤apprise you of the resolution I have formed, to decline being considered among the number of those out of ⑥whom a choice is to be made.

🔖 **문법분석**

[분사구문] (As) the period … being (is) not far distant, and the time arrived ~, it appears … that
…: ①(종속절) ~할 시간이 멀지 않았으며, ② ~할 시간이 도달한 지금, ④(주절) that ~은 ③~인 것 같다 /
⑤ apprise A of B: A에게 B를 알리다 / decline + ing(동명사): ~것을 사양하다 /
⑥ whom은 be made의 목적격 관계대명사: 선출 대상이 될 몇 사람 중에 포함되는 것

🔖 **본문해석**

Friends and Citizens(친구들과 동포시민 여러분):
The period for a new election of a citizen to administer the executive government of the United States being not far distant(미국 행정부를 관리할 한 시민을 새로 선출할 시기가 이제 멀지 않았으며), **and the time actually arrived**(~할 때가 실제로 도달한 지금은) **when your thoughts must be employed in designating the person who is to be clothed with that important trust**(또 여러분 각자가 그처럼 중요한 신임을 받을 사람의 선출에 대해 생각해야), **it appears to me proper**(적절한 시점이라고 생각하며), **especially as it may conduce to a more distinct expression of the public voice**(특히 그러한 결심은 일반 국민의 의견을 더욱 분명히 표현하게 하는 데 기여할 수 있다고 봅니다), **that I should now apprise you**(여러분께 알리는 데) **of the resolution I have formed, to decline being considered among the number of those out of whom a choice is to be made**(그러한 선출 대상이 될 몇 사람 중에 포함되는 것을 사양하기로 한 나의 결심을).

🔖 **단어분석**

- **administer** [ædmínistər, əd-] v. —vt. ① 관리하다, 지배[통치]하다. ②『~+목 / +목+전+명』(법령·의식을) 집행하다. ③ 베풀다, 주다, 공급하다(to). ④『+목+전+명』(약 따위를) 복용시키다. ⑤『+목+목 / +목+전+명』(사람에게 타격 따위를) 가하다, ~을 과하다, 지우다, 강제하다. ⑥ 【법률】 (유산을) 관리[처분]하다. / **employ** [emplɔ́i] vt. ①『~+목/ +목+as보/ +목+전+명』(사람을) 쓰다, 고용하다; (아무에게) 일을 주다. ②『+목+전+명』「보통 수동태 또는 재귀용법」~에 종사하다, ~에 헌신하다. / **designate** [dézignèit] vt. ① 가리키다, 지시[지적]하다, 표시[명시]하다, 나타내다. ②『+목+보』~라고 부르다(call), 명명하다. ③『+목+전+명/ +목+as보』지명하다, 임명[선정]하다(to; for); 지정하다. / **clothe** [klouð] vt. (p., pp. ~d [-ðd], (고어·문어) clad [klæd]) ① ~에게 옷을 주다. ②『+목+전+명』(비유) 싸다, 덮다; (말로) 표현하다. ③『~목/ +목+전+명』~에게 옷을 입히다. ④『+목+전+명』(권력·영광 따위를) 주다(with). / **conduce** [kəndjúː s] vi. +전+명』 도움이 되다, 이바지[공헌]하다, (어떤 결과로) 이끌다(to; toward). / **apprise, apprize** [əpráiz] vt. ~에 알리다, ~에 통고[통지]하다. /

✸ 다음 글을 읽고 물음에 답하시오. [1~4]

Friends and Citizens:

The period for a new election of a citizen to administer the executive government of the United States ①**being not** far distant, and the time actually ②**arrived** when your thoughts must be employed in designating the person who is to be clothed with that important trust, it appears to me proper, especially as **it** may ③**conduce** a more distinct expression of the public voice, that I should now apprise you of the resolution I have formed, to decline ④**being** considered among the number of those ⑤**out of** whom a choice is to be made.

1. 위 글의 종류는?

① delay   ② encouragement
③ rejection   ④ appreciation
⑤ consolation

2. 위 글의 밑줄 친 ①~⑤ 중, 문법적으로 어색한 것은?

①   ②   ③   ④   ⑤

3. 위 글의 밑줄 친 'it'가 가리키는 것은?

① a new election
② the person
③ the public voice
④ the resolution
⑤ the number

4. 위 글과 일치하지 <u>않은</u> 것은?

① 행정부의 새로운 선거가 임박했다.
② 중요한 믿음을 갖은 자를 선택해야 한다.
③ 작가는 지금의 자신의 소신을 밝힐 적기라 생각한다.
④ 자신이 내린 결단을 통보하는 자리이다.
⑤ 자신을 후보자 중 한 명으로 선택해준 것에 대해 감사한다.

1. ③   2. ③   3. ④   4. ⑤

동영상 강좌 http://youtu.be/T8xeLuL3SeE

I beg you, at the same time, to ①do me the justice to be assured that this resolution has ②not been taken without a strict regard to all the considerations ③ appertaining to the relation which binds a dutiful citizen to his country; and that ④ in withdrawing the tender of service, which ⑤silence in my situation might imply, ⑥I am influenced by no diminution of zeal for your future interest, no deficiency of grateful respect for your past kindness, but am supported by a full conviction that the step is compatible with both.

The acceptance of, and continuance hitherto in, the office ⑦to which your suffrages have twice called me have been ⑧a uniform sacrifice of inclination to the opinion of duty and to a deference for what appeared to be your desire. I constantly hoped that ⑨it would have been much earlier in my power, consistently with motives ⑩which I was not at liberty to disregard, ⑪to return to that retirement from which I had been reluctantly drawn. The strength of my inclination to do ⑫this, previous to the last election, had even led to the preparation of an address to declare it to you; but mature reflection on the then perplexed and critical posture of our affairs with foreign nations, and the unanimous advice of persons entitled to my confidence, impelled me to abandon the idea.

🖋 문법분석

① ～간곡히 부탁하다
② not A without B: 반드시 B하여 A한 / 엄격히 숙고한 후에 결심하게 된
③ ～에 속하는
④ service(임기를) the tender(퇴임서) in withdrawing(철회할 때) - [의역] 아무런 움직임을 취하지 아니한 데서
⑤ silence in my situation might imply: 제 상황에서의 침묵이 암시하는, [의역] 이미 짐작한 분도 있을 것으로 사료되는)
⑥ 여러분의 미래이익에 대하 나의 감소된 열정에 영향을 받아서, [직역] 국민 여러분의 향후 이익에 대한 나의 열정이 줄어서가 아니고 / I am influenced by no A(diminution) ～, no B(deficiency of) ～, but C(am supported by) ～: A나 B가 아닌 C에 의해 영향을 받았다 / both는 no diminution ～와 no deficiency of ～ 둘을 가리킴
⑦ your suffrages have twice called me to the office: which의 선행사는 the office - 두 번씩이나 나에게 맡겨주신 직책
⑧ inclination to the opinion ～and to a deference: ～의 여론과 ～의 존경심에 따른
⑨ it는 퇴임을 가리킴 - 훨씬 일찍 되었어야 했길
⑩ 거절할 만큼 자유롭지 않은(뜻을 따르기 위해 불가피하게 접었던)
⑪ 제가 억지로 끌려간 곳으로부터의 은퇴(은퇴의 뜻을 떨칠 수 없었던 곳으로부터) / I had been reluctantly drawn from that retirement /

⑫ this은 '사임'을 뜻함

🖋 본문해석

I beg you, at the same time, to do me the justice to be assured(국민 여러분께서 헤아려 주실 것을 간곡히 부탁드리고자 합니다) **that this resolution has not been taken**(이러한 결심을 하게 되었음을) **without a strict regard to all the considerations appertaining to the relation which binds a dutiful citizen to his country**(책임 있는 국민의 한 사람으로서 국가에 대한 책무와 관련된 모든 요소를 엄격하게 숙고한 후에); **and that in withdrawing the tender of service**(아무런 움직임을 취하지 아니한 데서), **which silence in my situation might imply**(이미 짐작한 분도 있을 것으로 사료됩니다), **I am influenced by no diminution of zeal for your future interest**(국민 여러분의 향후 이익에 대한 나의 열정이 줄어서도 아니고), **no deficiency of grateful respect for your past kindness**(지금까지 나에게 보내 주신 국민 여러분의 애정에 대한 감사와 존경이 없어서도 아니며), **but am supported by a full conviction that the step is compatible with both**(오로지 그런 결정이 양쪽 모두에게 부합되는 순전한 양심에 의한 것이었습니다).

The acceptance of, and continuance hitherto in(수락하고 지금까지 수행하여 온 것은), **the office to which your suffrages have twice called me**(국민 여러분께서 투표로써 두 번씩이나 나에게 맡겨주신 대통령직을) **have been a uniform sacrifice of inclination to the opinion of duty**(오로지 국가에 대한 의무를 다할 것을 요구하는 여론과) **and to a deference for what appeared to be your desire**(국민 여러분의 뜻을 따르기 위하여). **I constantly hoped**(지속적으로 바랐습니다) **that it would have been much earlier in my power**(오히려 지금보다 더 일찍 대통령직에서 퇴임하고자), **consistently with motives which I was not at liberty to disregard**(국민 여러분의 뜻을 따르기 위하여 불가피하게 접었던), **to return to that retirement from which I had been reluctantly drawn**(은퇴의 뜻을 떨칠 수 없었으며). **The strength of my inclination to do this, previous to the last election**(사실, 지난 대통령 선거 전에는 퇴임하고자 하는 나의 욕심이 강한 나머지), **had even led to the preparation of an address to declare it to you**(국민 여러분께 드릴 고별 연설문까지 준비한 바 있습니다); **but mature reflection on**(심사숙고한 끝에) **the then perplexed and critical posture of our affairs with foreign nations**(그러나, 당시 외국과의 복잡하고 중요한 상황과), **and the unanimous advice of persons entitled to my confidence**(주변의 한결 같은 만류를), **impelled me to abandon the idea**(퇴임의 뜻을 접게 되었습니다).

🖋 단어분석

- **appertain** [æ̀pərtéin] vi. 속하다(to); 관련되다(relate)(to). / **tender** [téndəːr] n. ① a) 제출, 제공, 신청; / **withdraw** [wiðdrɔ́ː, wiə-] v. (-drew [-drúː]; -drawn [-drɔ́ːn]) ─vt. (제의·신청 등을) 철회하다; 취소하다; (소송을) 취하하다 / **diminution** [dìmənjúːʃən] n. ① U 감소, 감손, 축소; 저감(低減); C 감소액[량], 분]. / **deficiency** [difíʃənsi] n. U,C 결핍, 부족, 결여; 영양부족, 영양소 결핍; U,C 결손; 결함; C 부족분[액·량]. [opp] sufficiency. / **conviction** [kənvíkʃən] n. ① U,C 신념, 확신. [SYN.] ⇨ CONFIDENCE. ② U 설득(력), 설득행위. ③ U 죄의 자각, 양심의 가책. / **hitherto** [hìðərtúː] ad. 지금까지(는), 지금까지로 봐서는 (아직). / **suffrage** [sʌ́frid3] n. U 찬성투표; 동의, 찬성. / **deference** [défərəns] n. U 복종; 존경, 경의(to), / **disregard** [dìsrigáːrd] vt. 무시하다, 문제시하지 않다; 경시하다 (ignore). [SYN.] ⇨ NEGLECT. / **confidence** [kánfidəns / kɔ́n-] n. U ① (남에 대한) 신용, 신뢰. [SYN.] ⇨ BELIEF. ② C 속내 말; 비밀, 내밀한 일. ③ (자기에 대한) 자신, 확신. [opp.] diffidence. ④ 대담, 사기. /

동영상 강좌 http://youtu.be/Fx1wfDuskOl

❋ 다음 글을 읽고 물음에 답하시오. [5~10]

I beg you, at the same time, to ①**do me the justice** to be assured that this resolution has not been taken without a strict regard to all the considerations appertaining/appertaining to the relation which binds a dutiful citizen to his country; and that in ㉠**withdrawing** the tender of service, which silence in my situation might imply, I am influenced by ②**no diminution of zeal** for your future interest, ③**no deficiency of grateful respect** for your past kindness, but am supported by a full conviction that the step is ㉡ **compatible** with Ⓐ**both**.

The acceptance of, and continuance hitherto in, the office from which/to which your suffrages have twice called me have been a ④**uniform sacrifice of inclination** to the opinion of duty and to a ㉢**deference** for what appeared to be your desire. I constantly hoped that Ⓑ**it would have been much earlier** in my power, consistently with motives which I was ⑤**not at liberty to disregard**, to return to that retirement from which I had been reluctantly drawn. The strength of my inclination to do Ⓑ**this**, previous to the last election, had even led to the preparation of an address to declare it to you; but mature ㉣**reflection** on the then perplexed and critical posture of our affairs with foreign nations, and the unanimous advice of persons entitled for/entitled to my confidence, impelled me to ㉤**accept** the idea.

5. 위 글에 나타난 지은이의 심정은?

① pleased　　② sorry
③ sad　　　　④ cool
⑤ impatient

6. 위 글에서 밑줄 친 ①~⑤ 중, 각각의 우리 말 번역이 어색한 것은?

① do me the justice (저의 마음을 헤아려주다.)
② no diminution of zeal (열정이 감소되지 않음)
③ no deficiency of grateful respect (감사와 존경심이 없어서가 아님)
④ uniform sacrifice of inclination (오로지 희생하는 정신)
⑤ not at liberty to disregard (자유를 기구하여)

7. 위 글의 네모상자 안의 적절한 단어를 고르시오.

① appertaining　　from which　entitled for
② appertaining　　to which　　entitled to
③ appertaining to　to which　　entitled for
④ appertaining to　from which　entitled to
⑤ appertaining to　to which　　entitled to

8. 위 글에서 밑줄 친 Ⓐ가 가리키는 것을 쓰시오

_____
_____
_____

9. 위 글에서 밑줄 친 ㉠~㉤중, 문맥상 어색한 단어는?

①　　②　　③　　④　　⑤

10. 위 글의 내용과 일치하는 것은?

① 작가는 자신의 결정을 간곡하게 이해를 구한다.

② 작가는 두 번씩이나 직책을 거부했다.

③ 작가는 미래에 대한 열정이 떨어졌다.

④ 작가는 노구으로 쇠약하여 공직을 떠나려 한다.

⑤ 작가의 고집으로 인해 주위 참모들은 괴로웠다.

I b_____ you, at the same time, to do me the j_____ to be assured(국민 여러분께서 헤아려 주실 것을 간곡히 부탁드리고자 합니다) that this r_____ has not been taken(이러한 결심을 하게 되었음을) w_____ a strict regard to all the considerations a to the relation which binds a dutiful citizen to his country(책임 있는 국민의 한 사람으로서 국가에 대한 책무와 관련된 모든 요소를 엄격하게 숙고한 후에); and that in w_____ the tender of service(아무런 움직임을 취하지 아니한 데서), which silence in my situation might imply(이미 짐작한 분도 있을 것으로 사료됩니다), I am influenced by no d_____ of zeal for your future interest(국민 여러분의 향후 이익에 대한 나의 열정이 줄어서도 아니고), no d_____ of grateful respect for your past kindness(지금까지 나에게 보내주신 국민 여러분의 애정에 대한 감사와 존경이 없어서도 아니며), but am supported by a full c_____ that the step is compatible with both(오로지 그런 결정이 양쪽 모두에게 부합되는 순전한 양심에 의해 것이었습니다).

The acceptance of, and continuance hitherto in(수락하고 지금까지 수행하여 온 것은), the office to which your s_____ have twice called me(국민 여러분께서 투표로써 두 번씩이나 나에게 맡겨주신 대통령직을) have been a uniform s_____ of inclination to the opinion of duty(오로지 국가에 대한 의무를 다할 것을 요구하는 여론과) and to a d_____ for what appeared to be your desire(국민 여러분의 뜻을 따르기 위하여). I constantly hoped(지속적으로 바랬습니다) that it would have been much earlier in my power(오히려 지금 보다 더 일찍 대통령직에서 퇴임하고자), c_____ with motives which I was not at liberty to disregard(국민 여러분의 뜻을 따르기 위하여 불가피하게 접었던), to return to that retirement from which I had been r_____ drawn(은퇴의 뜻을 떨칠 수 없었으며). The strength of my inclination to do this, previous to the last election(사실, 지난 대통령 선거 전에는 퇴임하고자 하는 나의 욕심이 강한 나머지), had even led to the preparation of an address to declare it to you(국민 여러분께 드릴 고별 연설문까지 준비한 바 있습니다); but m_____ reflection on(심사숙고한 끝에) the then p_____ and c_____ posture of our affairs with foreign nations(그러나 당시 외국과의 복잡하고 중요한 상황과), and the u_____ advice of persons entitled to my confidence(주변의 한결 같은 만류를), i_____ me to abandon the idea(퇴임의 뜻을 접게 되었습니다).

동영상 강좌 http://youtu.be/QuApwzvvD54

I rejoice that the state of your concerns, ①external as well as internal, ②no longer ③renders the pursuit of inclination incompatible with the sentiment of duty or propriety, and am persuaded, ④whatever partiality may be retained for my services, that, in the present circumstances of our country, you will not disapprove my determination to retire.

⑤The impressions with which I first undertook the arduous trust were explained on the proper occasion. In the discharge of this trust, I will only say that I have, with good intentions, ⑥contributed towards the organization and administration of the government the best exertions of which a very fallible judgment was capable. ⑦Not unconscious in the outset of the inferiority of my qualifications, ⑧experience in my own eyes, perhaps still more in the eyes of others, has strengthened the motives to diffidence of myself; and every day ⑨ the increasing weight of years admonishes me more and more that the shade of retirement is ⑩as necessary to me as it will be welcome. ⑪Satisfied that if any circumstances have given peculiar value to my services, they were temporary, I have the consolation to believe that, while choice and prudence invite me to quit the political scene, patriotism does not forbid it.

🔖 본문해석

① B as well as A: A뿐만 아니라 B도 - 국내외의

② 더 이상 ~않는

③ 의무감에 맞지 않는 기분에 따르는(의무감을 쫓는)

④ 어떠한 편견이 제 공직기간 동안 계속 되었을지라도(부적절한 국가에 대한 의무를 저버리는 것으로)

⑤ I first undertook the arduous trust with the impressions 네가 이 막중한 책무를 처음 맡았을 때의 감회는

⑥ contribute towards B A: A를 B에 기여하다 / a very fallible judgment was capable of the best exertion 아주 잘못된 판단이 최고의 전력을 다했다. [의역] 잘못된 판단을 내렸다.

⑦ (Though I was) Not unconscious ~, 처음부터 나의 능력이 부족함을 모르지 아니하였으나

⑧ experience (in my own eyes, perhaps still more in the eyes of others) has strengthened the motives to diffidence of myself. 제 스스로의 경험은 능력의 부족함을 더욱 절감하게 만들었다

⑨ the increasing weight ~admonishes me ~that ~더 더욱 힘든 무게감이 저로 하여금 ~하도록 훈계합니다.

⑩ 앞으로 환영받듯 저에게도 필요한(국민 여러분께서도 환영하리라)

⑪ (Because I am) Satisfied that ~, I have the consolation ~

동영상 강좌 http://youtu.be/QuApwzvvD54

🔖 본문해석

I rejoice that the state of your concerns, external as well as internal(이제 국내외 상황에 대한 국민 여러분의 염려가), no longer renders the pursuit of inclination incompatible with the sentiment of duty or propriety(더 이상의 의무감에서 해방되어), and am persuaded(믿게 되었다(설득되었다)), whatever partiality may be retained for my services(부적절하거나 국가에 대한 의무를 저버리는 것으로), that, in the present circumstances of our country(우리나라의 현 상황에서), you will not disapprove my determination to retire(나의 퇴임 결심을 국민 여러분께서 반대하지 아니할 것으로 믿게 되었습니다).

The impressions with which I first undertook the arduous trust(내가 이 막중한 책무를 처음 맡았을 때의 감회는) were explained on the proper occasion(적절한 자리에서 이미 밝힌 바 있습니다). In the discharge of this trust(이제 이 책무를 두고 물러나면서), I will only say(국민 여러분께 드리고자 하는 말씀은) that I have, with good intentions, contributed towards the organization and administration of the government the best exertions(내가 정부의 조직과 운영을 위하여 선의로써 최선의 노력을 다하였으나) of which a very fallible judgment was capable(그 과정에 잘못된 판단을 내린 부분도 있을 수 있다는 것입니다). Not unconscious in the outset of the inferiority of my qualifications(처음부터 나의 능력이 부족함을 모르지 아니하였으나), experience in my own eyes(나 스스로 처음의 의지에도 불구하고), perhaps still more in the eyes of others(나의 부족함은 국민 여러분의 눈에는 더욱 선명하게 보였으리라 생각됩니다), has strengthened the motives to diffidence of myself(능력의 부족함을 더욱 절감하게 되었으며); and every day the increasing weight of years admonishes me more and more that the shade of retirement(또한, 대통령직을 수행한 해가 쌓일수록 나의 부족함에 대한 자책의 무게가 날로 커지면서) is as necessary to me as it will be welcome(이를 국민 여러분께서도 환영하시리라 믿습니다). Satisfied that if any circumstances have given peculiar value to my services(지금까지 내가 대통령직을 수행함으로써 국가에 조금이나마 도움이 된 바가 있다면 그것으로 충분히 만족하며), they were temporary(그것들이 일시적이었던), I have the consolation to believe that(믿으며 이를 위안으로 삼고자 합니다), while choice and prudence invite me to quit the political scene, patriotism does not forbid it(정계를 떠나고자 하는 내 선택이 주의와 분별의 잣대에 비추어 바람직할 뿐 아니라 애국심의 잣대에 비추어서도 그릇되지 아니한 선택이라).

🪶 단어분석

- **rejoice** [ridʒɔ́is] v. —vi. ① 『+전+명/ +to do/ +that절』 기뻐하다, 좋아하다, 축하하다(at; in; over; on). —vt. 기쁘게 하다, 즐겁게 하다. / **render** [réndə: r] v. —vt. ① 『+목+보』 ~로 만들다, ~이 되게 하다. ② a) 『~+목/ +목+전+명』 (보답으로서) 주다, 갚다, ~에 보답하다. / **propriety** [prəpráiəti] n. ① U 타당, 적당. ② U 예의바름, 예모, 교양; (pl.) 예의 범절. / **partiality** [pà: rʃiǽləti] n. U 편파, 불공평, 치우침; (a ~) 특별히 좋아함(fondness), 편애(for; to); U 부분성, 국부성. / **retain** [ritéin]vt. ① 보류하다, 보유[유지]하다. [SYN.] ⇨ KEEP. ② (변호사·사환을) 고용하다. ③ (폐지하지 않고) 존속시키다; 계속 사용[실행]하다. ④ 잊지 않고 있다. / **fallible** [fǽləbəl]a. 틀리기 쉬운, 틀리지 않을 수 없는; (사람이) 속기 쉬운 / **diffidence** [dífidəns] n. U ① 자신 없음, 망설임, 사양. [opp] confidence. ② 암띰, 수줍음(modesty). / **admonish** [ædmániʃ, əd- -món-] v. —vt. ① 『~+목 / +목+to do / +목+전+명 / +목+that 절』 (아무를) 훈계하다, 타이르다(reprove), 깨우치다; 충고하다, (아무에게) 권고하다(advise). [SYN.] ⇨ ADVISE. ② 『+목+전+명 / +목+that 절』 경고하다(warn), (위험 등을) ㊉ ~의 주의를 촉구하다(of). —vi. 훈계[경고]를 주다. / **consolation** [kànsəléiʃən / kɔ̀n-] n. ① U 위로, 위안. ② C 위안이 되는 것[사람]. / **prudence** [prú: dəns] n. U ① 신중, 세심, 사려, 분별, 빈틈없음. ② 검약(frugality).

동영상 강좌 http://youtu.be/-qN9Q0aniKM

❋ 다음 글을 읽고 물음에 답하시오. [11~15]

I rejoice that the state of your concerns, external as well as internal, no longer renders the pursuit of inclination ①**incompatible** with the sentiment of duty or propriety, and am persuaded, whatever ②**partiality** may be retained for my services, that, in the present circumstances of our country, you will not disapprove my determination to retire.

The impressions with which I first undertook the ③**arduous** trust were explained on the proper occasion. Ⓐ**In the discharge of this trust**, I will only say that I have, with good intentions, contributed towards the organization and administration of the government Ⓑ**the best exertions of which a very fallible judgment was capable**. Not ④**conscious** in the outset of the inferiority of my qualifications, experience in my own eyes, perhaps still more in the eyes of others, has strengthened the motives to ⑤**diffidence** of myself; and every day the increasing weight of years admonishes me more and more that the shade of retirement is as necessary to me as it will be welcome. Satisfied that if any circumstances have given peculiar value to my services, they were temporary, I have the consolation to believe that, while choice and prudence invite me to quit the political scene, patriotism does not forbid Ⓒ**it**.

11. 위 글의 제목으로 가장 적절한 것은?

① the Politics: the Power and the Mortality
② the Sentiment of Quitting the Political Scene
③ Out of the Political Scene: Longing and Aspiration
④ The Presidency: Not easy to be
⑤ Not arduous, But happy

12. 위 글에서 밑줄 친 ①~⑤ 중, 문맥상 단어의 쓰임이 <u>어색한</u> 것은?

①   ②   ③   ④   ⑤

13. 위 글의 밑줄 친 Ⓐ가 암시하는 것은?

① re-election   ② disappointment
③ responsibility   ④ retirement
⑤ sacrifice

14. 위 글에서 밑줄 친 Ⓑ의 올바른 우리말 번역은?

① 잘못된 판단을 수정하고자 최선을 다했다.
② 잘못된 판단은 누구의 탓도 아니다.
③ 잘못된 판단을 내린 부분이 있었다.
④ 누구나 최선을 다하면 된다.
⑤ 판단을 내릴 능력만으로 최선을 다한 것이다.

15. 위 글의 밑줄 친 Ⓒ가 가리키는 것은?

① 정계를 떠나는 것   ② 선택과 신중함
③ 애국심   ④ 나의 공식생활
⑤ 대통령직

I r_____ that the state of your concerns, e_____ as well as i_____(이제 국내외 상황에 대한 국민 여러분의 염려가), no longer r_____ the pursuit of inclination i_____ with the sentiment of duty or propriety(더 이상의 의무감에서 해방되어), and am persuaded(믿게 되었다(설득되었다)), whatever partiality may be r_____ for my services(부적절하거나 국가에 대한 의무를 저버리는 것으로), that, in the present circumstances of our country(우리나라의 현 상황에서), you will not d_____ my determination to retire(나의 퇴임 결심을 국민 여러분께서 반대하지 아니할 것으로 믿게 되었습니다).

The impressions with which I first undertook the a_____ trust(내가 이 막중한 책무를 처음 맡았을 때의 감회는) were explained on the proper occasion(적절한 자리에서 이미 밝힌 바 있습니다). In the d_____ of this trust(이제 이 책무를 두고 물러나면서), I will only say(국민 여러분께 드리고자 하는 말씀은) that I have, with good intentions, contributed towards the organization and administration of the government the best e_____(내가 정부의 조직과 운영을 위하여 선의로써 최선의 노력을 다하였으나) of which a very f_____ judgment was capable(그 과정에 잘못된 판단을 내린 부분도 있을 수 있다는 것입니다). Not u_____ in the outset of the inferiority of my qualifications(처음부터 나의 능력이 부족함을 모르지 아니하였으나), experience in my own eyes(나 스스로 처음의 의지에도 불구하고), perhaps still more in the eyes of others(나의 부족함은 국민 여러분의 눈에는 더욱 선명하게 보였으리라 생각됩니다), has s_____ the motives to diffidence of myself(능력의 부족함을 더욱 절감하게 되었으며); and every day the increasing weight of years a_____ me more and more that the shade of retirement(또한, 대통령직을 수행한 해가 쌓일수록 나의 부족함에 대한 자책의 무게가 날로 커지면서) is as necessary to me as it will be welcome(이를 국민 여러분께서도 환영하시리라 믿습니다). Satisfied that if any circumstances have given p_____ value to my services(지금까지 내가 대통령직을 수행함으로써 국가에 조금이나마 도움이 된 바가 있다면 그것으로 충분히 만족하며), they were temporary(그것들이 일시적이었던), I have the c_____ to believe that(믿으며 이를 위안으로 삼고자 합니다), while choice and p_____ invite me to quit the political scene, p_____ does not forbid it(정계를 떠나고자 하는 내 선택이 주의와 분별의 잣대에 비추어 바람직할 뿐 아니라 애국심의 잣대에 비추어서도 그릇되지 아니한 선택이리라).

11. ② 12. ④ unconscious 13. ③
14. ③ 15. ①

동영상 강좌 http://youtu.be/cJspxYXYLvA

①In looking forward to the moment which is intended to terminate the career of my public life, my feelings do not ②permit me to suspend the deep acknowledgment of that debt of gratitude ③which I owe to my beloved country for the many honors ④it has conferred upon me; ⑤still more for the steadfast confidence with which it has supported me; and ⑥for the opportunities I have thence enjoyed of manifesting my inviolable attachment, by services faithful and persevering, though in usefulness unequal to my zeal. ⑦If benefits have resulted to our country from these services, let it always be remembered to your praise, and ⑧as an instructive example in our annals, that under circumstances in which the passions, agitated in every direction, were liable to mislead, amidst appearances sometimes dubious, vicissitudes of fortune often discouraging, in situations in which not unfrequently want of success has countenanced the spirit of criticism, the constancy of your support was the essential prop of the efforts, and a guarantee of the plans by which they were effected. ⑨Profoundly penetrated with this idea, I shall carry it with me to my grave, ⑩as a strong incitement to unceasing vows that heaven may continue to you the choicest tokens of its beneficence; ⑪that your union and brotherly affection may be perpetual; that the free Constitution, which is the work of your hands, may be sacredly maintained; that its administration in every department may be stamped with wisdom and virtue; that, in fine, the happiness of the people of these States, under the auspices of liberty, may be made complete by ⑫so careful a preservation and so prudent a use of this blessing as will acquire to them the glory of recommending ⑬it to the applause, the affection, and adoption of every nation which is yet a stranger to it.

📝 **문법분석**

① Before I look forward to: ～을 앞두고
② 감사를 빚의 깊은 인식을 미루는 것을 허락하다. [의역] 감사를 표할 기회를 미루다.
③ owe A to B: A는 B 덕분이다. owe의 목적어는 that debt of gratitude
④ confer A upon B: it(my beloved country) has conferred the many honors upon me 사랑하는 조국 이 나에게 부여해 준 수많은 영예
⑤ still more 변함없이 더 더욱 / it(my beloved country) has supported me with the steadfast confidence 저에게 확고한 신뢰로
⑥ I have thence the opportunities of manifesting my inviolable attachment 그렇게 때문에 제가 조국 에 대한 애정을 표현할 기회를 누리다 / by services (which are) faithful and persevering 나름의 충 직하고 끈질긴 직무 수행을 통하여 / thought (they(services) are) in usefulness unequal to my zeal. 나의 열의에 비하면
⑦ [조건절] A result from B: A는 B로 인한 결과이다. 나의 직무 수행으로 국익에 도움된 바가 있다면 / let[사역동사] it(our country) always be[원형동사] remembered[수동형] to your praise 이는 결코 나

의 공이 아니다(여러분이 받을 칭찬)

⑧ as[전치사] an instructive example in our annals 우리 역사에 교훈이 되는 예로서 / that[an instructive example과 동격절] ~in which the passions[관계대명사절의 주어], (which are) agitated ~, were[동사] liable to mislead[목적어인 vicissitudes를 수식], amidst appearances (which are) sometimes dubious, vicissitudes ~, in situations in which ~criticism, the constance[that절의 주어] of your support was[동사] the essential prop of the efforts[보어], and a guarantee ~effected[보어] /

⑨ [분사구문] (Because I am) Profoundly ~이러한 생각을 바탕으로 / I shall[주어의 의지] carry it with me to my grave 바르는 간절한 마음을 무덤까지 가져가고자 합니다.

⑩ as[전치사, ~로써] a strong ~that[unceasing vows와 동격절] heaven ~its[heaven] beneficence; 하늘이 멈춤 없이 여러분들에게 자비의 정선된 징표인 끝없는 공약의 강한 흥분으로서 [의역] 신의 가호가 국민 여러분과 함께하고] /

⑪ unceasing vows that ~beneficence; that ~perpetual; that ~maintained; that ~virtue; that ~: that의 계속 연결되는 동격절

⑫ so + 형용사 + a/an + 단수명사: 너무나 세심한 보존과 신중한 활용 / so ~as ···: ···한 만큼 ~한

⑬ it는 liberty를 가리킴

동영상 강좌 http://youtu.be/cJspxYXYLvA

📖 본문해석

In looking forward to the moment which is intended to terminate the career of my public life(내 공직생활의 마지막으로 기록될 퇴임식을 앞두고), **my feelings do not permit me to suspend the deep acknowledgment of that debt of gratitude**(감사를 표할 기회를 더 이상 미룰 수 없음을 널리 헤아려 주시기 바랍니다) **which I owe to my beloved country for the many honors it has conferred upon me**(사랑하는 조국이 나에게 부여해 준 수많은 영예와); **still more for the steadfast confidence with which it has supported me**(확고한 신뢰에 대하여); **and for the opportunities I have thence enjoyed of manifesting my inviolable attachment**(끈질긴 직무 수행을 통하여 조국에 대한 애정을 표현할 기회를 누릴 수 있었던 데 대하여), **by services faithful and persevering**(나름의 충직하고 끈질긴 직무 수행을 통하여), **though in usefulness**(또 나의 열의에 비하여) **unequal to my zeal**(나라에 도움이 된 바는 크지 않았지만). **If benefits have resulted to our country from these services**(나의 직무 수행으로 국익에 도움이 된 바가 있었다면), **let it always be remembered to your praise**(이는 결코 나의 공이 아니며), **and as an instructive example in our annals**(우리의 역사에 교훈이 되는 예로서), **that under circumstances in which the passions, agitated in every direction, were liable to mislead**(갖가지 서로 다른 열정과 성공에 대한 갈망으로 인하여 흔히 일어날 수 있는 실망스러운 상황의 변화에 대하여), **amidst appearances sometimes dubious, vicissitudes of fortune often discouraging**(비난의 화살을 퍼부을 수도 있는 불안한 상황 속에서), **in situations in which not unfrequently want of success has countenanced the spirit of criticism**(가끔 성공의 탐욕이 비판정신을 묵인한 위치에서), **the constancy of your support was the essential prop of the efforts**(여러분의 지속적인 지지는 그 노력의 꼭 필요한 지지대였고), **and a guarantee of the plans by which they were effected**(그 계획에 의해 완성된 보장). **Profoundly penetrated with this idea**(이러한 생각을 바탕으로), **I shall carry it with me to my grave**(바라는 간절한 마음을 무덤까지 가져가고자 합니다.), **as a strong incitement to unceasing vows that heaven may continue to you the choicest tokens of its**

beneficence(신의 가호가 국민 여러분과 함께하고); **that your union and brotherly affection may be perpetual**(국민 여러분의 결속과 형제애가 영원하며); **that the free Constitution, which is the work of your hands, may be sacredly maintained**(국민 여러분의 손으로 만든 자유헌법이 신성하게 보존되고); **that its administration in every department may be stamped with wisdom and virtue**(헌법의 집행이 모든 부처에서 현명하고 가치 있게 이루어지며); **that, in fine**(마지막으로), **the happiness of the people of these States, under the auspices of liberty**(자유의 보호 아래에서 자유의 축복을 소중히 지키고), **may be made complete by so careful a preservation and so prudent a use of this blessing as will acquire to them the glory**(미합중국 국민의 행복이 완전해지기를) **of recommending it to the applause, the affection**(자유를 찬미하고, 사랑하고, 또 얻을 수 있도록 함으로써), **and adoption of every nation which is yet a stranger to it**(신중하게 사용하여 아직 자유를 알지 못하는 모든 국가로 하여금).

🔖 단어분석

- **terminate** [tə́ːrmənèit]v. —vt. 끝내다; ～의 최후를 마무리하다, 종결시키다; 해고하다; 한정하다, 경계를 짓다. —vi. ① 끝나다, 그치다, 종결하다(in). [SYN.] ⇨ END. / **permit** [pəːrmít] v. (-tt-) —vt. ① 『～+목/ +목+to do/ +목+목』 허락하다, 허가하다, 인가하다. / **suspend** [səspénd] v. —vt. ① 『～+목/ +목+전+명』 (매)달다, 걸다. ② 중지하다, 일시 정지하다, 한때 멈추다, 연기하다. ③ 『～+목/ +목+전+명』 정직[정학]시키다, ～의 특권을 일시 정지시키다. / **gratitude** [grǽtətjùːd] n. U 감사, 보은의 마음; 사의(謝儀). / **confer** [kənfɔ́ːr] v. (-rr-) —vt. ① 『+목+전+명』 (칭호·학위 등을) 수여하다, (영예 등을) 증여하다, (은혜 등을) 베풀다. ② 『폐어』 「명령형」 (비교) 참조하라(compare)(略: cf.). —vi. 『+전+명』 의논하다, 협의하다(together; with). / **thence** [ðens] ad. (고어) 그렇기 때문에; (문어) 거기서부터; (고어) 그 때부터. / **manifest** [mǽnəfèst]v. —vt. ① 명백히 하다; 명시하다; (감정을) 드러내다. ② 증명하다; / **inviolate** [inváiəlit] a. 범하여지지 않은, 손상되지 않은; 더럽혀지지 않은; 신성한. / **annals** [ǽnəlz] n. pl. ① 연대기, 연대표. ② 역사적인 기록, 역사. / **agitate** [ǽdʒətèit] -v. —vt. ① 심하게 움직이다, 흔들어대다. ② 쑤석거리다, 동요시키다; (물결·액체를) 휘젓다. ③ (마음·사람을) 동요시키다, 들먹이다, 흥분시키다 / **liable** [láiəb-əl]a. ① 책임을 져야 할, 지변[지급]할 책임이 있는. ② 부과되어야 할, (～할 것을) 면할 수 없는(to; to do); ～할 의무가[책임이] 있는. ③ 자칫하면 ～하는, (까딱하면) ～하기 쉬운(to do) / **vicissitude** [visísətjùːd] n. C 변화, 변천; U (고어·시어) 순환, 교체; (pl.) 흥망, 성쇠 / **countenance** [káuntənəns] vt. ～에게 호의를 보이다; (은근히) 장려[지지]하다; 후원하다; 묵인하다 / **constancy** [kánstənsi / kɔ́n-] n. U ① 불변성, 항구성. ② 지조 견고; 절조, 성실; 정절. / **prop** [prɑp / prɔp] n. ① 지주(支柱), 버팀목, 버팀대. ② 지지자, 후원자, 의지(가 되는 사람). / **effect** [ifékt] vt. ① (변화 등을) 가져오다, 초래하다. ② 실행하다; (목적 따위를) 성취하다, 완수하다. / **penetrate** [pénətrèit] v. —vt. ① 꿰뚫다, 관통하다, 침입하다. ② (빛·목소리 따위가) ～을 통과하다, 지나가다. ③ ～에 스며들다; ～에 침투하다. / **incitement** [insáitmənt] n. U,C 격려, 고무, 선동, 자극; 자극물, 동기. / **choice** [tʃɔis] a. (choicer; choicest) ① 고르고 고른, 정선한; 【미국】 (쇠고기가) 상등의. ② 가리는, 까다로운. / **beneficence** [bənéfəsəns] n. ① U 선행, 은혜; 자선; 덕행. ② C 자선 행위; 시혜물(施惠物)(gift). / **brotherly** [brʌ́ðərli] a. 형제의; 형제다운; 우정이 두터운, 친숙한. / **perpetual** [pərpétʃuəl] a. ① 영구의, 영속하는, 종신의. ② 부단한, 끊임없는, 중지하지 않는. [SYN.] ⇨ CONTINUAL / **stamp** [stæmp] v. —vt. ① ～에 인지를 붙이다, ～에 우표를 붙이다. ② 『+목+전+명』 ～에 날인하다, ～에 도장을 찍다; ～에 ―을 누르다(with). ③ 『+목+전+명』 (마음 등에) (인상·생각 등을) 새겨넣다(with); (인상 등이) (마음 등에) 새겨들다(on, onto). / **auspice** [ɔ́ːspis] n. ① (새점(占)에 의한) 전조, (특히) 길조. ② (pl.) 후원, 찬조, 보호.

✳ 다음 글을 읽고 물음에 답하시오. [16~20]

①**In looking forward to the moment which is intended to terminate the career of my public life,** ②**my feelings do not permit me to suspend the deep acknowledgment of that debt of gratitude which I owe to my beloved country** for the many honors it has conferred upon me; still more for the steadfast confidence with which it has supported me; and for the opportunities ③**I have thence enjoyed of manifesting my inviolable attachment,** by services faithful and persevering, though in usefulness unequal to my zeal. If benefits have resulted to our country from these services, ④**let it always be remembered to your praise,** and as an instructive example in our annals, that under circumstances in which the passions, agitated in every direction, were liable to mislead, amidst appearances sometimes dubious, vicissitudes of fortune often discouraging, in situations in which ⑤**not unfrequently want of success has countenanced the spirit of criticism,** the constancy of your support was the essential prop of the efforts, and a guarantee of the plans by which they were effected. Profoundly penetrated with this idea, Ⓐ**I shall carry it with me to my grave,** as a strong incitement to unceasing vows that heaven may continue to you the choicest tokens of its beneficence; that your union and brotherly affection may be perpetual; that the free Constitution, which is the work of your hands, may be sacredly maintained; that its administration in every department may be stamped with wisdom and virtue; that, in fine,

the happiness of the people of these States, under the auspices of liberty, may be made complete by so careful a preservation and so prudent a use of this blessing as will acquire to them the glory of recommending Ⓑ**it** to the applause, the affection, and adoption of every nation which is yet a stranger to it.

16. 위 글에 나타난 연설자의 심정은?

① happy   ② gloomy
③ miserable   ④ transient
⑤ urgent

17. 위 글의 밑줄 친 ①~⑤가 각각 뜻한 것과 거리가 먼 것은?

① resignation   ② appreciation
③ satisfaction   ④ wish
⑤ happiness

18. 위 글에서 밑줄 친 Ⓐ가 암시하는 것은?

① oblivion   ② unforgettableness
③ death   ④ complaint
⑤ excitement

19. 위 글에서 밑줄 친 Ⓑ가 가리키는 것은?

① a preservation
② a use of this blessing
③ the glory
④ the happiness of the people of these States
⑤ every nation

20. 위 글과 일치하지 않은 것은?

① 작가는 공직생활을 마무리하려 한다.
② 작가는 모든 행위는 국민의 지지에서 시작되었다.
③ 신의 축복과 가호를 기원하고 있다.
④ 다른 국가들도 동참하기를 호소한다.
⑤ 자신의 업적이 역사에 영원하길 바라고 있다.

337

In looking forward to the m_____ which is intended to t_____ the career of my public life(내 공직생활의 마지막으로 기록될 퇴임식을 앞두고), **my feelings do not p_____ me to suspend the deep acknowledgment of that debt of g_____**(감사를 표할 기회를 더 이상 미룰 수 없음을 널리 헤아려 주시기 바랍니다) **which I owe to my beloved country for the many honors it has c_____ upon me**(사랑하는 조국이 나에게 부여해 준 수많은 영예와); **still more for the s_____ confidence with which it has supported me**(확고한 신뢰에 대하여); **and for the opportunities I have thence enjoyed of m_____ my inviolable attachment**(끈질긴 직무 수행을 통하여 조국에 대한 애정을 표현할 기회를 누릴 수 있었던 데 대하여), **by services faithful and p_____**(나름의 충직하고 끈질긴 직무 수행을 통하여), **though in usefulness**(또 나의 열의에 비하여) u_____ **to my zeal**(나라에 도움된 바는 크지 않았지만). / **If benefits have resulted to our country from these services**(나의 직무 수행으로 국익에 도움이 된 바가 있었다면), **let it always be remembered to your p_____**(이는 결코 나의 공이 아니며), **and as an instructive example in our a_____**(우리의 역사에 교훈이 되는 예로서), **that under circumstances in which the passions, a_____ in every direction, were liable to mislead**(갖가지 서로 다른 열정과 성공에 대한 갈망으로 인하여 흔히 일어날 수 있는 실망스러운 상황의 변화에 대하여), **amidst appearances sometimes d_____, vicissitudes of fortune often discouraging**(비난의 화살을 퍼부을 수도 있는 불안한 상황 속에서), **in situations in which not unfrequently want of success has c_____ the spirit of criticism**(가끔 성공의 탐욕이 비판정신을 묵인한 위치에서), **the constancy of your support was the essential prop of the efforts**(여러분의 지속적인 지지는 그 노력의 꼭 필요한 지지대였고), **and a guarantee of the plans by which they were effected**(그 계획에 의해 완성된 보장). / **Profoundly p_____ with this idea**(이러한 생각을 바탕으로), **I shall carry it with me to my grave**(바라는 간절한 마음을 무덤까지 가져가고자 합니다.), **as a strong incitement to unceasing vows that heaven may continue to you the choicest t_____ of its beneficence**(신의 가호가 국민 여러분과 함께하고); **that your union and brotherly affection may be p_____**(국민 여러분의 결속과 형제애가 영원하며); **that the free Constitution, which is the work of your hands, may be s_____ maintained**(국민 여러분의 손으로 만든 자유 헌법이 신성하게 보존되고); **that its administration in every department may be stamped with wisdom and virtue**(헌법의 집행이 모든 부처에서 현명하고 가치 있게 이루어지며); **that, in fine**(마지막으로), **the happiness of the people of these States, under the a_____ of liberty**(자유의 보호 아래에서 자유의 축복을 소중히 지키고), **may be made complete by so careful a preservation and so p_____ a use of this blessing as will acquire to them the glory**(미합중국 국민의 행복이 완전해지기를) **of recommending it to the a_____, the a_____**(자유를 찬미하고, 사랑하고, 또 얻을 수 있도록 함으로써), **and a_____ of every nation which is yet a stranger to it**(신중하게 사용하여 아직 자유를 알지 못하는 모든 국가로 하여금).

16. ① 17. ⑤ 18. ② 19. ④ 20. ⑤

Here, perhaps, ①I ought to stop. But a solicitude for your welfare, which ② cannot end but with my life, and the apprehension of danger, ③natural to that solicitude, urge me, on an occasion like the present, ④to offer to your solemn contemplation, and to recommend to your frequent review, some sentiments ⑤which are the result of much reflection, of no inconsiderable observation, and which appear to me all-important to the permanency of your felicity as a people. These will be offered to you with the more freedom, ⑥as you can only see in them the disinterested warnings of a parting friend, who can possibly have no personal motive ⑦to bias his counsel. ⑧Nor can I forget, ⑨as an encouragement to it, your indulgent reception of my sentiments on a former and not dissimilar occasion.

⑩Interwoven as is the love of liberty with every ligament of your hearts, no recommendation of mine is necessary to fortify or confirm the attachment.

🖎 문법분석

① ought to = should ～하고 싶다. ～해야만 하다. / a solicitude(주어) urge(동사)로 이루어진 문장 / urge + 목적어 + to 부정사: '목적어'가 'to 부정사' 하도록 재촉하다

② 나의 목숨이 다할 때까지 멈출 수 없는

③ danger, (which is) natural to ～자연스레 수반되는 위험

④ to offer to ～and to recommend ～, some sentiments: offer의 목적어는 sentiments임.

⑤ which are the result of much reflection, of no inconsiderable observation(형용사구) and which appear to me로 구성된 문장

⑥ 국민여러분이 물러나려는 친구의 사욕 없는 진언을 알 수만 있다면 / as = if로 해석하면 됨.

⑦ bias는 동사로 쓰여 his counsel = a parting friend's counsel

⑧ Nor로 문장이 도치됨 = or I can not forget: forget의 목적어는 your indulgent reception

⑨ 용기를 내어

⑩ 도치된 문장 As[Because] the love of liberty is interwoven with every ligament of your hearts: 국민 여러분의 마음속에 이미 자유에 대한 사랑이 깊이 뿌리내리고 있기 때문에

동영상 강좌 http://youtu.be/A2ZzJJiLEt8

🖎 본문해석

Here, perhaps, I ought to stop(어쩌면 이쯤에서 이 고별사를 맺는 것도 좋을 듯싶습니다). **But a solicitude for your welfare, which cannot end but with my life**(그러나, 나의 목숨이 다할 때까지 멈출 수 없는 국민 여러분의 복리에 대한 염려와), **and the apprehension of danger, natural to that solicitude**(그러한 염려에 자연스럽게 수반되는 위험에 대한 걱정으로 인하여), **urge me, on an occasion like the present**(현재와 같은 상황에서 ～제안하도록 저를 촉구합니다), **to offer to your solemn contemplation, and to recommend to your frequent review**(몇 가지 소견

339

을 심사와 숙고 끝에), **some sentiments which are the result of much reflection, of no inconsiderable observation**(이를 국민 여러분께서 신중하게 숙고하여 주시기 바랍니다), **and which appear to me all-important to the permanency of your felicity as a people**(국민 여러분의 행복이 영원하기 위하여 더없이 중요하다고 판단되는). **These will be offered to you with the more freedom**(여러분들에게 부담 없이 드리려 합니다), **as you can only see in them the disinterested warnings of a parting friend**(국민 여러분의 판단을 흐리게 할 이유가 전혀 없는 벗으로서), **who can possibly have no personal motive to bias his counsel**(아무런 부담과 사심도 없이 드리는 충언입니다). **Nor can I forget, as an encouragement to it, your indulgent reception**(나의 소견을 너그러이 받아주셨던 일을 기억하고 용기를 내어 드리는 말씀이기도 합니다) **of my sentiments on a former and not dissimilar occasion**(지금과는 다른 자리였지만 이전에도).

Interwoven as is the love of liberty with every ligament of your hearts(국민 여러분의 마음속에 이미 자유에 대한 사랑이 깊이 뿌리내리고 있기 때문에), **no recommendation of mine is necessary to fortify or confirm the attachment**(굳이 나의 충언으로 이를 확인하거나 강화하고자 할 필요는 없을 것입니다).

🖉 **단어분석**

- **solicitude** [səlísətjùː d] n. U 근심, 우려(care), 염려(concern)(about); 갈망; 열심; 배려(for); (pl.) 걱정 거리. / **apprehension** [æ̀prihénʃən] n. U (종종 pl.) 염려, 우려, 불안, 걱정(aboutː). / **solemn** [sáləm / sɔ́l-]a. ① 엄숙한, 근엄한. ② 장엄한, 장중한. ③ 엄연한, 중대한 / **contemplation** [kɑ̀ntəmpléiʃən / kɔ̀ntem-] n. U ① 주시, 응시; 정관(靜觀). ② 숙고, 심사(深思), 명상, 관조(觀照). ③ 기대, 예기, 의도, 계획. / **inconsiderable** [ˈinkənsídərəbəl] a. 적은; 중요치 않은, 하잘 것 없는. / **felicity** [filísəti] n. C 경사; U 더없는 행복(bliss); U (표현의) 교묘함; C 적절한 표현. / **disinterested** [disíntəristid, -rèst-] a. 사욕이 없는, 청렴[공평]한; (미국구어) 무관심한, 흥미를 갖지 않는. / **bias** [báiəs] vt. (-s-, ((영국)) -ss-) 편견을 갖게 하다, 한쪽으로 치우치게[기울게] 하다; (전극에) 바이어스를 걸다 / **indulgent** [indʌ́ldʒənt] a. 멋대로 하게 하는, 눈감아 주는, 관대한(to). / **dissimilar** [dissímələr] a. 닮지 않은, 다른(to; from). / **ligament** [lígəmənt] n. 줄, 끈, 띠; 〚해부학〛 인대(靭帶); (고어) 연줄, 기반(羈絆) /

✻ 다음 글을 읽고 물음에 답하시오. [21~25]

Here, perhaps, I ought to stop. But a solicitude for your welfare, which cannot end but with my life, and the apprehension of danger, natural to that solicitude, urge me, on an occasion like the present, **offering/to offer** to your solemn contemplation, and to recommend to your frequent review, some sentiments which are the result of much reflection, of no inconsiderable observation, and which appear to me all-important to the permanency of your felicity as a people. These will be offered to you with the more freedom, as you can only see in Ⓐ**them** the disinterested warnings of a **parted/parting** friend, who can possibly have no personal motive to bias his counsel. Nor can I forget, as an encouragement to it, your indulgent reception of my sentiments on a former and not dissimilar occasion.

Interweaving/Interwoven as is the love of liberty with every ligament of your hearts, no recommendation of mine is necessary to fortify or confirm the attachment.

21. 위 글에 나타난 작가의 심정으로 가리키는 단어와 거리가 먼 것은?

① solicitude ② apprehension
③ parting ④ bias
⑤ attachment

22. 위 글에서 작가가 강조하는 핵심은?

① your welfare
② solemn contemplation
③ no inconsiderable observation
④ more freedom
⑤ disinteresting warnings

23. 위 글의 네모상자 안의 올바른 단어는?

① offering parted Interweaving
② to offer parted Interwoven
③ offering parting Interweaving
④ to offer parting Interwoven
⑤ offering parting Interwoven

24. 위 글에서 밑줄 친 Ⓐ가 가리키는 것은?

① disinterested warnings
② Americans
③ some sentiments
④ your hearts
⑤ the attachment

25. 위 글과 일치하지 않은 것은?

① 작가는 이쯤에서 고별사를 맺고 싶어 한다.
② 작가는 국민 여러분의 복리에 대한 염려한다.
③ 국민 여러분의 신중한 숙고를 바란다.
④ 국민의 판단을 흐리게 했던 벗으로서 유감을 표명한다.
⑤ 국민의 뿌리 깊은 신뢰로 충언을 확인하고 싶지 않다.

21. ④ 22. ① 23. ④ 24. ③ 25. ④

동영상 강좌 http://youtu.be/WHytC0MZGUg

①The unity of government which constitutes you one people is also now dear to you. ② It is justly so, ③for it is ④a main pillar in the edifice of your real independence, the support of your tranquility at home, your peace abroad; of your safety; of your prosperity; of that very liberty which you so highly prize. But ⑤as it is easy to foresee that, from different causes and from different quarters, ⑥much pains will be taken, many artifices employed to weaken in your minds the conviction of this truth; ⑦as this is the point in your political fortress against which the batteries of internal and external enemies will be most constantly and actively (though often covertly and insidiously) directed, it is of infinite moment that you should properly ⑧estimate the immense value of your national union to your collective and individual happiness; ⑨that you should cherish a cordial, habitual, and immovable attachment to it; ⑩accustoming yourselves to think and speak of it as of the palladium of your political safety and prosperity; watching for its preservation with jealous anxiety; discountenancing whatever may suggest even a suspicion that it can in any event be abandoned; and indignantly frowning upon the first dawning of ⑪every attempt to alienate any portion of our country from the rest, or to enfeeble the sacred ties which now link together the various parts.

🖎 문법분석

① constitute A B: A를 B로 구성하다.

② It = the unity of government / justly 당연하게 / so = dear to you / 그것은 그럴만한 봐

③ for = because

④ a main pillar of your safety, of your prosperity, and that very liberty로 구성된 문장

⑤ as = though: 예측이 쉬울지라도

⑥ much pains will be taken, many artifices (will be) employed to ~: 많은 고통이 따를 것이고, 많은 술수가 여러분의 마음 속 진실의 양심을 약화시키고자 쓰일 것입니다.

⑦ as = because / against which는 관계대명사절을 받음 = the batteries of ~enemies will be constantly ~directed against your political fortress: 국내외의 적들의 포문은 계속해서 적극적으로 여러분의 정치적 보루의 급소를 / it is of infinite moment = it is infinitely momentous(형용사구) 아주 중요한

⑧ estimate A to B: B에 대해 A를 평가하다

⑨ (it is of infinite moment) that you should cherish ~/ it = your national union(연방정부)

⑩ accustoming ~; watching ~; discountenancing ~; and indignantly frowning: ~습관을 기르고; ~감시하고; ~반대하고; ~분연히 눈살을 찌푸리다(반대하다).

⑪ every attempt to alienate ~, or to enfeeble ~: 소원케 하거나 약화시키려고 하는 기도

본문해석

The unity of government which constitutes you one people is also now dear to you(여러분을 한 국민으로 구성케 하는 통일된 정부는 지금 여러분에게 소중합니다.). **It is justly so**(그것은 그럴 만한 바), **for it is a main pillar**(하나의 큰 기둥이 되기 때문입니다) **in the edifice of your real independence**(여러분의 진정한 독립의 전당에서), **the support of your tranquility at home, your peace abroad**(여러분의 국내 안온과 대외 화친과); **of your safety; of your prosperity**(여러분의 안전과 번영); **of that very liberty which you so highly prize**(여러분이 매우 소중하게 여기는 자유를 떠받치는). / **But as it is easy to foresee that**(쉽게 예견될 뿐 아니라), **from different causes and from different quarters**(여러 가지 운동과 여러 진영에서), **much pains will be taken**(많이 애쓸 것이고), **many artifices employed to weaken in your minds the conviction of this truth**(이 같은 진실에 대한 여러분의 확신을 약화시키기 위해); **as this is the point in your political fortress**(여러분의 정치적 보루의 급소이기 때문입니다) **against which the batteries of internal and external enemies will be most constantly and actively (though often covertly and insidiously) directed**(그것은 국내외 적들의 공격이 끊임없이 또 적극적으로(때로는 은밀하고도 교활하게) 그 포문을 집중시킬), **it is of infinite moment**(무한히 중요합니다) **that you should properly estimate the immense value of your national union to your collective and individual happiness**(여러분이 국민의 집단 및 개인적 행복에 대한 국민총화의 무한히 큰 가치를 올바르게 평가해야 하고); **that you should cherish a cordial, habitual, and immovable attachment to it**(또 그 가치에 대해 늘 마음으로부터 우러나는 부동한 애착심을 품으면서); **accustoming yourselves to think and speak of it as of the palladium of your political safety and prosperity**(그것을 여러분의 정치적 안정과 번영의 수호자로 늘 생각하고 말하는 습관을 기르고); **watching for its preservation with jealous anxiety**(경각심을 갖고 그것을 유지하도록 감시하고); **discountenancing whatever may suggest even a suspicion that it can in any event be abandoned**(그것이 어떻든 파기될지도 모른다는 의구심을 보여주는 모든 것에 반대하고); **and indignantly frowning upon the first dawning of every attempt**(바로 그 시초에 분연히 반대의 뜻을 표시해야 하는 것이) **to alienate any portion of our country from the rest**(우리나라의 일부 지역을 여타 지역들과 소원케 하거나), **or to enfeeble the sacred ties which now link together the various parts**(혹은 현재 여러 지역을 하나로 연결하는 신성한 결속을 약화시키려는 기도에 대해).

단어분석

- **pillar** [pílər] n. ① 기둥; 표주(標柱), 기념주; 대각(臺脚). ② 기둥 모양의 것; 불기둥; 물기둥; / **edifice** [édəfis] n. (큰) 건축물, 건물, 전당; (추상적인) 구성물, 조직; (사상의) 체계 / **tranquil** [trǽŋkwil] a. (more ~, ~(l)er; most ~, ~(l)est) 조용한, 평온한, (마음·바다 따위가) 차분한, 편안한, 평화로운. / **prize** [praiz] vt. ①『~+목/ +목+as보』높이 평가하다, 존중하다; 소중히 여기다. ② 평가하다. / **support** [səpɔ́ːrt] n. U ① 버팀, 지지, 유지. ② C 지지자[물]; 지주(支柱), 받침기둥; 의지가 되는 것 (of). ③ 원조, 후원, 고무, 옹호; 찬성. ④ 양육, 부양; (재정적인) 유지; 생활비. / **quarter** [kwɔ́ːrtər] n. (특수한) 방면, 통(通), (정보 등의) 출처(source). (pl.) 숙소, 거처, 주소. (pl.)『군사』진영, 병사(兵舍). (함선 내의) 부서, 배치. / **artifice** [áːrtəfis] n. U 고안(考案), 교묘한 솜씨; C 책략, 술책. / **fortress** [fɔ́ːrtris] n. ① 요새(지); 성채. ②「일반적」안전 견고한 곳 / **battery** [bǽtəri] n.①『군사』포열(砲列); 포병 중대; 포대; (군함의) 비포(備砲). / **insidious** [insídiəs] a.틈을 엿보는, 음험한, 교

343

활한, 방심할 수 없는(treacherous); / **immense** [iméns] a. ① 막대한(enormous, vast), 무한한, 헤아릴 수 없는; 광대한, 끝없는; 거대한. [SYN.] ⇨ HUGE. ② (구어) 멋진, 훌륭한. / **cherish** [tʃériʃ] vt. ① 소중히 하다. ② 귀여워하다, 소중히 기르다. / **cordial** [kɔ́ːrdʒəl / -diəl] a. ① 충심으로부터의, 따뜻한, 성심성의의; 친절한, 간곡한. ② 기운을 돋우는; 강심성(强心性)의. **Palladium** [pəléidiəm] n. (pl. -dia [-diə], ~s) ① Pallas 여신상(특히 Troy의). ② U,C (p-) 수호신[물]; 보장. / **jealous** [dʒéləs] a. ① 질투심이 많은, 투기가 강한(of). ② 시샘하는, 선망하는(envious)(of). / **discountenance** [diskáuntənəns] vt. ① 면목을 잃게 하다, 창피를 주다, 쩔쩔매게 하다. ② (계획 따위에) 찬성하지 않다, ~을 승인하지 않다. / **indignant** [indígnənt] n.분개한, 성난(at; over; with). ⑪~ly —ad. 분연히. / **frown** [fraun] v. —vi. ① 『~/ +전+명』 눈살을 찌푸리다, 얼굴을 찡그리다, 뚱한 표정을 짓다 / **alienate** [éiljənèit, -liə-] vt. 『~+목 / +목+전+명』 ① 멀리하다, 소원(疎遠)케 하다(from); 이간하다, 불화(不和)케 하다(from); 소외하다, 따돌리다(from). ② 딴 데로 돌리다; 양도[매각]하다. / **enfeeble** [infíːbəl, en-] vt. 약하게 하다

❋ 다음 글을 읽고 물음에 답하시오. [26~30]

The unity of government which constitutes you one people is also now dear to you. It is justly so, for ①**it** is a main pillar in the edifice of your real independence, the support of your tranquility at home, your peace abroad; of your safety; of your prosperity; of that very liberty which you so highly prize. But as it is easy to foresee that, from different causes and from different quarters, much pains will be taken, many artifices employed to weaken in your minds the conviction of this truth; as this is the point in _____ against which the batteries of internal and external enemies will be most constantly and actively (though often covertly and insidiously) directed, ②**it** is of infinite moment that you should properly estimate the immense value of your national union to your collective and individual happiness; that you should cherish a cordial, habitual, and immovable attachment to ③**it**; accustoming yourselves to think and speak of ④**it** as of the palladium of your political safety and prosperity; watching for its preservation with jealous anxiety; discountenancing whatever may suggest even a suspicion that ⑤**it** can in any event be abandoned; and indignantly frowning upon the first dawning of every attempt to alienate any portion of our country from the rest, or to enfeeble the sacred ties which now link together the various parts.

26. 위 글의 작가가 주장하는 것은?

① real independence
② the unity of government
③ the tranquility in mind
④ the preparation against enemies' potential batteries
⑤ jealous anxiety in any event

27. 위 글의 밑줄 친 ①~⑤ 중, 가리키는 대상이 <u>다른</u> 것은?

①   ②   ③   ④   ⑤

28. 위 글의 밑줄 친 빈칸에 적절한 표현 어구는?

① your political fortress
② the last escaping exit
③ the genuine compromise
④ your enemy's weak point
⑤ the world's peace

29. 위 글에 따라 다음 중, 나머지 넷과 의미가 <u>다른</u> 것은?

① independence
② prosperity
③ artifice
④ cordial
⑤ jealous anxiety

30. 위 글과 일치하지 <u>않은</u> 것은?

① 정부의 통합은 여러분을 한 국민으로 구성한다.

② 국내의 안정이 국외의 평화보다 더 중요하다.

③ 다른 여러 요인과 진영은 우리의 단합을 해치려 한다.

④ 국가의 통합을 집단적이고 개인적인 행복의 무한한 가치로 올바르게 평가하는 것이 중요하다.

⑤ 경각심을 늘 갖고, 국가의 신성한 결속을 약화시키는 어떠한 기대에 대한 분연히 반대하자.

For this ①you have every inducement of sympathy and interest. ②Citizens, by birth or choice, of a common country, that country has a right to concentrate your affections. The name of American, which belongs to you in your national capacity, must always exalt the just pride of patriotism ③more than any appellation derived from local discriminations. ④With slight shades of difference, you have the same religion, manners, habits, and political principles. ⑤You have in a common cause fought and triumphed together; ⑥the independence and liberty you possess are the work of joint counsels, and joint efforts of common dangers, sufferings, and successes.

But these considerations, ⑦however powerfully they address themselves to your sensibility, are greatly outweighed by those which apply more immediately to your interest. Here every portion of our country finds the most commanding motives for carefully guarding and preserving the union of the whole.

🖋 문법분석

① 여러분은 모든 동기를 갖고 있다. [의역] 여러분은 충분한 이유를 갖고 있다.
② (As you are) Citizens 〜, that country 〜. 여러분은 출생 또는 선택에 의해 같은 나라의 시민이 되었으므로, 이 나라를 집중적으로 사랑할 의미를 갖습니다.
③ more than any appellation (which is) derived from 〜: 지방의 차별에 기인하는 어떠한 명칭보다도
④ (Though there are) With slight shades of difference,
⑤ You have (in a common) fought and triumphed together; have + p.p and p.p 여러분은 공통의 대의 하에 함께 싸워 승리했습니다.
⑥ the independence and liberty (that) you possess are
⑦ however + 형용사/부사 + 주어 + 동사: 아무리 〜일지라도(양보절): 아무리 스스로 강한 호소력을 가진다 할지라도

🖋 본문해석

For this you have every inducement of sympathy and interest(이를 위해 여러분은 동정과 관심을 불러일으켜야 할 충분한 이유를 갖고 있습니다). **Citizens, by birth or choice, of a common country**(여러분은 출생 또는 선택에 의해 같은 나라의 시민이 되었으며), **that country has a right to concentrate your affections**(이 나라를 집중적으로 사랑할 의무를 갖습니다). **The name of American, which belongs to you in your national capacity**(여러분의 국민자격을 나타내는 미국인이란 호칭은), **must always exalt the just pride of patriotism**(더 의로운 애국적 긍지를 높여주어야 합니다) **more than any appellation derived from local discriminations**(언제나 지방의 차이에 기인하는 어떠한 명칭보다도). **With slight shades of difference**(일부 차이는 있으나), **you have the same religion, manners, habits, and political principles**(여러분은 동일한 종교와 예절과 관습과 정치의 원칙을 갖고 있습니다). **You have in a common cause fought and triumphed together**(여러분은 공통의 대의 하에 함께 싸워 승리했습니다); **the independence and liberty you possess**(여러분이 누리는 독립과 자유는) **are the work of joint counsels, and joint efforts of common dangers, sufferings, and successes**(공동 회의와 공동 노력, 공통된 위험과 고난과 성공의 소산입니다).

But these considerations, however powerfully they address themselves to your sensibility(그러나, 이러한 사실이 국민 여러분의 이성에 아무리 강력한 호소력을 가진다 할지라도), are greatly outweighed(크게 압도될 수밖에 없습니다) by those which apply more immediately to your interest(국민 여러분의 이익에 직결되는 문제 앞에서는). Here(바로 이 점 때문에) every portion of our country(연방을 구성하는 각 지역들) finds the most commanding motives for carefully guarding and preserving the union of the whole(연방을 수호하고 유지하고자 더욱 노력하여야 하는 것입니다).

🖎 단어분석

- **inducement** [indjúː smənt] n. U,C 유인(誘引), 유도, 권유, 장려; 유인(誘因), 동기, 자극(to); / †**sympathy** [símpəθi] n. U ① U,C 동정, 헤아림; (종종 pl.) 조위(弔慰), 문상, 위문. [opp] antipathy. ② (종종 pl.) 호의, 찬성, 동감, 공명; 〖심리학〗 공감. / †**affection** [əfékʃən] n. ① U,C 애정, 호의 (for; toward(s)); (pl.) 애착, 연모. ② U 감정, 감동, 정의. [SYN.] ⇨ FEELING. ③ U 영향. / **exalt** [igzɔ́ː lt] v. ─vt. 『～+목/ +목+전+명』 (명예·품위 따위를) 높이다; (관직·신분 따위를) 올리다, 승진시키다; 칭찬하다, 찬양하다; 몹시 기쁘게 하다, 의기양양케 하다; (어조·색조 따위를) 강하게 하다, 강렬하게[짙게] 하다; ～의 활동을[효과를] 강화하다. ─vi. 마음을 고양시키다. / †**patriotism** [péitriətìzəm / pǽt-] n. U 애국심. / **appellation** [æ̀pəléiʃən] n. 명칭, 호칭. / **discrimination** [diskrìmənéiʃən] n. U ① 구별; 식별(력), 판별(력), 안식(in). ② (고어) C 상위점. ③ 차별, 차별 대우. / †**principle** [prínsəpəl] n. ① 원리, 원칙, (물리·자연의) 법칙. [SYN.] ⇨ THEORY. ② 근본 방침, 주의. ③ U 행동 원리, 정의; (pl.) 도의, 절조. ④ 본질, 소인(素因). / **outweigh** [àutwéi] vt. ～보다 무겁다; ～보다 중요하다; ～보다 가치가[세력이] 있다. / **commanding** [kəmǽndiŋ / -máː nd-] a. 지휘하는; 위풍당당한; 전망이 좋은; 유리한 장소를 차지한.

For this you have every inducement of sympathy and interest. Ⓐ**Citizens**, by birth or choice, of a common country, that country has a right to concentrate your affections. The name of American, which ①**belongs to** you in your national capacity, must always ②**exalt** the just pride of patriotism more than any appellation derived from local discriminations. With slight shades of difference, you have the same religion, manners, habits, and political principles. You have in a ③**common** cause fought and triumphed together; the independence and liberty you possess are the work of joint counsels, and joint efforts of common dangers, sufferings, and successes.

But these considerations, however ④**powerful** they address themselves to your sensibility, are greatly outweighed by those which ⑤**apply** more immediately to your interest. Here every portion of our country finds the most commanding motives for carefully guarding and preserving the union of the whole.

31. 위 글에서 작가가 강조한 어휘가 관계가 적은 것은?

① a common country
② your affection
③ national capacity
④ local discriminations
⑤ commanding motives

32. 위 글의 밑줄 친 Ⓐ의 조건으로 적절하지 않은 것은?

① common birth
② same interest
③ same appellation
④ same political principles
⑤ common successes

33. 위 글에서 밑줄 친 ①~⑤ 중, 어법이나 문맥상 어색한 단어는?

①　　②　　③　　④　　⑤

34. 위 글에 나타난 단어의 쓰임이 우리말 표현으로 어색한 것은?

① belong to ~속하다
② inducement 유인, 장려
③ appellation 명칭, 호칭
④ commanding 전망이 좋은
⑤ exalt 올리다

35. 위 글의 내용과 일치하지 않은 것은?

① 국가는 당신이 사랑을 집중할 권리를 갖는다.
② 애국심을 고양시켜야만 한다.
③ 종교, 예의, 습과 그리고 정치적 원칙은 차이가 없다.
④ 독립과 자유는 공동의 노력을 통해서 얻어진 소산이다.
⑤ 연방을 구성하는 각 지역들은 연방을 수호하고 유지하고자 더욱 노력하여야만 한다.

31. ④　32. ②　33. ④ powerful
34. ④　35. ③

동영상 강좌 http://youtu.be/1N31N5Oh72I

The North, in an unrestrained intercourse with the South, ①protected by the equal laws of a common government, finds in the productions of the latter great additional resources of maritime and commercial enterprise and precious materials of manufacturing industry. The South, in the same intercourse, ②benefiting by the agency of the North, ③sees its agriculture grow and its commerce expand. ④Turning partly into its own channels the seamen of the North, ⑤it finds its particular navigation invigorated; and, while it contributes, in different ways, to nourish and increase the general mass of the national navigation, it looks forward to the protection of a maritime strength, ⑥to which itself is unequally adapted. ⑦The East, in a like intercourse with the West, already finds, and in the progressive improvement of interior communications by land and water, will more and more find a valuable vent for ⑧the commodities which it brings from abroad, or manufactures at home. ⑨The West derives from the East supplies requisite to its growth and comfort, and, ⑩what is perhaps of still greater consequence, it must ⑪of necessity ⑫ owe the secure enjoyment of indispensable outlets for its own productions to the weight, influence, and the future maritime strength of the Atlantic side of the Union, directed by an indissoluble community of interest as one nation. ⑬Any other tenure by which the West can hold this essential advantage, whether derived from its own separate strength, or from an apostate and unnatural connection with any foreign power, must be intrinsically precarious.

📝 문법분석

① (under which both are) protected by 보호되는 가운데 / the latter(후자) = the South(남부)

② benefiting by 〜의해 혜택을 얻고 있는, benefit(자동사)

③ see(지각동사) its(남부) agriculture grow(원형동사) and its commerce expand

④ Turning A into B: Turning the seamen of the North partly into its own channels 북부의 해운업은 기본 항로를 남부와 일부 활용함으로써

⑤ find A(its particular navigation) B(invigorated): 해상 운송량이 증가하는 효과를 거두다

⑥ 전치사+관계대명사: where itself is unequally adapted: 불리한 여건에 대해

⑦ The East 〜finds, and 〜will more and more find 〜. 구문임.

⑧ the commodities which it brings from abroad: brings의 목적어는 the commodities

⑨ The West derives (from the East) supplies (which are) requisite to its growth and comfort: 서부는 동부로부터 성장과 편의에 필요한 제품을 공급받는다.

⑩ 삽입 부사구: 어쩌면 이보다 더 중요한 것은

⑪ of necessity = necessarily

⑫ own A to B: A는 B 덕분이다

⑬ Any other tenure must be intrinsically precarious: 다른 권리는 빈약할 수밖에 없다고 할 것입니다.

🔖 **본문해석**

The North(북부는), **in an unrestrained intercourse with the South**(남부와의 자유로운 교류를 통하여), **protected by the equal laws of a common government**(공통의 정부의 평등한 법률로 보호받는 가운데), **finds in the productions of the latter great additional resources of maritime and commercial enterprise and precious materials of manufacturing industry**(남부의 산물로부터 해상업과 무역업에 필요한 추가적인 자원과 제조업에 사용되는 귀중한 소재를 확보하고 있습니다). **The South, in the same intercourse**(남부 역시), **benefiting by the agency of the North**(활발한 공업 활동이 이루어지는 북부와의 자유로운 교류를 통하여), **sees its agriculture grow**(농업이 성장하고) **and its commerce expand**(상업이 확대되는 효과를 거두고 있습니다). **Turning partly into its own channels the seamen of the North**(북부의 해운업은 기존 항로를 남부와의 교류에 일부 활용함으로써), **it finds its particular navigation invigorated**(해상 운송량이 증가하는 효과를 거두고 있으며); **and, while it contributes, in different ways, to nourish and increase the general mass of the national navigation**(이것이 전국적인 해상운송의 총량을 증가시키는 데 다양한 방식으로 기여하고 있으나), **it looks forward to the protection of a maritime strength**(해상력을 보호받기를 희망하고 있습니다.), **to which itself is unequally adapted**(불리한 여건에 있는). **The East, in a like intercourse with the West**(동부 역시 서부와의 자유로운 교류를 통하여), **already finds, and in the progressive improvement of interior communications by land and water**(국내 육상교통과 수상교통이 점진적으로 개선됨에 따라), **will more and more find a valuable vent for the commodities which it brings from abroad, or manufactures at home**(해외에서 수입하거나 국내 업체에서 생산된 제품을 판매할 귀중한 시장을 이미 확보하고 있으며). **The West derives from the East supplies requisite to its growth and comfort**(서부는 동부로부터 성장과 편의에 필요한 제품을 공급받고 있는데), **and, what is perhaps of still greater consequence**(어쩌면 이보다 더 중요한 것은), **it must of necessity owe the secure enjoyment of indispensable outlets for its own productions**(서부의 산물을 판매할 수 있는 귀중한 시장을 확보하고 있다는 점입니다) **to the weight, influence, and the future maritime strength of the Atlantic side of the Union**(연방의 대서양 연안 지역의 힘과, 영향력과, 미래의 해상력에 힘입어), **directed by an indissoluble community of interest as one nation**(한 국가로서 서로 분리할 수 없는 공동체의 이해에 따라). **Any other tenure**(다른 권리는) **by which the West can hold this essential advantage**(얻을 수 있는 이점은), **whether derived from its own separate strength, or from an apostate and unnatural connection with any foreign power**(이에 비하면 서부가 그 자체의 역량이나 외국과의 부자연스러운 연계를 통하여), **must be intrinsically precarious**(빈약할 수밖에 없다고 할 것입니다).

🔖 **단어분석**

- **unrestrained** [ʌ̀nristréind] a. 억제되지 않은, 무제한의, 제멋대로의, 자유로운. / **maritime** [mǽrətàim]a. ① 바다의, 해상의; 해사(海事)의, 해운의; 해상 무역의. [cf.] marine. ② 해변의, 해안의; 해안에 사는[서식하는]; 바다에 접한 / **intercourse** [íntərkɔ̀ːrs] n. U ① (인간의) 교제, 교섭, 왕래. ② (국가 간의) 교통, 거래. / **benefit** [bénəfit] v. —vt. ～의 이(利)가 되다; ～에게 이롭다. —vi. 『+전+명』 이익을 얻다(by; from). / **navigation** [næ̀vəgéiʃən] n. U ① 운항, 항해; 항해[항공]술[학], 항법(航法). ② 「집합적」 선박(shipping). / **invigorate** [invígərèit] vt. 원기[활기]를 돋구다, 북돋다. / **nourish** [nə́ːriʃ, nʌ́r-]vt. ① 『～+목/ +목+전+명』 ～에 자양분을 주다, 기르다, 살지게 하다. ② 육성하다, 조성하다

(promote). ③ (희망·원한·노염 등을) 마음에 품다(cherish). / **requisite** [rékwəzit] a. 필요한, 없어서는 안될, 필수의(needful)(to; for). [SYN.] ⇨ NECESSARY / **indispensable** [ìndispénsəbəl] a. ① 불가결의, 없어서는 안 될, 절대 필요한, 긴요한(to; for). [SYN.] ⇨ NECESSARY. ② (의무·약속 등을) 게을리[기피]할 수 없는. / **tenure** [ténjuə: r]n. ① U,C (부동산·지위·직분 등의) 보유; 보유권; C 보유기간; U 보유조건[형태]. ② 재직기간, 임기; U (대학교수 등의) 종신 재직권. / **apostate** [əpásteit, -tit / əpóstit, -eit] a. 신앙을 버린; 탈당[변절]한. / **intrinsic, -sical** [intrínsik], [-əl] a. (가치·성질 따위의) 본질적인, 본래 갖추어진, 고유의(inherent) (to; in); 〖해부학·의학〗 내재성[내인성]의. [opp.] extrinsic(al). / **precarious** [prikέəriəs] a. ① 불확실한, 믿을 수 없는, 불안정한; 위험한, 불안(不安)한(생활 따위). [SYN.] ⇨ UNCERTAIN. ② 지레짐작의, 근거 없는(가설·추측 따위).

✷ 다음 글을 읽고 물음에 답하시오. [36~40]

The North, in an unrestrained intercourse with the South, protected by the equal laws of a common government, finds in the productions of the ①**former** great additional resources of maritime and commercial enterprise and precious materials of manufacturing industry. The South, in the same intercourse, benefitted/benefiting by the agency of the North, sees its agriculture grow and its commerce expand/expanding. Turning partly into its own channels the seamen of the North, it finds its particular navigation invigorated/invigorating; and, while it contributes, in different ways, to nourish and increase the general mass of the national navigation, it looks forward to the protection of a maritime strength, to which ②**itself** is unequally adapted. The East, in a like intercourse with the West, already finds, and in the progressive improvement of interior communications by land and water, will more and more find a valuable vent for the commodities which it brings from abroad, or manufactures at home. The West derives from the East supplies ③**requisite** to its growth and comfort, and, what is perhaps of still greater consequence, it must of necessity owe the secure enjoyment of ④ **indispensable** outlets for its own productions for/to the weight, influence, and the future maritime strength of the Atlantic side of the Union, directed by an indissoluble community of interest as one nation. Any

other tenure by which the West can hold this essential advantage, whether derived from its own separate strength, or from an apostate and unnatural connection with any foreign power, must be intrinsically ⑤ **precarious**.

36. 위 글의 주제로 가장 적절한 것은?

① The South must open its door wider to the West.

② The intercourse between two areas is essentially indispensable.

③ The West ought to avoid its independent survival.

④ The trade at home and abroad is necessary at the present.

⑤ To be prosperous in the Union, more products must be produced.

37. 위 글의 밑줄 친 ①~⑤중, 문맥상 단어의 쓰임이 어색한 것은?

①　　②　　③　　④　　⑤

38. 위 글에서 네모상자 안의 적절한 단어는?

① benefitted　expand　invigorated　for
② benefiting　expanding　invigorated　for
③ benefitted　expanding　invigorating　for
④ benefitting　expand　invigorated　to
⑤ benefitted　expand　invigorating　to

39. 위 글을 다음과 같이 요약할 때, 빈칸 Ⓐ, Ⓑ에 각각 적절한 단어는?

> The ___Ⓐ___ of the Union brings about more ___Ⓑ___ .

① development   weakness
② growth   survival
③ politics   development
④ integration   prosperity
⑤ collapse   wars

40. 위 글의 내용과 일치하지 <u>않은</u> 것은?

① 서부지역은 남부로부터 해상업과 무역업에 필요한 추가적인 자원을 확보할 수 있다.
② 남부지역은 서부와의 활발한 교류를 통하여 농업이 성장하고 상업이 확대되는 효과를 거둔다.
③ 남부의 해운업은 북부와 교류에 활용함으로써 행상운송의 총량을 증가시키는데 기여한다.
④ 서부는 동부로부터 성장과 편의에 필요한 제품을 공급받는다.
⑤ 서부는 그 자체의 역량이나 외국과의 연계에 빈약할 수밖에 없다.

36. ②   37. ① latter   38. ④   39. ④
40. ③

①While, then, every part of our country thus feels an immediate and particular interest in union, (S)all the parts combined (V)cannot fail to find in the united mass of means and efforts (O)greater strength, greater resource, proportionably greater security from external danger, a less frequent interruption of their peace by foreign nations; and, what is of inestimable value, ②they must (V)derive from union (O)an exemption from those broils and wars between themselves, which so frequently afflict neighboring countries not tied together by the same governments, which their own rival ships alone would be sufficient to produce, but which opposite foreign alliances, attachments, and intrigues would stimulate and embitter. ③Hence, likewise, they will avoid the necessity of those overgrown military establishments which, under any form of government, are inauspicious to liberty, and which are to be regarded as particularly hostile to republican liberty. In this sense ④it is that your union ought to be considered as a main prop of your liberty, and that the love of the one ought to endear to you the preservation of the other.

🖊 문법분석

① While ~in union[부사절, ~하는 동안], [주절] all the parts (combined 결속된[후치수식]) cannot fail to(반드시 ~하다) find greater strength, greater resource, proportionably greater security, (and) a less frequent interruption;

② they(all the parts 모든 지역들) must derive an exemption / which(계속적인 용법) so frequently afflict ~, which their own rival ships ~, but which opposite foreign alliances ~would(~일 것이다) ~.

③ those overgrown military establishments which are ~, and which ~.

④ it[가주어] is that 주어 + 동사, and that 주어 + 동사.

🖊 본문해석

While, then(그렇다면), **every part of our country thus feels an immediate and particular interest in union**(우리나라의 모든 지역들이 이같이 연방에 대해 즉각적이고도 특수한 관심을 갖는 한), **all the parts combined**(연방 하에 결속된 여러분의 모든 지역은) **cannot fail to find**(어김없이 이룩할 수 있습니다) **in the united mass of means and efforts**(수단과 노력을 한데 뭉침으로써) **greater strength, greater resource, proportionably greater security from external danger**(보다 큰 힘, 보다 훌륭한 기략, 따라서 외부 위험으로부터의 보다 큰 안보), **a less frequent interruption of their peace by foreign nations**(국내평화에 대한 외국 간섭의 축소를); **and, what is of inestimable value**(그리고 무한히 소중한 것은), **they must derive from union an exemption from those broils and wars between themselves**(그들(각 주)이 연방을 지킴으로써 그들 상호간에 분쟁과 전쟁을 일으키는 일이 없도록 해야 한다는 것입니다), **which so frequently afflict neighboring countries not tied together by the same governments**(한 정부 밑에 뭉쳐 있지 못한 이웃 나라들은 번번이 이런 분쟁과 전쟁과 전쟁의 재난을 겪고 있습니다), **which their own rival ships alone would be sufficient to produce**(이러한 분쟁은 그들이 서로 적대시하기만 해도 일어나기 마련이며), **but which opposite foreign alliances, attachments, and intrigues would stimulate and embitter**(또 외세와의 동맹, 결탁 또는 음모는 이러한 분쟁을 자극하고 격화시키게 될 것입니다). **Hence, likewise,**

they will avoid the necessity of those overgrown military establishments which, under any form of government, are inauspicious to liberty(지나치게 큰 군사기관(군부)은 어떤 정부 하에서건 자유를 위해 이롭지 못하며), **and which are to be regarded as particularly hostile to republican liberty**(또 특히 공화정적 자유를 위해서는 해로운 것으로 간주되어야 할 것입니다). **In this sense**(이러한 목적으로) **it is that your union ought to be considered as a main prop of your liberty**(여러분의 연방은 여러분의 자유의 대들보로 간주되어야 하며), **and that the love of the one ought to endear to you the preservation of the other**(또 여러분의 연방에 대한 사랑은 여러분에게 자유보존의 가치를 고양시켜야 합니다).

📎 **단어분석**

- **interruption** [ìntərʌ́pʃən] n. U,C 가로막음; 방해, 훼사(毁事), 중지, 중절; (교통의) 불통 / **inestimable** [inéstəməbəl] a. 평가[계산]할 수 없는; 헤아릴 수 없는; 헤아릴 수 없을 만큼 큰(존귀한); 더없이 귀중한. / **derive** [diráiv] v. —vt. ① 『+목+전+명』 끌어내다(from); 손에 넣다, 획득하다(from). ② 『+목+전+명』 ~의 기원을[유래를] 찾다(from); 「종종 수동태」 ~에서 나와 있다, ~에서 시작하다(from). / **proportionable** [prəpɔ́ːrʃənəbəl] a. 균형되게 할 수 있는, 비례시킬 수 있는(to); 균형이 잡힌, 조화된 (to). / **inestimable** [inéstəməbəl] a. 평가[계산]할 수 없는; 헤아릴 수 없는; 헤아릴 수 없을 만큼 큰(존귀한); 더없이 귀중한 / **exemption** [igzémpʃən] n. U,C (의무 등의) 면제(from); 면제되는 사람[것]; (소득) 공제. / **broil** n. (문어) 싸움, 말다툼, 소동 / **afflict** [əflíkt] vt. 『~+목 / +목+전+명』 괴롭히다 (distress). [SYN.] ⇨ TORMENT. / **intrigue** [intríːg] n. ① U,C 음모, 밀모(密謀); 술책. ② C 정사, 밀통, 간통(with). / **stimulate** [stímjəlèit] v. —vt. ① 『~+목/ +목+to do/ +목+전+명』 자극하다, 활발하게 하다; 북돋우다(incite); 격려[고무]하다; ~의 격려가 되다. ② (커피·주류 따위로) 흥분시키다; 〖의학·생리〗 (기관(器官) 따위를) 자극하다. / **embitter** [imbítər] vt. (약 따위를) 더 쓰게 하다; 몹시 기분 나쁘게 하다; 한층 더 비참하게[나쁘게] 하다; 분격(憤激)[실망]시키다. / **inauspicious** [ìnɔːspíʃəs] a. 불길한, 상서롭지 않은, 재수 없는; 불행한, 불운한. / hence [hens] ad. ① 그러므로; 「동사를 생략하여」 이 사실에서 ~이 유래하다. ② 지금부터, 금후; (고어) 이 자리에서. / **likewise** [láikwàiz] ad. ① 똑같이, 마찬가지로. ② 또한, 게다가 또(moreover, also, too). / **endear** [endíər] vt. +목+전+명』 애정을 느끼게[그립게] 하다; 「재귀적」 (남에게) 사랑받다. /

①These considerations (∨)speak a persuasive language to every reflecting and virtuous mind, and (∨)exhibit the continuance of the Union as a primary object of patriotic desire. ②Is there a doubt whether a common government can embrace so large a sphere? Let experience solve it. ③To listen to mere speculation in such a case were criminal. ④We are authorized to hope that a proper organization of the whole with the auxiliary agency of governments for the respective subdivisions, will afford a happy issue to the experiment. ⑤It is well worth a fair and full experiment. ⑥With such powerful and obvious motives to union, affecting all parts of our country, while experience shall not have demonstrated its impracticability, there will always be reason to distrust the patriotism of those who in any quarter may endeavor to weaken its bands.

📃 문법분석

① These considerations speak 간접목적어 to 직접목적어, and exhibit 목적어 as 전치사구.

② Is there a doubt + 목적어[whether ～]?

③ [명사절] To ～[부사구] in such a case [동사] were [보어] criminal.

④ We are authorized to hope[동사] that[목적어절] a proper organization of the whole[주어] with the auxiliary ～subdivisions[부사구], will afford[동사] a happy issue[목적어] to the experiment.

⑤ It is well worth ～: ～할 충분한 가치가 있다.

⑥ [부사구] With such ～to union, affecting all parts of our country[union을 수식], [부사절] while ～its impracticability, [주절] there will always be reason [형용사구] to distrust the patriotism of those who(～하는 사람들) ～to weaken its bands(연방의 결속을 약화시키려는).

📃 본문해석

These considerations speak a persuasive language(설득력 있는 말로 주장합니다) **to every reflecting and virtuous mind**(깊은 사려와 덕을 갖춘 모든 국민들에게), **and exhibit**(보여주다) **the continuance of the Union**(연방의 지속이) **as a primary object of patriotic desire**(최고의 애국임을). **Is there a doubt**(일말의 의구심이 있습니까) **whether a common government can embrace so large a sphere**(공통의 정부가 그런 넓은 영역을 감당할 수 있는지)? **Let experience solve it**(경험을 통해 그 의구심이 자연스레 풀리도록 합시다). **To listen to mere speculation in such a case were criminal**(단순한 추측에 귀를 기울이는 것은 범죄와 다를 바 없습니다). **We are authorized to hope** (우리는 충분히 희망할 수 있습니다) **that a proper organization of the whole**(정부를 전체적으로 적절히 조직하면) **with the auxiliary agency of governments for the respective subdivisions**(정부 내 각 부문을 보조하는 각 부처들과 더불어), **will afford a happy issue to the experiment**(이러한 실험에서 좋은 결과가 나올 것임을). **It is well worth a fair and full experiment**(이는 공정하고 완전하게 실험을 할 충분한 가치가 있는 일입니다). **With such powerful and obvious motives to union**(연방을 향한 강력하고 분명

한 동기가), **affecting all parts of our country**(우리나라 모든 지역에 미치고 있다면), **while experience shall not have demonstrated its impracticability**(경험을 통해 연방이 실효성 없는 것으로 증명되는 일이란 있을 수 없겠지만), **there will always be reason to distrust the patriotism**(주장하는 애국심을 불신할 이유는 항상 있다 하겠습니다) **of those who in any quarter may endeavor to weaken its bands**(어느 지역에서나 연방의 유대를 약화시키려는 자들이).

📎 **단어분석**

- **reflecting** 사려 깊은 / †**virtuous** [və́ː rtʃuəs] a. ① 덕이 높은, 덕행이 있는, 고결한. ② 정숙한, 절개 있는. / ‡**exhibit** [igzíbit] v. —vt. ① 전람[전시]하다, 출품하다, 진열하다, 공개하다. [SYN.] ⇨ SHOW. ② (징후·감정 등을) 나타내다, 보이다, 드러내다, 표시하다. / ‡**primary** [práimeri, -məri] a. ① 첫째의, 제1의, 수위의, 주요한. [cf.] secondary. ② 최초의, 처음의, 본래의. ③ 원시적인, 근원적인. ④ 제1차적인, 근본적인. ⑤ 기초적인, 초보적인. / ‡**mere** [miər] a. (mérer; mérest) ① 단순한, ~에 불과한, 단지[다만, 그저] ~에 지나지 않는. ② (폐어) 전적인, 다른 어떤 것도 아닌, 순전한. / ‡ **speculation** [spèkjəléiʃ-ən] n. ① U 사색, 숙고, 심사, 고찰. ② (사색에 의한) 결론, 의견. ③ 추측, 억측. ④ 이론; 공론(空論). ⑤ U C 투기, 사행. / †**authorize** [ɔ́ː θəràiz] vt. ①『+목+to do』~에게 권한을 주다, 위임하다(empower). ② 인가[허가]하다. ③ 정당하다고 인정하다. / †**respective** [rispé ktiv] a. 각각의, 각기의, 각자의(보통 복수명사를 수반함). / **impracticability** [impræktikəbíləti] n. U 비실제성(非實際性), 실행 불능; C 실행할 수 없는 일. / **quarter** 방면; 지역, 지방(地方); (도시의) 지구, ~거리(district). / ‡**endeavor**, 【영국】 —our [endévər] v. —vt.『+to do』~하려고 노력하다, 애쓰다, ~을 시도하다. [SYN.] ⇨ TRY. —vi. ①『~ / +전+명』노력하다, 애쓰다(at doing; after). ② 시도하다.

동영상 강좌 http://youtu.be/wzGJZ9KF5Cs

✳ 다음 글을 읽고 물음에 답하시오. [41~45]

These considerations speak a persuasive language to every reflecting and virtuous mind, and exhibit the continuance of ①the Union as a primary object of patriotic desire. Is there a doubt whether ②a common government can embrace so large a sphere? Let experience solve Ⓐit. To listen to mere speculation in such a case were criminal. We are authorized to hope that a proper organization of ③the whole with the auxiliary agency of governments for ④the respective subdivisions, will afford a happy issue to Ⓑthe experiment. It is well worth a fair and full experiment. With such powerful and obvious motives to union, affecting all parts of ⑤our country, while experience shall not have demonstrated its impracticability, there will always be reason to distrust the patriotism of those who in any quarter may endeavor to weaken its bands.

41. 위 글의 제목으로 가장 적절한 표현은?

① Lift Up Our Patriotism
② The Continuance of the Union
③ Now, The Time for Experiment
④ The Strategy of defeating Enemy
⑤ The Way of Organizing Governments

42. 위 글의 밑줄 친 ①~⑤ 중, 가리키는 것이 나머지 넷과 다른 것은?

①   ②   ③   ④   ⑤

43. 위 글의 밑줄 친 Ⓑ가 가리키는 것은?

① a persuasive language
② patriotic desire
③ mere speculation
④ a proper organization of the whole governments
⑤ those who try to weaken its bands

44. 위 글의 밑줄 친 Ⓐ가 가리키는 것은?

① a persuasive language
② a doubt
③ a common government
④ criminal
⑤ impracticability

45. 위 글과 일치하지 <u>않은</u> 것은?

① 연방의 지속이 최고의 애국심이다.
② 단순한 추측에 귀를 기울이는 것은 범죄이다.
③ 각 부처들과의 적절한 조화는 희망을 낳을 수 있다.
④ 경험을 통해 실험의 비효율성이 나타날 가능성이 있다.
⑤ 연방의 유대를 약화시키려는 자들을 불신하자.

41. ② 42. ④ 43. ④ 44. ② 45. ④

동영상 강좌 http://youtu.be/rrijf4XR90w

①<u>In</u> contemplating the causes which may disturb our Union, it occurs as matter of serious concern that any ground should have been furnished for characterizing parties by geographical discriminations, Northern and Southern, Atlantic and Western; ② <u>whence</u> designing men may endeavor to excite a belief that there is a real difference of local interests and views. ③(s)<u>One</u> of the expedients of party (a)<u>to acquire</u> influence within particular districts (v)<u>is to</u> misrepresent the opinions and aims of other districts. ④<u>You</u> cannot shield yourselves too much against the jealousies and heartburnings which spring from these misrepresentations; ⑤<u>they</u> tend to render <u>alien</u> to each other <u>those who</u> ought to be bound together by fraternal affection. The inhabitants of our Western country have lately had a useful lesson on this head; ⑥(s)<u>they have seen</u>, in the negotiation by the Executive, and <u>in the unanimous ratification</u> by the Senate, <u>of the treaty</u> with Spain, and <u>in the universal satisfaction</u> at that event, throughout the United States, ⑦(o)<u>a decisive proof how unfounded were the suspicions propagated</u> among them of a policy ⑧<u>in the General Government and in the Atlantic States unfriendly to their interests in regard to the Mississippi;</u> ⑨<u>they have been witnesses to</u> the formation of two treaties, that with Great Britain, and that with Spain, <u>which secure</u> to them everything they could desire, in respect to our foreign relations, towards confirming their prosperity. Will it not be their wisdom ⑩<u>to rely for the preservation of these advantages on the Union</u> by which they were procured ? ⑪<u>Will they not henceforth be deaf</u> to those advisers, if such there are, who would sever them from their brethren and connect them with aliens?

📝 **문법분석**

① In contemplating the causes which[관계대명사절] ~Union, it[가주어] as ~[전치사절] that [진주어] ~should have been furnished[과거의 유감] ~Atlantic and Western;

② whence[앞 문장을 받아서, 그러므로] designing men[주어] ~excite a belief that[a belief와 동격절] there is a ~interests and views.

③ One of the expedients of party[주어] to acquire influence [목적 부사구] within particular districts is to misrepresent[동사] the opinions and aims of other districts[목적어].

④ cannot too ~: 아무리 ~해도 지나치지 않다. / the jealousies and heartburnings which spring from these misrepresentations; 이러한 왜곡에서 비롯되는 시기와 원한에 대해서는

⑤ render[make] A B: A를 B로 만들다: render alien (to each other) those who ~.

⑥ in the unanimous ratification (by the Senate) of the treaty with Spain: 상원에 의한 스페인과의 만장일치의 조약비준에서 /

⑦ they have seen[현재완료 경험] A[a decisive proof] B[how unfounded were the suspicions propagated]: A가 B라는 사실을 보았다.

⑧ A[in the General ~States] unfriendly to(~대해 비우호적인) their interests in regard to the

Mississippi;

⑨ they have been witnesses to: ～목격해 왔다. / the formation of two treaties, that[지시대명사] with Great Britain, and that with Spain: 그것은 영국과 스페인과의 조약 / which secure (to them) everything (they could desire): secure의 목적어 everything /

⑩ to rely (for the preservation of these advantages) on the Union / by which they(=these advantages) ～?

⑪ [부정 의문문] 이제부터는 귀를 닫아야 하지 않겠습니까?

동영상 강좌 http://youtu.be/rrijf4XR90w

📎 본문해석

In contemplating the causes which may disturb our Union(우리의 연방을 해칠 수도 있는 명분들을 살펴보면), **it occurs as matter of serious concern**(심각한 우려의 대상이 되고 있습니다) **that any ground should have been furnished for characterizing parties by geographical discriminations, Northern and Southern, Atlantic and Western**(남부와 북부, 대서양 연안과 서부 등 지리적 차이를 구실로 삼아 파벌을 조장하려 한다는 점이); **whence designing men**(이러한 구실을 고안한 자들은) **may endeavor to excite a belief**(믿도록 충동질할 수 있습니다) **that there is a real difference of local interests and views**(각 지역 간에 이해관계와 견해에 큰 차이가 있다고). **One of the expedients of party to acquire influence within particular districts**(특정 지역에서 영향력을 획득하려는 세력이 쓰는 편법 중에는) **is to misrepresent the opinions and aims of other districts**(다른 지역의 의견과 목표를 왜곡하는 수법이 있습니다). **You cannot shield yourselves too much**(아무리 경계해도 지나치지 않습니다) **against the jealousies and heartburnings which spring from these misrepresentations**(이러한 왜곡에서 비롯되는 시기와 원한에 대해서는); **they tend to render alien to each other**(서로 남남으로 만드는 경향이 있습니다) **those who ought to be bound together by fraternal affection**(이러한 시기와 원한은 형제애로 함께 뭉쳐야 할 사람들을). **The inhabitants of our Western country have lately had a useful lesson**(서부 지역 주민들은 최근 좋은 교훈을 얻었습니다) **on this head**(이와 관련하여); **they have seen**(보았습니다), **in the negotiation**(협상을 성실하게 진행하고) **by the Executive**(연방 행정부가), **and in the unanimous ratification by the Senate**(상원이 이를 만장일치로 비준하고), **of the treaty with Spain**(스페인과 조약 체결을), **and in the universal satisfaction at that event**(합중국 전체가 이를 만족스럽게 받아들인 데서), **throughout the United States, a decisive proof how unfounded were the suspicions propagated**(가지고 있을 것이라는 의심이 얼마나 근거가 없는 것이었는지 그 결정적 증거를) **among them of a policy in the General Government and in the Atlantic States unfriendly to their interests in regard to the Mississippi**(연방 정부와 대서양 연안 각 주가 미시시피에 대한 서부 각 주의 이해관계에 비우호적인 정책을); **they have been**(서부 주민들은) **witnesses**(목격했습니다) **to the formation of two treaties**(두 개의 조약), **that with Great Britain, and that with Spain**(즉 영국과 스페인과의 조약이 체결되는 것도), **which secure to them everything they could desire**(원하는 모든 것들을 확보해 준), **in respect to our foreign relations**(대외관계에 있어서), **towards confirming their prosperity**(서부 각 주가 그 번영을 확고히 하기 위해). **Will it not be their wisdom to rely**(의존하는 것이 지혜로운 일이 아니겠습니까?) **for the preservation of these advantages**(이러한 이익을 지키기 위해) **on the Union by which they were procured**(그 이익을 확보해 준 연방에)? **Will they not henceforth be deaf to those advisers**(이제부터는 귀를 닫아야 하지 않겠습니까?), **if such there are, who would sever them from their brethren**(형제들과

361

의 관계를 단절시키면서) **and connect them with aliens**(이방인들과 연결할 것을 조언하는 자들의 말에)**?**

📎 단어분석

- ✝**disturb** [distə́ːrb] v. —vt. ① (휴식·일·생각 중인 사람을) 방해하다; ～에게 폐를 끼치다. ② ～의 마음을 어지럽게 하다; 불안하게 하다. ③『～+목/ +목+전+명』(행위·상태를) 저해하다, 막다. ④ 혼란시키다; 휘저어 놓다. ⑤ (평화·질서·휴식을) 어지럽히다, 교란하다. ⑥ (권리를) 침해하다. / ✝**whence** [hwens]ad., conj. ①「의문사」 a) 어디서. [opp.] whither. b) 어찌하여, 왜. ②「관계사」 a) ～하는. b) (～하는) 거기서부터; (～하는[한]) 그 곳에. ③「앞 문장을 받아서」 그러므로(and thence), 그리하여. / ✝**expedient** [ikspíːdiənt] n. 수단, 방편, 편법, 임기(응변)의 조처. / **misrepresent** [mìsreprizént] v. —vt. 잘못 전하다; 거짓 설명을 하다; 허위로 대표하다; 대표 임무를 다하지 못하다. —vi. 허위 진술을 하다. / ✝**shield** [ʃiːld] v. —vt. ①『～+목/ +목+전+명』 감싸다, 보호하다(protect); 수호하다, 막다. ② 가리다, 차폐하다, 숨기다. / cannot ～too 아무리 ～해도 지나치지 않다 / **heartburn** [-bə̀ːrn] n. U ① 가슴앓이(cardialgia, pyrosis). ② 질투, 시기. / ✝**render** [réndər] v. —vt. ①『+목+보』 ～로 만들다, ～이 되게 하다. ② a)『～+목/ +목+전+명』 (보답으로서) 주다, 갚다, ～에 보답하다. b) / ✝**fraternal** [frətə́ːrn-əl] a. 형제의; 형제 같은[다운], 우애의. / ✝**ratification** [ræ̀təfikéiʃ-ən] n. U,C 비준(批准), 시인, 재가; / ✝**treaty** [tríːti] n. ① 조약, 협정, 맹약; 조약 문서. ② (개인 간의) 약정, 약속; U 협상, 교섭. / ✝**propagate** [prápəgèit / prɔ́p-] v. —vt. ① 번식시키다, 늘[불]리다. ② 널리 펴다, 선전 [보급]하다. ③ (빛·소리 따위를) 전파하다, 전하다. ④ (성질 따위를) 유전시키다, 전염시키다. / **secure** [sikjúər]v. —vt. ①『～+목/ +목+전+명』 안전하게 하다, 굳게 지키다, 굳게 하다(against). ② 확실하게 하다, 확고히 하다. / ✝**procure** [proukjúər, prə-] v. —vt. ①『～+목/ +목+목/ +목+전+명』 획득하다, (필수품을) 조달하다. ② (드물게) (남의 손을 빌려) 야기하다, 초래하다. / ✝**henceforth, -forward** [hènsfɔ́ːrə, ´-´] [-fɔ́ːrwərd] ad. 이제부터는, 금후, 이후. / ✝**sever** [sévəːr] v. —vt. ①『～+목/ +목+전+명』 절단하다, 끊다(from). ②『～+목/ +목+전+명』 떼다, 가르다. [SYN.] ⇨ SEPARATE. ③『～+목/ +목+전+명』 ～의 사이를 떼다, 이간시키다(A and B, A from B). / ✝**brethren** [bréðrən] n. pl. (종교상의) 형제, 동일 교회[교단]원; 동일 조합원, 동업자; 동포. ★혈족상의 형제에는 쓰지 않음. /

In contemplating the causes which may disturb our Union, it occurs as matter of serious concern that any ground should have been furnished for characterizing parties by geographical discriminations, Northern and Southern, Atlantic and Western; whence Ⓐ **designing men** may endeavor to excite a belief that there is a real difference of local interests and views. One of the expedients of party to acquire influence within particular districts is to misrepresent the opinions and aims of other districts. Ⓑ**You cannot shield yourselves too much against the jealousies and heartburnings** which spring from these misrepresentations; they tend to render alien to each other those who ought to be bound together by fraternal affection. The inhabitants of our Western country have lately had a useful lesson on this head; Ⓒ**they** have seen, in the negotiation by the Executive, and in the unanimous ratification by the Senate, of the treaty with Spain, and in the universal satisfaction at that event, throughout the United States, a decisive proof how unfounded were the suspicions propagated among them of a policy in the General Government and in the Atlantic States unfriendly to their interests in regard to the Mississippi; they have been witnesses to the formation of two treaties, that with Great Britain, and that with Spain, which secure to them everything they could desire, in respect to our foreign relations, towards confirming their prosperity. Will it not be their wisdom to rely for the preservation of these advantages on the Union by which they were procured ? Will they not

henceforth be deaf to those advisers, if such there are, who would sever them from their brethren and connect them with aliens?

46. 위 글을 주제는 무엇인가?

① It's always important to establish the treaties with foreign countries.
② Be on alert against the severance
③ The time of persuading others different from us always comes often.
④ The continuance of the Union originates from brethren affection.
⑤ The misinterpretation by the Western country would be more serious.

47. 위 글의 밑줄 친 Ⓐ가 가리키는 것은?

① geographical discriminations
② our Union
③ characterizing parties
④ local interests and views
⑤ foreign policy-makers

48. 위 글의 밑줄 친 Ⓑ의 올바른 우리말 번역은?

① 여러분이 그 시기와 원한에 대해선 스스로를 방어할 수 없다.
② 여러분이 그 시기와 원한에 대히 경계는 이미 때가 늦었다.
③ 여러분은 그 시기와 원한에 대해 이해심을 발휘해야만 한다.
④ 여러분이 그 시기와 원한에 대해서 아무리 경계해도 지나치지 않다.
⑤ 여러분이 그 시기와 원한에 대해 스스로를 위로해야 한다.

49. 위 글에서 밑줄 친 ⓒ가 가리키는 것은?

① these misrepresentations
② the whole people of the Union
③ the residents along the Atlantic States
④ the representatives between two countries
⑤ the inhabitants of our Western country

50. 위 글과 일치하지 않은 것은?

① 남부와 북구, 대서양과 서부 등 지리적 차이를 구실로 삼아 파벌을 조장하려 하고 있다.
② 특정 지역에서 영향력을 획득하려는 세력은 다른 지역의 의견과 목표를 왜곡하는 수법을 쓰고 있다.
③ 시기와 원한은 형제애로 함께 뭉쳐야 할 사람들을 서로 남남으로 만드는 경향이 있다.
④ 서부 주민들은 영국과 스페인과의 조약에서 불평등을 직접 목격했다.
⑤ 형제들과의 관계를 단절시키려는 사람들의 말엔 귀를 닫아도 무방하다.

46. ② 47. ③ 48. ④ 49. ⑤ 50. ④

①To the efficacy and permanency of your Union, a government for the whole is indispensable. No alliance, ②however strict, between the parts can be an adequate substitute; they must inevitably experience ③the infractions and interruptions which all alliances in all times have experienced. ④Sensible of this momentous truth, you have improved upon your first essay, by the adoption of a constitution of ⑤government better calculated than your former for an intimate union, and for the efficacious management of your common concerns. ⑥This government, the offspring of our own choice, uninfluenced and unawed, adopted upon full investigation and mature deliberation, completely free in its principles, in the distribution of its powers, uniting security with energy, and containing within itself a provision for its own amendment, has a just claim to your confidence and your support. ⑦Respect for its authority, compliance with its laws, acquiescence in its measures, are duties enjoined by the fundamental maxims of true liberty. The basis of our political systems is the right of the people to make and to alter their constitutions of government. But ⑧the Constitution which at any time exists, till changed by an explicit and authentic act of the whole people, is sacredly obligatory upon all. The very idea of the power and the right of the people to establish government presupposes the duty of every individual to obey the established government. ⑨All obstructions to the execution of the laws, all combinations and associations, under whatever plausible character, with the real design to direct, control, counteract, or awe the regular deliberation and action of the constituted authorities, are destructive of this fundamental principle, and of fatal tendency. ⑩They serve to organize faction, to give it an artificial and extraordinary force; to put, in the place of the delegated will of the nation the will of a party, often a small but artful and enterprising minority of the community; and, according to the alternate triumphs of different parties, to make the public administration the mirror of the ill-concerted and incongruous projects of faction, rather than the organ of consistent and wholesome plans digested by common counsels and modified by mutual interests.

📎 본문해석

① [부사구] ～하기 위해서: 연방의 효능과 영속을 위해서
② 아무리 ～일지라도: 아무리 단단할지라도
③ all alliances (in all times) experienced the infractions and interruptions.
④ (As you are) Sensible of ～,
⑤ government better calculated than your former: 과거의 것보다 더 잘 구상된 정부
⑥ [주어] This government, [동격] the offspring of our own choice, [부사구] uninfluenced and unawed, [과거분사] adopted upon full investigation and mature deliberation, [부사구] completely

free in its principles, [부사구] in the distribution of its powers, [분사구문] uniting security with energy, and containing within itself a provision for its own amendment, [본동사] has a just claim to your confidence and your support.

⑦ [주어] Respect ~, compliance ~, (and) acquiescence ~,

⑧ [주어] the Constitution [관계대명사] which at any time[부사구], exists[동사], till changed[과거분사] by an explicit and authentic act of the whole people, is[본동사] sacredly ~.

⑨ All obstructions[주어] to the execution ~, all combinations and associations[부사구], under whatever plausible character[부사구, ~그 구실이 아무리 그럴듯하더라도] with the real design to ~deliberation and action ~authorities[부사구] are[본동사] destructive of ~and of fatal tendency.

⑩ They serve to organize ~, to give ~; to put, ~the community; to make ~.

동영상 강좌 http://youtu.be/Q6w0TP59Jdo

📝 **본문해석**

To the efficacy and permanency of your Union(연방의 효능과 영속을 위해서는), **a government for the whole is indispensable**(한 통합정부가 절대로 필요합니다). **No alliance**(어떠한 동맹도), **however strict**(그것이 아무리 단단하더라도), **between the parts**(지역들 간에) **can be an adequate substitute**((통합정부를) 적절하게 대신할 수 없습니다); **they must inevitably experience**(불가피하게 경험할 것이 틀림없습니다) **the infractions and interruptions which all alliances in all times have experienced**(어느 시대에서나 겪은 협정위반과 해체를). **Sensible of this momentous truth**(이 중요한 진실을 잘 인식한), **you have improved upon your first essay**(여러분의 첫 시도의 결과를 개선했습니다), **by the adoption of a constitution of government better calculated than your former**(과거의 것보다 더 잘 구상된 정부에 관한 헌법을 채택함으로써) **for an intimate union**(여러분은 친밀한 병합과), **and for the efficacious management of your common concerns**(공동 관심사의 효과적인 관리를 위해). **This government**(본 정부는), **the offspring of our own choice**(우리 자신의 선택의 소산), **uninfluenced and unawed**(우리가 어떠한 영향도 받지 않고 어떠한 압력에도 굴하지), **adopted upon full investigation and mature deliberation**(충분한 연구 조사와 신중을 기한 숙고 하에 채택한 것이며), **completely free in its principles**(그 원칙들이 완전히 자유롭게 정해졌고), **in the distribution of its powers**(권력이 자유롭게 분산되고), **uniting security with energy**(안보와 정력을 결합하고), **and containing within itself a provision for its own amendment**(자체 내에 자체의 개정 규정을 포함하고 있는 바), **has a just claim to your confidence and your support**(이 같은 본 정부는 여러분의 신임과 지지를 마땅히 받을 만 합니다). **Respect for its authority**(그 권위를 존중하고), **compliance with its laws**(그 법을 준수하고), **acquiescence in its measures**(그 조처에 순종하는 것), **are duties enjoined by the fundamental maxims of true liberty**(진정한 자유의 기본 원리에 따라 부과되는 의무입니다). **The basis of our political systems**(우리 정치 제도의 기본은) **is the right of the people to make and to alter their constitutions of government**(국민들이 그들의 정부 기구를 만들고 변경하는 권리에 있습니다.). **But the Constitution which at any time exists**(존재하는 이 헌법은), **till changed by an explicit and authentic act of the whole people**(그러나 모든 국민들에 의한 명백하고도 인증된 조치에 의해 수정될 때까지), **is sacredly obligatory upon all**(모든 사람들에게 신성한 의무를 부과합니다). **The very idea of the power and the right of the people**(정부를 설치할 수 있는 국민의 권한과 권리에 관한 개념 그 자체는) **to establish government presupposes the duty of every individual to obey the established**

government(이렇게 설치된 정부에 순종해야 하는 모든 개인의 의무를 전제로 합니다). **All obstructions to the execution of the laws**(법 집행에 대한 모든 방해), **all combinations and associations**(모든 정부기관들(단체와 협회)), **under whatever plausible character**(그 구실이 아무리 그럴듯하더라도), **with the real design to direct, control, counteract, or awe**(유도하거나 통제하거나 방해하거나 두렵게하는 진정한 의도를 가지고) **the regular deliberation and action of the constituted authorities**(제정된 권위의 일상적 숙고와 행동), **are destructive of this fundamental principle, and of fatal tendency**(이 근본적인 원칙과 중대한 경향을 파괴하는 것입니다). **They serve to organize faction**(그들은 당파를 조직합니다), **to give it an artificial and extraordinary force**(그것에 인위적 엄청난 무력을 주고자); **to put, in the place of the delegated will of the nation**(국가를 대표하는 의지에 반하여) **the will of a party**(한 파벌에 의지를 강조합니다), **often a small but artful and enterprising minority of the community**(종종 공동체의 작지만 교활하고 모험적인 소수인); **and, according to the alternate triumphs of different parties**(그리고 다른 파벌과의 번갈아 가며 승리함에 따라), **to make the public administration the mirror of the ill-concerted and incongruous projects of faction**(공공행정을 파벌의 사악하게 타협하고 모순된 계획을 반영시키기 위해), **rather than the organ of consistent and wholesome plans digested by common counsels and modified by mutual interests**(공동 회의로 숙고되고 상호 이익에 의해 수정된 지속적이고 전체적인 계획안의 기관이기 보다는).

📖 **단어분석**

- † **efficacy** [éfəkəsi] n. U 효험, 효력, 유효. / **permanency** [pə́ːrmənənsi] n. ① U =PERMANENCE. ② C 영속적(永續的)인 사람[것, 지위], 종신관(終身官). / ╫ **indispensable** [ìndispénsəbəl] a. ① 불가결의, 없어서는 안 될, 절대 필요한, 긴요한(to; for). / † **alliance** [əláiəns] n. C,U 동맹; 맹약(盟約); 「집합적」 동맹국[자]; 결혼, 결연; 인척 관계; 협력, 제휴, 협조; / ╫ **strict** [strikt]a. ① 엄격한, 엄한(about a matter; with a person). ② 엄밀한, 정밀한. ③ 진정한, 순전한; 완전한. / ╫ **adequate** [ǽdikwit] a. ① (어떤 목적에) 어울리는, 적당한, 충분한; (직무를 다할) 능력이 있는, 적임의(to; for). / ╫ **substitute** [sʌ́bstitjùːt] v. —vt. ① 『~+목/ +목+전+명』 대용(代用)하다, 바꾸다(for); ~을 대리케 하다(for). ② 【화학】 치환하다. —vi. 『+전+명』 ~을 대신하다, 대리하다(for); 【화학】 치환하다. / **inevitable** [inévitəbəl] a. ① 피할 수 없는, 면할 수 없는, 부득이한. ② (논리적으로 보아) 필연의. ③ (이야기의 줄거리 따위가) 납득이 가는, 지당한. / ╫ **essay** [ései] n. ① 수필, (문예상의) 소론(小論), 시론(詩論); 평론. ② [+eséi] 시도, 시험(at; in); 시도의 (to (do); at). / † **adoption** [ədɔ́pʃən, ədɔ́p-] n. U,C 채용, 채택; 양자결연; (입후보자의) 공천; (외래어의) 차용. / **infraction** [infrǽkʃən] n. U 위반; 침해; C 위반 행위; / † **momentous** [mouméntəs] a. 중대한, 중요한, 쉽지 않은 / **efficacious** [èfəkéiʃəs] a. 의도된 효과가 있는, (약·치료 따위가) 효험[효능]이 있는, / ╫ **offspring** [ɔ́ːfspriŋ] n. (pl. ~(s)) ① 「집합적」 자식, 자녀; 자손, 후예. ② (하나의) 자식, 자손. ③ 생겨난 것, 소산(fruit), 결과(result) (of). / **unawed** [ʌnɔ́ːd] a. 두려워하지 않는, 태연한. / ╫ **provision** [prəvíʒən] n. U ① 예비, 준비, 설비(for; against). ② 공급, 지급; 지급량(量);(pl.) 양식, 식량; 저장품. ③ C 【법률】 규정, 조항(clause). / ╫ **amendment** [əméndmənt] n. ① U,C 변경, 개선, 교정(矯正), 개심. ② (법안 등의) 수정(안), 보정, 개정. / † **compliance, -ancy** [kəmpláiəns], [-i] n. U ① 승낙, 응낙. ② 고분고분함; 굴종, 추종; 맹종, 순종. / **acquiescence** [æ̀kwiésəns] n. U 묵낙, (어쩔 수 없는) 동의(in; to). / † **enjoin** [endʒɔ́in] vt. ①『+목+전+명/ +목+to do/ +that절』 ~에게 명령하다, (침묵·순종 따위를) 요구하다(demand); (행동 따위를) 강요하다(on, upon). ②『+목+전+명』 【법률】 ~을 금하다, ~에게 —하는 것을 금하다(prohibit)(from). / **presuppose** [prìːsəpóuz] vt. 미리 가정[예상]하다; 필요조건으로 예상하다, 전제로 하다; ~의 뜻을

포함하다. [SYN.] ⇨ PRESUME. / ⊤ **obey** [oubéi] v. —vt. ～에 복종하다, ～에 따르다; ～의 명령 [가르침, 소원]에 따르다; (이성 따위)에 따라 행동하다, (힘·충동)대로 움직이다; (기계 장치가) ～에 반응 하다. —vi. 복종하다, 말을 잘 듣다(to). / † **obstruction** [əbstrʌ́kʃən] n. ① U 폐색(閉塞), 차단, 〖의 학〗 폐색(증); 방해; 장애, 지장(to); 의사 방해(특히 의회의). / † **plausible** [plɔ́ː zəbəl] a. ① (이유·구 실 따위가) 그럴듯한, 정말 같은. ② 그럴 듯한 말을 하는, 말 재주가 좋은. / **artful** [áː rtfəl] a. ① 교 묘한, 기교를 부린. ② 기교를 부리는, 교활한. / † **enterprising** [éntərpràiziŋ] a. 기업심[모험심]이 왕성 한; (매우) 진취적인, 모험적인. / † **alternate** [ɔ́ː ltərnit, ǽl-] a. ①번갈아 하는, 교호(交互)의, 교체[교 대]의. ② 서로 엇갈리는, 하나 걸러의. / **ill-concerted** 사악한 타협의 / **incongruous** [inkʌ́ŋgruəs / -kɔ́ ŋ-] a. 일치[조화]하지 않는(with); 어울리지 않는, 부조리한 (태도 따위), 앞뒤가 안 맞는(이야기); / **⁑ organ** [ɔ́ː rgən] n. (정치적인) 기관; 기관지(紙·誌). / † **digest** [didʒést, dàid-] v. —vt. ① 소화하다, 삭이다. ② 요약하다, 간추리다; (압축하여) 정리[분류]하다. /

❊ 다음 글을 읽고 물음에 답하시오. [51~55]

To the efficacy and permanency of your Union, a government for the whole is indispensable. No alliance, however strict, between the parts can be an adequate substitute; Ⓐ**they** must inevitably experience the infractions and interruptions which all alliances in all times have experienced. Sensible of this momentous truth, you have improved upon your first essay, by the adoption of a constitution of government better calculated than your former for an intimate union, and for the efficacious management of your common concerns. This government, _____, uninfluenced and unawed, adopted upon full investigation and mature deliberation, completely free in its principles, in the distribution of its powers, uniting security with energy, and containing within itself a provision for its own amendment, ①**have** a just claim to your confidence and your support. Respect for its authority, compliance with its laws, acquiescence in its measures, ②**are** duties enjoined by the fundamental maxims of true liberty. The basis of our political systems is the right of the people to make and to alter their constitutions of government. But the Constitution which at any time exists, till changed by an explicit and authentic act of the whole people, ③**is** sacredly obligatory upon all. The very idea of the power and the right of the people to establish government ④**presupposes** the duty of every individual to obey the established government. All obstructions to the execution of the laws, all combinations and associations, under whatever plausible character, with the real design to direct, control, counteract, or awe the regular deliberation and action of the constituted authorities, ⑤**are** destructive of this fundamental principle, and of fatal tendency. They serve to organize faction, to give it an artificial and extraordinary force; to put, in the place of the delegated will of the nation the will of a party, often a small but artful and enterprising minority of the community; and, according to the alternate triumphs of different parties, to make the public administration the mirror of the ill-concerted and incongruous projects of faction, rather than the organ of consistent and wholesome plans digested by common counsels and modified by mutual interests.

51. 위 글의 주제는 무엇인가?

① Vicious fractions sometimes is necessary for the stronger unification.
② People have the right to try to amend and distribute the power.
③ The constitution should be changed by the whole people.
④ People should be on alert whenever there are obstructions.
⑤ Union must be protected from any trials.

52. 위 글에서 밑줄 친 Ⓐ가 의미하는 것은?

① the parts
② your Union
③ constitutional administrations
④ alliance between the parts
⑤ infractions and interruptions

53. 위 글의 밑줄 친 ①~⑤ 중, 어법상 어색한 것은?

①   ②   ③   ④   ⑤

54. 위 글의 빈칸에 가장 적절한 표현은?

① the opportunity by God's blessing
② the offspring of our own choice
③ the experience through long historical adversity
④ the counterpart against ill-concerted fractions
⑤ the system to have to be amended and changed by people at any time

55. 위 글의 내용과 일치하지 <u>않은</u> 것은?

① 연방의 효능과 영속을 위해서는 하나의 통합정부가 절대로 필요하다.
② 우리 자신의 선택의 소산인 이 정부는 충분한 숙고와 성숙한 고찰을 바탕으로 자유 원칙에 의해 구성되었다.
③ 권위존중, 그 법의 준수와 그에 순종하는 것은 진정한 자유의 기본 원리에 따라 부관된 의무이다.
④ 당파를 조장하여 무력으로 국가의 의지에 반하는 행위는 사악하고 모순된 것이다.
⑤ 국민의 의무는 사악한 존재를 파악하여 알리고 그들의 존재를 없애는 것이 하나의 주어진 의무이다.

51. ⑤   52. ④   53. 53. ① have → has
54. ②   55. ⑤

동영상 강좌 http://youtu.be/ichC7BJMkRc

However combinations or associations of the above description may now and then answer popular ends, they are likely, in the course of time and things, to become potent engines, by which cunning, ambitious, and unprincipled men will be enabled to subvert the power of the people and to usurp for themselves the reins of government, destroying afterwards the very engines which have lifted them to unjust dominion.

Towards the preservation of your government, and the permanency of your present happy state, it is requisite, not only that you steadily discountenance irregular oppositions to its acknowledged authority, but also that you resist with care the spirit of innovation upon its principles, however specious the pretexts. One method of assault may be to effect, in the forms of the Constitution, alterations which will impair the energy of the system, and thus to undermine what cannot be directly overthrown. In all the changes to which you may be invited, remember that time and habit are at least as necessary to fix the true character of governments as of other human institutions; that experience is the surest standard by which to test the real tendency of the existing constitution of a country; that facility in changes, upon the credit of mere hypothesis and opinion, exposes to perpetual change, from the endless variety of hypothesis and opinion; and remember, especially, that for the efficient management of your common interests, in a country so extensive as ours, a government of as much vigor as is consistent with the perfect security of liberty is indispensable.

🖎 본문해석

However combinations or associations of the above description(그러나 위에서 설명드린 조직과 단체는) **may now and then answer popular ends**(때때로 대중적 목적을 답할지 모를지라도), **they are likely, in the course of time and things**(시간과 사건의 과정 속에서), **to become potent engines**(강력한 동력이 되고자), **by which**(그것에 의해) **cunning, ambitious, and unprincipled men**(교활하고 야망적이고 원칙이 없는 사람들은) **will be enabled to subvert the power of the people and to usurp for themselves the reins of government**(국민의 권력을 전복시키고 그들 스스로 정부의 지배권을 강탈하고 할 것입니다.), **destroying afterwards the very engines which have lifted them to unjust dominion**(이후에 자신들은 부당한 통제로 올려놓았던 바로 그 동력을 파괴하면서).

Towards the preservation of your government, and the permanency of your present happy state(여러분의 정부 보존과 여러분의 현재의 행복한 상태의 영원함을 향하여), **it is requisite**(반드시 필요합니다), **not only that you steadily discountenance irregular oppositions to its acknowledged authority**(여러분이 연방의 인정된 권위에 대한 비정상적인 반대에 꾸준히 대적하는 것뿐만 아니라), **but also that you resist with care the spirit of innovation upon its principles**(연방의 원칙을 변경하려는 태도에 주의 깊게 저항하는 것), **however specious the pretexts**(아무리 그럴듯하더라도). **One method of assault**(한 가지 공격 방법은) **may be to effect, in the forms of the Constitution, alterations which will impair the energy of the system**(우리 제도의 활력을 손상시킬 헌법 개정의 형태를 취하며), **and thus to undermine**

what cannot be directly overthrown(이는 직접적으로 전복할 수 없는 것을 약화 시킬 수 있습니다). **In all the changes to which you may be invited**(여러분은 어떤 변화에 참여하도록 요청받았을 때는), **remember that time and habit are at least as necessary**(시간과 관습이 최소한 필요한 것을 점을 명심해야 합니다) **to fix the true character of governments as of other human institutions**(정부의 진정한 성격을 정하기 위해서는 다른 인간제도의 경우와 마찬가지로); **that experience is the surest standard**(경험이 가장 확실한 표준이라는 점) **by which to test the real tendency of the existing constitution of a country**(한 나라의 현존하는 구조의 진정한 경향을 시험하는 데는); **that facility in changes**(손쉽게 변경하면), **upon the credit of mere hypothesis and opinion**(단순한 가설과 견해만을 믿고), **exposes to perpetual change**(끝없는 변경을 하게 된다는 점을), **from the endless variety of hypothesis and opinion**(끝없는 다양한 가설과 의견으로부터); **and remember, especially**(특히 명심해야 합니다), **that for the efficient management of your common interests**(공동의 관심사를 효과적으로 관리하기 위해서는), **in a country so extensive as ours**(우리나라와 같이 광대한 국가에서), **a government of as much vigor as is consistent with the perfect security of liberty**(자유의 완전한 확보에 적합할 만큼 활력에 찬 정부가) **is indispensable**(절대로 필요하다는 점을).

🝆 단어분석

- **subvert** [səbvə́ːrt] vt. 뒤엎다, 멸망시키다, 파괴하다, (종교·주의 따위를) 타파하다. / † **usurp** [juːsə́ːrp, -zə́ːrp] v. —vt. (권력·지위 등을) 빼앗다, 찬탈하다, 강탈[횡령]하다. —vi. 범하다, 침해하다 (encroach) (upon, on). / † **rein** [rein] n. ① (종종 pl.) 고삐. ② U,C 통어하는 수단; 구속(력). ③ (pl.) 지배권, 지휘권. / † **dominion** [dəmínjən] n. ① U 지배[통치]권[력], 주권. ② U,C 지배, 통제(over); / † **requisite** [rékwəzit] a. 필요한, 없어서는 안 될, 필수의(needful)(to; for). [SYN.] ➩ NECESSARY. / **discountenance** [diskáuntənəns] vt. ① 면목을 잃게 하다, 창피를 주다, 쩔쩔매게 하다. ② (계획 따위에) 찬성하지 않다, ～을 승인하지 않다. / **specious** [spíːʃəs] a. 허울[외양]만 좋은, 진실같은; 그럴 듯한(plausible); 가면을 쓴. / † **pretext** [príːtekst] n. 구실, 핑계(for). / ‡ **effect** [ifékt] vt. ① (변화 등을) 가져오다, 초래하다. / ‡ **overthrow** [òuvərəróu] v. (-threw [-ərúː]; -thrown [-əróun]) —vt. ① 뒤집어 엎다, 타도하다, 무너뜨리다; 헐다, 파괴하다; (정부 따위를) 전복시키다, (제도 등을) 폐지하다. / † **undermine** [ʌndərmáin] vt. ① (명성 따위를) 음험한 수단으로 훼손하다, 몰래 손상시키다. / **as of** ～와 마찬가지로 / ‡ **facility** [fəsíləti] n. U,C ① 쉬움, 평이[용이함]. ② 재주 (dexterity), 능숙(skill), 유창(fluency); 재능. / † **hypothesis** [haipɑ́θəsis / -pɔ́θə-] n. (pl. -ses [-sìːz]) 가설(假說), 가정(假定); 전제; 단순한 추측, 억측. [SYN.] ➩ THEORY. / ‡ **vigor, 【영국】 vigour** [vígər] n. U ① 활기, 정력, 체력, 활력. ② 힘, 생기, 기운, 강도(強度), 세기. / † **consistent** [kənsístənt] a. ① (의견·행동·신념 등이) (～와) 일치 [조화·양립]하는(with). / ‡ **indispensable** [indispénsəbəl] a. ① 불가결의, 없어서는 안 될, 절대 필요한, 긴요한(to; for). [SYN.] ➩ NECESSARY.

동영상 강좌 http://youtu.be/l3cEAmJHDD4

※ 다음 글을 읽고 물음에 답하시오. [56~60]

However combinations or associations of the above description may now and then answer popular ends, Ⓐ**they** are likely, in the course of time and things, to become potent engines, ①**by which** cunning, ambitious, and unprincipled men will be enabled to subvert the power of the people and to usurp for themselves the reins of government, destroying afterwards the very engines ②**which** have lifted them to unjust dominion.

Towards the _____Ⓑ_____ of your government, and the _____Ⓒ_____ of your present happy state, it is requisite, not only that you steadily discountenance irregular oppositions to its acknowledged authority, but also that you resist with care the spirit of innovation upon its principles, however specious the pretexts. One method of assault may be to effect, in the forms of the Constitution, alterations ③**which** will impair the energy of the system, and thus to undermine what cannot be directly overthrown. In all the changes ④**which** you may be invited, remember that time and habit are at least as necessary to fix the true character of governments as of other human institutions; that experience is the surest standard ⑤**by which** to test the real tendency of the existing constitution of a country; that facility in changes, upon the credit of mere hypothesis and opinion, exposes to perpetual change, from the endless variety of hypothesis and opinion;

and remember, especially, that for the efficient management of your common interests, in a country so extensive as ours, a government of as much vigor as is consistent with the perfect security of liberty is indispensable.

56. What is being mainly told about?
① Understand what oppositions have claims for their existence.
② Experience that is the surest standard may be changed.
③ Remember the resistance confrontation to the irregular oppositions.
④ Respect the endless variety of hypothesis and opinion.
⑤ Please, accept all the changes to which you may be invited.

57. 위 글의 밑줄 친 ①~⑤ 중, 어법상 어색한 것은?
① ② ③ ④ ⑤

58. 위 글의 밑줄 친 빈칸 Ⓑ, Ⓒ의 적절한 단어는?
① overthrow   revolution
② mortality   continuation
③ reconstruction   improvement
④ power   repetition
⑤ preservation   permanency

373

59. 위 글의 밑줄 친 Ⓐ와 관계가 <u>적은</u> 것은?

① unprincipled men

② destroying unjust dominion

③ discountenancing irregular oppositions

④ the pretexts are specious

⑤ mere hypothesis and opinion

60. 위 글과 일치하지 <u>않은</u> 것은?

① 교활하고 야망적인 사람들은 자신들이
 만든 통제를 스스로 파괴한다.

② 연방의 인정된 권위에 대한 비정상적인
 것에 대적하자.

③ 위선자들의 공격 중 한 방법은 헌법을
 존속시키는 것이다.

④ 어떤 변화에 대한 참여를 요구받았을 때,
 시간과 관습이 필요하다.

⑤ 반대자들의 공격은 끝없는 다양한 가설
 의 의견이다.

56. ③   57. ④ which → to which
58. ⑤   59. ③   60. ③

Liberty itself will find in such a government, with powers properly distributed and adjusted, its surest guardian. It is, indeed, little else than a name, where the government is too feeble to withstand the enterprises of faction, to confine each member of the society within the limits prescribed by the laws, and to maintain all in the secure and tranquil enjoyment of the rights of person and property.

I have already intimated to you the danger of parties in the State, with particular reference to the founding of them on geographical discriminations. Let me now take a more comprehensive view, and warn you in the most solemn manner against the baneful effects of the spirit of party generally.

This spirit, unfortunately, is inseparable from our nature, having its root in the strongest passions of the human mind. It exists under different shapes in all governments, more or less stifled, controlled, or repressed; but, in those of the popular form, it is seen in its greatest rankness, and is truly their worst enemy.

📖 본문해석

Liberty itself will find(자유 그 자체는 ～가 될 것이다) **in such a government, with powers properly distributed and adjusted**(권력이 적절히 분산되고 조정되는 그 같은 정부에서), **its surest guardian**(가장 확실한 수호자). **It is**(정부는), **indeed**(사실), **little else than a name**(명목 이상의 아무것도 아닙니다), **where the government is too feeble to withstand the enterprises of faction**(정부가 너무나 허약해서 파당적인 시도에 견딜 수 없고), **to confine each member of the society within the limits prescribed by the laws**(사회의 각 구성원을 법이 제정한 제한 속에 가두어 놓을 수 없고), **and to maintain all in the secure and tranquil enjoyment of the rights of person and property**(모두가 인권과 재산을 안전하고도 조용한 가운데 계속 누릴 수 없는).

I have already intimated to you the danger of parties in the State(저는 이미 여러분에게 연방정부에서 여러 정당의 위험성을 넌지시 비추었습니다), **with particular reference to the founding of them on geographical discriminations**(지리적 차별 하에 그들의 생성에 특히 언급하면서). **Let me now take a more comprehensive view**(지금 더욱 포괄적인 고려하겠습니다), **and warn you in the most solemn manner**(가장 진지하게 여러분에 알려드리겠습니다) **against the baneful effects of the spirit of party generally**(일반적으로 정당정신의 파괴적인 효과에 대한).

This spirit, unfortunately, is inseparable from our nature(이 정신은 안타깝게도 우리 정부의 특성과 분리되어 있지 않습니다), **having its root in the strongest passions of the human mind**(인간의 마음의 가장 강한 열정에 뿌리를 두고 있습니다). **It exists under different shapes in all governments**(그것은 모든 정부에서 다른 형태 하에 존재합니다), **more or less stifled, controlled, or repressed**(다소간 억압되고 통제되거나 제진된); **but, in those of the popular form**(그러나 대중적인 형태의 정부에서), **it is seen in its greatest rankness, and is truly their worst enemy**(그것은 가장 썩은 것으로 보이며 진정 그들의 가장 나쁜 적입니다).

📖 단어분석

- ⳇ **feeble** [fiː bəl] (-bler; -blest) ① 연약한, 약한, 힘없는. [SYN.] ⇨ WEEK. ② 박약한, 나약한, 기

력이 없는; 저능의. ③ (빛·효과 따위가) 약한, 미약한 / ‡ **withstand** [wiðstǽnd, wiθ-] vt. (-stood [-stúd]) —vt. ① ~에 저항하다, ~에 반항[거역]하다. ② (곤란 등에) 잘 견디다, 버티다. —vi. (시어) 반항[저항]하다; 잘 견디다, 버티다. [OE with against]. / ‡ **enterprise** [éntərpràiz] n. ① 기획, 계획(특히 모험적인). ② U,C 기업(체) ③ U 진취적인 정신, 기업심[열]; 모험심. / **confine** [kənfáin] v. —vt. ① 『+목+전+명』 제한하다, 한하다(to; within). ② 가둬 넣다, 감금하다(in; within); 들어박히게 하다 (to). / ‡ **prescribe** [priskráib] v. —vt. ①『~+목/ +목+전+명/ +wh.절/ +wh. to do』 규정하다, 지시하다, 명하다(order). ② (약을) 처방하다; (요법을) 권하다. ③ 〖법률〗 시효로 하다, ~을 시효에 의해 취득[소멸]하다. / † **tranquil** [trǽŋkwil] a. (more ~, ~(l)er; most ~, ~(l)est) 조용한, 평온한, (마음·바다 따위가) 차분한, 편안한, 평화로운. / ‡ **intimate** [íntəmèit] vt. ~+목 / +목+전+명 / +that절』 ① 넌지시 비추다, 암시하다 (hint). [SYN.] ⇨ SUGGEST. ② 공표하다. / ‡ **solemn** [sáləm / sɔ́l-]a. ① 엄숙한, 근엄한. ② 장엄한, 장중한. ③ 엄연한, 중대한. ④ 진지한, 엄숙한. [SYN.] ⇨ GRAVE. / **baneful** [béinfəl] a. 파괴적[치명적]인, (고어) 해로운, 유독한. / † **stifle** [stáif-əl] v. —vt. ①『~+목/ +목+전+명』 ~을 숨 막히게 하다, 질식(사)시키다(by; with). ② (불평 따위를) 짓누르다; / **repress** [riprés] vt. 억누르다; 저지[제지]하다; (반란 등을) 진압하다; 〖유전학〗 (유전자를) 억제하다. / **rank** a. ① 무성한 ② 순전한, 지독한(나쁜 의미로). / **sharpen** [ʃáː rp-ən] v. —vt. ① 날카롭게 하다 ② 격심하게[강하게] 하다. / ‡ **revenge** [rivéndʒ] n. U ① 보복, 복수(vengeance) ② 원한, 유한(遺恨), 복수심. / † **dissension, -tion** [disénʃən] n. U 의견 차이; C 불화(의 씨); (pl.) 알력, 분쟁. / **perpetrate** [pə́ː rpətrèit] vt. (나쁜 짓·죄를) 행하다, 범하다. / † **horrid** [hɔ́ː rid, hár-] a. ① 무서운. [SYN.] ⇨ HORRIBLE. / **enormity** [inɔ́ː rməti] n. ① U 무법; (특히) 극악(極惡); C 중대한 범죄 ② (구어) (문제·일 등의) 거대[광대]. / **despotism** [déspətìzəm] n. ① U 독재 폭정. ② C 전제국, 독재군주국. /

"Funeral Oration(추도사)"

by Pericles 페리클레스(아테네 정치가 BC 431)

[난이도 ★★★★★]

동영상 강좌 http://youtu.be/BO_wytV0yUk

Most of my predecessors in this place have commended him who made this speech part of the law, telling us that it is well that it should be delivered at the burial of those who fall in battle. For myself, I should have thought that the worth which had displayed itself in deeds would be sufficiently rewarded by honors also shown by deeds; such as you now see in this funeral prepared at the people's cost.

🖎 본문해석

Most of my predecessors in this place(이곳 아테네의 대부분의 제 선배님들은) **have commended him who made this speech part of the law**(이 추도사를 법의 일부로 만들었던 그를 칭송해 왔습니다), **telling us that it is well that it should be delivered at the burial of those who fall in battle**(전쟁에서 죽은 사람들의 장례식에서 이것이(추도사가) 낭송되는 것은 적절하다고 우리에게 말씀하십니다). **For myself**(저로서), **I should have thought**(저는 생각이 짧았습니다) **that the worth which had displayed itself in deeds**(행동으로 보여준 가치는) **would be sufficiently rewarded by honors also shown by deeds**(국가를 위해 목숨을 바친 명예로 인해 충분히 보상을 받을 것입니다); **such as**(이를테면) **you now see in this funeral prepared at the people's cost**(여러분은 그 사람들의 희생을 추모하기 위한 이 장례식에서 지금 목격하고 있는 것입니다).

🖎 문법분석

Most of[대부분] my predecessors in this place[이곳, 아테네] have commended[현재완료의 계속, ~칭찬해 오고 있다] him who[관계 대명사] made A[this speech] B[part of the law][make A B: 5형식, A를 B로 만들다, 이 연설(추도사)을 법의 일부로 만들었다], telling us[and have told us] that it[가주어] is well[형용사, 적절한] that[진주어] it[=this speech, 추도사] should be delivered[it가 주어이므로 수동태, 이것이 낭송되어져야 하다] at[전치사, 장소] the burial[매장식에서, 장례식에서] of those who fall in battle[전쟁에서 죽은 사람들]. For myself[for+재귀대명사], I should have thought[should + have + p.p:(과거를 후회, 유감)~했어야만 했다] that the worth which[관계대명사] had displayed[과거완료시제] itself[죽음] in deeds[죽음을 행동으로 보여준 가치, 목숨을 바친] would[과거시제, ~일 것이다] be sufficiently[부사, rewarded를 수식] rewarded[주어 the worth가 사물이므로 '수동태'] by honors (which were) also shown by deeds[행동으로 보여준 명예]; such as[말의 계속을 재촉하는 용법] you now see[목격하다, 경험하다] in this funeral (which is) prepared at the people's cost(사람들의 희생을 추모하기 위해 준비된 장례식에서).

🖎 단어분석

† **predecessor** [prédisèsər] n. 전임자([opp.] successor); 선배; 선행자; / † **commend** [kəménd] vt. ① 칭찬하다(praise). ② 권하다. ③ 위탁하다(to). / ‡ **burial** [bériəl] n. 매장, 매장식. / ‡ **deed** [diː d] n. ① 행위, 소위(所爲). [SYN.] ⇨ ACT. ② 실행; U,C 사실(reality). ③ 공훈, 공적. / ‡ **sufficient** [səfíʃənt] a. ① 충분한, 족한(for). [cf.] deficient. [SYN.] ⇨ ENOUGH. / ‡ **reward** [riwɔ́ː rd] v. ―

vt. ① ～에게 보답하다; 보수를[상을] 주다(for; with). ② (행위에) 앙갚음하다, 보복하다, 벌하다. —vi. 보답하다. /

📗 동의어/반의어

commend v. acclaim[əkléim], applaud[əplɔ́ːd], compliment[kámpləmənt], extol[ikstóul], praise[preiz], advocate[ǽdvəkit], approve[əprúːv], endorse[endɔ́ːrs]승인하다, 선전하다, promote[prəmóut], recommend[rèkəménd, commit[kəmít], confide[kənfáid], entrust[entrʌ́st] **ant**. criticize[krítisàiz], condemn[kəndém] withhold[wiðhóul]

And I could have wished that the reputations of many brave men were not to be imperiled in the mouth of a single individual, to stand or fall according as he spoke well or ill. For it is hard to speak properly upon a subject where it is even difficult to convince your hearers that you are speaking the truth. On the one hand, the friend who is familiar with every fact of the story may think that some point has not been set forth with that fullness which he wishes and knows it to deserve; on the other, he who is a stranger to the matter may be led by envy to suspect exaggeration if he hears anything above his own nature.

📗 본문해석

And I could have wished(그리고 저는 소망했던 것 같습니다) **that the reputations of many brave men were not to be imperiled in the mouth of a single individual**(～ 많은 용맹스런 사람들의 명성이 한 개인의 입을 통해 위험에 빠지지 않기를), **to stand or fall according as he spoke well or ill**(그가 칭송이나 험담을 하는 것에 따라 명예롭거나 불명예스런). **For it is hard to speak properly upon a subject**(왜냐하면 ～한 주제에 관해 적절히 말하기는 어렵기 때문입니다) **where it is even difficult to convince your hearers that you are speaking the truth**(여러분의 청중에게 당신이 지금 진실을 말하고 있다고 납득시키기가 아주 어려운). **On the one hand**(한편으로), **the friend who is familiar with every fact of the story may think**(그 이야기의 분명한 진실에 알고 있는 그 친구는 ～라고 생각할 것 같습니다) **that some point has not been set forth with that fullness which he wishes and knows it to deserve**(그가 그럴만하다고 바라고 아는 것이 그렇게 완벽하게 언급되지 않았다); **on the other**(다른 한편으로), **he who is a stranger to the matter**(그 문제에 생소한 그는) **may be led by envy to suspect exaggeration**(과장됨을 의심하는 부러움에 사로잡힐 것 같습니다) **if he hears anything above his own nature**(만일 그가 자신을 과장하는 것을 듣는다면).

📗 문법분석

And I could have wished[～이었을는지도 모른다(현재에서 본 과거의 추측]. that the reputations of many brave men[많은 용맹한 사람들의 명성] were not to[be to의 용법 중, 가능(～하고 싶어 하지 않다)] be imperiled in the mouth of a single individual[한 개인의 말을 통해 위험에 빠지는], to stand or fall[살거나 죽거나, 명예롭거나 불명예스런] according as[접속사, ～에 따라] he spoke well or ill[칭찬이나 험담하다]. For[접속사=because] it[가주어] is hard to speak[진주어] properly upon a subject[한 주제에 관해 적절히 말하다] where[관계부사] it[가주어] is even difficult to convince[진주어, convince A that B: A를 B로 납득시키다.] your hearers that you are speaking the truth. On the one hand, the friend who[주격 관계대명사, 그 모든 진실을 알고 있는 친구] is familiar with every fact of the story may think that some point has not been set forth[핵심이 빠져있다] with that fullness[with+명사=부사구, 아주 완전히] which[관계대명사의 선행사는 some point] he wishes and knows it to deserve[그럴만한 가치가 있다]; on the other (hand)[다른 한편으로], he who is a stranger to the matter[그 문제를 모르는 친구] may be led by envy to suspect exaggeration[과장됨을 알면서도 은근히 좋아하는 뜻] if he hears anything above his own nature.

📖 단어분석

⌘ **reputation** [rèpjətéiʃ-ən] n. U,C ① 평판, 세평. ② 명성, 신망, 호평. / **imperil**[impéril] vt. (생명·재산 따위를) 위태롭게 하다, 위험하게 하다(endanger). / **according as** (conj.) (~함)에 따라서; ~에 응해서 (뒤에 clause) / ⌘ **convince** [kənvíns] vt. +목+전+명/ +목+that절』 ~에게 납득시키다 / ♣ **set forth** (1) 출발하다: (2) 진열하다, 설명하다 / ⌘ **suspect** [səspékt] v. —vt. ① 『+목+to be 보/ +(that)절』 ~이 아닌가 의심하다 / ⌘ **exaggeration**[igzæ̀dʒəréiʃən] n. ① U 과장, ② C 과장적 표현. /

📖 동의어/반의어

imperil v. compromise[kámprəmàiz], endanger[endéindʒər], hazard[hǽzərd], jeopardize[dʒépərdàiz], risk[risk] ant. protect[prətékt]

exaggeration n. hyperbole[haipə́: rbəli, overstatement[òuvərstéitmənt], aggrandizement[əgrǽ ndaimənt], embellishment[imbéliʃmənt], enhancement[enhǽnsmənt] ant. understatement[ʌndərsté imənt] minimizing[mínəmàiziŋ]

For men can endure to hear others praised only so long as they can severally persuade themselves of their own ability to equal the actions recounted: when this point is passed, envy comes in and with it incredulity. However, since our ancestors have stamped this custom with their approval, it becomes my duty to obey the law and to try to satisfy your several wishes and opinions as best I may.

📖 본문해석

For men can endure to hear others praised(왜냐하면 사람들은 다른 사람들이 칭찬받는 것을 듣는 것을 감수할 수 있기 때문이다) **only so long as they can severally persuade themselves of their own ability to equal the actions recounted**(단지 열거되는 그 행위에 필적하는 그들 행위에 여러 번 설득당하는 동안): **when this point is passed**(이런 시점이 지나갔을 때), **envy comes in and with it incredulity** (부러움은 불신으로 바뀌게 됩니다). **However, since our ancestors have stamped this custom with their approval**(그러나 우리의 조상님들은 이러한 관습을 묵인하셨기에), **it becomes my duty to obey the law and to try to satisfy your several wishes and opinions as best I may**(제가 최선을 다해 법을 준수하면서 여러분의 여러 소망과 의견을 만족시키고자 노력하는 것이 저의 임무임을 말씀드립니다).

📖 문법분석

"Funeral Oration(추도사)"

by Pericles 페리클레스(아테네 정치가 BC 431)

For[=because] men can endure to hear others praised[others와 praised는 수동형 관계, 칭찬받은 사람들] only so long as[접속사, 단지 ~하는 동안만] they can severally persuade themselves of[납득당하다] their own ability to[to부정사의 형용사적 용법, ~할 능력] equal the actions (which are) recounted: when[접속사, =after] this point is passed, envy comes in and with it[=envy] incredulity (comes). However, since[접속사, 완료형, ~이후로 내내] our ancestors have stamped this custom with their approval[이런 관습을 그들의 승인으로 받아 드리다(묵인하다)], it[가주어] becomes my duty to obey[진주어] the law and to try to satisfy your several wishes and opinions as best I may[추도사에서 최선을 다해 전쟁터에서 죽어간 영웅들을 기린다는 뜻].

📖 단어분석

✝ **endure** [endjúər] v. —vt. ① 『~+목/ +-ing/ +to do』 (사람·물건이) 견디다, 인내하다; 「주로 부정문」 ~을 참다. [SYN.] ⇨ BEAR. ② (고난 따위를) 경험하다, 받다. / ✝ **equal** [íː kwəl] vt. ① 『~+목/ +목+전+명』 ~과 같다; ~에 필적하다, ~에 못지않다. / ✝ **recount** [rikáunt] vt. 자세히 얘기하다 차례대로 얘기하다; 하나하나 열거하다. / **incredulity**[inkridjúː ləti] n. U 쉽사리 믿지 않음, 의심이 많음, 회의심. / **✱✱stamp**[stæmp] v. (마음 등에) (인상·생각 등을) 새겨 넣다(with);

📖 동의어/반의어

endure v. abide, continue, outlast, persist, remain, bear, suffer, survive, tolerate, undergo **ant**. decay enjoy

---

I shall begin with our ancestors: it is both just and proper that they should have the honor of the first mention on an occasion like the present. They dwelt in the country without break in the succession from generation to generation, and handed it down free to the present time by their valor. And if our more remote ancestors deserve praise, much more do our own fathers, who added to their inheritance the empire which we now possess, and spared no pains to be able to leave their acquisitions to us of the present generation.

📖 본문해석

I shall begin with our ancestors(저희 조상님들의 이야기로 시작하려 합니다): **it is both just and proper that they should have the honor of the first mention on an occasion like the present**(그들이 현재와 같은 추도식을 우선 명예로 언급해야 함이 옳고 적절하다 사료됩니다). **They dwelt in the country without break in the succession from generation to generation**(그들은 연속된 세대 간의 계승에서 휴식 없이 이 나라를 떠나지 않으셨고), **and handed it down free to the present time by their valor**(그들의 용맹함으로 기꺼이 현재 우리에게 물려 주셨습니다). **And if our more remote ancestors deserve praise**(그리고 만일 우리의 오랜 조상님들을 칭송하고자 한다면), **much more do our own fathers, who added to their inheritance the empire which we now possess**(지금 우리가 간직하고 있는 제국을 물려주시고), **and spared no pains to be able to leave their acquisitions to us of the present generation**(현 우리 세대에 그들의 유산을 물려주시고자 고통을 감내하신 우리 아버님들을 먼저 칭송하는 것이 도리일 것입니다).

🖊 문법분석

I shall[결의의 객관적인 표현, 꼭 ~한다] begin with[~로 시작하다] our ancestors: it[가주어] is both just and proper[both A and B: A와 B 모두] that[진주어] they should have the honor of the first mention on[~에 관한 우선적인 언급] an occasion like[전치사, ~같은 때] the present[오늘, 현재]. They[=our ancestors] dwelt[dwell의 과거형] in the country without break[휴식 없이] in the succession from generation to generation[연속된 세대교체], and handed it[=the succession] down[물려주다] free[부사로 hand it down을 수식, 기꺼이] to[전치사로 방향, ~으로] the present time by their valor[그들의 용맹함으로]. And if[조건절, 만일 ~라면] our more remote ancestors[오랜 조상님들] deserve praise, much more do[=deserve praise] our own fathers, who added[add의 목적어는 the empire, add A to B: A를 B에 더하다] to their inheritance the empire which[관계대명사] we now possess[목적어는 the empire], and (who) spared no pains to be able to leave A[their acquisitions] B[to us of the present generation][leave A to B: B에게 A를 물려주다].

🖊 단어분석

†**mention**[ménʃən] n. ① U 기재(記載), 언급, 진술, 이름을 듦. / †**dwell**[dwel] vi. (p., pp. dwelt [-t], dwelled [-d, -t]) ① 『+전+명』 살다, 거주하다(live)(at; in; near; on; among). / †**succession** [səksé ʃən] n. ① U,C 연속; 연속물. [SYN.] ⇨ SERIES. / ⁑**free**[friː] a. (freer [fríː ər]; freest [fríː ist]) ① 자유로운; 속박 없는. ② 구애되지[얽매이지] 않는. / †**valor**, 【영국】 -lour [vǽlər] n. U 용기, 용맹. [관련어] valiant —a. / †**inheritance**[inhéritəns] n. ① U 〖법률〗 상속, 계승. / †**acquisition**[æ̀ kwəzíʃən] n. ① U 취득, 획득; 습득, 손에 넣은 물건;

🖊 동의어/반의어

succession n. chain[tʃein], order[ɔ́ː rdər], progression[prəgréʃən], sequence[síː kwəns], series[sí-əriː z]

inheritance n. bequest[bikwést], birthright[bɔ́ː rərài]장자 상속권, endowment[endáumənt], estate[isté it], heritage[héritidʒ], legacy[légəsi]

acquisition n. gain[gein], accumulation[əkjùː mjəléiʃən] appropriation[əpròupriéiʃən], procurement [proukjúər, prə-], asset[ǽset], belonging[bilɔ́(ː)ŋiŋ], possession[pəzéʃən], property[prápərti]
ant. loss[lɔ(ː)s]

Lastly, there are few parts of our dominions that have not been augmented by those of us here, who are still more or less in the vigor of life; while the mother country has been furnished by us with everything that can enable her to depend on her own resources whether for war or for peace. That part of our history which tells of the military achievements which gave us our several possessions, or of the ready valor with which either we or our fathers stemmed the tide of Hellenic or foreign aggression, is a theme too familiar to my hearers for me to dilate on, and I shall therefore pass it by.

🖋 본문해석

Lastly, there are few parts of our dominions that have not been augmented by those of us here(끝으로 이곳에 있는 ~우리에게 확고부동한 우리의 관할권 지역들이 있습니다), **who are still more or less in the vigor of life**(여전히 다소 정렬적인 삶을 살고 있는); **while the mother country has been furnished by us with everything that can enable her to depend on her own resources whether for war or for peace**(조국이 우리에 의해 전쟁 시든 평화 시든 자원에 의존할 수 있게 모든 것을 제공받는 동안). **That part of our history**(우리 역사의 그 부분은) **which tells of the military achievements which gave us our several possessions**(우리에게 여러 소유권을 가져다준 군사적 업적이나), **or of the ready valor with which either we or our fathers stemmed the tide of Hellenic or foreign aggression**(우리나 우리의 아버지들이 그리스나 외세의 침공의 여파를 준비된 용맹으로 저지했던 것을 기록하는), **is a theme too familiar to my hearers for me to dilate on**(여러분들에게 너무나 친숙하여 제가 부연 설명할 필요가 없는 주제이기에), **and I shall therefore pass it by**(그 이야기는 피하려 합니다).

🖋 문법분석

Lastly, there are A[few] parts of our dominions that have B[not] been augmented by those of us here[few와 not으로 부정에 부정이 됨, 강한 긍정으로 해석, 이곳에 있는 우리가 더 이상의 논쟁할 필요가 없는 우리 주권의 영토], who are still more or less[다소간] in the vigor of life; while[접속사, ~하는 동안] A[the mother country] has been furnished by us B[with everything][A는 B를 제공받다] that can enable her to depend on her own resources whether[접속사, ~이든 아니든] (it is) for war or for peace. That part of our history[주어] which tells of the military achievements which gave us our several possessions, or (which tells) of the ready valor with which[선행사는 the ready valor] either we or our fathers stemmed the tide of Hellenic or foreign aggression (with the ready valor), is[본동사] a theme A[too] familiar to my hearers for me B[to][부분부정, 너무 ~해서 ~할 수 없는] dilate on, and I shall[단순미래, ~할 것이다] therefore pass it by.

🖋 단어분석

† **dominion** [dəmínjən] n. ① U 지배[통치]권[력], 주권. ② U,C 지배, 통제(over); / ‡ **furnish** [fə́ːrniʃ] v. 공급하다, 제공하다, 주다, 비치하다, 갖추다, 설비하다. / ‡ **stem** v. (-mm-) ─vt. (반대 따위를) 저지하다, (흐름을) 막다; / **Hellenic** [helíːnik] n. U 그리스어족 / **dilate** [dailéit, di-] v. ─vi. 상세히 설명[부연]하다(on, upon). /

🖋 동의어/반의어

dominion n. authority[əθɔ́ːriti], jurisdiction[dʒùərisdíkʃən], supremacy[səpréməsi], domain[douméin], empire[émpaiər], kingdom[kíŋdəm], land[lænd]

※ 다음 글을 읽고 물음에 답하시오. [01~08]

Most of my predecessors in this place have commended Ⓐ**him** who made this speech part of the law, **telling** us that ①**it** is well that ②**it** should be delivered at the burial of those who fall in battle. For myself, I (1)**should have thought** that the worth which had displayed itself in deeds would be sufficiently rewarded by honors also shown by deeds; such as you now see in this funeral prepared at the people's cost. And I (2)**could have wished** that the reputations of many brave men were not to be imperiled in the mouth of a single individual, to stand or fall according as he spoke well or ill. For ③**it** is hard to speak properly upon a subject where ④**it** is even difficult to convince your hearers that you are speaking the truth. _____Ⓑ_____, the friend who is (3)**familiar with every fact of the story** may think that some point has not been set forth with that fullness which he wishes and knows it to deserve; on the other, he who is a stranger to the matter may be led by envy to suspect exaggeration if he hears (4)**anything above his own nature**. For men can endure to hear others praised only so long as they can severally persuade themselves of their own ability to equal the actions recounted: when this point is passed, (5)**envy comes in and with it incredulity**. _____Ⓒ_____, since our ancestors have stamped this custom with their approval/disapproval, ⑤**it** becomes my duty to obey the law and to try to satisfy your several wishes and opinions as best I may. I shall begin with our ancestors: it is both just and proper that they should have the honor of the first mention on an occasion like the present. They dwelt in the country without break in the success/succession from generation to generation, and handed it down free to the present time by their valor. And if our more close/remote ancestors deserve praise, much more do our own fathers, who added to their inheritance the empire which we now possess, and spared no pains to be able to leave their acquisitions to us of the present generation.

1. 위 글의 주제로 가장 적절한 것은?

① It's essential to take care of audiences who are not likely to believe what the addressor say about.

② It's the time we had to fight against the enemies who objects to our tradition.

③ It's the holy duty we should take arms up and go into battles.

④ It cannot too admire the dead in wars like our ancestors's heritage.

⑤ It's not easy to follow up the predecessors' inheritance.

2. 위 글에서 밑줄 친 Ⓐ가 가리키는 것은?

① who rules the nation
② who addresses in the national events
③ who is one of our predecessors
④ who is a warrior with valor in wars
⑤ who is one of audiences in funeral

3. 위 글에서 밑줄 친 ①~⑤ 중, 어법상 쓰임이 <u>다른</u> 것은?

①　　　②　　　③　　　④　　　⑤

4. 위 글에서 밑줄 친 (1)~(5)의 우리말 번역이 어색한 것은?

① (1) 생각했어야만 했다. 즉, 생각지 못함.
② (2) 소망했던 것 같다.
③ (3) 그 이야기의 진실을 알고 있는
④ (4) 자신에 대한 진심
⑤ (5) 질투가 불신으로 바뀜

5. 위 글에서 작가의 조상에 대한 태도는?

① challenge　　　② grievance
③ obedience　　　④ indifference
⑤ argumentation

6. 위 글에서 밑줄 친 빈칸 ⑧, ⓒ에 적절한 단어는?

① Therefore　　　Meanwhile
② On the one hand　However
③ Likewise　　　Nevertheless
④ For example　　As a result
⑤ Additionally　　As a matter of fact

7. 위 글에서 네모상자 안의 적절한 단어는?

① approval　　　success　　　close
② disapproval　　success　　　remote
③ approval　　　succession　　close
④ disapproval　　succession　　remote
⑤ approval　　　succession　　remote

8. 위 글과 일치하지 <u>않은</u> 것은?

① 국가를 위해 목숨을 바친 명예로 인해 충분히 보상을 받을 것입니다.
② 많은 용맹스런 사람들의 명성이 한 개인의 입을 통해 위험에 빠지지 않기를 바랍니다.
③ 열거되는 그 행위에 필적하는 그들 행위에 여러 번 설득당하는 동안 사람들은 감수할 수 있습니다.
④ 현재와 같은 추도식을 우선 명예로 언급해야 함이 옳고 적절하다 사료됩니다.
⑤ 현 우리 세대에 그들의 유산을 물려주시고자 고통을 감내하신 먼 조상님들에게 먼저 칭송하는 것이 도리일 것입니다

동영상 강좌 http://youtu.be/UVzkvjXAZUA

1. ④　2. ②　3. ② 지시대명사[this address] / 나머지는 가주어　4. ④
5. ③　6. ②　7. ⑤　8. ⑤

But what was the road by which we reached our position, what the form of government under which our greatness grew, what the national habits out of which it sprang; these are questions which I may try to solve before I proceed to my panegyric upon these men; since I think this to be a subject upon which on the present occasion a speaker may properly dwell, and to which the whole assemblage, whether citizens or foreigners, may listen with advantage.

📖 **본문해석**

But what was the road by which we reached our position(그러나 우리가 현재의 위치에 도달한 것은 무엇 때문입니까), **what the form of government under which our greatness grew**(우리의 위대함이 정부의 형태에서 발전하도록 한 것은 무엇이었나요), **what the national habits out of which it sprang**(그것이(정부가) 국가의 기질 밖으로 겉돌게 한 것은 무엇이었나요); **these are questions which I may try to solve before I proceed to my panegyric upon these men**(이런 것들이 제가 이분들에게 찬사를 하기 전 풀고자 하는 문제들입니다); **since I think this to be a subject upon which on the present occasion a speaker may properly dwell**(저는 이것이 현재의 상황 하에서 연설자가 적절히 숙고해야 할 주제라 생각하고), **and to which the whole assemblage, whether citizens or foreigners, may listen with advantage**(시민이든 외국인이든 이곳에 모인 전 군중들이 옳게 귀 기울여야 할 주제라 생각하기 때문입니다).

📖 **문법분석**

But what was the road by which[관계대명사의 선행사는 the road] we reached our position (by the road), what (was) the form of government under which[관계대명사의 선행사는 the form of government] our greatness grew (under the form of government), what (was) the national habits out of which[관계대명사의 선행사는 the national habits] it sprang (out of the national habits); these are questions which I may try to solve[목적어는 questions] before I proceed to[to를 수반하여, ~로 나아가다] my panegyric upon these men[조국을 위해 목숨을 바친 사람들]; since[=because] I think this to be a subject upon which[관계대명사의 선행사는 a subject] on the present occasion[현재의 상황 하에서] a speaker may properly dwell (upon a subject), and to which the whole assemblage, whether[접속사로 삽입절] citizens or foreigners[시민이든 외국인이든], may listen (to a subject) with advantage[with+명사=부사구, 편의상, 이점을 갖고].

📖 **단어분석**

spring [spriŋ]v. (sprang [spræŋ], sprung [sprʌŋ]; sprung) —vi. ① 『+부/+전+명』 튀다(leap), 도약하다, 뛰어넘다, 뛰어오르다(jump). [SYN.] ⇨ JUMP. / †proceed** [prousíː d] vi. ① 『~ / +전+명』 앞으로 나아가다, (~에) 이르다(to) [SYN.] ⇨ ADVANCE. / **panegyric** [pæ̀nədʒírik, -dʒái-] n. 찬사; 과장된[형식적인] 칭찬의 말(upon). / †**assemblage** [əsémblidʒ] n. 집단; 집합, 집회;

📖 **동의어/반의어**

advantage n. benefit[bénəfit], blessing[blésiŋ], boon[buː n], privilege[prívəlidʒ], allowance[əláuəns], edge[edʒ], handicap[hǽndikæ̀p], odds[ɑdz/ɔdz], gain[gein], interest[íntərist], profit [práfit]
ant. curse[kəː rs], disadvantage[dìsədvǽntidʒ]

Our constitution does not copy the laws of neighboring states; we are rather a pattern to others than imitators ourselves. Its administration favors the many instead of the few; this is why it is called a democracy. If we look to the laws, they afford equal justice to all in their private differences; if no social standing, advancement in public life falls to reputation for capacity, class considerations not being allowed to interfere with merit; nor again does poverty bar the way, if a man is able to serve the state, he is not hindered by the obscurity of his condition.

🖋 본문해석

Our constitution does not copy the laws of neighboring states(우리의 헌법은 이웃나라의 법을 모방하지 않습니다); **we are rather a pattern to others than imitators ourselves**(우리는 모방자가 아닌 오히려 다른 사람들에게 귀감이 됩니다). **Its administration favors the many instead of the few**(우리나라의 행정조직은 소수대신 다수를 선호합니다); **this is why it is called a democracy**(이것이 민주주의라 불리는 이유입니다). **If we look to the laws**(만일 우리가 법에 의지한다면), **they afford equal justice to all in their private differences**(법은 서로 다른 모두에게 동등한 정의를 제공합니다); **if no social standing**(만일 사회적 신분이 없다면), **advancement in public life falls to reputation for capacity**(국민들 사이에서 출세는 능력 있는 명성을 추구하여), **class considerations not being allowed to interfere with merit**(장점에 방해를 허락지 않는 계급의 중요성이 인식되게 됩니다); **nor again does poverty bar the way**(또한 다시금 가난이 그 길을 방해하지 않습니다), **if a man is able to serve the state**(만일 누군가가 국가에 봉사할 수 있다면), **he is not hindered by the obscurity of his condition**(그는 자신의 낮은 신분으로 인한 방해를 받지 않습니다).

🖋 문법분석

Our constitution does not copy the laws of neighboring states; we are rather a pattern to others[오히려 다른 사람에게 귀감이 됨] than imitators[모방자가 아닌] ourselves[우리 스스로]. Its administration favors the many instead of the few; this is why[~라는 결과] it is called a democracy. If we look to[의지하다] the laws, they afford[~할 여유가 있다] equal justice to all in their private differences [서로 다른 개인들]; if (there is) no social standing, advancement in public life falls to[시작하다] reputation for capacity[명성을 추구], class considerations[계급의 중요성] not being allowed to interfere with[방해하다] merit; nor again does[도치됨] poverty[or again poverty does not] bar[방해하다] the way, if a man is able to serve the state, he is not hindered by[~로 방해 받지 않다] the obscurity of his condition[자시의 낮은 신분].

🖋 단어분석

⊩ **constitution**[kὰnstətjú: ʃən / kɔ̀n-] n. ① U 구성(構成), 조성; 구조, 조직(of); 본질, 골자. ② U,C (국가의 구성으로서의) 정체; (국가 조직을 규정하는) 헌법. / **imitator**[ímitèitər] n. 모방자, 모조자. / ⊩ **pattern** [pǽtərn] n. ① 모범, 본보기, 귀감. / **administration**[ædmìnəstréiʃən, əd-] n. U 행정, 통치; 행정 [통치] 기간[임기]. / ⊩ **standing**[stǽndiŋ] n. C,U 입장, 지위, 신분; C,U 명성, 평판. / ⊩ **interfere**[ìntərfíər] vi. ① 『~ / +전+명』 간섭하다, 말참견하다(in). ② 『~ / +전+명』 훼방 놓다, 방해하다; 저촉하다;

해(害)치다(with). ③『～ / +전+명』(이해 따위가) 충돌[대립]하다(with). / ✝ **poverty**[pávərti] n. U ① 가난, 빈곤([opp.] wealth). ② 결핍, 부족(of; in). ③ 열등, 빈약. / ✝ **hinder**[híndər] v. —vt.『～+목 / +목+전+명』① 방해하다, 훼방하다(in). ② ～의 방해를 하다; 지체케 하다, 늦게 하다. / ✝ **obscurity** [əbskjúərəti] n. U,C ① 어두컴컴함; 어둑한 곳. ② 불명료; 모호한 점, 난해한 곳. ③ 세상에 알려지지 않음; 무명(인); 낮은 신분; 궁벽한 땅. /

🖉 **동의어/반의어**

interfere v. butt[bʌt] in, disrupt[disrʌ́pt], intervene[intərvíː n], intrude[intrúː d], meddle[médl, hinder[híndər], impede[impíː d], interrupt[intərʌ́p], obstruct[əbstrʌ́kt]
ant. aid[eid]

The freedom which we enjoy in our government extends also to our ordinary life. There, far from exercising a jealous surveillance over each other, we do not feel called upon to be angry with our neighbor for doing what he likes, or even to indulge in those injurious looks which cannot fail to be offensive, although they inflict no positive penalty. But all this ease in our private relations does not make us lawless as citizens. Against this fear is our chief safeguard, teaching us to obey the magistrates and the laws, particularly such as regard the protection of the injured, whether they are actually on the statute book, or belong to that code which, although unwritten, yet cannot be broken without acknowledged disgrace.

🖉 **본문해석**

The freedom which we enjoy in our government extends also to our ordinary life(우리 정부에서 우리가 누리고 있는 자유는 일상적인 생활에까지 또한 미칩니다). **There, far from exercising a jealous surveillance over each other**(서로에 대한 질투어린 감시에 개의치 않고) **we do not feel called upon**(그의 방문에 겁먹을 필요도 없습니다) **to be angry with our neighbor for doing what he likes**(우리는 그가 좋아하는 것을 한다고 이웃에게 화를 내서), **or even to indulge in those injurious looks which cannot fail to be offensive**(또는 심지어 불쾌한 그런 해가 되는 모습을 보인다고), **although they inflict no positive penalty**(비록 그들이 실제적인 처벌을 가하지 않더라도). **But all this ease in our private relations does not make us lawless as citizens**(그러나 우리의 개인 관계에서 모든 이 여유는 시민으로서 우리가 법이 필요 없는 것은 아닙니다). **Against this fear is our chief safeguard, teaching us to obey the magistrates and the laws**(우리의 주요한 안전장치는 이런 두려움에 반해 우리에게 법을 준수하는 것을 가르치고 있습니다), **particularly such as regard the protection of the injured**(특히 이를테면 약자를 보호하는 것입니다), **whether they are actually on the statute book**(법이 실제로 성문법으로 존재하든), **or belong to that code which, although unwritten, yet cannot be broken without acknowledged disgrace**(또는 비록 성문화되어있진 않지만, 인식된 불명예 없인 파기될 수 없는 법규에 속하든지).

🖉 **문법분석**

The freedom which we enjoy[목적어는 the freedom] in our government extends also to[～까지 미치

다] our ordinary life. There, far from[=without] exercising a jealous surveillance over each other, we do not feel called upon[방문을 받은 느낌을 가질 필요가 없다] to be angry[to부정사의 원인, ～화를 낸다 해서] with our neighbor for doing what he likes, or even to indulge in[to부정사의 원인, ～즐긴다 해서] those injurious looks which <u>cannot fail to</u>[=can] be offensive, although they inflict no positive penalty. But all this ease in our private relations does not make us lawless[법을 지킬 필요가 없다] as citizens. Against this fear[전치사구] is[동사] our chief safeguard[주어], teaching[동사] us to obey the magistrates and the laws, particularly such as[특히 이를테면] (and teaching us to) regard the protection of the injured, whether[접속사, ～인지 아닌지] they are actually on the statute book [성문법이든], or belong to that code which, although unwritten[성문법이 아닐지라도], yet <u>cannot be broken</u>[=keep] <u>without acknowledged disgrace</u>[법의 파기가 인정된 경우를 제외하고].

🖰 단어분석

‡ **extend**[iksténd] v. —vt. (영토 등을) 확장하다, 확대하다; (세력 따위를) 펴다, 미치다; / ‡ **jealous**[dʒéləs] a. ① 질투심이 많은, 투기가 강한(of). ② 시샘하는, 선망하는(envious)(of). / **surveillance**[sərvéiləns, -ljəns] n. U 감시; 감독. / † **injurious**[indʒúəriəs] a. ① 해가 되는, 유해한(to). ② 불법의, 부정한. / ‡ **offensive**[əfénsiv] a. ① 불쾌한, 싫은; 마음에 걸리는. ② 무례한, 화가 나는; 모욕적인. / ‡ **indulge**[indʌ́ldʒ] —vi. ① 『+전+명』 (취미·욕망 따위에) 빠지다, 탐닉하다(in); 즐기다, 마음껏 누리다(in). / ‡ **inflict**[inflíkt] vt. ～+목 / +목+전+명』 ① (타격·상처·고통 따위를) 주다, 입히다, 가하다(on). ② (형벌 따위를) 과하다(on). / ‡ **penalty**[pénəlti] n. ① U,C 형, 형벌, 처벌. ② 벌금, 과료(科料), 위약금. ③ 벌, 인과 응보, 천벌, 재앙. / ‡ **ease**[iːz] n. U ① 안락, 편안; 경제적으로 걱정이 없음; 여유. ② 평정(平靜), 안심. ③ 한가, 태평. ④ 홀가분함, 쇄락(灑落). / † **safeguard**[séifgàːrd] n. ① U 보호, 호위; C 보호물, 안전 장치; 보장 조항[규약]; U,C (유혹 따위의) 방위(수단)(against). / ‡ **obey**[oubéi] v. —vt. ～에 복종하다, ～에 따르다; ～의 명령[가르침, 소원]에 따르다 / ‡ **magistrate**[mǽdʒəstrèit, -trit] n. ① (사법권을 가진) 행정 장관, 지사, 시장. ② 치안 판사 / † **statute**[stǽtʃuːtn]. 법령, 성문법, 법규; 정관(定款), 규칙 (of). [SYN.] ⇨ LAW. / ‡ **acknowledge**[æknálidʒ, ik- / -nɔ́l-] vt. ①『～+목 / +목+as 보 / +목+ to be 보 / + that 절 / +-ing / +목+done』 인정하다, 승인하다, 용인하다, 자인(自認)하다, 고백하다. / ‡ **disgrace**[disgréis] n. ① U 창피, 불명예, 치욕; C 망신거리. [cf.] dishonor, shame. ② U 눈밖에 남; 인기 없음.

🖰 동의어/반의어

injurious a. damaging[dǽmidʒiŋ], deleterious[dèlətíəriəs], destructive[distrʌ́ktiv], detrimental[dètrəméntl], harmful[háːrmfəl, defamatory[difǽmətɔ̀ːri], denigrating[dénigrèitiŋ], slanderous[slǽnd-ərəs / sláːn-

동영상 강좌 http://youtu.be/M12WLV9SCQE

✱ 다음 글을 읽고 물음에 답하시오. [9~15]

 Lastly, there are few parts of our dominions that have not been augmented by those of us here, who are still more or less in the vigor of life; while the mother country has been furnished by us with everything that can enable her to depend on her own resources whether for war or for peace. That part of our history which tells of the military achievements which gave us our several possessions, or of the ready valor with which either we or our fathers stemmed the tide of Hellenic or foreign aggression, is a theme too familiar to my hearers for me to dilate on, and I shall therefore pass Ⓐit by. But what was the road by which we reached our position, what the form of government under which our greatness grew, what the national habits out of which it sprang; these are questions which I may try to solve before I proceed to my panegyric upon Ⓑthese men; since I think this to be a subject upon which on the present occasion a speaker may properly dwell, and in which/to which the whole assemblage, whether citizens or foreigners, may listen with advantage.

Our constitution does not copy the laws of neighboring states; we are rather a pattern to others than imitators ourselves. Its administration favors the many instead of the few; this is because/why it is called a democracy. If we look to the laws, they afford equal justice to all in their private differences; _____, advancement in public life falls to reputation for capacity, class considerations not being allowed to interfere/interfere with merit; nor again does poverty bar the way, if a man is able to serve the state, he is not hindered by the obscurity of his condition. The freedom which we enjoy in our government extends also to our ① **ordinary** life. There, far from exercising a ②**jealous** surveillance over each other, we do not feel called upon to be angry with our neighbor for doing what he likes, or even to indulge in those ③**injurious** looks which cannot fail to be ④**lenient**, although they inflict no ⑤**positive** penalty. But all this ease in our private relations does not make us lawless as citizens. Against this fear is our chief safeguard, teaching us to obey the magistrates and the laws, particularly such as regard the protection of the injured, whether they are actually on the statute book, or belong to that code which, although unwritten, yet cannot be broken without acknowledged disgrace.

9. 위 글의 제목으로 가장 적절한 것은?

① The ways of keeping our national dominion
② Why must Law exist?
③ How much should we give the heros our tribute?
④ Class isn't needed on the present.
⑤ Rigid government is needed for the stronger nation.

10. 위 글에서 밑줄 친 Ⓐ가 가리키는 것은?

① part of our history
② the ready valor

③ the road

④ war

⑤ our position

② because there are many wars

③ if no social standing

④ if there are many chances to make business

⑤ if the country expands its sovereignty

11. 글에서 밑줄 친 ⑧가 가리키는 것은?

① who must have national respect

② who are gathered here

③ who keep the law well

④ who are addressing the audiences

⑤ who are leaders in the government

14. 위 글에서 밑줄 친 ①~⑤ 중, 문맥상 단어의 쓰임이 <u>어색한</u> 것은?

①   ②   ③   ④   ⑤

15. 위 글과 일치하지 <u>않은</u> 것은?

① 작가는 몇 가지 문제를 먼저 해결하고 다음 단계로 넘어가려한다.

② 우리의 법은 다른 나라 것을 모방하여 이젠 다른 나라의 귀감이 되고 있다.

③ 국민들 사이에 사회적 신분이 없다면, 국민들은 명성을 얻기 위해 더 많은 노력을 기울일 것이다.

④ 지금 우리가 누리고 있는 자유는 일상생활에까지 영향을 끼친다.

⑤ 법은 반드시 필요하다.

12. 위 글에서 네모상자 안의 적절한 단어는?

① in which   because   interfere

② in which   why   interfere

③ to which   because   interfere with

④ to which   why   interfere with

⑤ to which   because   interfere with

13. 위 글에서 밑줄 친 빈칸에 적절한 표현은?

① though the public life is rich

9. ②   10. ①   11. ①   12. ④   13. ③

14. ④ lenient → offensive   15. ②

Further, we provide plenty of means for the mind to refresh itself from business. We celebrate games and sacrifices all the year round, and the elegance of our private establishments forms a daily source of pleasure and helps to banish the spleen; while the magnitude of our city draws the produce of the world into our harbour, so that to the Athenian the fruits of other countries are as familiar a luxury as those of his own.

🔖 본문해석

Further, we provide plenty of means for the mind to refresh itself from business(더욱이, 우리는 국민들에게 일상으로부터 지친 마음에 활력을 돌아주는 많은 방식을 제공하고 있습니다). **We celebrate games and sacrifices all the year round**(우리는 1년 내내 경기대회와 제물의식을 거행합니다), **and the elegance of our private establishments forms a daily source of pleasure and helps to banish the spleen**(그리고 우리의 사설기관의 기품은 일상의 기쁨의 근원을 형성하며 우울한 마음을 쫓아내는 데 도움을 줍니다); **while the magnitude of our city draws the produce of the world into our harbour**(우리 도시의 웅장함은 전 세계의 농산물이 우리 항구로 유입되게 합니다), **so that to the Athenian the fruits of other countries are as familiar a luxury as those of his own**(그리하여 아테네 시민에 이르기까지 다른 나라들의 과일은 그의 과일처럼 익숙한 고급품입니다).

🔖 문법분석

Further[부사로 문장 전체 수식, 그 위에, 게다가], we provide plenty of means[많은 수단] for the mind[국민들] to refresh itself[=the mind] from business[장사로 지친 마음에 활력을 주다]. We celebrate[행하다] games[경기] and sacrifices[의식] all the year round[년 중], and the elegance of our private establishments[사설기관] forms[=make, create] a daily source of pleasure and helps to banish the spleen; while[접속사, ~하는 동안] the magnitude of our city draws[유입시키다] the produce[농산물] of the world into our harbour[항구 안으로], so that[접속사로 결과, 그리하여] to the Athenian[아테네 사람들에게 까지] the fruits of other countries are as familiar a luxury as those[=fruits] of his own[as+형용사+단수명사+as: ~만큼 …한]

🔖 단어분석

game: (pl.) (특히 고대 그리스·로마의) 경기회, 경연회, 투기회 / ⨪ **celebrate** [sélǝbrèit] v. —vt. ① 『~+목/ +목+전+명』 (식을 올려) 경축하다; (의식·제전을) 거행하다. ②『+목+전+명』 (용사·훈공 따위를) 찬양하다(praise), 기리다. / ⨪ **elegance**, —**gancy**[éligǝns], [-i] n. (pl. -gances; -cies) ① U 우아, 고상, 기품. ② U 정확[적확]함, 간결함. / ⨪ **establishment**[istǽbliʃmǝnt] n. ① U 설립, 창립; 설치. ② C (사회) 시설(학교·병원·상점·회사·여관 따위), (공공 또는 사설의) 시설물. / ⨪ **banish**[bǽniʃ] vt. 『~+목/ +목+전+명』 ① 추방하다, 유형에 처하다; 내쫓다. ② (아무를) 멀리하다; (근심 따위를) 떨어버리다. / **spleen**[spli ː n] n.① 『해부학』 비장(脾臟), 지라. ② U 울화, 기분이 언짢음; 심술, 악의(malice); 원한(grudge), 유한; U (고어) 우울(melancholy), 낙담(dejection). / ⨪ **magnitude**[mǽgnǝtjùː d] n. U ① (길이·규모·수량) 크기, 양. ② 중대(성), 중요함; 위대함, 고결. / ⨪ **harbor**, 【영국】-bour [háː rbǝr] n. ① 항구, 배가 닿는 곳. ★harbor는 주로 항구의 수면을, port는 도시를 중요시한 구별. ② 피난처, 잠복처, 은신처. / ⨪ **Athenian**[ǝθíː niǝn] a., n. 아테네의, 아테네 사람. / ⨪ **luxury**[lʌ́kʃǝri] n. U ① 사치, 호사. ② C (종

종 pl.) 사치품, 고급품.

🔖 **동의어/반의어**

elegance n. beauty[bjúːti], dignity[dígnəti], grace[greis], grandeur[grǽndʒər], polish[páliʃ], refinement[rifáinmənt] ant. vulgarity[vʌlgǽrəti] 야비, 무례한 언동

banish v. deport[dipɔ́ːrt], eject[idʒékt], evictevict [ivíkt], exile[égzail], expatriate[ekspéitrièt] 국외로 추방하다, expel[ikspél] ant. welcome[wélkəm]

If we turn to our military policy, there also we differ from our antagonists. We throw open our city to the world, and never by alien acts exclude foreigners from any opportunity of learning or observing, although the eyes of an enemy may occasionally profit by our liberality; trusting less in system and policy than to the native spirit of our citizens; while in education, where our rivals from their very cradles by a painful discipline seek after manliness, at Athens we live exactly as we please, and yet are just as ready to encounter every legitimate danger. In proof of this it may be noticed that the Lacedaemonians do not invade our country alone, but bring with them all their confederates; while we Athenians advance unsupported into the territory of a neighbor, and fighting upon a foreign soil usually vanquish with ease men who are defending their homes.

🔖 **본문해석**

If we turn to our military policy(만일 우리군 정책으로 눈을 돌려본다면), **there also we differ from our antagonists**(우리는 적들과 또한 다릅니다). **We throw open our city to the world**(우리는 전 세계로 문을 활짝 열어 놓고 있습니다), **and never by alien acts exclude foreigners from any opportunity of learning or observing**(이질적 행위로 인한 외국인들이 배우고 관찰할 기회를 배제하지 않습니다), **although the eyes of an enemy may occasionally profit by our liberality**(비록 적들의 눈엔 우리의 관대함이 때때로 이득으로 보일 수도 있습니다); **trusting less in system and policy than to the native spirit of our citizens**(체제와 정책에서 보다 우리 국민들의 타고난 정신력을 더 믿고 있기 때문입니다); **while in education, where our rivals from their very cradles by a painful discipline seek after manliness**(교육에서도 우리의 적대국들은 요람에서부터 고통적인 원칙에 의해 용맹성을 추구하는 반면), **at Athens we live exactly as we please**(아테네에서 우린 원하는 대로 살고 있습니다), **and yet are just as ready to encounter every legitimate danger**(그리고 이제 모든 정당한 위험에 받아들일 준비가 되어 있습니다). **In proof of this**(이 증거로) **it may be noticed**(~알려져 있습니다) **that the Lacedaemonians do not invade our country alone**(스파르타는 단독으로 우리나라를 침공하지 못하고), **but bring with them all their confederates**(모든 연합군을 모아야만 합니다); **while we Athenians advance unsupported into the territory of a neighbor**(반면 우리 아테네인들은 지원 없이 이웃영토로 진군합니다), **and fighting upon a foreign soil usually vanquish with ease men who are defending their homes**(외국 영토에의 전투는 자신의 고향을 지키고자 하는 적군을 쉽게 추방시킵니다).

If we turn to[~방향을 돌리다] our military policy, there also we differ from[~와 다른] our antagonists[적군]. We throw open our city to the world, and never by alien acts exclude foreigners from[exclude A from B: A를 B로부터 배제하다] any opportunity of learning or observing, although [양보절, 비록 ~일지라도] the eyes of an enemy may occasionally profit by our liberality; trusting less in system and policy than to the native spirit of our citizens[trusting to ~더 신임하고 있는]; while in education, where our rivals from their very cradles by a painful discipline seek after[추구 하다] manliness, at Athens we live exactly as we please[우리가 원하는 대로], and yet are just as ready to[기꺼이 ~할 준비가 된] encounter every legitimate danger. In proof of this it may be noticed that the Lacedaemonians do not invade our country alone, but bring with them[=Lacedaemonians, 스파르타인] all their confederates; while[접속사, ~하는 동안] we Athenians advance unsupported into the territory of a neighbor, and fighting upon a foreign soil usually vanquish with ease[부사구=easily] men who are defending their homes.

📝 단어분석

† **antagonist**[æntǽgənist] n. ① 적수, 적대자, 반대자. [SYN.] ⇨ OPPONENT. / **throw open** (1) (문 따위를) 열어 젖히다. (2) 공개하다, 개방하다(to). / † **alien**[éiljən, -liən] a. ① 외국의, 이국(異國)의 (foreign); 외국인의. ② 성질이 다른, 이질의(from). / ‡ **exclude** [iksklúːd] vt. ① 『~+목/ +목+전+명 』 못 들어오게 하다, 배척하다, 제외[배제]하다([opp] include); 몰아내다, 추방하다; (특히 출산이나 부화 때에) 방출하다; 빼다(omit)(from). ② 고려하지 않다, 무시하다; (증거 따위를) 받아들이지 않다, / **liberality**[lìbərǽləti] n. U 너그러움, 관대 / **manliness** ─n. U 남성적임, 용감, 과단. / ‡ **encounter**[enkáuntər] v. ─vt. ① ~와 우연히 만나다, 마주치다, 조우하다. ② (적과) 교전하다, ~와 맞서다, ~에 대항 하다. ③ (곤란·반대·위험 등에) 부닥치다. / † **legitimate**[lidʒítəmit] a. ① 합법의, 적법의; 옳은, 정당한. [opp.] illegitimate. [SYN.] ⇨ LAWFUL. ② 본격적인, 정통의, 정계(正系)의; 적출의. / † **confederate**[kənfédərit] n. ① 동맹자, 연합자; 동맹국, 연합국. / † **vanquish**[vǽŋkwiʃ, vǽn-] vt. ~에게 이기다, 정복하다; (감정 등을) 극복하다.

📝 동의어/반의어

exclude v. ban[bæn], bar[baːr], blackball[blǽk-bɔ̀ːl], boycott[bɔ́ikat], ostracize[ástrəsàiz]국외로 추 방하다, prohibit[prouhíbit], eliminate[ilímənèit], except[iksépt], omit[oumít] ant. admit[ædmít] include[inklúːd]

legitimate a. authentic[ɔːθéntik], genuine[dʒénjuin], verifiable[vérəfàiəbəl], logical[ládʒikəl], reasonable[ríːz-ənəb-əl], sound[saund], correct[kərékt], tenable[ténəb-əl], appropriate[əpróuprièit], proper[prápər], lawful[lɔ́ːfəl], legal[líg-əl], licensed[láis-ənst], rightful[ráitfəl] ant. fraudulent[frɔ́ː dʒulənt], irrational[irǽʃənəl], unsuitable[ʌnsúːtəbəl] illicit[illísit]

Our united force was never yet encountered by any enemy, because we have at once to attend to our marine and to dispatch our citizens by land upon a hundred different services; so that, wherever they engage with some such fraction of our strength, a success against a detachment is

magnified into a victory over the nation, and a defeat into a reverse suffered at the hands of our entire people. And yet if with habits not of labor but of ease, and courage not of art but of nature, we are still willing to encounter danger, we have the double advantage of escaping the experience of hardships in anticipation and of facing them in the hour of need as fearlessly as those who are never free from them.

📖 본문해석

Our united force was never yet encountered by any enemy(우리의 연합군은 아직까지 한 번도 어떠한 적과 마주친 적이 없었습니다), **because we have at once to attend to our marine and to dispatch our citizens by land upon a hundred different services**(이것이 우리가 즉시 해군력에 집중해야만 하고 우리 시민들을 육로로 많은 다른 임무지역으로 파견해야 하는 이유입니다); **so that, wherever they engage with some such fraction of our strength**(다른 방어지역이 우리 군의 파견대와 연동을 할 땐 언제나), **a success against a detachment is magnified into a victory over the nation**(파견에 대비된 성공은 조국에 대한 승리를 확실하게 합니다), **and a defeat into a reverse suffered at the hands of our entire people**(그리고 반대쪽 진영은 우리 전 국민의 통제 하에 받는 패배는 배가됩니다.). **And yet**(그럼에도 불구하고) **if with habits not of labor but of ease, and courage not of art but of nature**(만일 힘들이지 않는 여유로운 기질과 인위적인 아닌 타고난 용기로), **we are still willing to encounter danger**(우리가 여전히 기꺼이 위험에 대적할 수 있다면), **we have the double advantage of escaping the experience of hardships in anticipation**(우리는 예상된 힘든 경험을 피하고) **and of facing them in the hour of need as fearlessly as those who are never free from them**(죽기 살기의 사람들처럼 용맹하게 필요한 시간 안에 그들과 대적할 갑절의 이점을 갖게 됩니다).

📖 문법분석

Our united force <u>was never yet encountered</u>[경험, 아직 대적한 경험이 없다] by any enemy, because we have <u>at once</u>[즉시] to <u>attend to</u>[주의를 기울이다] our marine and to dispatch our citizens <u>by land</u>[육로로] <u>upon a hundred different services</u>[많은 다른 방어지역들로]; so that[접속사, 그리하여], wherever[복합 관계부사, 언제든지] they[=a hundred different services] <u>engage with</u>[연동작전을 펴다] some such fraction of our strength[몇몇 파견대], a <u>success against a detachment</u>[파견으로 인한 성공] is magnified into a victory over the nation[승리로 우뚝 서다], and a defeat (is magnified) into a reverse suffered at the hands of our entire people. And yet if with habits not <u>of labor</u>[of+명사=형용사구] but <u>of ease</u>[=easy], and courage not <u>of art</u>[=artful] but <u>of nature</u>[=natural], we are still willing to encounter danger, we have the double advantage[두 배의 이점] of escaping the experience of hardships in anticipation[선제공격] and of facing them[=hardships] in the hour of need as fearlessly as[~처럼 …한] those who are never free from them[=hardships][죽기 살기로 용맹한].

📖 단어분석

⚟ **dispatch, des**—[dispǽtʃ] v. —vt. ① (편지·사자 등을) 급송하다; 급파[특파]하다; 파병하다. ② (일 따위를) 급히 해치우다. / ⚟ **fraction**[frǽkʃ-ən] n. ① 파편, 단편. / ⚟ **magnify**[mǽgnəfài] v. —vt. ① (렌즈 따위로) 확대하다; 크게 보이게 하다. ② 과장하다. / ⚟ **hardship**[hάː rdʃip] n. ① (종종 pl.) 고난, 고초, 신고, 곤란, 곤궁. [SYN.] ⇨ SUFFERING. ② 곤경; 어려운 일. / ⚟ **anticipation**[æntisəpéiʃən] n. U,C ① 예기, 예감, 예상, 내다봄, 기대. ② 선제 행동, 선수; 예방. /

동영상 강좌 http://youtu.be/OIDxJNS60yE

Nor are these the only points in which our city is worthy of admiration. We cultivate refinement without extravagance and knowledge without effeminacy; wealth we employ more for use than for show, and place the real disgrace of poverty not in owning to the fact but in declining the struggle against it. Our public men have, besides politics, their private affairs to attend to, and our ordinary citizens, though occupied with the pursuits of industry, are still fair judges of public matters; for, unlike any other nation, regarding him who takes no part in these duties not as unambitious but as useless, we Athenians are able to judge at all events if we cannot originate, and, instead of looking on discussion as a stumbling-block in the way of action, we think it an indispensable preliminary to any wise action at all.

본문해석

Nor are these the only points in which our city is worthy of admiration(또한 우리 도시가 칭찬할 가치는 이것만이 아닙니다). **We cultivate refinement without extravagance and knowledge without effeminacy**(우리는 사치 없는 세련미와 나약하지 않은 지식을 발전시켜 왔습니다); **wealth we employ more for use than for show**(우리는 보여주기 위한 것이 아닌 이용하기 위해 더 많은 부를 사용하고 있습니다), **and place the real disgrace of poverty not in owning to the fact but in declining the struggle against it**(그리고 우리는 빈곤의 사실을 인정할 때가 아닌 빈곤에 대항하는 투지가 감소할 때 빈곤의 진정한 불명예의 본질을 밝힙니다). **Our public men have, besides politics, their private affairs to attend to**(우리 국민들은 정치 이외에 보살펴야 할 사생활이 있고), **and our ordinary citizens, though occupied with the pursuits of industry, are still fair judges of public matters**(우리 평범한 시민들은 비록 산업발달에 몰입할지라도 대중적인 문제에 대해 여전히 공정한 판단을 내리시는 분들입니다); **for, unlike any other nation, regarding him who takes no part in these duties not as unambitious but as useless**(이러한 의무에 참여하지 않는 사람을 야망적이 아닌 무용지물로 간주할 때, 다른 나라 국민들과 달리), **we Athenians are able to judge at all events if we cannot originate**(만일 우리가 창작할 수 없을지라도, 우리 아테네 사람들은 모든 일에 판단할 능력을 갖추고 있습니다), **and, instead of looking on discussion as a stumbling-block in the way of action**(그리고 행동으로 옮기는 와중에 장애물을 방관하기보다), **we think it an indispensable preliminary to any wise action at all**(우리는 모든 일에 그것(장애물)을 어떤 현명한 행동에 대한 필수적인 준비단계라 생각합니다).

"Funeral Oration(추도사)"

by Pericles 페리클레스(아테네 정치가 BC 431)

📖 문법분석

Nor are these[도치문=Or these are not] the only points in which our city is worthy of[~에 가치 있는] admiration (in the only point). We cultivate[=grow, develop] refinement without extravagance[사치 없는 품위] and knowledge without effeminacy[나태 없는 지식] wealth we employ[목적어는 wealth] more for use than for show[전시보다는 실용적인], and place[=judge 판단하다] the real disgrace of poverty not in owning to[인정하다] the fact[가난하다는 사실] but in declining the struggle against it[=the fact]. Our public men have, besides[=in addition to, along with 더불어] politics, their private affairs to attend to[주의를 기울이다], and our ordinary citizens, though (they are) occupied with[몰두하다] the pursuits of industry, are still fair judges of public matters; for, unlike any other nation, (as we are) regarding[regard A as B: A를 B로 간주하다] him who takes no part in these duties not as unambitious but as useless, we Athenians are able to judge at all events[모든 업무에서] if[=though] we cannot originate, and, instead of looking on[방관하다] discussion as a stumbling-block in the way of action[일이 진행되는 도중에, 실행에 옮기는], we think A[it] B[an indispensable preliminary] to any wise action at all.[think A B: A를 B로 생각하다]

📖 단어분석

‡ **worthy** [wɔ́ːrði] a. (-thier; -thiest) ① 훌륭한, 존경할 만한, 가치 있는 / ‡ **admiration** [æ̀dməréiʃən] n. U ① 감탄, 칭찬(of; for); 찬탄 / ‡ **cultivate** [kʌ́ltəvèit] vt. ① (땅을) 갈다, 경작하다; (재배 중인 작물·밭을) 사이갈이하다. [SYN.] ⇨ TILL. ② 재배하다; (물고기·진주 등을) 양식하다; (세균을) 배양하다. [SYN.] ⇨ GROW. ③ (재능·정신 따위를) 신장하다, 계발[연마]하다 / ‡ **refinement** [rifáinmənt] n. U ① 정련, 정제, 순화. ② 세련, 고상, 우아, 품위 있음. ③ 정밀, 정교; 극치. / **extravagance, —cy** [ikstrǽvəgəns], [-i] n. ① U 사치, 무절제, 방종. ② C 낭비, 방종한 언행 / **effeminacy** [ifémənəsi] n. U 여성적임, 나약, 유약, 기력이 없음, 우유부단. / ‡ **disgrace** [disgréis] n. ① U 창피, 불명예, 치욕 / own —vi. 『+전+명』 인정하다, (~을) 자백하다(to). / **unambitious** [ʌ̀næmbíʃəs] a. 공영심이 없는, 야심이 없는; 눈에 띄지 않는, 수수한. / ‡ **originate** [ərídʒənèit] v. —vt. ① 시작하다, 근원이 되다, 일으키다. / **look on**: ~방관하다 / **stúmbling blòck** 방해물, 장애물. / ‡ **indispensable** [ìndispénsəbəl] a. ① 불가결의, 없어서는 안 될, 절대 필요한, 긴요한(to; for) / ‡ **preliminary** [prilímənèri / -nəri] a. ① 예비의, 준비의; 임시의; 시초의. ② 서문의. /

📖 동의어/반의어

admiration n. esteem[istíːm], regard[rigáːrd], respect[rispékt], adoration[æ̀dəréiʃən], praise[preiz], reverence[révərəns], veneration[vènəréiʃən], amazement[əméizmənt], awe[ɔː], wonder[wʌ́ndəːr] ant. contempt[kəntémpt] disdain[disdéin]

🎬 동영상 강좌 http://youtu.be/bZmTpUt6x5s

Again, in our enterprises we present the singular spectacle of daring and deliberation, each carried to its highest point, and both united in the same persons; although usually decision is the fruit of ignorance, those, who best know the difference between hardship and pleasure and yet are never tempted to shrink from danger. In generosity we are equally singular, acquiring our friends by conferring, not by receiving, favours. Yet, of course, the doer of the favo is the firmer friend of the two, in order by continued kindness to keep the recipient in his debt; while the debtor feels less keenly from the very consciousness that the return he makes will be a payment, not a free gift. And it is only the Athenians, who, fearless of consequences, confer their benefits not from calculations of expediency, but in the confidence of liberality.

📝 본문해석

Again, in our enterprises we present the singular spectacle of daring and deliberation(다시 말씀드리자면, 우리의 계획에서 우리는 용맹과 숙고의 유일한 장관을 제시합니다), **each carried to its highest point**(각각은 정점으로 향해 이동합니다), **and both united in the same persons**(그리고 이 둘은 같은 개인 안에서 융합됩니다); **although usually decision is the fruit of ignorance**(비록 평상시의 결단이 무지의 소산일지라도), **those, who best know the difference between hardship and pleasure and yet are never tempted to shrink from danger**(이분들은 고난과 기쁨의 차이점을 가장 잘 아시고 위험으로부터 움츠리는 유혹을 결코 받지 않습니다). **In generosity we are equally singular, acquiring our friends by conferring, not by receiving, favors**(일반적으로 말하자면, 우리는 호의를 받는 것이 아닌 베푸는 것으로 친구를 얻는 동등한 유일물입니다). **Yet, of course, the doer of the favor is the firmer friend of the two**(그러나, 물론, 호의를 베푸는 자는 둘 중에 더 강인한 친구입니다), **in order by continued kindness to keep the recipient in his debt**(계속된 친절로 그 수혜자를 자신의 은혜 속에 유지시키기 위해서); **while the debtor feels less keen from the very consciousness that the return he makes will be a payment, not a free gift**(반면 수혜자는 자신의 보답이 공짜선물이 아닌 보상이 될 것이라는 바로 그 의식으로부터 덜 민감하게 됩니다). **And it is only the Athenians, who, fearless of consequences, confer their benefits not from calculations of expediency, but in the confidence of liberality**(결과에 연연하지 않고 사리추구의 속셈이 아닌 관대한 자신감에서 자신들의 은혜를 베푸는 사람은 다름 아닌 바로 아테네 국민들입니다).

📝 문법분석

Again[강조하여 말하자면], in our enterprises[국가적 계획] we present[제시하다] the singular spectacle of daring and deliberation, each[=daring or deliberation] (is가 생략) carried to its highest point[최 정점으로 향하는], and both[=daring or deliberation] (are) united in the same persons; [양보절]although usually decision is the fruit of ignorance[무지의 산물(소산)], (it is)[강조용법으로 봄] those[바로 그 사람들(아테네 국민들) 입니다], who best know the difference between hardship and pleasure and yet are never tempted to shrink from danger. In generosity[=Generally speaking] we are equally singular, (who is[관계대명사+동사 생략]) acquiring our friends by conferring, not by receiving, favours. Yet, of course, the doer of the favor is the firmer friend of the two, in order by continued kindness to[~하기 위해서] keep[keep A in B: A를 B 안에 유지시키다] the recipient in his debt; while[접속사, 반면] the debtor feels less keen[feel+형용사: 덜 민감해지다] from the very consciousness that the return (that) he makes[목적어는 return: 그가 베푼 답례] will be a payment, not a free gift. And [강조용법: ~한 것은 바로 아테네 국민이다] it is only the Athenians, who, fearless of consequences[결과에 두려워하지 않고, 결과에 연연하지 않고], confer their benefits[자신의

"Funeral Oration(추도사)"

by Pericles 페리클레스(아테네 정치가 BC 431)

은덕을 베풀다] not from calculations of expediency[사욕이 아닌], but in the confidence of liberality [관대한 자신감에서].

🔖 단어분석

‡ enterprise [éntərprəiz] n. ① 기획, 계획(특히 모험적인). ② U,C 기업(체), 사업; 기업경영. ③ U 진취적인 정신, 기업심[열]; 모험심. / singular [síŋgjələ：r] a. ① 유일한[의], 단독의, 독자의. ② 개개의, 따로따로의(separate), 각자의(individual). ③ 보통이 아닌, 뛰어난, 비범한(unusual). / ‡ spectacle [spéktək-əl]n. 광경, 미관, 장관, 기관(奇觀); 비참한 광경. / ‡ daring [déəriŋ] n. U 대담 무쌍, 호담(豪膽). a 대담한, 용감한; 앞뒤를 가리지 않는. / † deliberation [dilibəréiʃən] n. U 숙고; 신중, 침착. / ‡ tempt [tempt]vt. ① ～의 마음을 끌다, 유혹하다, 부추기다. ②『+목+to do』～할 기분이 나게 하다, 꾀다. / † generosity [dʒènərásəti / -rɔ́s-] n. U 관대, 아량; 고결. / ‡ acquire [əkwáiər] vt. 손에 넣다, 획득하다; (버릇·기호·학력 따위를) 몸에 익히다, 습득하다. [SYN.] ⇨ GET. / † confer [kənfɔ́：r] v. (-rr-) — vt. (칭호·학위 등을) 수여하다, (영예 등을) 증여하다, (은혜 등을) 베풀다. / recipient [risípiənt] n. 수납자, 수령인; 수용자 / † keenly [kí：nli] ad. 날카롭게, 격심하게, 예민하게; 열심히, 빈틈없이. / ‡ payment [péimənt] n. ① U 지불, 납부, 납입. ② 보수, 보상 / ‡ calculation [kæ̀lkjəléiʃən] n. ① U 계산(하기), C 계산(의 결과); 셈; 계산법. / expediency, -ence [ikspí：diənsi], [-əns] n. ① U 편의, 형편 좋음; (타산적인) 편의주의; (악랄한) 사리(私利)추구. ② C 방편, 편법. / liberality [libərǽləti] n. U 너그러움, 관대, 관후; 활수함, 인색하지 않음

🔖 동의어/반의어

spectacle n. curiosity [kjùəriásəti], marvel[má：rv-əl], phenomenon[finámənàn / -nɔ́mən], sight[sait], wonder[wʌ́ndə：r], demonstration[dèmənstréiʃən], display[displéi], exhibition[èksəbíʃən], presentation[prèzəntéiʃən] production[prədʌ́kʃən]

tempt v. bait[beit], entice[entáis], inveigle[invíː gəl], invite[inváit], lure[luər], tantalize[tǽntəlàiz] 감질나게하여 괴롭히다 ant. repel[ripél] 쫓아 버리다, 격퇴하다.

confer v. accord[əkɔ́ː rd], award[əwɔ́ː rd], bestow[bistóu], give[giv], grant[grænt, grɑː nt], consult[kənsʌ́lt], converse[kənvɔ́ː rs], deliberate[dilíbərèit], parley[pɑ́ː rli] 회담하다, 교섭[담판]하다. ant. withdraw[wiðdrɔ́ː , wiə-] 움츠리다, 회수하다

In short, I say that as a city we are the school of Hellas, while I doubt if the world can produce a man who, where he has only himself to depend upon, is equal to so many emergencies, and graced by so happy a versatility, as the Athenian. And that this is no mere boast thrown out for the occasion, but plain matter of fact, the power of the state acquired by these habits proves. For Athens alone of her contemporaries is found when tested to be greater than her reputation, and alone gives no occasion to her assailants to blush at the antagonist by whom they have been worsted, or to her subjects to question her title by merit to rule.

🔖 본문해석

In short(요약하자면), **I say that as a city we are the school of Hellas**(도시국가로서 우리는 헬라스학파

라고 말씀드립니다), **while I doubt if the world can produce a man who, where he has only himself to depend upon**(자신만을 의지할 수 있는 곳에서), **is equal to so many emergencies**(너무나 많은 위기를 감당해내고), **and graced by so happy a versatility, as the Athenian**(너무나 행복한 재능을 부여받은 아테네 국민 같은 사람을 세상은 만들어낼 수 있을지 저는 의심이 듭니다). **And that this is no mere boast thrown out for the occasion**(기회가 있을 때 내뱉는 단순한 자랑이 아닙니다), **but plain matter of fact**(그러나 분명한 사실은), **the power of the state acquired by these habits proves**(이러한 국민성으로 획득된 국가의 힘은 그것을 입증하고도 남습니다). **For Athens alone of her contemporaries is found when tested to be greater than her reputation**(왜냐하면 동시대의 유일한 아테네만이 명성보다 더 큰 존재로 입증되었고), **and alone gives no occasion to her assailants to blush at the antagonist by whom they have been worsted, or to her subjects to question her title by merit to rule**(아테네만이 그들을 패배시켰던 적을 당황시키기 위해 적에게, 또는 아테네란 도시 명칭이 통치할 수 있을지 의심하는 백성들에겐 어떠한 기회도 주지 않습니다).

📑 문법분석

In short[=shortly speaking, in a word], I say that as[전치사: ～로써] a city we are the school[학파] of Hellas, while I doubt if[접속사=whether(명사절): ～인지 아닌지 의심하다] the world can produce a man who, where he has only himself to depend upon, is equal to[～를 감당하다] so many emergencies, and (who is) graced by so happy a versatility[so+형용사+단수명사: 너무나 행복한 재능을 부여받은], as[전치사: ～처럼] the Athenian. And that this is no mere boast thrown out for the occasion[기회가 있을 던지는 단순한 자랑], but plain matter of fact[=as a matter of fact], the power of the state (which was) acquired by these habits proves[목적어는 that임: 도치문]. For[=because] Athens(단수: 아테네수도를 일컫음) alone of her contemporaries is found when tested to be greater than her reputation, and (Athens) alone gives no occasion to[～에게 빈틈을 보이지 않다] her assailants to blush at the antagonist by whom[목적격 관계대명사] they have been worsted (by the antagonist)[그들을 패배시킨 적이 있는 적), or to her subjects[백성들] to question her title by merit to rule[아테네 도시국가의 직함이 통치할 능력이 있는지 의심함].

📑 단어분석

⚇ **emergency** [imə́ːrdʒənsi] n. U,C 비상[돌발] 사태, 위급, 위급한 경우. / ⚇ **grace** vt. ① 『～+목/+목+전+명』 우미[우아]하게 하다, 아름답게 꾸미다; ～에게 영광을 주다(with). / † **versatile** [və́ːrsətl / -tàil] a. ① 재주가 많은, 다예(多藝)한, 다능의, 융통성 있는, 다방면의. ② (드물게) (감정·기질 등이) 변하기 쉬운, 변덕스러운. / ⚇ **mere** [miər] a. (mérer; mérest) ① 단순한, ～에 불과한, 단지[다만, 그저] ～에 지나지 않는. ② (폐어) 전적인, 다른 어떤 것도 아닌, 순전한. / ⚇ **boast** [boust] n. 자랑(거리); 허풍. / † **Athens** [ǽθinz] n. 아테네(그리스의 수도). / ⚇ **contemporary** [kəntémpərèri / -pərəri] n. ① 동시대[동연대]의 사람; 동기생(at school); 동갑내기. / ⚇ **reputation** [rèpjətéiʃ-ən] n. U,C ① 평판, 세평. ② 명성, 신망, 호평. / † **assailant** [əséilənt] n. 공격자; 가해자; 적. / ⚇ **blush** [blʌʃ] v. —vi. ① 『～/ +보/ +부/ +전+명』 얼굴을 붉히다, (얼굴이 ～으로) 빨개지다(at ; for ; with). ② 『+전+명/ +to do』 부끄러워하다[지다] (at ; for). / † **antagonist** [æntǽgənist] n. ① 적수, 적대자, 반대자. [SYN.] ⇨ OPPONENT. / ✲✲**worst** [wəːrst] vt. 패배하게 하다, 무찌르다. / ⚇ **merit** [mérit] n. ① U,C 우수함, 가치; 장점, 취할 점. [SYN.] ⇨ WORTH. ② (보통 pl.) 공적, 공로, 훈공 / ✲✲**rule** [ruːl] v. —vt. ① 다스리다, 통치[관리]하다. [SYN.] ⇨ GOVERN. ② 「보통 수동태」 지도[설득]하다. 억제하다.

🐟 동의어/반의어

emergency n. accident, contingency, crisis, exigency, strait, urgency a. life-supporting, maintaining sustaining

versatile a. adaptable, all-purpose, multifaceted, multipurpose ant. limited

reputation n. character, fame, name, position, prestige, rank, standing status

---

동영상 강좌 http://youtu.be/bSkD59JNhRs

Rather, the admiration of the present and succeeding ages will be ours, since we have not left our power without witness, but have shown it by mighty proofs; and far from needing a Homer for our panegyrist, or other of his craft whose verses might charm for the moment only for the impression which they gave to melt at the touch of fact, we have forced every sea and land to be the highway of our daring, and everywhere, whether for evil or for good, have left imperishable monuments behind us. Such is the Athens for which these men, in the assertion of their resolve not to lose her, nobly fought and died; and well may every one of their survivors be ready to suffer in her cause.

🐟 본문해석

Rather(오히려), **the admiration of the present and succeeding ages will be ours**(현재와 앞으로 계속될 세대의 칭송은 우리가 받게 될 것입니다), **since we have not left our power without witness**(왜냐하면 우리는 증거 없이 우리의 힘을 남겨 놓지 않았기 때문입니다), **but have shown it by mighty proofs**(그러나 우리는 그것(우리의 힘)을 강력한 증거와 입증해 왔기 때문입니다); **and far from needing a Homer for our panegyrist**(서사시인 호머도 필요치 않으며), **or other of his craft whose verses might charm for the moment only for the impression which they gave to melt at the touch of fact**(또는 호머의 다른 기교적인 운문이 지금 이 순간에 호머의 운문이 주었던 감동을 진실의 햇불로 누그러트리는 유혹도 필요치 않으므로), **we have forced every sea and land to be the highway of our daring**(우리는 모든 삼라만상이 우리의 거침없는 용맹성이 되지 않을 수 없었고), **and everywhere, whether for evil or for good, have left imperishable monuments behind us**(선이든 악이든 모든 곳이 우리 뒤에 불멸의 기념비를 세워 놓았습니다(우리를 칭송하고 있습니다)). **Such is the Athens for which these men, in the assertion of their resolve not to lose her, nobly fought and died**(이러한 칭송은 아테네를 잃지 않으려는 그들의 결의에 찬 단언 속에서, 이런 전사들이 고결하게 싸우고 순직한 아테네의 것입니다); **and well may every one of their survivors be ready to suffer in her cause**(그리고 생존자 개개인이 아테네의 대의 속에서 돌아가신 분들을 애도하는 고통은 당연합니다).

🐟 문법분석

Rather, the admiration of the present and succeeding ages will be ours[소유대명사=the admiration], since[현재완료의 계속=because] we have not left our power without witness, but have shown it[=our power] by mighty proofs; and far from[이외에] needing a Homer for our panegyrist, or other of his craft whose verses might charm for the moment only for the impression which they gave[목적어는 the impression] to melt at the touch of fact, we have forced every sea and land to be the highway of our daring[force A to B: 삼라만상이 우리의 용맹성에 감탄하다], and everywhere, whether[삽입 부사절: 선이든 악이든지] (our daring is) for evil or for good, have left imperishable monuments behind us. Such[그러한 칭송을 받을 자격은 바로 아테네를 일컬음] is the Athens for which[관계대명사: 선행사는 the Athens] these men[아테네를 위해 순국한 전사들], in the assertion of their resolve not to lose her, nobly fought and died (for the Athens); and [도치문: every ～survivors may well be ready to ～]well may every one of their survivors be ready to suffer in her cause.

🔖 단어분석

† succeeding [səksíː diŋ] a. 계속되는, 다음의, 계속 일어나는. / **panegyrist** [pǽnədʒírist, -dʒái-, -́-́-]
n. 찬사의 글을 쓰는 사람; 상찬자(賞讚者), 찬양자. / **† verse** [vəː rs] n. ① 운문, 시(詩). [cf.] prose. ★ poetry에 비해서 내용보다 시형(詩形)을 문제로 함. / **† charm** [tʃɑː rm] —vi. ① 매력적이다, 매력을 갖다. ② 마법을 걸다. / **† melt** [melt] v. (～ed [méltid]; ～ed, molten [móultən]) —vi. ①『～/ +전+명』녹다, 용해하다. ②『+부/ +전+명』서서히 사라지다. / **imperishable** [impériʃəbəl] a. 불멸의, 불후의 (indestructible), 영속적인(everlasting). / **† assertion** [əsə́ː rʃən] n. U 단언, 주장; C (자기 개인의) 언설 (言說). / **＊＊cause** [kɔː z] n. U,C ① 원인([opp.] effect); 이유(reason); 까닭, 근거, 동기(for). [SYN.] ⇨ ORIGIN. ② 주의, 주장; 대의, 큰 목적(object), ～(을 위한) 운동(for; of).

🔖 동의어/반의어

succeeding v. accomplish[əkάmpliʃ], achieve[ətʃíː v], flourish[flɔ́ː riʃ], prosper[práspər], ensue[ensúː], follow[fάlou], replace[ripléis], supersede[sùː pəərsíː d], supplant[səplǽnt] 밀어내다
ant. fail[feil] precede[prisíː d] 앞서다

assertion n. avowal[əvάuəl], contention[kənténʃən], declaration[dèkləréiʃən], proclamation[prὰkləméiʃə], pronouncement[prənάunsmənt], statement[stéitmənt] ant. denial[dináiəl]

Indeed if I have dwelt at some length upon the character of our country, it has been to show that our stake in the struggle is not the same as theirs who have no such blessings to lose, and also that the panegyric of the men over whom I am now speaking might be by definite proofs established. That panegyric is now in a great measure complete; for the Athens that I have celebrated is only what the heroism of these and their like have made her, men whose fame, unlike that of most Hellenes, will be found to be only commensurate with their deserts. And if a test of worth be wanted, it is to be found in their closing scene, and this not only in cases in which it set the final seal upon their merit, but also in those in which it gave the first intimation of their having any.

🔖 본문해석

Indeed if I have dwelt at some length upon the character of our country(실제로 만일 제가 우리 조국의 이런 기질 토대 위에서 오래 살아 왔다면), **it has been to show that our stake in the struggle is not**

"Funeral Oration(추도사)"

by Pericles 페리클레스(아테네 정치가 BC 431)

the same as theirs who have no such blessings to lose(이 전투에서의 우리의 이해관계는 잃을 축복이 없는 적국의 그들의 것과 다르고), **and also that the panegyric of the men over whom I am now speaking might be by definite proofs established**(그리고 또한 제가 지금 말하고 있는 이분들에 대한 칭송은 분명한 증거로 확립된 것 을 보여주고 있습니다). **That panegyric is now in a great measure complete**(그 찬양은 위대한 척도에서 더할 나위가 없습니다); **for the Athens that I have celebrated is only what the heroism of these and their like have made her**(왜냐하면 제가 기리는 아테네는 이들과 그들의 비슷한 장렬함만 만든 것이기 때문입니다), **men whose fame, unlike that of most Hellenes, will be found to be only commensurate with their deserts**(대부분의 그리스 사람의 명성과 다른, 명성을 소유한 사람들은 그들의 공적에 단지 상응하는 것이 될 것입니다). **And if a test of worth be wanted**(그리고 만일 증거가 필요하다면), **it is to be found in their closing scene**(그 증거는 그들의 마지막 무대에서 발견될 것이고), **and this not only in cases in which it set the final seal upon their merit**(이것은 그들의 공적을 결정적으로 하는 경우에 발견될 뿐만 아니라), **but also in those in which it gave the first intimation of their having any**(그것이 그들이 어떠한 공적을 갖고 있다는 첫 번째 암시를 한 경우에서도 발견되어질 것입니다).

📝 문법분석

Indeed if I have dwelt at some length[오랜 기간] upon the character of our country, it[가주어] has been to show that[진주어] our stake in the struggle is not the same as theirs[=their state: 그들의 이해관계에 속한 사람들] who have no such blessings to lose, and also that the panegyric of the men over whom[목적격 관계대명사] I am now speaking (over men)[제가 지금 말하고 있는 분들에 대한 칭송] might be by definite proofs established. That panegyric is now [삽입구]in a great measure complete[보어인 형용사]; for[=because] the Athens that I have celebrated[목적어는 the Athens] is only what the heroism of these and their like[이들과 그들의 비슷한 장렬함] have made her[made A[her] B[what]: 5형식], men whose fame[명성을 갖은 사람들], unlike[전치사] that[=fame] of most Hellenes, will be found to be only commensurate with[단지 ~에 상응하는] their deserts. And if a test of worth (should) be wanted, it is to be[found A[in their closing scene], and this not only (is to be found) B[in cases] in which it set the final seal upon their merit, but also (is to be found) C[in those (cases)] in which it gave the first intimation of their having any (merit).

📝 단어분석

at some length 상당히 자세하게[길게]. / ✝**stake** [steik] n. 이해(관계) (interest), (개인적) 관여. / ✝**establish** [istǽbliʃ] vt. ① 확립하다, 설치[설립]하다, 개설[창립]하다, (제도·법률 등을) 제정하다. ② (선례·습관·소신·요구·명성 등을) 확립하다, 확고히 굳히다, 일반에게 확인시키다, 수립하다. / ✱✱**measure** [méʒə: r]n. ① U 치수, 분량; 크기, 무게, 길이, 말수(斗數). ② U,C 한도, 한계, 정도; 표준, 적도(適度). / ✝**heroism** [hérouìzəm] n. U 영웅적 자질, 장렬, 의열(義烈); C 영웅적 행위. / ✝**fame** [feim] n. U ① 명성, 명예, 성망. ② 평판, 풍문; (고어) 세평, 소문. / **commensurate** [kəménʃərit] a. 같은 양[면적, 크기]의, 동연(同延)의(with), 같은 시간의; 비례한, 균형이 잡힌, 상응한(to; with); =COMMENSURABLE / **desert** [dizɔ́: rt] n. ① 상[벌]을 받을 만한 가치[자격], 공과(功過); (종종 pl.) 당연한 보답, 응분의 상[벌]. ② 공적(merit); 미덕. / **set the seal on** ~을 결정적인 것으로 하다. / **intimation** [intəméiʃən] n. U,C 암시, 넌지시 비춤 (hint); 통지, 통고, 발표.

동영상 강좌 http://youtu.be/YTUjvCyf9GU

동의어/반의어

establish v. found[faund], initiate[iníʃièit], institute[ínstətjùː t], organize[ɔ́ː rgənàiz], ensconce[inskáns] 몸을 편히 앉히다, install[instɔ́ː l], settle[sétl], situate[sítʃuèit], authenticate[ɔː θéntikèit] 입증하다, confirm[kənfɔ́ː rm], prove[pruː v], validate[vǽlədèit], verify[vérəfài]   ant. dissolve[dizálv], uproot[ʌprúː t] disprove[disprúː v]

For there is justice in the claim that steadfastness in his country's battles should be as a cloak to cover a man's other imperfections; since the good action has blotted out the bad, and his merit as a citizen more than outweighed his demerits as an individual. But none of these allowed either wealth with its prospect of future enjoyment to unnerve his spirit, or poverty with its hope of a day of freedom and riches to tempt him to shrink from danger.

본문해석

For there is justice in the claim that steadfastness in his country's battles should be as a cloak to cover a man's other imperfections(왜냐하면 조국의 전쟁에서 불변의 신념은 한 개인의 다른 결함을 덮어주는 망토로서의 역할이 되어야한다는 주장은 당연하기 때문입니다) ; **since the good action has blotted out the bad**(선행이 악행을 섬멸했기 때문에), **and his merit as a citizen more than outweighed his demerits as an individual**(그리고 한 시민으로서 그의 공적이 한 개인으로서의 결점을 훨씬 능가했기 때문입니다). **But none of these allowed either wealth with its prospect of future enjoyment to unnerve his spirit**(그러나 이런 어떠한 것도 그의 용기를 잃게 하는 미래의 향락의 측면에서 부를 허락하지 않았거나-부로 인해 사기가 떨어지는 일), **or poverty with its hope of a day of freedom and riches to tempt him to shrink from danger**(그를 위험으로부터 움츠리게 유혹하는 하루의 자유와 부의 바람에서 결핍을 허락하지 않았습니다).

문법분석

For[=Because] there is justice in the claim[~라 주장하는 것은 당연하다] that steadfastness in his country's battles should be as a cloak[~로서의 역할을 하다] to cover a man's other imperfections; since[접속사: ~이후로 계속해서] the good action has blotted out the bad (action), and his merit as [전치사: ~로서 a citizen more than outweighed[~능가한 것 이상이었다] his demerits as an individual. But none of these allowed either[either A or B: A나 B중 어느 하나] wealth with its prospect of future enjoyment to unnerve his spirit[부로 인해 사기가 떨어지는 것], or poverty[wealth 와 대조를 이룸] with its hope of a day of freedom and riches[단 하루 편하고자하는 부족한 정신] to tempt him to shrink from danger.

단어분석

† **steadfast** [stédfæ̀st, -fəst] a. 확고 부동한, 고정된, (신념 등) 불변의, 부동의. / † cloak [klouk] n. ① (보통 소매가 없는) 외투, 망토. ② 덮는 것(covering), 가면. ③ 구실(pretext), 은폐하는 수단. / †

imperfection [ìmpərfékʃən] n. ① U 불완전(성). ② C 결함, 결점 / **blot out** ⇨—vt. (글자·기억을) 지우다, 없애다; (적·도시 등을) 진멸하다. / ⸷ **merit** [mérit] n. ① U,C 우수함, 가치; 장점, 취할 점. [SYN.] ⇨ WORTH. ② (보통 pl.) 공적, 공로, 훈공 / **demerit** [di : mérit] n. 결점, 결함, 단점 / **outweigh** [àutwéi] vt. ～보다 무겁다; ～보다 중요하다; ～보다 가치가[세력이] 있다. / **unnerve** [ʌnnə́ : rv] vt. (아무의) 용기를[기력을, 결단력을, 확신을] 잃게 하다, 무기력화하다. / ⸷ **enjoyment** [endʒɔ́imənt] n. ① C 즐거움, 기쁨; 유쾌. ② U 향락; 향유, 향수(享受). / ⸷ **prospect** [práspekt / prɔ́s-] n. ① 조망(眺望), 전망; 경치. ② 예상, 기대; (종종 pl.) (장래의) 가망 / ⸷ **poverty** [pávərti / pɔ́v-] n. U ① 가난, 빈곤([opp.] wealth). ② 결핍, 부족(of; in). / ⸷ **shrink** [ʃriŋk] v. (shrank [ʃræŋk], shrunk [ʃrʌŋk]; shrunk, shrunken [ʃrʌ́ŋkən]) —vi. ① 『～/ +전+명/ +부』 (천 따위가) 오그라들다. (수량·가치 등이) 줄다(up; away). ② 『+전+명/ +부』 움츠리다(up), 겁내다, 위축되다(at) /

📝 동의어/반의어

steadfast a. constant[kánstənt], faithful[féiθfəl], firm[fə : rm], staunch[stɔ : ntʃ], unfailing[ʌnféiliŋ], unwavering[ʌnwéivəriŋ ant. vacillating[væsəlèitiŋ

unnerve v. frighten[fráitn], intimidate[intímədèit], scare[skɛə : r], upset[ʌpsét], worry[wə́ : ri] ant. assure[əʃúər]

prospect n. chance[tʃæns], likelihood[láiklihùd], possibility[pàsəbíləti], probability[pràbəbíləti], anticipation[æntìsəpéiʃən], expectation[èkspektéiʃən], hope[houp], promise[prámis], prospects[práspekts] clients[kláiənts], customers[kʌ́stəmərs], outlook[áutlùk], scene[si : n], view[vju :] v. explore[iksplɔ́ : r], investigate[invéstəgèit] search[sə : rtʃ]

poverty n. destitution[dèstətjù : ʃən], impoverishment[impávəriʃmənt], indigence,[índidʒəns] penury[pénjəri], privation[praivéiʃən], dearth[də : rθ], insufficiency[insəfíʃənsi], meagerness[mí : gə : rnis], paucity[pɔ́ : səti], scarcity[skɛ́ə : rsəti]

ant. wealth[welθ] abundance[əbʌ́ndəns]

No, holding that vengeance upon their enemies was more to be desired than any personal blessings, and reckoning this to be the most glorious of hazards, they joyfully determined to accept the risk, to make sure of their vengeance, and to let their wishes wait; and while committing to hope the uncertainty of final success, in the business before them they thought fit to act boldly and trust in themselves. Thus choosing to die resisting, rather than to live submitting, they fled only from dishonour, but met danger face to face, and after one brief moment, while at the summit of their fortune, escaped, not from their fear, but from their glory.

📝 본문해석

No(그렇습니다), **holding that vengeance upon their enemies was more to be desired than any personal blessings**(그들의 적에 대한 복수심은 어떤 개인의 저주 보다 더 바람직했다는 생각과), **and reckoning this to be the most glorious of hazards**(그리고 이것이 모험 중에서 가장 영광스러운 것으로 생각하였던), **they joyfully determined to accept the risk, to make sure of their vengeance, and to let their wishes wait**(그들은 기꺼이 위험을 무릅 쓰기로, 그들의 복수를 반드시 하기로, 그리고 그들의 소망이 실현되기를 결심했습니다); **and while committing to hope the uncertainty of final success**(그리고 마지

막 성공의 불확실성을 기대는 것 대신), **in the business before them**(그들 앞에 놓여있는 상황에서) **they thought fit to act boldly and trust in themselves**(그들은 용감히 일어서 그들 자신을 믿는 것만이 옳다고 생각했습니다). **Thus choosing to die resisting, rather than to live submitting**(그리하여 굴복하여 목숨을 건지니 차라리 저항하다 죽을 것을 선택한), **they fled only from dishonour, but met danger face to face**(그들은 불명예로부터 빠져나와 전면으로 위험과 대적했습니다), **and after one brief moment**(그리고 마지막 순간에), **while at the summit of their fortune**(마지막 목숨이 있는 동안에도), **escaped, not from their fear, but from their glory**(그들은 두려움이 아닌 그들의 영광을 바라지 않았습니다).

🐚 문법분석

No[앞 문장이 부정이므로: '그렇습니다'로 해석], holding[=thinking] that vengeance upon their enemies was more to be desired than any personal blessings, and reckoning[=considering] this to be the most glorious of hazards, they joyfully determined [A]to accept the risk, [B]to make sure of their vengeance, and [C]to let their wishes wait; and while   committing[분사구문: =they committed] to hope the uncertainty of final success, in the business before them[그들 앞에 놓여있는 상황 하에서] they thought[think A B: B를 A를 생각하다] fit to act boldly and trust in themselves. Thus choosing[분사구문: After they chose] to die resisting, rather than[~라기 보다는] to live submitting, they fled (not) only from dishonour, but (also) met danger face to face, and after one brief moment[찰나의 순간 이후, 마지막 순간에], while (they were) at the summit of their fortune[그들의 행운의 정상에 있는, 마지막 목숨이 있는], escaped, not from their fear, but from their glory[영광으로부터 탈출하다=[의역] 영광을 바라지 않았다].

🐚 단어분석

hold 생각하다; (을) ~라고 생각하다, 평가하다; 판정하다 / ✝**vengeance** [véndʒəns] n. U,C 복수, 원수 갚기, 앙갚음. / ✝**blessing** [blésiŋ] n. ① 축복(의 말); 식전[식후]의 기도. ②「반어적」저주(하기). / ✝**reckon** [rék-ən] v. —vt. ①『+목+(to be)보/ +목+전+명』(~로) 보다, 간주하다(consider), 판단[단정]하다, 평가하다(as; for). ② (구어) 생각하다(특히 ((미국에서는 삽입적으로도 쓰임)); (영국속어) 좋다고[가망 있다고] 생각하다. / ✝**glorious** [glɔ́ː riəs] a. ① 영광스러운, 명예[영예]로운. ② 영광에 넘치는, 이름 높은. / ✝**hazard** [hǽzərd] n. ① 위험, 모험; 위험요소; 운에 맡기기; 우연, 운. [SYN.] ⇨ DANGER. / ✝**commit** [kəmít] vt. (-tt-) ①『+목+전+명』위임하다, 위탁하다; 회부하다. ②『+목+전+명』(기록·기억· 처분·망각 등에) 맡기다, 부치다(to). /

🐚 동의어/반의어

<u>**vengeance**</u> n. reprisal[ripráiz-əl, retaliation[ritæ̀liéiʃ-ən], v.   avenge[əvéndʒ], punish[pʌ́niʃ], repay[ri ː péi], retaliate[ritǽlièit], vindicate[víndəkèit] ant. pardon[pɑ́ː rdn] forgive[fəː rgív]

<u>**glorious**</u> a. gorgeous[gɔ́ː rdʒəs], magnificent[mægnífəsənt], marvelous[mɑ́ː rv-ələs], superb[suː pə ː rb], splendid[spléndid], consummate[kənsʌ́mət] 완전한, divine[diváin], sublime[səbláim], lustrous[lʌ́strəs], transcendent[trænséndənt], bright[brait], brilliant[bríljənt], radiant[réidiənt], resplendent[rispléndənt] ant. terrible[térəb-əl] dull[dʌl]

"Funeral Oration(추도사)"

by Pericles 페리클레스(아테네 정치가 BC 431)

동영상 강좌 http://youtu.be/AY3mlf6mwfA

Athena Mourning. So died these men as became Athenians. You, their survivors, must determine to have as unfaltering a resolution in the field, though you may pray that it may have a happier issue. And not contented with ideas derived only from words of the advantages which are bound up with the defence of your country, though these would furnish a valuable text to a speaker even before an audience so alive to them as the present, you must yourselves realize the power of Athens, and feed your eyes upon her from day to day, till love of her fills your hearts; and then, when all her greatness shall break upon you, you must reflect that it was by courage, sense of duty, and a keen feeling of honor in action that men were enabled to win all this, and that no personal failure in an enterprise could make them consent to deprive their country of their valor, but they laid it at her feet as the most glorious contribution that they could offer.

🖊 본문해석

Athena Mourning(아테네는 애도합니다). **So died these men as became Athenians**(이분들은 아테네인이 되고자 목숨을 바쳤습니다). **You, their survivors, must determine to have as unfaltering a resolution in the field**(생존자 여러분들도 전장에서 단호한 결심을 하신 것이 틀림없습니다), **though you may pray that it may have a happier issue**(비록 그 결심이 행운이 있기를 기도했을지라도). **And not contented with ideas derived only from words of the advantages which are bound up with the defence of your country**(여러분의 조국수호와 결부된 단지 몇 마디의 편의에 기인한 생각에 만족하지 않고), **though these would furnish a valuable text to a speaker even before an audience so alive to them as the present**(비록 현재와 같이 그들에게 너무나 생생했던 것처럼 청중들 앞에서 조차 이러한 생각이 연설자에게 어떤 귀중한 연설주제를 줄 것을 바랄지라도), **you must yourselves realize the power of Athens**(여러분들은 아테네의 국력을 절감하고 있음이 틀림없습니다), **and feed your eyes upon her from day to day, till love of her fills your hearts**(그리고 조국의 사랑이 여러분의 가슴을 가득 채울 때까지, 언제나 여러분은 조국에 만족했음이 틀림없습니다); **and then, when all her greatness shall break upon you**(그러므로 모든 조국의 위대함이 여러분들에게 밀려오게 될 때), **you must reflect that it was by courage, sense of duty, and a keen feeling of honor in action that men were enabled to win all this**(이것은 시민들이 이 모든 것을 쟁취하도록 한 행동에서 용기, 의무감, 그리고 명예심으로 성취된 것이라 여러분은 분명 생각할 것입니다), **and that no personal failure in an enterprise could make them consent to deprive their country of their valor**(그리고 모험적인 전쟁에서 어떠한 개인적인 실패(희생)도 그들로 하여금 용맹한 그들의 조국을 앗아가는 것을 용납할 수 없게 했습니다), **but they laid it at her feet as the most glorious contribution that they could offer**(그러나 그들은 그것(개인적인 희생)이 그들이 줄 수 있었던 가장 영광스런 공헌으로서 조국의 발아래에 깔아 놓았습니다).

🖊 문법분석

Athena (is) Mourning. So died these men as became Athenians[so A as B: B처럼 A한: 아테네 시민이 되는 것과 같이 목숨을 받친 것입니다]. You, their survivors, must[조동사: ~임에 틀림없다] determine to have as unfaltering a resolution[as(so)+형용사+a/an+단수명사: 아주 단호한 결단력] in the field, though you may pray that it may have a happier issue[신의 가오를 바라다]. And [분사구문] (Because they were) not contented with ideas derived only from words of the advantages which are bound up with the defence of your country, though these would furnish a valuable text to a speaker[연설자에게도 말할 주제를 제공하다] even before an audience so alive to them as the present [지금처럼 그들에게도 너무나 생생했던 것처럼], [주어]you must yourselves realize the power of Athens, and feed your eyes upon her[조국에 대해 만족하다] from day to day, till[접속사: ~까지 계속해서] love of her fills your hearts; and then, when all her greatness shall break upon you[~로 밀려오다], you must reflect that it was by courage, sense of duty, and a keen feeling of honor in action that[동격접속사] men were enabled to win all this, and (you must reflect) that no personal failure in an enterprise[군사작전] could make them consent to deprive their country of their valor, but they laid it at her feet as[전치사: ~처럼] the most glorious contribution that[관계대명사] they could offer[목적어는 the most glorious contribution].

🔖 단어분석

‡ **mourn** [mɔːrn] v. —vi. 『+전+명』 ① 슬퍼하다, 한탄하다(for; over). ② 죽음을 애통해하다(grieve); 조상(弔喪)하다, 애도하다. / **unfaltering** [ʌnfɔ́ːltəriŋ] a. 비틀거리지[흔들리지] 않는, 확고한; 주저하지 않는, 단호한. / ‡ **derive** [diráiv] v. —vt. ① 『+목+전+명』 끌어 내다(from); 손에 넣다, 획득하다(from). ② 『+목+전+명』 ~의 기원을[유래를] 찾다(from) / ‡ **advantage** [ædvǽntidʒ, -váːn-, əd-] n. ① U 유리, 이익; 편의. [SYN.] ⇨ PROFIT. ② U 우세, 우월(of something to someone). ③ C 이점, 장점. / ‡ **furnish** [fɔ́ːrniʃ] v. —vt. ① 『~+목/ +목+전+명/ +목+목』 (필요한 물건을) 공급하다, 제공하다, 주다. / **✻✻feed** [fiːd] v. (p., pp. fed [fed]) ④ 『~+목/ +목+전+명』 ~에게 즐거움을 주다; 만족시키다(gratify). / ♣**break on [upon]** ~에 돌연 나타나다; (파도가) ~으로 밀려오다; ~이 분명해지다. / ‡ **deprive** [dipráiv] vt. ① 『+목+전+명』 ~에게서 빼앗다, 박탈하다(of). [SYN.] ⇨ ROB. /

🔖 동의어/반의어

mourn v. grieve[griːv], lament[ləmént], languish[lǽŋgwiʃ], pine[pain], sorrow[sárou, sɔ́ːr] ant. rejoice[ridʒɔ́is]

unfaltering a. constant[kánstənt], dependable[dipéndəbl], reliable[riláiəb-əl], steady[stédi], unwavering[ʌnwéivəriŋ], endless[éndlis], enduring[indjúəriŋ], inexhaustible[inigzɔ́ːstəbəl], infallible[infǽləbəl], perfect[pɔ́ːrfikt], unerring[ʌnɔ́ːriŋ] ant. inconstant[inkánstənt], finite[fáinait], fallible[fǽləbəl]

advantage n. benefit[bénəfit], blessing[blésiŋ], boon[buːn], privilege[prívəlidʒ], odds[adz/ɔdz], allowance[əláuəns], edge[edʒ], handicap[hǽndikæ̀p], gain[gein], interest[íntərist], profit[práfit] ant. curse[kəːrs] disadvantage[dìsədvǽntiddʒ]

furnish v. equip[ikwíp], gear[giər], outfit[áutfit], provide[prəváid], rig[rig], stock[stak/stɔk] supply[səplái]

For this offering of their lives made in common by them all they each of them individually received that renown which never grows old, and for a sepulcher, not so much that in which their bones have been deposited, but that noblest of shrines wherein their glory is laid up to be eternally remembered upon every occasion on which deed or story shall call for its commemoration. For heroes have the whole earth for their tomb; and in lands far from their own, where the column with its epitaph declares it, there is enshrined in every breast a record unwritten with no tablet to preserve it, except that of the heart.

🔖 본문해석

For this offering of their lives made in common by them all(그들 모두의 똑같은 희생으로) **they each of them individually received that renown which never grows old**(결코 퇴색되지 않을 명성을 그들 개개인은 받으셨습니다), **and for a sepulcher, not so much that in which their bones have been deposited**(그들의 유해가 안치된 무덤이라서가 아닌), **but that noblest of shrines**(가장 숭고한 사당으로서) **wherein their glory is laid up to be eternally remembered upon every occasion on which deed or story shall call for its commemoration**(전사들의 행동과 이야기로 기념식이 열린 땐 늘 이곳에서 그들의 영광은 영원히 기억될 것입니다). **For heroes have the whole earth for their tomb**(왜냐하면 영웅들은 그들 묘지로 전 대지를 감싸 안았기 때문입니다); **and in lands far from their own**(그들 자신의 고향에서 멀리 떨어진 대지에서), **where the column with its epitaph declares it**(비문 기둥이 그것을 선언하는 곳에서), **there is enshrined in every breast a record unwritten with no tablet to preserve it, except that of the heart**(용기 있는 자들의 기록은 제외하더라도, 기록을 보존할 평판에 써진 기록은 모든 사람들의 가슴 마다 소중히 간직되어 있습니다).

🔖 문법분석

For[전치사: ∼을 위해서] this offering of their lives[헌신: 국가에 목숨을 바침] made in common by them all[그들 모두에 의해: 전장에서 순국한 전사들] they each of them[그들 각각] individually received that renown which[관계대명사] never grows[목적어는 that renown] old, and for a sepulcher, not so much that[부사구: 그래서가 아닌] in which[관계대명사:=where 선행사는 a sepulcher] their bones have been deposited[유해가 안치되어 있는], but that[not A but B용법: that[지시대명사]] noblest of shrines wherein[전치사+관계대명사=in which용법] their glory is laid up[저장되어 있다, 놓여 있다] to be eternally remembered upon every occasion[전치사구: 언제나] on which deed or story shall call for its commemoration[그들의 공적을 기념할 때]. For[=because] heroes have the whole earth for their tomb[영웅들을 전 지역에서 기리다]; and in lands far from their own, where[관계부사: ∼인 곳에서] the column with its epitaph declares it[비문에 새겨진 영웅들의 명성], there is enshrined[주어는 a record] in every breast[모든 사람들의 가슴마다] a record unwritten with no tablet to preserve it[=a record], except[전치사: ∼제외하고] that[=a record] of the heart.

🔖 단어분석

† **offering** [ɔ́(ː)fəriŋ, áf-] n. C,U ① (신에의) 공물, 제물, 봉납(물). ② (교회에의) 헌금, 헌납. ③ 선물(gift). ④ 신청, 제공; 팔 물건, 매물(賣物). / † **renown** [rináun] n. U 명성, 영명(令名). / † **sepulcher**, 【영국】 —chre [sépəlkər] n. ① 묘, 무덤; 매장소 / ǂ **deposit** [dipázit / -póz-] v. —vt. ① 아래에 놓다, 두다; (알을) 낳다. ② 침전시키다, 가라앉히다, 퇴적시키다. / ǂ **wherein** [hwɛərín] ad. (문어) ① 「의문사」 어디에, 어떤 점에서. ② 「관계사」 그 중에, 그 곳에, 그 점에서(in which). / ǂ **occasion** [əkéiʒən] n. ① (특정한) 경우, 때(on), 시(時); 일. ② (∼할) 기회, 호기(好機) (for), 알맞은 때. [SYN.] ⇨ OPPORTUNITY. ③ 중요한 때, 경사스러운 때; 축전(祝典), 행사. ④ U 이유, 근거; 유인(誘因), 원인. /

♣**lay up** (1) 저축[저장]하다; 쓰지 않고 두다. / †**commemoration** [kəmèməréiʃən] n. U 기념, 축하; C 기념식[축제], 축전; 기념물; (C-) 【영국】 Oxford 대학 기념 축제. / ‡**column** [káləm / kɔ́l-] n. ① 기둥, 원주, 지주; 기둥 모양의 물건. / †**epitaph** [épətæ̀f, -tɑ̀ː f] n. 비명(碑銘), 비문, 묘비명 / **enshrine** [enʃráin] vt. ~+목/ +목+전+명』 ① (성당에) 모시다, 안치하다; 신성한 것으로 소중히 하다, (마음에) 간직하다(in). / ‡**tablet** [tǽblit] n. ① 평판(平板), 명판(銘板), 기념 액자, 패(牌). ② 작고 납작한 조각(비누·캔디 등). / ⁑**heart** [hɑː rt] n. ① 심장. ② 용기, 기운. 용기 있는 자, 우수한 사람

🛡 **동의어/반의어**

deposit v. drop[drɑp], lay[lei], precipitate[prisípətèit] 거꾸로 떨어뜨리다, set[set], accumulate[əkjúː mjəlèit], amass[əmǽs], bank[bæŋk], save[seiv], store[stɔː r] n. alluvium[əlúː viəm] 충적층, 충적토, sediment[sédəmənt] 퇴적물, silt[silt], collateral[kəlǽtərəl], down payment[daun péimənt] (할부금의) 첫 지불액, earnest money[ɔ́ː rnist mʌ́ni] 계약금 ant. disperse[dispɔ́ː rs] scatter[skǽtə r]

commemoration n. carnival[káː rnəvəl], feast[fiː st], festival[féstəvəl], gala[gáː lə], jubilee[dʒúː bəlìː], party[páː rti], festivity[festívəti], merrymaking[mérimèikiŋ], revelry[rév-əlri], ceremony[sérəmòuni],   commemoration[kəmèməréiʃən],   observance[əbzɔ́ː rvəns],   ritual[rítʃu-əl] solemnization[sàləmnizéiʃən]

Duties of American Citizenship

by Theodore Roosevelt

[난이도 ★★★★★]

동영상 강좌 http://youtu.be/eL7BgoRmIBQ

January 26, 1883; Buffalo, New York

Of course, in one sense, the first essential for a man's being a good citizen is his possession of the home virtues of which we think when we call a man by the emphatic adjective of manly

🖎 해석기법

①**Of course**(물론), ②**in one sense**(어떤 의미에서), ③**the first essential for a man's being a good citizen**(훌륭한 시민이 되는 사람의 첫 필수적인 조건은) ⑤**is his possession of the home virtues of which we think**(우리가 생각하는 것은 그가 갖고 있는 가정에 대한 덕망을 소유하고 있느냐는 것입니다) ④**when we call a man by the emphatic adjective of manly** (우리가 그 사람을 명확한 형용사를 사용해 '남자답다'라고 부를 때).

🖎 문법분석

in one[a = any 어떤] sense / the first[수사 앞에 정관사 the를 붙임, 형용사] essential[명사] / we think of (the home virtue)s[which[관계 대명사]의 선행] when [5형식문장]we call a man[A] by the emphatic adjective of manly[B]의 문장구조임. - of + 형용사 = 형용사구[남자다운]

🖎 단어분석

⧾ **essential** [isénʃəl] a. 필수의, 불가결한 / ⧾ **emphatic** [imfǽtik, em-] a. 명확한; 단호한 / ⧾ **adjective** [ǽdʒiktiv] n. 형용사. / ⧾ **manly** [mǽnli] a. (-lier; -liest) 남자다운, 씩씩한. /

🖎 동의어/반의어

emphatic a. assertive[əsə́ː rtiv], forceful[fɔ́ː rsfəl], insistent[insístənt], intense[inténs], vigorous[vígərəs], impassioned[impǽʃənd], stressed[stresd], resounding[rizáundiŋ], underscored [ʌ̀ndərskɔ́ː rd] ant. irresolute[iré zəlùː t]

No man can be a good citizen who is not a good husband and a good father, who is not honest in his dealings with other men and women, faithful to his friends and fearless in the presence of his foes, who has not got a sound heart, a sound mind, and a sound body; exactly as no amount of attention to civil duties will save a nation if the domestic life is undermined, or there is lack of the rude military virtues which alone can assure a country's position in the world.

🖎 해석기법

①**No man can be a good citizen**(어떠한 남자도 ②~은 훌륭한 시민이 될 수 없습니다) ②**who is not a good husband and a good father**(훌륭한 남편이나 아버지가 아닌 사람), **who is not honest in his** dealings with other men and women(다른 사람들과 거래할 때 정직하지 않은 사람), **faithful to his friends and fearless in the presence of his foes**(친구들에게 신용이 없는 사람), **who has not got a sound heart, a sound mind, and a sound body**(건전한 심성, 건전한 마음과 건전한 신체 갖지 않은 사람); / ③**exactly as no amount of attention to civil duties will save a nation**(시민으로서의 의무에 전혀 관심을 기울이지 않는 것은 국가를 구해낼 수 없는 것과 마찬가지 입니다) ①**if the domestic life is undermined**(만일 가정생활이 손상되어 있거나), **or** ②**there is lack of the rude military virtues which alone can assure a country's position in the world**(세계에서 한 국가의 위상을 홀로 보장할 수 있는 강인한 군기가 부족하다면).

📜 문법분석

no man[전체 부정, 어떠한 남자도 ~가 아닌] / a good citizen who[주격 관계대명사, ~라는 훌륭한 시민], ~, (who is not) faithful[신용이 없는] ~, who[선행사 a good citizen을 수식] ~; exactly as[접속사, 정확히 ~인 것처럼] ~if[조건절, 만일 ~라면] ~is undermined['손상시키다'의 수동태, 손상되다], or there[유도부사, 도치문: ~가 있다] is lack[불가산명사, ~부족한 것] of the rude military virtues[강인한 군기] which[관계대명사]

📜 단어분석

‡ **faithful** [féiəfəl] a. 충실한, 성실한, 믿을 수 있는(reliable)(to). SINCERE. / ‡ **fearless** [fiərlis] a. 두려움을 모르는 / ‡ **foe** [fou] n. (시어·문어) 적, 원수; 적군 / **sound** [saund]a. 건전한, 정상적인 [SYN.] ⇨ HEALTHY. / ⁂**attention** [əténʃən] n. U 주의, 유의; 주의력. / ‡ **domestic** [douméstik] a. 가정의, 사육되어 길든(tame). [opp] wild. 국내의, 자국의. [opp] foreign. / † **undermine** [ʌndərmáin] vt. (명성 따위를) 음험한 수단으로 훼손하다 / ‡ **virtue** [vɔ́ːrtʃuː] n. ① U 미덕, 덕, 덕행, 선행. [opp.] vice. ② C (어떤 특수한) 덕, 미점, 미덕

In a free republic the ideal citizen must be one willing and able to take arms for the defense of the flag, exactly as the ideal citizen must be the father of many healthy children.

📜 해석기법

①**In a free republic**(자유 공화국에서) ②**the ideal citizen must be one willing and able to take arms for the defense of the flag**(이상적인 시민은 자국의 국기를 방어하기 위해 무기를 기꺼이 들거나 들 수 있는 사람이어야만 한다), ③**exactly as the ideal citizen must be the father of many healthy children** (그 이상적 시민이 많은 건강한 아이들의 아버지임에 틀림없는 것과 같은 이치이다).

📜 문법분석

[부사구] In a free republic [주어] the ideal citizen ~one (who is) willing[기꺼이 ~하다] and able [할 수 있다] to take arms[무기를 들다] / exactly as[접속사, 틀림없이 ~인 것과 같다]

📜 단어분석

‡ **willing** [wíliŋ] a. 「서술적」 기꺼이 ~하는(to do). / ‡ **arm** [ɑːrm] n. ① (보통 pl.) 무기, 병기. / ‡ **defense** [diféns, dːˈfens] n. U,C 방어

동의어/반의어

willing a. acquiescent[æ̀kwiésənt], amenable [əmíː nəbəl], deliberate[dilíbərit] ant. reluctant[rilʌ́ktənt] involuntary[inʌ́ləntèri]

A race must be strong and vigorous; it must be a race of good fighters and good breeders, else its wisdom will come to naught and its virtue be ineffective; and no sweetness and delicacy, no love for and appreciation of beauty in art or literature, no capacity for building up material prosperity can possibly atone for the lack of the great virile virtues.

해석기법

A race must be strong and vigorous(국민은 강하고 강건해야만 합니다); **it must be a race of good fighters and good breeders**(국민은 훌륭한 전사나 훌륭한 양육자가 되어야만 합니다), **else its wisdom will come to naught and its virtue be ineffective**(그렇지 않으면 국민의 지혜는 무가치하게 되고 그 미덕은 비효율적이 될 것입니다); **and no sweetness and delicacy**(어떠한 달콤함과 정교함), **no love for and appreciation of beauty in art or literature**(어떤 예술과 문학에서의 미의 사랑과 인식), **no capacity for building up material prosperity**(물질적 번영을 건설할 어떠한 능력은) **can possibly atone for the lack of the great virile virtues**(아주 강인한 덕망의 부족으로 인해 채워지지 못할 가능성이 있습니다).

문법분석

good fighters[국가를 위한 전사] good breeders[가정을 위한 부모 역할]을 말함 / (or) else[그렇지 않으면] / come to[~가 되다, become의 뜻] / its virtue (will) be ineffective / no[형용사로 전체 부정, 어떤 ~도 아닌]

단어분석

race [reis]n. ① 인종, 종족; (the ~) 인류(human ~). ★ 민족학적으로는 ethnic group [stock]이라는 과학적 명칭을 사용함. ② (문화상의 구별로) 민족, 국민. [SYN.] ⇨ NATION. / **‡ vigorous [vígərəs] a. ① 정력 왕성한, 원기 왕성한, 활발한, 박력 있는, 강건한. [SYN.] ⇨ STRONG. ② 강력한; 강경한, 단호한. / **† breeder** [bríː də: r] n. ① 종축(種畜), 번식하는 동물[식물]. ② 양육[사육]자; 품종 개량가, 육종가; 발기인, 장본인. ③ (불만 따위의) 씨, 원인. / **‡ naught, nought** [nɔː t, nɑː t] a. 파멸한, 망한; (고어) 무가치한, 무용의; 사악한. / **ineffective** [ìniféktiv] a. 무효의, 효과 없는(ineffectual); 쓸모 없는, 무력한, 무능한; (예술품이) 감명을 주지 않는. / **† delicacy** [délikəsi] n. U ① 섬세(함), 정치(精緻), (기계 따위의) 정교함; (취급의) 정밀함. ② 우미, 우아함. / **‡ appreciation** [əpriː ʃiéiʃən] n. U ① (올바른) 평가, 판단, 이해; 진가의 인정. ② 감상, 음미; 비평. / **‡ literature** [lítərətʃər, -tʃùər] n. U ① 문학, 문예. ② 문학 연구; 작가 생활, 저술. / **‡ capacity** [kəpǽsəti] n. U,C ① 수용량; (최대) 수용능력. ② 용적, 용량; 〖물리〗 열[전기] 용량; 〖컴퓨터〗 용량. ③ 능력, 재능. / ****material** [mətí-əriəl]a. ① 물질의, 물질에 관한(physical); 구체적인, 유형의. ② 육체상의[적인](corporeal); 감각적인, 관능적인. [opp.] spiritual. ③ 세속적인, 비속한. / **‡ prosperity** [prɑspérəti / prɔs-] n. ① U 번영, 번창, 융성; 성공; 행운, 부유. [opp.] adversity. ② (pl.) 번영의 상태, 부유한 처지. / **† atone** [ətóun] v. —vi. ① 속죄[보상]하다(for). ② (실

책 등의) 벌충을 하다(for). / **virile** [vírəl, víraíl] a. 힘찬, 남성다운 / † **virtue** [və́ːrtʃuː] n. ① U 미덕, 덕, 덕행, 선행. [opp.] vice ⇨ CARDINAL VIRTUES. ② C (어떤 특수한) 덕, 미점, 미덕

🔖 동의어/반의어

vigorous a. dynamic [dainǽmik], energetic[ènərdʒéti, exuberant[igzúːbərənt], spirited[spíritid] , vital[váitl, hardy[háːrdi], powerful[páuərfəl], robust[roubʌ́st, róubʌs], strong[strɔ(ː)ŋ, strɑŋ] ant. passive[pǽsiv] a. ① 수동의, 활동적이 아닌, 활기가 없는; 반응이 없는.; frail [freil] a. ① 무른, 부서지기 쉬운; (체질이) 약한. [SYN.] ⇨ WEAK. ② 덧없는. /

delicacy n. dainty[déinti], luxury[lʌ́kʃəri], tidbit[tídbìt], elegance[éligəns], exquisiteness[ikskwízit, ékskwi-], fineness [fáinnis], discrimination[diskrìmənéiʃən], sensitivity[sènsətívəti], ant. coarseness[kɔːrsnis]] , insensibility[insènsəbiləti] resilience[rizíljəns, -liəns]

동영상 강좌 http://youtu.be/wvdNsroDkLk

But this is aside from my subject, for what I wish to talk of is the attitude of the American citizen in civic life. It ought to be axiomatic in this country that every man must devote a reasonable share of his time to doing his duty in the Political life of the community.

🔖 해석기법

But this is aside from my subject(그러나 이것은 제 주제와는 별개입니다), **for what I wish to talk of is the attitude of the American citizen in civic life**(왜냐하면 제가 말씀 드리고 싶은 것은 사회생활에서 미 국민의 마음가짐에 관한 것이기 때문입니다). **It ought to be axiomatic in this country that every man must devote a reasonable share of his time to doing his duty in the Political life of the community**(모든 국민들이 합리적으로 배분된 시간을 공동체의 정치적 삶에서 자신의 의무를 다하는 것에 헌신해야만 하는 것은 이 국가에서 반드시 필요한 자명한 사실입니다).

🔖 문법분석\

this[앞에서 언급한 국민의 강인한 정신] / for[접속사 because의 뜻으로 계속적인 용법, 왜냐하면 ～이기 때문이다] / what I wish to talk of[전치사 of의 목적어는 what으로 주어[명사절]이다] / It[가주어] ought to[should, 권고, 훈계, 유감] / that[진주어] every man ～/ devote A[a reasonable share of his time] B[to, 전치사] doing ～: A를 B에 헌신하다. /

🔖 단어분석

♣**aside from** 【미국】 ～은 차치하고; ～을 제외하고 / † **attitude** [ǽtitjùːd] n. ① (사람·물건 등에 대한) 태도, 마음가짐. ② 자세(posture), 몸가짐, 거동. / **axiomatic, —ical** [æ̀ksiəmǽtik], [-əl] a. 자명한 /

🔖 동의어/반의어

attitude n. opinion[əpínjən] n. C 의견 / outlook [áutlùk] n. 사고방식, 견해. / perspective [pəːrspéktiv] n.전망; 시각, 견지 / stance [stæns] (육체적, 정신적인) 자세 / viewpoint [vjúːpɔ̀int] n. 견해, 견

지, 관점(point of view) / bearing [bέəriŋ] n. U,C 태도(manner), 거동, 행동거지 / demeanor[dimíː nər] n. U 태도; 품행, 행실 / manner [mǽnəːr] n. ① 방법, 방식, 투. [SYN.] ⇨ METHOD. ② 태도, 거동, 모양; 훌륭한 태도. ③ (pl.) 예절, 예의, 법식에 맞는 예법. / posture [pástʃər / pós-] n. ① U 자세, 자태. ② 젠체하는 태도. ③ (정신적) 태도, 마음가짐.

No man has a right to shirk his political duties under whatever plea of pleasure or business; and while such shirking may be pardoned in those of small cleans it is entirely unpardonable in those among whom it is most common – in the people whose circumstances give them freedom in the struggle for life.

🔖 해석기법

No man has a right to shirk his political duties under whatever plea of pleasure or business(아무도 쾌락과 사업 핑계가 무엇이든 자신의 정치적 의무를 회피할 권리는 갖고 있지 않습니다); **and while such shirking may be pardoned in those of small cleans**(그리고 그러한 회피가 약간의 청소[핑계]을 대는 사람에게 용서가 될지 모르나) **it is entirely unpardonable in those among whom it is most common – in the people whose circumstances give them freedom in the struggle for life**(대게 그들의 상황이 힘든 생계에서 자유를 받은 사람들에 속하는 사람들에겐 전혀 용서되지 않는 것입니다).

🔖 문법분석

No man[Nobody 아무도 ∼할 수 없는] a right to shirk[부사의 형용사적 용법, ∼회피할 권리] under[∼ 하에서] whatever[복합관계대명사, 무엇이든지] plea ∼(is가 생략됨). / while[접속사, ∼반면에] such shirking[그러한 회피] may[가능성의 조동사, ∼일지 모른다] be pardoned[수동태로, 용서받다] in those of small cleans[약간의 핑계를 대는 사람에게] / those among whom it is most common[일반적인 사람들] - in the people ∼[자유가 허락된 사람들]

🔖 단어분석

∗∗**pleasure** [pléʒər] n. ① U 기쁨, 즐거움(enjoyment); 쾌감, 만족(satisfaction). ② 즐거운 일, 유쾌한 일. ③ 오락, 위안, 즐거움. / † **plea** [pliː] n. ① 탄원, 청원(entreaty); 기원. ② 변명(excuse); 구실, 핑계(pretext). / **shirk** [ʃəːrk] v. —vt. 『∼+목/ +-ing』 (책임 등을) 회피하다; 기피하다. / ‡ **pardon** [páːrdn] vt. ① 용서하다(forgive). ② 『∼+목/ +목+전+명』 관대히 봐주다(tolerate). / ‡ **circumstance** [sə́ːrkəmstæns / -stəns] n. ① (보통 pl.) 상황, 환경; 주위의 사정. ② (pl.) (경제적인) 처지, 생활 형편. ③ C 사건(incident), 사실(fact). ④ U 부대 상황; 상세한 내용, 제목. / **struggle** [strʌ́g-əl] n. ① 버둥질. ② 노력, 고투. ③ 싸움, 전투, 투쟁. [cf.] fight. / ∗∗**common** [kámən / kóm-] a. (∼er, more ∼; ∼est, most ∼) ① (둘 이상에) 공통의, 공동의, 공유(共有)의. ② 협동의, 협력의. ③ 공유(公有)의, 공공의, 공중의. ④ a) 일반의; 만인의, 일반적으로 보급되어 있는. b) 보통의, 일반적인, 평범한, 흔히 있는, 자주 일어나는. [opp.] rare. ⑤ 비속한, 품위 없는, 하치의.

🔖 동의어/반의어

pleasure n. diversion[divə́ːrʒən, -ʃən, dai-], enjoyment[endʒóimənt], entertainment[èntərtéinmənt], fun[fʌn], fancy[fǽnsi], inclination[inklənéiʃən], preference[préfərəns], will[wil], bliss[blis], delight[diláit], elation[iléiʃən], joy[dʒɔi] , gratification[græ̀təfikéiʃən, hedonism[híː dənìzəm, satisfaction [sæ̀tisfǽkʃ-ən] ant. duty[djúː ti], torment[tɔ́ː rment], abstinence[ǽbstənəns], [-si] n. ① U 절제, 금욕, 금주(from).

pardon v. absolve[æbzálv], excuse[ikskjúː z], forgive[fə rgív] , acquit[əkwít], clear[kliər], exonerate [igzánəreît] n. absolution[æ̀bsəlúː ʃən], grace[greis], mercy[mə́ː rsi], amnesty[ǽmnəsti], clemency[klémənsi], leniency [líː niənci] ant. blame[bleim], punish[pʌ́niʃ], revenge[rivéndʒ] punishment[pʌ́niʃmənt]

circumstance n. case[keis], condition[kəndíʃən], estate[istéit], situation[sìtʃuéiʃ-ən], state[steit], event[ivént], happening[hǽpəniŋ], incident[ínsədənt], occurrence[əkɔ́ː rəns, əkʌ́r-], ceremony[sérəmò uni / -məni], formality[fɔː rmǽləti], pageantry[pǽdʒəntri], pomp[pɑmp / pɔmp]

In so far as the community grows to think rightly, it will likewise grow to regard the young man of means who shirks his duty to the State in time of peace as being only one degree worse than the man who thus shirks it in time of war.

📎 해석기법

In so far as the community grows to think rightly(사회가 올바르게 생각하는 한), **it will likewise grow ⑥to regard ②the young man of means who shirks his duty to the State ①in time of peace as being only one degree worse than ④the man who thus shirks it ③in time of war**(평화 시 자신의 의무를 국가에게 대신 돌리려는 교묘한 젊은이들은 전쟁 시 자신의 의무를 피하는 자 보다 약간 더 나쁜 사람으로 똑같이 간주될 것이다).

📎 문법분석

In so far as[접속사, ～하는 한, as long as] grows[become～가 되다], it[가주어] ～to regard[진주어] A[the young～] B[as ～war]: A를 B로 간주하다. / the young man of means[of+명사=형용사구: 모든 수단을 강구하는(교묘한) 젊은이들] / (the young man) being only one degree worse than[비교급, 단지 1도 나쁜, 거의 같은]

📎 단어분석

♯ **likewise** [láikwàiz] ad. ① 똑같이, 마찬가지로. ② 또한, 게다가 또(moreover, also, too). / ***regard** [rigáː rd] v.『+목+as보』 ～을 (―로) 생각하다[여기다] (as). / **shirk** [ʃə rk] v. ―vt.『～+목/ +-ing』 (책임 등을) 회피하다; 기피하다. / ***degree** [digríː] n. ① 정도; 등급, 단계. [SYN.] ⇨ RANK. ② 계급, 지위; 칭호, 학위. ③ (온도·각도·경위도 따위의) 도(度)(부호°); 『수학』 차(次); 『음악』 음계상의 도(度); 『문법』 급(級)(형용사·부사의 비교의). / ♯ **means** [miː nz] n. pl. ①「단·복수취급」 수단, 방법; 기관. ②「복수취급」 자력(資力), 재산, 수입.

📎 동의어/반의어

regard v. consider[kənsídər], judge[dʒʌ́dʒ], rate[reit], think[θiŋk] , view[vjuː], admire[ædmáiər, əd-], esteem,[istíː m] honor[ánər / ɔ́n-], respect[rispékt], revere[rivíə r] , contemplate[kántəmplèit], observe[əbzɔ́ː rv], scan[skæn], scrutinize[skrúː t-ənàiz] ant. disregard[dìsrigáː rd], scorn,[skɔː rn], neglect[niglékt], disrespect[dìsrispékt]

---

shirk v. avoid[əvɔ́id], dodge[dɑdʒ / dɔdʒ], evade[ivéid], loaf[louf], malinger[məlíŋgəː r] vi. (특히 군인 등이) 꾀병을 부리다.

means n. formula[fɔ́ː rmjələ], method[méəəd], mode[moud], procedure[prəsíː dʒər], way[wei], fortune[fɔ́ː rtʃ-ən], riches[rítʃiz] , wealth[welə] ant. end[end] poverty[pávərti / pɔ́v-]

A great many of our men in business, or of our young men who are bent on enjoying life (as they have a perfect right to do if only they do not sacrifice other things to enjoyment), rather plume themselves upon being good citizens if they even vote; yet voting is the very least of their duties, Nothing worth gaining is ever gained without effort.

🔖 해석기법

①**A great many of our men in business**(사업하는 많은 국민들), **or of our young men who are bent on enjoying life**(또는 삶을 즐기는데 열중하는 많은 우리 젊은이들) (②**as they have a perfect right to do if only they do not sacrifice other things to enjoyment**(만일 그들이 쾌락을 위한 나쁜 일에 빠지지 않는 경우, 그들이 즐길 완벽한 권리를 갖듯이), ④**rather plume themselves upon being good citizens**(훌륭한 시민이 됨을 아주 자랑스러워합니다) ③**if they even vote**(만일 그들이 투표까지 한다면); yet voting is the very least of their duties(그러나 투표는 그들 의무의 가장 적은 부분입니다). **Nothing worth gaining is ever gained without effort**(노력 없이 아무것도 얻어질 수는 없는 것이니까요).

🔖 문법분석

A great ~in business, or (a great many) of[주어] who[주격 관계 대명사] are bent on enjoying life [삶에 열중하다] / as[접속사, ~같이] ~do[=enjoy life] if only[~한 경우에만] ~enjoyment, rather plume themselves upon[~을 자랑하다] ~; the very least[극히 작은 영역]. Nothing worth gaining[worth ~ing, ~할 가치가 있는]

🔖 단어분석

⚕ **bend** [bend] v. (p., pp. bent [bent]) —vt. 『+목+전+명』 (눈·걸음을) 딴 데로 돌리다(to; toward(s)); (마음·노력·정력 따위를) 기울이다; 쏟다(on; to; toward). / ⚕ **sacrifice** [sǽkrəfàis]v. —vt. ① 『+목+전+명』 희생하다, 제물로 바치다; 단념[포기]하다(for; to). / ⚕ **plume** [pluː m] vt. 『~+목/ +목+전+명』 깃털로 장식하다; 빌려 입은 옷으로 차려입다. ♣~ oneself 몸을 치장하다.

🔖 동의어/반의어

sacrifice n. oblation[əbléiʃən], offering[ɔ́ː fəriiŋ], tribute[tríbjuː t], concession[kənséʃən] renunciation[rinʌnsiéiʃ-ən] 포기, 체념, loss[lɔ́ː s], reduction[ridʌ́kʃən] v. immolate[iməlèit], forego[fɔ́ː rgóu] 선행하다, forfeit [fɔ́ː rfit] 몰수되다, relinquish[rilíŋkwiʃ], renounce[rináuns] 포기하다 ant. acquisition[ӕkwəzíʃən], gain[gein], withhold[wiðhóuld]

You can no more have freedom without striving and suffering for it than you can win success as a banker or a lawyer without labor and effort, without self-denial in youth and the display of a ready and alert intelligence in middle age.

🪶 해석기법

You can no more have freedom without striving and suffering for it(당신은 자유를 얻기 위한 노력과 고통 없이는 자유를 얻을 수 없는 것과 같습니다) **than you can win success as a banker or a lawyer without labor and effort**(당신이 노동과 노력 없이 은행가나 법률가로 성공할 수 없듯이), **without self-denial in youth and the display of a ready and alert intelligence in middle age**(젊은 시절 자제하지 못한다면 중년의 나이에 준비되고 방심 않는 지성을 보여주지 못하는 것과 마찬가지).

🪶 문법분석

no ~than ~: --- 이 아닌 것은 ~이 아닌 것과 같다. / suffering for it[=freedom] / and (without) the display ~

🪶 단어분석

self-denial [sélfdináiəl] n. U 극기; 금욕(禁慾); 무사(無私). / **ready**[réadi] a. (readier; -iest) ① 준비가 된(for); (언제든지 ~할) 채비를 갖춘; 각오가 되어 있는(to do). ② 금방에라도 ~할 것 같은(to do). ③ 즉석에서의, 당장에 응(應)하는; 재빠른; 교묘한(at). [SYN.] ⇨ QUICK. / **alert**[əlɔ́ːrt] a. ① 방심 않는, 정신을 바짝 차린, 빈틈없는(watchful). / **intelligence**[intélədʒəns] n. U ① 지성, 이지; 이해력, 사고력, 지능; 지혜, 총명. ② 정보, 보도

🪶 동의어/반의어

alert a. attentive[əténtiv], conscious[kánʃəs], mindful[máindfəl], vigilant[vídʒələnt] , watchful[wátʃfəl] ant. oblivious[əblíviəs], lethargic[leθáːrdʒik]혼수 상태의, 둔감한

The people who say that they have not time to attend to politics are simply saying that they are unfit to live in a free community.

🪶 해석기법

The people who say that they have not time to attend to politics(정치에 관심을 둘 시간이 없다고 말하는 사람들은) **are simply saying that they are unfit to live in a free community**(그들이 자유 공동체 사회에서 사는데 걸맞지 않다고 단순히 말하고 있는 것이 됩니다).

🪶 문법분석

The people who[주격 관계대명사] say that[접속사] / have not[=don't have] / ~attend to[주의하다] ~ are[동사] ~saying that[접속사] they are unfit[맞지 않는]

🔖 단어분석

₊₊attend [əténd] v. —vt. ① ~에 출석하다. ②『~+목/ +목+전+명』(문어) (결과로서) ~을 수반하다. ③ ~와 동행[동반]하다, 수행하다, ~을 섬기다. [SYN.] ⇨ ACCOMPANY. ④ ~을 시중들다, 왕진하다, (병자를) 간호하다; (고객을) 응대하다. ⑤ (고어) ~에 주의하다, 소중하게 간직하다. —vi.『+전+명』① 출석하다(at). ② 시중들다, 섬기다(on, upon). ③ 보살피다, 돌보다, 간호하다(on, upon; to). ④ 주의하다, 경청하다(to).

🔖 동의어/반의어

unfit a. unhealthy[ʌnhéləi], incapable[inkéipəbəl], incompetent[inkámpətənt], unqualified[ʌnkwáləfàid], improper[imprápər], inappropriate[inəpróupriit], unsuitable[ʌnsúː təbəl]

ant. fit[fit], competent[kámpətənt] apt[æpt]

free a. emancipated[imǽnsəpèit], liberated[líbərèit], autonomous[ɔː tánəməs], independent[indipéndənt], separate[sépərit], sovereign[sáv-ərin], complimentary[kàmpləméntəri], gratis[gréitis]

❋ 다음 글을 읽고 물음에 답하시오. [1~3]

Of course, in one sense, the first essential for a man's being a good citizen is his possession of the home virtues of which we think when we call a man by the emphatic adjective of manly. No man can be a good citizen who is not a good husband and a good father, who is not honest in his dealings with other men and women, faithful to his friends and fearless in the presence of his foes, who has not got a sound heart, a sound mind, and a sound body; exactly as no amount of attention to civil duties will save a nation _____, or there is lack of the rude military virtues which alone can assure a country's position in the world. In a free republic the ideal citizen must be one willing and able to take arms for the defense of the flag, exactly as the ideal citizen must be the father of many healthy children. A race must be strong and vigorous; it must be a race of good fighters and good breeders, else its wisdom will come to naught and its virtue be ineffective; and no sweetness and delicacy, no love for and appreciation of beauty in art or literature, no capacity for building up material prosperity can possibly atone for the lack of the great virile virtues.

1. 위 글의 주제로 가장 적절한 것은?

① We all have to be ideal citizens for the sake of material prosperity.
② As long as one has a good attitude on the nation, it doesn't matter how much he think of his family and friends.
③ To be a great businessman, one should learn much of social relationship.
④ The nation always goes beyond the home.
⑤ A ideal citizen takes the first step in the domestic affection.

2. 위 글의 밑줄 친 빈칸에 가장 적절한 표현은?

① if one doesn't have his family
② though the nation is weak
③ if the domestic life is undermined
④ as if a ideal citizen has a great amount of experiences
⑤ if the social environment doesn't match with that of the world

3. 위 글과 일치하지 않은 것은?

① 훌륭한 시민의 첫 필수조건은 가정에 대한 덕망을 소유하고 있느냐고 판단될 수 있다.
② 훌륭한 남편이자 아버지만이 이상적인 시민의 자격을 갖출 수 있다.
③ 위기 시에 국가보다 가족을 먼저 보살펴야만 한다.
④ 국민은 훌륭한 전사나 양육자가 되어야만 한다.

⑤ 물질만 추구하는 번영은 결국엔 소멸할 수밖에 없다.

✸ 다음 글을 읽고 물음에 답하시오. [4~6]

But this is aside for/aside from my subject, for what I wish to talk of is the attitude of the American citizen in civic life. It ought to be axiomatic in this country that every man must devote a reasonable share of his time doing/to doing his duty in the Political life of the community. No man has a right to shirk his political duties under whatever/whenever plea of pleasure or business; and while such shirking may be pardoned in those of ①**small** cleans it is entirely unpardonable in those among whom it is most common–in the people whose circumstances give them ②**freedom** in the struggle for life. In so far as the community grows to think ③**rightly**, it will likewise grow to regard the young man of means who shirks his duty to the State in time of peace as being only one degree ④**better** than the man who thus shirks it in time of war. A great many of our men in business, or of our young men who are bent on ⑤ **enjoying** life (as they have a perfect right to do if only they do not sacrifice other things to enjoyment), rather plume themselves upon being good citizens if they

even vote; yet voting is the very least of their duties, Nothing worth gaining is ever gained without effort.

4. 위 글에서 네모상자 안의 적절한 단어를 고르시오.

① aside for   doing   whatever
② aside from   doing   whenever
③ aside for   doing   whenever
④ aside from   to doing   whatever
⑤ aside for   to doing   whatever

5. 위 글에서 밑줄 친 ①~⑤ 중, 문맥상 단어의 쓰임이 어색한 것은?

①   ②   ③   ④   ⑤

6. 위 글과 일치하는 것은?

① 작가는 시민생활에서 국민의 마음가짐이 무엇보다 중요하다고 강조한다.
② 모든 국민은 합리적으로 할당된 시간에 자신의 업무에 충실해야만 한다.
③ 정치적 의무는 때때로 회피할 권리를 지닌다.
④ 힘든 생계에서 자유를 얻은 사람은 정치적 의무에 면제를 받는다.
⑤ 이상적 시민의 투표권은 가장 큰 영향을 끼친다.

1. ⑤   2. ③   3. ③   4. ④
5. ④ better → worse   6. ①

Their place is under a despotism; or if they are content to do nothing but vote, you can take despotism tempered by an occasional plebiscite, like that of the second Napoleon.

🔖 해석기법

Their place is under a despotism(그들의 터전은 독제권력 하에 놓여 있거나); **or if they are content to do nothing but vote**(만일 그들이 단지 선거에만 만족한다면), **you can take despotism tempered by an occasional plebiscite, like that of the second Napoleon**(당신은 제2차 나폴레옹 독제와 같이 가끔 있는 국민투표에 단련된 독제를 선택할 수 있다).

🔖 문법분석

do[강조용법=really] nothing but[=only 단지] vote[투표하다] / take despotism (which is) tempered by [～의해 단련된 독재를 선택하다] / like that[=despotism]

🔖 단어분석

despotism [déspətìzəm] n. U 독재, 전제; 전제 정치; 폭정. / †**content** [kəntént] a. 「서술적」 (～에) 만족하는, 감수하는(with); / †**temper** [témpə：r] v. —vt. ① 『～+목/ +목+전+명』 부드럽게 하다, 진정시키다, 누르다, 경감하다. / **plebiscite** [plébəsàit, -sit] n. (국가적 중요 문제에 관한) 국민[일반] 투표 (referendum).

🔖 동의어/반의어

despotism n. despot[déspət], dictator[díkteitər], oppressor, totalitarian[toutをləté-əriən, overlord[óuvərlɔ̀：rd], slave driver, taskmaster[tをskmをstə：r] 공사감독, 혹사하는 사람 ant. slave[sleiv]

In one of Lowell's magnificent stanzas about the Civil War he speaks of the fact which his countrymen were then learning, that freedom is not a gift that tarries long in the hands of cowards: nor yet does it tarry long in the hands of the sluggard and the idler, in the hands of the man so much absorbed in the pursuit of pleasure or in the pursuit of gain, or so much wrapped up in his own easy home life as to be unable to take his part in the rough struggle with his fellow men for political supremacy.

🔖 해석기법

In one of Lowell's magnificent stanzas about the Civil War(내란에 관한 로웰의 웅장한 서사시중 하나에서) **he speaks of the fact which his countrymen were then learning**(그 당시 자신의 국민들이 알고 있었던 사실은), **that freedom is not a gift that tarries long in the hands of cowards**(자유란 겁쟁이들의 권력 안에서 오랫동안 기다리는 선물이 아니라는 사실입니다): **nor yet does it tarry long in the hands of the sluggard and the idler**(또한 자유란 나태하거나 게으름뱅이의 권력 하에서 ～오래 기다리지 않는 것입니다), **in the hands of the man so much absorbed in the pursuit of pleasure or in the pursuit of gain**(쾌락과 이익을 추구하는데 너무나 열중하는 사람의 권력 하에서), **or so much wrapped**

Duties of American Citizenship

by Theodore Roosevelt

up in his own easy home life as to be unable to take his part in the rough struggle with his fellow men for political supremacy(정치적 패권을 위해 동료들과 힘든 투쟁에 참여할 수 없어서 자신의 쉬운 가정생활에 너무 몰두하는 사람의 권력 하에서는).

📝 문법분석

one of 복수명사[~중에 하나] / the fact which[관계대명사] ~that[접속사, the fact와 동격 ~라는 사실] ~in the hands[권력 하에서] ~; nor yet[또한 그러나] does[nor로 인해 도치된 문장] ~the man (who is) so much absorbed in[~에 너무 몰두하는 사람] ~, or (the man who is) so much wrapped up[~에 침묵하는 사람] ~as to[~하기 위해서] ~take his part in[~에 참여하다]

📝 단어분석

⍭ **magnificent** [mægnífəsənt] a. ① 장대한(grand), 장엄한, 장려한. ② 당당한, 훌륭한, (생각 따위가) 고상한, 격조 높은. ③ 엄청난, 막대한. / ⍭ **stanza** [stǽnzə]n. 운율』 (시의) 연(聯) / **tarry** [tǽri] v. —vi. ① 체재하다, 묵다(at; in; on). ② 시간이 걸리다, 늦어지다; 주저하다. ③ 기다리다(for). —vt. ~을 기다리다. / ⍭ **coward** [káuərd] n. 겁쟁이; 비겁한 자; / **sluggard** [slʌ́gəːrd] n. 게으름쟁이, 빈둥거리는 사람, 나태자(懶怠者). / **idler** [áidlər] n. 게으름뱅이; / ⍭ **supremacy** [səpréməsi, su(ː)-] n.패권; 우위, 우월.

📝 동의어/반의어

supremacy n. ascendancy[əséndənsi], dominance[dámənəns], preeminence[priémənəns], superiority[supìərió(ː)rəti]

If freedom is worth having, if the right of self-government is a valuable right, then the one and the other must be retained exactly as our forefathers acquired them, by labor, and especially by labor in organization, that is in combination with our fellows who have the same interests and the same principles.

📝 해석기법

If freedom is worth having(만일 자유가 쟁취할 가치가 있다면), **if the right of self-government is a valuable right**(자치정부의 권리가 귀중한 권리라면), **then the one and the other**(그때 전자와 후자는) **must be retained exactly as our forefathers acquired them**(~ 우리의 조상들이 그것들을 얻었던 방식대로 보존되어야만 합니다), **by labor, and especially by labor in organization, that is in combination with our fellows who have the same interests and the same principles**(같은 이익과 원칙을 갖는 동료들과 결합되어 있는 조직체서 특히 노력에 의해).

📝 문법분석

worth ~ing[~할 가치가 있는] / the one[전자: 자유] and the other[후자, 자치정부의 권리] / ~exactly as[접속사: ~와 같이] ~them[=freedom, right of self-government] ~that[관계대명사]

📝 단어분석

⁑**valuable** [vǽljuːəbəl, -ljəbəl] a. ① 귀중한, 귀한, 소중한. ② 값비싼. / ⍭ **retain** [ritéin]vt. 보류하다,

보유[유지]하다. [SYN.] ⇨ KEEP. / ‡ **forefather** [fɔ́ːrfɑ̀ːðər] n. (보통 pl.) 조상, 선조(ancestor). / ‡ **acquire** [əkwáiər] vt. ① 손에 넣다, 획득하다; (버릇·기호·학력 따위를) 몸에 익히다, 습득하다. [SYN.] ⇨ GET. ② (재산·권리 등을) 취득하다. /

We should not accept the excuse of the business man who attributed his failure to the fact that his social duties were so pleasant and engrossing that he had no time left for work in his office; nor would we pay much heed to his further statement that he did not like business anyhow because he thought the morals of the business community by no means what they should be, and saw that the great successes were most often won by men of the Jay Gould stamp.

🔖 해석기법

We should not accept the excuse of the business man(우리는 ～장사꾼의 변명을 받아들여서는 안 됩니다) **who attributed his failure to the fact that his social duties were so pleasant and engrossing that he had no time left for work in his office**(자신의 실패는 그의 사회적 의무가 너무나 호감이 가고 매력적이어서 자신의 업무를 할 시간이 없었다는 사실을 탓으로 돌리는); **nor would we pay much heed to his further statement that he did not like business anyhow**(또는 그는 어쨌든 장사를 싫어했어라는 말에 우리가 주의를 기울이지 않고 했다는 사실에) **because he thought the morals of the business community by no means what they should be**(그는 장사의 도덕성은 결코 존재하지 않을 거라고 생각했고), **and saw that the great successes were most often won by men of the Jay Gould stamp**(큰 성공은 Jay Gould stamp 직원들만의 몫이라 보는 것 때문에).

🔖 문법분석

attribute A to B: A를 B의 탓으로 돌리다. ～the fact that[동격절: ～라는 사실] / so A[pleasant and engrossing] that 절[너무 ～해서 …하다] / nor would[도치문: = or we would not] we pay much heed to[더 주의를 기울이다] his further statement that he did not like business anyhow[그는 어쨌든 장사를 싫어했어라는 이후의 말] / because he though A[the morals ～community] by no means[=never] B[what they should be, they=morals, 도덕성이 있어야만 하는]: A를 B로 생각하다.

🔖 단어분석

✱✱pleasant [pléznt] a. (more ～, ～er; most ～, ～est)(중심적인 뜻: 유쾌한 기분이 되게 하는). ① (사물이) 즐거운, 기분 좋은, 유쾌한. ② (날씨가) 좋은. ③ 호감이 가는, 상냥한; 쾌활한. / **engrossing** [engróusiŋ] a. 마음을 빼앗는, 몰두시키는. / ‡ **heed** [hiːd] n. U 주의(attention), 유의(regard); 배려, 조심. / **statement** [stéitmənt] n. 명세서; (사업) 보고(서). / ‡ **anyhow** [énihàu] ad. ① 아무리 해도. ② 어떤 식[방법]으로든, 어떻게든; 여하튼, 좌우간, 어쨌든. ③ 적당히 얼버무려, 아무렇게나. / ‡ **moral** [mɔ́ː( )r-əl, mǽr-]a. ① 도덕(상)의, 윤리(상)의, 도덕[윤리]에 관한. ② 덕육적인, 훈계[교육]적인. /

🔖 동의어/반의어

engrossing a. absorbing[æbsɔ́ːrbiŋ], captivating[kǽptəvèitiŋ], engaging[engéidʒiŋ], fascinating[fǽsənèitiŋ], interesting[íntəristiŋ], obsessive [əbsésiv] ant. boring

It is just the same way with politics. It makes one feel half angry and half amused, and wholly contemptuous, to find men of high business or social standing in the community saying that they really have not got time to go to ward meetings, to organize political clubs, and to take a personal share in all the important details of practical politics; men who further urge against their going the fact that they think the condition of political morality low, and are afraid that they may be required to do what is not right if they go into politics.

🔖 해석기법

It is just the same way with politics(그것은 정치와 아주 흡사합니다). **It makes one feel half angry and half amused, and wholly contemptuous**(그것은 사람을 어느 정도 분노하게 하거나 기쁘게도 만들며 아주 모욕감을 갖게도 합니다), **to find men of high business or social standing in the community saying**(～ 말하는 높은 직위의 기업가나 사회적 덕망이 높은 사람들을 찾기 위해서) **that they really have not got time to go to ward meetings, to organize political clubs, and to take a personal share in all the important details of practical politics**(그들은 감독회의에 가거나 정치클럽을 조직하거나 실질적 정치의 모든 중요한 세부사항에서 개인적 이득을 챙길 시간이 정말로 없다고); **men who further urge against their going the fact that they think the condition of political morality low**(그들은 정치적 도덕성의 상황이 낮다고 생각하는 사실과), **and are afraid that they may be required to do what is not right if they go into politics**(만일 그들이 정치에 입문한다면 옳지 않은 것을 요구받을지 모른다고 염려하는 사실에 대해 역설하는 사람들).

🔖 문법분석

the same as[with] ～와 같은 / makes[사역동사] + one[목적어] + feel[원형동사] half[부사] angry[형용사, 목적격보어] / to find men (of high business[of+명사=형용사구] or (of) social standing[of+명사=형용사구]) ～saying[의 주어는 men] / (to find) men who further urge against[～대해 역설[반대]하다] their going the fact[그들이 ～라는 사실로 들어가는 것] that[접속사] they think A[the condition ～] B[low]: A를 B라고 생각하다 / † morality [mɔ(ː)rǽləti, mɑr-] n. ① U 도덕(성), 도의(성); U (개인 또는 특정 사회의) 덕성, 윤리성. ② 선악, 정사(正邪). ③ U 품행, 행실; (남녀간의) 풍기.

🔖 단어분석

half [hæf, hɑːf] ad. ① 절반, 반쯤. ② 불완전하게, 어중간하게, 적당히, 되는 대로. ③ 얼마쯤, 어느 정도; 거의, 몹시. / † **contemptuous** [kəntémptʃuəs] a. 모욕적인, 남을 얕보는, (～을) 경멸하는(of). [SYN.] ⇨ CONTEMPTIBLE. / † **ward** [wɔːrd] n. ① U 보호; 감독, 감시; 억류, 연금. ② 「집합적」보호[감독]자들. / **low** [lou] a. ① 낮은(키·고도·온도·위도·평가 따위). [opp.] high. ② (신분·태생이) 낮은(humble), 비천한, 하층의. ③ 저급의, 상스러운; 추접[외설]한. / † **urge** [əːrdʒ] v. —vt. ①『～+목/ +목+전+명/ +목+부』좨치다, 재촉하다, 노력하게 하다. —vi. ① 주장[요구, 반대 의견 등]을 역설하다. / † **morality** [mɔ(ː)rǽləti, mɑr-] n. ① U 도덕(성), 도의(성); U (개인 또는 특정 사회의) 덕성, 윤리성. ② 선악, 정사(正邪).

🔖 동의어/반의어

contemptuous a. arrogant[ǽrəgənt], condescending[kàndiséndiŋ] 생색내는, disdainful[disdéinfəl], haughty[hɔ́ːti], scornful[skɔ́ːrnfəl] ant. gracious[gréiʃəs] 호의적인, 정중한, accommodating[əkámədèitiŋ], amiable[éimiəbəl]

✳ 다음 글을 읽고 물음에 답하시오. [7~9]

Ⓐ**You can no more have freedom without striving and suffering for it than you can win success as a banker or a lawyer without labor and effort**, without self-denial in youth and the display of a ready and ① **alert** intelligence in middle age. The people who say that they have not time to attend to politics are simply saying that they are ②**fit** to live in a free community. Their place is under a despotism; or if they are ③**content** to do nothing but vote, you can take despotism tempered by an occasional plebiscite, like that of the second Napoleon. In one of Lowell's magnificent stanzas about the Civil War he speaks of the fact which his countrymen were then learning, that Ⓑ**freedom** is not a gift that tarries long in the hands of cowards: nor yet does it tarry long in the hands of the sluggard and the idler, in the hands of the man so much ④**absorbed** in the pursuit of pleasure or in the pursuit of gain, or so much wrapped up in his own ⑤**easy** home life as to be unable to take his part in the rough struggle with his fellow men for political supremacy.

---

7. 위 글에서 밑줄 친 Ⓐ의 의미와 같은 것은?

① Freedom needs more effort and labor than success as a banker.

② Not only does freedom need effort, but also suffering.

③ Both freedom and success are required with striving and effort.

④ There are some different gap between freedom and success.

⑤ Freedom and success are that we should attain to.

8. 위 글에서 밑줄 친 ①~⑤ 중, 문맥상 단어 쓰임이 <u>어색한</u> 것은?

①   ②   ③   ④   ⑤

9. 위 글에서 밑줄 친 Ⓑ를 방해하는 것이 <u>아닌</u> 것은?

① cowards

② sluggard

③ the man in the pursuit of pleasure

④ the man in his own easy home life

⑤ the man to take his part in the rough struggle

✳ 다음 글을 읽고 물음에 답하시오. [10~13]

If freedom is worth having, if the right of self-government is a valuable right, then Ⓐ **the one and the other** must be retained exactly as our forefathers acquired them, by labor, and especially by labor in organization, that is in combination with our fellows who have the same interests and the same principles.

We should not accept the excuse of the business man who attributed his failure for/to the fact that his social duties were so pleasant and engrossing that he had no time left for work in his office; nor/or would we pay much heed to his further statement that he did not like business anyhow because he thought the morals of the business community by no means what they should be, and saw that the great successes were most often won by men of the Jay Gould stamp. It is just the same way with politics. It makes one feel half angry and half amused, and wholly contemptuous, to find men of high business or social standing in

---

the community saying that they really have not got time to go to ward meetings, to organize political clubs, and to take a personal share in all the important details of practical politics; men who further urge against their going the fact that they think the condition of political morality high/low, and are afraid that they may be required to do what is not right if they go into politics.

10. 위 글의 주제로 가장 적절한 것은?

① The success of business should be based on politics.
② We should be careful of people saying some excuses.
③ Business and politics are the same.
④ To be successful in politics we should start in politics first.
⑤ Politics is so attractive we had better go into politics.

11. 위 글에서 밑줄 친 Ⓐ의 'the one'과 'the other'가 가리키는 것은?

① one person and the other person
② we and our forefathers
③ freedom and forefathers
④ freedom and the right of self-government
⑤ organization and combination

12. 위 글의 네모상자 안의 적절한 단어?

① for	nor	high
② to	nor	low
③ for	nor	low
④ to	or	high
⑤ for	or	low

13. 위 글의 분위기는?

① It's in the mood of understanding readers with many examples.
② It's very difficult for us to understand the article.
③ The author is blaming for business and politics.
④ The mood is exciting and encouraging.
⑤ Its atmosphere is complicated but relaxing.

6. ①   7. ③   8. ② fit → unfit
9. ⑤   10. ③   11. ④   12. ②   13. ①

The first duty of an American citizen, then, is that he shall work in politics; his second duty is that he shall do that work in a practical manner; and his third is that it shall be done in accord with the highest principles of honor and justice.

🖋 해석기법

The first duty of an American citizen, then, is that he shall work in politics(미국 시민의 첫째 의무는 그렇다면 시민이 정치에 참여하게 하는 것입니다); **his second duty is that he shall do that work in a practical manner**(그의 두 번째 임무는 실리적인 방식에서 정치에 참여하는 것입니다); **and his third is that it shall be done in accord with the highest principles of honor and justice**(그리고 그의 세 번째 임무는 정치가 명예와 정의의 가장 고결한 원칙에 따라 행해져야 하는 것입니다).

🖋 문법분석

shall[말하는 사람의 의지] ～하게 하는 것이다 / do = work / his third (duty) is that[접속사, 보어로서 명사절] it[=politics] shall be done[be worked] in accord with[～에 일치하여, 따라]

🖋 단어분석

⚓ **practical** [prǽktikəl] a. ① 실제의, 실제상의; 실리상의. [cf.] speculative, theoretical. 경험이 풍부한, 경험 있는. / ⚓ **principle** [prínsəpəl] n. ① 원리, 원칙, (물리·자연의) 법칙. [SYN.] ⇨ THEORY. ② 행동 원리, 정의; (pl.) 도의, 절조. / ⚓**honor**, 【영국】 -our [ánər / ɔ́n-] n. 명예, 영예; 영광.

🖋 동의어/반의어

principle n. law[lɔː], regulation[règjəléiʃ-ən] rule[ruː l], axiom[ǽksiəm] 자명한 이치, 격언, postulate[pástʃəlèit], precept[príː sept] 교훈, 격언, 법칙, belief[bilíː f], creed[kriː d] 신조, tenet[ténət, tíː -], ethics[éθiks] 윤리, integrity[intégrəti], morality[mɔ(ː)rǽləti], reason [ríː z-ən], standards[stǽndəː rds], grounds[graunds], motive[móutiv], rationale [rὰʃənǽl] 근본적 이유, ant. immorality

---

Of course, it is not possible to define rigidly just the way in which the work shall be made practical. Each man's individual temper and convictions must be taken into account. To a certain extent his work must be done in accordance with his individual beliefs and theories of right and wrong.

🖋 해석기법

Of course(물론), **it is not possible to define rigidly just the way in which the work shall be made practical**(그 일이(정치가) 실용적이 되게 하려는 방식을 아주 정확히 정의하는 것을 불가능합니다). **Each man's individual temper and convictions must be taken into account**(각 개인의 성격과 양심이 고려되어져야만 합니다). **To a certain extent**(어느 정도까지) **his work must be done in accordance with his individual beliefs and theories of right and wrong**(그의 정치활동은 개인적 신념과 옳고 그릇된 이론에 부응하여 행해져야만 합니다).

Duties of American Citizenship

🔖 문법분석

it[가주어] is not possible[형용사] (for us)[의미상의 주어] to define[진주어] ~/ take A into account[=consideration]: A를 고려하다 /

🔖 단어분석

† **rigid** [rídʒid] a. ① 굳은, 단단한, 휘어지지 않는. [opp.] pliable, soft. / ‡ **temper** [témpə：r] n. ① a) 기질, 천성, 성질. [cf.] disposition. / ‡ **conviction** [kənvíkʃən] n. ① U,C 신념, 확신. [SYN.] ⇨ CONFIDENCE. ② 양심의 가책. / † **accordance** [əkɔ́：rdəns] n. U 일치, 조화; 부합; 수여. / ‡ **theory** [θí：əri]n. ① 학설, 설(說), 논(論), (학문상의) 법칙.

🔖 동의어/반의어

rigid a. fixed [fikst], hard[ha：rd], stiff[stif], tense[tens], adamant[ǽdəmənt], unyielding[ʌnjí：ldiŋ], obdurate[ábdjurit], uncompromising[ʌnkámprəmàiziziŋ], austere[ɔ：stíər], harsh[ha：rʃ], severe[sivíə：r], stern[stə：rn], strict[strikt] ant. supple[sʌ́pəl], flexible[fléksəbəl], lenient[lí：niənt]

To a yet greater extent it must be done in combination with others, he yielding or modifying certain of his own theories and beliefs so as to enable him to stand on a common ground with his fellows, who have likewise yielded or modified certain of their theories and beliefs.

🔖 해석기법

To a yet greater extent(이제 더 큰 범위로 볼 때) **it must be done in combination with others**(그것은 다른 사람들과 연계하여 행해져야만 합니다), **he yielding or modifying certain of his own theories and beliefs**(그는 어떠한 자신만의 이론과 신념을 제시하고 수정할 것입니다) **so as to enable him to stand on a common ground with his fellows**(자신이 ~동료들과 함께 공통의 토대 위에 설 수 있도록 하기 위해서), **who have likewise yielded or modified certain of their theories and beliefs**(어떠한 그들의 이론과 신념도 마찬가지로 제시되어 수정된).

🔖 문법분석

To a yet greater extent[이제 ~라는 더 큰 범위에서] it ~/ [분사구문] (as he is) he yielding or modifying ~so as to[~하기 위해서]

🔖 단어분석

‡ **combination** [kàmbənéiʃən / kɔ̀m-] n. U,C ① 결합, 짝맞추기; 연합, 공동(동작); (색 등의) 배합. / ‡ **extent** [ikstént] n. ① U 넓이, 크기, 길이. ② 광활한 지역. ③ C 정도; 범위, 한계, 한도. / ‡ **likewise** [láikwàiz] ad. ① 똑같이, 마찬가지로. ② 또한, 게다가 또(moreover, also, too). / ‡ **yield** [ji：ld] v. —vi. ① 생기게 하다, 산출(産出)하다(produce); (이익 따위를) 가져오다. [SYN.] ⇨ CROP. / ‡ **modify** [mádəfai / mɔ́d-]v. —vt. ① 수정[변경]하다. ② 완화하다, 조절[제한]하다.

---

common a. collective[kəléktiv], communal[kəmjú： nl], public[pʌ́blik], customary[kʌ́stəmèri], familiar[fəmíljər], frequent[frí： kwənt], routine[ru： tí： n], average[ǽvəridʒ], conventional[kənvé nʃənəl]

There is no need of dogmatizing about independence on the one hand or party allegiance on the other. There are occasions when it may be the highest duty of any man to act outside of parties and against the one with which he has himself been hitherto identified; and there may be many more occasions when his highest duty is to sacrifice some of his own cherished opinions for the sake of the success of the party which he on the whole believes to be right.

📎 해석기법

There is no need of dogmatizing about independence on the one hand or party allegiance on the other(한편으로 무소속이거나 다른 한편으로 정당에 충실하다고 단정 지을 필요는 없습니다). ④**There are occasions**(~인 경우도 있습니다) ③**when it may be the highest duty**(~ 가장 숭고한 의무가 될 수도 있는 때) ①**of any man to act outside of parties**(누군가가 정당에 소속되지 않고 활동하는 것과) ②**and against the one with which he has himself been hitherto identified**(그가 지금껏 소속되었던 정당에 반대하여 활동하는 것이); **and there may be many more occasions**(많은 ~도 있을 수 있습니다) **when his highest duty is to sacrifice some of his own cherished opinions for the sake of the success of the party which he on the whole believes to be right**(그의 숭고한 의무가 어떤 자기 자신의 소중한 의견이 그가 전반적으로 옳다고 믿는 정당의 성공에 희생을 당하는 경우).

📎 문법분석

on the other (hand)[다른 한편으로] / There are occasions[~인 경우(기회)도 있다] / when it[가주어] may ~of any man[의미상의 주어] to act[진주어] ~and (any man to act) against the one[=party] / ~been hitherto identified (with the one 정당과 동일시하다)[which 관계대명사의 선행사는 the one] / sacrifice A[희생시키다] for the sake of[~을 위하여] the success of the party which[관계대명사] he on the whole[전반적으로] believes[의 목적어는 the success of the party]

📎 단어분석

dogmatize [dɔ́(：)gmətàiz, dάg-] vi.,vt. 독단적으로 단정하다[말하다] / †allegiance [əlí： dʒəns] n. U,C 충실 / ☨occasion [əkéiʒən] n. ① (특정한) 경우, 때(on), 기회 / ☨hitherto [hìðərtú：] ad. 지금까지(는), / ☨identify [aidéntəfài] v. —vt. (~와) 동일시하다 / ☨sacrifice [sǽkrəfàis]v. —vt. 희생하다, 제물로 바치다; 단념[포기]하다.

📎 동의어/반의어

allegiance n. devotion[divóuʃən], faithfulness[féiθfəlnis], fealty [fí： əlti], fidelity[fidéləti], ant. treachery[trétʃ-əri] 배반

Duties of American Citizenship

by Theodore Roosevelt

I do not think that the average citizen, at least in one of our great cities, can very well manage to support his own party all the time on every issue, local and otherwise; at any rate if he can do so he has been more fortunately placed than I have been.

📎 **해석기법**

I do not think that the average citizen, at least in one of our great cities(적어도 큰 대도시에 사는 일반 시민이), **can very well manage to support his own party all the time on every issue, local and otherwise**(지역적이거나 다른 모든 문제에 늘 자신의 정당을 전적으로 지지한다고 저는 생각지 않습니다) ; **at any rate if he can do so he has been more fortunately placed than I have been**(아무튼 만일 그가 그렇게 할 수 있다면 그는 제 상황보다 더 좋은 상황에 있는 것입니다).

📎 **문법분석**

manage to[가까스로 ～하다] ～on every issue, (which is) local and otherwise[some other issues]; if [조건절, 만일 ～라면] he can do so[=support ～otherwise] ～placed[현재의 상황] that I have been (placed) /

📎 **단어분석**

╪ **average** [ǽvəridʒ] a. 평균의; 보통의. / ╪ **otherwise** [ʌ́ðərwàiz] a. ① 「서술용법」 딴 것의, 다른. ② 「한정용법」 만약 그렇지 않다면 ～인[일지도 모르는]. / ⁎⁎**place** [pleis] v. ─vt. 직위에 앉히다; 임명하다; /

📎 **동의어/반의어**

<u>average</u> a. mediocre[miː dióukəː r], passable[pǽsəbəl] ant. unusual[ʌnjúː ʒuəl], exception[iksépʃən] extreme[ikstríː m]

On the other hand, I am fully convinced that to do the best work people must be organized; and of course an organization is really a party, whether it be a great organization covering the whole nation and numbering its millions of adherents, or an association of citizens in a particular locality, banded together to win a certain specific victory, as, for instance, that of municipal reform.

📎 **해석기법**

On the other hand(다른 한편으로), **I am fully convinced**(저는 ～가 완전히 이해가 갑니다) **that to do the best work**(최고의 일을 하기 위해서) **people must be organized**(사람들은 체계적이어야만 합니다); **and of course an organization is really a party**(물론 조직이 진정한 정당입니다), **whether it be a great organization covering the whole nation and numbering its millions of adherents**(그것이 전국적이고 수백만 지지자들로 구성된 조직이든), **or an association of citizens in a particular locality, banded together to win a certain specific victory**(어떤 특정한 승리를 쟁취하기 위해 함께 결속된 특정 지역에

근거한 시민협회든 간에), **as, for instance, that of municipal reform**(예를 들어, 도시개혁 조직과 같은).

🖎 문법분석

to do[to부정사의 목적, ∼하기 위해서] ∼, whether[접속사] it (should) be a great organization (which is) covering ∼and (which is) numbering ∼in a particular locality, (who are) banded together

---

🖎 단어분석

† **adherent** [ǽdhíərənt] n. 지지자, 신봉자 / ✱✱**number** [nʌ́mbəːr] v. —vt. 구성원으로[요소로] 간주하다(among; in; with). / ‡ municipal [mjuːnísəp-əl]a. 시(市)의, 도시의, 자치 도시의, 시정(市政)

※ 다음 글을 읽고 물음에 답하시오. [14~21]

The first duty of an American citizen, then, is that he shall work in politics; his second duty is that he shall do that work in a practical manner; and his third is that it shall be done ①**in accord with** the highest principles of honor and justice. Of course, it is not possible to define rigidly just the way in which the work shall be made practical. Each man's individual temper and convictions must be taken ②**in account**. To a certain extent his work must be done ③**in accordance with** his individual beliefs and theories of right and wrong. To a yet greater extent it must be done ④**in combination with** others, he is yielding/yielding or modifying certain of his own theories and beliefs so as to enable him to stand on a common ground with his fellows, who have likewise yielded or modified certain of their theories and beliefs. There is no need of dogmatizing about independence ⑤**on the one hand** or party allegiance on the other. There are occasions when it may be the highest duty of any man to act outside of parties and against the one which/with which he has himself been hitherto identified; and there may be many more occasions when his highest duty is to sacrifice some of his own cherished opinions for the sake of the success of the party for which/which he on the whole believes to be right. I do not think that the average citizen, at least in one of our great cities, can very well manage to support his own party all the time on every issue, local and otherwise; at any rate if he can do Ⓐ**so** he has been more fortunately placed than I have been. On the other hand, I am fully convinced that to do the best work

_____; and of course an organization is really a party, whether it be a great organization covering the whole nation and numbering its millions of adherents, or an association of citizens in a particular locality, banded together to win a certain specific victory, as, for instance, Ⓑ **that** of municipal reform.

14. 위 글의 주제로 가장 적절한 것은?

① Just one party should be existed covering all the nation.
② One's opinion should be extended to all the others' spectrum until it covers all opinions.
③ If one party is chosen, one must not change it to another.
④ To be ideal citizens, we should not participate in any organizations.
⑤ To take part in politics, one should be in any kind of proper organization.

15. 위 글에서 밑줄 친 ①~⑤ 중, 쓰임이 <u>어색한</u> 것은?

①   ②   ③   ④   ⑤

16. 위 글에서 네모상자 안의 적절한 단어는?

① is yielding	which	for which
② yielding	with which	for which
③ is yielding	with which	which
④ yielding	which	which
⑤ yielding	with which	which

17. 위 글에서 밑줄 친 ⒶⒶ가 가리키는 것은?

① not to think

② to support his own party

③ to be an average citizen

④ to be local and otherwise

⑤ to manage his own party

18. 위 글에서 밑줄 친 빈칸에 가장 적절한 표현은?

① people must be organized

② people must rise up and be assembled together

③ people must be independent

④ politics should be guaranteed in freedom

⑤ people must elect great leaders

19. 위 글에서 밑줄 친 ⒷⒷ가 가리키는 것은?

① association

② adherents

③ locality

④ a certain specific victory

⑤ a party

20. 위 글에서 미국 시민의 '의무'와 일치하지 않은 것은?

① it should be taken part in politics.

② it should be done in practical manner.

③\ it should be in accordance with the highest principles of honor and justice.

④ it should be in coordination with other's opinions.

⑤ it should be in party allegiance.

21. 위 글과 일치하지 않은 것은?

① 체계를 갖춘 정당이 이상적이라 주장한다.

② 지역 정당을 변함없이 지지해야 이득이 된다.

③ 자신의 소중한 의견이 정당의 성공을 위해 희생이 될 수도 있다.

④ 다른 사람의 이론과 신념도 나의 것과 같이 제시되고 수정될 수 있다.

⑤ 시민의 정치참여는 실리적인 방식에서 이루어져야만 한다.

Duties of American Citizenship

by Theodore Roosevelt

Somebody has said that a racing-yacht, like a good rifle, is a bundle of incompatibilities; that you must get the utmost possible sail power without sacrificing some other quality if you really do get the utmost sail power, that, in short you have got to make more or less of a compromise on each in order to acquire the dozen things needful; but, of course, in making this compromise you must be very careful for the sake of something unimportant not to sacrifice any of the great principles of successful naval architecture.

🔖 해석기법

Somebody has said ①that a racing-yacht, like a good rifle, is a bundle of incompatibilities(누군가가 말하기를 좋은 소총같이 요트경기도 여러 각기 다른 특성들을 갖고 있습니다); **②that you must get the utmost possible sail power without sacrificing some other quality**(당신은 다른 특성을 희생시키는 것 없이 최고 가능성 있는 항해 동력을 얻어야만 합니다) **if you really do get the utmost sail power**(만일 당신이 진정 최고의 항해 동력을 갖고자 원한다면), **③that, in short**(간략히 말해) **you have got to make more or less of a compromise on each in order to acquire the dozen things needful**(당신은 필요한 여러 가지를 획득하기 위해서 각각의 특성에 대해 약간의 타협(조화)을 해야만 합니다); **④but, of course, in making this compromise**(그러나 물론 타협을 시도할 때) **you must be very careful for the sake of something unimportant not to sacrifice any of the great principles of successful naval architecture** (당신은 성공을 위한 배 구조의 어떠한 위대한 원칙을 희생시키지 않기 위해 중요하지 않은 것에 주의를 기울여야만 합니다. - 성공적인 항해를 위해).

🔖 문법분석

Somebody ①has said[현재완료 경험] that[접속사, 목적어인 명사절] ~, like[전치사, ~같이] ~, is ~ of incompatibilities[각기 다른 특성들] ② ~if you really do[강조용법, 진정으로] ~, ③ ~more or less of [부사, 다소간, 약간] a compromise on each (quality)[각각의 특성들과 조화] ~; ④ ~in making[부사구, when you make] ~for the sake of[~을 위하여] ~not to[~하지 않기 위해서] ~of successful naval architecture(성공을 위한 배 구조의)

🔖 단어분석

⚓ **bundle** [bʌ́ndl] n. ① 묶음, 묶은 것. / **a racing-yacht** 요트경기 / **incompatibility** [inkəmpæ̀təbíləti] n. U,C 양립하지 않음, 성격의 불일치; / ⚓ **utmost** [ʌ́tmòust / -məst] a. 최고도의, 극도의, 극단의. / ⚓ **sacrifice** [sǽkrəfàis]v.—vt. 희생하다, 단념[포기]하다(for; to). / ⚓ **compromise** [kɑ́mprəmàiz] n. U,C 타협, 화해, 양보. / ⚓ **architecture** [ɑ́ːrkətèktʃər] n. U 구조, 구성, 설계, 체계. /

🔖 동의어/반의어

<u>compromise</u> n. arbitration[ɑ̀ːrbitréiʃən], concession[kənséʃən], mediation[mìːdiéiʃ-ən] 중재, negotiation[nigòuʃiéiʃən] v. risk[risk], discredit[diskrédit], endanger[endéindʒər], jeopardize[dʒépərdàiz] ant. disagreement[disəgríːmənt]

<u>successful</u> a. flourishing [fláːriʃiŋ], fortunate[fɔ́ːrtʃ-ənit], prosperous[prɑ́spərəs], thriving[θráiviŋ], eminent[émənənt], famous[féiməs], important[impɔ́ːrtənt], notable[nóutəbl-ə], conquering[kɑ́ŋkər / kɔ́ŋ], triumphant[traiʌ́mfənt], victorious[viktɔ́ːriəs], effective[iféktiv], fruitful[frúːtfəl], productive [prədʌ́ktiv] ant. failing[féiliŋ], obscure[əbskjúər], unsuccessful[ʌ̀nsəksésfəl, futilefutile [fjúːtl, -tail]

Well, it is about so with a man's political work. He has got to preserve his independence on the one hand; and on the other, unless he wishes to be a wholly ineffective crank, he has got to have some sense of party allegiance and party responsibility, and he has got to realize that in any given exigency it may be a matter of duty to sacrifice one quality, or it may be a matter of duty to sacrifice the other.

🖎 해석기법

Well, it is about so with a man's political work(음, 그것(요트경기)은 한 사람의 정치적 행위와의 그런 것(조화를 이루는 일)에 관한 것과 같습니다). **He has got to preserve his independence on the one hand**(그는 한편으론 자신의 독립성을 유지해야만 합니다); **and on the other, unless he wishes to be a wholly ineffective crank**(그리고 다른 한편으론 자신이 전반적으로 비효율적인 변덕쟁이가 되기를 바라지 않는 한), **he has got to have some sense of party allegiance and party responsibility**(그는 당에 복종과 책임감을 가져야만 합니다), **and he has got to realize**(그리고 그가 깨달아야만 하는 것은) **that in any given exigency**(어느 닥쳐온 위기상황에서) **it may be a matter of duty to sacrifice one quality, or it may be a matter of duty to sacrifice the other**(한 특성이나 다른 특성을 희생하는 것이 의무적인 문제(의무로 제기된 위기)가 될 수도 있다는 것입니다).

🖎 문법분석

it[=a racing-yacht] is about[=like] so[making this compromise) with ~. ~; and on the other (hand)[다른 한편으로], unless[접속사, ~하지 않으면] ~, he has got to[=have to] ~, in any given exigency[when it is in ~] it ~a matter of duty[=a dutiful matter, 형용사구가 됨] to sacrifice the other (quality).

🖎 단어분석

☦ **preserve** [prizə́ːrv] v. —vt. ① 보전하다, 유지하다. / ✝ **crank** [kræŋk] n. 변덕, 괴짜 / **allegiance**[əlíːdʒəns] n. 충성, 충절; 충실; / **exigency, -gence**[éksədʒənsi]긴급한 경우, 긴급사태; / ☦ **responsibility**[rispànsəbíləti/-spɔ̀n-] n. ① U 책임, 책무, 의무(of; for). [SYN.] ⇨ DUTY.

🖎 동의어/반의어

<u>preserve</u> v. conserve[kənsə́ːrv], reserve[rizə́ːrv], save[seiv], spare[spɛəːr], maintain[meintéin], perpetuate[pə(ː)rpétʃuèit], sustain[səstéin], shield[ʃiːld], shelter[ʃéltəːr], uphold[ʌdphóuld], harbor[háːrbər], safeguard[séifgàːrd,

n. reservation[rèzəːrvéiʃ-ən], retreat[riːtríːt], sanctuary[sǽŋktʃuèri] ant. waste[weist], abolish[əbáliʃ]

<u>exigency</u> n. demands[dimǽndz] exigence[éksədʒəns], urgency[ə́ːrdʒənsi], difficulty[dífikλlti], crisis[kráisis], needs[niːdz], emergency[iməːrdʒənsi] predicament [pridíkəmənt]